THE HARBRACE ANTHOLOGY OF POETRY

THE HARBRACE ANTHOLOGY OF POETRY

SENIOR EDITORS

JON C. STOTT

RAYMOND E. JONES

RICK BOWERS

CONTRIBUTING EDITORS

GLENN BURGER

WILLIAM CONNOR

KATHERINE KOLLER

JAMES NELSON

DAPHNE READ

GLENNIS STEPHENSON

BRUCE STOVEL

University of Alberta

HARCOURT
BRACE
CANADA

Harcourt Brace & Company, Canada

Toronto Montreal Orlando Fort Worth San Diego
Philadelphia London Sydney Tokyo

Canadian Cataloguing in Publication Data

Main entry under title:

The Harbrace anthology of poetry

Includes bibliographical references and index.

ISBN 0-7747-3353-5

1. English poetry. 2. American poetry. 3. Canadian poetry (English).* I. Stott, Jon C., 1939-   .
II. Jones, Raymond E. III. Bowers, Rick.

PN6101.H3 1994   821.008   C94-930109-4

Editorial Director: *Heather McWhinney*
Acquisitions Editor: *Heather McWhinney*
Developmental Editors: *Deborah Adamczyk, Dianne Horton*
Editorial Assistant: *Debra Jarrett-Chase*
Director of Publishing Services: *Steve Lau*
Editorial Manager: *Liz Radojkovic*
Editorial Co-ordinator: *Marcel Chiera*
Production Manager: *Sue-Ann Becker*
Production Co-ordinator: *Denise Wake*
Copy Editor: *Cy Strom*
Cover and Interior Design: *Landgraff Design Associates*
Typesetting and Assembly: *True to Type Inc.*
Printing and Binding: *Best Book Manufacturers*

Cover Art: *French Doors I* by Joseph Plaskett. Courtesy of Bau-Xi Gallery, Toronto and Vancouver, Canada.

♾ This book was printed in Canada on acid-free paper.

2 3 4 5   98 97 96 95

PREFACE

"We imagine ourselves, we create ourselves, we touch ourselves into being with words, words that are important to us," writes native North American author Gerald Vizenor. One means by which we imagine or create ourselves is through the reading of literature.

The Harbrace Anthology of Literature uses three approaches to encourage its readers in this activity. First, it presents significant and representative works from the increasingly widening canon of literature in English. Second, it provides strategies to assist readers in their appreciation of works of literature. Third, by introducing readers to the language of literature, both simple and complex, and by suggesting methods for articulating responses, it provides opportunities to explore literature and to respond to language in its rich and varied forms.

Although no anthology can include all of its readers' favourite works, the editors have attempted to make their selections as varied and diverse as possible. Thus, *The Harbrace Anthology of Literature* offers many contemporary poems, plays, and short stories, by men and women alike, from a variety of cultures and backgrounds, in addition to many of those works that have always formed an integral part of the accepted canon of literature in English. It also includes a large sampling of English Canadian literature in the belief that Canadian students should have the opportunity to experience the major works of their literary tradition both on their own terms and within the larger context of literature written in English.

Individual works in *The Harbrace Anthology of Literature* mirror the diversity of backgrounds and interests of Canadian students as well as reflecting an expanded canon. The poems, plays, and short stories reveal many of the characteristic themes and artistic techniques of their authors; they also reflect the cultural and social contexts in which they were written. In particular they embody, as the eighteenth-century poet Alexander Pope observed, "what oft was thought but ne'er so well expressed." Most readers of this anthology will find its works speaking directly to them and addressing their most deeply felt concerns.

The Harbrace Anthology of Literature is organized by genre, beginning with poetry. Its poetry selections span eleven hundred years, the longest period of the three genres presented in the anthology. It continues with drama and concludes with short stories, the most recent of the three genres to develop. Selections within each genre are chronological, according to the birth dates of their authors. Following a selection, its date of publication is printed in parentheses on the right; when it differs significantly and is known, the date of composition appears in parentheses on the left. Such an organizational pattern, based on chronology rather than on pedagogical or theoretical concerns, invites a broad range of responses to a work, unencumbered by artificial or purely technical groupings based on content or theme. It does, of course, implicitly suggest an historical continuity in literature: that works from a specific period often have technical and thematic similarities; and that earlier works and authors can influence later ones.

The General Introduction considers the reading of literature both as a personal, necessary lifelong activity and as a discipline. It explores how reading poems, plays, and short stories allows individuals to understand their own lives and responses to literature in relation to those of other people. It also demonstrates how readers can engage more deeply with a text, experiencing it more fully and relating it more completely to their own lives.

The introduction to each genre focuses directly on the characteristics and conventions of the genre, using examples from the literature presented in *The Harbrace Anthology of Literature*. Discussions of individual characteristics are intended not to offer explanations or explications, but to indicate ways in which authors have used the various elements of the genre. For the reader, an awareness of these characteristics may assist in engagement with the text and lead to a broader range of responses.

Each work or, in the case of poetry, each group of poems by the same author is prefaced by a brief headnote establishing a biographical and literary context. The headnote may also touch on technique or theme. Explanatory footnotes identify historical, fictional, and mythological personages, literary and artistic works, real and fictional places, and terms not usually found in standard dictionaries. This material provides resources to assist readers in the personal creation of meaning — not to impose a critical viewpoint or to force interpretation in a specific, narrow direction.

Reading literature invites writing about it. The chapter entitled "Writing Essays about Literature" explores some of the challenges that writing about literature poses, without prescribing a recipe or rigid format for writing. It offers constructive suggestions to assist readers and writers in articulating responses — intellectual, aesthetic, or emotional — to works of literature.

The Glossary offers definitions of key terms, providing for readers both an awareness of essential concepts and a standard vocabulary for use in discussing literature.

The compilation of this anthology was a co-operative venture of the ten colleagues whose names appear on the title page; however, no book, even one developed by ten people, is ever created in a vacuum. During the planning, compiling, writing, and editing stages of *The Harbrace Anthology of Literature*, many people offered suggestions and made valuable comments. We wish to acknowledge the contributions and suggestions of our colleagues from the University of Alberta and reviewers from other universities: Claude G. Arnold, Richard Arnold, Diana Austin, William Benzie, William Blackburn, Sylvia Bowerbank, Mervin Butovsky, George J. Casey, Lorelei Cederstrom, Diane T. Edwards, Ian W. Fairclough, James Hart, Ron

Johnson, W.B. Lambert, Edward Lobb, T.J. Matheson, Lee McLeod, Craig W. McLuckie, Edward Mullaly, Victor A. Neufeldt, Andrew Parkin, Victor Ramraj, Constance Rooke, Eric J. Savoy, John F. Secker, Tony Steele, S. Warren Stevenson, J.E. Svilpis, Peter A. Taylor, B.F. Tyson, Paul S. Upton, Aritha van Herk, Lorraine York, and Edward R. Zietlow. As well, we thank Heather McWhinney, Nancy Ennis, Dianne Horton, Deborah Adamczyk, Marcel Chiera, Debra Jarrett-Chase, Graeme Whitley, and Michael Young at Harcourt Brace. These people have made this a better anthology; the responsibility for its limitations is our own.

PUBLISHER'S NOTE TO STUDENTS AND INSTRUCTORS

This textbook is a key component of your course. If you are the instructor of this course, you undoubtedly considered a number of texts carefully before choosing this as the one that would work best for your students and you. The authors and publishers spent considerable time and money to ensure its high quality, and we appreciate your recognition of this effort and accomplishment. Please note the copyright statement.

If you are a student, we are confident that this text will help you to meet the objectives of your course. It will also become a valuable addition to your personal library.

Since we want to hear what you think about this book, please be sure to send us the stamped reply card at the end of the text. Your input will help us to continue to publish high-quality books for your courses.

A NOTE ON THE HARBRACE ANTHOLOGIES OF POETRY, DRAMA, AND SHORT FICTION

The success of *The Harbrace Anthology of Literature* provides the publisher with an ideal opportunity to print individual anthologies of each of the three genres presented in *The Harbrace Anthology of Literature*. These are *The Harbrace Anthology of Poetry*, *The Harbrace Anthology of Drama*, and *The Harbrace Anthology of Short Fiction*. The new one-genre anthologies will offer greater choice to instructors teaching courses in these individual genres. Each of the one-genre anthologies incorporates the following elements from *The Harbrace Anthology of Literature*:
- the general introduction to literature
- the introduction to the specific genre
- the glossary of literary terms
- the chapter on writing essays about literature
- the index.

Each of the anthologies also contains the entire table of contents for *The Harbrace Anthology of Literature*. This will give instructors who choose to use one or more of the one-genre anthologies the opportunity to refer to all works in the other anthologies.

ACKNOWLEDGEMENTS

ALLEN, WOODY: *God*. From *Without Feathers* by Woody Allen. Copyright © 1972, 1973, 1974, 1975 by Woody Allen. Reprinted by permission of Random House, Inc..

AMMONS, A.R.: "Dunes" is reprinted from *The Selected Poems, 1951-1977*, by A.R. Ammons, by permission of W.W. Norton & Company, Inc. Copyright © 1977, 1975, 1974, 1972, 1971, 1970, 1966, 1965, 1964, 1955 by A.R. Ammons.

ANONYMOUS MEDIEVAL LYRICS: "Western Wind" from *Early English Lyrics*, 1967, published by October House. Copyright © 1966 and reprinted by permission of Sidgwick and Jackson Limited.

ANONYMOUS MEDIEVAL LYRICS: "I Sing of a Maiden," "Sunset on Calvary," "Alison," and "The Cuckoo Song" from *One Hundred Middle English Lyrics*, edited by R.D. Stevick (Indianapolis: The Bobbs-Merrill Company/Macmillan Publishing Company, 1964).

ANONYMOUS MEDIEVAL POPULAR BALLADS: "Sir Patrick Spens," "Get Up and Bar the Door," "Lord Randall," "The Twa Corbies," and "The Birth of Robin Hood." Reprinted from Arthur Quiller-Couch, editor. *The Oxford Book of Ballads* (London: Oxford University Press, 1910).

ARNOLD, MATTHEW: "Isolation: To Marguerite" and "Dover Beach" by Matthew Arnold. Reprinted from C.B. Tinker and H.F. Lowry, editors. *Arnold: Poetical Works* (Oxford: Oxford University Press, 1950).

ATWOOD, MARGARET: "Progressive Insanities of a Pioneer," "The Animals in That Country," "Further Arrivals," and "you fit into me." From Margaret Atwood's *Selected Poems 1966-1984*, copyright©Margaret Atwood, 1990, reprinted by permission of Oxford University Press Canada. "Variations on the Word *Love*," "A Women's Issue," and "Interlunar." From Margaret Atwood's *Selected Poems 1966-1984*, copyright © Margaret Atwood 1990, reprinted by permission of Oxford University Press Canada. "The Resplendent Quetzal." From *Dancing Girls* by Margaret Atwood. Used by permission of the Canadian Publishers, McClelland & Stewart, Toronto.

AUDEN, W.H.: "Musée des Beaux Arts," "The Unknown Citizen," "In Memory of William Butler Yeats," and "The Shield of Achilles." From W. H. Auden, *Collected Shorter Poems 1927–1957* (London: Faber and Faber, 1966). Reprinted with the permission of Faber and Faber Limited. "After Reading a Child's Guide to Modern Physics" and "Lullaby." From Edward Mendelson, editor. *Collected Poems of W.H. Auden* (London: Faber and Faber, 1976). Reprinted with the permission of Faber and Faber Limited.

BARTHELME, DONALD: "Jaws." Reprinted by permission of the Putnam Publishing Group from *Forty Stories* by Donald Barthelme. Copyright © 1988 by Donald Barthelme.

BEHN, APHRA: "Song (*Amyntas* led me to a Grove)" and *The Rover*. Reprinted from Montague Summers, editor. *The Works of Aphra Behn* (6 vols.) (London: Heinemann, 1915).

BENNETT, LOUISE: " Colonization in Reverse." Reprinted from Louise Bennett, *Jamaica Labrish* (Sangster's, 1966), with the permission of the author.

BETJEMAN, JOHN: "In Westminster Abbey" and "Upper Lambourne." From *John Betjeman's Collected Poems*, enlarged edition (London: John Murray, 1970), compiled by the Earl of Birkenhead. Reprinted by permission of John Murray Publishers.

BIRNEY, EARLE: "Vancouver Lights," "Anglosaxon Street," "Mappemounde," and "Bushed." From *The Collected Poems of Earle Birney*, 2 vols., by Earle Birney. Used by permission of the Canadian Publishers, McClelland & Stewart, Toronto.

BLAKE, WILLIAM: Songs of Innocence: "The Lamb," "The Little Black Boy," "The Chimney Sweeper," "Holy Thursday," and "Nurse's Song," and Songs of Experience: "The Tyger," "The Chimney Sweeper," "Holy Thursday," "Nurse's Song," "The Sick Rose," "London," and "Auguries of Innocence" reprinted from David V. Erdman, editor. *The Complete Poetry and Prose of William Blake*, revised edition (New York: Doubleday, 1962).

BRADSTREET, ANNE: "The Author to her Book," "To my Dear and loving Husband," and "Upon the burning of our house, July 10, 1966." Reprinted from Robert Hutchinson, editor. *Poems of Anne Bradstreet* (New York: Dover Publications, 1969).

BRAND, DIONNE: "Eurocentric." From Dionne Brand, *Chronicles of the Hostile Sun* (Stratford, Ontario: Williams-Wallace, 1984). Copyright © 1984 Dionne Brand. Reprinted by permission of Williams-Wallace Publishers.

BURNS, ROBERT: "To A Mouse: On Turning Her Up in Her Nest, with the Plough, November, 1785" and "Holy Willie's Prayer." Reprinted from James Kinsley, editor. *The Poems and Songs of Robert Burns* (Oxford: Clarendon Press, 1968).

BYRON, GEORGE GORDON, LORD: "She Walks in Beauty," "Who kill'd John Keats?", and "On This Day I Complete My Thirty-Sixth Year." Reprinted from Robert F. Gleckner, editor. *The Poetical Works of Byron* (Boston: Houghton Mifflin, 1975).

CARVER, RAYMOND: "Cathedral." From *Cathedral* by Raymond Carver. Copyright © 1983 by Raymond Carver. Reprinted by permission of Alfred A. Knopf, Inc.

CATHER, WILLA: "Paul's Case." Reprinted from *Willa Cather's Collected Short Fiction, 1892-1912*, edited by Virginia Faulkner, introduction by Mildred R. Bennett, by permission of University of Nebraska Press. Copyright © 1965, 1970 by the University of Nebraska Press.

CHAUCER, GEOFFREY: "General Prologue" and "The Miller's Prologue and Tale." Reprinted from Robinson, F.N. (Editor). *The Works of Geoffrey Chaucer*. Copyright © 1957 by Houghton Mifflin Company. Used with permission.

CHEEVER, JOHN: "Goodbye, My Brother." Copyright 1951 by John Cheever. Reprinted from *The Stories of John Cheever*, by permission of Alfred A. Knopf, Inc.

CHOPIN, KATE: "The Story of an Hour" by Kate Chopin reprinted from *The Complete Works of Kate Chopin*, vol. 1 (Baton Rouge: Louisiana State University Press, 1969).

CLARKE, AUSTIN C.: "The Motor Car." From *When He Was Free and Young and He Used to Wear Silks* by Austin C. Clarke. Reprinted by permission of Harold Ober Associates Incorporated. Copyright © 1971, 1972, 1973 by Austin C. Clarke.

COHEN, LEONARD: "I Have Not Lingered in European Monasteries." "For E.J.P.," and "Suzanne Takes You Down." From *Selected Poems 1950–1975* by Leonard Cohen. Used by permission of the Canadian Publishers, McClelland & Stewart, Toronto.

COLERIDGE, SAMUEL TAYLOR: "Kubla Khan," "Frost at Midnight," and "The Rime of the Ancient Mariner." Reprinted from Ernest Hartley Coleridge, editor. *Coleridge: The Complete Poetical Works* (Oxford: Oxford University Press, 1912).

CONRAD, JOSEPH: "An Outpost of Progress" by Joseph Conrad reprinted from *The Medallion Edition of the Works of Joseph Conrad*, vol. 1 (London: Gresham Publishing, 1925).

CRANE, STEPHEN: "The Open Boat" by Stephen Crane reprinted from *The Open Boat and Other Stories* (London: Heinemann, 1898).

CREELEY, ROBERT: "Ballad of the Despairing Husband" and "The Rhythm." From Robert Creeley, *Collected Poems of Robert Creeley, 1945–1975* (Berkeley: University of California Press, 1983). Copyright © 1983 The Regents of the University of California. Reprinted by permission of the University of California Press.

CUMMINGS, E.E.: "anyone lived in a pretty how town," "it may not always be so; and i say," "in Just-spring," and "next to of course god america i." Reprinted from *Complete Poems, 1913–1962*, by E.E. Cummings, by permission of Liveright Publishing Corporation. Copyright © 1923, 1925, 1931, 1935, 1938, 1939, 1940, 1944, 1945, 1946, 1947, 1948, 1949, 1950, 1951, 1952, 1953, 1954, 1955, 1956, 1957, 1958, 1959, 1960, 1961, 1962 by the Trustees for the E.E. Cummings Trust. Copyright © 1961, 1963, 1968 by Marion Morehouse Cummings.

DE LA MARE, WALTER: "The Listeners" from *The Complete Poems of Walter de la Mare* (London: Faber and Faber, 1969). Reprinted with the permission of The Literary Trustees of Walter de la Mare and The Society of Authors as their representative.

DICKINSON, EMILY: "There's a certain Slant of light," "I'm Nobody! Who are you?", "The Soul selects her own Society," "A Bird came down the Walk — ," "I heard a Fly buzz — when I died — ," "I started early — took my Dog — ," and "As imperceptibly as Grief." Reprinted by permission of the publishers and the Trustees of Amherst College from *The Poems of Emilly Dickinson*, Thomas H. Johnson, editor, Cambridge, MA: The Belknap Press of Harvard University Press, Copyright 1951, © 1955, 1979, 1983 by the President and Fellows of Harvard College.

DONNE, JOHN: "The Ecstasy." Reprinted from A.J. Smith, editor. *John Donne: The Complete English Poems* (Harmondsworth: Penguin, 1971).

DUNCAN, ROBERT: "Bending the Bow" and "My Mother Would Be a Falconress." From Robert Duncan: *Bending the Bow*. Copyright © 1968 by Robert Duncan. Reprinted by permission of New Directions Publishing Corporation.

ELIOT, T.S.: "The Hollow Men," "Journey of the Magi," "The Love Song of J. Alfred Prufrock," and "Preludes." From T.S. Eliot, *The Complete Poems and Plays 1909–1950* (London: Faber and Faber, 1971). Reprinted with the permission of Faber and Faber Limited.

FAULKNER, WILLIAM: "A Rose for Emily." Copyright 1930 and renewed 1958 by William Faulkner. Reprinted from *Collected Stories of William Faulkner*, by permission of Random House, Inc.

FERLINGHETTI, LAWRENCE: "Constantly Risking Absurdity." From Lawrence Ferlinghetti: *A Coney Island of the Mind*. Copyright © 1958 by Lawrence Ferlinghetti. Reprinted by permission of New Directions Publishing Corporation.

FRENCH, DAVID: *Leaving Home* by David French (Toronto: New Press, 1972). Copyright © 1972 by David French. Reproduced with the permission of Stoddart Publishing Co. Limited, 34 Lesmill Rd., Don Mills, Ontario, Canada.

FROST, ROBERT: "Stopping by Woods on a Snowy Evening," "After Apple-Picking," "Design," "An Old Man's Winter Night," "Acquainted with the Night," and "For Once, Then, Something." From *The Poetry of Robert Frost* edited by Edward Connery Lathem. Copyright 1923, 1928 © 1964 by Lesley Frost Ballantine. Reprinted by permission of Henry Holt and Company.

FUGARD, ATHOL: *"MASTER HAROLD" . . . and the boys*. From *"MASTER HAROLD" . . . and the boys* by Athol Fugard. Copyright © 1982 by Athol Fugard. Reprinted by permission of Alfred A. Knopf, Inc.

GALLANT, MAVIS: "My Heart Is Broken." Reprinted by permission of Georges Borchardt Inc. for the author. Copyright © 1957 by Mavis Gallant.

GILMAN, CHARLOTTE PERKINS: "The Yellow Wallpaper" by Charlotte Perkins Gilman reprinted from *The Charlotte Perkins Gilman Reader*, vol.1 (New York: Pantheon, 1980).

GINSBERG, ALLEN: "A Supermarket in California" by Allen Ginsberg from *Collected Poems 1947–1980* by Allen Ginsberg. Copyright © 1984 by Allen Ginsberg. Reprinted by permission of HarperCollins Publishers Inc.

GRAVES, ROBERT: "The Cool Web" and "The Naked and the Nude." From Robert Graves, *New Collected Poems* (London: A.P. Watt, 1977). Reprinted with the permission of A.P. Watt Ltd. on behalf of The Trustees of the Robert Graves Copyright Trust.

GRAY, THOMAS: "Elegy Written in a Country Church-Yard." Reprinted from H.W. Starr and J.R. Hendrickson, editors. *The Complete Poems of Thomas Gray* (Oxford: Clarendon Press, 1966).

GUNN, THOM: "On the Move," "To Yvor Winters, 1955," and "Moly" by Thom Gunn. From *Selected Poems 1950–1975* (London: Faber and Faber, 1979). Reprinted by permission of Faber and Faber Limited.

HARDY, THOMAS: "Hap," "The Darkling Thrush," "New Year's Eve," "The Convergence of the Twain," "The Ruined Maid," and "Afterwards." Reprinted from James Gibson, editor. *The Complete Poems of Thomas Hardy* (London: Macmillan, 1976).

HAWTHORNE, NATHANIEL: "My Kinsman, Major Molineux" by Nathaniel Hawthorne reprinted from *Centenary Edition of the Works of Nathaniel Hawthorne*, vol. XI (Columbus, OH: Ohio State University Press).

HEANEY, SEAMUS: "Personal Helicon" and "Death of a Naturalist" from Seamus Heaney, *Selected Poems 1965–1975* (London: Faber and Faber, 1981). Reprinted by permission of Faber and Faber Limited. "The Singer's House," "The Harvest Bow," "The Otter," and "Casualty" from Seamus Heaney, *Field Work* (London: Faber and Faber, 1980). Reprinted by permission of Faber and Faber Limited.

HECHT, ANTHONY: "The Dover Bitch." From *Collected Earlier Poems* by Anthony Hecht. Copyright © 1990 by Anthony E. Hecht. Reprinted by permission of Alfred A. Knopf, Inc.

HEMINGWAY, ERNEST: "A Clean, Well-Lighted Place." Reprinted with persmission of Charles Scribner's Sons, an imprint of Macmillan Publishing Company from *The Short Stories of Ernest Hemingway* by Ernest Hemingway. Copyright 1933 by Charles Scribner's Sons; renewal copyright © 1961 by Mary Hemingway.

HODGINS, JACK: "The Concert Stages of Europe." From *The Barclay Family Theatre* by Jack Hodgins. Copyright © 1981 by Jack Hodgins. Reprinted by permission of Macmillan of Canada, A Division of Canada Publishing Corporation.

HOGAN, LINDA: "The Sand Roses." From *Seeing Through the Sun* by Linda Hogan (Amherst: University of Massachusetts Press, 1985), copyright © 1985 by Linda Hogan. Reprinted by permission of the University of Massachusetts Press.

HOPKINS, GERARD MANLEY: "Pied Beauty," Sonnet 65, "The Windhover," and "God's Grandeur." Reprinted from W.H. Gardiner and N.H. Mackenzie, editors. *The Poems of Gerald Manley Hopkins* (Oxford: Oxford University Press, 1967).

HOUSMAN, A.E.: "Loveliest of trees, the cherry now," "When I was one-and-twenty," and "To an Athlete Dying Young." From *Collected Poems*. Reprinted by permission of The Society of Authors as the literary representative of the Estate of A.E. Housman and Jonathan Cape Ltd., publishers of A.E. Housman's *Collected Poems*.

HUGHES, TED: "Wind," "Pike," and "Hawk Roosting" by Ted Hughes from *Selected Poems 1957–1967*. Copyright © 1972 by Ted Hughes. Reprinted by permission of HarperCollins Publishers Inc.

JAMES, HENRY: "The Real Thing" by Henry James. Reprinted from Leon Edel, editor. *The Complete Tales of Henry James*, vol. 8 (New York: Lippincott, 1963).

JOHNSON, PAULINE: "The Derelict" by Pauline Johnson reprinted from *The Moccasin Maker* (Toronto: Ryerson, 1913).

JONSON, BEN: "Song: To Celia," "Queen and huntress," "Come, my Celia," and "On My First Son." Reprinted from Harry Levin, editor. *Ben Jonson: Selected Works* (New York: Random House, 1938).

JOYCE, JAMES: "The Dead" from *The Dubliners* by James Joyce. Copyright 1916 by B.W. Huebsch. Definitive text copyright © 1967 by the Estate of James Joyce. Used by permission of Viking Penguin, a division of Penguin Books USA, Inc.

KEATS, JOHN: "Ode to a Nightingale," "Ode on a Grecian Urn," "To Autumn," "La Belle Dame sans Merci," "When I have fears," "On First Looking into Chapman's Homer," and Sonnet: "Bright star!" reprinted from H.W. Garrod, editor. *The Poetical Works of John Keats* (Oxford: Clarendon Press, 1958).

KLEIN, A.M.: "Heirloom" and "Portrait of the Poet as Landscape" by A.M. Klein. From *A. M. Klein: Complete Poems, parts 1 and 2*, edited by Zailig Pollock. Copyright © 1990 by University of Toronto Press. Reprinted by permission of University of Toronto Press.

LARKIN, PHILIP: "Church Going," "Lines of a Young Lady's Photograph Album," "Toads," "An Arundel Tomb," and "Next, Please" by Philip Larkin are reprinted from *The Less Deceived* by permission of the Marvel Press, England.

LAURENCE, MARGARET: "The Loons." From *A Bird in the House* by Margaret Laurence. Reprinted by permission of the Canadian Publishers, McClelland & Stewart, Toronto.

LAWRENCE, D.H.: "Piano" and "Snake." From *The Complete Poems of D. H. Lawrence* (London: Heinemann, 1964, 1972). Reprinted with the permission of Laurence Pollinger Limited, Authors' Agents, and the Estate of Frieda Lawrence Ravagli. "The Horse Dealer's Daughter." From *The Complete Short Stories of D. H. Lawrence* (London: Heinemann, 1955). Reprinted with the permission of Laurence Pollinger Limited, Authors' Agents, and the Estate of Frieda Lawrence Ravagli.

LAYTON, IRVING: "The Birth of Tragedy" and "Keine Lazarovich, 1870–1959." From *Collected Poems* by Irving Layton. Used by permission of the Canadian Publishers, McClelland & Stewart, Toronto.

LePAN, DOUGLAS: "A Country Without a *Mythology*" by Douglas LePan. From *Weathering It* by Douglas LePan. Used by permission of the Canadian Publishers, McClelland & Stewart, Toronto.

LESSING, DORIS: "A Woman on a Roof." Copyright © 1963 Doris Lessing. Reprinted by permission of Jonathan Clowes Ltd, London, on behalf of Doris Lessing.

LEVERTOV, DENISE: "The Ache of Marriage" and "What Were They Like?" From Denise Levertov: *Poems 1960–1967*. Copyright © 1964, 1966 by Denise Levertov Goodman. Reprinted by permission of New Directions Publishing Corporation.

LIVESAY, DOROTHY: "Bartok and the Geranium" and "The Three Emilys" by Dorothy Livesay. Reprinted from *Collected Poems: The Two Seasons* (Toronto: McGraw-Hill Ryerson, 1972). Copyright © and reprinted with the permission of Dorothy Livesay.

LOWELL, ROBERT: "Skunk Hour" from *Life Studies* by Robert Lowell. Copyright © 1956, 1959 by Robert Lowell. Renewal copyright © 1981, 1986, 1987 by Harriet W. Lowell, Caroline Lowell and Sheridan Lowell. Reprinted by permission of Farrar, Straus and Giroux, Inc. "After the Surprising Conversion" in *Lord Weary's Castle* copyright 1946 and renewed 1974 by Robert Lowell, reprinted by permission of Harcourt Brace Jovanovich, Inc.

MacEWEN, GWENDOLYN: "Dark Pines Under Water." From Gwendolyn MacEwen, *The Shadow-Maker* (Toronto: Macmillan, 1969). Reprinted with the permission of the author's family. "The Real Enemies" reprinted by permission of Mosaic Press, 1252 Speers Rd., Units 1 & 2, Oakville, Ontario, L6L 5N9, from *The T. E. Lawrence Poems*. "But." From *Afterworlds* by Gwendolyn MacEwen. Used by permission of the Canadian Publishers, McClelland & Stewart, Toronto.

MANSFIELD, KATHERINE: "Bliss" by Katherine Mansfield reprinted from *Bliss and Other Stories* (New York: Knopf, 1931).

MARLOWE, CHRISTOPHER: *Doctor Faustus*. Reprinted from *The Plays of Christopher Marlowe* (Cleveland and New York: World Publishing, 1962).

McGRATH, ELIZABETH: "Fogbound in Avalon." Reprinted by permission; © 1980 The New Yorker Magazine, Inc.

MILTON, JOHN: "How soon hath Time" from John Milton: *Complete Poems and Major Prose*, edited by Merritt Y. Hughes (New York: Macmillan Publishing Company, 1985).

MILTON, JOHN: "When I consider how my light is spent," "On the Late Massacre in Piedmont," "Methought I saw my late espousèd saint," "Lycidas." Reprinted from D. Masson, editor. *The Poetical Works of John Milton* (London: Macmillan, 1891).

MOURÉ, ERIN: "Miss Chatelaine" and "The Producers." From Erin Mouré, *Furious* (Toronto: House of Anansi, 1987). These selections were reproduced with the permission of Stoddart Publishing Co. Limited, 34 Lesmill Rd., Don Mills, Ontario, Canada. "Bends" and "Safety." From Erin Mouré, *Domestic Fuel* (Toronto: House of Anansi, 1985). These selections were reproduced with the permission of Stoddart Publishing Co. Limited, 34 Lesmill Rd., Don Mills, Ontario, Canada.

MUKHERJEE, BHARATI: "The Tenant." From *The Middleman and Other Stories.* Copyright © 1988 by Bharati Mukherjee. Reprinted by permission of Penguin Books Canada Limited.

MUNRO, ALICE: "Mrs. Cross and Mrs. Kidd." From *The Moons of Jupiter* by Alice Munro. Copyright © 1983 by Alice Munro. Reprinted by permission of Macmillan of Canada, A Division of Canada Publishing Corporation.

NOWLAN, ALDEN: "The Bull Moose." From *An Exchange of Gifts* (Toronto: Irwin, 1985). Copyright © by Alden Nowlan. This selection was reproduced with the permission of Stoddart Publishing Co. Limited, 34 Lesmill Rd., Don Mills, Ontario, Canada.

O'CONNOR, FLANNERY: "Everything that Rises Must Converge" from *Everything that Rises Must Converge* by Flannery O'Connor. Copyright © 1965 by the Estate of Mary Flannery O'Connor. Reprinted by permission of Farrar, Straus and Giroux, Inc.

OLSON, CHARLES: "Maximus, to himself" by Charles Olson. From George Butterick, editor. *The Maximus Poems* (Berkeley: University of California Press, 1983). Copyright © 1983 The Regents of the University of California. Reprinted by permission of the University of California Press.

ONDAATJE, MICHAEL: "Elizabeth," "White Dwarfs," "Letters and Other Worlds," and "Bearhug." From *There's a Trick with a Knife I'm Learning to Do: Poems 1963–1978* by Michael Ondaatje. Used by permission of the Canadian Publishers, McClelland & Stewart, Toronto. "The Cinnamon Peeler," "To a Sad Daughter," and "When you drive the Queensborough roads at midnight." From *Secular Love* (Toronto: Coach House, 1984). Copyright © 1984 and reprinted by permission of the author.

OODGEROO OF THE TRIBE NOONUCCAL, CUSTODIAN OF THE LAND MINJERRIBAH: "Nona" and "We Are Going" by Oodgeroo of the tribe Noonuccal. Reprinted from *My People* (Milton, Queensland: The Jacaranda Press, 1964) with the permission of The Jacaranda Press.

OWEN, WILFRED: "Strange Meeting," "Anthem for Doomed Youth," and "*Dulce et Decorum Est.*" From Jon Stallworthy, editor. *The Complete Poems and Fragments*, vol. 1 (London: The Hogarth Press, 1983). Reprinted with the permission of the Estate of Wilfred Owen and The Hogarth Press.

PAGE, P.K.: "The Stenographers," "Stories of Snow," and "Photos of a Salt Mine" copyright © P.K. Page. Reprinted with the permission of the author from *The Glass Air: Selected Poems* (Toronto: Oxford University Press, 1985).

PINTER, HAROLD: *The Homecoming.* Copyright © 1965 Harold Pinter. Reprinted by permission of Faber and Faber Limited.

PLATH, SYLVIA: "Daddy," "Lady Lazarus," and "Spider." From *Ariel* by Sylvia Plath (London: Faber and Faber, 1966). Reprinted by permission of Faber and Faber Limited.

POLLOCK, SHARON: *Blood Relations* from *Blood Relations and Other Plays.* Reprinted by permission of NeWest Publishers Limited, Edmonton.

POPE, ALEXANDER: "The Rape of the Lock." Reprinted from Geoffrey Tillotson, editor. *The Rape of the Lock and Other Poems*, vol. 2 of *The Poems of Alexander Pope*, 3rd edition (London: Methuen, 1962). Excerpt from "Essay on Man," Epistle II. Reprinted from Maynard Mack, editor. *An Essay on Man*, vol. 3 of *The Poems of Alexander Pope*, 3rd edition (London: Methuen, 1962). Reprinted with the permission of Routledge Publishers.

PORTER, KATHERINE ANN: "Rope" from *Flowering Judas and Other Stories*, copyright 1930 and renewed 1958 by Katherine Ann Porter, reprinted by permission of Harcourt Brace Jovanovich, Inc.

POUND, EZRA: "An Immorality." From Ezra Pound: *Collected Earlier Poems.* Copyright © 1976 by the Trustees of the Ezra Pound Literary Property Trust. Reprinted by permission of New Directions Publishing Corporation. "The Seafarer," "Ancient Music," "In a Station of the Metro," "The River Merchant's Wife: A Letter," and "There died a myriad." From Ezra Pound: *Personae.* Copyright 1926 by Ezra Pound. Reprinted by permission of New Directions Publishing Corporation.

PRATT, E.J.: "From Stone to Steel" and "The Truant" by E.J. Pratt from *E. J. Pratt: Complete Poems*, edited by Sandra Djwa and R.G. Moyles, copyright © 1989 University of Toronto Press. Reprinted by permission of University of Toronto Press.

PURDY, AL: "The Country North of Belleville" and "Lament for the Dorsets." From *Being Alive: Poems 1958–78* by Al Purdy. Used by permission of the Canadian Publishers, McClelland & Stewart, Toronto.

RICH, ADRIENNE: "Aunt Jennifer's Tigers," "Living in Sin," "Snapshots of a Daughter-in-Law," "Diving into the Wreck," and "Transit." Reprinted from *The Fact of a Doorframe, Poems Selected and New, 1950–1984*, by Adrienne Rich, by permission of W.W. Norton & Company, Inc. Copyright © 1984 by Adrienne Rich. Copyright © 1975, 1978 by W.W. Norton & Company, Inc. Copyright © 1981 by Adrienne Rich.

ROBERTS, SIR CHARLES G.D. "Tantramar Revisited," "The Potato Harvest," "The Winter Fields," and "The Herring Weir" by Sir Charles G.D. Roberts. Reprinted from *The Collected Poems of Sir Charles G. D. Roberts* (Wolfville, N.S.: The Wombat Press, 1985). Copyright © by Mary Pacey and Lady Joan Roberts. Reprinted by permission of The Wombat Press.

ROBINSON, EDWIN ARLINGTON: "Richard Cory" from *The Children of the Night* by Edwin Arlington Robinson (New York: Charles Scribner's Sons, 1897). "Mr. Flood's Party" from *Collected Poems* by Edwin Arlington Robinson. Copyright 1921 by Edwin Arlington Robinson, renewed 1949 by Ruth Nivison. "Eros Turannos" from *Collected Poems* by Edwin Arlington Robinson. Copyright 1916 by Edwin Arlington Robinson, renewed 1944 by Ruth Nivison.

ROCHESTER, JOHN WILMOT, EARL OF: "A Satire against Mankind." Reprinted from David M. Vieth, editor. *The Complete Poems of John Wilmot, Earl of Rochester.* Copyright © 1968 and reprinted with the permission of Yale University Press.

SPENDER, STEPHEN: "The Truly Great" and "An Elementary School Classroom in a Slum" from Stephen Spender, *Collected Poems 1928–1953* (London: Faber and Faber, 1955). Reprinted by permission of Faber and Faber Limited.

STEVENS, WALLACE: "The Idea of Order at Key West," "Sunday Morning," "Thirteen Ways of Looking at a Blackbird," and "Study of Two Pears." From *The Collected Poems of Wallace Stevens* by Wallace Stevens. Copyright 1923 and renewed 1951 by Wallace Stevens. Reprinted by permission of Alfred A. Knopf, Inc.

SWIFT, JONATHAN: "A Description of the Morning" and "A Satirical Elegy on the Death of a Late Famous General." Reprinted from Harold Williams, editor. *The Poems of Jonathan Swift*, 3rd edition (Oxford: Clarendon Press, 1958).

TAN, AMY: "Two Kinds." Reprinted by permission of The Putnam Publishing Group from *The Joy Luck Club* by Amy Tan. Copyright © 1989 by Amy Tan.

TAYLOR, EDWARD: "Upon a Spider Catching a Fly" and "Huswifery" reprinted with permission from *The Poems of Edward Taylor*. Copyright © 1960, 1988 by Donald E. Stanford.

THOMAS, DYLAN: "And Death Shall Have No Dominion," "The Force That through the Green Fuse Drives the Flower," "The Hunchback in the Park," "Fern Hill," "In My Craft or Sullen Art," and "Do Not Go Gentle into That Good Night" by Dylan Thomas. From *Dylan Thomas: The Poems* (London: J.M. Dent, 1971). Reprinted by permission of David Higham Associates.

UPDIKE, JOHN: "A & P." From *Pigeon Feathers and Other Stories* by John Updike. Copyright © 1962 by John Updike. Reprinted by permission of Alfred A. Knopf, Inc. Originally appeared in *The New Yorker*.

VANDERHAEGHE, GUY: "Cages." From *Man Descending* by Guy Vanderhaeghe. Copyright © 1982 by Guy Vanderhaeghe. Reprinted by permission of Macmillan of Canada, A Division of Canada Publishing Corporation.

WADDINGTON, MIRIAM: "Conserving" from Miriam Waddington's *Collected Poems*, copyright © Miriam Waddington 1986. Reprinted by permission of Oxford University Press Canada.

WALKER, ALICE: "Everyday Use" from *In Love & Trouble: Stories of Black Women*, copyright © 1973 by Alice Walker, reprinted by permission of Harcourt Brace Jovanovich, Inc.

WEBB, PHYLLIS: "Marvell's Garden" and "The Glass Castle" by Phyllis Webb. From Sharon Thesen, editor. *The Vision Tree: Selected Poems* (Vancouver: Talonbooks, 1982, 1985). Copyright © 1982 and reprinted with the permission of Phyllis Webb. "Treblinka Gas Chamber" from *Wilson's Bowl* by Phyllis Webb (Toronto: Coach House Press, 1980). Copyright © 1980 and reprinted with the permission of the author.

WELTY, EUDORA: "Why I Live at the P.O." from *A Curtain of Green and Other Stories*, copyright © 1941 and renewed 1969 by Eudora Welty, reprinted by permission of Harcourt Brace Jovanovich, Inc.

WHITMAN, WALT: "One's-Self I Sing," "Out of the Cradle Endlessly Rocking," "There Was a Child Went Forth," and "When Lilacs Last in the Dooryard Bloom'd" from *Leaves of Grass: Comprehensive Reader's Edition*, edited by Harold W. Blodgett and Sculley Bradley, reprinted by permission of New York University Press. Copyright © 1965 by New York University.

WIEBE, RUDY: "Chinook Christmas." From *The Angel of the Tar Sands and Other Stories* by Rudy Wiebe. Used by permission of the Canadian Publishers, McClelland & Stewart, Toronto.

WILDE, OSCAR: *The Importance of Being Earnest*. Reprinted from R. Ross, editor. *The First Collected Edition of the Works of Oscar Wilde*, vol. 3 (London: Dawson of Pall Mall, 1969).

WILLIAMS, TENNESSEE: *Cat on a Hot Tin Roof.* Copyright 1954, 1955, 1971, 1975 by Tennessee Williams. Reprinted by permission of New Directions Publishing Corporation. Canadian rights.

WILLIAMS, WILLIAM CARLOS: "Portrait of a Lady," "Tract," "The Red Wheelbarrow," and "Spring and All." From William Carlos Williams: *The Collected Poems of William Carlos Williams, 1909–1939*, vol. 1. Copyright 1938 by New Directions Publishing Corporation. Reprinted by permission of New Directions Publishing Corporation.

WINCHELSEA, ANNE FINCH, COUNTESS OF: "The Introduction." Reprinted from Denys Thompson, editor. *Anne Finch, Countess of Winchelsea: Selected Poems*. Copyright © 1987 and reprinted with the permission of Carcanet Press Ltd.

WINTERS, YVOR: "By the Road to the Air-Base" and "The Slow Pacific Swell." From Yvor Winters: *The Collected Poems of Yvor Winters*. Copyright 1943 by New Directions Publishing Corporation. Reprinted by permission of New Directions Publishing Corporation.

WORDSWORTH, WILLIAM: "Michael: A Pastoral Poem," "Lines Composed a Few Miles above Tintern Abbey," "Composed upon Westminster Bridge, September 3, 1802," Sonnet: "It is a beauteous evening, calm and free," "London, 1802," Sonnet: "The world is too much with us," and "I wandered lonely as a cloud." Reprinted from Ernest de Selincourt, editor. *The Poetical Works of Wordsworth*, new edition, revised (Oxford: Oxford University Press, 1953).

YEATS, WILLIAM BUTLER: "The Second Coming," "Easter 1916," "Sailing to Byzantium," "Among School Children," "Crazy Jane Talks with the Bishop," "Lapis Lazuli." "The Circus Animals' Desertion," and "The Old Men Admiring Themselves in the Water." Reprinted from *The Poems of William Butler Yeats* (London: Macmillan, 1933).

CONTENTS

SHORT FICTION

INTRODUCTION

"*P*art of the beauty of all literature," commented novelist and short story writer F. Scott Fitzgerald, is that "you discover that your longings are universal longings, that you're not lonely and isolated from anyone. You belong." Sharing experience through the creation and reception of stories, poems, and plays is a very old, basic, and necessary human activity, as necessary to human existence as food, shelter, and clothing. The literary critic Northrop Frye further emphasized the importance of literature, observing that "whenever a society is reduced to the barest primary requirements of food and sex and shelter, the arts, including poetry, stand out sharply in relief as ranking with those primary requirements." The need to bring order, through language and stories, to human experience seems to be fundamental to all societies and cultures.

While some literature may simply entertain or allow escape from everyday lives, the works that ultimately stay with their readers are those that challenge, engage, or make demands. Well-crafted literature invites its readers to laugh, to cry, to wonder, to analyze, to explore, to understand.

Throughout our lives, we seek to understand ourselves, our emotions, our experiences, and our relationships with others. We also attempt to define our connections to larger social and cultural institutions. One way that we can do so is through literature, for works of literature are the records of individual response to the world in which we live.

Because of our own experiences, we are able to understand the self-doubts and uncertainties expressed in T.S. Eliot's "The Love Song of J. Alfred Prufrock," the mixed emotions of love and hate of the title characters in William Shakespeare's *Antony and Cleopatra*, the social obligations and friendships in Alice Munro's "Mrs. Cross and Mrs. Kidd," and the anguish of Phyllis Webb's "Treblinka Gas Chamber." The specific experiences may be different from our own, but we recognize similarities in the thoughts and emotions of the characters; examination and reflection may lead to clearer insights into our own lives.

Because works of literature are often demanding, they offer great rewards. Readers come to fuller awareness of themselves and others. They discover both the uniqueness and the universality of human experience; they explore both their own world and worlds they may never otherwise see. Through critical response to literature, readers question a work, examine their relationship to the author, consider the author's role, and develop an appreciation of the work, both on its own terms and as an expression of the author's vision of life. Readers may also explore a work in the context of its times, whether social, historical, or ideological.

Until fairly recently, much of the literature studied in English courses was chosen from a list of works deemed important by a majority of critics and scholars, a list referred to as the canon of English literature. Like most of these critics and scholars, most of the writers were white, male, and British or of British descent. The list usually began with the anonymous creator of the Anglo-Saxon epic "Beowulf" and ended with such earlier twentieth-century writers as T.S. Eliot, W.H. Auden, and Dylan Thomas. Because it included very few works by women, members of ethnic minorities, or writers from the British colonies, however, it could not be said to reflect the diversity of writing in English.

The past 25 years have seen a remarkable change in our society as a whole: the recognition of the equal place of all people in it, regardless of gender or ethnic origin. As a consequence, many literary scholars and critics have vigorously sought to expand the canon so that it speaks to everyone. They have demanded the inclusion of the many voices whose stories, poems, and dramas are worthy of study, both on their own merits and because of the insights they offer into a very large segment of the population of the English-speaking world. Such critics have argued that literature should certainly present universal human concerns but should also help readers understand how gender, cultural background, and social position influence responses to life. The works in this anthology reflect this expanded canon.

Reading and reflecting on works of literature reveal human similarities as well as differences. Aphra Behn's drama *The Rover* makes us aware of the position of women in the male-dominated upper-class English society of the late seventeenth century. Athol Fugard's *"MASTER HAROLD" . . . and the boys* delineates the political and racial tensions of mid-twentieth-century South Africa. The poetry of Oodgeroo of the tribe Noonuccal (Kath Walker) reveals a modern Australian aboriginal woman examining her people's past and its troubled relationships with both government and newcomers.

Readers who come actively to such works with an open, questioning mind will be able to join with their authors in making explicit the implicit. They will appreciate that an author has used language connotatively, choosing words that, in addition to their dictionary meanings, suggest a range of emotions, ideas, or associations. They will recognize the symbolic nature of actions, characters, and objects. As the German literary critic Wolfgang Iser has commented, literary texts are incomplete; they contain gaps that readers fill in or bridge to create meaning. Readers anticipate, make inferences, draw conclusions; in short, they actively work with the language of a piece of literature to arrive at meaning.

Reading for meaning is a very personal act. It is not simply a matter of paraphrasing or summarizing a story or play, of transforming poetry into prose, or of examining literary technique or metaphorical language. Each reader is unique and will, therefore, respond differently — perhaps slightly, perhaps dramatically — to a work. A Dubliner will no doubt react differently to James Joyce's "The Dead" than will a Winnipegger; a man about to retire will react differently to Shakespeare's *The Tempest* than will a young woman who has just left home for first-year college or university; a woman will react differently to Margaret Atwood's "The Resplendent Quetzal" than will a man. People who have read widely in each of these three authors or who have a well-developed knowledge of literature would likely have a different and broader interpretation of these three works than someone who seldom reads. Readers draw on personal experience, knowledge, and awareness of both specific literature and literary techniques to appreciate and interpret a literary work.

There is no one simple process for interpreting literature; different readers develop different approaches, some of which will be more useful for some works than for others. That said, interpretation of a literary work begins with the words of the text themselves. Readers question the choice and arrangement of details and ponder their significance. Such active inquiry may commence on reading the title or during a first reading. Individual interpretation will change with each rereading as readers observe more details, acquire more information about them, and perceive new relationships among them.

Readers bring their own experiences to their interpretation of literature. Basing interpretation on the words of the text, they can compare and contrast their own responses to life with those of authors and characters. Readers who have had intense family conflicts will be able to make inferences about the domestic arguments in Eudora Welty's "Why I Live at the P.O." Reciprocally, interpretation of literature can enrich experiences of life. Younger readers will not have had the experiences of the elderly women in Alice Munro's "Mrs. Cross and Mrs. Kidd," but a reading of that story may bring empathy towards the elderly people in their lives. Recalling personal experience while reading a work for the first time can assist in its interpretation.

Readers also bring considerable literary experience to their reading of literature: an understanding of the ways in which authors use language and the general patterns of the major literary genres (poetry, drama, and fiction), awareness of important themes, and, frequently, familiarity with other works by the same writer. For example, knowledge of Shakespeare's use of blank verse, his creation of patterns of imagery, and the nature of his tragic heroes will make study of *Antony and Cleopatra* more rewarding. Reflection on the myths surrounding men and women will aid in the interpretation of Adrienne Rich's "Diving into the Wreck." Readers draw on what they already know and on critical literature to expand their interpretation of a literary work.

While readers bring considerable knowledge and experience to a literary work, they must also be conscious of the creative intelligence behind the selection and arrangement of its elements. General techniques and genre characteristics, as well as cultural or other forces at play during the writing, may influence some of the selection and arrangement, but most choices arise from the author's purpose in writing the work. Although readers may not find this purpose apparent on first reading, speculation on purpose, based on attention to details and their sequence, may reveal potentially deeper meanings in a work.

Understanding is enhanced as readers acquire more relevant background information and apply it to the text. Knowledge of the actual people and literary or mythological characters mentioned in the text, of allusions to historical events and episodes in other works, and of geographical or architectural settings will clarify their function in a work. In "Fogbound in Avalon," for example, Annie, the narrator, reads a magazine article about the painter Edvard Munch. Examining that artist's works may reveal a clearer picture of Annie's state of mind.

Literary works often reflect events and conflicts in the lives of their authors; awareness of such personal details can enhance a reader's understanding of how and why authors have written as they have. For example, James Joyce, in "The Dead," William Wordsworth, in "Tintern Abbey," and Amy Tan, in "Two Kinds," drew on facts from their own lives. What is perhaps most interesting is the way in which an author has taken such raw materials of life and shaped them to meet the needs of the work.

Literary works are also products of the times in which they were written, for nearly all writers have been sensitive to and influenced by the literary, intellectual, political, and social forces around them. Ernest Hemingway's attitude towards the rejection by many of traditional moral and religious values during and after World War I helps to explain the actions of the two waiters and the elderly man in "A Clean, Well-Lighted Place." Familiarity with Margaret Atwood's musings on being a woman writer will enrich interpretations of her poetry and such short stories as "The Resplendent Quetzal."

Finally, readers should remember that just as it is impossible to understand completely another person or even oneself, so there is no such thing as a final, complete, or totally correct interpretation of a work of literature. To successive readings of a work readers bring different frames of mind, other personal experiences, new literary or other factual knowledge, and greater familiarity with the work. Thus, with each reading, fuller, more rewarding, and potentially new interpretations are possible.

To assist readers in the creation of meaning, the introductions to the three genres in this anthology — poetry, drama, and short stories — discuss technical aspects of literary works. Headnotes and footnotes provide information about authors and their works and about names, places, and obscure terms mentioned in the texts. The Glossary defines terms frequently used in discussing literature.

Critical response to literature often involves writing about poems, stories, and dramas. Through writing, readers explore the parts and the whole of a work, examine their previous interpretations and test their validity, evaluate the significance of relationships among parts of a work, and create new meanings. Of course, new interpretations may not be final ones; indeed, they may be modified several times during the writing process. Exploration of apparently contradictory information may provide fresh insights into a work. If, in creating an interpretation, the writer has based the statements on the text, has provided evidence and not ignored contradictory evidence, and has argued logically and clearly, then the interpretation is valid. For those seeking assistance in the writing of interpretive essays, the chapter entitled "Writing Essays about Literature" offers a number of suggestions and guidelines.

What are the rewards of becoming active readers and interpreters? An answer can be found by returning to this introduction's opening discussion of essential human needs. Poems, plays, and short stories are artistic and articulate responses to life that offer emotional, intellectual, and imaginative nourishment to their readers. Anthologies such as this provide exposure to literature that enhances the readers' knowledge of themselves and the world outside of themselves. Such experiences can lead to self-discovery and a life-long love of reading.

POETRY

INTRODUCTION TO POETRY

DEFINING POETRY

*N*o one can state definitely how poetry began, but we know that it existed as an oral medium long before writing developed. Perhaps it originated in primitive religious rituals; people probably used rhythmical, repetitive chants to placate angry gods, to beseech them for success in the hunt or in battle, or to honour them for food and victories received. Furthermore, the rhythm of these chants probably exercised an almost hypnotic power, arousing the appropriate feelings of awe or fear in those who listened. Even today, poetry continues to arouse and express religious feelings, for it is prominent in the sacred texts and hymns of many religions.

Poetry, however, has served many other purposes. It instilled pride in nations, celebrating in the lofty language of epics the great deeds of their heroes. Poetry also became a major feature of important public ceremonies, such as coronations, inaugurations, and victory celebrations. Poetry was not, of course, limited to official and public events. Primarily in the form of **ballads** and other songs, poetry has entertained and expressed the feelings of ordinary people, the "folk." As well, the development of a tradition of writing poetry, either instead of or in addition to reciting it, allowed poetry to serve even more functions because it was now available whenever anyone wanted to read it, and not only when a bard recited it. Poetry could, among other things, entertain and inform in printed collections, express gratitude in dedications to books, celebrate passion in love letters, and honour the memory of the dead on monuments and tombstones. In short, throughout history, whenever people have wanted to give elevated verbal expression to deeds or ideas, whenever they have wanted to make memorable their thoughts, whenever they have wanted to convey their feelings, they have turned to poetry.

Poetry was once a major form of entertainment, providing stories, jokes, descriptions, and reflections. Novels, movies, and television have now replaced many of its storytelling functions, but poetry is everywhere in the modern world. Parents continue to recite it to their children, who delight in the rollicking metres of nursery rhymes. Teenagers and adults who listen to music often listen to poetry, for it exists in the lyrics of many popular songs. They also meet poetry in commercials on television and radio, for advertisers rely on its ability to linger in the memory when they devise slogans to sell products. People still mark special occasions with it, expressing their feelings through greeting-card verse that ranges in mood from the sentimental to the humorously bawdy. Of course, numerous magazines still include poetry, and book publishers prominently display it in their catalogues. What is more, in an age that often demands elaborate spectacles in its public entertainments, poetry readings enjoy remarkable popularity.

Defining poetry, however, is like wrestling with Proteus: just when we think we have pinned it into submission, it changes shape, like the ancient Greek god, and eludes us. Poetry, that is, is so varied in form and content that comprehensive definitions always seem inadequate. Nevertheless, some of the most accomplished poets have tried to identify the essence of their art. Many have emphasized the emotional and intellectual depth of poetry. William Wordsworth said that "poetry is the spontaneous overflow of powerful feelings" and that "poetry is the breath and finer spirit of all knowledge. . . . " Emily Dickinson emphasized emotional response: "If I read a book and it makes my whole body so cold no fire can ever warm me I know that is poetry. If I feel physically as if the top of my head were taken off, I know that is poetry." Percy Bysshe Shelley defined poetry as "the record of the best and happiest moments of the happiest and best minds." Similarly, Matthew Arnold declared: "Poetry is simply the most beautiful, impressive and wisely effective mode of saying things, and hence its importance." Twentieth-century poets have given their own cast to such ideas. Wallace Stevens stressed the metaphysical: "Poetry is a search for the inexplicable." Adrienne Rich has emphasized poetry's power, its ability to condense and communicate significant meaning: "Poetry is above all a concentration of the *power* of language, which is the power of our ultimate relationship to everything in the universe. It is as if forces we can lay claim to in no other way, become present to us in sensuous form." Robert Frost was more colourful: "Poetry is a way of taking life by the throat." The Canadian poet Irving Layton has described it as a way of bridging mundane reality and the world of imagination, a process that creates a separate world: "Mercifully, all poetry, in the final analysis, is about poetry itself; creating through its myriad forms a world in which the elements of reality are sundered; are, as it were, preserved for a time in suspension."

Instead of defining poetry through its connections to feelings, ideas, and actions, however, some writers have tried to look at the aesthetic and technical elements of the craft. Edgar Allan Poe called poetry "*the Rhythmical Creation of Beauty.*" Samuel Taylor Coleridge avoided both the emphasis on refined feelings or ideas and the insistence on beauty when he stressed verbal craftsmanship in this equation:"poetry = the best words in their best order." Throughout the twentieth century, writers have returned to this concept of craftsmanship in their definitions. Dylan Thomas, for instance, described the task of creating poetry as "constructing a formally watertight compartment of words." Frost defined poetry even more simply as "a performance in words." Wallace Stevens probably went as far as possible in dissociating the poet's task from that described in definitions stressing ethical thought, declaring: "Poetry is poetry, and one's objective as a poet is to achieve poetry precisely as one's objective in music is to achieve music."

The precise nature of the poetic achievement is, as these disparate definitions suggest, very much open to debate. Poetry does not seem to depend upon content: poems may be about beauty or ugliness, refined feelings or base ones, matters of perpetual importance or of transient interest. Neither is any single technical feature, such as rhyme, rhythm, or division into lines with ragged right margins, the determinant: it is possible for a good poem to exhibit none of these features. Probably the best we can do is to describe poetry as a concentrated form of literary expression. Poetry is evocative, often rhythmical, language that describes or comments on ideas and experiences and that evokes feelings about them. In poetry the manner of expression is as important as the matter.

POETRY AND LITERARY READING

Because each word in a poem is charged with meaning and feeling to a degree rarely possible in prose, reading poetry may require patience. One reading is simply not sufficient to allow readers to engage with the text, to sense all of its intellectual, emotional, and aesthetic resources. Literary reading demands rereading. As the general Introduction makes clear, no single reading procedure is adequate in all circumstances. In fact, theorists do not agree on how poems work and how they should be read. Competing theories emphasize different elements of the relationships between poet, reader, and poem. Nevertheless, readers who are aware of the various biographical, historical, and theoretical contexts may find their reading of a poem more meaningful and, therefore, more enjoyable.

Understanding biographical and cultural contexts may at first seem to be a separate area of study, but these contexts can be vital in constructing meaning. Many critics and theorists, that is, insist that poems do not exist in isolation from the poets who wrote them or apart from the societies in which the poets lived. Personal feelings and experiences shape what poets write and how they write. In turn, their feelings and experiences, if not directly shaped by cultural situations, have often been influenced by the social and moral assumptions of their societies. No one argues that readers must know everything about a poet's life to enjoy a poem. Many critics do suggest, however, that an understanding of a poet's life and artistic ideas may provide information that will help readers to understand the mind and verbal habits of the poet and thus better to construct meaning when reading poetry. The poet's gender and attitudes to gender, for example, may be crucial. The American poet Adrienne Rich says, "I had been taught that poetry should be 'universal,' which meant of course, non-female." In her own poems, therefore, she seeks to express her feelings as a female whose views and experiences may be distinct from those previously celebrated as universal.

Similarly, some critics claim that an understanding of cultural history is sometimes essential. First, literary conventions and habits of expression change from generation to generation; understanding these may help in the understanding of works written during an earlier period. Second, what people of any age write reflects their connection to the dominant culture of their time. Literature may thus openly express attitudes officially sanctioned by a given society. This is the belief of Thomas Carlyle, who saw poetry as a mirror of the spirit of an age: "The history of a nation's poetry is the essence of its history, political, scientific, religious." Of course, as Marxist and other theorists concerned with class and economic factors note, poetry may also seek, often covertly, to subvert the dominant culture. In developing meaning, the contemporary reader may thus require an understanding of the sometimes latent assumptions within a poem.

Many other theorists downplay the significance of such contexts. For some of these, poetry is an artifact, like a Greek vase, that exists separate from the reader and must be understood on its own terms. For others, poetry is more of a tool kit or an Erector set that the reader plays with, constructing and reconstructing meaning. One group argues for the realization of a final meaning inherent in the work; the other argues that no single meaning can be inherent in the work and, instead, stresses the process of reading rather than the results. The more traditional theorists point out that the word *poetry* comes from a Greek root meaning "thing made" and that a poet is a "maker." They see poems as carefully constructed, unified artifacts, and they argue that the reader needs to note the contribution of all of the parts of a work to discover its inherent meaning. For example, some of these theorists argue that a poem's basic structure is a set of binary oppositions, such as life and death or virtue and sin, and that meaning comes when the poem "privileges," or gives approval to, one set of these oppositions. They believe that the reader's task in understanding a poem is to locate the structure of binary oppositions. Those who look at poetry more as the tool kit that the reader uses take differing approaches. Some have extended this notion of binary oppositions, arguing that every literary work actually contains not only oppositions but also contradictions and that, therefore, no poem can have a determinate meaning. They contend that a work "deconstructs" itself, saying two contradictory things at once. Finally, another group of theorists concentrates on the reader's involvement with poems, arguing that the work itself contains no meaning: a poem is simply a series of squiggles on the page until the reader engages with the text and actively creates meaning from it. The reader not only "decodes" individual words — deciding, for example, that the letters *d-o-g* refer to a particular kind of animal — but also, because of previous personal and literary experiences, associates particular ideas and attitudes with each word decoded: when faced with the word *dog*, some readers will envision a slavering attack beast, whereas others will envision a friendly lapdog. Although many poems use what Wolfgang Iser calls "response-inviting structures," devices that encourage readers to read in particular ways, these devices cannot possibly limit readers to one single response. Because each person's experiences and associations are different, each will read a given poem differently.

Although the competition between rival theories may suggest to some readers that a poem means anything a given reader thinks it means, all theories imply that literary understanding begins with close attention to words. Many theories stress that poetry is a playful use of language, even in poems about serious matters, and that a playful attitude in reading, an attitude that brings all of a person's associations and experiences to bear on each word, makes it easier to discover or construct meaning.

In truth, few readers are concerned about competing theories when first reading a poem; instead, most readers ordinarily want to construct at least a provisional meaning as soon as possible. Such readers may find some guidelines useful as the basis for beginning a significant reading of a work.

Because poetry is an art that depends upon achieving the maximum effect from each word, readers need to understand both the **denotations**, or dictionary meanings of words, and the **connotations**, or implications, of these words. Some words, that is, carry extra meaning: they have negative or positive associations that may influence interpretation. We may think positively about an adult who is *childlike*, but negatively about one who is *childish*. We may also have different attitudes about speakers who use colloquial language and speakers who consistently use elaborate, formal language. Sensitivity to words and their nuances is an important step in meaningful reading.

Traditionally, readers have also found useful a number of basic questions about the content and form of a poem. The first questions focus on the speaker in the poem: Who is the speaker? To whom is he or she speaking? What are the circumstances? These questions may not be very important in a poem like Tennyson's "The Eagle," but they are crucial considerations in dramatic monologues like Browning's "The Bishop Orders His Tomb at Saint Praxed's Church" and Louise Bennett's "Colonization in Reverse," in which an understanding of the speaker's character and the context in which he or she is speaking is necessary to make the poem meaningful. Another question concerns the arrangement of content: How is the poem organized to develop its ideas? The order in which details are presented can influence our attitudes towards them and our understanding of the development of major ideas within the poem. In Browning's "My Last Duchess," the duke's description of the fate of his last wife precedes his discussion of arrangements for a new bride, making him seem especially arrogant, cynical, and brutal. In Sonnet 73, Shakespeare emphasizes both the narrator's age and the brevity of time by arranging images that imply death in a sequence that moves from larger to smaller measures of time: he moves from a season, to a day, to the moment when a fire is dying out.

Readers may also find it useful to ask questions about the technical elements of a poem: How do techniques or elements such as rhythm, sound devices, images, and diction influence our understanding? The purpose of examining techniques is not to catalogue them but to understand their role in shaping our ideas and feelings within the poem as a whole. For example, readers who notice the difference in rhythm in the first and final sections of Marvell's "To His Coy Mistress" can determine how it influences their understanding of the narrator's attitudes towards traditional ideals of court-ship and his own growing sense of urgency. Finally, readers often find it useful to consider literary contexts: How does this poem compare to other poems, especially those with similar forms, those from the same period, and those about similar subjects? An understanding of conventions of form or subject matter and of literary "schools" or literary periods enables readers to place the work in a literary and historical context that can be helpful in understanding the poem. Shakespeare's Sonnet 130, "My mistress' eyes are nothing like the sun," for instance, is far more meaningful to readers who understand something of the Petrarchan tradition of love sonnets and have read some English love sonnets by such poets as Wyatt and Surrey.

FIGURATIVE LANGUAGE (1):
IMAGERY, SIMILE, METAPHOR, CONCEIT

Poetry is a sensual medium. Sound, discussed later, and imagery, the subject of this section, appeal to the senses, stimulating an imaginative body of impressions, feelings, and ideas. These may be new, or they may be familiar, but the sensory appeals of poetry give them an immediacy that directly involves readers.

At its most basic level, **imagery** is language that creates images, or pic-tures, in the imagination. Some poems, like "The Red Wheelbarrow," by William Carlos Williams, rely almost exclusively on verbal pictures. Most poems, however, use imagery to develop statements about feelings and ideas. The opening section of Wordsworth's "Lines Composed a Few Miles above Tintern Abbey" creates a picture of the scene, describing such things as "These hedgerows, hardly hedgerows, / Little lines of sportive wood run wild. . . . " In this way, the narrator impresses on readers the power the set-ting holds over him as a scene of "beauteous forms." Although the roots of the word suggest a visual element, imagery is not exclusively visual; it fre-quently makes appeals to touch, taste, and sound. In the final stanza of "To Autumn," for example, Keats describes the "music" of autumn, with such sound images as "Then in a wailful choir the small gnats mourn / Among the river sallows. . . . " In "Dover Beach," Arnold uses sound imagery to convey "The eternal note of sadness": he describes "the grating roar / Of pebbles" flung back and forth by the waves.

Images, like all appeals to the senses, can evoke emotional reactions, but they also can be a medium of intellectual discourse. In "Eurocentric," for example, Dionne Brand criticizes the political and cultural ethnocentrism of North Americans through a catalogue of images. By juxtaposing atrocities, such as "blacks lynched in the american way," and elements of life in third-world countries, such as "rain, on a beach in the caribbean," she attacks the failure of North Americans to see the world as it really is. Images most frequently give concrete form to ideas and feelings, however, by compelling readers to understand one idea in terms of another. This linking of objects or ideas is the basis of most figurative language, language that goes beyond the literal denotation of the words by imaginatively extending their meaning.

The most common figures of speech are similes and metaphors. Both tend to give concrete form to abstract ideas or to make the unfamiliar clearer and more forceful by linking it to something familiar. **Simile** expresses similarity between things and always uses such linking terms as *like, as, than,* or *as if.* Keats, in "On First Looking into Chapman's Homer," conveys the magnitude of his feelings of discovery with a simile that connects his reactions upon reading a book to a rarer but more public experience: "Then felt I like some watcher of the skies / When a new planet swims into his ken." In the opening simile of T.S. Eliot's "The Love Song of J. Alfred Prufrock," the narrator provides a clue to his own emotional numbness by saying that "the evening is spread out against the sky / Like a patient etherized upon a table." P.K. Page does much the same thing when she describes the secretaries in "The Stenographers" as being "taut as net curtains / stretched upon frames." **Metaphor** compares by equating things. In Shakespeare's Sonnet 73, the metaphor in which the boughs become "Bare ruined choirs" creates a sense of collapse and destruction because it implicitly equates the trees in late autumn and abandoned, ruined churches. In "The Flea," John Donne's narrator uses metaphor as part of his strategy of seduction, aggrandizing the flea: "This flea is you and I, and this / Our marriage bed and marriage temple is." In "The Ache of Marriage," Denise Levertov uses a far less romantic comparison to show the consuming power of that ache within: "It is leviathan."

Not every comparison is as brief as those just discussed. More elaborate and extended comparisons, whether similes or metaphors, are called **conceits**. The **Petrarchan conceit**, developed by those who followed the example of the Italian Petrarch, the poet who popularized the sonnet form, uses rather conventional extended comparisons, as in Wyatt's "My galley . . . ," which compares the lover to a ship at sea, or Surrey's "Love that doth reign . . . ," which personifies love as a military leader. More original and startling comparisons are called **metaphysical conceits** because they were developed by the so-called **metaphysical poets** of the seventeenth century, who linked physical with metaphysical or spiritual elements in their images. John Donne's "Valediction: Forbidding Mourning" contains the most famous of these, his comparison of separated lovers to "stiff twin compasses."

FIGURATIVE LANGUAGE (2):
PERSONIFICATION, APOSTROPHE, METONYMY,
SYNECDOCHE, SYMBOL, MOTIF

Other figurative devices also link ideas. **Personification** gives human qualities to abstractions or to things that do not possess them. Thus, William Wordsworth, in "The world is too much with us," suggests the sensuousness of nature through personification: "The Sea that bares her bosom to the moon." In Sonnet 7, on the other hand, Milton makes an abstraction concrete: his personification, "Time, the subtle thief of youth," emphasizes the narrator's feelings that he is a victim who has unwittingly been robbed of his youth. In one of his odes, John Keats personifies an object, an ancient Greek urn, as a "sylvan historian," suggesting that it can tell much about life. Personification often develops through **apostrophe**, a direct address to a thing or abstraction, as in Shelley's "O wild West Wind, thou breath of Autumn's being" or Donne's "Death, be not proud." Apostrophe is not always part of personification because the device also includes direct addresses to an absent or dead person, as in Wordsworth's "Milton! thou shouldst be living at this hour." In either case, it gives immediacy and concreteness to people, events, and ideas.

Two other linking devices are frequently used to condense complex experiences into images. **Metonymy**, or "substitute naming," uses an associated idea to name something. In "London, 1802," for example, Wordsworth talks of "altar, sword, and pen," instead of the clergy, soldiers, and authors, in order to suggest concretely both the people and the function of those people. A related device is **synecdoche**, in which a part stands for the whole, or the whole stands for the part. It is most evident in such expressions as "All hands on deck!" in which *hands* stands for *sailors*, and in the prayer for "daily bread," in which *bread* stands for all food. Shakespeare uses it in the opening line of Sonnet 29, "When, in disgrace with fortune and men's eyes," in which *eyes* stands for humanity's social and moral judgements. In Eliot's "Prufrock," synecdoche, evident in the naming of a part instead of the whole crab or lobster, suggests the narrator's lack of a fully developed identity: "I should have been a pair of ragged claws / Scuttling across the floors of silent seas." Synecdoche is most shockingly apparent, however, in the vision of death in Marvell's "To His Coy Mistress," which reduces the woman's morality to sexual organs: " . . . then worms shall try / That long preserved virginity, / And your quaint honour turn to dust."

The linking device that many readers find most difficult to grasp is **symbolism**. *Symbol* comes from the Greek "to throw together." A symbol throws together objects, people, or actions and a meaning that is not necessarily inherent in them. Symbols fall into two major categories, conventional symbols and contextual symbols. **Conventional symbols** are those that traditionally carry a particular meaning. Sometimes, the symbol is conventional only within a given culture. A cross, for example, means something quite different to Christians in North America than to Buddhists in China. The rose, to cite another example, traditionally suggests love or beauty in Western culture. Such conventional symbols may be the basis of relatively simple ideas: "Gather ye rosebuds while ye may," the opening line of Herrick's "To the Virgins, To Make Much of Time," develops the *carpe diem* ("seize the day") idea of living for the moment because, like the rose, youth and beauty fade. They may also develop more complex and even ambiguous ideas, as in William Blake's "The Sick Rose," in which the rose suggests ideas of love but leaves open to speculation the exact nature of that love and of the worm that destroys it. Not all conventional symbols are limited to a specific culture. Some seem to be universal, having appeared so frequently and for such a long time in the literatures of various cultures that their meanings seem to be natural. These are known as **archetypes**. One such archetype is the description of the sun's movement from sunrise to sunset to symbolize aging in human beings. This archetype appears in such different works as Herrick's "To the Virgins, To Make Much of Time," where it reinforces the idea that youth must live for the moment, and Earle Birney's "Bushed," where it suggests the rapidly approaching death of the trapper.

Readers acquire understanding of conventional symbols by familiarity with a large number of works using them. In Frost's "Stopping by Woods on a Snowy Evening," for example, repetition of the last line, "And miles to go before I sleep," puts such additional stress on both *miles* and *sleep* that these words imply more than they literally say. Readers familiar with other poems that use either a journey or sleep as a symbol can see this poem as using the conventional archetypal symbol of a journey towards death, an additional implication that coexists with its surface meaning of a journey on a winter's night.

Contextual symbols, however, become symbolic only within the context of a given work; they may not have the same symbolic meaning, or even any symbolic meaning, in different work. For example, the tiger symbolizes, among other things, fierceness and destructiveness in Blake's "The Tyger," but it symbolizes the repressed dreams of a conventional woman in Adrienne Rich's "Aunt Jennifer's Tigers." Sometimes the accumulation of details creates a contextual symbol, as it does in Shelley's "Ozymandias," in which the ruined statue of the pharaoh gradually becomes a general symbol of mutability and the vanity of human desires. Such contextual symbols are not always obvious: during an initial reading, they may seem to be simply a part of the concrete description or narrative movement of the poem. This is why rereading is important. With each rereading, a poem becomes more familiar, and its details, patterns, and emphases — the elements that create contextual symbols — become more apparent.

With each rereading, as well, the links to other poems and the connecting links within the poem itself become more apparent. Any poem using an archetype, for example, is using an element that occurs in many works.

Understanding the archetype in one poem thus helps in understanding others. Archetypes and symbols are not the only recurring elements, of course. Images, characters, objects, settings, situations, or themes may recur in many works; these recurring elements are called **motifs**. The *carpe diem* theme, for example, is a thematic motif, whether or not it is expressed by the archetype of the setting sun. Elements can also be repeated to link the parts of an individual work. Linda Hogan's "The Sand Roses," for example, contains numerous references to stones and roses. Such recurring elements within an individual work, whether recurring words, phrases, images, situations, or themes, are also sometimes called motifs, although they are more generally called **leitmotifs**. Readers who note such recurring devices will be able to respond more completely to the poem, to link together its various parts, to connect the poem to other works and to situations outside the poem itself, and to construct more meaning.

IRONY, PARADOX, OXYMORON

Simile, metaphor, symbol, and other devices of figurative language discussed above link images to feelings and ideas, but they do not always forge their links in the way that we may at first expect. Sometimes another device, irony, twists the connections. **Irony** is a discrepancy between appearance and reality, expectation and result, or surface meaning and implied meaning. Traditionally, critics have described three major kinds of irony: dramatic irony, situational irony, and verbal irony. Dramatic irony, a device found more frequently in drama and fiction than in poetry, is the discrepancy between what a character says or does and what the reader knows to be the truth of the situation. Situational irony, which is also inherent in dramatic irony, presents a situation in which the result is the reverse of what a character or speaker expected. Verbal irony reverses the denotation of words so that a given statement actually means the opposite of what it says literally, as when we call "graceful" someone who has just tripped.

Whatever its form, irony is a device that is often integral to the **theme**, the central idea developed by a poem. In "Ozymandias," for example, both verbal irony, the boast that Ozymandias makes about his greatness, and situational irony, the image of a shattered statue upon whose base the boastful words are carved, reverse the pharaoh's intention: instead of celebrating glorious, lasting achievements, both the words and the statue make a moving statement about mutability and the impermanence of human achievement. Similarly, in Margaret Atwood's "Progressive Insanities of a Pioneer," the language of measurement and geometry, normally a sign of logic and control, reverses itself to reveal the mad egocentricity of the pioneer. Unable to recognize nature for what it is, he tries to impose his vision on it and stands "a point / on a sheet of green paper / proclaiming himself the centre." His failure of vision eventually leads to his defeat by the very forces he sought to dominate. Irony can also be a powerful device for political comment and protest. Wilfred Owen deliberately uses the juxtaposition of the title phrase in "*Dulce et Decorum Est*" and the scene of a soldier dying in a gas attack to reverse the wartime propaganda that called it glorious for the young to die for their country.

Two other devices found frequently in poetry depend upon an unusual link of expression and idea. **Paradox** is a statement that seems contradictory on the surface but contains a truth on deeper examination. Among the most famous of paradoxes is Wordsworth's statement that "The Child is father of the Man," a claim that is biologically absurd but psychologically profound: the statement concisely expresses the idea that the experiences of childhood shape adult lives. Paradox often serves to convey complex spiritual and psychological truths, as in Donne's Holy Sonnet XIV ("Batter my heart"), which concludes with a notable and shocking set of paradoxes about the narrator's relationship with God:

> *Take me to you, imprison me, for I*
> *Except you enthral me, never shall be free,*
> *Nor ever chaste, except you ravish me.*

A related device is **oxymoron**, a word whose Greek roots imply "sharp stupidity" or "wise foolishness." Oxymoron contains a contradiction: it links opposites in the surface expression in order to defamiliarize or make unusual the connections we expect. Thus, Milton describes hell as having "darkness visible" and Emily Dickinson, in "There's a certain Slant of light," speaks of "Heavenly Hurt."

LINE LENGTH, METRE, AND RHYTHM

Two things immediately distinguish poetry from prose: the look upon the page and the sound when read aloud. The distinctive look of most poetry comes from its organization into lines. In most English poems written before the twentieth century, the line lengths were dependent upon **metre**. English, with its stressed syllables (indicated by ∕) and unstressed syllables (indicated by ⌣), naturally creates rhythm, the flow of rising and falling sounds, but poetry organizes rhythm, as prose and common speech do not. Metre, a word derived from the Greek "to measure," measures the organization of repeated stressed and unstressed syllables, giving names to the rhythmic patterns within a poem.

At various times and in various places, different systems of measurement have been used. French poetry, for example, counts only syllables. The same is true of the Japanese haiku, a form sometimes adopted by writers in English: it contains three lines of five, seven, and five syllables, respectively. Anglo-Saxon, or Old English, poetry, on the other hand, is accentual: it measures only the stresses in a given line and does not count the unstressed syllables. Furthermore, it organizes the stresses by placing two in each half, or hemistich, of a line, by having three stresses share an **alliterative** sound, and by separating each half with a **caesura**, or pause. A few poets have tried to use this form with modern English. In "Anglosaxon Street," for example, Earle Birney graphically indicates the hemistichs by using a wide space for each caesura:

Dáwn drízzle ended *dámpness steáms from*

blótching bríck and *blánk plásterwaste*

    The most common system for measuring poetry in modern English, however, considers both the **accents** and the number of syllables in a line. The base of the system is the **foot**, a unit consisting of one or more syllables, usually with one stressed. Repetition of the pattern of stressed and unstressed syllables found within a given foot creates a regular **rhythm**, and each of the various regular rhythms has a name based on the pattern within the foot and the number of feet composing the line. Figure 1 lists the names and shows the patterns of the metrical feet. The dominant rhythm in a poem will probably be one of the first four patterns: the others are normally variations within a regular rhythm. Figure 2 names the various line lengths according to the number of feet in each. A process called **scansion** indicates graphically the metre of a poem. This process requires the marking of all stressed and unstressed syllables and the clear division of feet from each other by means of a vertical line. Scansion graphically shows, for example, that the opening line of Shakespeare's Sonnet 73 is iambic pentameter, a pattern formed from five iambic feet:

That tíme | of yéar | thou máyst | in mé | behóld

Figure 1. *The Metrical Feet*

NOUN	ADJECTIVE	PATTERN	EXAMPLE
iamb	iambic	˘ /	remote
trochee	trochaic	/ ˘	joker
anapest	anapestic	˘ ˘ /	interrupt
dactyl	dactylic	/ ˘ ˘	heavenly
spondee	spondiac	/ /	heartbreak
pyrrhic	pyrrhic	˘ ˘	in the
amphibrach	amphibrachic	˘ / ˘	soprano
amphimacer (or cretic)	amphimacric	/ ˘ /	first and last

Figure 2. *Line Lengths*

NUMBER OF FEET IN LINE	NAME OF LINE LENGTH
1	monometer
2	dimeter
3	trimeter
4	tetrameter
5	pentameter
6	hexameter
7	heptameter
8	octameter

RHYTHMIC VARIATION

Poets do not always write according to strict metre. They frequently introduce variations within their lines not only to avoid the potential monotony of a regular metre but also to emphasize particular words or ideas. For example, in the last line of Sonnet 73, Shakespeare substitutes a spondee for the iamb in the final foot:

> To love | that well | which thou | must leave | ere long

This substitution creates three stressed syllables in a row. Generally, a sequence of stressed syllables slows the movement of a line, whereas a sequence of unaccented syllables quickens the flow. Here, the rhythmic flow slows down, emphasizing these last words, which summarize the idea of the brief time remaining to the narrator.

While it is common to vary rhythm within lines by using metrical feet that deviate from the dominant pattern and by adding extra feet or extra syllables to a line, poets can affect the flow of their lines in other ways. One is by judicious use of the caesura, or pause (indicated in scansion by two vertical lines). Because the most emphatic positions in any unit of expression (line, phrase, sentence, paragraph) are first, at the end, and second, the beginning, the caesura creates emphasis by increasing the number of these positions. In Tennyson's "Ulysses," for example, the caesura effectively halts the flow of the lines to emphasize tedium:

> How dull | it is | to pause, || to make | an end,
>
> To rust | unburn|ished, || not | to shine | in use!

In the first line, "pause" immediately precedes a pause, and "end" comes at the end of the line, the meaning of both words thus being effectively reinforced by their position. In the second line, the caesura comes in the middle of a foot, disrupting the regular flow and creating an oral counterpoint to it. Strictly speaking, that is, metre expresses the division into feet according to the stresses of syllables, and this line is a perfectly regular iambic line. Dramatic reading of it, however, provides a different sense of how the line flows. If we consider the caesura as creating a pause that divides this line into two units, we would scan this line for reading by marking it as consisting of an iamb, amphibrach, amphimacer, and iamb:

> To rust | unburnished, ‖

> not to shine | in use!

The dramatic, interpretive rhythm exists simultaneously with the regular metre. The interpretive rhythm insists on a pause, accentuating the contrast between the sedentary state and the active one that follows; the conventional metre pulls the reader forward in expectation of completing the iambic pattern. Interpretive rhythm could also make the contrast between the two parts of the line even more emphatic: when "not to shine" is read as an anapest, the two unaccented syllables quicken the pace, indicating joy, and place an even more meaningful and emphatic stress on *shine*.

In the lines just quoted, Tennyson uses **end-stopped lines**, lines that terminate with a natural pause. Such lines are usually indicated by punctuation, which reinforces this pause. Poets often vary the flow of their lines by using run-on lines, or **enjambment** (from the French for "striding over"). Tennyson uses enjambment throughout "Ulysses":

> I can|not rest | from trav|el; ‖ I | will drink

> Life to | the lees.

Because of the caesura in the middle of a foot in the first line and the shift to trochee in the first foot of the second line, the key words *I, drink, Life,* and *lees* are all accented and are all visually, grammatically, or by strict measure in positions of emphasis, at the beginning or end of a unit. The enjambment, however, creates a variation in the rhythmic flow, linking the last part of the first line to the first part of the second line: although the iambic pentameter pattern is completed with *drink*, the reader cannot pause at the end of the line because the idea is incomplete; instead, the reader must continue until the completion of the idea in the middle of the second line.

BEYOND SCANSION: FREE VERSE AND SHAPED VERSE

Not every poem displays a dominant rhythm that can be scanned like those in the preceding examples. Some poems are written in **free verse** or *vers* *libre*, terms popularized by Ezra Pound, among others. Pound compared the conventional patterns of regularly repeated metrical feet to the monotonous beat of a metronome. He argued that the lines of a poem should be free from the conventional system, that, instead, lines should follow the more natural patterns evident in spoken language and music. (Incidentally, free verse should not be confused with **blank verse**, a form popular in Elizabethan England, which usually means an unrhymed line of iambic pentameter.) Other writers, however, may organize lines by meaning. In "The Country North of Belleville," for example, Al Purdy intensifies the irony of defeat by placing each stage of the farmers' recognition of futility in a separate line:

> *without grandeur or self deception in*
> > *noble struggle*
> *of being a fool —*

Margaret Atwood is even subtler in her description of the man standing in a field in "Progressive Insanities of a Pioneer":

> *with no walls, no borders*
> *anywhere; the sky no height*
> *above him, totally un-*
> *enclosed*

She divides the lines to place words suggesting measurement and logical calculation in emphatic positions. Furthermore, she breaks up the word "unenclosed" to emphasize the ironic discrepancy between the pioneer's perception that he is "enclosed," which leads him to shout insanely that he wants out, and the reader's understanding that nothing actually encloses him.

Line length may also graphically reflect meaning. George Herbert's "Altar" arranges lines to form a picture that represents the central idea of the poem. Lines in such shaped verse convey meaning, but they must be seen on the page to be fully appreciated. Much the same is true of concrete poetry, a form popular in the 1960s and early 1970s. In some concrete poems, however, the lines forming the picture may be letters or other typographical elements that can have no meaning on their own. Meaning exists entirely in the picture as a whole.

RHYME AND STANZA FORM

Many poems, especially those written before the twentieth century, link lines by more than subject matter and rhythm: they use **rhyme**, the repetition of accented vowels and all syllables following the accented vowel. **Single rhymes**, or **masculine rhymes**, repeat only the last syllable of words: *know, go; delight, fight*. **Double rhymes**, also called **feminine rhymes** or **trochaic rhymes**, repeat identical sounds in both an accented syllable and the following unaccented syllable: *kissing, missing; seasons, reasons*. **Triple rhymes**, or **dactylic rhymes**, also occur: *tenderly, slenderly; scornfully, mournfully*. Rhymes most frequently occur as **end rhymes**, in which the rhyming words are at the end of lines. **Internal rhymes** operate within lines, as in this example from "The Rime of the Ancient Mariner": "And every *day*, for food or *play*."

All the examples so far have been **exact rhymes** or **true rhymes**. In some cases, poets use **near rhyme** (also known as **slant, off, imperfect**, or **oblique** rhyme), a rhyme that approximates rather than exactly repeats a sound: *bridge, hedge; still, wheel; tucker, supper*. Slant rhyme usually depends on similarity of the final consonant, but it can include such imperfect rhymes as *flew* and *boot*, which rhyme the vowel but not the consonant. Another form is **eye rhyme**, or **sight rhyme**, in which words spelled similarly but pronounced differently are treated as rhymes. In some cases, as with Shakespeare's rhyming of *proved* and *loved*, the words may have been pronounced similarly at the time the poem was written. In other cases, such as Coleridge's rhyming of *prow* and *blow* in "The Rime of the Ancient Mariner," the rhymes are purely visual.

Rhyme can be a mnemonic device, something that helps poets, listeners, and readers to remember a work, but it is also an important structural device that helps to group lines into meaningful sections. The normal grouping of lines is called the **stanza**. Figure 3 provides the general names for stanzas according to the number of lines they contain. Stanzas are infinitely variable, but a number of poetic forms specify the precise number of lines the stanza can contain and the pattern of rhymes, known as the rhyme scheme, that those lines must follow.

Figure 3. *Names of Stanzas and Line Groupings*

NUMBER OF LINES	NAME
2	couplet
3	tercet
	(triplet when all three lines rhyme together)
4	quatrain
5	quintet
6	sestet
7	septet
8	octave

Figure 4 names and describes the most notable of these fixed forms. We describe rhyme schemes by using a separate letter for each end rhyme. Thus, we indicate a stanza in which the first and fourth lines and the second and third lines rhyme by the formula *a b b a*. Sometimes, however, we must resort to a more complex description because line lengths vary. In these cases, we describe a stanza by indicating its predominant rhythm and by noting with each letter of the rhyme scheme the number of feet in that line. Consider the opening stanza of "Sir Patrick Spens," which we could describe as predominantly iambic with a rhyme scheme of *4a, 3b, 4c, 3b*:

The king | sits in | Dunferm | line town	*a* (4 feet)
Drinking | the blude- | red wine;	*b* (3 feet)
"O whare | will I get | a skee | ly skipper	*c* (4 feet)
To sail | this new ship | o' mine?"	*b* (3 feet)

This pattern is known as ballad measure; many other patterns also have names, and knowing these can simplify the description.

Stanzas depend upon a few basic patterns in their rhymes. **Couplets** are pairs of rhyming lines: *a a b b*. Heroic couplets are in iambic pentameter. If the idea expressed by the couplet is completed within the compass of the two lines, the couplet is a **closed couplet**. **Triplets** or **tercets** consist of three lines, rhymed or unrhymed. A **quatrain** is any group of four lines, rhymed or unrhymed; it is the most common form in English poetry. A **sestet** is a unit of six lines, whereas an **octave** is one of eight lines.

These last three — the quatrain, the sestet, and the octave — are important terms in describing one of the most pervasive and highly controlled of poetic forms, the **sonnet**. The **Italian** or **Petrarchan sonnet** is a fourteen-line iambic pentameter form usually rhyming *abba abba cdecde* (but the last six lines have many variations in rhyme scheme). The Italian sonnet develops an idea in the octave, and then uses a **volta**, or turn (often signalled by such words as "yet" or "but"), before concluding that idea in the sestet. The **English** or **Shakespearean sonnet** is an iambic pentameter poem rhyming *abab cdcd efef gg*. It consists of three quatrains and a heroic couplet. Its turn of thought occurs in the couplet and must be more compressed and concentrated than that in an Italian sonnet. A Spenserian sonnet is similar, except that it rhymes *abab bcbc cdcd ee*. A fourth variation is the **Miltonic sonnet**. It follows the Italian form, but it does not pause after the octave.

Some stanzaic forms can be very complicated, requiring the poet to possess exceptional skill in order both to meet the technical requirements of the form and to produce a work that is moving or interesting. For example, Dylan Thomas's "Do Not Go Gentle into That Good Night" and Theodore Roethke's "The Waking" are built on a medieval French form called the **villanelle**: this nineteen-line form requires five tercets and one quatrain, contains only two rhymes, and uses two refrains that must appear in a specified order.

Line length, rhythm, rhyme, and stanzaic form contribute to the development of thought and feeling. Whether the work is in free verse or follows a restrictive form like that of the villanelle, these elements emphasize

Figure 4. *Notable Fixed and Complex Forms*

NUMBER OF LINES IN POEM OR STANZA	NAME AND DESCRIPTION
3	TERZA RIMA: tercets of iambic pentameter with linked rhymes (*aba bcb cdc* . . .)
4	COMMON MEASURE: a quatrain in iambic metre, with the first and third lines having four iambic feet and the second and fourth having three iambic feet (*abcb*)
	BALLAD STANZA: similar to common measure but the four lines can be in any metre, with four metrical feet in the first and third and three in the second and fourth lines (*abcb*)
6	ITALIAN SESTET: six lines of iambic pentameter (*abcabc*)
	SICILIAN SESTET: six lines of iambic pentameter (*ababab*)
	HEROIC SESTET: six lines of iambic pentameter (*ababcc*)
7	RIME ROYAL: seven lines of iambic pentameter (*ababbcc*)
8	OTTAVA RIMA: eight lines of iambic pentameter (*abababcc*)
	ITALIAN OCTAVE: eight lines of iambic pentameter (*abbaabba*)
	SICILIAN OCTAVE: eight lines of iambic pentameter (*abababab*)
9	SPENSERIAN STANZA: nine lines rhyming *ababbcbcc* with the first eight in iambic pentameter and the last in iambic hexameter (which is called an Alexandrine)
10	ENGLISH (KEATSIAN) ODE: Three ten-line iambic pentameter stanzas, each with the same rhyme scheme (*ababcdecde*)
14	SONNET: fourteen iambic pentameter lines
	ENGLISH (SHAKESPEAREAN) SONNET: (*abab cdcd efef gg*)
	SPENSERIAN SONNET (*abab bcbc cdcd ee*)
	PETRARCHAN (ITALIAN) SONNET (*abba abba cde cde* or *abba abba cdcdcd*)
19	VILLANELLE: nineteen lines of any length, divided into five tercets and one quatrain; built on two rhymes and two refrains (shown by superscripts [R1] and [R2], both of which end with the *a* rhyme ($a^{R1}ba^{R2}aba^{R1}aba^{R2}aba^{R1}aba^{R2}aba^{R1}a^{R2}$)

certain words and create links between words and groups of lines. Readers who note these emphases are not only better able to appreciate the craft of the poet, but they are better able to understand the textures of a poem's ideas and to feel its emotional shadings.

SOUND AND SOUND DEVICES

The rhythmic flow of a line of poetry is not entirely a matter of rhythm patterns, caesurae, and run-on lines; the choice of words, their very sounds, can make a line flow more swiftly or slowly. In "An Essay on Criticism," a work not included in this anthology, Alexander Pope argued that "the sound must seem an echo to the sense," and illustrated how word choice and placement can make a strict iambic rhythm seem ponderously slow or light and quick:

> When Ajax strives some rock's vast weight to throw,
> The line too labors, and the words move slow;
> Not so, when swift Camilla scours the plain,
> Flies o'er th' unbending corn and skims along the main.

In the first of these lines, Pope slows the reading of the line by using a number of monosyllabic words and cacophony, harsh or unpleasant sounding language, produced here by a sequence of consonants that are relatively difficult to pronounce together. In the third and fourth lines, he quickens the pace with a careful placement of polysyllabic words and the use of euphony, or pleasant sounding language with pleasing combinations of vowels and consonants.

Several other sound devices affect a poem's pace and meaning; sometimes these are instrumental in conveying the tone, which is the speaker's attitude towards the subject and the audience (both the audience implied by the context, as in a dramatic monologue, and the audience actually reading or listening to the poem). One of the most notable of these is **alliteration**, the repetition of initial consonants. In Donne's Holy Sonnet XIV, for example, the b sound is repeated when the speaker pleads that God "bend / Your force, to break, blow, burn, and make me new." Alliteration tends to emphasize words, giving them extra force and linking them as a unit. Here, the b sound emphasizes the violence of the action Donne requests of God and suggests that it will require all of God's force to save the speaker. Alliteration, therefore, suggests both the difficulty of the task and the intensity of the speaker's desire for renewal. It can, of course, be used for gentler effects, as in Christina Rossetti's "Song": "When I am dead, my dearest, / Sing no sad songs for me." In this case, the heaviness of the d sounds in the first line suggests the sadness normally associated with death, but the softness of the s sounds in the second line lightens the mood to indicate the speaker's contrary feeling. Furthermore, the alliteration surrounds the word *no*, a word that in scansion receives an accent, or heavy beat, creating a contrast that emphasizes the word and its idea even more.

Repetition of sound is also central to assonance and consonance. **Assonance** is the repetition of vowel sounds, as in the *i* sound of "swift Camilla" and "skims" in Pope's lines quoted above. **Consonance** is the repetition of consonant sounds within or at the end of words, as with the repeated *l* sounds in the last line of Archibald Lampman's "Winter Evening": "Glittering and still shall come the awful night."

One other important device is **onomatopoeia**, or imitative harmony, in which a word imitates or echoes a sound, as in "clip clop" to suggest the movement of horses, or as in the word *break* in Donne's alliterative "break, blow, bend" quoted above, or as in this famous example from a long poem that does not appear in this anthology, Tennyson's *The Princess* (1847): "The moan of doves in immemorial elms, / And murmuring of innumerable bees." Here *moan* and *murmur* imitate natural sounds, and alliteration of the *m* heightens and extends the effect throughout both lines.

Although it has been necessary to examine them separately, sound devices most frequently work together. In the final line of Shakespeare's Sonnet 73, "To love that well which thou must leave ere long," discussed earlier to show meaningful variation in metre, alliteration links *love*, *leave*, and *long*, emphasizing these three important words. Moreover, the two major terms, *love* and *leave*, are further linked and intensified by internal slant rhyme. Finally, consonance links *love* and *well*, uniting these words into a single concept. A similar careful attention to sound is evident in such modern poems as Oodgeroo's "Nona," which euphoniously describes a young naked girl: "Nona the lithe and lovely, / Liked by all." As in the example from Shakespeare, alliteration is the major linking device. Assonance further links *lithe* and *Liked*, and consonance joins *Liked* and *all* to emphasize the idea of universal popularity. Rhythm and line length further emphasize this idea in three ways. First, the line containing them is set apart by pauses (indicated by the commas before and at the end of the line). Second, the linked words are at the beginning and end of the line, where they stand out because of these pauses. Third, these words receive the only accents in this line, the shortest, and thus most noticeable, line in the poem. This concern for sound is thematically purposeful. When it becomes clear later in the poem that the men and women do not see the same thing when they look at the girl, the short line gains retrospective irony. Its seemingly innocent celebration of beauty and popularity, that is, becomes open to a variety of interpretations because it clearly implies that "Like" may have significantly, even ominously, different meanings for the women and men. Readers who notice such uses of sound gain a greater appreciation of the resources and technical demands of the craft of poetry, but they also gain something personally enriching. Sensitivity to sound enables readers to respond more fully to the nuances of language and, thus, to be more open to both emotional stimulation and intellectual meaning in their reading.

POETRY AND PLEASURE

The preceding sections have explored only the major technical elements that make poetry such a complex literary form. Poems can use these techniques in inexhaustible combinations. Poems, however, are much more than compilations of techniques, and reading poetry is more than cataloguing techniques. Poems express the deepest feelings, the most moving thoughts, the heartiest laughter, the most scathing denunciations that people throughout the ages have felt. Poems are expressions of unique personalities and bear the marks of originating in particular social, cultural, and historical contexts, but poems are open to all readers who take the time to open themselves to them, who listen to the rhythms and the sounds, who imaginatively perceive the imagery. The more readers discover about a poem, its context, and literature and poetry in general, the more they can extend their appreciation and enjoyment of poetry. The key to such appreciation and enjoyment, however, is to forget that a poem is a work of "serious literature" that must be studied. Readers need to approach the poem in the same way they approach music, plays, short stories, and novels; they should, that is, be willing to be entertained, be open to new sensations and ideas, be ready to be teased and puzzled, be eager to enter into the imaginative life of the poem. This willingness allows readers to experience an array of emotions and ideas they may not otherwise have. Reading poetry in this way can thus become an act of self-revelation that makes readers more deeply aware of their own humanity. Such reading does not, however, lock us into ourselves. Because poetry originates in another's mind and voice and because it touches on nearly universal experiences and feelings, such reading can connect us to other human beings. It can also make the moments of reading moments of pleasure. That, in itself, is a worthwhile reason for reading poetry.

ANONYMOUS
THE SEAFARER

TRANSLATED BY EZRA POUND

*B*ecause Old English poetry was originally composed for oral performance, it works with a limited and highly conventionalized poetic vocabulary incorporating many easily remembered formulaic phrases. As noted in the Introduction to Poetry, its metre depended on a four-stress line linked by alliteration. However, this verse is also rich in metaphoric language, including specially coined compounds called *kennings* (for example, "whale's acre" for "sea," *The Seafarer*, line 60). The themes of Old English poetry reflect the heroic ideals of the warrior class that formed its audience, overlaid with a renunciatory Christian stoicism introduced by the conversion of Anglo-Saxon society in the seventh century. In the warrior's lonely struggle against overwhelming forces and realization of the impermanence of worldly possessions, only heroic ideals (especially loyalty to one's lord, whether on earth or in heaven) were beyond the reach of evil. *The Seafarer* is characteristic of Old English poetry in its vivid account of the difficulties and dangers of the sea voyage, its melancholy lament for the transitory nature of earthly prosperity and happiness, and its larger image of life as a sea journey redeemed only by the joy in heaven.

Pound's version of *The Seafarer* is neither complete nor strictly accurate as a translation. Pound sought to return to what he (and a number of other scholars of his day) took to be the original pre-Christian poem (see note to line 76). But his motivation in translating is as much personal and poetic as it is scholarly. He is interested less in rendering each word or local meaning exactly than he is in mapping the sounds, rhythm, and diction of Old English poetry, in reproducing its musicality and in rediscovering the roots of English verse (see note to line 88).

Compare Pound's opening five and a half lines with the Old English original, reproduced below with scansion guides and a literal translation. Regularity of rhythm was especially important in Old English poetry, with each line broken into two verses or half-lines: || marks the caesura or break between verses; / marks primary stress; \, secondary stress; and x, an unstressed syllable. A primary stress mark in parentheses indicates a point where the accompanying harp would have provided the stress.

Mæg ic be me sylfum ‖ soðgied   wrecan,

I can   about myself   a true story   recite,

siþas   secgan, ‖   hu ic geswincdagum

(my) travels   narrate,   how I in days of toil

earfoðhwile ‖   oft   þrowade,

time of hardship   often   suffered,

bitre breostceare ‖ gebiden   hæbbe,

bitter breastcare   (I) have   experienced,

gecunnad in   ceole   ‖   cearselda   fela,

have known on (board) ship   abodes of care   many,

atol   yþa   gewealc. ‖   þær mec oft bigeat

terrible waves   rolling.

The Seafarer

FROM THE ANGLO-SAXON
May I for my own self song's truth reckon,
Journey's jargon, how I in harsh days
Hardship endured oft.
Bitter breast-cares have I abided,
5   Known on my keel many a care's hold,
And dire sea-surge, and there I oft spent
Narrow nightwatch nigh the ship's head
While she tossed close to cliffs. Coldly afflicted,
My feet were by frost benumbed.
10   Chill its chains are; chafing sighs
Hew my heart round and hunger begot
Mere-weary mood. Lest man know not

That he on dry land loveliest liveth,
List how I, care-wretched, on ice-cold sea,
15   Weathered the winter, wretched outcast
Deprived of my kinsmen;
Hung with hard ice-flakes, where hail-scur flew,
There I heard naught save the harsh sea
And ice-cold wave, at whiles the swan cries,
20   Did for my games the gannet's clamour,
Sea-fowls' loudness was for me laughter,
The mews' singing all my mead-drink.
Storms, on the stone-cliffs beaten, fell on the stern
In icy feathers; full oft the eagle screamed
With spray on his pinion.
25   Not any protector
May make merry man faring needy.
This he little believes, who aye in winsome life
Abides 'mid burghers some heavy business,
Wealthy and wine-flushed, how I weary oft
30   Must bide above brine.
Neareth nightshade, snoweth from north,
Frost froze the land, hail fell on earth then,
Corn of the coldest. Nathless there knocketh now
The heart's thought that I on high streams
35   The salt-wavy tumult traverse alone.
Moaneth alway my mind's lust
That I fare forth, that I afar hence
Seek out a foreign fastness.
For this there's no mood-lofty man over earth's midst,
40   Not though he be given his good, but will have in his
          youth greed;
Nor his deed to the daring, nor his king to the faithful
But shall have his sorrow for sea-fare
Whatever his lord will.
He hath not heart for harping, nor in ring-having
45   Nor winsomeness to wife, nor world's delight
Nor any whit else save the wave's slash,
Yet longing comes upon him to fare forth on the water.
Bosque taketh blossom, cometh beauty of berries,
Fields to fairness, land fares brisker,

50   All this admonisheth man eager of mood,
       The heart turns to travel so that he then thinks
       On flood-ways to be far departing.
       Cuckoo calleth with gloomy crying,
       He singeth summerward, bodeth sorrow,
55   The bitter heart's blood. Burgher knows not —
       He the prosperous man — what some perform
       Where wandering them widest draweth.
       So that but now my heart burst from my breastlock,
       My mood 'mid the mere-flood,
60   Over the whale's acre, would wander wide.
       On earth's shelter cometh oft to me,
       Eager and ready, the crying lone-flyer,
       Whets for the whale-path the heart irresistibly,
       O'er tracks of ocean; seeing that anyhow
65   My lord deems to me this dead life
       On loan and on land, I believe not
       That any earth-weal eternal standeth
       Save there be somewhat calamitous
       That, ere a man's tide go, turn it to twain.
70   Disease or oldness or sword-hate
       Beats out the breath from doom-gripped body.
       And for this, every earl whatever, for those speaking
              after —
       Laud of the living, boasteth some last word,
       That he will work ere he pass onward,
75   Frame on the fair earth 'gainst foes his malice,
       Daring ado, . . . [1]
       So that all men shall honour him after
       And his laud beyond them remain 'mid the English,
       Aye, for ever, a lasting life's-blast,

---

1 "It seems most likely that a fragment of the original poem, clear through about the first thirty lines and thereafter increasingly illegible, fell into the hands of a monk with literary ambitions, who filled in the gaps with his own guesses and 'improvements.'" To strip away these "improvements" Pound rejected half of line 76 ("against the Devil"), read "Angles" (i.e., "English") for angels in line 78, and omitted the religious final part. In Pound's words he "stopped translating before the passage about the soul and the longer lines beginning 'Mickle is the fear of the Almighty,' and ending in a dignified but platitudinous address to the Deity: 'World's elder, eminent creater, in all ages, amen.'" [Quotations from Pound's note on textual degeneracy accompanying the first publication of his translation in A.R. Orage's weekly New Age (30 November 1911)].

Delight 'mid the doughty.

80   Days little durable,

And all arrogance of earthen riches,

There come now no kings nor Cæsars

Nor gold-giving lords like those gone.

Howe'er in mirth most magnified,

85 Whoe'er lived in life most lordliest,

Drear all this excellence, delights undurable!

Waneth the watch, but the world holdeth.

Tomb hideth trouble. The blade is layed low.[2]

Earthly glory ageth and seareth.

90 No man at all going the earth's gait,

But age fares against him, his face paleth,

Grey-haired he groaneth, knows gone companions,

Lordly men, are to earth o'ergiven,

Nor may he then the flesh-cover, whose life ceaseth,

95 Nor eat the sweet nor feel the sorry,

Nor stir hand nor think in mid heart,

And though he strew the grave with gold,

His born brothers, their buried bodies

Be an unlikely treasure hoard.

(c. 970–990)   (Pound trans. 1911)

---

2 *note that the sound of Old English* **blæd is gehnæged** produces Pound's "The blade is layed low" rather than the literally correct "glory is humbled."

GEOFFREY CHAUCER

(c.1340–1400)

orn into a well-to-do merchant family in the City of London, Chaucer spent most of his adult life in public service to the king and his court. He was variously a soldier, a member of diplomatic missions abroad, a justice of the peace, a member of Parliament, and for many years a controller of customs. In his early poetry — including a succession of dream visions and the polished verse romance Troilus and Criseyde *— Chaucer translated the refined forms of French and Italian courtly poetry into his own idiom. In the process he was instrumental in transforming native English verse (organized by stress and alliteration) in the light of Continental practice (organized by regularity of line length and rhyme). From the late 1380s until his death in 1400, he worked on his most famous and innovative literary creation,* The Canterbury Tales.

INTRODUCTION TO THE CANTERBURY TALES

he *Canterbury Tales* are notable for their diversity of styles and genres, featuring everything from romance and philosophy to beast fable and bawdy folktale. Equally important is Chaucer's idea of grouping the tales within the fictional frame of the Canterbury pilgrimage. The detailed portraits of the pilgrims in the General Prologue provide a vivid description of and commentary upon late-medieval English society. Following his description of the individual pilgrims, the narrator recounts how the idea of a series of Canterbury tales originated. The same night these pilgrims were gathered together at the Tabard Inn, Harry Bailey, their host, proposed a storytelling contest to while away the time of the pilgrimage. Each pilgrim was to tell two stories on the way to Canterbury, and two coming back. Harry Bailey would be the judge, and the winner of the contest would receive a free supper back at the Tabard at the other pilgrims' expense. The next morning as they prepare to begin their journey, the Host asks the Knight, the Prioress, and the Clerk to draw straws in order to see who will begin the storytelling. However, this attempt at social decorum falls apart after the Knight's tale, when the drunken Miller insists upon matching the Knight's elevated story of chivalric romance with his own bawdy "legend and a life of a carpenter and his wife." In the end, Harry Bailey's game of storytelling also gives way to a more serious view of pilgrimage. For *The Canterbury Tales* finish not back at the Tabard as planned, but just outside Canterbury when the Parson tells his penitential tale in prose about the seven deadly sins. The idea of pilgrimage itself, then, embodies the tension between transcendent and carnivalesque approaches to life and art that animate the *Tales* as a whole.

Throughout, Chaucer uses the pilgrimage frame to consider the ironic relationship of tale-teller and tale, to comment on the social and ideological differences between the pilgrims, and ultimately to explore the validity and usefulness of fiction in mirroring the human condition.

from The Canterbury Tales
General Prologue

Whan that Aprill with his shoures soote
The droghte of March hath perced to the roote,
And bathed every veyne in swich licour
Of which vertu engendered is the flour;
5   Whan Zephirus eek with his sweete breeth
Inspired hath in every holt and heeth
The tendre croppes, and the yonge sonne
Hath in the Ram his halve cours yronne,
And smale foweles maken melodye,
10   That slepen al the nyght with open ye
(So priketh hem nature in hir corages);
Thanne longen folk to goon on pilgrimages,
And palmeres for to seken straunge strondes,
To ferne halwes, kowthe in sondry londes;
15   And specially from every shires ende
Of Engelond to Caunterbury they wende,
The hooly blisful martir for to seke,
That hem hath holpen whan that they were seeke.
    Bifil that in that seson on a day,
20   In Southwerk at the Tabard as I lay
Redy to wenden on my pilgrymage

1 his shoures soote: its sweet, gentle showers. *3 swich licour:* such liquid. *4 vertu:* potency. *5 Zephirus:* the west wind. *8 Ram:* the zodiacal house of Aries (the Ram). *11 hem:* them. *hir corages:* their hearts. *13 palmeres:* professional pilgrims, whose emblem was a palm frond, meant to signify that they had been to the Holy Land. *strondes:* shores. *14 fern halwes:* distant holy places. *kowthe:* known. *17 martir:* St. Thomas à Becket, martyred in Canterbury Cathedral in 1170.

To Caunterbury with ful devout corage,
At nyght was come into that hostelrye
Wel nyne and twenty in a compaignye,
25 Of sondry folk, by aventure yfalle
In felaweshipe, and pilgrimes were they alle,
That toward Caunterbury wolden ryde.
The chambres and the stables weren wyde,
And wel we weren esed atte beste.
30 And shortly, whan the sonne was to reste,
So hadde I spoken with hem everichon
That I was of hir felaweshipe anon,
And made forward erly for to ryse,
To take oure wey ther as I yow devyse.
35   But nathelees, whil I have tyme and space,
Er that I ferther in this tale pace,
Me thynketh it acordaunt to resoun
To telle yow al the condicioun
Of ech of hem, so as it semed me,
40 And whiche they weren, and of what degree,
And eek in what array that they were inne;
And at a knyght than wol I first bigynne.
        A KNYGHT ther was, and that a worthy man,
That fro the tyme that he first bigan
45 To riden out, he loved chivalrie,
Trouthe and honour, fredom and curteisie.
Ful worthy was he in his lordes werre,
And therto hadde he riden, no man ferre,
As wel in cristendom as in hethenesse,
50 And evere honoured for his worthynesse.
At Alisaundre he was whan it was wonne.
Ful ofte tyme he hadde the bord bigonne
Aboven alle nacions in Pruce;
In Lettow hadde he reysed and in Ruce,

---

25 *by aventure yfalle:* fallen by chance. *29 esed atte beste:* accommodated in the best
way. *35 nathelees:* nonetheless. *36 pace:* go, proceed. *40 degree:* social rank. *46 trouthe:* integrity.
honour: good reputation. *fredom:* generosity. *curteisie:* refinement of manners. *51 Alisaundre:*
Alexandria, captured and held briefly by European crusaders in 1365. English knights in the
fourteenth century did campaign in all the places mentioned in lines 51–66. *52 bord bigonne:* sat
in the place of honour at banquets. *53 Pruce:* Prussia. *54 Lettow:* Lithuania. *reysed:* ridden on
raids. *Ruce:* Russia.

55   No Cristen man so ofte of his degree.
      In Gernade at the seege eek hadde he be
      Of Algezir, and riden in Belmarye.
      At Lyeys was he and at Satalye,
      Whan they were wonne; and in the Grete See
60   At many a noble armee hadde he be.
      At mortal batailles hadde he been fiftene,
      And foughten for oure feith at Tramyssene
      In lystes thries, and ay slayn his foo.
      This ilke worthy knyght hadde been also
65   Somtyme with the lord of Palatye
      Agayn another hethen in Turkye.
      And everemoore he hadde a sovereyn prys;
      And though that he were worthy, he was wys,
      And of his port as meeke as is a mayde.
70   He nevere yet no vileynye ne sayde
      In al his lyf unto no maner wight.
      He was a verray, parfit gentil knyght.
      But, for to tellen yow of his array,
      His hors were goode, but he was nat gay.
75   Of fustian he wered a gypon
      Al bismotered with his habergeon,
      For he was late ycome from his viage,
      And wente for to doon his pilgrymage.
          With hym ther was his sone, a yong SQUIER,
80   A lovyere and a lusty bacheler,
      With lokkes crulle as they were leyd in presse.
      Of twenty yeer of age he was, I gesse.
      Of his stature he was of evene lengthe,
      And wonderly delyvere, and of greet strengthe.
85   And he hadde been somtyme in chyvachie

56–57 Gernade . . . Algezir: Granada and Algeciras, cities in Spain controlled at this time by Moslems. ***Belmarye:*** Morocco (Benmarin), along with Tlemcen ("Tramyssene"), Moorish kingdoms in North Africa. *58 Lyeys . . . Satalye:* Ayash and Atalia in modern Turkey. *59 Grete See:* the Mediterranean. *64 ilke:* same. *65 Palatye:* Balat in modern Turkey, in 1365 bound by treaty to the Christian kingdom of Cyprus. *67 sovereyn prys:* outstanding reputation. *69 port:* bearing, behaviour. *70 vileynye:* rudeness. *71 no maner wight:* any sort of person. *72 verray:* true. *parfit:* perfect. *gentil:* noble. *75 fustian:* coarse cloth. *gypon:* tunic. *76 bismotered with his habergeon:* stained by his coat of mail. *81 crulle:* curled. *presse:* press (curler). *83 evene lengthe:* moderate height. *84 delyvere:* agile. *85 in chyvachie:* on cavalry expeditions.

In Flaundres, in Artoys, and Pycardie,
And born hym weel, as of so litel space,
In hope to stonden in his lady grace.
Embrouded was he, as it were a meede
90   Al ful of fresshe floures, whyte and reede.
Syngynge he was, or floytynge, al the day;
He was as fressh as is the month of May.
Short was his gowne, with sleves longe and wyde.
Wel koude he sitte on hors and faire ryde.
95   He koude songes make and wel endite,
Juste and eek daunce, and weel purtreye and write.
So hoote he lovede that by nyghtertale
He sleep namoore than dooth a nyghtyngale.
Curteis he was, lowely, and servysable,
100   And carf biforn his fader at the table.

. . . .

Ther was also a Nonne, a PRIORESSE,
That of hir smylyng was ful symple and coy;
120   Hire gretteste ooth was but by Seinte Loy;
And she was cleped madame Eglentyne.
Ful weel she soong the service dyvyne,
Entuned in hir nose ful semely,
And Frenssh she spak ful faire and fetisly,
125   After the scole of Stratford atte Bowe,
For Frenssh of Parys was to hire unknowe.
At mete wel ytaught was she with alle:
She leet no morsel from hir lippes falle,
Ne wette hir fyngres in hir sauce depe;
130   Wel koude she carie a morsel and wel kepe
That no drope ne fille upon hire brest.
In curteisie was set ful muchel hir lest.

---

86 Flaundres . . . Pycardie: military expeditions in Flanders and parts of northern France, part of the Hundred Years War (1337–1453) between England and France. **89 embrouded:** embroidered. **meede:** meadow. **96 juste:** joust. **eek:** also. **99 lowely:** modest. **servysable:** attentive. **100 carf:** carved. **119 symple:** unaffected. **coy:** reserved. **120 Seinte Loy:** St Eligius (588–629), a handsome, genteel French saint, especially popular among fashionable court circles of the day (hence a mild oath). **121 cleped:** called. **Eglentyne:** a typical romance heroine's name. **122 service dyvyne:** liturgy. **123 entuned in hir nose:** apparently the correct way to sing Gregorian chant. **124 fetisly:** elegantly. **125 scole of Stratford atte Bowe:** the Prioress has learned Anglo-Norman French, a provincial dialect spoken in England since the Norman Conquest, rather than the more fashionable Parisian French now current at the English court. **132 lest:** pleasure.

Hir over-lippe wyped she so clene
That in hir coppe ther was no ferthyng sene
135   Of grece, whan she dronken hadde hir draughte.
Ful semely after hir mete she raughte.
And sikerly she was of greet desport,
And ful plesaunt, and amyable of port,
And peyned hire to countrefete cheere
140   Of court, and to been estatlich of manere,
And to ben holden digne of reverence.
But, for to speken of hire conscience,
She was so charitable and so pitous
She wolde wepe, if that she saugh a mous
145   Kaught in a trappe, if it were deed or bledde.
Of smale houndes hadde she that she fedde
With rosted flessh, or milk and wastel-breed.
But soore wepte she if oon of hem were deed,
Or if men smoot it with a yerde smerte;
150   And al was conscience and tendre herte.
Ful semyly hir wympul pynched was,
Hir nose tretys, hir eyen greye as glas,
Hir mouth ful smal, and therto softe and reed;
But sikerly she hadde a fair forheed;
155   It was almoost a spanne brood, I trowe;
For, hardily, she was nat undergrowe.
Ful fetys was hir cloke, as I was war.
Of smal coral aboute hire arm she bar
A peire of bedes, gauded al with grene,
160   And theron heng a brooch of gold ful sheene,
On which ther was first write a crowned A,
And after *Amor vincit omnia.*

. . . .

---

134 ferthyng: speck. **136 raughte:** reached. **137 sikerly:** certainly. *greet desport:* excellent
deportment. **139 contrefete cheere:** imitate the manners. **140 estatlich:** dignified. **141 digne:**
worthy. **147 wastel-breed:** expensive white bread: the poor ate black bread, and meat only on rare
occasions; moreover, this was a period of particular hardship for the poor that had led to the
Peasants' Revolt of 1381. **149 yerde:** yardstick. **152 tretys:** well-shaped, aristocratic. **155 spanne
brood:** a handspan in length. **159 peire of bedes:** rosary. *gauded:* divided by large beads. **162 Amor
vincit omnia:** "Love conquers all"; the phrase can apply to divine or earthly love.

445 A good WIF was ther OF biside BATHE,
But she was somdel deef, and that was scathe.
Of clooth-makyng she hadde swich an haunt,
She passed hem of Ypres and of Gaunt.
In al the parisshe wif ne was ther noon
450 That to the offrynge bifore hire sholde goon;
And if ther dide, certeyn so wrooth was she,
That she was out of alle charitee.
Hir coverchiefs ful fyne weren of ground;
I dorste swere they weyeden ten pound
455 That on a Sonday weren upon hir heed.
Hir hosen weren of fyn scarlet reed,
Ful streite yteyd, and shoes ful moyste and newe.
Boold was hir face, and fair, and reed of hewe.
She was a worthy womman al hir lyve:
460 Housebondes at chirche dore she hadde fyve,
Withouten oother compaignye in youthe, —
But therof nedeth nat to speke as nowthe.
And thries hadde she been at Jerusalem;
She hadde passed many a straunge strem;
465 At Rome she hadde been, and at Boloigne,
In Galice at Seint-Jame, and at Coloigne.
She koude muchel of wandrynge by the weye.
Gat-tothed was she, soothly for to seye.
Upon an amblere esily she sat,
470 Ywympled wel, and on hir heed an hat
As brood as is a bokeler or a targe;
A foot-mantel aboute hir hipes large,
And on hir feet a paire of spores sharpe.
In felaweshipe wel koude she laughe and carpe.
475 Of remedies of love she knew per chaunce,
For she koude of that art the olde daunce.

. . . .

---

446 *scathe:* unfortunate. 447 *haunt:* skill. 448 *Gaunt:* Ypres and Ghent (in modern Belgium) were renowned cloth-making centres. 450 *offrynge:* during mass the people went to the altar with their offerings. 453 *coverchiefs:* kerchiefs. *of ground:* in texture. 457 *moyste:* supple. 460 *at chirche dore:* in the Middle Ages the actual marriage vows were said at the door, after which the couple entered the church for mass. 461 *withouten:* not counting. 463 *Jerusalem:* Jerusalem, Rome, Boulogne (in France), St. James of Compostella (in Galicia in northwestern Spain), and Cologne (in Germany) were celebrated places of pilgrimage. 468 *gat-tothed:* teeth set apart were thought to indicate a lascivious nature. 471 *bokeler or a targe:* terms for shields.

545   The MILLERE was a stout carl for the nones;
      Ful byg he was of brawn, and eek of bones.
      That proved wel, for over al ther he cam,
      At wrastlynge he wolde have alwey the ram.
      He was short-sholdred, brood, a thikke knarre;
550   Ther was no dore that he nolde heve of harre,
      Or breke it at a rennyng with his heed.
      His berd as any sowe or fox was reed,
      And therto brood, as though it were a spade.
      Upon the cop right of his nose he hade
555   A werte, and theron stood a toft of herys,
      Reed as the brustles of a sowes erys;
      His nosethirles blake were and wyde.
      A swerd and bokeler bar he by his syde.
      His mouth as greet was as a greet forneys.
560   He was a janglere and a goliardeys,
      And that was moost of synne and harlotries.
      Wel koude he stelen corn and tollen thries;
      And yet he hadde a thombe of gold, pardee.
      A whit cote and a blew hood wered he.
565   A baggepipe wel koude he blowe and sowne,
      And therwithal he broghte us out of towne.

      . . . .

      The REVE was a sclendre colerik man.
      His berd was shave as ny as ever he kan;
      His heer was by his erys ful round yshorn;
590   His top was dokked lyk a preest biforn
      Ful longe were his legges and ful lene,
      Ylyk a staf, ther was no calf ysene.
      Wel koude he kepe a gerner and a bynne;
      Ther was noon auditour koude on him wynne.

---

545 carl: churl, fellow. **548 ram:** the prize at country contests. **549 knarre:** knot (as in
wood). **550 nolde:** would not. **heve of harre:** lift off its hinges. **554 cop:** top ridge. **556 brustles:**
bristles. **557 nosethirles:** nostrils. **560 janglere:** windbag. **goliardeys:** teller of dirty
stories. **561 harlotries:** obscenities. **562 tollen thries:** take his toll or percentage thrice. **587 Reve:**
manager of an estate or farm. **colerik:** choleric, peevish. **593 gerner:** granary.

595   Wel wiste he by the droghte and by the reyn
         The yeldynge of his seed and of his greyn.
         His lordes sheep, his neet, his dayerye,
         His swyn, his hors, his stoor, and his pultrye
         Was hoolly in this Reves governynge,
600   And by his covenant yaf the rekenynge,
         Syn that his lord was twenty yeer of age.
         Ther koude no man brynge hym in arrerage.
         Ther nas baillif, ne hierde, nor oother hyne,
         That he ne knew his sleighte and his covyne;
605   They were adrad of hym as of the deeth.
         His wonyng was ful faire upon an heeth;
         With grene trees yshadwed was his place.
         He koude bettre than his lord purchace.
         Ful riche he was astored pryvely:
610   His lord wel koude he plesen subtilly,
         To yeve and lene hym of his owene good,
         And have a thank, and yet a cote and hood.
         In youthe he hadde lerned a good myster;
         He was a wel good wrighte, a carpenter.
615   This Reve sat upon a ful good stot,
         That was al pomely grey and highte Scot.
         A long surcote of pers upon he hade,
         And by his syde he baar a rusty blade.
         Of Northfolk was this Reve of which I telle,
620   Biside a toun men clepen Baldeswelle.
         Tukked he was as is a frere aboute,
         And evere he rood the hyndreste of oure route.

         . . . .

         (c. 1390)

---

597 *neet:* cattle. 598 *stoor:* livestock. 602 *arrerage:* arrears. 603 *nas:* was not. *baillif:* manager of a
farm. *hierde:* herdsman. *hyne:* farm labourer. 604 *covyne:* treachery. 606 *wonyng:*
dwelling. 611 *lene:* lend. 612 *cote and hood:* payment of clothing (i.e., reward). 613 *myster:*
craft. 615 *stot:* farm horse. 616 *pomely:* dappled. *highte:* called. 617 *surcote of pers:* dark blue outer
coat. 621 *tukked:* having his long coat hitched up. *frere:* friar. 622 *hyndreste:* last. *route:* company.

The Miller's Prologue

Heere folwen the wordes bitwene the Hoost and the
Millere.

Whan that the Knyght had thus his tale ytoold,
3110 In al the route nas ther yong ne oold
That he ne seyde it was a noble storie,
And worthy for to drawen to memorie;
And namely the gentils everichon.
Oure Hooste lough and swoor, "So moot I gon,
3115 This gooth aright; unbokeled is the male.
Lat se now who shal telle another tale;
For trewely the game is wel bigonne.
Now telleth ye, sir Monk, if that ye konne
Somwhat to quite with the Knyghtes tale."
3120 The Millere, that for dronken was al pale,
So that unnethe upon his hors he sat,
He nolde avalen neither hood ne hat,
Ne abyde no man for his curteisie,
But in Pilates voys he gan to crie,
3125 And swoor, "By armes, and by blood and bones,
I kan a noble tale for the nones,
With which I wol now quite the Knyghtes tale."
Oure Hooste saugh that he was dronke of ale,
And seyde, "Abyd, Robyn, my leeve brother;
3130 Som bettre man shal telle us first another.
Abyd, and lat us werken thriftily."
    "By Goddes soule," quod he, "that wol nat I;
For I wol speke, or elles go my wey."
Oure Hoost answerde, "Tel on, a devel wey!
3135 Thou art a fool; thy wit is overcome."

3110 *route:* company. *nas:* was not. 3113 *gentils:* gentlefolk. 3115 *unbokeled is the male:* untied is the
money bag (i.e., the game is well begun). 3119 *quite:* match. 3121 *unnethe:* scarcely. 3122 *nolde:*
would not. *avalen:* take off. 3124 *Pilates voys:* Pontius Pilate was played as a loud, ranting villain
in the medieval English mystery plays (i.e., cycles of biblical drama). 3125 *by armes, and by blood
and bones:* by the arms, blood, bones of Christ.

"Now herkneth," quod the Millere, "alle and some!
But first I make a protestacioun
That I am dronke, I knowe it by my soun;
And therfore if that I mysspeke or seye,

3140   Wyte it the ale of Southwerk, I you preye.
For I wol telle a legende and a lyf
Bothe of a carpenter and of his wyf,
How that a clerk hath set the wrightes cappe."
        The Reve answerde and seyde, "Stynt thy clappe!

3145   Lat be thy lewed dronken harlotrye.
It is a synne and eek a greet folye
To apeyren any man, or hym defame,
And eek to bryngen wyves in swich fame.
Thou mayst ynogh of othere thynges seyn."

3150   This dronke Millere spak ful soone ageyn
And seyde, "Leve brother Osewold,
Who hath no wyf, he is no cokewold.
But I sey nat therfore that thou art oon;
Ther been ful goode wyves many oon,

3155   And evere a thousand goode ayeyns oon badde.
That knowestow wel thyself, but if thou madde.
Why artow angry with my tale now?
I have a wyf, pardee, as wel as thow;
Yet nolde I, for the oxen in my plogh,

3160   Take upon me moore than ynogh,
As demen of myself that I were oon;
I wol bileve wel that I am noon.
An housbonde shal nat been inquisityf
Of Goddes pryvetee, nor of his wyf.

3165   So he may fynde Goddes foyson there,
Of the remenant nedeth nat enquere."
        What sholde I moore seyn, but this Millere
He nolde his wordes for no man forbere,
But tolde his cherles tale in his manere.

3140 wyte it: blame it on. **3143 set the wrightes cappe:** made a fool of the carpenter. **3144 stynt thy clappe:** stop your noisy talk. **3145 lewed:** ignorant. **harlotrye:** ribaldry. **3147 apeyren:** injure. **3152 cokewold:** cuckold. **3165 foyson:** plenty. **3169 cherles:** churl's, low-born fellow's.

3170 M'athynketh that I shal reherce it heere.
And therfore every gentil wight I preye,
For Goddes love, demeth nat that I seye
Of yvel entente, but for I moot reherce
Hir tales alle, be they bettre or werse,
3175 Or elles falsen som of my mateere.
And therfore, whoso list it nat yheere,
Turne over the leef and chese another tale;
For he shal fynde ynowe, grete and smale,
Of storial thyng that toucheth gentillesse,
3180 And eek moralitee and hoolynesse.
Blameth nat me if that ye chese amys.
The Millere is a cherl, ye knowe wel this;
So was the Reve eek and othere mo,
And harlotrie they tolden bothe two.
3185 Avyseth yow, and put me out of blame;
And eek men shal nat maken ernest of game.

The Miller's Tale

Heere bigynneth the Millere his tale.

Whilom ther was dwellynge at Oxenford
A riche gnof, that gestes heeld to bord,
And of his craft he was a carpenter.
3190 With hym ther was dwellynge a poure scoler,
Hadde lerned art, but al his fantasye
Was turned for to lerne astrologye,
And koude a certeyn of conclusiouns,
To demen by interrogaciouns,
3195 If that men asked hym in certein houres

3171 *wight:* person. **3173** *moot:* must. **3176** *list:* desires. **3177** *chese:* choose. **3179** *storial:* historical, true. **3187** *whilom:* once. *Oxenford:* Oxford. **3188** *gnof:* churl. **3191** *art:* the arts curriculum at the university. *fantasye:* fancy. **3193** *certeyn of conclusiouns:* a certain number of astrological operations. **3194** *demen by interrogaciouns:* to determine by scientific calculations.

Whan that men sholde have droghte or elles shoures,
Or if men asked him what sholde bifalle
Of every thyng; I may nat rekene hem alle.
   This clerk was cleped hende Nicholas.
3200   Of deerne love he koude and of solas;
And therto he was sleigh and ful privee,
And lyk a mayden meke for to see.
A chambre hadde he in that hostelrye
Allone, withouten any compaignye,
3205   Ful fetisly ydight with herbes swoote;
And he hymself as sweete as is the roote
Of lycorys, or any cetewale.
His Almageste, and bookes grete and smale,
His astrelabie, longynge for his art,
3210   His augrym stones layen faire apart,
On shelves couched at his beddes heed;
His presse ycovered with a faldyng reed;
And al above ther lay a gay sautrie,
On which he made a-nyghtes melodie
3215   So swetely that all the chambre rong;
And *Angelus ad virginem* he song;
And after that he song the Kynges Noote.
Ful often blessed was his myrie throte.
And thus this sweete clerk his tyme spente
3220   After his freendes fyndyng and his rente.
   This carpenter hadde wedded newe a wyf,
Which that he lovede moore than his lyf;
Of eighteteene yeer she was of age.
Jalous he was, and heeld hire narwe in cage,
3225   For she was wylde and yong, and he was old,
And demed hymself been like a cokewold.
He knew nat Catoun, for his wit was rude,

3199 *hende:* courteous, handy (adroit). 3200 *deerne:* secret. *solas:* satisfaction (of sexual desire). 3201 *sleigh:* sly. *privee:* secretive. 3205 *fetisly ydight:* elegantly furnished. *swoote:* sweet. 3207 *cetewale:* zedoary (a spice resembling ginger). 3208 *Almageste:* title of Ptolemy's book on astrology. 3209 *astrelabie:* astrolabe. *longynge for:* belonging to. 3212 *presse:* cupboard. *faldyng:* coarse woollen cloth. 3213 *sautrie:* psaltery (harp). 3216 *Angelus ad virginem:* "The Angel to the Virgin [Mary]," a hymn on the angel's Annunciation of the coming birth of Jesus (to a virgin whose husband was a carpenter). 3220 *after his freendes fyndyng:* according to what his friends provided. *rente:* income. 3227 *Catoun:* a collection of Latin proverbs, attributed to Cato, used as an elementary school text.

That bad man sholde wedde his simylitude.
Men sholde wedden after hire estaat,
3230 For youthe and elde is often at debaat.
But sith that he was fallen in the snare,
He moste endure, as oother folk, his care.
　Fair was this yonge wyf, and therwithal
As any wezele hir body gent and smal.
3235 A ceynt she werede, barred al of silk,
A barmclooth eek as whit as morne milk
Upon hir lendes, ful of many a goore.
Whit was hir smok, and broyden al bifoore
And eek bihynde, on hir coler aboute,
3240 Of col-blak silk, withinne and eek without.
The tapes of hir white voluper
Were of the same suyte of hir coler;
Hir filet brood of silk, and set ful hye.
And sikerly she hadde a likerous ye;
3245 Ful smale ypulled were hire browes two,
And tho were bent and blake as any sloo.
She was ful moore blisful on to see
Than is the newe pere-jonette tree,
And softer than the wolle is of a wether.
3250 And by hir girdel heeng a purs of lether,
Tasseled with silk, and perled with latoun.
In al this world, to seken up and doun,
There nys no man so wys that koude thenche
So gay a popelote or swich a wenche.
3255 Ful brighter was the shynyng of hir hewe
Than in the Tour the noble yforged newe.
But of hir song, it was as loude and yerne
As any swalwe sittynge on a berne.

3231 *sith:* since. 3234 *gent:* delicate. *smal:* slender. 3235 *ceynt:* belt. 3236 **barmclooth:**
apron. 3237 *lendes:* loins. *goore:* flounce. 3238 *smok:* undergarment. *broyden:*
embroidered. 3241 *tapes:* ribbons. *voluper:* cap. 3242 *suyte of:* colour as. 3243 *filet:*
headband. 3244 *sikerly:* truly. *likerous:* flirtatious. 3245 *ypulled:* plucked. 3246 *sloo:* sloe (a plum-
like fruit). 3248 **newe pere-jonette tree:** early pear tree; elsewhere in medieval literature the pear
tree (because of its succulent and swelling fruit) is a symbol of awakening
sexuality. 3249 *wether:* sheet (ram). 3250 *girdel:* belt. 3251 *perled:* adorned. *latoun:*
brass. 3253 *thenche:* imagine. 3254 *popelote:* little doll. 3256 *Tour:* Tower of London (the mint).
noble: gold coin. 3257 *yerne:* lively.

Therto she koude skippe and make game,

3260   As any kyde or calf folwynge his dame.

Hir mouth was sweete as bragot or the meeth,

Or hoord of apples leyd in hey or heeth.

Wynsynge she was, as is a joly colt,

Long as a mast, and upright as a bolt.

3265   A brooch she baar upon hir lowe coler,

As brood as is the boos of a bokeler.

Hir shoes were laced on hir legges hye.

She was a prymerole, a piggesnye,

For any lord to leggen in his bedde,

3270   Or yet for any good yeman to wedde.

    Now, sire, and eft, sire, so bifel the cas,

That on a day this hende Nicholas

Fil with this yonge wyf to rage and pleye,

Whil that hir housbonde was at Oseneye,

3275   As clerkes ben ful subtile and ful queynte;

And prively he caughte hire by the queynte,

And seyde, "Ywis, but if ich have my wille,

For deerne love of thee, lemman, I spille."

And heeld hire harde by the haunchebones,

3280   And seyde, "Lemman, love me al atones,

Or I wol dyen, also God me save!"

And she sproong as a colt dooth in the trave,

And with hir heed she wryed faste awey,

And seyde, "I wol nat kisse thee, by my fey!

3285   Why, lat be," quod she, "lat be, Nicholas,

Or I wol crie 'out, harrow' and 'allas'!

Do wey youre handes, for youre curteisye!"

    This Nicholas gan mercy for to crye,

And spak so faire, and profred him so faste,

3290   That she hir love hym graunted atte laste,

And swoor hir ooth, by seint Thomas of Kent,

3261 bragot: ale. **meeth:** mead. **3262 heeth:** heather. **3263 wynsynge:** skittish. **3268 prymerole:** primrose. **piggesnye:** "pig's eye," the name of a flower used as a term of endearment. **3269 leggen:** lay. **3273 rage:** romp, sport (sexually). **3274 Oseneye:** Osney, a town just outside Oxford. **3275 queynte:** clever. **3276 queynte:** pleasing thing (i.e., female genitalia). **3278 spille:** die. **3282 trave:** frame for holding a horse to be shod. **3291 Thomas of Kent:** St. Thomas à Becket, whose shrine is the object of the Canterbury pilgrimage.

That she wol been at his comandement,
Whan that she may hir leyser wel espie.
"Myn housbonde is so ful of jalousie

3295   That but ye wayte wel and been privee,
I woot right wel I nam but deed," quod she.
"Ye moste been ful deerne, as in this cas."
    "Nay, therof care thee noght," quod Nicholas.
"A clerk hadde litherly biset his whyle,

3300   But if he koude a carpenter bigyle."
And thus they been accorded and ysworn
To wayte a tyme, as I have told biforn.
    Whan Nicholas had doon thus everideel,
And thakked hire aboute the lendes weel,

3305   He kiste hire sweete and taketh his sawtrie,
And pleyeth faste, and maketh melodie.
    Thanne fil it thus, that to the paryssh chirche,
Cristes owene werkes for to wirche,
This goode wyf went on an haliday.

3310   Hir forheed shoon as bright as any day,
So was it wasshen whan she leet hir werk.
Now was ther of that chirche a parissh clerk,
The which that was ycleped Absolon.
Crul was his heer, and as the gold it shoon,

3315   And strouted as a fanne large and brode;
Ful streight and evene lay his joly shode.
His rode was reed, his eyen greye as goos.
With Poules wyndow corven on his shoos,
In hoses rede he wente fetisly.

3320   Yclad he was ful smal and proprely
Al in a kirtel of a lyght waget;
Ful faire and thikke been the poyntes set.
And therupon he hadde a gay surplys

3293 *leyser:* opportunity. 3295 *privee:* discreet. 3299 *litherly biset his whyle:* wasted his
time. 3304 *thakked:* patted. 3308 *wirche:* work. 3309 *haliday:* holy day. 3311 *leet:*
left. 3315 *strouted:* stretched out. 3316 *shode:* parted hair. 3317 *rode:* complexion. 3318 *Poules
wyndow:* it was high fashion at the time to have designs cut into the upper leather of shoes,
through which the bright-coloured hose could be seen; the effect, then, would be like the
elaborate stained glass windows of St. Paul's Cathedral in London. 3320 *smal:* daintily, in close-
fitting clothes. 3321 *kirtel:* tunic. *waget:* light blue. 3322 *poyntes:* laces.

As whit as is the blosme upon the rys.
3325   A myrie child he was, so God me save.
Wel koude he laten blood and clippe and shave,
And maken a chartre of lond or acquitaunce.
In twenty manere koude he trippe and daunce
After the scole of Oxenforde tho,
3330   And with his legges casten to and fro,
And pleyen songes on a smal rubible;
Therto he song som tyme a loud quynyble;
And as wel koude he pleye on a giterne.
In al the toun nas brewhous ne taverne
3335   That he ne visited with his solas,
Ther any gaylard tappestere was.
But sooth to seyn, he was somdeel squaymous
Of fartyng, and of speche daungerous.
    This Absolon, that jolif was and gay,
3340   Gooth with a sencer on the haliday,
Sensynge the wyves of the parisshe faste;
And many a lovely look on hem he caste,
And namely on this carpenteris wyf.
To looke on hire hym thoughte a myrie lyf,
3345   She was so propre and sweete and likerous.
I dar wel seyn, if she hadde been a mous,
And he a cat, he wolde hire hente anon.
This parissh clerk, this joly Absolon,
Hath in his herte swich a love-longynge
3350   That of no wyf took he noon offrynge;
For curteisie, he seyde, he wolde noon.
    The moone, whan it was nyght, ful brighte shoon,
And Absolon his gyterne hath ytake,
For paramours he thoghte for to wake.
3355   And forth he gooth, jolif and amorous,
Til he cam to the carpenteres hous

3324 *rys:* branch. 3325 *child:* young man. 3326 *laten blood . . . shave:* being a parish clerk was a part-time occupation, and barbers were also surgeons. 3331 *rubible:* rebeck, a kind of fiddle. 3332 *quynyble:* high treble. 3333 *giterne:* cithern, a guitar-like stringed instrument. 3336 *gaylard tappestere:* merry barmaid. 3337 *somdeel squaymous:* somewhat squeamish. 3338 *daungerous:* fastidious. 3347 *hente:* seized. 3354 *for paramours:* for the sake of love.

A litel after cokkes hadde ycrowe,
And dressed hym up by a shot-wyndowe
That was upon the carpenteris wal.
3360   He syngeth in his voys gentil and smal,
"Now, deere lady, if thy wille be,
I praye yow that ye wole rewe on me,"
Ful wel acordaunt to his gyternynge.
This carpenter awook, and herde him synge,
3365   And spak unto his wyf, and seyde anon,
"What! Alison! herestow nat Absolon,
That chaunteth thus under oure boures wal?"
And she answerde hir housbonde therwithal,
"Yis, God woot, John, I heere it every deel."
3370   This passeth forth; what wol ye bet than weel?
Fro day to day this joly Absolon
So woweth hire that hym is wo bigon.
He waketh al the nyght and al the day;
He kembeth his lokkes brode, and made hym gay;
3375   He woweth hire by meenes and brocage,
And swoor he wolde been hir owene page;
He syngeth, brokkynge as a nyghtyngale;
He sente hire pyment, meeth, and spiced ale,
And wafres, pipyng hoot out of the gleede;
3380   And, for she was of town, he profred meede.
For som folk wol ben wonnen for richesse,
And somme for strokes, and somme for gentillesse.
        Somtyme, to shewe his lightnesse and maistrye,
He pleyeth Herodes upon a scaffold hye.
3385   But what availleth hym as in this cas?
She loveth so this hende Nicholas
That Absolon may blowe the bukkes horn;
He ne hadde for his labour but a scorn.
And thus she maketh Absolon hire ape,

3358 *dressed hym:* stationed himself. *shot-wyndowe:* hinged window. 3362 *rewe:* have
pity. 3375 *meenes:* go-betweens. *brocage:* agents. 3377 *brokkynge:* trilling. 3378 *pyment:* spiced,
sweetened wine. 3379 *wafres:* cakes. *gleede:* fire. 3380 *meede:* money. 3382 *for strokes:* by
force. 3383 *lightnesse:* agility. *maistrye:* skill. 3384 *Herodes:* the part of Herod was played as a
roaring bully in medieval mystery plays. 3389 *ape:* fool, dupe.

3390 And al his ernest turneth til a jape.
Ful sooth is this proverbe, it is no lye,
Men seyn right thus, "Alwey the nye slye
Maketh the ferre leeve to be looth."
For though that Absolon be wood or wrooth,
3395 By cause that he fer was from hire sight,
This nye Nicholas stood in his light.
    Now ber thee wel, thou hende Nicholas,
For Absolon may waille and synge "allas."
And so bifel it on a Saterday,
3400 This carpenter was goon til Osenay;
And hende Nicholas and Alisoun
Acorded been to this conclusioun,
That Nicholas shal shapen hym a wyle
This sely jalous housbonde to bigyle;
3405 And if so be the game wente aright,
She sholde slepen in his arm al nyght,
For this was his desir and hire also.
And right anon, withouten wordes mo,
This Nicholas no lenger wolde tarie,
3410 But dooth ful softe unto his chambre carie
Bothe mete and drynke for a day or tweye,
And to hir housbonde bad hire for to seye,
If that he axed after Nicholas,
She sholde seye she nyste where he was,
3415 Of al that day she saugh hym nat with ye;
She trowed that he was in maladye,
For for no cry hir mayde koude hym calle,
He nolde answere for thyng that myghte falle.
    This passeth forth al thilke Saterday,
3420 That Nicholas stille in his chambre lay,
And eet and sleep, or dide what hym leste,
Til Sonday, that the sonne gooth to reste.
This sely carpenter hath greet merveyle

3390 *jape:* joke. 3392 *nye slye:* nigh (at hand) sly one. 3393 *ferre leeve:* distant love. *looth:*
disliked. 3394 *wood:* crazy. 3404 *sely:* innocent, simple, foolish. 3414 *nyste:* did not
know. 3416 *trowed:* believed.

Of Nicholas, or what thyng myghte hym eyle,
3425 And seyde, "I am adrad, by Seint Thomas,
It stondeth nat aright with Nicholas.
God shilde that he deyde sodeynly!
This world is now ful tikel, sikerly.
I saugh to-day a cors yborn to chirche
3430 That now, on Monday last, I saugh hym wirche.
    "Go up," quod he unto his knave anoon,
"Clepe at his dore, or knokke with a stoon.
Looke how it is, and tel me boldely."
    This knave gooth hym up ful sturdily,
3435 And at the chambre dore whil that he stood,
He cride and knokked as that he were wood,
"What! how! what do ye, maister Nicholay?
How may ye slepen al the longe day?"
    But al for noght, he herde nat a word.
3440 An hole he foond, ful lowe upon a bord,
Ther as the cat was wont in for to crepe,
And at that hole he looked in ful depe,
And at the laste he hadde of hym a sight.
This Nicholas sat evere capyng upright,
3445 As he had kiked on the newe moone.
Adoun he gooth, and tolde his maister soone
In what array he saugh this ilke man.
    This carpenter to blessen hym bigan,
And seyde, "Help us, seinte Frydeswyde!
3450 A man woot litel what hym shal bityde.
This man is falle, with his astromye,
In some woodnesse or in som agonye.
I thoghte ay wel how that it sholde be!
Men sholde nat knowe of Goddes pryvetee.
3455 Ye, blessed by alwey a lewed man
That noght but oonly his bileve kan!

3428 *tikel:* unstable, ticklish. 3429 *cors:* corpse. 3444 *capyng:* gaping. 3445 *kiked:*
stared. 3449 *seinte Frydeswyde:* St. Frideswide, patron saint of Oxford and noted for her healing
power. 3450 *woot:* knows. 3456 *bileve:* creed.

So ferde another clerk with astromye;
He walked in the feeldes, for to prye
Upon the sterres, what ther sholde bifalle,
3460   Til he was in a marle-pit yfalle;
He saugh nat that. But yet, by seint Thomas,
Me reweth soore of hende Nicholas.
He shal be rated of his studiyng,
If that I may, be Jhesus, hevene kyng!
3465   Get me a staf, that I may underspore,
Whil that thou, Robyn, hevest up the dore.
He shal out of his studiyng, as I gesse" —
And to the chambre dore he gan hym dresse.
His knave was a strong carl for the nones,
3470   And by the haspe he haaf it of atones;
Into the floor the door fil anon.
This Nicholas sat ay as stille as stoon,
And evere caped upward into the eir.
This carpenter wende he were in despeir,
3475   And hente hym by the sholdres myghtily,
And shook hym harde, and cride spitously,
"What! Nicholay! what, how! what, looke adoun!
Awak, and thenk on Cristes passioun!
I crouche thee from elves and fro wightes.
3480   Therwith the nyght-spel seyde he anon-rightes
On foure halves of the hous aboute,
And on the thresshfold of the dore withoute:
"Jhesu Crist and seinte Benedight,
Blesse this hous from every wikked wight,
3485   For nyghtes verye, the white *pater-noster*!
Where wentestow, seinte Petres soster?"
    And atte laste this hende Nicholas
Gan for to sik soore, and seyde, "Allas!
Shal al the world be lost eftsoones now?"

3460 **marle-pit:** clay pit. 3463 *rated of:* scolded for. 3465 **underspore:** pry up. 3470 **haaf:** heaved.
atones: at once. 3476 **spitously:** vigorously. 3479 **crouche:** make the sign of the cross. **wightes:** (evil)
creatures. 3488 **sik:** sigh. 3489 **eftsoones now:** right now (i.e., a second time).

3490	This carpenter answerde, "What seystow?
	What! thynk on God, as we doon, men that swynke."
	This Nicholas answerde, "Fecche me drynke,
	And after wol I speke in pryvetee
	Of certeyn thyng that toucheth me and thee.
3495	I wol telle it noon oother man, certeyn."
	This carpenter goth doun, and comth ageyn,
	And broghte of myghty ale a large quart;
	And whan that ech of hem had dronke his part,
	This Nicholas his dore faste shette,
3500	And doun the carpenter by hym he sette.
	He seyde "John, myn hooste, lief and deere,
	Thou shalt upon thy trouthe swere me heere
	That to no wight thou shalt this conseil wreye;
	For it is Cristes conseil that I seye,
3505	And if thou telle it man, thou art forlore;
	For this vengeaunce thou shalt han therfore,
	That if thou wreye me, thou shalt be wood."
	"Nay, Crist forbede it, for his hooly blood!"
	Quod tho this sely man, "I nam no labbe;
3510	Ne, though I seye, I nam nat lief to gabbe.
	Sey what thou wolt, I shal it nevere telle
	To child ne wyf, by hym that harwed helle!"
	"Now John," quod Nicholas, "I wol nat lye;
	I have yfounde in myn astrologye,
3515	As I have looked in the moone bright,
	That now a Monday next, at quarter nyght,
	Shal falle a reyn, and that so wilde and wood,
	That half so greet was nevere Noes flood.
	This world," he seyde, "in lasse than an hour
3520	Shal al be dreynt, so hidous is the shour.
	Thus shal mankynde drenche, and lese hir lyf."
	This carpenter answerde, "Allas, my wyf!

3491 *swynke:* work. **3503** *wreye:* reveal. **3505** *forlore:* lost. **3509** *labbe:* blabbermouth. **3510** *nam nat lief to gabbe:* do not like to gab (gossip). **3512** *harwed helle:* the story of Christ's descent into hell between the Crucifixion and the Resurrection and his release of the good souls born before the Incarnation (i.e., his "Harrowing of Hell") was extremely popular in the Middle Ages and a subject frequently treated in the mystery plays. **3518** *Noes:* Noah's. **3520** *dreynt:* drowned.

And shal she drenche? allas, myn Alisoun!"
For sorwe of this he fil almoost adoun,
3525 And seyde, "Is ther no remedie in this cas?"
      "Why, yis, for Gode," quod hende Nicholas,
"If thou wolt werken after loor and reed.
Thou mayst nat werken after thyn owene heed;
For thus seith Salomon, that was ful trewe,
3530 'Werk al by conseil, and thou shalt nat rewe.'
And if thou werken wolt by good conseil,
I undertake, withouten mast and seyl,
Yet shal I saven hire and thee and me.
Hastow nat herd hou saved was Noe,
3535 Whan that oure Lord hadde warned hym biforn
That al the world with water sholde be lorn?"
      "Yis," quod this Carpenter, "ful yoore ago."
      "Hastou nat herd," quod Nicholas, "also
The sorwe of Noe with his felaweshipe,
3540 Er that he myghte gete his wyf to shipe?
Hym hadde be levere, I dar wel undertake
At thilke tyme, than alle his wetheres blake
That she hadde had a ship hirself allone.
And therfore, woostou what is best to doone?
3545 This asketh haste, and of an hastif thyng
Men may nat preche or maken tariyng.
      Anon go gete us faste into this in
A knedyng trogh, or ellis a kymelyn,
For ech of us, but looke that they be large,
3550 In which we mowe swymme as in a barge,
And han therinne vitaille suffisant
But for a day, — fly on the remenant!
The water shal aslake and goon away
Aboute pryme upon the nexte day.
3555 But Robyn may nat wite of this, thy knave,

3527 *after loore and reed:* according to learning and advice. 3540 *his wyf to shipe:* a reference to the comic scenes in the medieval mystery plays where Noah's wife refuses to enter the ark. 3541 *levere:* happier. 3542 *thilke:* that. 3544 *woostou:* do you know. 3547 *in:* house. 3548 *knedyng trogh:* large trough for kneading dough. *kymelyn:* large tub for brewing beer. 3550 *swymme:* float. 3551 *vitaille suffisant:* sufficient food (victuals).

Ne eek thy mayde Gille I may nat save;
Axe nat why, for though thou aske me,
I wol nat tellen Goddes pryvetee.
Suffiseth thee, but if thy wittes madde,
3560   To han as greet a grace as Noe hadde.
Thy wyf shal I wel saven, out of doute.
Go now thy wey, and speed thee heer-aboute.

      But whan thou hast, for hire and thee and me,
Ygeten us thise knedyng tubbes thre,
3565   Thanne shaltow hange hem in the roof ful hye,
That no man of oure purveiaunce spye.
And whan thou thus has doon, as I have seyd,
And hast oure vitaille faire in hem yleyd,
And eek an ax, to smyte the corde atwo,
3570   Whan that the water comth, that we may go,
And breke an hole an heigh, upon the gable,
Unto the gardyn-ward, over the stable,
That we may frely passen forth oure way,
Whan that the grete shour is goon away,
3575   Thanne shaltou swymme as myrie, I undertake,
As dooth the white doke after hire drake.
Thanne wol I clepe, 'How, Alison! how, John!
By myrie, for the flood wol passe anon.'
And thou wolt seyn, 'Hayl maister Nicholay!
3580   Good morwe, I se thee wel, for it is day.'
And thanne shul we be lordes al oure lyf
Of al the world, as Noe and his wyf.

      But of o thyng I warne thee ful right:
Be wel avysed on that ilke nyght
3585   That we ben entred into shippes bord,
That noon of us ne speke nat a word,
Ne clepe, ne crie, but be in his preyere;
For it is Goddes owene heeste deere.

      Thy wyf and thou moote hange fer atwynne;
3590   For that bitwixe yow shal be no synne,

3554 *pryme:* around 9 A.M. 3555 *wite:* know. 3566 *purveiaunce:* preparations. 3569 *atwo:* in two. 3571 *an heigh:* above. 3583 *o:* one. 3590 *no synne:* an allusion to the traditional teaching that there was no copulation on the ark.

Namoore in lookyng than ther shal in deede,
This ordinance is seyd. Go, God thee speede!
Tomorwe at nyght, whan men ben alle aslepe,
Into oure knedyng-tubbes wol we crepe,
3595   And sitten there, abidyng Goddes grace.
Go now thy wey, I have no lenger space
To make of this no lenger sermonyng.
Men seyn thus, 'sende the wise, and sey no thyng:'
Thou art so wys, it needeth thee nat teche.
3600   Go, save oure lyf, and that I the biseche."
    This sely carpenter goth forth his wey.
Ful ofte he seide "allas" and "weylawey,"
And to his wyf he tolde his pryvetee,
And she was war, and knew it bet than he,
3605   What al this queynte cast was for to seye.
But nathelees she ferde as she wolde deye,
And seyde, "Allas! go forth thy wey anon,
Help us to scape, or we been dede echon!
I am thy trewe, verray wedded wyf;
3610   Go, deere spouse, and help to save oure lyf."
    Lo, which a greet thyng is affeccioun!
Men may dyen of ymaginacioun,
So depe may impressioun be take.
This sely carpenter bigynneth quake;
3615   Hym thynketh verraily that he may see
Noees flood come walwynge as the see
To drenchen Alisoun, his hony deere.
He wepeth, weyleth, maketh sory cheere;
He siketh with ful many a sory swogh;
3620   He gooth and geteth hym a knedyng trogh,
And after that a tubbe and a kymelyn,
And pryvely he sente hem to his in,
And heng hem in the roof in pryvetee.
His owene hand he made laddres thre,

3605 *queynte cast:* ingenious plot. *3611 affeccioun:* emotion. *3612 ymaginacioun:*
fantasy. *3616 walwynge:* surging, billowing. *3618 sory cheere:* sad countenance. *3619 swogh:*
groan. *3626 balkes:* beams.

3625 To clymben by the ronges and the stalkes
Unto the tubbes hangynge in the balkes,
And hem vitailled, bothe trogh and tubbe,
With breed and chese, and good ale in a jubbe,
Suffisynge right ynogh as for a day.
3630 But er that he hadde maad al this array,
He sente his knave, and eek his wenche also,
Upon his nede to London for to go.
And on the Monday, whan it drow to nyght,
He shette his dore withoute candel-lyght,
3635 And dressed alle thyng as it sholde be.
And shortly, up they clomben alle thre;
They seten stille wel a furlong way.
   "Now, *Pater-noster*, clom!" seyde Nicholay,
And "clom," quod John, and "clom," seyde Alisoun.
3640 This carpenter seyde his devocioun,
And stille he sit, and biddeth his preyere,
Awaitynge on the reyn, if he it heere.
   The dede sleep, for wery bisynesse,
Fil on this carpenter right, as I gesse,
3645 About corfew-tyme, or litel moore;
For travaille of his goost he groneth soore,
And eft he routeth, for his heed myslay.
Doun of the laddre stalketh Nicholay,
And Alisoun ful softe adoun she spedde;
3650 Withouten wordes mo they goon to bedde,
Ther as the carpenter is wont to lye.
Ther was the revel and the melodye;
And thus lith Alison and Nicholas,
In bisynesse of myrthe and of solas,
3655 Til that the belle of laudes gan to rynge,
And freres in the chauncel gonne synge.
   This parissh clerk, this amorous Absolon,

3628 jubbe: large container, jug. **3638 Pater-noster, clom:** say the Lord's Prayer and be quiet. **3645 corfew-tyme:** curfew, about dusk. **3646 travaille of his goost:** suffering of his spirit, mental anguish. **3647 routeth:** snores. **3655 laudes:** the first service of the day, before daybreak.

That is for love alwey so wo bigon,
Upon the Monday was at Oseneye
3660   With compaignye, hym to disporte and pleye,
And axed upon cas a cloisterer
Ful prively after John the carpenter;
And he drough hym apart out of the chirche,
And seyde, "I noot, I saugh hym heere nat wirche
3665   Syn Saterday; I trowe that he be went
For tymber, ther oure abbot hath hym sent;
For he is wont for tymber for to go,
And dwellen at the grange a day or two;
Or elles he is at his hous, certeyn.
3670   Where that he be, I kan nat soothly seyn."
        This Absolon ful joly was and light,
And thoghte, "Now is tyme to wake al nyght;
For sikirly I saugh hym nat stirynge
Aboute his dore, syn day bigan to sprynge.
3675   So moot I thryve, I shal, at cokkes crowe,
Ful pryvely knokken at his wyndowe
That stant ful lowe upon his boures wal.
To Alison now wol I tellen al
My love-longynge, for yet I shal nat mysse
3680   That at the leeste wey I shal hire kisse.
Som maner confort shal I have, parfay.
My mouth hath icched al this longe day;
That is a signe of kissyng atte leeste.
Al nyght me mette eek I was at a feeste.
3685   Therfore I wol go slepe an houre or tweye,
And al the nyght thanne wol I wake and pleye."
        Whan that the firste cok hath crowe, anon
Up rist this joly lovere Absolon,
And hym arraieth gay, at poynt-devys.
3690   But first he cheweth greyn and lycorys,
To smellen sweete, er he hadde kembd his heer.

3661 upon cas: by chance. **3663 drough:** drew. **3668 grange:** outlying farm. **3674 syn:** since. **3675 thryve:** thrive (succeed). **3677 boures:** bedroom's. **3684 me mette:** I dreamed. **3688 rist:** rises. **3689 araieth gay:** dresses handsomely. **at poynt-devys:** in every detail. **3690 greyn:** Grain of Paradise (cardamon seed).

Under his tonge a trewe-love he beer,
For therby wende he to ben gracious.
He rometh to the carpenteres hous,
3695   And stille he stant under the shot-wyndowe —
Unto his brest it raughte, it was so lowe —
And softe he cougheth with a semy soun:
"What do ye, hony-comb, sweete Alisoun,
My faire byrd, my sweete cynamome?
3700   Awaketh, lemman myn, and speketh to me!
Wel litel thynken ye upon my wo,
That for youre love I swete ther I go.
No wonder is thogh that I swelte and swete;
I moorne as dooth a lamb after the tete.
3705   Ywis, lemman, I have swich love-longynge,
That lik a turtel trewe is my moornynge.
I may nat ete na moore than a mayde."
    "Go fro the wyndow, Jakke fool," she sayde;
"As help me God, it wol nat be 'com pa me."
3710   I love another — and elles I were to blame —
Wel bet than thee, by Jhesu, Absolon.
Go forth thy wey, or I wol caste a ston,
And lat me slepe, a twenty devel wey!"
    "Allas," quod Absolon, "and weylawey,
3715   That trewe love was evere so yvel biset!
Thanne kysse me, syn it may be no bet,
For Jhesus love, and for the love of me."
    "Wiltow thanne go thy wey therwith?" quod she.
    "Ye, certes, lemman," quod this Absolon.
3720   "Thanne make thee redy," quod she, "I come anon."
And unto Nicholas she seyde stille,
"Now hust, and thou shalt laughen al thy fille."
    This Absolon doun sette hym on his knees
And seyde, "I am a lord at alle degrees;

3692 *trewe-love:* a four-leafed sprig of herb-paris (in the shape of a fourfold true-love knot). 3693 *wende:* thought. 3696 *raughte:* reached. 3697 *semy:* small, gentle. 3700 *lemman:* sweetheart. 3706 *turtel:* turtledove. 3709 *'com pa me':* "come kiss me." 3722 *hust:* be quiet.

3725 For after this I hope ther cometh moore.
Lemman, thy grace, and sweete bryd, thyn oore!"
The wyndow she undoth, and that in haste.
"Have do," quod she, "com of, and speed the faste,
Lest that oure neighebores thee espie."
3730 This Absolon gan wype his mouth ful drie.
Derk was the nyght as pich, or as the cole,
And at the wyndow out she putte hir hole,
And Absolon, hym fil no bet ne wers,
But with his mouth he kiste hir naked ers
3735 Ful savourly, er he were war of this.
Abak he stirte, and thoughte it was amys,
For wel he wiste a womman hath no berd.
He felte a thyng al rough and long yherd,
And seyde, "Fy! allas! what have I do?"
3740 "Tehee!" quod she, and clapte the wyndow to,
And Absolon gooth forth a sory pas.
"A berd! a berd!" quod hende Nicholas,
"By Goddes corpus, this goth faire and weel."
This sely Absolon herde every deel,
3745 And on his lippe he gan for anger byte,
And to hymself he seyde, "I shal thee quyte."
Who rubbeth now, who froteth now his lippes
With dust, with sond, with straw, with clooth, with
      chippes,
But Absolon, that seith ful ofte, "Allas!"
3750 "My soule bitake I unto Sathanas,
But me were levere than al this toun," quod he,
"Of this despit awroken for to be.
Allas," quod he, "allas, I ne hadde ybleynt!"
His hoote love was coold and al yqueynt;
3755 For fro that tyme that he hadde kist hir ers,
Of paramours he sette nat a kers;
For he was heeled of his maladie.

3726 *oore:* grace. 3738 *long yherd:* long-haired. 3741 *a sory pas:* sadly. 3742 *a berd! a berd!:* a beard!
a trick! 3746 *quyte:* pay back (in revenge). 3747 *froteth:* rubs. 3752 *awroken:*
avenged. 3753 *ybleynt:* turned away. 3754 *yqueynt:* quenched.

Ful ofte paramours he gan deffie,
And weep as dooth a child that is ybete.
3760 A softe paas he wente over the strete
Until a smyth men cleped daun Gerveys,
That in his forge smythed plough harneys;
He sharpeth shaar and kultour bisily.
This Absolon knokketh al esily,
3765 And seyde, "Undo, Gerveys, and that anon."
"What, who artow?" "It am I, Absolon."
"What, Absolon! for Cristes sweete tree,
Why rise ye so rathe? ey, *benedicitee*!
Why eyleth yow? Som gay gerl, God it woot,
3770 Hath broght yow thus upon the viritoot.
By seinte Note, ye woot wel what I mene."
    This Absolon ne roghte nat a bene
Of al his pley; no word agayn he yaf;
He hadde moore tow on his distaf
3775 Than Gerveys knew, and seyde, "Freend so deere,
That hoote kultour in the chymenee heere,
As lene it me, I have therwith to doone,
And I wol brynge it thee agayn ful soone."
    Gerveys answerde, "Certes, were it gold,
3780 Or in a poke nobles alle untold,
Thou sholdest have, as I am trewe smyth.
Ey, Cristes foo! what wol ye do therwith?"
    "Therof," quod Absolon, "be as be may.
I shal wel telle it thee to-morwe day" —
3785 And caughte the kultour by the colde stele.
Ful softe out at the dore he gan to stele,
And wente unto the carpenteris wal.
He cogheth first, and knokketh therwithal
Upon the wyndowe, right as he dide er.

3761 *daun:* sir. 3763 *shaar:* ploughshare. *kultour:* vertical blade at the front of the plough (turf cutter). 3768 *rathe:* early. *benedicitee:* "(the Lord) bless you." 3770 *upon the viritoot:* colloquial phrase whose origin and meaning is obscure; probably means *astir.* 3771 *seint Note:* St. Neot of Glastonbury. 3772 *roght nat a bene:* cared not a bean (i.e., nothing). 3774 *tow on his distaf:* flax on his distaff (i.e., business at hand.) 3780 *poke:* bag.

3790   This Alison answerde, "Who is ther
That knokketh so? I warante it a theef."
    "Why, nay," quod he, "God woot, my sweete leef,
I am thyn Absolon, my deerelyng.
Of gold," quod he, "I have thee broght a ryng.
3795   My mooder yaf it me, so God me save;
Ful fyn it is, and therto wel ygrave.
This wol I yeve thee, if thou me kisse."
    This Nicholas was risen for to pisse,
And thoughte he wolde amenden al the jape;
3800   He sholde kisse his ers er that he scape.
And up the wyndowe dide he hastily,
And out his ers he putteth pryvely
Over the buttok, to the haunche-bon;
And therwith spak this clerk, this Absolon,
3805   "Spek, sweete byrd, I noot nat where thou art."
    This Nicholas anon leet fle a fart,
As greet as it had been a thonder-dent,
That with the strook he was almoost yblent;
And he was redy with his iren hoot,
3810   And Nicholas amydde the ers he smoot.
    Of gooth the skyn an hande-brede aboute,
The hoote kultour brende so his toute,
And for the smert he wende for to dye.
As he were wood, for wo he gan to crye,
3815   "Help! water! water! help, for Goddes herte!"
    This carpenter out of his slomber sterte,
And herde oon crien "water" as he were wood,
And thoughte, "Allas, now comth Nowelis flood!"
He sit hym up withouten wordes mo,
3820   And with his ax he smoot the corde atwo,
And doun gooth al; he foond neither to selle,
Ne breed ne ale, til he cam to the celle
Upon the floor, and ther aswowne he lay.
    Up stirte hire Alison and Nicholay,

3792 *leef:* beloved. **3795** *yaf:* gave. **3799** *amenden:* improve upon. *jape:* joke. **3807** *thonder-dent:* thunderstroke. **3808** *yblent:* blinded. **3812** *toute:* rump. **3818** *Nowelis:* Noah's. **3822** *celle:* floorboards.

3825 And criden "out" and "harrow" in the strete.
The neighebores, bothe smale and grete,
In ronnen for to gauren on this man,
That yet aswowne lay, bothe pale and wan,
For with the fal he brosten hadde his arm.
3830 But stonde he moste unto his owene harm;
For whan he spak, he was anon bore doun
With hende Nicholas and Alisoun.
They tolden every man that he was wood,
He was agast so of Nowelis flood
3835 Thurgh fantasie, that of his vanytee
He hadde yboght hym knedyng tubbes thre,
And hadde hem hanged in the roof above;
And that he preyed hem, for Goddes love,
To sitten in the roof, *par compaignye.*
3840   The folk gan laughen at his fantasye;
Into the roof they kiken and they cape,
And turned al his harm unto a jape.
For what so that this carpenter answerde,
It was for noght, no man his reson herde.
3845 With othes grete he was so sworn adoun
That he was holde wood in al the toun;
For every clerk anonright heeld with oother.
They seyde, "The man is wood, my leeve brother";
And every wight gan laughen at this stryf.
3850 Thus swyved was this carpenteris wyf,
For al his kepyng and his jalousye;
And Absolon hath kist hir nether ye;
And Nicholas is scalded in the towte.
This tale is doon, and God save al the rowte!

Herre endeth the Millere his tale

(c. 1390)

3827 **gauren:** stare. 3829 **brosten:** broken. 3835 **vanytee:** foolishness. 3839 **par compaignye:** to keep him company. 3845 **sworn adoun:** overcome by oaths. 3847 **anonright:** immediately. **heeld:** agreed. 3850 **swyved:** copulated with. 3852 **nether ye:** lower eye. 3854 **this tale is doon:** popular folktales of the type told by the Miller and the Reeve often have this kind of neatly pointed ending highlighting the ironic reversals of the plot.

ANONYMOUS MEDIEVAL POPULAR BALLADS

*T*hese popular folk songs are one of the oldest forms of poetic narrative. Traditionally they have depended for their transmission and preservation upon oral performance (not necessarily professional, and often with musical accompaniment). The ballad usually focuses on a single event, on action rather than character or feeling (as in the medieval lyric), and its form is characterized by a simple rhyme scheme and metre. Although individual ballads must once have originated with one person or group, every retelling reflects the different performer and the performer's audience (no doubt contributing to their continuing popularity). For this reason most ballads exist in a variety of versions, each slightly different from the next. While the selections that follow reflect the rich British tradition of ballad composition, many British ballads taken by immigrants to North America have been transformed by the new audiences and cultural influences encountered here (for example, African-American culture and the experience of the American frontier). Also, new ballads continue to appear — most recently in contemporary pop music and songs of protest.

Sir Patrick Spens

I

The king sits in Dunfermline town
Drinking the blude-red wine;
'O whare will I get a skeely[1] skipper
To sail this new ship o' mine?'

II

5   O up and spak an eldern knight,
Sat at the king's right knee:
'Sir Patrick Spens is the best sailor
That ever sail'd the sea.'

1 *skilful*

III

Our king has written a braid[2] letter,
10   And seal'd it with his hand,
And sent it to Sir Patrick Spens,
      Was walking on the strand.

IV

'To Noroway, to Noroway,
      To Noroway o'er the faem;[3]
15   The king's daughter o' Noroway,
      'Tis thou must bring her hame.'

V

The first word that Sir Patrick read
      So loud, loud laugh'd he;
the neist[4] word that Sir Patrick read
20   The tear blinded his e'e.[5]

VI

'O wha[6] is this has done this deed
      And tauld the king o' me,
To send us out, at this time o' year,
      To sail upon the sea?

VII

25   'Be it wind, be it weet,[7] be it hail, be it sleet,
      Our ship must sail the faem;
The king's daughter o' Noroway,
      'Tis we must fetch her hame.'

VIII

They hoysed their sails on Monenday morn
30   Wi' a' the speed they may;
They hae landed in Noroway
      Upon a Wodensday.

2 *broad.*
3 *foam.*
4 *next.*
5 *eye.*
6 *who.*
7 *wet.*

IX

'Mak ready, mak ready, my merry men a'!
    Our gude ship sails the morn.' —
35   'Now ever alack, my master dear,
        I fear a deadly storm.

X

'I saw the new moon late yestreen[8]
    Wi' the auld moon in her arm;
And if we gang to sea, master,
40   I fear we'll come to harm.'

XI

They hadna sail'd a league, a league.
    A league but barely three,
When the lift[9] grew dark, and the wind blew loud,
    And gurly[10] grew the sea.

XII

45   The ankers brak, and the topmast lap,[11]
    It was sic[12] a deadly storm:
And the waves cam owre the broken ship
    Till a' her sides were torn.

XIII

'O where will I get a gude sailor
50   To tak' my helm in hand,
Till I get up to the tall topmast
    To see if I can spy land?' —

XIV

'O here am I, a sailor gude,
    To tak' the helm in hand,
55   Till you go up to the tall topmast,
    But I fear you'll ne'er spy land.'

8 *yesterday evening.*
9 *sky.*
10 *stormy.*
11 *leapt, sprang free.*
12 *such.*

XV

He hadna gane a step, a step,
   A step but barely ane,[13]
When a bolt flew out of our goodly ship,
60   And the saut[14] sea it came in.

XVI

'Go fetch a web o' the silken claith,
   Another o' the twine,
And wap[15] them into our ship's side,
   And let nae the sea come in.'

XVII

65   They fetch d a web o' the silken claith,
   Another o' the twine,
And they wapp'd them round that gude ship's side,
   But still the sea came in.

XVIII

O laith, laith[16] were our gude Scots lords
70   To wet their cork-heel'd shoon,[17]
But lang or a' the play was play'd
   They wat their hats aboon.[18]

XIX

And mony was the feather bed
   That flatter'd[19] on the faem;
75   And mony was the gude lord's son
   That never mair cam hame.

XX

O lang, lang may the ladies sit,
   Wi' their fans into their hand,
Before they see Sir Patrick Spens
80   Come sailing to the strand!

---

13 *one.* **14** *salt.* **15** *wrap.* **16** *loath.* **17** *shoes.* **18** *above.* **19** *tossed afloat.*

XXI

And lang, lang may the maidens sit
  Wi' their gowd kames[20] in their hair,
A-waiting for their ain[21] dear loves!
  For them they'll see nae mair.

XXII

85   Half-owre, half-owre[22] to Aberdour,[23]
  'Tis fifty fathoms deep;
And there lies gude Sir Patrick Spens,
  Wi' the Scots lords at his feet!

Get Up and Bar the Door

I

It fell about the Martinmas time,[1]
  And a gay time it was then,
When our goodwife got puddings to make,
  And she's boil'd them in the pan.

II

5   The wind sae cauld blew south and north,
  And blew into the floor;
Quoth our goodman to our goodwife,
  'Gae out and bar the door.' —

III

'My hand is in my hussyfskap,[2]
10   Goodman, as ye may see;
An' it shou'dna be barr'd this hundred year,
  It's no be barr'd for me.'

20 *combs.*
21 *own.*
22 *halfway over.*
23 *Aberdeen.*

1 *the Feast of St. Martin (i.e., November 11).*
2 *housekeeping.*

IV

They made a paction 'tween them twa,
    They made it firm and sure,
15   That the first word whae'er shou'd speak,
    Shou'd rise and bar the door.

V

Then by there came two gentlemen,
    At twelve o'clock at night,
And they could neither see house nor hall,
20   Nor coal nor candle-light.

VI

'Now whether is this a rich man's house,
    Or whether is it a poor?'
But n'er a word wad³ ane o' them speak,
    For barring of the door.

VII

25   And first they ate the white puddings,
    And then they ate the black.
Tho' muckle⁴ thought the goodwife to hersel'
    Yet ne'er a word she spake.

VIII

Then said the one unto the other,
30   'Here, man, tak ye my knife;
Do ye tak aff the auld man's beard,
    And I'll kiss the goodwife.' —

IX

'But there's nae water in the house,
    And what shall we do than?' —
35   'What ails ye at the pudding-broo⁵
    That boils into the pan?'

3 *would.*
4 *much.*
5 *the water in which sausage puddings have been boiled.*

X

O up then started our goodman,
    And angry man was he:
'Will ye kiss my wife before my een,
40   And sca'd me wi' pudding-bree?'

XI

Then up and started our goodwife,
    Gied⁶ three skips on the floor:
'Goodman, you've spoken the foremost word!
    Get up and bar the door.'

Lord Randall

I

'O where hae ye been, Lord Randal, my son?
O where hae ye been, my handsome young man?' —
'I hae been to the wild wood; mother, make my bed soon,
For I'm weary wi' hunting, and fain¹ wald² lie down.'

II

5   'Where gat ye your dinner, Lord Randal, my son?
Where gat ye your dinner, my handsome young man?' —
'I dined wi' my true-love; mother, make my bed soon,
For I'm weary wi' hunting, and fain wald lie down.'

III

'What gat ye to your dinner, Lord Randal, my son?
10   What gat ye to your dinner, my handsome young man?' —
'I gat eels boil'd in broo';³ mother, make my bed soon,
For I'm weary wi' hunting, and fain wald lie down.'

6 *gave.*

1 *gladly.*
2 *would.*
3 *broth.*

IV

'What became of your bloodhounds, Lord Randal, my son?
What became of your bloodhounds, my handsome young
     man?' —
15 'O they swell'd and they died; mother make my bed soon,
For I'm weary wi' hunting, and fain wald lie down.'

V

'O I fear ye are poison'd, Lord Randal, my son!
O I fear ye are poison'd, my handsome young man!' —
'O yes! I am poison'd; mother, make my bed soon,
20 For I'm sick at the heart, and I fain wald lie down.'

The Twa Corbies

I

As I was walking all alane,
I heard twa corbies[1] making a mane:
The tane unto the tither did say,
'Whar sall we gane and dine the day?'

II

5 ' — In behint yon auld fail[2] dyke
I wot there lies a new-slain knight;
And naebody kens[3] that he lies there
But his hawk, his hound, and his lady fair.

III

'His hound is to the hunting gane,
10 His hawk to fetch the wild-fowl hame,
His lady's ta'en anither mate,
So we may mak' our dinner sweet.

1 *ravens.*
2 *turf.*
3 *knows.*

IV

'Ye'll sit on his white hause-bane,[4]
And I'll pike out his bonny blue e'en:
15   Wi' ae lock o' his gowden hair
We'll theek[5] our nest when it grows bare.

V

'Mony a one for him maks mane,
But nane sall ken whar he is gane:
O'er his white banes, when they are bare,
20   The wind sall blaw for evermair.'

The Birth of Robin Hood

I

O Willie's large o' limb and lith,[1]
   And come o' high degree,
And he is gane to Earl Richard,
   To serve for meat and fee.

II

5   Earl Richard had but ae daughter,
   Fair as a lily-flower,
And they made up their love-contract
   Like proper paramour.

III

It fell upon a simmer's nicht,[2]
10   Whan the leaves were fair and green,
That Willie met his gay ladie
   Intil[3] the wood alane.

4 *neckbone.*
5 *thatch.*

1 *joint.*
2 *summer's night.*
3 *in.*

IV

'O narrow is my gown, Willie,
That wont[4] to be sae wide;
15   And gane is a' my fair colour,
That wont to be my pride.

V

'But gin[5] my father should get word
What's past between us twa,
Before that he should eat or drink
20   He'd hang you o'er that wa'.

VI

'But ye'll come to my bower, Willie,
Just as the sun gaes down,
And kep[6] me in your arms twa,
And latna me fa' down.'

VII

25   O whan the sun was now gane down,
He's doen him till[7] her bower,
And there, by the lee[8] licht o' the moon,
Her window she lookit o'er.

VIII

Intill a robe o' red scarlet
30   She lap,[9] fearless o' harm;
And Willie was large o' lith and limb,
And keppit her in his arm.

IX

And they've gane to the gude green-wood,
And, ere the night was deen,[10]
35   She's born to him a bonny young son,
Amang the leaves sae green.

---

4 *used to be.* 5 *if.* 6 *keep.* 7 *went to.* 8 *pleasant.* 9 *lay.* 10 *done.*

X

Whan night was gane, and day was come,
    And the sun began to peep
Up and raise the Earl Richard
40   Out o' his drowsy sleep.

XI

He's ca'd upon his merry young men,
    By ane, by twa, and by three:
'O what's come o' my daughter dear,
    That she's nae come to me?

XII

45 'I dreamt a dreary dream last night,
    God grant it come to gude!
I dreamt I saw my daughter dear
    Drown in the saut sea flood.

XIII

'But gin my daughter be dead or sick,
50   Or yet be stown awa',
I mak a vow, and I'll keep it true,
    I'll hang ye ane and a'!'

XIV

They sought her back, they sought her fore,
    They sought her up and down;
55 They got her in the gude green-wood,
    Nursing her bonny young son.

XV

He took the bonny boy in his arms,
    And kist him tenderlie;
Says, 'Though I would your father hang,
60   Your mother's dear to me.'

XVI

He kist him o'er and o'er again:
  'My grandson I thee claim,
And Robin Hood in gude green-wood,
  And that shall be your name.'

XVII

65 And mony ane sings o' grass, o' grass,
  And mony ane sings o' corn,
And mony ane sings o' Robin Hood
  Kens[11] little whare he was born.

XVIII

It wasna in the ha', the ha',
70   Nor in the painted bower;
But it was in the gude green-wood,
  Amang the lily-flower.

11 *knows.*

Anonymous Medieval Lyrics

*M*edieval lyrics began as popular oral poetry and were frequently set to music. Even in the later Middle Ages, when composed and transmitted as written verse, the lyric changed little and remained highly conventionalized in form and content. In part, this manifests a widespread desire in the Middle Ages to relate the individual through the universal (distinguishing these poems from modern lyric poetry with its emphasis on personal experience). But the conventional nature of these poems also reflects the general nature of their themes — spring, the beauty of a lady, death, Christ's suffering for our sins. Such an emphasis on universality in theme and language, concentrating on fundamental human feelings rather than narrative (as in the ballad), can make difficult and complex situations more accessible and affective for the individual reader. "Sunset at Calvary," for example, focuses on the pain that a mother feels at the death of her child. By identifying in this way with a common situation from life, the poet can then communicate in profoundly human terms the anguish felt contemplating Christ's sacrifice in the Crucifixion.

Western Wind

> Western wind, when will thou blow,
> The small rain down can rain?
> Christ, if my love were in my arms
> And I in my bed again!

I Sing of a Maiden

> I synge of a mayden
> That is makeles:[1]
> Kyng of alle kynges
> To hir sone she ches.[2]

---

1 *spotless, matchless, mateless (a triple pun on the Virgin Mary's virtues).*
2 *chose.*

5 He cam also stille[3]
   Ther[4] his moder[5] was
   As dewe in Aprill
   That falleth on the gras.

   He cam also stille
10 To his modres bour[6]
   As dewe in Aprill
   That falleth on the flour.

   He cam also stille
   Ther his moder lay
15 As dewe in Aprill
   That falleth on the spray.

   Moder and mayden
   Was nevere non but she:
   Wel may swich[7] a lady
20 Goddes[8] moder be.

Sunset on Calvary

Now goth sonne under wode, — [1]
Me reweth,[2] Marie, thy faire rode.[3]
Now goth sonne under tree, —
Me reweth, Marie, thy sone and thee.

---

3 *as silently, as gently.* 4 *(there) where.* 5 *mother.* 6 *inner room, bedchamber.* 7 *such.* 8 *God's.*
1 *wood (i.e., the Cross).* 2 *pity.* 3 *face.*

The Cuckoo Song

Somer[1] is i-comen in,
Loude syng cuckow!
Groweth seed and bloweth[2] meed[3]
And spryngeth the wode[4] now.
5 Syng cuckow!
Ewe bleteth after lamb,
Loweth after calve cow;
Bullock sterteth,[5] bukke[6] farteth, —
Myrie syng cuckow!
10 Cuckow! Cuckow!
Wel syngest thou cuckow:
Ne swik[7] thou nevere now.
  Syng cuckow, now, syng cuckow!
  Syng cuckow, syng cuckow, now!

---

1 *summer.* **2** *blows (i.e., blooms).* **3** *meadow.* **4** *wood.* **5** *leaps.* **6** *buck.* **7** *cease.*

Alison

Bitwene March and Aperil,
Whan spray bigynneth to sprynge,
The litel fowel hath hir wyl
On hir lede[1] to synge.
5   I lyve in love-longynge
For semlokest[2] of alle thyng;
She may me blisse brynge:
I am in hir baundoun.[3]
    An hende hap[4] I have i-hent,[5]
10   I wot[6] from hevene it is me sent; —
From alle wommen my love is lent[7]
And light on Alysoun.

On hewe hir heer is faire ynough,
Hir browes broune, hir eyen blake,
15   Wyth lufsom[8] chere she on me lough,[9]
Wyth myddel smal and wel i-mak.

But she me wol to hire take
For-to ben hir owene make,[10]
Longe to lyve I wyl forsake
20   And feye[11] falle adoun.
    An hende hap I have i-hent,
I wot from hevene it is me sent; —
From alle wommen my love is lent
And light on Alysoun.

---

1 *in her language.* 2 *seemliest, fairest.* 3 *power.* 4 *a gracious chance.* 5 *received.* 6 *know.* 7 *gone.* 8 *lovely face.* 9 *smiled.* 10 *mate.* 11 *doomed (to die).*

25   Nyghtes whan I wende[12] and wake —
      For-thy myne wonges[13] waxen wan;
      Lady, al for thy sake
      Longyng is i-lent[14] me on.
      In world nis[15] non so witter[16] man
30   That al hir bountee[17] telle can:
      Hir swire[18] is whiter thanne the swan,
      And fairest[19] may in toun.
           An hende hap I have i-hent,
           I wot from hevene it is me sent; —
35   From alle wommen my love is lent
           And light on Alysoun.

      I am for wowyng al forwake,[20]
      Wery as water in wore;[21]
      Lest any reve me my make
40   I have i-yerned yore.[22]
      Bettre is tholen while[23] sore
      Thanne murnen[24] evermore.
      Geynest[25] under gore,
      Herkne to my roun:[26]
45   An hende hap I have i-hent,
           I wot from hevene it is me sent; —
           From alle wommen my love is lent
           And light on Alysoun.

---

12 *turn (and toss).* 13 *cheeks.* 14 *come upon.* 15 *is not.* 16 *wise.* 17 *excellence.* 18 *neck.* 19 *(she is the) fairest maid.* 20 *worn out with lying awake.* 21 *? pond, pool.* 22 *worried long since.* 23 *endure for a time.* 24 *mourn.* 25 *fairest in clothing (i.e., of all women).* 26 *round (i.e., song)*

SIR THOMAS WYATT

(1503–1542)

*W*yatt was born at Allington Castle in Kent. Educated at St. John's Col-
lege, Cambridge, he spent most of his adult life as a courtier and diplo-
mat in the service of Henry VIII. His missions abroad put him in touch with met-
rically complex and imagistically vivid verse forms, especially the sonnet, which he
introduced to England through translations and adaptations of Petrarch.

    The sonnet is a prescribed form (see Introduction to Poetry, p. 2). but it con-
tains much room for variety. In importing the sonnet to England, Wyatt modified
the standard patterns of contemplation, love, and rejection. These topics, of course,
were quite conventional: the Lover begs acceptance of the Lady through various met-
aphors of agony, disenchantment, and bliss; she, with studied disregard, rebuffs or
ignores his advances; such rejection only intensifies his next attempt. Wyatt refines
this classical regularity with the addition of directness and plain-speaking — attri-
butes which, though adopted from Italian models, are rendered as strictly "English"
in Wyatt's lyrical verse.

    Although he himself was renowned as a scholar, poet, and public figure,
Wyatt's verse did not enjoy a wide readership until the appearance of the anthology
of poems published by Richard Tottel in 1557. Popularly referred to as Tottel's
Miscellany, the volume included sonnets and lyrics by Wyatt and others, and
represents the "renaissance" of poetry in England.

They flee from me

THE LOVER SHEWETH HOW HE IS FORSAKEN OF SUCH AS HE
SOMETIME ENJOYED.

> They flee from me, that sometime did me seek,
> With naked foot stalking within my chamber:
> Once have I seen them gentle, tame, and meek,
> That now are wild, and do not once remember,
> 5   That sometime they have put themselves in danger
> To take bread at my hand; and now they range
>   Busily seeking in continual change.
>   Thanked be Fortune, it hath been otherwise
> Twenty times better; but once especial,

10   In thin array, after a pleasant guise,[1]
       When her loose gown did from her shoulders fall
       And she me caught in her arms long and small,[2]
       And therewithal so sweetly did me kiss,
       And softly said, 'Dear heart, how like you this?'
15   It was no dream; for I lay broad awaking:
       But all is turn'd now, through my gentleness,
       Into a bitter fashion of forsaking;
       And I have leave to go of her goodness;
       And she also to use new fangleness.
20   But since that I unkindly so am served:
       How like you this, what hath she now deserved?

(1520–30?)   (1557)

My galley charged with forgetfulness

THE LOVER COMPARETH HIS STATE TO A SHIP IN PERILOUS STORM
TOSSED ON THE SEA.

       My galley charged with forgetfulness,
       Through sharp seas, in winter nights, doth pass
       'Tween rock and rock; and eke[1] my foe, alas,
       That is my lord,[2] steereth with cruelness:
5   And every hour, a thought in readiness,
       As though that death were light in such a case.
       An endless wind doth tear the sail apace
       Of forced sighs and trusty fearfulness;
       A rain of tears, a cloud of dark disdain,
10   Have done the wearied cords great hinderance:

---

1 *usual manner of behaviour.*
2 *slender.*

1 *also.*
2 *i.e., Cupid.*

Wreathed with error, and with ignorance;
The stars[3] be hid that lead me to this pain;
  Drown'd is reason that should be my comfort,
  And I remain, despairing of the port.

(1520–30?)   (1557)

---

3 i.e., the lady's eyes.

HENRY HOWARD, EARL OF SURREY

(1517–1547)

*S*urrey was a member of the major aristocracy in the reign of Henry
VIII. A soldier and scholar, his short and tempestuous life at court was
invariably linked to the relative favour of his cousins Anne Boleyn and Catherine
Howard (wives of the king) as well as to his own military victories and setbacks.
As a poet, he is usually paired with Wyatt in establishing the sonnet form in Eng-
land, and Tottel's Miscellany (1557) was in fact titled Songs and Sonnets
written by the Right Honourable Lord Henry Howard late Earl of
Surrey and other.

His precedence on the title page was purely honorary, but Surrey was a gifted
innovator with poetic form and rhyme as well as the first English poet to publish
blank verse. His sonnets often carry extended metaphors with grace and suggestive-
ness. Fiercely proud and reactionary in temperament, he was accused of treason and
beheaded at the age of 30, a mere eight days before the death of the king.

Love that doth reign

Love that doth reign and live within my thought,
And built his seat within my captive breast,
Clad in the arms wherein with me he fought,
Oft in my face he doth his banner rest.
5 But she that taught me love and suffer pain,
My doubtful hope and eke[1] my hot desire
With shamefast[2] look to shadow and refrain,
Her smiling grace converteth straight to ire.
And coward love then to the heart apace
10 Taketh his flight, where he doth lurk and plain[3]
His purpose lost, and dare not show his face.
For my lord's guilt thus faultless bide I pain;
Yet from my lord shall not my foot remove.
Sweet is the death that taketh end by love.

(1542?)   (1557)

1 *also.*
2 *shamefaced.*
3 *complain.*

Alas! so all things

A COMPLAINT BY NIGHT OF THE LOVER NOT BELOVED.

Alas! so all things now do hold their peace!
Heaven and earth disturbed in no thing;
The beasts, the air, the birds their song do cease,
The nightès car the stars about doth bring.
5   Calm is the sea; the waves work less and less:
So am not I, whom love, alas! doth wring,
Bringing before my face the great increase
Of my desires, whereat I weep and sing,
In joy and woe, as in a doubtful ease.
10   For my sweet thoughts sometime do pleasure bring
But by and by, the cause of my disease[1]
Gives me a pang, that inwardly doth sting,
   When that I think what grief it is again,
   To live and lack the thing should rid my pain.

(1542?)   (1557)

---

1 i.e., lack of ease, discomfort.

EDMUND SPENSER

(1552–1599)

*S*penser stands with Shakespeare and Milton as one of the foremost poets
of the English Renaissance. He was in the employ of the Earl of Leicester
(Queen Elizabeth's favourite) and came to know Sir Philip Sidney, to whom in
1579 he dedicated his first important work, The Shepheardes Calendar.
Spenser was not merely a gentleman-poet, however, but a career civil servant who
went to Ireland in 1580 as secretary to Lord Grey of Wilton, and remained there
in minor government posts for the rest of his life, ever hopeful of preferment.
Although introduced at the court of Elizabeth I, worldly advancement was not
forthcoming. But his epitaph in Westminster Abbey proclaims him "Prince of
Poets," and his place in English letters is secured by his massive romantic epic The
Faerie Queene. Consciously archaic, allegorically complex, mythically sugges-
tive, Spenser's poetic world is rich, varied, and very much his own, as is his char-
acteristic use of language, rhyme, and rhythm in his sonnet sequence Amoretti, to
which the following poems belong.

Lyke as a huntsman

Lyke as a huntsman after weary chace,
Seeing the game from him escapt away,
Sits downe to rest him in some shady place,
With panting hounds beguiled of their pray:[1]
So, after long pursuit and vaine assay,
When I all weary had the chace forsooke,
The gentle deer returnd the selfe-same way,
Thinking to quench her thirst at the next brooke:
There she, beholding me with mylder looke,
Sought not to fly, but fearlesse still did bide;
Till I in hand her yet halfe trembling tooke,
And with her owne goodwill her fyrmely tyde.
    Strange thing, me seemd, to see a beast so wyld,
    So goodly wonne, with her owne will beguyld.

(1595)

1 prey.

One day I wrote her name upon the strand

One day I wrote her name upon the strand;
But came the waves, and washed it away:
Agayne, I wrote it with a second hand;
But came the tyde, and made my paynes his pray.[1]
5 Vayne man, sayd she, that doest in vaine assay
A mortall thing so to immortalize;
For I my selve shall lyke to this decay,
And eke[2] my name bee wyped out lykewize.
Not so, quod I; let baser things devize
10 To dy in dust, but you shall live by fame:
My verse your vertues rare shall éternize,
And in the hevens wryte your glorious name.
    Where, when as death shall all the world subdew,
    Our love shall live, and later life renew.

(1595)

1 *prey.*
2 *also.*

SIR WALTER RALEGH

(c. 1552–1618)

*R*alegh is perhaps best known for his colonization of Virginia and for popu-
larizing the use of tobacco in England. He was also friend and patron to
Edmund Spenser. Notoriously proud, ambitious, and ostentatious, he commanded
extremes of loyalty and hatred through the power of his public personality. Though
he was a favourite of Queen Elizabeth in the 1580s, Ralegh spent most of the final
fifteen years of his life imprisoned in the Tower by James I. While in the Tower,
Ralegh wrote the bulk of his voluminous History of the World. But he was a
poet as well as a man of action and confirmed skeptic, and his verse is characterized
by direct, unadorned, even bitter realism — seen especially in the haughty denunci-
ations of "The Lie." His is a hard-minded poetic vision that rejects easy idealiza-
tions. Released from prison in 1616 to lead the ill-fated Guiana expedition in
search of gold for the English treasury, Ralegh was tried on charges of reopening
hostilities with Spain and beheaded.

The Nymph's Reply[1]

If all the world and love were young,
And truth in every shepherd's tongue,
These pretty pleasures might me move
To live with thee and be thy love.

5   But time drives flocks from field to fold,
When rivers rage and rocks grow cold;
And Philomel[2] becometh dumb;
The rest complains of cares to come.

The flowers do fade, and wanton fields
10   To wayward winter reckoning yields:
A honey tongue, a heart of gall,
Is fancy's spring, but sorrow's fall.

1 reply to Christopher Marlowe's "The Passionate Shepherd to His Love."
2 nightingale (mythological).

Thy gowns, thy shoes, thy beds of roses,
Thy cap, thy kirtle, and thy posies,
15   Soon break, soon wither, soon forgotten, —
In folly ripe, in reason rotten.

Thy belt of straw and ivy buds,
Thy coral clasps and amber studs, —
All those in me no means can move
20   To come to thee and be thy love.

But could youth last, and love still breed;
Had joys no date, nor age no need;
Then those delights my mind might move
To live with thee and be thy love.

(1600)

The Lie[1]

Go, Soul, the body's guest,
   Upon a thankless arrant:[2]
Fear not to touch the best;
   The truth shall be thy warrant:
5   Go, since I needs must die,
   And give the world the lie.

Say to the court, it glows
   And shines like rotten wood;
Say to the church, it shows
10   What's good, and doth no good:
If church and court reply,
   Then give them both the lie.

---

1 to give "the lie" was the ultimate insult and challenge. It could be settled only by death.
2 errand.

Tell potentates, they live
   Acting by others' action;
Not loved unless they give,
   Not strong but by a faction:
If potentates reply,
Give potentates the lie.

Tell men of high condition,
   That manage the estate,
Their purpose is ambition,
   Their practice only hate:
And if they once reply,
Then give them all the lie.

Tell them that brave it most,
   They beg for more by spending,
Who, in their greatest cost,
   Seek nothing but commending:
And if they make reply,
Then give them all the lie.

Tell zeal it wants devotion;
   Tell love it is but lust;
Tell time it is but motion;
   Tell flesh it is but dust:
And wish them not reply,
For thou must give the lie.

Tell age it daily wasteth;
   Tell honour how it alters;
Tell beauty how she blasteth;
   Tell favour how it falters:
And as they shall reply,
Give every one the lie.

15

20

25

30

35

40

Tell wit how much it wrangles
   In tickle points of niceness;
Tell wisdom she entangles
   Herself in over-wiseness:
And when they do reply,
Straight give them both the lie.

Tell physic of her boldness;
   Tell skill it is pretension;
Tell charity of coldness;
   Tell law it is contention:
And as they do reply,
So give them still the lie.

Tell fortune of her blindness;
   Tell nature of decay;
Tell friendship of unkindness;
   Tell justice of delay:
And if they will reply,
Then give them all the lie.

Tell arts they have no soundness,
   But vary by esteeming;
Tell schools they want profoundness,
   And stand too much on seeming:
If arts and schools reply,
Give arts and schools the lie.

Tell faith it's fled the city;
   Tell how the country erreth;
Tell manhood shakes off pity;
   Tell virtue least preferreth:
And if they do reply,
Spare not to give the lie.

So when thou hast, as I
    Commanded thee, done blabbing, —
75 Although to give the lie
    Deserves no less than stabbing, —
Stab at thee he that will,
No stab the soul can kill.

(1593?)   (1608)

SIR PHILIP SIDNEY

(1554–1586)

*L*egend *almost overshadows the biographical facts of Sidney's life. He was a poet, scholar, patron-aristocrat, soldier, gentleman — the perfect Elizabethan courtier who died on the battlefield in defence of his country's ideals. It therefore comes almost as a relief that Ben Jonson (who elsewhere praises Sidney's poetry) told Drummond of Hawthronden, "Sir P. Sidney was no pleasant man in countenance, his face being spoiled with pimples." But, legend and anecdote aside, Sidney's contribution to English letters is substantial: his* Astrophel and Stella, *comprising 108 sonnets and eleven songs, is the first complete sonnet sequence in English; his* Defense of Poesy *is the first English book of literary criticism; his* Arcadia *is considered the most important English prose fiction prior to the rise of the novel in the eighteenth century. Sidney used the conventional Petrarchan subject of the contrary feelings of the lover, but he was a fresh and innovative sonneteer. As the following examples from* Astrophel and Stella *demonstrate, he projected a feeling of personal immediacy even within the stylized world of the love sonnet.*

Loving in truth

Loving in truth, and fain in verse my love to show,
That she, dear she! might take some pleasure of my pain;
Pleasure might cause her read, reading might make her
know,
Knowledge might pity win, and pity grace obtain:
5 I sought fit words to paint the blackest face of woe,
Studying inventions fine, her wits to entertain:
Oft turning others' leaves, to see if thence would flow
Some fresh and fruitful showers upon my sun-burn'd
brain.

But words came halting forth, wanting[1] invention's stay;
10   Invention, Nature's child, fled step-dame Study's blows,
And others' feet still seem'd but strangers in my way.
      Thus, great with child to speak, and helpless in my
          throes,
Biting my truant pen, beating myself for spite,
Fool! said my Muse to me, look in thy heart, and write.

(1581–83?)   (1591)

Having this day my horse

Having this day my horse, my hand, my lance,
Guided so well, that I obtain'd the prize,
Both by the judgment of the English eyes,
      And of some sent from that sweet en'my[1] France;
5   Horsemen, my skill in horsemanship advance;
Town-folks my strength; a daintier judge applies
His praise to sleight, which from good use doth rise:
      Some lucky wits impute it but to chance:

Others, because of both sides I do take
10   My blood from them who did excel in this,
Think Nature me a man of arms did make;
      How far they shot awry! the true cause is,
Stella look'd on, and from her heav'nly face,
Sent forth the beams which made so fair my race.

(1581–83?)   (1591)

1 lacking.

1 enemy (two syllables).

CHRISTOPHER MARLOWE

(1564–1593)

*B*orn the son of a Canterbury shoemaker, Christopher Marlowe received *the M.A. degree from Cambridge in 1587. Best known as a dramatic poet using blank verse, he demonstrated technical virtuosity in translating such classics as Ovid's* Amores *and the first book of Lucan's* Pharsalia. *His unfinished erotic narrative* Hero and Leander *is written in ironic and smooth rhyming couplets. Thus, the short pastoral verse entitled "The Passionate Shepherd to His Love" seems somewhat uncharacteristic. And yet, since at least the seventeenth century, it has been celebrated, and linked with Sir Walter Ralegh's skeptical "answer."*

Marlowe's mercurial career saw him gain prominence very early with the introduction of his "mighty line": the blank verse metre of Tamburlaine *(1587), which was to become the poetic medium of Shakespearean and Renaissance drama, as well as the measure of Milton's* Paradise Lost. *Surrey had used unrhymed decasyllables in translating the* Aeneid *some 35 years before, but his verse was meant to be stately and Latinate. It was Marlowe who made the measure distinctly English by demonstrating its directness, versatility, and power.*

The Passionate Shepherd to His Love

Come live with me, and be my love;
And we will all the pleasures prove
That hills and valleys, dales and fields,
Woods, or steepy mountain yields.

5 And we will sit upon the rocks,
Seeing the shepherds feed their flocks
By shallow rivers, to whose falls
Melodious birds sing madrigals.

And I will make thee beds of roses,
10 And a thousand fragrant posies;
A cap of flowers, and a kirtle
Embroidered all with leaves of myrtle;

A gown made of the finest wool
Which from our pretty lambs we pull;
15 Fair-lined slippers for the cold,
With buckles of the purest gold;

A belt of straw and ivy-buds,
With coral clasps and amber-studs:
And if these pleasures may thee move,
20 Come live with me, and be my love.

The shepherd-swains shall dance and sing
For thy delight each May-morning;
If these delights thy mind may move,
Then live with me, and be my love.

(1599)

WILLIAM SHAKESPEARE

(1564–1616)

*S*hakespeare was born in Stratford-on-Avon, probably a day or two previous to his christening on April 26, 1564. It is traditional that his birthday be celebrated on April 23, which is the feast day of St. George, England's patron saint. Much of Shakespeare's adult life was spent in London as an actor and playwright with the Globe Theatre.

Although celebrated as the foremost dramatist in the language, Shakespeare is also a sonneteer. His 154 sonnets were published in 1609 but were noted previously by Francis Meres, who in 1598 made mention of Shakespeare's "sugared sonnets among his private friends." The sonnets, however, are far from sugary. They are profound moral and aesthetic contemplations that adapt metaphors from the theatrical world and from the world of human emotions. Investigators have been fascinated by the biographical possibilities of Shakespeare's sonnets, but they are primarily metaphorical contemplations that probe the complexities of love, death, fame, and mutability.

Sonnets

18

Shall I compare thee to a summer's day?
Thou art more lovely and more temperate:
Rough winds do shake the darling buds of May,
And summer's lease hath all too short a date:
5   Sometime too hot the eye of heaven shines,
And often is his gold complexion dimm'd;
And every fair from fair sometime declines
By chance or nature's changing course untrimm'd;
But thy eternal summer shall not fade
10   Nor lose possession of that fair thou ow'st;[1]
Nor shall Death brag thou wander'st in his shade,
When in eternal lines to time thou grow'st:
    So long as men can breathe or eyes can see,
    So long lives this and this gives life to thee.

(1609)

---

1 *ownest.*

29

When, in disgrace with fortune and men's eyes,
I all alone beweep my outcast state,
And trouble deaf heaven with my bootless[1] cries,
And look upon myself and curse my fate,
5   Wishing me like to one more rich in hope,
Featured like him, like him with friends possess'd,
Desiring this man's art and that man's scope,
With what I most enjoy contented least;
Yet in these thoughts myself almost despising,
10   Haply I think on thee, and then my state,
Like to the lark at break of day arising
From sullen earth, sings hymns at heaven's gate;
      For thy sweet love remember'd such wealth brings
      That then I scorn to change my state with kings.

(1609)

55

Not marble, nor the gilded monuments
Of princes, shall outlive this powerful rime;
But you shall shine more bright in these contents
Than unswept stone besmear'd with sluttish time.
5   When wasteful war shall statues overturn,
And broils root out the work of masonry,
Nor Mars his sword nor war's quick fire shall burn
The living record of your memory.
'Gainst death and all-oblivious enmity
10   Shall you pace forth: your praise shall still find room
Even in the eyes of all posterity
That wear this world out to the ending doom.
      So, till the judgement that yourself arise,[1]
      You live in this, and dwell in lovers' eyes.

(1609)

---

1 *useless, futile.*

1 *i.e., "So until you arise from the dead on Judgement Day."*

73

That time of year thou mayst in me behold
When yellow leaves, or none, or few, do hang
Upon those boughs which shake against the cold,
Bare ruin'd choirs where late the sweet birds sang.
In me thou see'st the twilight of such day
As after sunset fadeth in the west;
Which by and by black night doth take away,
Death's second self, that seals up all in rest.
In me thou see'st the glowing of such fire
That on the ashes of his youth doth lie,
As the death-bed whereon it must expire,
Consumed with that which it was nourish'd by.
    This thou perceiv'st, which makes thy love more strong,
    To love that well which thou must leave ere long.

(1609)

116

Let me not to the marriage of true minds
Admit impediments. Love is not love
Which alters when it alteration finds,
Or bends with the remover to remove:
O, no! it is an ever-fixed mark,
That looks on tempests and is never shaken;
It is the star to every wandering bark,[1]
Whose worth's unknown, although his height be taken.
Love's not Time's fool,[2] though rosy lips and cheeks
Within his bending sickle's compass come;
Love alters not with his brief hours and weeks,
But bears it out even to the edge of doom.
    If this be error and upon me proved,
    I never writ, nor no man ever loved.

(1609)

1 *sailing ship.*
2 *i.e., victim.*

129

The expense of spirit in a waste of shame
Is lust in action; and till action, lust
Is perjured, murderous, bloody, full of blame,
Savage, extreme, rude, cruel, not to trust;
5   Enjoy'd no sooner but despised straight;
Past reason hunted, and no sooner had,
Past reason hated, as a swallow'd bait
On purpose laid to make the taker mad:
Mad in pursuit and in possession so;
10   Had, having, and in quest to have, extreme;
A bliss in proof,[1] and proved, a very woe;
Before a joy proposed; behind a dream.
    All this the world well knows; yet none knows well
    To shun the heaven that leads men to this hell.

(1609)

130

My mistress' eyes are nothing like the sun;
Coral is far more red than her lips' red:
If snow be white, why then her breasts are dun;
If hairs be wires, black wires grow on her head.
5   I have seen roses damask'd,[1] red and white,
But no such roses see I in her cheeks;
And in some perfumes is there more delight
Than in the breath that from my mistress reeks.
I love to hear her speak, yet well I know
10   That music hath a far more pleasing sound:
I grant I never saw a goddess go;
My mistress, when she walks, treads on the ground:
    And yet, by heaven, I think my love as rare
    As any she belied[2] with false compare.

(1609)

1 *i.e., during the experience.*

1 *mingled, variegated.*
2 *misrepresented.*

JOHN DONNE

(1572–1631)

ohn Donne was a talented young man hopeful of worldly advancement. Appointed private secretary to Sir Thomas Egerton in 1598, Donne ruined hope of further preferment in that household when his secret marriage to Sir Thomas's seventeen-year-old niece became public. But Donne's gifts of learning, intelligence, and social grace would not let him fade away from the public eye. On the encouragement of King James himself, Donne took holy orders and was appointed Dean of St. Paul's Cathedral, London, in 1621.

Next to nothing of Donne's literary output was published during his own lifetime. (The first edition of his collected poems appeared in 1633.) His brilliance as a "metaphysical" poet is a virtual rediscovery by twentieth-century criticism, and he is now recognized as one of the greatest English love poets. Donne's forceful exposition and bold metaphorical style also made him one of the greatest preachers of the seventeenth century, as well as a significant religious poet. He seemed singularly adept at uniting passion and intellect. And the two periods of "Jack Donne," lyrical poet, and "Doctor Donne," learned divine, into which Donne himself separated his life might not seem all that irreconcilable in light of the powerful rhetoric and deep meditational technique common to both.

Song

Go, and catch a falling star,
   Get with child a mandrake root,
Tell me, where all past years are,
   Or who cleft the Devil's foot,
5 Teach me to hear Mermaids singing,
   Or to keep off envy's stinging,
       And find
       What wind
Serves to advance an honest mind.

10 If thou be'st born to strange sights,
       Things invisible to see,
    Ride ten thousand days and nights,
       Till age snow white hairs on thee,
    Thou, when thou return'st, wilt tell me
15 All strange wonders that befell thee,
              And swear
              No where
    Lives a woman true, and fair.

    If thou find'st one, let me know,
20   Such a Pilgrimage were sweet;
    Yet do not, I would not go,
       Though at next door we might meet,
    Though she were true, when you met her,
    And last, till you write your letter,
25   Yet she
              Will be
    False, ere I come, to two, or three.

                                        (1633)

The Bait[1]

    Come live with me, and be my love,
    And we will some new pleasures prove
    Of golden sands, and crystal brooks,
    With silken lines, and silver hooks.

5   There will the river whispering run
    Warm'd by thy eyes, more than the Sun.
    And there th' enamour'd fish will stay,
    Begging themselves they may betray.

1 *a reply to Marlowe's "The Passionate Shepherd to His Love."*

When thou wilt swim in that live bath,
10 Each fish, which every channel hath,
Will amorously to thee swim,
Gladder to catch thee, than thou him.

If thou, to be so seen, be'st loth,
By Sun, or Moon, thou dark'nest both,
15 And if myself have leave to see,
I need not their light, having thee.

Let others freeze with angling reeds,
And cut their legs, with shells and weeds,
Or treacherously poor fish beset,
20 With strangling snare, or windowy net:

Let coarse bold hands, from slimy nest
The bedded fish in banks out-wrest,
Or curious traitors, sleeve-silk flies
Bewitch poor fishes' wand'ring eyes.

25 For thee, thou need'st no such deceit,
For thou thyself art thine own bait;
That fish, that is not catch'd thereby,
Alas, is wiser far than I.

(1633)

A Valediction: Forbidding Mourning

As virtuous men pass mildly away,
And whisper to their souls, to go,
Whilst some of their sad friends do say,
The breath goes now, and some say, no:

5   So let us melt, and make no noise,
           No tear-floods, nor sigh-tempests move,
       'Twere profanation of our joys
           To tell the laity our love.

       Moving of th' earth brings harms and fears,
10   Men reckon what it did and meant,
       But trepidation of the spheres,[1]
           Though greater far, is innocent.

       Dull sublunary lovers' love
           (Whose soul is sense) cannot admit
15   Absence, because it doth remove
           Those things which elemented it.

       But we by a love, so much refin'd,
           That ourselves know not what it is,
       Inter-assured of the mind,
20   Care less eyes, lips, and hands to miss.

       Our two souls therefore, which are one,
           Though I must go, endure not yet
       A breach, but an expansion,
           Like gold to aery thinness beat.

25   If they be two, they are two so
           As stiff twin compasses are two,
       Thy soul the fixed foot, makes no show
           To move, but doth, if th' other do.

       And though it in the centre sit,
30   Yet when the other far doth roam,
       It leans, and hearkens after it,
           And grows erect, as that comes home.

---

1 *in pre-Copernican cosmology, the shaking of the nine concentric spheres around the earth.*

Such wilt thou be to me, who must
   Like th' other foot, obliquely run;
35   Thy firmness draws my circle just,
   And makes me end, where I begun.

(1633)

The Canonization

For God's sake hold your tongue, and let me love;
   Or chide my palsy, or my gout,
My five grey hairs, or ruin'd fortune flout;
   With wealth your state, your mind with arts improve,
5   Take you a course, get you a place,
      Observe his Honour, or his Grace,
Or the King's real, or his stamped face
   Contemplate; what you will, approve,
   So you will let me love.

10 Alas, alas, who's injur'd by my love?
   What merchant's ships have my sighs drown'd?
Who says my tears have overflow'd his ground?
   When did my colds a forward spring remove?
      When did the heats which my veins fill
15   Add one more to the plaguy bill?[1]
Soldiers find wars, and lawyers find out still
   Litigious men, which quarrels move,
   Though she and I do love.

Call us what you will, we are made such by love;
20   Call her one, me another fly,
We're tapers too, and at our own cost die,
   And we in us find the Eagle and the Dove.
      The Phœnix riddle hath more wit
      By us; we two being one, are it.
25 So to one neutral thing both sexes fit,
   We die and rise the same, and prove
   Mysterious by this love.

1 *i.e., add one more name to the weekly list (bill) of plague victims.*

We can die by it, if not live by love,
  And if unfit for tombs and hearse
30 Our legend be, it will be fit for verse;
    And if no piece of Chronicle we prove,
      We'll build in sonnets pretty rooms;
      As well a well-wrought urn becomes
The greatest ashes, as half-acre tombs,
35   And by these hymns, all shall approve
  Us canonized for Love:

And thus invoke us; You whom reverend love
  Made one another's hermitage;
You, to whom love was peace, that now is rage;
40   Who did the whole world's soul contract, and drove
    Into the glasses of your eyes
    (So made such mirrors, and such spies,
That they did all to you epitomize,)
    Countries, Towns, Courts: beg from above
45   A pattern of your love!

(1633)

The Flea

Mark but this flea, and mark in this,
How little that which thou deny'st me is;
It suck'd me first, and now sucks thee,
And in this flea, our two bloods mingled be;
5 Though know'st that this cannot be said
A sin, nor shame, nor less of maidenhead,
    Yet this enjoys before it woo,
    And pamper'd swells with one blood made of two,
    And this, alas, is more than we would do.

10   Oh stay, three lives in one flea spare,
    Where we almost, yea more than married are.
    This flea is you and I, and this
    Our marriage bed, and marriage temple is;
    Though parents grudge, and you, we're met,
15   And cloistered in these living walls of jet.
      Though use make you apt to kill me,
      Let not to that, self murder added be,
      And sacrilege, three sins in killing three.

    Cruel and sudden, hast thou since
20   Purpled thy nail, in blood of innocence?
    Wherein could this flea guilty be,
    Except in that drop which it suck'd from thee?
    Yet thou triumph'st, and say'st that thou
    Find'st not thyself, nor me the weaker now;
25   'Tis true, then learn how false, fears be;
      Just so much honour, when thou yield'st to me,
      Will waste, as this flea's death took life from thee.

(1633)

Holy Sonnet VII

    At the round earth's imagin'd corners, blow
    Your trumpets, Angels, and arise, arise
    From death, you numberless infinities
    Of souls, and to your scatter'd bodies go,
5   All whom the flood did, and fire shall o'erthrow,
    All whom war, dearth, age, agues, tyrannies,
    Despair, law, chance, hath slain, and you whose eyes,
    Shall behold God, and never taste death's woe.

But let them sleep, Lord, and me mourn a space,
10   For, if above all these, my sins abound,
'Tis late to ask abundance of Thy grace,
When we are there; here on this lowly ground,
Teach me how to repent; for that's as good
As if Thou hadst seal'd my pardon, with Thy blood.

(1633)

Holy Sonnet X

Death be not proud, though some have called thee
Mighty and dreadful, for, thou art not so,
For, those, whom thou think'st, thou dost overthrow,
Die not, poor death, nor yet canst thou kill me.
5   From rest and sleep, which but thy pictures be,
Much pleasure, then from thee, much more must flow,
And soonest our best men with thee do go,
Rest of their bones, and soul's delivery.
Thou art slave to Fate, Chance, kings, and desperate men,
10   And dost with poison, war, and sickness dwell,
And poppy, or charms can make us sleep as well,
And better than thy stroke; why swell'st thou then?
One short sleep past, we wake eternally,
And death shall be no more; death, thou shalt die.

(1633)

Holy Sonnet XIV

Batter my heart, three-person'd God; for, you
As yet but knock, breathe, shine, and seek to mend;
That I may rise, and stand, o'erthrow me, and bend
Your force, to break, blow, burn and make me new.
5   I, like an usurp'd town, to another due,
Labour to admit you, but Oh, to no end,
Reason your viceroy in me, me should defend,
But is captiv'd, and proves weak or untrue.
Yet dearly I love you, and would be loved fain,
10 But am betroth'd unto your enemy:
Divorce me, untie, or break that knot again,
Take me to you, imprison me, for I
Except you enthral me, never shall be free,
Nor ever chaste, except you ravish me.

(1633)

The Ecstasy

Where, like a pillow on a bed,
    A pregnant bank swelled up, to rest
The violet's reclining head,
    Sat we two, one another's best;

5   Our hands were firmly cemented
    With a fast balm, which thence did spring,
Our eye-beams twisted, and did thread
    Our eyes, upon one double string;

So to' intergraft our hands, as yet
10   Was all our means to make us one,
And pictures in our eyes to get
    Was all our propagation.

As 'twixt two equal armies, Fate
    Suspends uncertain victory,
15   Our souls, (which to advance their state,
    Were gone out), hung 'twixt her, and me.

And whilst our souls negotiate there,
    We like sepulchral statues lay;
All day, the same our postures were,
20   And we said nothing, all the day.

If any, so by love refined,
    That he soul's language understood,
And by good love were grown all mind,
    Within convenient distance stood,

25   He (though he knew not which soul spake
    Because both meant, both spake the same)
Might thence a new concoction take,
    And part far purer than he came.

This ecstacy doth unperplex
30   (We said) and tell us what we love,
We see by this, it was not sex,
    We see, we saw not what did move:

But as all several souls contain
    Mixture of things, they know not what,
35   Love, these mixed souls doth mix again,
    And makes both one, each this and that.

A single violet transplant,
    The strength, the colour, and the size,
(All which before was poor, and scant,)
40   Redoubles still, and multiplies.

When love, with one another so
    Interinanimates two souls,
That abler soul, which thence doth flow,
    Defects of loneliness controls.

45   We then, who are this new soul, know,
          Of what we are composed, and made,
      For, th' atomies[1] of which we grow,
          Are souls, whom no change can invade.

      But O alas, so long, so far
50   Our bodies why do we forbear?
      They are ours, though they are not we, we are
          The intelligences, they the sphere.

      We owe them thanks, because they thus,
          Did us, to us, at first convey,
55   Yielded their forces, sense, to us,
          Nor are dross to us, but allay.

      On man heaven's influence works not so,
          But that it first imprints the air,
      So soul into the soul may flow,
60   Though it to body first repair.

      As our blood labours to beget
          Spirits, as like souls as it can,
      Because such fingers need to knit
          That subtle knot, which makes us man:

65   So must pure lovers' souls descend
          T' affections, and to faculties,
      Which sense may reach and apprehend,
          Else a great prince in prison lies.

      To our bodies turn we then, that so
70   Weak men on love revealed may look;
      Love's mysteries in souls do grow,
          But yet the body is his book.

1 *atoms.*

And if some lover, such as we,
   Have heard this dialogue of one,
75   Let him still mark us, he shall see
    Small change, when we'are to bodies gone.

(1633)

Elegy XIX

To His Mistress Going to Bed

Come, Madam, come, all rest my powers defy,
Until I labour, I in labour lie.
The foe oft-times having the foe in sight,
Is tired with standing though he never fight.
5   Off with that girdle, like heaven's Zone glistering,
But a far fairer world encompassing.
Unpin that spangled breastplate which you wear,
That th' eyes of busy fools may be stopt there.
Unlace yourself, for that harmonious chime
10   Tells me from you, that now it is bed time.
Off with that happy busk, which I envy,
That still can be, and still can stand so nigh.
Your gown going off, such beauteous state reveals,
As when from flowry meads th' hill's shadow steals.
15   Off with that wiry Coronet and show
The hairy Diadem which on you doth grow:
Now off with those shoes, and then safely tread
In this love's hallow'd temple, this soft bed.
In such white robes, heaven's Angels used to be
20   Receiv'd by men; thou Angel bring'st with thee

A heaven like Mahomet's[1] Paradise; and though
Ill spirits walk in white, we easily know,
By this these Angels from an evil sprite,
Those set our hairs, but these our flesh upright.
25   Licence my roving hands, and let them go,
Before, behind, between, above, below.
O my America! my new-found-land,
My kingdom, safeliest when with one man mann'd,
My Mine of precious stones, My Empery,
30   How blest am I in this discovering thee!
To enter in these bonds, is to be free;
Then where my hand is set, my seal shall be.
   Full nakedness! All joys are due to thee,
As souls unbodied, bodies uncloth'd must be,
35   To taste whole joys. Gems which you women use
Are like Atlanta's balls,[2] cast in men's views,
That when a fool's eye lighteth on a Gem,
His earthly soul may covet theirs, not them.
Like pictures, or like books' gay coverings made
40   For lay-men, are all women thus array'd;
Themselves are mystic books, which only we
(Whom their imputed grace will dignify)
Must see reveal'd. Then since that I may know,
As liberally, as to a Midwife, show
45   Thyself: cast all, yea, this white linen hence,
There is no penance due to innocence.
   To teach thee, I am naked first; why then
What needst thou have more covering than a man.

(1669)

---

1 *i.e., Muhammad's.*
2. *i.e., a distraction. Atalanta lost a race because of golden apples which were dropped in her way by her competitor (and suitor) Hippomenes.*

BEN JONSON

(1572–1637)

cholar, poet, playwright, classicist, and controversialist — Jonson's career consolidates the emergence of professional letters in the English Renaissance. He was the first English poet to publish his own works, in 1616, and his first play, Every Man in His Humour *(1598), included actor William Shakespeare in the cast. Master of the English plain style, Jonson, whose output was voluminous and various, held pride of place at the Mermaid Tavern where he presided over a club of aspiring poets known as the "sons of Ben."*

    Jonson was also a man of action who, while a soldier in Flanders, killed an enemy champion in hand-to-hand combat — a biographical fact that he gloried in relating to his host, William Drummond of Hawthornden. Argumentative, satirical, and pugnacious, Jonson was a professional writer who took his business seriously enough to insist on its critical appreciation in both the public playhouse and the private masquing house where he also triumphed as author. With stage architect Inigo Jones (a detested rival), Jonson prepared many lavish ceremonial masques for the court of James I, and was still a significant cultural spokesperson in the reign of Charles I.

Song: To Celia

Drink to me only with thine eyes,
    And I will pledge with mine;
Or leave a kiss within the cup,
    And I'll not look for wine.
5   The thirst that from the soul doth rise,
    Doth ask a drink divine;
But might I of Jove's nectar sup,
    I would not change for thine.

I sent thee late a rosy wreath,
10   Not so much honouring thee,
As giving it a hope that there
    It could not withered be.
But thou thereon didst only breathe,
    And sent'st it back to me;
15   Since when it grows, and smells, I swear,
    Not of itself, but thee.

(1616)

Queen and huntress[1]

Queen and huntress, chaste and fair,
Now the sun is laid to sleep,
Seated in thy silver chair,
State in wonted manner keep.
5   Hesperus[2] entreats thy light,
    Goddess excellently bright.

Earth, let not thy envious shade
Dare itself to interpose;
Cynthia's shining orb[3] was made
10 Heaven to clear, when day did close.
    Bless us then with wishèd sight,
    Goddess excellently bright.

Lay thy bow of pearl apart,
And thy crystal-shining quiver;
15 Give unto the flying hart
Space to breathe, how short soever;
    Thou that mak'st a day of night,
    Goddess excellently bright.

(1600)

Come, my Celia[1]

Come, my Celia, let us prove,
While we can, the sports of love.
Time will not be ours forever,
He at length our good will sever;
5 Spend not then his gifts in vain.
Suns that set may rise again;

---

1 *from act 5 of* Cynthia's Revels.
2 *evening star.*
3 *i.e., the Moon. "Cynthia" refers at once to the goddess of Roman myth and to Queen Elizabeth I.*

1 *from act 3 scene 7 of* Volpone.

But if once we lose this light,
'Tis with us perpetual night.
Why should we defer our joys?
10   Fame and rumour are but toys.
Cannot we delude the eyes
Of a few poor household spies?
Or his easier ears beguile,
Thus removèd by our wile?
15   'Tis no sin love's fruits to steal,
But the sweet thefts to reveal:
To be taken, to be seen,
These have crimes accounted been.

(1606)

On My First Son

Farewell, thou child of my right hand, and joy;
My sin was too much hope of thee, lov'd boy:
Seven years thou wert lent to me, and I thee pay,
Exacted by thy fate, on the just day.
5   O, could I lose all father,[1] now! for why,
Will man lament the state he should envy?
To have so soon scaped world's, and flesh's rage,
And, if no other misery, yet age!
Rest in soft peace, and ask'd, say here doth lie
10   BEN JONSON his best piece of poetry:
For whose sake henceforth all his vows be such,
As what he loves may never like too much.

(1603?)   (1616)

---

1 i.e., give up all gentle, fatherly thoughts.

ROBERT HERRICK

(1591–1674)

*H*errick was a clergyman from London who found himself at the age of 38
posted to the tiny vicarage of Dean Prior, Devonshire. There he per-
formed the social and religious rituals for a largely illiterate population, all the
while recording his own witty poetic observations on his flock. But his observations
are never condescending. His rural themes are consistently simple, often playful, but
seldom trivial: beauty, love, art, natural splendour, religious devotion. And his
speaking voice or persona — somewhat risqué for a bachelor country parson — no
doubt occasioned the final couplet in the first part of his collection: "To his book's
end this last line he'd have placed: / Jocund his Muse was, but his life was
chaste."

    Expelled from his vicarage in 1647 as a Royalist sympathizer, Herrick went
back to London where he published his verses in a single volume, Hesperides
(1648), comprising over fourteen hundred sacred and secular lyrics. After the
Puritan interregnum, Herrick was reinstated under Charles II and lived out the
end of his long life in Dean Prior.

Delight in Disorder

    A sweet disorder in the dresse
    Kindles in cloathes a wantonnesse.
    A lawne[1] about the shoulders thrown
    Into a fine distraction;
5   An erring lace, which here and there
    Enthralls the crimson stomacher;
    A cuffe neglectfull, and thereby
    Ribbands to flow confusedly;
    A winning wave (deserving note)
10   In the tempestuous petticote;
    A carelesse shooe-string, in whose tye
    I see a wilde civility; —
    Do more bewitch me than when art
    Is too precise in every part.

(1648)

---

1 *fine linen.*

To the Virgins, To Make Much of Time

Gather ye rose-buds while ye may,
  Old time is still a flying,
And this same flower that smiles to-day,
  To-morrow will be dying.

5   The glorious lamp of Heaven, the sun,
  The higher he's a getting,
The sooner will his race be run,
  And neerer he's to setting.

That age is best which is the first,
10   When youth and blood are warmer;
But being spent, the worse, and worst
  Times still succeed the former.

Then be not coy, but use your time,
  And while ye may, go marry;
15   For having lost but once your prime,
  You may for ever tarry.

(1648)

Upon Julia's Clothes

When as in silks my Julia goes,
Then, then, me thinks, how sweetly flowes
That liquefaction of her clothes.

Next, when I cast mine eyes and see
5   That brave vibration, each way free,
O how that glittering taketh me!

(1648)

GEORGE HERBERT

(1593–1633)

*G*eorge Herbert was born into an ancient and respected Welsh family. His brother Edward was the philosopher-statesman Lord Herbert of Cherbury, and another brother, Sir Henry, was Master of the Revels in England, whose job it was to censor and approve public entertainment during the Stuart reign. George was more private, if (it seems) no less ambitious. A scholar and ecclesiastic, he attained the position of Public Orator at Cambridge University but never received the place at court which he must surely have coveted. Instead, in 1629 he accepted a minor church living at Bemerton near Salisbury, where he lived out the rest of his short life in good works, holy contemplation, and poetic composition.

Herbert's poetry is sharply expressed, richly imaginative, and concrete. Here, a poem's shape expresses meaning, souls have voices, love speaks. Consistently devotional, his verse has an artistic originality and cleverness that mark it as among the most exalted of the "metaphysical" mode.

The Altar

A broken ALTAR, Lord, thy servant rears,
Made of a heart, and cemented with tears:
Whose parts are as thy hand did frame;
No workman's tool hath touch'd the same.
5   A   HEART   alone
Is   such   a   stone,
As   nothing   but
Thy   power   doth   cut.
Wherefore   each   part
10   Of   my   hard   heart
Meets   in   this   frame,
To   praise   thy   name:
That, if I chance to hold my peace,
These stones to praise thee may not cease.
15   O   let   thy   blessed   SACRIFICE   be   mine,
And   sanctify   this   ALTAR   to   be   thine.

(1633)

Prayer (I)

Prayer, the Church's banquet, Angel's age,
   God's breath in man returning to his birth,
   The soul in paraphrase, heart in pilgrimage,
   The Christian plummet sounding heaven and earth;

5   Engine against the Almighty, sinner's tower,
   Reversed thunder, Christ-side-piercing spear,
   The six-days'-world transposing in an hour,
   A kind of tune, which all things hear and fear;

Softness, and peace, and joy, and love, and bliss,
10   Exalted manna, gladness of the best,
   Heaven in ordinary, man well drest,
   The milky way, the bird of Paradise,

Church-bells beyond the stars heard, the soul's blood,
The land of spices, something understood.

(1633)

The Collar

I struck the board, and cried, No more;
   I will abroad.
What? shall I ever sigh and pine?
My lines and life are free; free as the road,
5   Loose as the wind, as large as store.[1]
   Shall I be still in suit[2]?
Have I no harvest but a thorn
To let me blood, and not restore

1 *abundance.*
2 *debt, dispute, as a suitor.*

What I have lost with cordial fruit?
10   Sure there was wine,
Before my sighs did dry it: there was corn,
            Before my tears did drown it.
        Is the year only lost to me?
        Have I no bays³ to crown it?
15 No flowers, no garlands gay? all blasted?
                    All wasted?
        Not so, my heart: but there is fruit
                And thou hast hands.
        Recover all thy sigh-blown age
20 On double pleasures: leave thy cold dispute
Of what is *fit, and not:* forsake thy cage,
            Thy rope of sands,
Which petty thoughts have made, and made to thee
        Good cable, to enforce and draw,
25   And be thy law,
While thou didst wink and wouldst not see.
                Away; take heed:
                I will abroad.
Call in thy death's-head there: tie up thy fears.
30   He that forbears
        To suit and serve his need
                Deserves his load.
But as I raved and grew more fierce and wild
                At every word,
35   Methought I heard one calling, *Child:*
            And I replied, *My Lord.*

(1633)

3 *bay leaves, classical poets' wreath.*

Love (III)

Love bade me welcome; yet my soul drew back,
    Guilty of dust and sin.
But quick-eyed Love, observing me grow slack
    From my first entrance in,
5 Drew nearer to me, sweetly questioning,
    If I lack'd any thing.

A guest, I answer'd, worthy to be here:
    Love said, You shall be he.
I the unkind, ungrateful? Ah, my dear,
10   I cannot look on thee.
Love took my hand, and smiling did reply,
    Who made the eyes but I?

Truth, Lord, but I have marr'd them: let my shame
    Go where it doth deserve.
15 And know you not, says Love, who bore the blame?
    My dear, then I will serve.
You must sit down, says Love, and taste my meat:
    So I did sit and eat.

(1633)

JOHN MILTON

(1608–1674)

*M*ilton was born into a middle-class London family. Prodigiously intellectual, he received a thorough education at St. Paul's School, London, and in Christ's College, Cambridge. Later, he travelled on the Continent where he met the aged and broken Galileo. Milton too would later survey the heavens, but as a blind poet with a self-proclaimed mandate to "justify the ways of God to men" (Paradise Lost I, 26).

Milton was also a public figure who held the position of Latin Secretary to Oliver Cromwell during the Puritan interregnum. His journalism on topical matters such as divorce, church government, and censorship, in addition to diplomatic and political matters, was prolific. He lived out his final days after the restoration of Charles II in humble circumstances. But it was during this time that Milton gained his immortal reputation as a poet. His poetry is celebrated for its profound spiritual and metaphorical sense of inquiry. Considered by many as the highest achievement in English non-dramatic verse, his epic Paradise Lost stands as testament to his genius.

How soon hath Time

How soon hath Time, the subtle thief of youth,
    Stolen on his wing my three-and-twentieth year!
    My hasting days fly on with full career,
    But my late spring no bud or blossom shew'th.
5 Perhaps my semblance might deceive the truth
    That I to manhood am arrived so near;
    And inward ripeness doth much less appear,
    That some more timely-happy spirits endu'th.[1]
Yet, be it less or more, or soon or slow,
10   It shall be still in strictest measure even
    To that same lot, however mean or high,
Toward which Time leads me, and the will of Heaven.
    All is,[2] if I have grace to use it so,
    As ever in my great Task-Master's eye.

(1632)   (1673)

1 *endows.*
2 *i.e., That is.*

Lycidas[1]

In this Monody the Author bewails a learned Friend,[2] unfortunately drowned in his
passage from Chester on the Irish Sea, 1637; and, by occasion, foretells the ruin
of our corrupted Clergy, then in their height.

Yet once more, O ye laurels, and once more,
Ye myrtles brown, with ivy never sere,[3]
I come to pluck your berries harsh and crude,
And with forced fingers rude
5   Shatter your leaves before the mellowing year.
Bitter constraint and sad occasion dear
Compels me to disturb your season due;
For Lycidas is dead, dead ere his prime,
Young Lycidas, and hath not left his peer.
10   Who would not sing for Lycidas? he knew
Himself to sing, and build the lofty rhyme.
He must not float upon his watery bier
Unwept, and welter to the parching wind,
Without the meed[4] of some melodious tear.
15   Begin, then, Sisters of the sacred well[5]
That from beneath the seat of Jove doth spring;
Begin, and somewhat loudly sweep the string.
Hence with denial vain and coy excuse:
So may some gentle Muse
20   With lucky words favour *my* destined urn,
And as he passes turn,
And bid fair peace to be my sable shroud!
For we were nursed upon the self-same hill,

1 *traditional pastoral name for a shepherd.*
2 *Edward King, a fellow student of Milton's acquaintance at Cambridge.*
3 *laurels, myrtles, ivy: evergreens associated with poetic inspiration and honour.*
4 *reward.*
5 *i.e., the nine sister Muses responsible for the flow of poetic inspiration.*

Fed the same flock, by fountain, shade, and rill;
25 Together both, ere the high lawns appeared
Under the opening eyelids of the Morn,
We drove a-field, and both together heard
What time the grey-fly winds her sultry horn,
Battening our flocks with the fresh dews of night,
30 Oft till the star that rose at evening bright
Toward heaven's descent had sloped his westering wheel.
Meanwhile the rural ditties were not mute;
Tempered to the oaten flute,
Rough Satyrs danced, and Fauns with cloven heel
35 From the glad sound would not be absent long;
And old Damœtas[6] loved to hear our song.

But, oh! the heavy change, now thou art gone,
Now thou art gone and never must return!
Thee, Shepherd, thee the woods and desert caves,
40 With wild thyme and the gadding vine o'ergrown,
And all their echoes, mourn.
The willows, and the hazel copses green,
Shall now no more be seen
Fanning their joyous leaves to thy soft lays.
45 As killing as the canker to the rose,
Or taint-worm to the weanling herds that graze,
Or frost to flowers, that their gay wardrobe wear,
When first the white-thorn blows;
Such, Lycidas, thy loss to shepherd's ear.
50 Where were ye, Nymphs,[7] when the remorseless deep
Closed o'er the head of your loved Lycidas?
For neither were ye playing on the steep
Where your old bards, the famous Druids,[8] lie,
Nor on the shaggy top of Mona high,
55 Nor yet where Deva spreads her wizard stream.[9]

---

6 *a traditional pastoral name which perhaps refers to a specific Cambridge don known to both Milton and King.*
7 *female nature spirits.*
8 *priestly class in ancient Britain.*
9 *Mona: isle of Anglesey; Deva: the river Dee in Cheshire that empties into the Irish Sea.*

Ay me! I fondly dream
"Had ye been there," . . . for what could that have done?
What could the Muse herself that Orpheus bore,[10]
The Muse herself, for her enchanting son,
60   Whom universal nature did lament,
When, by the rout that made the hideous roar,
His gory visage down the stream was sent,
Down the swift Hebrus to the Lesbian shore?[11]
Alas! what boots[12] it with uncessant care
65   To tend the homely, slighted, shepherd's trade,
And strictly mediate the thankless Muse?
Were it not better done, as others use,
To sport with Amaryllis in the shade,
Or with the tangles of Neæra's hair?[13]
70   Fame is the spur that the clear spirit doth raise
(That last infirmity of noble mind)
To scorn delights and live laborious days;
But the fair guerdon[14] when we hope to find,
And think to burst out into sudden blaze,
75   Comes the blind Fury with the abhorred shears,[15]
And slits the thin-spun life. "But not the praise,"
Phœbus[16] replied, and touched my trembling ears:
"Fame is no plant that grows on mortal soil,
Nor in the glistering foil
80   Set off to the world, nor in broad rumour lies
But lives and spreads aloft by those pure eyes
And perfect witness of all-judging Jove;
As he pronounces lastly on each deed,
Of so much fame in heaven expect thy meed."
85   O fountain Arethuse, and thou honoured flood,

---

10 *Orpheus: archetypal poet born of the muse Calliope.* 11 *decapitated by angered and overzealous celebrants, Orpheus's head floated down the river Hebrus to the isle of Lesbos.* 12 *profits.* 13 *Amaryllis, Neaera: pastoral names for pretty shepherdesses.* 14 *reward.* 15 *i.e., Atropos, the Fate who finally cuts off the thread of life.* 16 *i.e., Phoebus Apollo, god of poetry.*

Smooth-sliding Mincius, crowned with vocal reeds,[17]
That strain I heard was of a higher mood.
But now my oat[18] proceeds,
And listens to the Herald of the Sea,[19]
90   That came in Neptune's plea.
He asked the waves, and asked the felon winds,
What hard mishap hath doomed this gentle swain?
And questioned every gust of rugged wings
That blows from off each beakèd promontory.
95   They knew not of his story;
And sage Hippotades[20] their answer brings,
That not a blast was from his dungeon strayed:
The air was calm, and on the level brine
Sleek Panope[21] with all her sisters played.
100   It was that fatal and perfidious bark,
Built in the eclipse, and rigged with curses dark,
That sunk so low that sacred head of thine.
    Next, Camus,[22] reverend sire, went footing slow,
His mantle hairy, and his bonnet sedge,
105   Inwrought with figures dim, and on the edge
Like to that sanguine flower inscribed with woe.
"Ah! who hath reft," quoth he, "my dearest pledge?"
Last came, and last did go,
The Pilot of the Galilean Lake;[23]
110   Two massy keys he bore of metals twain
(The golden opes, the iron shuts amain).
He shook his mitred locks, and stern bespake: —
"How well could I have spared for thee, young swain,
Enow of such as, for their bellies' sake,

---

17 *Arethuse, a spring; Mincius, a river: Italian locations associated respectively with the great pasturul poets*
    Theocritus and Virgil.
18 *i.e., "oaten flute" (line 33).*
19 *Triton is Neptune's "herald of the sea."*
20 *god of winds.*
21 *a sea nymph: one of 50 sisters who were daughters of Nereus.*
22 *god of the river Cam upon which Cambridge University is situated.*
23 *i.e., St. Peter.*

115   Creep, and intrude, and climb into the fold!
Of other care they little reckoning make
Than how to scramble at the shearers' feast,
And shove away the worthy bidden guest.
Blind mouths! that scarce themselves know how to hold
120   A sheep-hook, or have learnt aught else the least
That to the faithful herdman's art belongs!
What recks it them? What need they? They are sped;
And, when they list, their lean and flashy songs
Grate on their scrannel[24] pipes of wretched straw;
125   The hungry sheep look up, and are not fed,
But, swoln with wind and the rank mist they draw,
Rot inwardly, and foul contagion spread;
Besides what the grim wolf with privy paw
Daily devours apace, and nothing said.
130   But that two-handed engine at the door
Stands ready to smite once, and smite no more."
    Return, Alpheus[25]; the dread voice is past
That shrunk thy streams; return Sicilian Muse,
And call the vales, and bid them hither cast
135   Their bells and flowerets of a thousand hues.
Ye valleys low, where the mild whispers use
Of shades, and wanton winds, and gushing brooks,
On whose fresh lap the swart star[26] sparely looks,
Throw hither all your quaint enamelled eyes,
140   That on the green turf suck the honeyed showers,
And purple all the ground with vernal flowers.
Bring the rathe[27] primrose that forsaken dies,
The tufted crow-toe, and pale jessamine,
The white pink, and the pansy freaked[28] with jet,
145   The glowing violet,
The musk-rose, and the well-attired woodbine,
With cowslips wan that hang the pensive head,
And every flower that sad embroidery wears;

24 *thin, meagre.*
25 *Arcadian river, symbol for gentle pastoral verse.*
26 *Sirius, the Dog Star of late summer.*
27 *early.*
28 *freckled.*

Bid amaranthus[29] all his beauty shed,

150   And daffadillies fill their cups with tears,

To strew the laureate hearse where Lycid lies.

For so, to interpose a little ease,

Let our frail thoughts dally with false surmise,

Ay me! whilst thee the shores and sounding seas

155   Wash far away, where'er thy bones are hurled;

Whether beyond the stormy Hebrides,[30]

Where thou perhaps under the whelming tide

Visit'st the bottom of the monstrous world;

Or whether thou, to our moist vows denied,

160   Sleep'st by the fable of Bellerus[31] old,

Where the great Vision of the guarded mount

Looks toward Namancos and Bayona's hold.[32]

Look homeward, Angel, now, and melt with ruth:

And, O ye dolphins, waft the hapless youth.

165   Weep no more, woeful shepherds, weep no more,

For Lycidas, your sorrow, is not dead,

Sunk though he be beneath the watery floor.

So sinks the day-star[33] in the ocean bed,

And yet anon repairs his drooping head,

170   And tricks his beams, and with new-spangled ore

Flames in the forehead of the morning sky:

So Lycidas sunk low, but mounted high,

Through the dear might of Him that walked the waves,

Where, other groves and other streams along,

175   With nectar pure his oozy locks he laves,

And hears the unexpressive nuptial song,

In the blest kingdoms meek of joy and love.

There entertain him all the Saints above,

In solemn troops, and sweet societies,

180   That sing, and singing in their glory move,

And wipe the tears for ever from his eyes.

Now, Lycidas, the shepherds weep no more;

---

29 *an imaginary flower that is always in bloom.*
30 *islands off the coast of Scotland that mark the northern boundary of the Irish Sea.*
31 *an imaginary giant supposed to be buried at Land's End, Cornwall.*
32 *Namancos, Bayona: locations on the coast of Spain, imagined as visible from St. Michael's Mount, Cornwall.*
33 *i.e., the sun.*

Henceforth thou art the Genius[34] of the shore,
In thy large recompense, and shalt be good
185   To all that wander in that perilous flood.

Thus sang the uncouth swain to the oaks and rills,
While the still morn went out with sandals grey:
He touched the tender stops of various quills,
With eager thought warbling his Doric lay:[35]
190   And now the sun had stretched out all the hills,
And now was dropt into the western bay.
At last he rose, and twitched his mantle blue:
To-morrow to fresh woods, and pastures new.

(1638)

When I consider how my light is spent

When I consider how my light is spent
Ere half my days in this dark world and wide,
And that one talent which is death to hide
Lodged with me useless, though my soul more bent
5   To serve therewith my Maker, and present
My true account, lest He returning chide,
"Doth God exact day-labour, light denied?"
I fondly ask. But Patience, to prevent
That murmur, soon replies, "God doth not need
10   Either man's work or his own gifts. Who best
Bear his mild yoke, they serve him best. His state
Is kingly: thousands at his bidding speed,
And post o'er land and ocean without rest;
They also serve who only stand and wait."

(1652?)   (1673)

34 i.e., protective local deity.
35 i.e., simple song.

On the Late Massacre in Piedmont[1]

Avenge, O Lord, thy slaughtered saints, whose bones
  Lie scattered on the Alpine mountains cold;
  Even them who kept thy truth so pure of old,
  When all our fathers worshiped stocks and stones,
5 Forget not: in thy book record their groans
  Who were thy sheep, and in their ancient fold
  Slain by the bloody Piemontese, that rolled
  Mother with infant down the rocks. Their moans
The vales redoubled to the hills, and they
10   To heaven. Their martyred blood and ashes sow
  O'er all the Italian fields, where still doth sway
The triple Tyrant[2]; that from these may grow
  A hundredfold, who, having learnt thy way,
  Early may fly the Babylonian woe.[3]

(1655)   (1673)

Methought I saw my late espousèd saint

Methought I saw my late espousèd saint
  Brought to me like Alcestis from the grave,[1]
  Whom Jove's great son to her glad husband gave,
  Rescued from Death by force, though pale and faint.

---

1 *the Piedmont region of northwestern Italy, bounded by France and Switzerland. On April 24, 1655, Italian troops massacred the Protestant Piedmontese for their dissenting views.*
2 *i.e., the pope, identified by his triple crown.*
3 *apocalyptic destruction; see Revelation 18.*

1 *in mythology, Alcestis (wife of Admetus) was rescued from the grave by Hercules, "Jove's great son."*

5   Mine, as whom washed from spot of child-bed taint
         Purification in the Old Law did save,
         And such as yet once more I trust to have
         Full sight of her in Heaven without restraint,
    Came vested all in white, pure as her mind.
10   Her face was veiled; yet to my fancied sight
         Love, sweetness, goodness, in her person shined
    So clear as in no face with more delight.
         But, oh! as to embrace me she inclined,
         I waked, she fled, and day brought back my night.

(1658)   (1673)

ANNE BRADSTREET

(c. 1612–1672)

Born in Northampton, England, Anne Bradstreet, unlike most young women of her day, read widely in classical and English poetry. When she was eighteen years old, she came to Massachusetts with her family and husband. While taking care of the family's frequent moves and raising eight children, she wrote a great deal of poetry and is recognized as one of the first important American poets. Although she wrote many long, complex works on theological subjects, she is best remembered for those poems that sensitively communicate her feelings and observations about her home and family.

The Author to her Book

Thou ill-form'd offspring of my feeble brain,
Who after birth did'st by my side remain,
Till snatcht from thence by friends[1], less wise than true
Who thee abroad, expos'd to publick view;
5   Made thee in raggs, halting to th' press to trudg,
Where errors were not lessened (all may judg)
At thy return my blushing was not small,
My rambling brat (in print) should mother call,
I cast thee by as one unfit for light,
10   Thy Visage was so irksome in my sight;
Yet being mine own, at length affection would
Thy blemishes amend, if so I could:
I wash'd thy face, but more defects I saw,
And rubbing off a spot, still made a flaw.
15   I stretcht thy joynts to make thee even feet,
Yet still thou run'st more hobling than is meet;
In better dress to trim thee was my mind,
But nought save home-spun Cloth, i'th' house I find.
In this array, 'mongst Vulgars[2] mayst thou roam

1 *a reference to her manuscript being taken to England.*
2 *ordinary, commonplace people.*

20   In Criticks hands, beware thou dost not come;
And take thy way where yet thou art not known,
If for thy Father askt, say, thou hadst none:
And for thy Mother, she alas is poor,
Which caus'd her thus to send thee out of door.

(1678)

To my Dear and loving Husband

If ever two were one, then surely we.
If ever man were lov'd by wife, then thee;
If ever wife was happy in a man,
Compare with me ye women if you can.
5   I prize thy love more than whole Mines of gold,
Or all the riches that the East doth hold.
My love is such that Rivers cannot quench,
Nor ought but love from thee, give recompence.
Thy love is such I can no way repay,
10   The heavens reward thee manifold I pray.
Then while we live, in love lets so persever,[1]
That when we live no more, we may live ever.

(1678)

---

1 *persevere.*

Upon the burning of our house, July 10, 1666

In silent night when rest I took,
For sorrow neer I did not look,
I waken'd was with thundring nois
And Piteous shreiks of dreadfull voice.
5   That fearfull sound of fire and fire,
Let no man know is my Desire.

I, starting up, the light did spye,
And to my God my heart did cry
To strengthen me in my Distresse
10   And not to leave me succourlesse.[1]
Then coming out beheld a space,
The flame consume my dwelling place.

And, when I could no longer look,
I blest his Name that gave and took,
15   That layd my goods now in the dust:
Yea so it was, and so 'twas just.
It was his own: it was not mine;
Far be it that I should repine.

He might of All justly bereft,
20   But yet sufficient for us left.
When by the Ruines oft I past,
My sorrowing eyes aside did cast,
And here and there the places spye
Where oft I sate, and long did lye.

1 *without help.*

25   Here stood that Trunk, and there that chest;
     There lay that store I counted best:
     My pleasant things in ashes lye,
     And them behold no more shall I.
     Under thy roof no guest shall sitt.
30   Nor at thy Table eat a bitt.

     No pleasant tale shall 'ere be told,
     Nor things recounted done of old.
     No Candle 'ere shall shine in Thee,
     Nor bridegroom's voice ere heard shall bee.
35   In silence ever shalt thou lye;
     Adeiu, Adeiu; All's vanity.

     Then streight I gin my heart to chide,
     And did thy wealth on earth abide?
     Didst fix thy hope on mouldring dust,
40   The arm of flesh didst make thy trust?
     Raise up thy thoughts above the skye
     That dunghill mists away may flie.

     Thou hast an house on high erect
     Fram'd by that mighty Architect,
45   With glory richly furnished,
     Stands permanent tho' this bee fled.
     It's purchaséd, and paid for too
     By him who hath enough to doe.

     A Prise so vast as is unknown,
50   Yet, by his Gift, is made thine own.
     Ther's wealth enough, I need no more;
     Farewell my Pelf,[2] farewell my Store.
     The world no longer let me Love,
     My hope and Treasure lyes Above.

                                        (1678)

2 *property, earthly possessions.*

ANDREW MARVELL

(1621–1678)

*A*ndrew Marvell was the son of a Yorkshire clergyman. He obtained his
B.A. at Trinity College, Cambridge, and proceeded to travel widely on the
Continent. Adept at learning, he absorbed French, Italian, Dutch, and Spanish —
languages important for an Englishman bent on a career in public service and
diplomacy. He was appointed assistant to Cromwell's Latin secretary, John Milton,
in 1658, and was later elected M.P. for Hull. It seems Marvell brought some
influence to bear upon securing the release and safety of Milton at the Restoration.
Throughout his career in public life, Marvell was prudent, honest, and commit-
tedly faithful to Puritan politics during and after the time of Cromwell's
administration.

But he was also a poet. His verses are smooth and urbane with a metaphysi-
cal quality of irony and control that reinvests conventional images with freshness.
Although overshadowed in reputation by Milton, Marvell creates lucid images of
nature and time with wit and precision. None of his poems was published in his
own lifetime.

To His Coy Mistress

Had we but world enough, and time,
This coyness, lady, were no crime.
We would sit down, and think which way
To walk, and pass our long love's day.
5   Thou by the Indian Ganges' side
Should'st rubies find: I by the tide
Of Humber would complain. I would
Love you ten years before the flood,
And you should, if you please, refuse
10   Till the conversion of the Jews;
My vegetable love should grow
Vaster than empires and more slow;
An hundred years should go to praise
Thine eyes, and on thy forehead gaze;
15   Two hundred to adore each breast,

But thirty thousand to the rest;
An age at least to every part,
And the last age should show your heart.
For, lady, you deserve this state,
20   Nor would I love at lower rate.
    But at my back I always hear
Time's winged chariot hurrying near,
And yonder all before us lie
Deserts of vast eternity.
25   Thy beauty shall no more be found,
Nor, in thy marble vault, shall sound
My echoing song: then worms shall try
That long preserved virginity,
And your quaint honour turn to dust,
30   And into ashes all my lust:
The grave's a fine and private place,
But none, I think, do there embrace.
    Now therefore, while the youthful hue
Sits on thy skin like morning dew,
35   And while thy willing soul transpires
At every pore with instant fires,
Now let us sport us while we may,
And now, like amorous birds of prey
Rather at once our time devour,
40   Than languish in his slow-chaped[1] power.
Let us roll all our strength and all
Our sweetness up into one ball,
And tear our pleasures with rough strife,
Thorough[2] the iron gates of life;
45   Thus, though we cannot make our sun
Stand still, yet we will make him run.

(1650–58?)   (1681)

---

1 i.e., slow-jawed, slow-chewing.
2 through.

The Garden

How vainly men themselves amaze,
To win the palm, the oak, or bays,[1]
And their incessant labours see
Crowned from some single herb, or tree,
5   Whose short and narrow-verged shade
Does prudently their toils upbraid,
While all the flowers, and trees, do close
To weave the garlands of repose!

Fair Quiet, have I found thee here,
10   And Innocence, thy sister dear?
Mistaken long, I sought you then
In busy companies of men.
Your sacred plants, if here below,
Only among the plants will grow;
15   Society is all but rude
To this delicious solitude.

No white nor red was ever seen
So amorous as this lovely green.
Fond lovers, cruel as their flame,
20   Cut in these trees their mistress' name:
Little, alas! they know or heed,
How far these beauties her exceed!
Fair trees! where'er your barks I wound,
No name shall but your own be found.

25   When we have run our passion's heat,
Love hither makes his best retreat.
The gods, who mortal beauty chase,
Still in a tree did end their race;
Apollo hunted Daphne so,
30   Only that she might laurel grow;
And Pan did after Syrinx speed,
Not as a nymph, but for a reed.

1 *classical trophies for military, civic, or poetic achievement.*

What wond'rous life is this I lead!
Ripe apples drop about my head;
35   The luscious clusters of the vine
Upon my mouth do crush their wine;
The nectarine, and curious peach,
Into my hands themselves do reach;
Stumbling on melons, as I pass,
40   Insnared with flowers, I fall on grass.

Meanwhile the mind, from pleasure less,
Withdraws into its happiness; —
The mind, that ocean where each kind
Does straight its own resemblance find; —
45   Yet it creates, transcending these,
Far other worlds, and other seas,
Annihilating all that's made
To a green thought in a green shade.

Here at the fountain's sliding foot,
50   Or at some fruit-tree's mossy root,
Casting the body's vest aside,
My soul into the boughs does glide:
There, like a bird, it sits and sings,
Then whets and combs its silver wings,
55   And, till prepared for longer flight,
Waves in its plumes the various light.

Such was that happy garden-state,
While man there walked without a mate:
After a place so pure and sweet,
60   What other help could yet be meet!
But 'twas beyond a mortal's share
To wander solitary there:
Two paradises 'twere in one,
To live in paradise alone.

65   How well the skilful gardener drew
Of flowers, and herbs, this dial[2] new,

2 *sundial.*

Where, from above, the milder sun
Does through a fragrant zodiac run,
And, as it works, the industrious bee
70 Computes its time as well as we!
How could such sweet and wholesome hours
Be reckoned but with herbs and flowers?

(1650–58?) (1681)

Bermudas

Where the remote Bermudas ride,
In the ocean's bosom unespied,
From a small boat, that rowed along,
The listening winds received this song.

5 "What should we do but sing his praise,
That led us through the watery maze,
Unto an isle so long unknown,
And yet far kinder than our own?
Where he the huge sea-monsters wracks,
10 That lift the deep upon their backs,
He lands us on a grassy stage,
Safe from the storms, and prelate's rage.
He gave us this eternal spring,
Which here enamels every thing,
15 And sends the fowls to us in care,
On daily visits through the air;
He hangs in shades the orange bright,
Like golden lamps in a green night,
And does in the pomegranates close,
20 Jewels more rich than Ormus[1] shows;

---

1 island in the Persian Gulf: renowned centre for the jewel trade.

He makes the figs our mouths to meet,
And throws the melons at our feet,
But apples plants of such a price,
No tree could ever bear them twice;
25   With cedars chosen by his hand,
From Lebanon, he stores the land,
And makes the hollow seas, that roar,
Proclaim the ambergrease[2] on shore;
He cast (of which we rather boast)
30   The Gospel's pearl upon our coast,
And in these rocks for us did frame
A temple where to sound his name.
Oh! let our voice his praise exalt,
'Till it arrive at heaven's vault,
35   Which, then (perhaps) rebounding, may
Echo beyond the Mexique Bay."[3]

Thus sung they, in the English boat,
A holy and a cheerful note,
And all the way, to guide their chime,
40   With falling oars they kept the time.

(1650–58?)   (1681)

2 *ambergris: valuable expectoration of sperm whales; used in making perfumes.*
3 *Gulf of Mexico.*

Aphra Behn

(1640–1689)

phra Behn was the first English woman to earn her living by writing. Her early years are shrouded in mystery; the first certain fact known about her is that in 1666, already a widow at the age of 26, she served as a spy in the Netherlands for the government of Charles II. She used her code name as a spy, Astrea, as her literary pseudonym when she turned to writing as a career in 1670. She became not only the first significant woman playwright in England, but also one of the most popular playwrights on the Restoration stage, writing nineteen plays, including her best-known comedy, The Rover (1677). She also wrote graceful lyric and occasional poems. Both her plays and her poems are written within the conventions established by the writers, all male, popular in the court circle. In her final years, she turned to prose fiction, yet another form in which she was the first important female author in English; her short novel Oroonoko; or, The Royal Slave (1688) is a powerful indictment of the slave trade and the British commercial ethos as hypocritical. No Puritan, she enjoyed the company of the wild rakes and wits at the court of Charles II, including the Earl of Rochester; her plays, short novels, and poems are as bawdy as those of the male writers in the court circle. For the most part a scandal in her time and to succeeding generations, her courage and ambition are now seen very differently: Virginia Woolf says in A Room of One's Own (1928): "All women together ought to let flowers fall upon the tomb of Aphra Behn, for it was she who earned them the right to speak their minds." The following untitled song appears in Behn's play The Dutch Lover (1673).

Song

Amyntas[1] led me to a Grove,
    Where all the Trees did shade us;
The Sun it self, tho it had strove,
    Yet could not have betray'd us.
5 The place secure from human Eyes,
    No other fear allows,
But when the Winds that gently rise
    Do kiss the yielding Boughs.

---

1 *a typical name for a shepherd in pastoral poetry*

Down there we sat upon the Moss,
10   And did begin to play
A thousand wanton Tricks, to pass
    The Heat of all the Day.
A many Kisses he did give,
    And I return'd the same:
15   Which made me willing to receive
    That which I dare not name.

His charming Eyes no aid requir'd,
    To tell their amorous Tale;
On her that was already fir'd,
20   'Twas easy to prevail.
He did but kiss, and clasp me round,
    Whilst they his thoughts exprest,
And laid me gently on the Ground;
    Oh! who can guess the rest?

(1673)

EDWARD TAYLOR

(c.1642–1729)

orn in Sketchley, England, Edward Taylor came to America in 1668, graduated from Harvard, and, from 1671 to 1729, served as a frontier clergyman in western Massachusetts. His poetry, which was not published until 1939, reflects the influence of English religious poets such as George Herbert. In addition to Prefatory Meditations, *a group of over 200 poems on theological subjects, he is also known for a series of short poems based on observations of everyday experiences. Because, like most Puritans, he saw the influence of God's power and will visible in the world around him, he frequently used common, domestic imagery to portray the relationship between the physical and spiritual worlds.*

Upon a Spider Catching a Fly

Thou sorrow, venom Elfe.
　　Is this thy play,
To spin a web out of thyselfe
　　To Catch a Fly?
5　　　　For Why?

I saw a pettish[1] wasp
　　Fall foule therein.
Whom yet thy Whorle pins[2] did not clasp
　　Lest he should fling
10　　　　His sting.

But as affraid, remote
　　Didst stand hereat
And with thy little fingers stroke
　　And gently tap
15　　　　His back.

---

1 *impatient, angry.*
2 *a pin that attaches a small flywheel to the spindle of a spinning wheel.*

Thus gently him didst treate
  Lest he should pet,
And in a froppish, waspish heate
  Should greatly fret
20   Thy net.

Whereas the silly Fly,
  Caught by its leg
Thou by the throate tookst hastily
  And 'hinde the head
25   Bite Dead.

This goes to pot, that not
  Nature doth call.
Strive not above what strength hath got
  Lest in the brawle
30   Thou fall.

This Frey seems thus to us.
  Hells Spider gets
His intrails spun to whip Cords thus
  And wove to nets
35   And sets.

To tangle Adams race
  In's stratigems
To their Destructions, spoil'd, made base
  By venom things
40   Damn'd Sins.

But mighty, Gracious Lord
  Communicate
Thy Grace to breake the Cord, afford
  Us Glorys Gate
45   And State.

We'l Nightingaile sing like
  When pearcht on high
In Glories Cage, thy glory, bright,
  And thankfully,
50   For joy.

(1939)

Huswifery[1]

Make me, O Lord, thy Spining Wheele compleate.
  Thy Holy Worde my Distaff[2] make for mee.
Make mine Affections thy Swift Flyers[3] neate
  And make my Soule thy holy Spoole to bee.
5   My Conversation make to be thy Reele[4]
  And reele the yarn thereon spun of thy Wheele.

Make me thy Loome then, knit therein this Twine:
  And make thy Holy Spirit, Lord, winde quills[5]:
Then weave the Web thyselfe. The yarn is fine.
10   Thine Ordinances[6] make my Fulling Mills.[7]
  Then dy the same in Heavenly Colours Choice,
  All pinkt with Varnisht Flowers of Paradise.

Then cloath therewith mine Understanding, Will,
  Affections, Judgment, Conscience, Memory
15   My Words, and Actions, that their shine may fill
  My wayes with glory and thee glorify.
  Then mine apparell shall display before yee
  That I am Cloathd in Holy robes for glory.

(1939)

---

1 *household activities.* 2 *a staff on which raw wool was wound.* 3 *part of a spinning machine that twists thread.* 4 *instrument on which spun thread is wound.* 5 *a hollow stem on which yarn is wound.* 6 *a decree of God.* 7 *machines on which newly woven cloth is cleaned and thickened.*

John Wilmot, Earl of Rochester

(1647–1680)

*J*ohn Wilmot was the most brilliant wit and rake at the court of Charles II. The son of a Cavalier general and war hero, he arrived at court at the age of seventeen, and soon made himself famous — and notorious — for his handsomeness, his wit and charm, his cynicism, his courage, his vitriolic lampoons and satires, and his dissoluteness. Though he married for love and had four children, his promiscuity was legendary, and at the end of his life he told his biographer that he was continually drunk for five years together. His life proclaimed his allegiance to the ideas of the contemporary philosopher Thomas Hobbes, who held that all moral laws are artificial social checks upon natural human desires. His relatively few poems, consisting mainly of some fine short lyric poems and several extended satires, were never published during his lifetime, yet he established the form that would dominate English poetry for the next hundred years or so: the poetic satire. The poems of Dryden, Swift, and Pope all clearly show the imprint of his wit, his shock tactics, and his inventive use of rhyming couplets. Sick and disillusioned, he became a pious Christian on his deathbed, under the influence of the Scottish divine Gilbert Burnet, at the age of 32.

A Satire Against Mankind

Were I (who to my cost already am
One of those strange, prodigious[1] creatures, man)
A spirit free to choose, for my own share,
What case of flesh and blood I pleased to wear,
5   I'd be a dog, a monkey, or a bear,
Or anything but that vain animal
Who is so proud of being rational.
    The senses are too gross, and he'll contrive
A sixth, to contradict the other five,
10   And before certain instinct, will prefer
Reason, which fifty times for one does err;
Reason, an *ignis fatuus*[2] in the mind,
Which, leaving light of nature, sense, behind,

---

1 *monstrous, unnatural.*
2 *will-o'-the-wisp, delusive light.*

Pathless and dangerous wandering ways it takes

15 Through error's fenny bogs and thorny brakes;[3]

Whilst the misguided follower climbs with pain

Mountains of whimseys, heaped in his own brain;

Stumbling from thought to thought, falls headlong down

Into doubt's boundless sea, where, like to drown,

20 Books bear him up awhile, and make him try

To swim with bladders of philosophy;

In hopes still to o'ertake th' escaping light,

The vapor dances in his dazzling[4] sight

Till, spent, it leaves him to eternal night.

25 Then old age and experience, hand in hand,

Lead him to death, and make him understand,

After a search so painful and so long,

That all his life he has been in the wrong.

Huddled in dirt the reasoning engine lies,

30 Who was so proud, so witty, and so wise.

    Pride drew him in, as cheats their bubbles[5] catch,

And made him venture to be made a wretch.

His wisdom did his happiness destroy,

Aiming to know that world he should enjoy.

35 And wit was his vain, frivolous pretense

Of pleasing others at his own expense,

For wits are treated just like common whores:

First they're enjoyed, and then kicked out of doors.

The pleasure past, a threatening doubt remains

40 That frights th' enjoyer with succeeding pains.

Women and men of wit are dangerous tools,

And ever fatal to admiring fools:

Pleasure allures, and when the fops escape,

'Tis not that they're belov'd, but fortunate,

45 And therefore what they fear at heart, they hate.

---

3 *thickets.*
4 *dazzled.*
5 *dupes.*

But now, methinks, some formal band[6] and beard
Takes me to task, Come on, sir; I'm prepared.
    "Then, by your favor, anything that's writ
Against this gibing, jingling knack called wit
50   Likes[7] me abundantly; but you take care
Upon this point, not to be too severe.
Perhaps my muse were fitter for this part,
For I profess I can be very smart
On wit, which I abhor with all my heart.
55   I long to lash it in some sharp essay,
But your grand indiscretion bids me stay
And turns my tide of ink another way.
    "What rage ferments in your degenerate mind
To make you rail at reason and mankind?
60   Blest, glorious man! to whom alone kind heaven
An everlasting soul has freely given,
Whom his great Maker took such care to make
That from himself he did the image take
And this fair frame in shining reason dressed
65   To dignify his nature above beast;
Reason, by whose aspiring influence
We take a flight beyond material sense,
Dive into mysteries, then soaring pierce
The flaming limits of the universe,
70   Search heaven and hell, find out what's acted there,
And give the world true grounds of hope and fear."
    Hold, mighty man, I cry, all this we know
From the pathetic pen of Ingelo,[8]
From Patrick's *Pilgrim*,[9] Sibbes' soliloquies,[10]
75   And 'tis this very reason I despise:
This supernatural gift, that makes a mite
Think he's the image of the infinite,
Comparing his short life, void of all rest,
To the eternal and the ever blest;

6 *wearer of a clergyman's band, i.e., a clergyman.*
7 *pleases.*
8 *Nathaniel Ingelo, clerical author of the religious romance* Bentivolio and Urania *(1660), popular at the time.*
9 *Simon Patrick, Bishop of Ely, wrote the Treaties of the Pilgrim (1644), a forerunner of Bunyan's* Pilgrim's Progress *(1678).*
10 *Richard Sibbes (1577–1635), a Puritan clergyman and author of many religious tracts.*

80 This busy, puzzling stirrer-up of doubt
    That frames deep mysteries, then finds 'em out,
    Filling with frantic crowds of thinking fools
    Those reverend bedlams,[11] colleges and schools;
    Borne on whose wings, each heavy sot can pierce
85 The limits of the boundless universe;
    So charming[12] ointments make an old witch fly
    And bear a crippled carcass through the sky.
    'Tis this exalted power, whose business lies
    In nonsense and impossibilities,
90 This made a whimsical philosopher
    Before the spacious world, his tub prefer,[13]
    And we have modern cloistered coxcombs who
    Retire to think, 'cause they have nought to do.
      But thoughts are given for action's government;
95 Where action ceases, thought's impertinent.
    Our sphere of action is life's happiness,
    And he who thinks beyond, thinks like an ass.
    Thus, whilst against false reasoning I inveigh,
    I own right reason, which I would obey:
100 That reason which distinguishes by sense
    And gives us rules of good and ill from thence,
    That bounds desires with a reforming will
    To keep 'em more in vigor, not to kill.
    Your reason hinders, mine helps to enjoy,
105 Renewing appetites yours would destroy.
    My reason is my friend, yours is a cheat;
    Hunger calls out, my reason bids me eat;
    Perversely, yours your appetite does mock:
    This asks for food, that answers, "What's o'clock?"
110 This plain distinction, sir, your doubt secures:[14]
    'Tis not true reason I despise, but yours.

11 *madhouses.*
12 *magical.*
13 *the Greek philosopher Diogenes lived in a tub and taught that virtue lies in the avoidance of all physical pleasure.*
14 *resolves, satisfies.*

Thus I think reason righted, but for man,
I'll ne'er recant; defend him if you can.
For all his pride and his philosophy,
115 'Tis evident beasts are, in their degree,
As wise at least, and better far than he.
Those creatures are the wisest who attain,
By surest means, the ends at which they aim.
If therefore Jowler[15] finds and kills his hares
120 Better than Meres[16] supplies committee chairs,
Though one's a statesman, th' other but a hound,
Jowler, in justice, would be wiser found.
You see how far man's wisdom here extends;
Look next if human nature makes amends:
125 Whose principles most generous are, and just,
And to whose morals you would sooner trust.
Be judge yourself, I'll bring it to the test:
Which is the basest creature, man or beast?
Birds feed on birds, beasts on each other prey,
130 But savage man alone does man betray.
Pressed by necessity, they kill for food;
Man undoes man to do himself no good.
With teeth and claws by nature armed, they hunt
Nature's allowance, to supply their want.
135 But man, with smiles, embraces, friendship, praise,
Inhumanly his fellow's life betrays;
With voluntary pains works his distress,
Not through necessity, but wantonness.
For hunger or for love they fight and tear,
140 Whilst wretched man is still in arms for fear.
For fear he arms, and is of arms afraid,
By fear to fear successively betrayed;
Base fear, the source whence his best passions came:
His boasted honor, and his dear-bought fame;
145 That lust of power, to which he's such a slave,
And for the which alone he dares be brave;

---

15 *a typical name for a hunting dog.*
16 *Sir Thomas Meres (1633–1715), member of Parliament and prominent politician.*

To which his various projects are designed;
Which makes him generous, affable, and kind;
For which he takes such pains to be thought wise,
And screws[17] his actions in a forced disguise,
Leading a tedius life in misery
Under laborious, mean hypocrisy.
Look to the bottom of his vast design,
Wherein man's wisdom, power, and glory join:
The good he acts, the ill he does endure,
'Tis all from fear, to make himself secure.
Merely for safety, after fame we thirst,
For all men would be cowards if they durst.
    And honesty's against all common sense:
Men must be knaves, 'tis in their own defence.
Mankind's dishonest; if you think it fair
Amongst known cheats to play upon the square,
You'll be undone.
Nor can weak truth your reputation save:
The knaves will all agree to call you knave.
Wronged shall he live, insulted o'er, oppressed,
Who dares be less a villain than the rest.
    Thus, sir, you see what human nature craves:
Most men are cowards, all men should be knaves.
The difference lies, as far as I can see,
Not in the thing itself, but the degree,
And all the subject matter of debate
Is only: Who's a knave of the first rate?

    All this with indignation have I hurled
At the pretending part of the proud world,
Who, swollen with selfish vanity, devise
False freedoms, holy cheats, and formal lies
Over their fellow slaves to tyrannize.
    But if in Court so just a man there be
(In Court a just man, yet unknown to me)
Who does his needful flattery direct,
Not to oppress and ruin, but protect

150
155
160
165
170
175
180

17 *deforms.*

(Since flattery, which way soever laid,
Is still a tax on that unhappy trade);
185   If so upright a statesman you can find,
Whose passions bend to his unbiased mind,
Who does his arts and policies apply
To raise his country, not his family,
Nor, whilst his pride owned[18] avarice withstands,
190   Receives close[19] bribes through friends' corrupted hands —
    Is there a churchman who on God relies;
Whose life, his faith and doctrine justifies?
Not one blown up with vain prelatic pride,[20]
Who, for reproof of sins, does man deride;
195   Whose envious heart makes preaching a pretense,
With his obstreperous, saucy eloquence,
To chide at kings, and rail at men of sense;
None of that sensual tribe whose talents lie
In avarice, pride, sloth, and gluttony;
200   Who hunt good livings,[21] but abhor good lives;
Whose lust exalted to that height arrives
They act adultery with their own wives,
And ere a score of years completed be,
Can from the lofty pulpit proudly see
205   Half a large parish their own progeny;
Nor doting bishop who would be adored
For domineering at the council board,[22]
A greater fop in business at fourscore,
Fonder of serious toys, affected more,
210   Than the gay, glittering fool at twenty proves
With all his noise, his tawdry clothes, and loves;
    But a meek, humble man of honest sense,
Who, preaching peace, does practice continence;
Whose pious life's a proof he does believe
215   Mysterious truths, which no man can conceive.

18 *acknowledged, open.*
19 *secret.*
20 *self-importance at holding high office in the church.*
21 *church appointments that carry an assured income.*
22 *meetings of the Privy Council, where matters of state are decided.*

If upon earth there dwell such God-like men,
I'll here recant my paradox to them,
Adore those shrines of virtue, homage pay,
And, with the rabble world, their laws obey.
220   If such there be, yet grant me this at least:
Man differs more from man, than man from beast.

(1680)

ANNE FINCH, COUNTESS OF WINCHELSEA

(1661–1720)

orn into a wealthy landed family, Anne Kingsmill became a maid of honour at the court of Charles II. There she met Colonel Heneage Finch, also a royal attendant and later the Earl of Winchelsea, and they married in 1684. When James II was forced from the throne in 1688, the Finches retired to a family estate in Kent. There she wrote most of her poems, influenced by the solitude and tranquillity of the country, and encouraged by her husband, who transcribed her poetry. The one volume she published during her lifetime, Miscellany Poems on Several Occasions, Written by a Lady, *appeared in 1713. She was befriended and admired by many of the leading writers of the age, including Pope, Swift, and Gay, and wrote in the forms admired at the time: verse drama, satire, odes, verse fables. Her poems were valued in their own day for their wit and delicacy of phrasing; later, the Romantic poet William Wordsworth frequently praised her observant treatment of rural subjects. Today, however, she is known for her more personal and introspective poems such as "The Introduction." She chose not to publish this preface to her work in her 1713* Miscellany — *for reasons that the poem itself makes abundantly clear. The poem invokes the Bible's authority in order to argue, daringly, that British women are "fallen," not because human nature is fallen, but because of the "mistaken rules" inculcated by their education.*

The Introduction

Did I my lines intend for public view,
How many censures would their faults pursue!
Some would, because such words they do affect,
Cry they're insipid, empty, incorrect.
5   And many have attained, dull and untaught,
The name of wit, only by finding fault.
True judges might condemn their want of wit;
And all might say, they're by a woman of writ;
Alas! a woman that attempts the pen,
10   Such an intruder on the rights of men,

Such a presumptuous creature is esteemed,
The fault can by no virtue be redeemed.
They tell us we mistake our sex and way;
Good breeding, fashion, dancing, dressing, play,
15 Are the accomplishments we should desire;
To write, or read, or think, or to enquire,
Would cloud our beauty, and exhaust our time,
And interrupt the conquests of our prime;
While the dull manage of a servile house[1]
20 Is held by some our utmost art and use.

Sure, 'twas not ever thus, nor are we told
Fables,[2] of women that excelled of old;
To whom, by the diffusive hand of heaven,
Some share of wit and poetry was given.
25 On that glad day, on which the Ark returned,[3]
The holy pledge, for which the land had mourned,
The joyful tribes attend it on the way,
The Levites[4] do the sacred charge convey,
Whilst various instruments before it play;
30 Here, holy virgins in the concert join,
The louder notes to soften and refine,
And with alternate verse complete the hymn divine.

Lo! the young poet,[5] after God's own heart,
By him inspired and taught the Muses' art,
35 Returned from conquest a bright chorus meets,
That sing his slain ten thousand in the streets.
In such loud numbers they his acts declare,
Proclaim the wonders of his early war,
That Saul upon the vast applause does frown,
40 And feel its mighty thunder shake the crown.
What can the threatened judgment now prolong?[6]
Half of the kingdom is already gone:
The fairest half, whose judgment guides the rest,
Have David's empire o'er their hearts confessed.

1 *a house full of servants.*
2 *falsehoods.*
3 *the Ark of the Covenant, restored to Jerusalem by David (see I Chronicles 15).*
4 *assistants to the priests.*
5 *David (see I Samuel 17–18).*
6 *avert, defer.*

45   A woman here leads fainting Israel on,
       She fights, she wins, she triumphs with a song,[7]
       Devout, majestic, for the subject fit,
       And far above her arms exalts her wit,
       Then to the peaceful, shady palm withdraws,
50   And rules the rescued nation with her laws.
           How are we fallen! fallen by mistaken rules,
       And Education's, more than Nature's fools;
       Debarred from all improvements of the mind,
       And to be dull, expected and designed,
55   And if some one would soar above the rest,
       With warmer fancy, and ambition pressed,
       So strong the opposing faction still appears,
       The hopes to thrive can ne'er outweigh the fears.
       Be cautioned, then, my Muse, and still retired;
60   Nor be despised, aiming to be admired;
       Conscious of wants, still with contracted wing,
       To some few friends, and to thy sorrows sing.
       For groves of laurel[8] thou wert never meant:
       Be dark enough thy shades, and be thou there content.

       (c. 1700)   (1903)

---

7 *Deborah led the Israelites to victory in battle and celebrated it in song (Judges 4–5).*
8 *the tree whose leaves were used to crown victorious poets in classical times.*

Jonathan Swift

(1677–1745)

*B*orn and educated in Ireland, Jonathan Swift came from a well-connected but poor Protestant family. After serving as a clergyman in Ireland, Swift settled in London in 1710 and became for four years the chief propagandist of the ruling Tory party, advocating peace in the War of the Spanish Succession and discrediting the Whig war hero, General John Churchill, Duke of Marlborough. Made dean of St. Patrick's Cathedral in 1713, Swift spent the rest of his life in semi-exile in Ireland. While there, he published his most famous work, Gulliver's Travels (1726), and his notorious tract "A Modest Proposal" (1729), a hardly modest proposal that the starving Irish sell their children to the English as food. His prose proves that simple words and straightforward sentences can have the intensity of poetry when used ironically; his poetry is distinctively unpoetic — satirical, parodic, down-to-earth, often shocking. Both the prose and the poetry mount an attack upon human complacency by parodying literary forms that take themselves all too seriously. Just as Gulliver's Travels is ostensibly a book of travel adventures and "A Modest Proposal" pretends to be an economic pamphlet, so Swift's poems make use of established genres to sharpen his satiric criticism of contemporary life: his poem on the death of the Duke of Marlborough is, as its title indicates, "A Satirical Elegy," while "A Description of the Morning" plays with the conventions of pastoral poetry — poetry which presents a nostalgic picture of the simple, natural life of shepherds.

A Description of the Morning

Now hardly[1] here and there an Hackney-Coach[2]
Appearing, show'd the Ruddy Morns Approach.
Now *Betty*[3] from her Masters Bed had flown,
And softly stole to discompose her own.
5   The Slipshod Prentice from his Masters Door,
Had par'd[4] the Dirt, and Sprinked round the Floor.
Now *Moll* had whirl'd her Mop with dext'rous Airs,
Prepar'd to Scrub the Entry and the Stairs.

1 *violently, suddenly.*
2 *a hired four-wheel coach, drawn by two horses.*
3 *a stock name for a maid-servant (Betty is thus an urban, low-life equivalent of Aurora, goddess of dawn, who in pastoral poetry leaves the bed of lover Tithonus each morning; the sprinkled floor, the air-stirring mop, and the street-vendors' cries also have pastoral counterparts).*
4 *reduced.*

The Youth with Broomy Stumps began to trace
10   The Kennel-Edge,[5] where Wheels had worn the Place.
The Smallcoal-Man[6] was heard with Cadence deep,
'Till drown'd in Shriller Notes of Chimney-Sweep,
Duns[7] at his Lordships Gate began to meet,
And Brickdust *Moll*[8] had Scream'd through half the Street.
15   The Turnkey[9] now his Flock returning sees,
Duly let out a Nights to Steal for Fees.
The watchful Bailiffs take their silent Stands,
And School-Boys lag with Satchels in their Hands.

(1709)

A Satirical Elegy on the Death of a Late Famous General

His Grace! impossible! what dead![1]
Of old age too, and in his bed!
And could that Mighty Warrior fall?
And so inglorious, after all!
5   Well, since he's gone, no matter how,
The last loud trump must wake him now:
And, trust me, as the noise grows stronger,
He'd wish to sleep a little longer.
And could he be indeed so old
10   As by the news-papers we're told?
Threescore, I think, is pretty high;
'Twas time in conscience he should die.

---

5 *the gutter's edge, where he looks for old nails that he can sell.*
6 *charcoal vendor.*
7 *bill collectors.*
8 *a woman selling powdered brick, used for cleaning knives.*
9 *the jailer, who lets his prisoners out at night so that they can steal in order to pay him the fees he exacts.*

1 *John Churchill, first Duke of Marlborough (1650–1722), general and statesman, generally considered one of the greatest commanders in military history.*

This world he cumber'd long enough;
He burnt his candle to the snuff;
15   And that's the reason, some folks think,
He left behind *so great a s---k.*
Behold his funeral appears,
Nor widow's sighs, nor orphan's tears,
Wont at such times each heart to pierce,
20   Attend the progress of his herse.
But what of that, his friends may say,
He had those honours in his day.
True to his profit and his pride,
He made them weep before he dy'd.

25   Come hither, all ye empty things,
Ye bubbles rais'd by breath of Kings;
Who float upon the tide of state,
Come hither, and behold your fate.
Let pride be taught by this rebuke,
30   How very mean a thing's a Duke;
From all his ill-got honours flung,[2]
Turn'd to that dirt from whence he sprung.

(1722)   (1764)

2 *Marlborough's many victories in the War of the Spanish Succession (1701–14) made him a national hero and earned him many honours, most notably his title and his estate, Blenheim Palace (named after his most famous victory).*

ALEXANDER POPE

(1688–1744)

*P*ope dominated English poetry during the first half of the eighteenth century. His greatest poems were satires, public statements that had the power to change the course of public events. Like most poets of his own and the previous age, Pope wrote primarily in heroic couplets (i.e., closed iambic pentameter couplets); unlike others, however, Pope lived on his earnings as a poet. He had to, since he faced two devastating handicaps. He was born into a Roman Catholic family, which meant that he was forbidden by law from attending university, holding public office, or even living in London. Even worse, when he was a boy he contracted tuberculosis of the spine, which stunted his growth (he was never more than about four-foot-eight in height), made his body crooked, and gave him almost constant pain during his adult life. Fortunately, however, he had kindly and well-to-do parents, who raised him just outside London and saw that he had a thorough education in classical literature. Pope's poetic career falls into three distinct phases. His early poems, up to about 1713, were witty and playful satires; The Rape of the Lock, first published in 1712, is the gem of these early poems and still his best-known work. During a middle period from roughly 1713 to 1726, he devoted himself to translating Homer's two great epics, the Iliad (completed in 1720) and the Odyssey (completed in 1726), and to producing an edition of Shakespeare's plays (1725). These projects gave him financial security, and from 1727 onward Pope again wrote his own poetry, but now of a much more sober nature: satires, including the autobiographical Epistle to Dr. Arbuthnot (1735) and The Dunciad (1728–43), a mock-epic celebrating the triumph of duncedom in contemporary Britain; moral essays in verse upon such topics as the proper use of riches; and his philosophical poem An Essay on Man, published anonymously in 1733–34.

The Rape of the Lock;
An Heroi-Comical Poem[1]

Nolueram, Belinda, tuos violare capillos,
Sed juvat hoc precibus me tribuisse tuis.
——MARTIAL[2]

TO
Mrs.[3] *ARABELLA FERMOR.*

MADAM,

I t will be in vain to deny that I have some Regard for this
Piece, since I Dedicate it to You. Yet You may bear me Witness,
it was intended only to divert a few young Ladies, who have
good Sense and good Humour enough, to laugh not only at their
5 Sex's little unguarded Follies, but at their own. But as it was
communicated with the Air of a Secret, it soon found its Way
into the World. An imperfect Copy having been offer'd to a
Bookseller, You had the Good-Nature for my Sake to consent
to the Publication of one more correct: This I was forc'd to before
10 I had executed half my Design, for the *Machinery* was entirely
wanting to compleat it.[4]

The *Machinery*, Madam, is a Term invented by the Criticks,
to signify that Part which the Deities, Angels, or Dæmons, are
made to act in a Poem: For the ancient Poets are in one respect
15 like many modern Ladies; Let an Action be never so trivial in
it self, they always make it appear of the utmost Importance.
These Machines I determin'd to raise on a very new and odd
Foundation, the *Rosicrucian*[5] Doctrine of Spirits.

1 Pope's title alludes to the poem's origin. A quarrel had developed between two prominent Roman Catholic families
when Robert, Lord Petre, cut off a lock from the head of Arabella Fermor, a celebrated beauty known as "Belle."
John Caryll, Pope's friend, urged Pope to write a poem that would restore good feelings. Pope's subtitle alludes to
the poem's genre: it is a mock-epic, and the well-known features of epic poems are comically transformed. The
combat of heroic warriors becomes the drawing-room war between the sexes; the rape of Helen becomes that of a
lock of hair; the arming of the hero for combat becomes the heroine's dressing and beautification for a social
engagement, and so on.
2 Pope's epigraph is slightly altered from the Roman satirist Martial: "I did not wish, Belinda, to profane your
locks, but it pleases me to have granted this to your prayers."
3 "Mrs." was used for ladies, whether married or single.
4 in its original (1712) form, the poem consisted of two cantos of 334 lines; as Pope explains, he expanded the poem
to five cantos in 1714 by adding the "machinery" (the supernatural agents found in epic poems).
5 an eccentric occult religion that originated in Germany early in the seventeenth century.

I know how disagreeable it is to make use of hard Words
before a Lady; but 'tis so much the Concern of a Poet to have
his Works understood, and particularly by your Sex, that You
must give me leave to explain two or three difficult Terms.

The *Rosicrucians* are a People I must bring You acquainted
with. The best Account I know of them is in a French Book
call'd *Le Comte de Gabalis*, which both in its Title and Size is
so like a *Novel*, that many of the Fair Sex have read it for one
by Mistake.[6] According to these Gentlemen, the four Elements[7]
are inhabited by Spirits, which they call *Sylphs, Gnomes, Nymphs*,
and *Salamanders*. The *Gnomes*, or Dæmons of Earth, delight in
Mischief; but the *Sylphs*, whose Habitation is in the Air, are the
best-condition'd Creatures imaginable. For they say, any Mortals
may enjoy the most intimate Familiarities with these gentle Spirits,
upon a Condition very easie to all true *Adepts*, an inviolate
Preservation of Chastity.

As to the following Canto's, all the Passages of them are
as Fabulous, as the Vision at the Beginning, or the Transformation
at the End; (except the Loss of your Hair, which I always mention
with Reverence.) The Human Persons are as Fictitious as the
Airy ones; and the Character of *Belinda*, as it is now manag'd,
resembles You in nothing but in Beauty.

If this Poem had as many Graces as there are in Your Person,
or in Your Mind, yet I could never hope it should pass thro'
the World half so Uncensured as You have done. But let its Fortune
be what it will, mine is happy enough, to have given me this
Occasion of assuring You that I am, with the truest Esteem,

Madam,

Your Most Obedient
Humble Servant.
A. POPE

CANTO I.

What dire Offence from am'rous Causes springs,
What mighty Contests rise from trivial Things,[8]
I sing — This Verse to *Caryll*, Muse! is due;
This, ev'n *Belinda* may vouchsafe to view:

6 in fact, Le Comte de Gabalis (1670), written by the Abbé de Montfaucon de Villars, is a facetious and
largely fictitious summary of Rosicrucianism that had been published as a novel when translated into English in
1680.
7 air, earth, water, and fire, according to traditional science.
8 like Homer, Virgil, and Milton, Pope begins his poem with a concise statement of its theme, immediately followed
by an invocation of the Muse.

5   Slight is the Subject, but not so the Praise,

If She inspire, and He approve my Lays.

      Say what strange Motive, Goddess! cou'd compel

A well-bred *Lord* t'assault a gentle *Belle*?[9]

Oh say what stranger Cause, yet unexplor'd,

10   Cou'd make a gentle *Belle* reject a *Lord*?

In Tasks so bold, can Little Men engage,

And in soft Bosoms dwells such mighty Rage?

      Sol thro' white Curtains shot a tim'rous Ray,

And Op'd those Eyes that must eclipse the Day;

15   Now Lapdog's give themselves the rowzing Shake,

And sleepless Lovers, just at Twelve, awake:

Thrice rung the Bell, the Slipper knock'd the Ground,[10]

And the press'd Watch return'd a silver Sound.[11]

Belinda still her downy Pillow prest,

20   Her Guardian *Sylph* prolong'd the balmy Rest.

'Twas he had summon'd to her silent Bed

The Morning-Dream that hover'd o'er her Head.[12]

A Youth more glitt'ring than a *Birth-night Beau*,[13]

(That ev'n in Slumber caus'd her Cheek to glow)

25   Seem'd to her Ear his winning Lips to lay,

And thus in Whispers said, or seem'd to say.

      Fairest of Mortals, thou distinguish'd Care

Of thousand bright Inhabitants of Air!

If e'er one Vision touch'd thy infant Thought,

30   Of all the Nurse and all the Priest have taught,[14]

Of airy Elves by Moonlight Shadows seen,

The silver Token,[15] and the circled Green,[16]

Or Virgins visited by Angel-Pow'rs,[17]

With Golden Crowns and Wreaths of heav'nly Flow'rs,

35   Hear and believe! thy own Importance know,

Nor bound thy narrow Views to Things below.

---

9 *again, like Virgil and Milton, before plunging into the action of his poem Pope asks questions about the causes of all that will follow.*

10 *ladies summoned their maids by ringing a hand-bell or by knocking on the floor with a high-heeled shoe.*

11 *England was famous for its "repeater" watches; when the stem was pressed, the watch chimed the most recent hour and quarter-hour.*

12 *epic heroes often receive warnings about coming events from the gods in dreams; cf. Eve's dream in* Paradise Lost *V.28–93.*

13 *a courtier splendidly dressed for the royal birthday.*

Some secret Truths from Learned Pride conceal'd,
To Maids alone and Children are reveal'd:
What tho' no Credit doubting Wits may give?
40 The Fair and Innocent shall still believe.
Know then, unnumber'd Spirits round thee fly,
The light *Militia* of the lower Sky;
These, tho' unseen, are ever on the Wing,
Hang o'er the *Box*,[18] and hover round the *Ring*.[19]
45 Think what an Equipage[20] thou hast in Air,
And view with scorn *Two Pages* and a *Chair*.[21]
As now your own, our Beings were of old,
And once inclos'd in Woman's beauteous Mold;
Thence, by a soft Transition, we repair
50 From earthly Vehicles[22] to these of Air.
Think not, when Woman's transient Breath is fled,
That all her Vanities at once are dead:
Succeeding Vanities she still regards,
And tho' she plays no more, o'erlooks the Cards.
55 Her Joy in gilded Chariots, when alive,
And Love of *Ombre*,[23] after Death survive.
For when the Fair in all their Pride expire,
To their first Elements[24] their Souls retire:
The Sprights[25] of fiery Termagants[26] in Flame
60 Mount up, and take a *Salamander's*[27] Name.
Soft yielding Minds to Water glide away,
And sip with *Nymphs*, their Elemental Tea.
The graver Prude sinks downward to a *Gnome*,
In search of Mischief still on Earth to roam.
65 The light Coquettes in *Sylphs* aloft repair,
And sport and flutter in the Fields of Air.
Know farther yet; Whoever fair and chaste

---

14 *the traditional promulgators of superstitions.* **15** *fairies were believed to skim off the cream from jugs of milk left standing overnight, leaving a coin as payment.* **16** *"fairy rings" (withered circles in grass) were thought to be caused by fairies dancing.* **17** *many saints were virgins to whom angels appeared in mystic visions (St. Theresa of Avila, for instance).* **18** *the theatre box, where the élite among playgoers sat.* **19** *a fashionable circular drive in Hyde Park.* **20** *carriage with horses and footmen.* **21** *sedan-chair, in which passengers were carried* **22** *meaning both carriages and bodies (the body is the vehicle of the soul).* **23** *a popular card game (see note 73).* **24** *traditionally, the four elements of all matter (earth, air, fire, water) had their counterparts in the four "humours" or fluids of the human body (black bile, yellow bile, blood, phlegm); one of these humours was supposed to dominate each person, determining his or her temperament.* **25** *spirits.* **26** *shrews.* **27** *salamanders were believed able to live in fire.*

Rejects Mankind, is by some *Sylph* embrac'd:
For Spirits, freed from mortal Laws, with ease
70   Assume what Sexes and what Shapes they please.[28]
What guards the Purity of melting Maids,
In Courtly Balls, and Midnight Masquerades,[29]
Safe from the treach'rous Friend, the daring Spark,[30]
The Glance by Day, the Whisper in the Dark;
75   When kind Occasion prompts their warm Desires,
When Musick softens, and when Dancing fires?
'Tis but their *Sylph*, the wise Celestials know,
Tho' *Honour* is the Word with Men below.
    Some Nymphs there are, too conscious of their Face,
80   For Life predestin'd to the *Gnomes* Embrace.
These swell their Prospects and exalt their Pride,
When Offers are disdain'd, and Love deny'd.
Then gay Ideas crowd the vacant Brain;
While Peers and Dukes, and all their sweeping Train,
85   And Garters, Stars, and Coronets[31] appear,
And in soft Sounds, *Your Grace*[32] salutes their Ear.
'Tis these that early taint the Female Soul,
Instruct the Eyes of young *Coquettes* to roll,
Teach Infant-Cheeks a bidden Blush to know,
90   And little Hearts to flutter at a *Beau*.
    Oft when the World imagine Women stray,
The *Sylphs* thro' mystick Mazes guide their Way,
Thro' all the giddy Circle they pursue,
And old Impertinence expel by new.
95   What tender Maid but must a Victim fall
To one Man's Treat,[33] but for another's Ball?
When *Florio* speaks, what Virgin could withstand,
If gentle *Damon* did not squeeze her Hand?
With varying Vanities, from ev'ry Part,
100   They shift the moving Toyshop of their Heart;
Where Wigs with Wigs, with Sword-knots[34] Sword-knots
     strive,
Beaus banish Beaus, and Coaches Coaches drive.

---

28 *as Milton had explained in* Paradise Lost *I.427–31.* **29** *masked balls.* **30** *fop or beau.* **31** *garters, stars, and coronets are all insignia of noble rank.* **32** *the courtesy title used to address a duke or duchess.* **33** *feast, entertainment.* **34** *ribbons tied to the hilt of a sword.*

This erring Mortals Levity may call,
Oh blind to Truth! the *Sylphs* contrive it all.

105 Of these am I, who thy Protection claim,
A watchful Sprite, and *Ariel* is my Name.
Late, as I rang'd the Crystal Wilds of Air,
In the clear Mirror of thy ruling *Star*
I saw, alas! some dread Event impend,
110 Ere to the Main this Morning Sun descend.
But Heav'n reveals not what, or how, or where:
Warn'd by thy *Sylph,* oh Pious Maid beware!
This to disclose is all thy Guardian can.
Beware of all, but most beware of Man!

115 He said; when *Shock,*[35] who thought she slept too long,
Leapt up, and wak'd his Mistress with his Tongue.
'Twas then *Belinda!* if Report say true,
Thy Eyes first open'd on a *Billet-doux*[36];
Wounds, Charms, and *Ardors,* were no sooner read,
120 But all the Vision vanish'd from thy Head.

And now, unveil'd, the *Toilet*[37] stands display'd,
Each Silver Vase in mystic Order laid.
First, rob'd in White, the Nymph intent adores
With Head uncover'd, the *Cosmetic* Pow'rs.
125 A heavn'ly Image in the Glass appears,
To that she bends, to that her Eyes she rears;
Th'inferior Priestess,[38] at her Altar's side,
Trembling, begins the sacred Rites of Pride.
Unnumber'd Treasures ope at once, and here
130 The various Off'rings of the World appear;
From each she nicely[39] culls with curious[40] Toil,
And decks the Goddess with the glitt'ring Spoil.
This Casket *India's* glowing Gems unlocks,
And all *Arabia* breathes from yonder Box.

35 *Belinda's lap-dop.*
36 *love-letter.*
37 *dressing table.*
38 *Belinda's maid Betty.*
39 *fastidiously.*
40 *careful.*

135   The Tortoise here and Elephant unite,
Transform'd to *Combs*, the speckled and the white.
Here Files of Pins extend their shining Rows,
Puffs, Powders, Patches, Bibles, Billet-doux.
Now awful[41] Beauty puts on all its Arms;
140   The Fair each moment rises in her Charms,
Repairs her Smiles, awakens ev'ry Grace,
And calls forth all the Wonders of her Face;
Sees by Degrees a purer Blush arise,
And keener Lightnings quicken in her Eyes.
145   The busy *Sylphs* surround their darling Care;
These set the Head, and those divide the Hair,
Some fold the Sleeve, whilst others plait the Gown;
And *Betty*'s prais'd for Labours not her own.

CANTO II.

Not with more Glories, in th' Etherial Plain,
The Sun first rises o'er the purpled Main,
Than issuing forth, the Rival of his Beams
Lanch'd on the Bosom of the Silver *Thames*.[42]
5   Fair Nymphs, and well-drest Youths around her shone,
But ev'ry Eye was fix'd on her alone.
On her white Breast a sparkling *Cross* she wore,
Which *Jews* might kiss, and Infidels adore.[43]
Her lively Looks a sprightly Mind disclose,
10   Quick as her Eyes, and as unfix'd as those:
Favours to none, to all she Smiles extends,
Oft she rejects, but never once offends.
Bright as the Sun, her Eyes the Gazers strike,
And, like the Sun, they shine on all alike.
15   Yet graceful Ease, and Sweetness void of Pride,
Might hide her Faults, if *Belles* had Faults to hide:

---

41 *awe-inspiring.*
42 *Belinda travels by boat up the Thames from London to Hampton Court Palace, the royal palace some ten kilometres upstream.*
43 *kissing or adoration of the cross marked conversion to Christianity.*

If to her share some Female Errors fall,
Look on her Face, and you'll forget 'em all.
 This Nymph, to the Destruction of Mankind,
20 Nourish'd two Locks, which graceful hung behind
In equal Curls, and well conspir'd to deck
With shining Ringlets the smooth Iv'ry Neck.
Love in these Labyrinths his Slaves detains,
And mighty Hearts are held in slender Chains.
25 With hairy Sprindges[44] we the Birds betray,
Slight Lines of Hair surprize the Finny Prey,
Fair Tresses Man's Imperial Race insnare,
And Beauty draws us with a single Hair.
 Th' Adventrous *Baron* the bright Locks admir'd,
30 He saw, he wish'd, and to the Prize aspir'd:
Resolv'd to win, he meditates the way,
By Force to ravish, or by Fraud betray;
For when Success a Lover's Toil attends,
Few ask, if Fraud or Force attain'd his Ends.
35 For this, ere *Phœbus*[45] rose, he had implor'd
Propitious Heav'n, and ev'ry Pow'r ador'd,
But chiefly *Love* — to *Love* an Altar built,
Of twelve vast *French* Romances,[46] neatly gilt.
There lay three Garters, half a Pair of Gloves;
40 And all the Trophies of his former Loves.
With tender *Billet-doux* he lights the Pyre,
And breathes three am'rous Sighs to raise the Fire.
Then prostrate falls, and begs with ardent Eyes
Soon to obtain, and long possess the Prize:
45 The Pow'rs gave Ear, and granted half his Pray'r,
The rest, the Winds dispers'd in empty Air.[47]
 But now secure[48] the painted Vessel glides,

---

44 *snares, traps; pronounced sprin-jez.*
45 *the sun.*
46 *notoriously long and idealized love stories, written by seventeenth-century French aristocrats and set in ancient Greece and Rome.*
47 *in epics, the gods frequently grant only half of a character's prayer, with the other half being abandoned to the winds.*
48 *free from care.*

The Sun-beams trembling on the floating Tydes,
While melting Musick steals upon the Sky,
50   And soften'd Sounds along the Waters die.
Smooth flow the Waves, the Zephyrs[49] gently play,
Belinda smil'd, and all the World was gay.
All but the *Sylph* — With careful Thoughts opprest,
Th'impending Woe sate heavy on his Breast.
55   He summons strait his Denizens of Air;
The lucid Squadrons round the Sails repair:[50]
Soft o'er the Shrouds[51] Aerial Whispers breathe,
That seem'd but *Zephyrs* to the Train beneath.
Some to the Sun their Insect-Wings unfold,
60   Waft on the Breeze, or sink in Clouds of Gold.
Transparent Forms, too fine for mortal Sight,
Their fluid Bodies half dissolv'd in Light.
Loose to the Wind their airy Garments flew,
Thin glitt'ring Textures of the filmy Dew;
65   Dipt in the richest Tincture of the Skies,
Where Light disports in ever-mingling Dies,
While ev'ry Beam new transient Colours flings,
Colours that change whene'er they wave their Wings.
Amid the Circle, on the gilded Mast,
70   Superior by the Head,[52] was *Ariel* plac'd;
His Purple Pinions opening to the Sun,
He rais'd his Azure Wand, and thus begun.
     Ye *Sylphs* and *Sylphids*,[53] to your Chief give Ear,
Fays, Fairies, Genii, Elves, and *Dæmons* hear![54]
75   Ye know the Spheres and various Tasks assign'd,
By Laws Eternal, to th' Aerial Kind.
Some in the Fields of purest *aether*[55] play,
And bask and whiten in the Blaze of Day.
Some guide the Course of wandring Orbs on high,
80   Or roll the Planets thro' the boundless Sky.

---

49 *gentle breezes.* **50** *gather.* **51** *ropes.* **52** *epic heroes are usually taller than their followers.* **53** *female sylphs.* **54** *the epic hero normally rallies his forces for action by a stirring speech which begins by addressing each of the ranks present in turn.* **55** *the air above the moon was considered pure and was known as the aether.*

Some less refin'd, beneath the Moon's pale Light
Pursue the Stars that shoot athwart the Night,
Or suck the Mists in grosser Air below,
Or dip their Pinions in the painted Bow,
85   Or brew fierce Tempests on the wintry Main,
Or o'er the Glebe[56] distill the kindly Rain.
Others on Earth o'er human Race preside,
Watch all their Ways, and all their Actions guide:
Of these the Chief the Care of Nations own,
90   And guard with Arms Divine the *British Throne.*
    Our humbler Province is to tend the Fair,
Not a less pleasing, tho' less glorious Care.
To save the Powder from too rude a Gale,
Nor let th' imprison'd Essences[57] exhale,
95   To draw fresh Colours from the vernal[58] Flow'rs,
To steal from Rainbows ere they drop in Show'rs
A brighter Wash;[59] to curl their waving Hairs,
Assist their Blushes, and inspire their Airs;
Nay oft, in Dreams, Invention we bestow,
100   To change a *Flounce,* or add a *Furbelo.*[60]
    This Day, black Omens threat the brightest Fair
That e'er deserv'd a watchful Spirit's Care;
Some dire Disaster, or by Force, or Slight,[61]
But what, or where, the Fates have wrapt in Night.
105   Whether the Nymph shall break *Diana's*[62] Law,
Or some frail *China* Jar receive a Flaw,
Or stain her Honour, or her new Brocade,
Forget her Pray'rs, or miss a Masquerade,
Or lose her Heart, or Necklace, at a Ball;
110   Or whether Heav'n has doom'd that *Shock* must fall.
Haste then ye Spirits! to your Charge repair;
The flutt'ring Fan be *Zephyretta's* Care;
The Drops[63] to thee, *Brillante,* we consign;

---

56 *farmland.* **57** *perfumes.* **58** *spring.* **59** *lotion, rinse.* **60** *ruffle.* **61** *sleight, trick.* **62** *Diana was the Roman goddess of chastity.* **63** *diamond earrings.*

And, *Momentilla*, let the Watch be thine;
115   Do thou, *Cripissa*, tend her fav'rite Lock;
Ariel himself shall be the Guard of *Shock*.
    To Fifty chosen *Sylphs*, of special Note,
We trust th'important Charge, the *Petticoat*:
Oft have we known that sev'nfold Fence to fail,
120   Tho' stiff with Hoops, and arm'd with Ribs of Whale.
Form a strong Line about the Silver Bound,
And guard the wide Circumference around.
    Whatever Spirit, careless of his Charge,
His Post neglects, or leaves the Fair at large,
125   Shall feel sharp Vengeance soon o'ertake his Sins,
Be stopt in *Vials*, or transfixt with *Pins*;
Or plung'd in Lakes of bitter *Washes* lie,
Or wedg'd whole Ages in a *Bodkin's*[64] Eye:
Gums and *Pomatums*[65] shall his Flight restrain,
130   While clog'd he beats his silken Wings in vain;
Or Alom-*Stypticks*[66] with contracting Power
Shrink his thin Essence like a rivell'd[67] Flower.
Or as *Ixion*[68] fix'd, the Wretch shall feel
The giddy Motion of the whirling Mill,[69]
135   In Fumes of burning Chocolate shall glow,
And tremble at the Sea that froaths below!
    He spoke; the Spirits from the Sails descend;
Some, Orb in Orb, around the Nymph extend,
Some thrid the mazy Ringlets of her Hair,
140   Some hang upon the Pendants of her Ear;
With beating Hearts the dire Event they wait,
Anxious, and trembling for the Birth of Fate.

---

64 *needle's.* **65** *ointments.* **66** *astringents to stop bleeding.* **67** *shrivelled, wrinkled.* **68** *in Greek mythology, Ixion was a king whose punishment for his attempt to seduce the goddess Hera was to be bound in hell to a perpetually turning wheel.* **69** *for beating chocolate.*

CANTO III.

Close by those Meads for ever crown'd with Flow'rs,
Where *Thames* with Pride surveys his rising Tow'rs,
There stands a Structure of Majestick Frame,[70]
Which from the neighb'ring *Hampton* takes it Name.
5 Here *Britain*'s Statesmen oft the Fall foredoom
Of Foreign Tyrants, and of Nymphs at home;
Here Thou, Great *Anna!*[71] whom three Realms obey,
Dost sometimes Counsel take — and sometimes *Tea*.
   Hither the Heroes and the Nymphs resort,
10 To taste awhile the Pleasures of a Court;
In various Talk th' instructive hours they past,
Who gave the *Ball*, or paid the *Visit* last:
One speaks the Glory of the *British Queen*,
And one describes a charming *Indian Screen*;
15 A third interprets Motions, Looks, and Eyes;
At ev'ry Word a Reputation dies.
Snuff, or the *Fan*, supply each Pause of Chat,
With singing, laughing, ogling, and all that.
   Mean while declining from the Noon of Day,
20 The Sun obliquely shoots his burning Ray;
The hungry Judges soon the Sentence sign,
And Wretches hang that Jury-men may Dine;
The Merchant from th'*Exchange*[72] returns in Peace,
And the long Labours of the *Toilette* cease —
25 *Belinda* now, whom Thirst of Fame invites,
Burns to encounter two adventrous Knights,
At *Ombre*[73] singly to decide their Doom;
And swells her Breast with Conquests yet to come.
Strait the three Bands prepare in Arms to join,

---

70 *Hampton Court Palace, largest of the royal palaces.*
71 *Queen Anne, ruler of England, Scotland, and Ireland.*
72 *the Royal Exchange in London's financial district, where merchants, bankers, and stockbrokers met to do business.*
73 *Belinda's card game mimics the epic games at which warriors relax and at the same time celebrate their heroic code; see Homer's* Iliad, *Book XXIII. Ombre (pronounced* om-ber, *from the Spanish* hombre, *meaning man) is played by three persons with 40 cards, the eights, nines, and tens being removed from the deck. Nine cards are dealt to each player, and nine tricks are played, with the highest card winning each. One player, called the "Ombre," undertakes to win more tricks than either of the other two and chooses which suit will be trumps.*

30 Each Band the number of the Sacred Nine.
Soon as she spreads her Hand, th' Aerial Guard
Descend, and sit on each important Card:
First *Ariel* perch'd upon a *Matadore*,[74]
Then each, according to the Rank they bore;
35 For *Sylphs*, yet mindful of their ancient Race,
Are, as when Women, wondrous fond of Place.[75]
    Behold, four *Kings* in Majesty rever'd,
With hoary Whiskers and a forky Beard;
And four fair *Queens* whose hands sustain a Flow'r,
40 Th' expressive Emblem of their softer Pow'r;
Four *Knaves* in Garbs succinct,[76] a trusty Band,
Caps on their heads, and Halberds[77] in their hand;
And Particolour'd Troops, a shining Train,
Draw forth to Combat on the Velvet Plain.
45   The skilful Nymph reviews her Force with Care;
Let Spades be Trumps! she said, and Trumps they were.[78]
    Now move to War her Sable *Matadores*,
In Show like Leaders of the swarthy *Moors*.
Spadillio[79] first, unconquerable Lord!
50 Led off two captive Trumps, and swept the Board.
As many more *Manillio*[80] forc'd to yield,
And march'd a Victor from the verdant Field.
Him *Basto*[81] follow'd, but his Fate more hard
Gain'd but one Trump and one *Plebeian* Card.
55 With his broad Sabre next, a Chief in Years,
The hoary Majesty of *Spades* appears;
Puts forth one manly Leg, to sight reveal'd;
The rest of his many-colour'd Robe conceal'd.
The Rebel-*Knave*, who dares his Prince engage,
60 Proves the just Victim of his Royal Rage.
Ev'n mighty *Pam*[82] that Kings and Queens o'erthrew,
And mow'd down Armies in the Fights of *Lu*,
Sad Chance of War! now, destitute of Aid,
Falls undistinguish'd by the Victor *Spade*!

---

74 *one of the three cards of highest value; they are, in order, the ace of spades, the two of the trump suit (when, as here, a black suit is trumps), the ace of clubs.* **75** *rank* **76** *girded up.* **77** *battle-axes attached to long spears.* **78** *cf. Genesis 1:3: "And God said, Let there be light; and there was light."* **79** *the ace of spades.* **80** *the two of spades.* **81** *the ace of clubs.* **82** *the knave of clubs, highest card in the game of Loo, or Lu.*

65   Thus far both Armies to *Belinda* yield;
Now to the *Baron* Fate inclines the Field.
His warlike *Amazon*[83] her Host invades,
Th' Imperial Consort of the Crown of *Spades*.
The *Club's* black Tyrant first her Victim dy'd,
70   Spite of his haughty Mien, and barb'rous Pride:
What boots the Regal Circle on his Head,
His Giant Limbs in State unwieldy spread?
That long behind he trails his pompous Robe,
And of all Monarchs only grasps the Globe?
75   The *Baron* now his *Diamonds* pours apace;
Th' embroider'd *King* who shows but half his Face,
And his refulgent[84] *Queen*, with Pow'rs combin'd,
Of broken Troops an easie Conquest find.
Clubs, Diamonds, Hearts, in wild Disorder seen,
80   With Throngs promiscuous strow the level Green.
Thus when dispers'd a routed Army runs,
Of *Asia's* Troops, and *Africk's* Sable Sons,
With like Confusion different Nations fly,
Of various Habit and of various Dye,
85   The pierc'd Battalions dis-united fall,
In Heaps on Heaps; one Fate o'erwhelms them all.
       The *Knave* of *Diamonds* tries his wily Arts,
And wins (oh shameful Chance!) the *Queen of Hearts*.
At this, the Blood the Virgin's Cheek forsook,
90   A livid Paleness spreads o'er all her Look;
She sees, and trembles at th' approaching Ill,
Just in the Jaws of Ruin, and *Codille*.[85]
And now, (as oft in some distemper'd State)
On one nice[86] *Trick* depends the gen'ral Fate.
95   An *Ace* of Hearts steps forth: The *King* unseen
Lurk'd in her Hand, and mourn'd his captive *Queen*.
He springs to Vengeance with an eager pace,
And falls like Thunder on the prostrate *Ace*.[87]

---

83 *the queen of spades.*
84 *shining, glorious.*
85 *if the Ombre failed to win more tricks than one of the other players, he or she was said to be given "codille" (from the Spanish for elbow).*
86 *precise.*
87 *when a black suit is trumps, the king, queen, and knave of a red suit outrank the ace; Belinda thus wins the trick and the game.*

The Nymph exulting fills with Shouts the Sky,
100   The Walls, the Woods, and long Canals reply.
        Oh thoughtless Mortals! ever blind to Fate,
Too soon dejected, and too soon elate!
Sudden these Honours shall be snatch'd away,
And curs'd for ever this Victorious Day.
105   For lo! the Board with Cups and Spoons is crown'd,
The Berries crackle, and the Mill[88] turns round.
On shining Altars of *Japan*[89] they raise
The silver Lamp; the fiery Spirits[90] blaze.
From silver Spouts the grateful[91] Liquors glide,
110   While *China*'s Earth[92] receives the smoking Tyde.
At once they gratify their Scent and Taste,
And frequent Cups prolong the rich Repast.
Strait hover round the Fair her Airy Band;
Some, as she sip'd the fuming Liquor fann'd,
115   Some, o'er her Lap their careful Plumes display'd,
Trembling, and conscious of the rich Brocade.
Coffee, (which makes the Politician wise,
And see thro' all things with his half-shut Eyes)
Sent up in Vapours to the *Baron*'s Brain
120   New Stratagems, the radiant Lock to gain.
Ah cease rash Youth! desist ere 'tis too late,
Fear the just Gods, and think of *Scylla*'s[93] Fate!
Chang'd to a Bird, and sent to flit in Air,
She dearly pays for *Nisus*' injur'd Hair!
125   But when to Mischief Mortals bend their Will,
How soon they find fit Instruments of Ill!
Just then, *Clarissa* drew with tempting Grace
A two-edg'd Weapon from her shining Case;
So Ladies in Romance assist their Knight,
130   Present the Spear, and arm him for the Fight.
He takes the Gift with rev'rence, and extends
The little Engine on his Fingers' Ends,

---

88 *the coffee-mill, which grinds coffee beans (the "Berries").* **89** *japanned or lacquered tables.* **90** *in spirit-lamps.* **91** *pleasing.* **92** *cups of china, i.e., fine earthenware.* **93** *according to legend, Scylla was the daughter of King Nisus, whose life and kingdom depended on a purple hair growing on his head. Scylla fell in love with King Minos, who was besieging her father's kingdom, and plucked out the hair and took it to Minos; he rejected it with horror, and she was turned into a sea-bird.*

This just behind *Belinda*'s Neck he spread,
As o'er the fragrant Steams she bends her Head:
135 Swift to the Lock a thousand Sprights repair,
A thousand Wings, by turns, blow back the Hair,
And thrice they twitch'd the Diamond in her Ear,
Thrice she look'd back, and thrice the Foe drew near.
Just in that instant, anxious *Ariel* sought
140 The close Recesses of the Virgin's Thought;
As on the Nosegay[94] in her Breast reclin'd,
He watch'd th' Ideas rising in her Mind,
Sudden he view'd, in spite of all her Art,
An Earthly Lover lurking at her Heart.
145 Amaz'd, confus'd, he found his Pow'r expir'd,
Resign'd to Fate, and with a Sigh retir'd.
      The Peer now spreads the glitt'ring *Forfex*[95] wide,
T'inclose the Lock; now joins it, to divide.
Ev'n then, before the fatal Engine clos'd,
150 A wretched *Sylph* too fondly interpos'd;
Fate urg'd the Sheers, and cut the *Sylph* in twain,
(But Airy Substance soon unites again)[96]
The meeting Points the sacred Hair dissever
From the fair Head, for ever and for ever!
155   Then flash'd the living Lightning from her Eyes,
And Screams of Horror rend th' affrighted Skies.
Not louder Shrieks to pitying Heav'n are cast,
When Husbands or when Lap-dogs breathe their last,
Or when rich *China* Vessels, fal'n from high,
160 In glittring Dust and painted Fragments lie!
      Let Wreaths of Triumph now my Temples twine,
(The Victor cry'd) the glorious Prize is mine!
While Fish in Streams, or Birds delight in Air,
Or in a Coach and Six the *British* Fair,

---

94 *corsage of flowers.*
95 *the Latin word for scissors.*
96 *just as Milton's Satan does when pierced by Michael's sword* (Paradise Lost VI.330–31).

165 As long as *Atalantis*[97] shall be read,
Or the small Pillow grace a Lady's Bed,
While *Visits* shall be paid on solemn Days,
When numerous Wax-lights in bright Order blaze,
While Nymphs take Treats, or Assignations give,
170 So long my Honour, Name, and Praise shall live!
    What Time wou'd spare, from Steel receives its date,
And Monuments, like Men, submit to Fate!
175 Steel cou'd the Labour of the Gods[98] destroy,
And strike to Dust th' Imperial Tow'rs of *Troy*;
Steel cou'd the Works of mortal Pride confound,
And hew Triumphal Arches to the Ground.
What Wonder then, fair Nymph! thy Hairs shou'd feel
180 The conqu'ring Force of unresisted Steel?

CANTO IV.

But anxious Cares the pensive Nmyph opprest,
And secret Passions labour'd in her Breast.
Not youthful Kings in Battel seiz'd alive,
Not scornful Virgins who their Charms survive,
5 Not ardent Lovers robb'd of all their Bliss,
Not ancient Ladies when refus'd a Kiss,
Not Tyrants fierce that unrepenting die,
Not *Cynthia* when her *Manteau's*[99] pinn'd awry,
E'er felt such Rage, Resentment and Despair,
10 As Thou, sad Virgin! for thy ravish'd Hair.
    For, that sad moment, when the *Sylphs* withdrew,
And *Ariel* weeping from *Belinda* flew,
Umbriel,[100] a dusky melancholy Spright,
As ever sully'd the fair face of Light,

---

97 The New Atalantis *(1709), by Delariver Manley, a popular novel consisting largely of thinly veiled accounts of scandals in high life.*
98 *Troy was believed to have been built by two gods, Apollo and Poseidon.*
99 *a loose robe or cloak.*
100 *a Gnome (see I.63–64); his name is from the Latin word* umbra, *meaning shadow.*

15   Down to the Central Earth, his proper Scene,[101]
      Repair'd to search the gloomy Cave of *Spleen*.[102]
          Swift on his sooty Pinions flitts the *Gnome*,
      And in a Vapour[103] reach'd the dismal Dome.
      No cheerful Breeze this sullen Region knows,
20   The dreadful *East*[104] is all the Wind that blows.
      Here, in a Grotto, sheltred close from Air,
      And screen'd in Shades from Day's detested Glare,
      She sighs for ever on her pensive Bed,
      Pain at her Side, and *Megrim*[105] at her Head.
25   Two Handmaids wait the Throne: Alike in Place,
      But diff'ring far in Figure and in Face.
      Here stood *Ill-nature* like an *ancient Maid*,
      Her wrinked Form in *Black* and *White* array'd;
      With store of Pray'rs, for Mornings, Nights, and Noons,
30   Her Hand is fill'd; her Bosom with Lampoons.
          There *Affectation* with a sickly Mien
      Shows in her Cheek the Roses of Eighteen,
      Practis'd to Lisp, and hang the Head aside,
      Faints into Airs, and languishes with Pride;
      On the rich Quilt sinks with becoming Woe,
35   Wrapt in a Gown, for Sickness, and for Show.[106]
      The Fair-ones feel such Maladies as these,
      When each new Night-Dress gives a new Disease.
          A constant *Vapour* o'er the Palace flies;
40   Strange Phantoms rising as the Mists arise;
      Dreadful, as Hermit's Dreams in haunted Shades,
      Or bright as Visions of expiring Maids.
      Now glaring Fiends, and Snakes on rolling Spires,[107]
      Pale Spectres, gaping Tombs and Purple Fires:
45   Now Lakes of liquid Gold, *Elysian*[108] Scenes,
      And Crystal Domes, and Angels in Machines.[109]
          Unnumber'd Throngs on ev'ry side are seen

---

101 *Umbriel's journey to the cave of Spleen imitates the epic hero's visit to the underworld in search of knowledge unavailable on earth; see Homer's* Odyssey, *Book XI, and Virgil's* Aeneid, *Book VI.* **102** *the spleen, thought to be the seat of the emotions in traditional medicine, became the name of a fashionable psychosomatic ailment of the rich and leisured; it consisted of ill temper, depression, and hypochondria.* **103** *suitably, since the desease known as "the spleen" was also called "the vapours" (see lines 39 and 59 of this canto).* **104** *the east wind was considered unhealthy; it was thought to provoke the spleen.* **105** *migraine headache.* **106** *ladies often received formal visits in bed.* **107** *spirals.* **108** *Elysium in Greek mythology was the abode of the blessed after death, and so a place of ideal happiness.* **109** *stage machinery.*

Of Bodies chang'd to various Forms by *Spleen*.[110]
Here living *Teapots* stand, one Arm held out,
50   One bent; the Handle this, and that the Spout:
A Pipkin[111] there like *Homer's Tripod*[112] walks;
Here sighs a Jar, and there a Goose-pye talks;
Men prove with Child, as powr'ful Fancy works,
And Maids turn'd Bottels, call aloud for Corks.
55   Safe past the *Gnome* thro' this fantastick Band,
A Branch of healing *Spleenwort*[113] in his hand.
Then thus addrest the Pow'r — Hail wayward Queen!
Who rule the Sex to Fifty from Fifteen,
Parents of Vapors and of Female Wit,
60   Who give th' *Hysteric* or *Poetic* Fit,
On various Tempers act by various ways,
Make some take Physick,[114] others scribble Plays;
Who cause the Proud their Visits to delay,
And send the Godly in a Pett, to pray.
65   A Nymph there is, that all thy Pow'r disdains,
And thousands more in equal Mirth maintains.
But oh! if e'er thy *Gnome* could spoil a Grace,
Or raise a Pimple on a beauteous Face,
Like Citron-Waters[115] Matrons' Cheeks inflame,
70   Or change Complexions at a losing Game;
If e'er with airy Horns[116] I planted Heads,
Or rumpled Petticoats, or tumbled Beds,
Or caus'd Suspicion when no Soul was rude,
Or discompos'd the Head-dress of a Prude,
75   Or e'er to costive[117] Lap-Dog gave Disease,
Which not the Tears of brightest Eyes could ease:
Hear me, and touch *Belinda* with Chagrin;
That single Act gives half the World the Spleen.
The Goddess with a discontented Air
80   Seems to reject him, tho' she grants his Pray'r.

---

110 *one symptom of the spleen was suffering from hallucinations.* 111 *a small earthen pot.* 112 *in the* Iliad
(XVIII.439 *ff.*), *Homer tells how Hephaistos made walking tripods (three-legged stools).* 113 *just as Aenease
carries a golden bough to guarantee safe passage through the underworld in the* Aeneid, *Umbriel carries a branch
of spleenwort, a ferm believed to protect one against the spleen.* 114 *medicine.* 115 *brandy flavoured with lemon
peel.* 116 *the traditional emblem of the cuckold.* 117 *constipated.*

A wondrous Bag with both her Hands she binds,
Like that where once *Ulysses* held the Winds;[118]
There she collects the Force of Female Lungs,
Sighs, Sobs, and Passions, and the War of Tongues.
85   A Vial next she fills with fainting Fears,
Soft Sorrows, melting Griefs, and flowing Tears.
The *Gnome* rejoicing bears her Gifts away,
Spreads his black Wings, and slowly mounts to Day.
  Sunk in *Thalestris'*[119] Arms the Nymph he found,
90   Her Eyes dejected and her Hair unbound.
Full o'er their Heads the swelling Bag he rent,
And all the Furies issued at the Vent.
Belinda burns with more than mortal Ire,
And fierce *Thalestris* fans the rising Fire.
95   O wretched Maid! she spread her Hands, and cry'd,
While *Hampton's* Ecchos, wretched Maid! reply'd)
Was it for this you took such constant Care
The *Bodkin*,[120] *Comb*, and *Essence* to prepare;
For this your Locks in Paper-Durance[121] bound,
100   For this with tort'ring Irons wreath'd around?
For this with Fillets[122] strain'd your tender Head,
And bravely bore the double Loads of Lead?[123]
Gods! shall the Ravisher display your Hair,
While the Fops envy, and the Ladies Stare!
105   *Honour* forbid! at whose unrival'd Shrine
Ease, Pleasure, Virtue, All, our Sex resign.
Methinks already I your Tears survey,
Already hear the horrid things they say,
Already see you a degraded Toast,[124]
110   And all your Honour in a Whisper lost!
How shall I, then, your helpless Fame defend?
'Twill then be Infamy to seem your Friend!
And shall this Prize, th' inestimable Prize,

---

118 *Aeolus, god of winds, gave Odysseus, or Ulysses, a bag containing all the winds that could prevent him from returning home; Odysseus's men opened the bag when he was asleep and the ensuing storms drove them far away (Odyssey X.19 ff.).* **119** *the name of a legendary warrior-queen of the Amazons.* **120** *a needle used as a hairpin.* **121** *inflated epic diction for curling papers, the papers that were wrapped around curling irons (the "tort'ring of line 100) to prepare the elaborate coiffures worn by women.* **122** *headbands.* **123** *the elaborate upright coiffures of ladies were arranged upon a wooden frame; strips of pliant lead attached to the frame kept the curls in place.* **124** *a woman whose health is often drunk by men.*

Expos'd thro' Crystal to the gazing Eyes,
115   And heighten'd by the Diamond's circling Rays,
On that Rapacious Hand for ever blaze?
Sooner shall Grass in *Hide*-Park *Circus*[125] grow,
And Wits take Lodgings in the Sound of *Bow;*[126]
Sooner let Earth, Air, Sea, to *Chaos* fall,
120   Men, Monkies, Lap-dogs, Parrots, perish all!
She said; then raging to *Sir Plume*[127] repairs,
And bids her *Beau* demand the precious Hairs:
(*Sir Plume*, of *Amber Snuff-box* justly vain,
And the nice Conduct of a *clouded*[128] *Cane*)
125   With earnest Eyes, and round unthinking Face,
He first the Snuff-box open'd, then the Case,
And thus broke out — "My Lord, why, what the Devil?
"Z — ds!"[129] damn the Lock! 'fore Gad, you must be civil!
"Plague on't! 'tis past a Jest — nay prithee, Pox!
130   "Give her the Hair" — he spoke, and rapp'd his Box.
It grieves me much (reply'd the Peer again)
Who speaks so well shou'd ever speak in vain.
But by this Lock, this sacred Lock I swear,
(Which never more shall join its parted Hair,
135   Which never more its Honours[130] shall renew,
Clipt from the lovely Head where late it grew)
That while my Nostrils draw the vital Air,
This Hand, which won it, shall for ever wear.
He spoke, and speaking, in proud Triumph spread
140   The long-contended Honours of her Head.
But *Umbriel*, hateful *Gnome!* forbears not so;
He breaks the Vial whence the Sorrows flow.
Then see! the *Nymph* in beauteous Grief appears,
Her Eyes half-languishing, half-drown'd in Tears;
145   On her heav'd Bosom hung her drooping Head,
Which, with a Sigh, she rais'd; and thus she said.

---

125 *the Ring (see I.44), where carriages kept the grass from growing.* 126 *within the sound of St. Mary-le-Bow in Cheapside, the unfashionable commercial quarter of London.* 127 *Sir George Browne, Arabella's kinsman, who chiefly fomented the quarrel.* 128 *mottled.* 129 *Zounds, a corrupted version of "God's wounds" — an oath expressing indignation.* 130 *beauties, graces (as well as honours); see also line 140 of this canto.*

For ever curs'd be this detested Day,[131]
Which snatch'd my best, my fav'rite Curl away!
Happy! ah ten times happy, had I been,
150   If *Hampton-Court* these Eyes had never seen!
Yet am not I the first mistaken Maid,
By Love of *Courts* to num'rous Ills betray'd.
Oh had I rather un-admir'd remain'd
In some lone Isle, or distant *Northern* Land;
155   Where the gilt *Chariot* never marks the Way,
Where none learn *Ombre*, none e'er taste *Bohea*![132]
There kept my Charms conceal'd from mortal Eye,
Like Roses that in Desarts bloom and die.
What mov'd my Mind with youthful Lords to rome?
160   O had I stay'd, and said my Pray'rs at home!
'Twas this, the Morning *Omens* seem'd to tell;
Thrice from my trembling hand the *Patch-box* fell;
The tott'ring *China* shook without a Wind,
Nay, *Poll* sate mute, and *Shock* was most Unkind!
165   A *Sylph* too warn'd me of the Threats of Fate,
In mystic Visions, now believ'd too late!
See the poor Remnants of these slighted Hairs!
My hands shall rend what ev'n thy Rapine spares:
These, in two sable Ringlets taught to break,
170   Once gave new Beauties to the snowie Neck.
The Sister-Lock now sits uncouth, alone,
And in its Fellow's Fate foresees its own;
Uncurl'd it hangs, the fatal Sheers demands;
And tempts once more thy sacrilegious Hands.
175   Oh hadst thou, Cruel! been content to seize
Hairs less in sight, or any Hairs but these!

131 *an imitation of Achilles's lament for Patroclus in the* Iliad *(XVIII.107 ff.).*
132 *a costly kind of tea.*

CANTO V.

She said: the pitying Audience melt in Tears,
But *Fate* and *Jove* had stopp'd the *Baron*'s Ears.
In Vain *Thalestris* with Reproach assails,
For who can move when fair *Belinda* fails?
5   Not half so fixt the *Trojan* cou'd remain,
While *Anna* begg'd and *Dido* rag'd in vain.[133]
Then grave *Clarissa* graceful wav'd her Fan;
Silence ensu'd, and thus the Nymph began.[134]
    Say, why are Beauties prais'd and honour'd most,
10   The wise Man's Passion, and the vain Man's Toast?
Why deck'd with all that Land and Sea afford,
Why Angels call'd, and Angel-like ador'd?
Why round our Coaches crowd the white-glov'd Beaus,
Why bows the Side-box[135] from its inmost Rows?
15   How vain are all these Glories, all our Pains,
Unless good Sense preserve what Beauty gains:
That Men may say, when we the Front-box grace,
Behold the first in Virtue, as in Face!
Oh! if to dance all Night, and dress all Day,
20   Charm'd the Small-pox,[136] or chas'd old Age away;
Who would not scorn what Huswife's Cares produce,
Or who would learn one earthly Thing of Use?
To patch, nay ogle, might become a Saint,
Nor could it sure be such a Sin to paint.
25   But since, alas! frail Beauty must decay,
Curl'd or uncurl'd, since Locks will turn to grey,
Since painted, or not painted, all shall fade,
And she who scorns a Man, must die a Maid;
What then remains, but well our Pow'r to use,
30   And keep good Humour still whate'er we lose?

---

133 *Aeneas, burdened with his divine mission of founding a new Troy, left Carthage and Queen Dido, despite her furious reproaches and the prayers of her sister Anna (Aeneid IV.296–449).* **134** *when Pope published his collected early poetry in 1717, he added Clarissa's speech to the five-canto Rape of 1714 in order, as he explained, "to open the moral of the poem, in a parody of the speech of Sarpedon to Glaucus in Homer"; Sarpedon's speech is an appeal to his comrade to earn in battle the honour they both enjoy as leaders (Iliad XII.371–96).* **135** *gentlemen preferred the side boxes at the theatre, ladies the front boxes facing the stage (see line 17 of this canto).* **136** *before vaccination, smallpox was common and deadly; the Lord Petre of this poem died of smallpox in 1713.*

And trust me, Dear! good Humour can prevail,
When Airs, and Flights, and Screams, and Scolding fail.
Beauties in vain their pretty Eyes may roll;
Charms strike the Sight, but Merit wins the Soul.
35   So spoke the Dame, but no Applause ensu'd;
Belinda frown'd, *Thalestris* call'd her Prude.
To Arms, to Arms! the fierce Virago[137] cries,
And swift as Lightning to the Combate flies.
All side in Parties, and begin th' Attack;
40   Fans clap, Silks russle, and tough Whalebones crack;
Heroes' and Heroins' Shouts confus'dly rise,
And base, and treble Voices strike the Skies.
No common Weapons in their Hands are found,
Like Gods they fight, nor dread a mortal Wound.
45   So when bold *Homer* makes the Gods engage,[138]
And heavn'ly Breasts with human Passions rage;
'Gainst *Pallas*,[139] *Mars*; *Latona*,[140] *Hermes* arms;
And all *Olympus* rings with loud Alarms.
Jove's Thunder roars, Heav'n trembles all around;
50   Blue *Neptune* storms, the bellowing Deeps resound;
Earth shakes her nodding Tow'rs, the Ground gives way;
And the pale Ghosts start at the Flash of Day!
      Triumphant *Umbriel* on a Sconce's[141] Height
Clapt his glad Wings, and sate to view the Fight:
55   Propt on their Bodkin Spears, the Sprights survey
The growing Combat, or assist the Fray.
      While thro' the Press enrag'd *Thalestris* flies,
And scatters Deaths around from both her Eyes,
A *Beau* and *Witling*[142] perish'd in the Throng,
60   One dy'd in *Metaphor*, and one in *Song*.
O cruel Nymph! a living Death I bear,
Cry'd *Dapperwit*,[143] and sunk beside his Chair.
A mournful Glance Sir *Fopling* upwards cast,
Those Eyes are made so killing — was his last:

---

137 *man-like woman, female warrior.* **138** *see the* Iliad *XX.91 ff.* **139** *Pallas Athena, the Greek goddess of war (also the goddess of wisdom).* **140** *the mother of the Greek deities Apollo and Artemis.* **141** *candlestick attached to the wall.* **142** *a tiny wit.* **143** *like "Sir Fopling" in the next line, a type-name for a fop and would-be wit in Restoration comic plays.*

65   Thus on *Meander's*[144] flow'ry Margin lies
        Th' expiring Swan, and as he sings he dies.[145]
            When bold Sir *Plume* had drawn *Clarissa* down,
        Chloe stept in, and kill'd him with a Frown;
        She smil'd to see the doughty Hero slain,
70   But at her Smile, the Beau reviv'd again.
            Now *Jove* suspends his golden Scales in Air,[146]
        Weighs the Men's Wits against the Lady's Hair;
        The doubtful Beam long nods from side to side;
        At length the Wits mount up, the Hairs subside.
75   See fierce *Belinda* on the *Baron* flies,
        With more than usual Lightning in her Eyes;
        Nor fear'd the Chief th'unequal Fight to try,
        Who sought no more than on his Foe to die.
        But this bold Lord, with manly Strength indu'd,
80   She with one Finger and a Thumb subdu'd:
        Just where the Breath of Life his Nostrils drew,
        A Charge of *Snuff* the wily Virgin threw;
        The *Gnomes* direct, to ev'ry Atome just,
        The pungent Grains of titillating Dust.
85   Sudden, with starting Tears each Eye o'erflows,
        And the high Dome re-ecchoes to his Nose.
            Now meet thy Fate, incens'd *Belinda* cry'd,
        And drew a deadly *Bodkin* from her Side.
        (The same,[147] his ancient Personage to deck,
90   Her great great Grandsire wore about his Neck
        In three *Seal-Rings*; which after, melted down,
        Form'd a vast *Buckle* for his Widow's Gown:
        Her infant Grandame's *Whistle* next it grew,
        The *Bells* she gingled,[148] and the *Whistle* blew;
95   Then in a *Bodkin* grac'd her Mother's Hairs,
        Which long she wore, and now *Belinda* wears.)
            Boast not my Fall (he cry'd) insulting Foe!

144 *a celebrated winding river in Asia Minor.*
145 *swans were believed to sing beautifully only as they died.*
146 *an epic convention when a decisive battle is about to take place; see the* Iliad *VIII.87 ff. and the* Aeneid
    XII.725 ff.
147 *what follows is a parody of epic descriptions of a hero's armour and its descent through the generations in his
    family.*
148 *jingled.*

Thou by some other shalt be laid as low.
Nor think, to die dejects my lofty Mind;
All that I dread, is leaving you behind!
Rather than so, ah let me still survive,
And burn in *Cupid*'s Flames, — but burn alive.
   Restore the Lock! she cries; and all around
Restore the Lock! the vaulted Roofs rebound.
Not fierce *Othello* in so loud a Strain
Roar'd for the Handkerchief that caus'd his Pain.
But see how oft Ambitious Aims are cross'd,
And Chiefs contend 'till all the Prize is lost!
The Lock, obtain'd with Guilt, and kept with Pain.
In ev'ry place is sought, but sought in vain:
With such a Prize no Mortal must be blest,
So Heav'n decrees! with Heav'n who can contest?
   Some thought it mounted to the Lunar Sphere,
Since all things lost on Earth, are treasur'd there.[149]
There Heroes' Wits are kept in pondrous Vases,
And Beaus' in *Snuff-boxes* and *Tweezer-Cases.*
There broken Vows, and Death-bed Alms are found,
And Lovers' Hearts with Ends of Riband[150] bound;
The Courtier's Promises, and Sick Man's Pray'rs,
The Smiles of Harlots, and the Tears of Heirs,
Cages for Gnats, and Chains to Yoak a Flea;
Dry'd Butterflies, and Tomes of Casuistry.[151]
   But trust the Muse — she saw it upward rise,
Tho' mark'd by none but quick Poetic Eyes:
(So *Rome*'s great Founder to the Heav'ns withdrew,
To *Proculus* alone confess'd in view.)[152]
A sudden Star, it shot thro' liquid[153] Air,
And drew behind a radiant *Trail of Hair.*
Not *Berenice*'s[154] Locks first rose so bright,
The Heav'ns bespangling with dishevel'd Light.

---

149 *in a striking episode in* Orlando Furioso *(1532), the chivalric epic by the Italian poet Ariosto, the hero's lost wits are found on the moon, where all things that are lost on earth may be found.* **150** *ribbon.* **151** *casuistry, the branch of theology which studies the application of general ethical rules to particular cases, had become a synonym for hair-splitting rationalization.* **152** *Romulus, the founder and first king of Rome, disappeared from earth in the midst of a storm; the senator Proculus affirmed that Romulus had ascended to the heavens.* **153** *clear, transparent.* **154** *Berenice, wife of King Ptolemy III of ancient Egypt, vowed to sacrifice her hair to the gods if her husband returned safe from battle; upon his return, she placed her hair in the temple of Aphrodite, but the next day it had disappeared and was believed to have become a constellation.*

The *Sylphs* behold it kindling as it flies,
And pleas'd pursue its Progress thro' the Skies.
   This the *Beau-monde*[155] shall from the *Mall*[156] survey,
And hail with Musick its propitious Ray.
135   This, the blest Lover shall for *Venus* take,
And send up Vows from *Rosamonda*'s Lake.[157]
This *Partridge*[158] soon shall view in cloudless Skies,
When next he looks thro' *Galileo*'s Eyes;[159]
And hence th' Egregious Wizard shall foredoom
140   The Fate of *Louis*, and the Fall of *Rome*.
   Then cease, bright Nymph! to mourn thy ravish'd Hair
Which adds new Glory to the shining Sphere!
Not all the Tresses that fair Head can boast
Shall draw such Envy as the Lock you lost.
145   For, after all the Murders of your Eye,
When, after Millions slain, your self shall die;
When those fair Suns shall sett, as sett they must,
And all those Tresses shall be laid in Dust;
This Lock, the Muse shall consecrate to Fame,
150   And mid'st the Stars inscribe *Belinda*'s Name!

(1714)

---

155 *fashionable world.*
156 *Pall Mall, a walk laid out by Charles II in St. James's Park.*
157 *a pond in St. James's Park considered to be the haunt of unhappy lovers; it was named after Rosamund Clifford (died 1177), known as "Fair Rosamond," mistress of Henry II, who was, according to legend, made to drink poison by his queen.*
158 *a quack astrologer of the time, who predicted every year that the pope and King Louis XIV of France would fall from power that year (see line 140).*
159 *i.e., a telescope; Galileo constructed the first telescope in 1609.*

An Essay on Man

From EPISTLE II[1]

Know then thyself, presume not God to scan;
The proper study of Mankind is Man.
Plac'd on this isthmus of a middle state,
A being darkly wise, and rudely[2] great:
5   With too much knowledge for the Sceptic[3] side,
With too much weakness for the Stoic's[4] pride,
He hangs between; in doubt to act, or rest,
In doubt to deem himself a God, or Beast;
In doubt his Mind or Body to prefer,
10   Born but to die, and reas'ning but to err;
Alike in ignorance, his reason such,
Whether he thinks too little, or too much:
Chaos of Thought and Passion, all confus'd;
Still by himself abus'd, or disabus'd;
15   Created half to rise, and half to fall;
Great lord of all things, yet a prey to all;
Sole judge of Truth, in endless Error hurl'd:
The glory, jest, and riddle of the world!
    Go, wond'rous creature! mount where Science guides,
20   Go, measure earth, weigh air, and state the tides;
Instruct the planets in what orbs to run,
Correct old Time, and regulate the Sun;
Go, soar with Plato[5] to th' empyreal sphere,[6]
To the first good, first perfect, and first fair;
25   Or tread the mazy round his follow'rs trod,

1 *Epistle I of Pope's philosophical poem has considered man's identity in relation to the universe, arguing that human life is simply one link in a divinely ordered Great Chain of Being; this excerpt begins Epistle II, in which Pope treats human identity considered in itself. Epistle III deals with man's relation to society and Epistle IV with man's relation to happiness.*
2 *turbulently, roughly.*
3 *the Skeptic philosophers of ancient Greece doubted man's ability to gain any real or true knowledge.*
4 *the Stoic philosophers of Greece and Rome believed that men could learn not to feel pleasure or pain, and so could attain a god-like state.*
5 *the most idealistic of ancient Greek philosophers, whose works present an idealistic vision of the universe as centred upon humanity.*
6 *in traditional cosmology, the outermost sphere of the universe, where God is thought to abide and where Plato's ideal forms are assumed to be.*

And quitting sense call imitating God;[7]
As Eastern priests in giddy circles run,
And turn their heads to imitate the Sun.
Go, teach Eternal Wisdom how to rule —
30   Then drop into thyself, and be a fool!

(1733)

---

7 the Neoplatonists (classical and Renaissance followers of Plato's doctrines) advocated the suppression of bodily sensation in order to enjoy divine visions.

THOMAS GRAY

(1716–1771)

*T*homas Gray, a shy scholar, wrote very few poems — but among them is *one of the best-known and most-loved poems in the language, his* Elegy Written in a Country Church-Yard *(or, as it is usually called, Gray's* Elegy*). Gray spent his entire adult life as a scholar at Cambridge University; he was known as one of the most learned men in Europe, and helped create scholarly interest in Welsh, Old Norse, and medieval English poetry. Gray published his* Elegy *in 1751. His shyness led him to turn down the position of Poet Laureate when he was offered it in 1757; although named Professor of Modern History at Cambridge, he was unable to deliver a single lecture. Nevertheless, as soon as his* Elegy *was published, he became recognized as the greatest lyric poet of the age. His contemporary Samuel Johnson memorably sums up the poem's appeal: "The* Church-Yard *abounds with images which find a mirror in every mind, and with sentiments to which every bosom returns an echo."*

Elegy Written in a Country Church-Yard

The Curfew tolls the knell of parting day,
The lowing herd wind slowly o'er the lea,[1]
The plowman homeward plods his weary way,
And leaves the world to darkness and to me.

5 Now fades the glimmering landscape on the sight,
And all the air a solemn stillness holds,
Save where the beetle wheels his droning flight,
And drowsy tinklings lull the distant folds;

Save that from yonder ivy-mantled tow'r
10 The mopeing owl does to the moon complain
Of such, as wand'ring near her secret bow'r,
Molest her ancient solitary reign.

1 *open field, grassland.*

Beneath those rugged elms, that yew-tree's shade,
Where heaves the turf in many a mould'ring heap,
15   Each in his narrow cell for ever laid,
The rude² Forefathers of the hamlet sleep.

The breezy call of incense-breathing Morn,
The swallow twitt'ring from the straw-built shed,
The cock's shrill clarion, or the ecchoing horn,
20   No more shall rouse them from their lowly bed.

For them no more the blazing hearth shall burn,
Or busy houswife ply her evening care:
No children run to lisp their sire's return,
Or climb his knees the envied kiss to share.

25   Oft did the harvest to their sickle yield,
Their furrow oft the stubborn glebe³ has broke;
How jocund did they drive their team afield!
How bow'd the woods beneath their sturdy stroke!

Let not Ambition mock their useful toil,
30   Their homely joys, and destiny obscure;
Nor Grandeur hear with a disdainful smile,
The short and simple annals of the poor.

The boast of heraldry, the pomp of pow'r,
And all that beauty, all that wealth e'er gave,
35   Awaits alike th' inevitable hour.
The paths of glory lead but to the grave.

Nor you, ye Proud, impute to These the fault,
If Mem'ry o'er their Tomb no Trophies raise,
Where thro' the long-drawn isle⁴ and fretted vault
40   The pealing anthem swells the note of praise.

Can storied urn or animated bust
Back to its mansion call the fleeting breath?
Can Honour's voice provoke the silent dust,
Or Flatt'ry sooth the dull cold ear of Death?

2 *uneducated.*
3 *soil.*
4 *aisle.*

45   Perhaps in this neglected spot is laid
Some heart once pregnant with celestial fire,
Hands, that the rod of empire might have sway'd,
Or wak'd to extasy the living lyre.

But Knowledge to their eyes her ample page
50   Rich with the spoils of time did ne'er unroll;
Chill Penury repress'd their noble rage,[5]
And froze the genial[6] current of the soul.

Full many a gem of purest ray serene,
The dark unfathom'd caves of ocean bear:
55   Full many a flower is born to blush unseen,
And waste its sweetness on the desert air.

Some village-Hampden,[7] that with dauntless breast
The little Tyrant of his fields withstood;
Some mute inglorious Milton here may rest,
60   Some Cromwell guiltless of his country's blood.

Th' applause of list'ning senates to command,
The threats of pain and ruin to despise,
To scatter plenty o'er a smiling land,
And read their hist'ry in a nation's eyes.

65   Their lot forbad: nor circumscrib'd alone
Their growing virtues, but their crimes confin'd;
Forbad to wade through slaughter to a throne,
And shut the gates of mercy on mankind,

The struggling pangs of conscious truth to hide,
70   To quench the blushes of ingenuous shame,
Or heap the shrine of Luxury and Pride
With incense kindled at the Muse's flame.

5 *rapture, ardour.*
6 *creative.*
7 *John Hampden (1594–1643), member of Parliament who defended the rights of the people against Charles I and became a leader of the Puritan cause in the Civil War.*

Far from the madding[8] crowd's ignoble strife,
Their sober wishes never learn'd to stray;
75 Along the cool sequester'd vale of life
They kept the noiseless tenor of their way.

Yet ev'n these bones from insult to protect
Some frail memorial still erected nigh,
With uncouth rhimes and shapeless sculpture deck'd,
80 Implores the passing tribute of a sigh.

Their name, their years, spelt by th' unletter'd muse,
The place of fame and elegy supply:
And many a holy text around she strews,
That teach the rustic moralist to die.

85 For who to dumb Forgetfulness a prey,
This pleasing anxious being e'er resign'd,
Left the warm precincts of the chearful day,
Nor cast one longing ling'ring look behind?

On some fond breast the parting soul relies,
90 Some pious drops the closing eye requires;
Ev'n from the tomb the voice of Nature cries,
Ev'n in our Ashes live their wonted Fires.

For thee, who mindful of th' unhonour'd Dead
Dost in these lines their artless tale relate;
95 If chance,[9] by lonely contemplation led,
Some kindred Spirit shall inquire thy fate,

Haply some hoary-headed Swain[10] may say,
'Oft have we seen him at the peep of dawn
'Brushing with hasty steps the dews away
100 'To meet the sun upon the upland lawn.

'There at the foot of yonder nodding beech
'That wreathes its old fantastic roots so high,
'His listless length at noontide wou'd he stretch,
'And pore upon the brook that babbles by.

8 *frenzied, maddened.*
9 *by chance.*
10 *shepherd.*

105   'Hard by yon wood, now smiling as in scorn,
     'Mutt'ring his wayward fancies he wou'd rove,
     'Now drooping, woeful wan, like one forlorn,
     'Or craz'd with care, or cross'd in hopeless love.

     'One morn I miss'd him on the custom'd hill,
110   'Along the heath and near his fav'rite tree;
     'Another came; nor yet beside the rill,
     'Nor up the lawn, nor at the wood was he,

     'The next with dirges due in sad array
     'Slow thro' the church-way path we saw him borne.
115   'Approach and read (for thou can'st read) the lay,
     'Grav'd on the stone beneath yon aged thorn.'

The EPITAPH.

HERE rests his head upon the lap of Earth
A Youth to Fortune and to Fame unknown,
Fair Science[11] *frown'd not on his humble birth,*
120   *And Melancholy mark'd him for her own.*

Large was his bounty, and his soul sincere,
Heav'n did a recompence as largely send:
He gave to Mis'ry all he had, a tear,
He gain'd from Heav'n ('twas all he wish'd) a friend.

125   *No farther seek his merits to disclose,*
Or draw his frailties from their dread abode,
(There they alike in trembling hope repose)
The bosom of his Father and his God.

(1751)

11 *learning.*

WILLIAM BLAKE

(1757–1827)

*B*orn in London, William Blake studied art at the Royal Academy as a
boy before serving an apprenticeship to an engraver. His first collection of
poems, Poetic Sketches *(1783), indicated his departure from the neoclassical
conventions which had dominated the eighteenth century. However,* Songs of
Innocence and Experience *(1794), illustrated by his own hand-painted
engravings, marked the first flowering of his genius. Lyrics revealing the influence
of Elizabethan and seventeenth-century English poetry, they present "two contrast-
ing states of the human mind." Many are companion poems, using the lives and
views of children to symbolize innocence and experience. During the 1790s, Blake
was influenced by radical political, religious, and philosophical currents prevalent
in England and wrote in his poems about tyranny and oppression, the power of
"God & his Priest & King," as they affected the lives of common people, especially
children. He celebrated the visionary powers of the imagination in a series of "Pro-
phetic Books" written after the publication of the* Songs. *Complex and often
obscure, they develop a philosophy in which human life is seen as progressing from
the initial innocence of childhood, to the complexity and pain of experience, and
finally to a higher, more fulfilled innocence. "Auguries of Innocence," written
around 1803 and published posthumously, reveals the symbolic connections between
small, apparently insignificant objects and actions and the universe at large. Rela-
tively ignored during his lifetime and in the 50 years after his death, Blake's works
have been studied seriously during the twentieth century, and he is now recognized
as one of the greatest romantic poets.*

The Lamb

  Little Lamb who made thee
  Dost thou know who made thee
 Gave thee life & bid thee feed.
 By the stream & o'er the mead;[1]
5 Gave thee clothing of delight,
 Softest clothing wooly bright;
 Gave thee such a tender voice,
 Making all the vales rejoice!
  Little Lamb who made thee
10 Dost thou know who made thee

---

1 *meadow.*

Little Lamb I'll tell thee,
Little Lamb I'll tell thee!
He is called by thy name,
For he calls himself a Lamb:
15   He is meek & he is mild,
He became a little child:
I a child & thou a lamb,
We are called by his name.
    Little Lamb God bless thee.
20   Little Lamb God bless thee.

(1789)

The Little Black Boy

My mother bore me in the southern wild,
And I am black, but O! my soul is white;
White as an angel is the English child:
But I am black as if bereav'd[1] of light.

5   My mother taught me underneath a tree
And sitting down before the heat of day,
She took me on her lap and kissed me,
And pointing to the east began to say.

Look on the rising sun: there God does live
10   And gives his light, and gives his heat away.
And flowers and trees and beasts and men recieve
Comfort in morning joy in the noon day.

And we are put on earth a little space,
That we may learn to bear the beams of love,
15   And these black bodies and this sun-burnt face
Is but a cloud, and like a shady grove.

1 *deprived.*

For when our souls have learn'd the heat to bear
The cloud will vanish we shall hear his voice.
Saying: come out from the grove my love & care,
20   And round my golden tent like lambs rejoice.

Thus did my mother say and kissed me,
And thus I say to little English boy.
When I from black and he from white cloud free,
And round the tent of God like lambs we joy:

25   Ill shade him from the heat till he can bear,
To lean in joy upon our fathers knee.
And then I'll stand and stroke his silver hair,
And be like him and he will then love me.

(1789)

The Chimney Sweeper

When my mother died I was very young,
And my father sold me while yet my tongue,
Could scarcely crey weep weep weep weep.
So your chimneys I sweep & in soot I sleep.

5   Theres little Tom Dacre, who cried when his head
That curl'd like a lambs back, was shav'd, so I said.
Hush Tom never mind it, for when your head's bare,
You know that the soot cannot spoil your white hair.

And so he was quiet, & that very night,
10   As Tom was a sleeping he had such a sight,
That thousands of sweepers Dick, Joe Ned & Jack
Were all of them lock'd up in coffins of black,

And by came an Angel who had a bright key,
And he open'd the coffins & set them all free.
15   Then down a green plain leaping laughing they run
And wash in a river and shine in the Sun.

Then naked & white, all their bags left behind,
They rise upon clouds, and sport in the wind.
And the Angel told Tom if he'd be a good boy,
20   He'd have God for his father & never want joy.

And so Tom awoke and we rose in the dark
And got with our bags & our brushes to work.
Tho' the morning was cold, Tom was happy & warm,
So if all do their duty, they need not fear harm.

(1789)

Holy Thursday[1]

Twas on a Holy Thursday their innocent faces clean
The children walking two & two in red & blue & green
Grey headed beadles walkd before with wands as white as
          snow
Till into the high dome of Pauls[2] they like Thames waters
          flow

5   O what a multitude they seemd these flowers of London
          town
Seated in companies they sit with radiance all their own
The hum of multitudes was there but multitudes of lambs
Thousands of little boys & girls raising their innocent
          hands

Now like a mighty wind they raise to heaven the voice of
          song
10   Or like harmonious thunderings the seats of heaven
          among
Beneath them sit the aged men wise guardians of the poor
Then cherish pity, lest you drive an angel from your door

(1789)

1 in the Anglican tradition, the Thursday 40 days after Easter, when Christ is said to have ascended to heaven.
2 St. Paul's Cathedral, London.

Nurse's[1] Song

When the voices of children are heard on the green
And laughing is heard on the hill,
My heart is at rest within my breast
And every thing else is still

5　　Then come home my children, the sun is gone down
And the dews of night arise
Come come leave off play, and let us away
Till the morning appears in the skies

No no let us play, for it is yet day
10　　And we cannot go to sleep
Besides in the sky, the little birds fly
And the hills are all covered with sheep

Well well go & play till the light fades away
And then go home to bed
15　　The little ones leaped & shouted & laugh'd
And all the hills ecchoed

(c. 1784)   (1789)

The Tyger

Tyger Tyger, burning bright,
In the forests of the night;
What immortal hand or eye,
Could frame thy fearful symmetry?

5　　In what distant deeps or skies!
Burnt the fire of thine eyes?
On what wings dare he aspire?
What the hand, dare sieze the fire?

1 *woman hired to care for a young child.*

And what shoulder, & what art,
10   Could twist the sinews of thy heart?
And when thy heart began to beat,
What dread hand? & what dread feet?

What the hammer? what the chain?
In what furnace was thy brain?
15   What the anvil? what dread grasp,
Dare its deadly terrors clasp?

When the stars threw down their spears
And water'd heaven with their tears;
Did he smile his work to see?
20   Did he who made the Lamb make thee?

Tyger Tyger burning bright,
In the forests of the night:
What immortal hand or eye,
Dare frame thy fearful symmetry?

(1790–92)   (1794)

The Chimney Sweeper

A little black thing among the snow:
Crying weep, weep, in notes of woe!
Where are thy father & mother? say?
They are both gone up to the church to pray.

5   Because I was happy upon the heath,[1]
And smil'd among the winters snow:
They clothed me in the clothes of death,
And taught me to sing the notes of woe.

---

1 open countryside containing scrubby vegetation.

And because I am happy, & dance & sing,
10   They think they have done me no injury:
And are gone to praise God & his Priest & King
Who make up a heaven of our misery.

(1790–92)   (1794)

Holy Thursday

Is this a holy thing to see,
In a rich and fruitful land,
Babes reducd to misery,
Fed with cold and usurous hand?

5   Is that trembling cry a song?
Can it be a song of joy?
And so many children poor?
It is a land of poverty!

And their sun does never shine.
10   And their fields are bleak & bare.
And their ways are fill'd with thorns.
It is eternal winter there.

For where-e'er the sun does shine,
And where-e'er the rain does fall:
15   Babe can never hunger there,
Nor poverty the mind appall.

(1794)

Nurse's Song

When the voices of children, are heard on the green
And whisprings are in the dale:
The days of my youth rise fresh in my mind,
My face turns green and pale.

5   Then come home my children, the sun is gone down
And the dews of night arise
Your spring & your day, are wasted in play
And your winter and night in disguise.

(1794)

The Sick Rose

O Rose thou art sick.
The invisible worm,
That flies in the night
In the howling storm:

5   Has found out thy bed
Of crimson joy:
And his dark secret love
Does thy life destroy.

(1794)

London

I wander thro' each charter'd[1] street,
Near where the charter'd Thames does flow.
And mark in every face I meet
Marks of weakness, marks of woe.

5   In every cry of every Man,
In every Infants cry of fear,
In every voice: in every ban,
The mind-forg'd manacles I hear

How the Chimney-sweepers cry
10   Every blackning Church appalls,
And the hapless Soldiers sigh
Runs in blood down Palace walls

But most thro' midnight streets I hear
How the youthful Harlots curse
15   Blasts the new-born Infants tear
And blights with plagues the Marriage hearse.

(1794)

Auguries[1] of Innocence

To see a World in a Grain of Sand
And a Heaven in a Wild Flower
Hold Infinity in the palm of your hand
And Eternity in an hour
5   A Robin Red breast in a Cage
Puts all Heaven in a Rage
A dove house filld with doves & Pigeons

1 *protected as private property.*

1 *signs, foretellings, or prophecies.*

Shudders Hell thro all its regions
A dog starvd at his Masters Gate
10 Predicts the ruin of the State
A Horse misusd upon the Road
Calls to Heaven for Human Blood
Each outcry of the hunted Hare
A fibre from the Brain does tear
15 A Skylark wounded in the wing
A Cherubim[2] does cease to sing
The Game Cock[3] clipd & armd for fight
Does the Rising Sun affright
Every Wolfs & Lions howl
20 Raises from Hell a Human Soul
The wild deer wandring here & there
Keeps the Human Soul from Care
The Lamb misusd breeds Public strife
And yet forgives the Butchers Knife
25 The Bat that flits at close of Eve
Has left the Brain that wont Believe
The Owl that calls upon the Night
Speaks the Unbelievers fright
He who shall hurt the little Wren
30 Shall never be belovd by Men
He who the Ox to wrath has movd
Shall never be by Woman lovd
The wanton Boy that kills the Fly
Shall feel the Spiders enmity
35 He who torments the Chafers[4] sprite
Weaves a Bower in endless Night
The Catterpiller on the Leaf
Repeats to thee thy Mothers grief
Kill not the Moth nor Buttefly
40 For the Last Judgment draweth nigh

2 *an angel.*
3 *gamecocks had their wings clipped and their spurs tipped with metal.*
4 *beetle.*

He who shall train the Horse to War
Shall never pass the Polar Bar[5]
The Beggers Dog & Widows Cat
Feed them & thou wilt grow fat
45   The Gnat that sings his Summers song
Poison gets from Slanders tongue
The poison of the Snake & Newt
Is the sweat of Envys Foot
The Poison of the Honey Bee
50   Is the Artists Jealousy
The Princes Robes & Beggars Rags
Are Toadstools on the Misers Bags
A truth thats told with bad intent
Beats all the Lies you can invent
55   It is right it should be so
Man was made for Joy & Woe
And when this we rightly know
Thro the World we safely go
Joy & Woe are woven fine
60   A Clothing for the soul divine
Under every grief & pine
Runs a joy with silken twine
The Babe is more than swadling Bands
Throughout all these Human Lands
65   Tools were made & Born were hands
Every Farmer Understands
Every Tear from Every Eye
Becomes a Babe in Eternity
This is caught by Females bright
70   And returnd to its own delight
The Bleat the Bark Bellow & Roar
Are Waves that Beat on Heavens Shore
The Babe that weeps the Rod beneath
Writes Revenge in realms of death

5 *Polaris, the North Star.*

75   The Beggars Rags fluttering in Air
      Does to Rags the Heavens tear
      The Soldier armd with Sword & Gun
      Palsied strikes the Summers Sun
      The poor Mans Farthing is worth more
80   Than all the Gold on Africs Shore
      One Mite wrung from the Labrers hands
      Shall buy & sell the Misers Lands
      Or if protected from on high
      Does that whole Nation sell & buy
85   He who mocks the Infants Faith
      Shall be mock'd in Age & Death
      He who shall teach the Child to Doubt
      The rotting Grave shall neer get out
      He who respects the Infants faith
90   Triumphs over Hell & Death
      The Childs Toys & the Old Mans Reasons
      Are the Fruits of the Two seasons
      The Questioner who sits so sly
      Shall never know how to Reply
95   He who replies to words of Doubt
      Doth put the Light of Knowledge out
      The Strongest Poison ever known
      Came from Caesars Laurel Crown[6]
      Nought can deform the Human Race
100   Like to the Armours iron brace
      When Gold & Gems adorn the Plow
      To peaceful Arts shall Envy Bow
      A Riddle or the Crickets Cry
      Is to Doubt a fit Reply
105   The Emmets[7] Inch & Eagles Mile
      Make Lame Philosophy to smile
      He who Doubts from what he sees

6 *although Julius Caesar refused the crown of kingship and instead wore a laurel crown, many people believed he ruled tyranically.*
7 *ant.*

Will neer Believe do what you Please
If the Sun & Moon should doubt
110   Theyd immediately Go out
To be in a Passion you Good may do
But no Good if a Passion is in you
The Whore & Gambler by the State
Licencd build that Nations Fate
115   The Harlots cry from Street to Street
Shall weave Old Englands winding Sheet[8]
The Winners Shout the Losers Curse
Dance before dead Englands Hearse
Every Night & every Morn
120   Some to Misery are Born
Every Morn & every Night
Some are Born to sweet delight
Some are Born to sweet delight
Some are Born to Endless Night
125   We are led to Believe a Lie
When we see not Thro the Eye
Which was Born in a Night to perish in a Night[9]
When the Soul Slept in Beams of Light
God Appears & God is Light
130   To those poor Souls who dwell in Night
But does a Human Form Display
To those who Dwell in Realms of day

(c. 1803)   (1863)

8 *cloth used to wrap a corpse.*
9 *see Jonah 4:10.*

ROBERT BURNS

(1759–1796)

*M*ore than any other major writer in English, Robert Burns is a "people's poet," and that for many reasons. For one, he was the son of a poor farmer in southwestern Scotland; unlike other poets, during his boyhood and most of his adult life the self-educated Burns put in hard workdays on subsistence-level farms. For another reason, Burns turned his back on formal English poetry and wrote in the forms of Scottish folk-poetry and in Scots, the dialect spoken by Scottish peasants. For another thing, his flagrant sexuality (he acknowledged fathering nine illegitimate children during his brief life), his bouts of drunkenness, and his defiance of the righteous elders of the Presbyterian Scottish Kirk all embody the ordinary person's instinctive rebellion against stern authority. And, finally, Burns is a people's poet because he appeals to vast numbers who are not students of literature: almost everyone who speaks English knows his most famous songs, and every New Year's Eve Burns is commemorated when people join to sing the best known of them all, "Auld Lang Syne."

To a Mouse, *On Turning Her Up in Her Nest, with the Plough, November, 1785.*

Wee, sleeket,[1] cowran, tim'rous *beastie,*
O, what a panic's in thy breastie!
Thou need na start awa sae hasty,
    Wi' bickering brattle![2]
5   I wad be laith[3] to rin an' chase thee,
    Wi' murd'ring *pattle*![4]

1 *sleek.*
2 *scampering haste.*
3 *loath.*
4 *plough-staff.*

I'm truly sorry Man's dominion
Has broken Nature's social union,
An' justifies that ill opinion,
   Which makes thee startle,
At me, thy poor, earth-born companion,
   An' *fellow-mortal*!

I doubt na, whyles,[5] but thou may *thieve;*
What then? poor beastie, thou maun[6] live!
A *daimen-icker*[7] in a *thrave*[8]
   'S a sma' request:
I'll get a blessin wi' the lave,[9]
   An' never miss't!

Thy wee-bit *housie*, too, in ruin!
It's silly[10] wa's the win's are strewin!
An' naething, now, to big[11] a new ane,
   O' foggage[12] green!
An' bleak *December's winds* ensuin,
   Baith snell[13] an' keen!

Thou saw the fields laid bare an' wast,
An' weary *Winter* comin fast,
An' cozie here, beneath the blast,
   Thou thought to dwell,
Till crash! the cruel *coulter*[14] past
   Out thro' thy cell.

That wee-bit heap o' leaves an' stibble,
Has cost thee monie a weary nibble!
Now thou's turn'd out, for a' thy trouble,
   But[15] house or hald,[16]
To thole[17] the Winter's *sleety dribble*,
   An' *cranreuch*[18] cauld!

---

5 *sometimes.* 6 *must.* 7 *occasional ear.* 8 *twenty-four sheaves.* 9 *rest.* 10 *puny.* 11 *build.* 12 *coarse grass.* 13 *bitter* 14 *plough-blade.* 15 *without.* 16 *holding (i.e., property)* 17 *endure.* 18 *hoarfrost.*

But Mousie, thou art no thy-lane,[19]
In proving *foresight* may be vain:
The best laid schemes o' *Mice* an' *Men*,
40   Gang aft agley,[20]
An' lea'e us nought but grief an' pain,
    For promis'd joy!

Still, thou art blest, compar'd wi' *me*!
The *present* only toucheth thee:
45   But Och! I *backward* cast my e'e,
    On prospects drear!
An' *forward*, tho' I canna *see*,
    I *guess* an' *fear*!

(1786)

Holy Willie's Prayer

And send the Godly in a pet to pray —
POPE.[1]

Argument

Holy Willie[2] was a rather oldish batchelor Elder in the parish of Mauchline, and much and justly famed for that polemical chattering which ends in tippling Orthodoxy, and for that Spiritualized Bawdry which refines to Liquorish[3] Devotion. — In a Sessional process with a gentleman in Mauchline, a Mr. Gavin Hamilton, Holy Willie, and his priest, father Auld, after full hearing in the Presbytry of Ayr, came off but second best; owing partly to the oratorical powers of Mr. Robt. Aiken, Mr. Hamilton's Counsel; but chiefly to Mr. Hamilton's being one of the most irreproachable and truly respectable characters in the country. — On losing his Process, the Muse overheard him at his devotions as follows —

---

19 *not alone.*
20 *go oft awry.*

1 *Burns's epigraph is drawn from* The Rape of the Lock *IV.64.*
2 *as Burns explains, William Fisher, a self-righteous elder of the Scottish Kirk, had accused Burns's friend and patron Gavin Hamilton of neglecting to attend church and other misdemeanours; Hamilton was exonerated.*
3 *lecherous, but also a pun suggesting a fondness for alcohol.*

O Thou that in the heavens does dwell!
Wha, as it pleases best thysel,
Sends ane to heaven and ten to h-ll,[4]
    A' for thy glory!
5   And no for ony gude or ill
      They've done before thee. —

I bless and praise thy matchless might,
When thousands thou has left in night,
That I am here before thy sight,
10   For gifts and grace,
A burning and a shining light
      To a' this place. —

What was I, or my generation,[5]
That I should get such exaltation?
15   I, wha deserv'd most just damnation,
      For broken laws
Sax[6] thousand years ere my creation,
      Thro' Adam's cause!

When from my mother's womb I fell,
20   Thou might hae plunged me deep in hell,
To gnash my gooms, and weep, and wail,
      In burning lakes,
Where damned devils roar and yell
      Chain'd to their stakes. —

25   Yet I am here, a chosen sample,
To shew thy grace is great and ample:
I'm here, a pillar o' thy temple
      Strong as a rock,
A guide, a ruler and example
30   To a' thy flock. —

4 *as a Calvinist, Willie believes that he is one of the elect predestined for grace, no matter what his behaviour in this life.*
5 *birth.*
6 *six.*

O L—d thou kens[7] what zeal I bear,
When drinkers drink, and swearers swear,
And singin' there, and dancin' here
    Wi' great an' sma';
35   For I am keepet by thy fear,
    Free frae them a'. —

But yet — O L—d — confess I must —
At times I'm fash'd[8] wi' fleshly lust;
And sometimes too, in warldly trust[9]
40   Vile Self gets in;
But thou remembers we are dust
    Defil'd wi' sin. —

O L—d — yestreen[10] — thou kens; — wi' Meg —
Thy pardon I sincerely beg!
45   O may't ne'er be a living plague,
    To my dishonor!
And I'll ne'er lift a lawless leg
    Again upon her. —

Besides, I farther maun[11] avow,
50   Wi' Leezie's lass, three times — I trow[12] —
But L—d, that friday I was fou[13]
    When I cam near her;
Or else, thou kens, thy servant true
    Wad never steer[14] her. —

55   Maybe thou lets this fleshy thorn
Buffet thy servant e'en and morn,
Lest he o'er proud and high should turn,
    That he's sae gifted;
If sae, thy hand maun e'en be borne
60   Untill thou lift it. —

---

7 *knowest.* **8** *troubled.* **9** *as an elder, Willie was entrusted with handling church funds.* **10** *last night.* **11** *must.* **12** *believe.* **13** *drunk.* **14** *molest.*

L—d bless thy Chosen in this place,
For here thou has a chosen race:
But G-d, confound their stubborn face,
  And blast their name,
65 Wha bring thy rulers to disgrace
  And open shame. —

L—d mind Gaun Hamilton's deserts!
He drinks, and swears, and plays at cartes,[15]
Yet has sae mony taking arts
70 Wi' Great and Sma',
Frae G-d's ain priest the people's hearts
  He steals awa. —

And when we chasten'd him therefore,
Thou kens how he bred sic a splore,[16]
75 And set the warld in a roar
  O' laughin at us:
Curse thou his basket and his store,
  Kail[17] and potatoes. —

L—d hear my earnest cry and prayer
80 Against that Presbytry of Ayr!
Thy strong right hand, L—d, make it bare
  Upon their heads!
L—d visit them, and dinna spare,
  For their misdeeds!

85 O L—d my G-d, that glib-tongu'd Aiken![18]
My very heart and flesh are quaking
To think how I sat, sweating, shaking,
  And p-ss'd wi' dread,
While Auld wi' hingin[19] lip gaed[20] sneaking
90 And hid his head!

15 *cards.*
16 *riot, uproar.*
17 *cabbage.*
18 *for Robert Aiken and Father Auld (line 89), see Burns's own headnote to the poem.*
19 *hanging.*
20 *went.*

L—d, in thy day o' vengeance try him!
L—d visit him that did employ him!
And pass not in thy mercy by them,
    Nor hear their prayer;
95 But for thy people's sake destroy them,
    And dinna spare!

But L—d, remember me and mine
Wi' mercies temporal and divine!
That I for grace and gear[21] may shine,
100   Excell'd by nane!
And a' the glory shall be thine!
    AMEN! AMEN!

(1789)

21 *possessions, wealth.*

WILLIAM WORDSWORTH

(1770–1850)

*orn in Cockermouth, near the English Lake District, William Words-
worth attended Cambridge University and then travelled widely in
Europe, spending a year in France during the Revolution. There he fathered an ille-
gitimate child, Caroline, referred to indirectly in his sonnet "It is a Beauteous Eve-
ning." In 1798, with his friend Samuel Taylor Coleridge, he published* Lyrical
Ballads, *a collection in which, as Coleridge stated, Wordsworth gave "the charm
of novelty to things of everyday." In the Preface to the 1800 edition, written in
response to criticism of the first edition, Wordsworth explained the theory underly-
ing his poems. Reacting in part against the dominant poetic tastes and conventions
of the eighteenth century, he stated that the poems were created from "emotion recol-
lected in tranquillity," an idea illustrated in "Tintern Abbey," and later in "I
Wandered Lonely as a Cloud." As seen in "Michael," he chose as his subjects
"incidents and situations of common life," presented in "language really used by
men." In 1802, influenced in part by his reading of John Milton, who is
addressed in "London, 1802," Wordsworth wrote a number of sonnets considered
by many critics to be the finest to have appeared since the seventeenth century.
Wordsworth's reputation increased steadily during his lifetime, and, in 1843, he
was appointed Poet Laureate. He is now recognized not only as one of the greatest of
the romantics and a major English poet, but as one who, in his portrayal of com-
mon people and nature, radically altered the course of English poetry in the nine-
teenth century.*

Lines

COMPOSED A FEW MILES ABOVE TINTERN ABBEY,[1] ON REVISITING
THE BANKS OF THE WYE DURING A TOUR. JULY 13, 1798

Five years have past; five summers, with the length
Of five long winters! and again I hear
These waters, rolling from their mountain-springs
With a soft inland murmur. — Once again
5   Do I behold these steep and lofty cliffs,
That on a wild secluded scene impress

---

1 *a ruined Cistercian abbey located on the Wye River, Wales.*

Thoughts of more deep seclusion; and connect
The landscape with the quiet of the sky.
The day is come when I again repose

10   Here, under this dark sycamore, and view
These plots of cottage-ground, these orchard-tufts,
Which at this season, with their unripe fruits,
Are clad in one green hue, and lose themselves
'Mid groves and copses. Once again I see

15   These hedge-rows, hardly hedge-rows, little lines
Of sportive wood run wild: these pastoral farms,
Green to the very door; and wreaths of smoke
Sent up, in silence, from among the trees!
With some uncertain notice, as might seem

20   Of vagrant dwellers in the houseless woods,
Or of some Hermit's cave, where by his fire
The Hermit sits alone.

                  These beauteous forms,
Through a long absence, have not been to me
As is a landscape to a blind man's eye:

25   But oft, in lonely rooms, and 'mid the din
Of towns and cities, I have owed to them
In hours of weariness, sensations sweet,
Felt in the blood, and felt along the heart;
And passing even into my purer mind,

30   With tranquil restoration: — feelings too
Of unremembered pleasure: such, perhaps,
As have no slight or trivial influence
On that best portion of a good man's life,
His little, nameless, unremembered, acts

35   Of kindness and of love. Nor less, I trust,
To them I may have owed another gift,
Of aspect more sublime; that blessed mood,
In which the burthen of the mystery,
In which the heavy and the weary weight

40   Of all this unintelligible world,
Is lightened: — that serene and blessed mood,
In which the affections gently lead us on, —

Until the breath of this corporeal frame
And even the motion of our human blood
45 Almost suspended, we are laid asleep
In body, and become a living soul:
While with an eye made quiet by the power
Of harmony, and the deep power of joy,
We see into the life of things.
        If this
50 Be but a vain belief, yet, oh! how oft —
In darkness and amid the many shapes
Of joyless daylight; when the fretful stir
Unprofitable, and the fever of the world,
Have hung upon the beatings of my heart —
55 How oft, in spirit, have I turned to thee,
O sylvan Wye! thou wanderer thro' the woods,
How often has my spirit turned to thee!
  And now, with gleams of half-extinguished thought,
With many recognitions dim and faint,
60 And somewhat of a sad perplexity,
The picture of the mind revives again:
While here I stand, not only with the sense
Of present pleasure, but with pleasing thoughts
That in this moment there is life and food
65 For future years. And so I dare to hope,
Though changed, no doubt, from what I was when first
I came among these hills; when like a roe
I bounded o'er the mountains, by the sides
Of the deep rivers, and the lonely streams,
70 Wherever nature led: more like a man
Flying from something that he dreads than one
Who sought the thing he loved. For nature then
(The coarser pleasures of my boyish days,
And their glad animal movements all gone by)
75 To me was all in all. — I cannot paint
What then I was. The sounding cataract
Haunted me like a passion: the tall rock,
The mountain, and the deep and gloomy wood,
Their colours and their forms, were then to me
80 An appetite; a feeling and a love,

That had no need of a remoter charm,
By thought supplied, nor any interest
Unborrowed from the eye. — That time is past,
And all its aching joys are now no more,
85   And all its dizzy raptures. Not for this
Faint I, nor mourn nor murmur; other gifts
Have followed; for such loss, I would believe,
Abundant recompense. For I have learned
To look on nature, not as in the hour
90   Of thoughtless youth; but hearing often-times
The still, sad music of humanity,
Nor harsh nor grating, though of ample power
To chasten and subdue. And I have felt
A presence that disturbs me with the joy
95   Of elevated thoughts; a sense sublime
Of something far more deeply interfused,
Whose dwelling is the light of setting suns,
And the round ocean and the living air,
And the blue sky, and in the mind of man:
100   A motion and a spirit, that impels
All thinking things, all objects of all thought,
And rolls through all things. Therefore am I still
A lover of the meadows and the woods,
And mountains; and of all that we behold
105   From this green earth; of all the mighty world
Of eye, and ear, — both what they half create,
And what perceive; well pleased to recognise
In nature and the language of the sense
The anchor of my purest thoughts, the nurse,
110   The guide, the guardian of my heart, and soul
Of all my moral being.
                                        Nor perchance,
If I were not thus taught, should I the more
Suffer my genial spirits to decay:
For thou art with me here upon the banks
115   Of this fair river; thou my dearest Friend,[2]

---

2 *Wordsworth's sister, Dorothy.*

My dear, dear Friend; and in thy voice I catch
The language of my former heart, and read
My former pleasures in the shooting lights
Of thy wild eyes. Oh! yet a little while
120   May I behold in thee what I was once,
My dear, dear Sister! and this prayer I make,
Knowing that Nature never did betray
The heart that loved her; 'tis her privilege,
Through all the years of this our life, to lead
125   From joy to joy: for she can so inform
The mind that is within us, so impress
With quietness and beauty, and so feed
With lofty thoughts, that neither evil tongues,
Rash judgments, nor the sneers of selfish men,
130   Nor greetings where no kindness is, nor all
The dreary intercourse of daily life,
Shall e'er prevail against us, or disturb
Our cheerful faith, that all which we behold
Is full of blessings. Therefore let the moon
135   Shine on thee in thy solitary walk;
And let the misty mountain-winds be free
To blow against thee: and, in after years,
When these wild ecstasies shall be matured
Into a sober pleasure; when thy mind
140   Shall be a mansion for all lovely forms,
Thy memory be as a dwelling-place
For all sweet sounds and harmonies; oh! then,
If solitude, or fear, or pain, or grief,
Should be thy portion, with what healing thoughts
145   Of tender joy wilt thou remember me,
And these my exhortations! Nor, perchance —
If I should be where I no more can hear
Thy voice, nor catch from thy wild eyes these gleams
Of past existence — wilt thou then forget
150   That on the banks of this delightful stream
We stood together; and that I, so long
A worshipper of Nature, hither came

Unwearied in that service: rather say
With warmer love — oh! with far deeper zeal
155   Of holier love. Nor wilt thou then forget
That after many wanderings, many years
Of absence, these steep woods and lofty cliffs,
And this green pastoral landscape, were to me
More dear, both for themselves and for thy sake!

(1798)

Michael

A PASTORAL POEM

If from the public way you turn your steps
Up the tumultuous brook of Green-head Ghyll,[1]
You will suppose that with an upright path
Your feet must struggle; in such bold ascent
5   The pastoral mountains front you, face to face.
But, courage! for around that boisterous brook
The mountains have all opened out themselves,
And made a hidden valley of their own.
No habitation can be seen; but they
10   Who journey thither find themselves alone
With a few sheep, with rocks and stones, and kites[2]
That overhead are sailing in the sky.
It is in truth an utter solitude;
Nor should I have made mention of this Dell
15   But for one object which you might pass by,
Might see and notice not. Beside the brook
Appears a straggling heap of unhewn stones!
And to that simple object appertains
A story — unenriched with strange events,

1 located in the Lake District of northwestern England.
2 a bird of prey.

20   Yet not unfit, I deem, for the fireside,
      Or for the summer shade. It was the first
      Of those domestic tales that spake to me
      Of Shepherds, dwellers in the valleys, men
      Whom I already loved; — not verily
25   For their own sakes, but for the fields and hills
      Where was their occupation and abode.
      And hence this Tale, while I was yet a Boy
      Careless of books, yet having felt the power
      Of Nature, by the gentle agency
30   Of natural objects, led me on to feel
      For passions that were not my own, and think
      (At random and imperfectly indeed)
      On man, the heart of man, and human life.
      Therefore, although it be a history
35   Homely and rude, I will relate the same
      For the delight of a few natural hearts;
      And, with yet fonder feeling, for the sake
      Of youthful Poets, who among these hills
      Will be my second self when I am gone.

40   Upon the forest-side in Grasmere Vale[3]
      There dwelt a Shepherd, Michael was his name;
      An old man, stout of heart, and strong of limb.
      His bodily frame had been from youth to age
      Of an unusual strength: his mind was keen,
45   Intense, and frugal, apt for all affairs,
      And in his shepherd's calling he was prompt
      And watchful more than ordinary men.
      Hence had he learned the meaning of all winds,
      Of blasts of every tone; and oftentimes,
50   When others heeded not, He heard the South
      Make subterraneous music, like the noise
      Of bagpipers on distant Highland hills.
      The Shepherd, at such warning, of his flock

---

3 *village in the Lake District.*

Bethought him, and he to himself would say,
55 'The winds are now devising work for me!'
And, truly, at all times, the storm, that drives
The traveller to a shelter, summoned him
Up to the mountains: he had been alone
Amid the heart of many thousand mists,
60 That came to him, and left him, on the heights.
So lived he till his eightieth year was past.
And grossly that man errs, who should suppose
That the green valleys, and the streams and rocks,
Were things indifferent to the Shepherd's thoughts.
65 Fields, where with cheerful spirits he had breathed
The common air; hills, which with vigorous step
He had so often climbed; which had impressed
So many incidents upon his mind
Of hardship, skill or courage, joy or fear;
70 Which, like a book, preserved the memory
Of the dumb animals, whom he had saved,
Had fed or sheltered, linking to such acts
The certainty of honourable gain;
Those fields, those hills — what could they less? had laid
75 Strong hold on his affections, were to him
A pleasurable feeling of blind love,
The pleasure which there is in life itself.

His days had not been passed in singleness.
His Helpmate was a comely matron, old —
80 Though younger than himself full twenty years.
She was a woman of a stirring life,
Whose heart was in her house: two wheels she had
Of antique form; this large, for spinning wool;
That small, for flax; and, if one wheel had rest,
85 It was because the other was at work.
The Pair had but one inmate in their house,
An only Child, who had been born to them
When Michael, telling o'er his years, began
To deem that he was old, — in shepherd's phrase,
90 With one foot in the grave. This only Son,

With two brave sheep-dogs tried in many a storm,
The one of an inestimable worth,
Made all their household. I may truly say,
That they were as a proverb in the vale
95   For endless industry. When day was gone,
And from their occupations out of doors
The Son and Father were come home, even then,
Their labour did not cease; unless when all
Turned to the cleanly supper-board, and there
100   Each with a mess of pottage[4] and skimmed milk,
Sat round the basket piled with oaten cakes,
And their plain home-made cheese. Yet when the meal
Was ended, Luke (for so the Son was named)
And his old Father both betook themselves
105   To such convenient work as might employ
Their hands by the fire-side; perhaps to card
Wool for the Housewife's spindle, or repair
Some injury done to sickle, flail, or scythe,
Or other implement of house or field.

110   Down from the ceiling, by the chimney's edge,
That in our ancient uncouth country style
With huge and black projection overbrowed
Large space beneath, as duly as the light
Of day grew dim the Housewife hung a lamp;
115   An aged utensil, which had performed
Service beyond all others of its kind.
Early at evening did it burn — and late,
Surviving comrade of uncounted hours,
Which, going by from year to year, had found,
120   And left, the couple neither gay perhaps
Nor cheerful, yet with objects and with hopes,
Living a life of eager industry.
And now, when Luke had reached his eighteenth year,
There by the light of this old lamp they sate,

4 *thick, mainly vegetable soup.*

125 Father and Son, while far into the night
The Housewife plied her own peculiar work,
Making the cottage through the silent hours
Murmur as with the sound of summer flies.
This light was famous in its neighbourhood,
130 And was a public symbol of the life
That thrifty Pair had lived. For, as it chanced,
Their cottage on a plot of rising ground
Stood single, with large prospect, north and south,
High into Easedale, up to Dunmail-Raise,[5]
135 And westward to the village near the lake;
And from this constant light, so regular,
And so far seen, the House itself, by all
Who dwelt within the limits of the vale,
Both old and young, was named THE EVENING STAR.

140 Thus living on through such a length of years,
The Shepherd, if he loved himself, must needs
Have loved his Helpmate; but to Michael's heart
This son of his old age was yet more dear —
Less from instinctive tenderness, the same
145 Fond spirit that blindly works in the blood of all —
Than that a child, more than all other gifts
That earth can offer to declining man,
Brings hope with it, and forward-looking thoughts,
And stirrings of inquietude, when they
150 By tendency of nature needs must fail.
Exceeding was the love he bare to him,
His heart and his heart's joy! For often-times,
Old Michael, while he was a babe in arms,
Had done him female service, not alone
155 For pastime and delight, as is the use
Of fathers, but with patient mind enforced
To acts of tenderness; and he had rocked
His cradle, as with a woman's gentle hand.

And in a later time, ere yet the Boy
160 Had put on boy's attire, did Michael love,

---

5 *located in the Lake District.*

Albeit of a stern unbending mind,
To have the Young-one in his sight, when he
Wrought in the field, or on his shepherd's stool
Sate with a fettered sheep before him stretched
165   Under the large old oak, that near his door
Stood single, and, from matchless depth of shade,
Chosen for the Shearer's covert from the sun,
Thence in our rustic dialect was called
The CLIPPING TREE,[6] a name which yet it bears,
170   There, while they two were sitting in the shade.
With others round them, earnest all and blithe,
Would Michael exercise his heart with looks
Of fond correction and reproof bestowed
Upon the Child, if he disturbed the sheep
175   By catching at their legs, or with his shouts,
Scared them, while they lay still beneath the shears.

And when by Heaven's good grace the boy grew up
A healthy Lad, and carried in his cheek
Two steady roses that were five years old;
180   Then Michael from a winter coppice cut
With his own hand a sapling, which he hooped
With iron, making it throughout in all
Due requisites a perfect shepherd's staff,
And gave it to the Boy; wherewith equipt
185   He as a watchman oftentimes was placed
At gate or gap, to stem or turn the flock;
And, to his office prematurely called,
There stood the urchin, as you will divine,
Something between a hindrance and a help;
190   And for this cause not always, I believe,
Receiving from his Father hire of praise;
Though nought was left undone which staff, or voice,
Or looks, or threatening gestures, could perform.

But soon as Luke, full ten years old, could stand
195   Against the mountain blasts; and to the heights,
Not fearing toil, nor length of weary ways,

---

6 *tree under which the sheep were shorn.*

He with his Father daily went, and they
Were as companions, why should I relate
That objects which the Shepherd loved before
200   Were dearer now? that from the Boy there came
Feelings and emanations — things which were
Light to the sun and music to the wind;
And that the old Man's heart seemed born again?

Thus in his Father's sight the Boy grew up:
205   And now, when he had reached his eighteenth year,
He was his comfort and his daily hope.

While in this sort the simple household lived
From day to day, to Michael's ear there came
Distressful tidings. Long before the time
210   Of which I speak, the Shepherd had been bound
In surety[7] for his brother's son, a man
Of an industrious life, and ample means;
But unforeseen misfortunes suddenly
Had prest upon him; and old Michael now
215   Was summoned to discharge the forfeiture,
A grievous penalty, but little less
Than half his substance. This unlooked-for claim
At the first hearing, for a moment took
More hope out of his life than he supposed
220   That any old man ever could have lost.
As soon as he had armed himself with strength
To look his trouble in the face, it seemed
The Shepherd's sole resource to sell at once
A portion of his patrimonial fields.
225   Such was his first resolve; he thought again,
And his heart failed him. 'Isabel,' said he,
Two evenings after he had heard the news.
'I have been toiling more than seventy years,
And in the open sunshine of God's love
230   Have we all lived; yet, if these fields of ours
Should pass into a stranger's hand, I think

7 *a legal guarantee or promise.*

That I could not lie quiet in my grave.
Our lot is a hard lot; the sun himself
Has scarcely been more diligent than I;
235   And I have lived to be a fool at last
To my own family. An evil man
That was, and made an evil choice, if he
Were false to us; and, if he were not false,
There are ten thousand to whom loss like this
240   Had been no sorrow. I forgive him; — but
'Twere better to be dumb than to talk thus.

When I began, my purpose was to speak
Of remedies and of a cheerful hope.
Our Luke shall leave us, Isabel; the land
245   Shall not go from us, and it shall be free;
He shall possess it, free as is the wind
That passes over it. We have, thou know'st,
Another kinsman — he will be our friend
In this distress. He is a prosperous man,
250   Thriving in trade — and Luke to him shall go,
And with his kinsman's help and his own thrift
He quickly will repair this loss, and then
He may return to us. If here he stay,
What can be done? Where every one is poor,
255   What can be gained?'
            At this the old Man paused,
And Isabel sat silent, for her mind
Was busy, looking back into past times.
There's Richard Bateman, thought she to herself,
He was a parish-boy, at the church-door
260   They made a gathering for him, shillings, pence,
And halfpennies, wherewith the neighbours bought
A basket, which they filled with pedlar's wares;
And, with this basket on his arm, the lad
Went up to London, found a master there,
265   Who, out of many, chose the trusty boy
To go and overlook his merchandise
Beyond the seas; where he grew wondrous rich,
And left estates and monies to the poor,

And, at his birth-place, built a chapel floored
270   With marble, which he sent from foreign lands.
These thoughts, and many others of like sort,
Passed quickly through the mind of Isabel,
And her face brightened. The old Man was glad,
And thus resumed: — 'Well, Isabel! this scheme
275   These two days has been meat and drink to me.
Far more than we have lost is left us yet.
— We have enough — I wish indeed that I
Were younger; — but this hope is a good hope.
Make ready Luke's best garments, of the best
280   Buy for him more, and let us send him forth
To-morrow, or the next day, or to-night:
    If he *could* go, the Boy should go to-night.'

    Here Michael ceased, and to the fields went forth
With a light heart. The Housewife for five days
285   Was restless morn and night, and all day long
Wrought on with her best fingers to prepare
Things needful for the journey of her son.
But Isabel was glad when Sunday came
To stop her in her work: for, when she lay
290   By Michael's side, she through the last two nights
Heard him, how he was troubled in his sleep:
And when they rose at morning she could see
That all his hopes were gone. That day at noon
She said to Luke, while they two by themselves
295   Were sitting at the door, 'Thou must not go:
We have no other Child but thee to lose,
None to remember — do not go away,
For if thou leave thy Father he will die.'
The Youth made answer with a jocund voice;
300   And Isabel, when she had told her fears,
Recovered heart. That evening her best fare
Did she bring forth, and all together sat
Like happy people round a Christmas fire.

With daylight Isabel resumed her work;
305 And all the ensuing week the house appeared
As cheerful as a grove in Spring: at length
The expected letter from their kinsman came,
With kind assurances that he would do
His utmost for the welfare of the Boy;
310 To which, requests were added, that forthwith
He might be sent to him. Ten times or more
The letter was read over; Isabel
Went forth to show it to the neighbours round;
Nor was there at that time on English land
315 A prouder heart than Luke's. When Isabel
Had to her house returned, the old Man said,
'He shall depart to-morrow.' To this word
The Housewife answered, talking much of things
Which, if at such short notice he should go,
320 Would surely be forgotten. But at length
She gave consent, and Michael was at ease.

Near the tumultuous brook of Greenhead Ghyll,
In that deep valley, Michael had designed
To build a Sheep-fold; and, before he heard
325 The tidings of his melancholy loss,
For this same purpose he had gathered up
A heap of stones, which by the streamlet's edge
Lay thrown together, ready for the work.
With Luke that evening thitherward he walked:
330 And soon as they had reached the place he stopped,
And thus the old Man spake to him: — 'My son,
To-morrow thou wilt leave me: with full heart
I look upon thee, for thou art the same
That wert a promise to me ere thy birth,
335 And all thy life hast been my daily joy.
I will relate to thee some little part
Of our two histories; 'twill do thee good
When thou art from me, even if I should touch
On things thou canst not know of. — After thou
340 First cam'st into the world — as oft befalls

To new-born infants — thou didst sleep away
Two days, and blessings from thy Father's tongue
Then fell upon thee. Day by day passed on,
And still I loved thee with increasing love.
345 Never to living ear came sweeter sounds
Than when I heard thee by our own fireside
First uttering, without words, a natural tune;
While thou, a feeding babe, didst in thy joy
Sing at thy Mother's breast. Month followed month,
350 And in the open fields my life was passed
And on the mountains; else I think that thou
Hadst been brought up upon thy Father's knees.
But we were playmates, Luke: among these hills,
As well thou knowest, in us the old and young
355 Have played together, nor with me didst thou
Lack any pleasure which a boy can know.'
Luke had a manly heart; but at these words
He sobbed aloud. The old Man grasped his hand,
And said, 'Nay, do not take it so — I see
360 That these are things of which I need not speak.
— Even to the utmost I have been to thee
A kind and a good Father: and herein
I but repay a gift which I myself
Received at others' hands; for, though now old
365 Beyond the common life of man, I still
Remember them who loved me in my youth.
Both of them sleep together: here they lived,
As all their Forefathers had done; and, when
At length their time was come, they were not loth
370 To give their bodies to the family mould.
I wished that thou shouldst live the life they lived,
But 'tis a long time to look back, my Son,
And see so little gain from threescore years.
These fields were burthened when they came to me;
375 Till I was forty years of age, not more
Than half of my inheritance was mine.
I toiled and toiled; God blessed me in my work,
And till these three weeks past the land was free.
— It looks as if it never could endure

380   Another Master. Heaven forgive me, Luke,
      If I judge ill for thee, but it seems good
      That thou shouldst go.'
            At this the old Man paused;
      Then, pointing to the stones near which they stood,
      Thus, after a short silence, he resumed:
385   'This was a work for us; and now, my Son,
      It is a work for me. But, lay one stone —
      Here, lay it for me, Luke, with thine own hands.
      Nay, Boy, be of good hope; — we both may live
      To see a better day. At eighty-four
390   I still am strong and hale; — Do thou thy part;
      I will do mine. — I will begin again
      With many tasks that were resigned to thee:
      Up to the heights, and in among the storms,
      Will I without thee go again, and do
395   All works which I was wont to do alone,
      Before I knew thy face. — Heaven bless thee, Boy!
      Thy heart these two weeks has been beating fast
      With many hopes; it should be so — yes — yes —
      I knew that thou couldst never have a wish
400   To leave me, Luke: thou hast been bound to me
      Only by links of love: when thou art gone,
      What will be left to us! — But I forget
      My purposes. Lay now the corner-stone,
      As I requested; and hereafter, Luke,
405   When thou art gone away, should evil men
      Be thy companions, think of me, my Son,
      And of this moment; hither turn thy thoughts,
      And God will strengthen thee: amid all fear
      And all temptation, Luke, I pray that thou
410   May'st bear in mind the life thy Fathers lived,
      Who, being innocent, did for that cause
      Bestir them in good deeds. Now, fare thee well —
      When thou return'st, thou in this place wilt see
      A work which is not here: a covenant[8]

8 *an agreement or pledge between two parties.*

415 'Twill be between us; but, whatever fate
Befall thee, I shall love thee to the last,
And bear thy memory with me to the grave.'

The Shepherd ended here; and Luke stooped down,
And, as his Father had requested, laid
420 The first stone of the Sheep-fold. At the sight
The old Man's grief broke from him; to his heart
He pressed his Son, he kissèd him and wept;
And to the house together they returned.
— Hushed was that House in peace, or seeming peace,
425 Ere the night fell: — with morrow's dawn the Boy
Began his journey, and, when he had reached
The public way, he put on a bold face;
And all the neighbours, as he passed their doors,
Came forth with wishes and with farewell prayers,
430 That followed him till he was out of sight.

A good report did from their Kinsman come,
Of Luke and his well-doing: and the Boy
Wrote loving letters, full of wondrous news,
Which, as the Housewife phrased it, were throughout
435 'The prettiest letters that were ever seen.'
Both parents read them with rejoicing hearts.
So, many months passed on: and once again
The Shepherd went about his daily work
With confident and cheerful thoughts; and now
440 Sometimes when he could find a leisure hour
He to that valley took his way, and there
Wrought at the Sheep-fold. Meantime Luke began
To slacken in his duty; and, at length,
He in the dissolute city gave himself
445 To evil courses: ignominy and shame
Fell on him, so that he was driven at last
To seek a hiding-place beyond the seas.

There is a comfort in the strength of love;
'Twill make a thing endurable, which else

450   Would overset the brain, or break the heart:
      I have conversed with more than one who well
      Remember the old Man, and what he was
      Years after he had heard this heavy news.
      His bodily frame had been from youth to age
455   Of an unusual strength. Among the rocks
      He went, and still looked up to sun and cloud,
      And listened to the wind; and, as before,
      Performed all kinds of labour for his sheep,
      And for the land, his small inheritance.
460   And to that hollow dell from time to time
      Did he repair, to build the Fold of which
      His flock had need. 'Tis not forgotten yet
      The pity which was then in every heart
      For the old Man — and 'tis believed by all
465   That many and many a day he thither went,
      And never lifted up a single stone.

         There, by the Sheep-fold, sometimes was he seen
      Sitting alone, or with his faithful Dog,
      Then old, beside him, lying at his feet.
470   The length of full seven years, from time to time,
      He at the building of this Sheep-fold wrought,
      And left the work unfinished when he died.
      Three years, or little more, did Isabel
      Survive her Husband: at her death the estate
475   Was sold, and went into a stranger's hand.
      The Cottage which was named THE EVENING STAR
      Is gone — the ploughshare has been through the ground
      On which it stood; great changes have been wrought
      In all the neighbourhood: — yet the oak is left
480   That grew beside their door; and the remains
      Of the unfinished Sheep-fold may be seen
      Beside the boisterous brook of Greenhead Ghyll.

                                          (1800)

Composed upon Westminster Bridge,[1] September 3, 1802

Earth has not anything to show more fair:
Dull would he be of soul who could pass by
A sight so touching in its majesty:
This City now doth, like a garment, wear
5   The beauty of the morning; silent, bare,
Ships, towers, domes, theatres, and temples lie
Open unto the fields, and to the sky;
All bright and glittering in the smokeless air.
Never did sun more beautifully steep
10   In his first splendour, valley, rock, or hill;
Ne'er saw I, never felt, a calm so deep!
The river glideth at his own sweet will:
Dear God! the very houses seem asleep;
And all that mighty heart is lying still!

(1802)   (1807)

It is a beauteous evening, calm and free

It is a beauteous evening, calm and free,
The holy time is quiet as a Nun
Breathless with adoration; the broad sun
Is sinking down in its tranquillity;
5   The gentleness of heaven broods o'er the Sea:
Listen! the mighty Being is awake,
And doth with his eternal motion make
A sound like thunder — everlastingly.
Dear Child![1] dear Girl! that walkest with me here,
10   If thou appear untouched by solemn thought,

---

1 *a bridge over the Thames River in London, England.*

1 *Wordsworth's illegitimate daughter, Caroline.*

Thy nature is not therefore less divine:
Thou liest in Abraham's bosom[2] all the year;
And worshipp'st at the Temple's inner shrine,
God being with thee when we know it not.

(1802)   (1807)

London, 1802

Milton! thou shouldst be living at this hour:
England hath need of thee: she is a fen
Of stagnant waters: altar, sword, and pen,
Fireside, the heroic wealth of hall and bower,
5   Have forfeited their ancient English dower
Of inward happiness. We are selfish men;
Oh! raise us up, return to us again;
And give us manners, virtue, freedom, power.
Thy soul was like a Star, and dwelt apart;
10   Thou hadst a voice whose sound was like the sea:
Pure as the naked heavens, majestic, free,
So didst thou travel on life's common way,
In cheerful godliness; and yet thy heart
The lowliest duties on herself did lay.

(1802)   (1807)

The world is too much with us

The world is too much with us; late and soon,
Getting and spending, we lay waste our powers:
Little we see in Nature that is ours;
We have given our hearts away, a sordid boon!

---

2 *heavenly rest, peace. Cf. Luke 16:22–23.*

5   This Sea that bares her bosom to the moon;
The winds that will be howling at all hours,
And are up-gathered now like sleeping flowers;
For this, for everything, we are out of tune;
It moves us not. — Great God! I'd rather be
10 A Pagan suckled in a creed outworn;
So might I, standing on this pleasant lea,
Have glimpses that would make me less forlorn;
Have sight of Proteus[1] rising from the sea;
Or hear old Triton[2] blow his wreathèd horn.

(c. 1802)   (1807)

I wandered lonely as a cloud

I wandered lonely as a cloud
That floats on high o'er vales and hills,
When all at once I saw a crowd,
A host, of golden daffodils;
5   Beside the lake, beneath the trees,
Fluttering and dancing in the breeze.

Continuous as the stars that shine
And twinkle on the milky way,
They stretched in never-ending line
10 Along the margin of a bay:
Ten thousand saw I at a glance,
Tossing their heads in sprightly dance.

The waves beside them danced; but they
Out-did the sparkling waves in glee:
15 A poet could not but be gay,
In such a jocund company:
I gazed — and gazed — but little thought
What wealth the show to me had brought:

1 *Greek sea deity who had the power of prophecy.*
2 *Greek sea deity who was half-man and half-fish and who had the power to calm the ocean.*

For oft, when on my couch I lie
20   In vacant or in pensive mood,
They flash upon that inward eye
Which is the bliss of solitude;
And then my heart with pleasure fills,
And dances with the daffodils.

(1804)   (1807)

SAMUEL TAYLOR COLERIDGE

(1772–1834)

orn in the small town of Ottery St. Mary, Devonshire, Samuel Taylor Coleridge grew up in London, an intelligent, but very lonely, unhappy child. He studied at Cambridge, spent a year in the army, and interested himself in radical politics. In 1797, he met William Wordsworth, and a year later the two published Lyrical Ballads. *Coleridge's contributions were poems written on supernatural or romantic subjects, designed to create in the reader what he called "that willing suspension of disbelief for the moment, which constitutes poetic faith." Of these poems, the best known is "The Rime of the Ancient Mariner." Adapting the traditional ballad stanza, which had become popular during the last half of the eighteenth century, he drew on his voluminous reading in folklore and science to create the account of the title figure's symbolic journey of sin, guilt, repentance, and redemption, and the effect its retelling has on the somewhat self-satisfied wedding guest. Also written during this period were "Kubla Khan," which Coleridge said was based on an opium-induced dream, and "Frost at Midnight," a descriptive-meditative poem in which the speaker, regarding his sleeping infant son, recalls his own childhood. Although Coleridge continued to write poetry throughout his life, his most noted later work is* Biographia Literaria *(1817), a combination of autobiography, philosophy, and literary criticism.*

Kubla Khan[1]

> In Xanadu[2] did Kubla Khan
> A stately pleasure-dome decree:
> Where Alph, the sacred river, ran
> Through caverns measureless to man
> 5   Down to a sunless sea.
> So twice five miles of fertile ground
> With walls and towers were girdled round:
> And there were gardens bright with sinuous rills,
> Where blossomed many an incense-bearing tree;
> 10   And here were forests ancient as the hills,
> Enfolding sunny spots of greenery.

1 *thirteenth-century emperor of China. He was the grandson of Genghis Khan and a patron of the arts.*
2 *Shang-tu, a city founded by Kubla Khan, on the site of modern Beijing.*

But oh! that deep romantic chasm which slanted
Down the green hill athwart a cedarn cover![3]
A savage place! as holy and enchanted
15   As e'er beneath a waning moon was haunted
By woman wailing for her demon-lover!
And from this chasm, with ceaseless turmoil seething,
As if this earth in fast thick pants were breathing,
A mighty fountain momently was forced:
20   Amid whose swift half-intermitted burst
Huge fragments vaulted like rebounding hail,
Or chaffy grain beneath the thresher's flail:
And 'mid these dancing rocks at once and ever
It flung up momently the sacred river.
25   Five miles meandering with a mazy motion
Through wood and dale the sacred river ran,
Then reached the caverns measureless to man,
And sank in tumult to a lifeless ocean:
And 'mid this tumult Kubla heard from far
30   Ancestral voices prophesying war!
     The shadow of the dome of pleasure
     Floated midway on the waves
     Where was heard the mingled measure
     From the fountain and the caves.
35   It was a miracle of rare device,
A sunny pleasure-dome with caves of ice!

     A damsel with a dulcimer
     In a vision once I saw:
     It was an Abyssinian maid,
40   And on her dulcimer she played,
     Singing of Mount Abora.[4]
     Could I revive within me
     Her symphony and song,
     To such a deep delight 'twould win me,
45   That with music loud and long,
I would build that dome in air,
That sunny dome! those caves of ice!

3 *covered by cedar trees.*
4 *possibly Mt. Amara, in Abyssinia, now Ethiopia.*

And all who heard should see them there,
And all should cry, Beware! Beware!
50   His flashing eyes, his floating hair!
Weave a circle round him thrice,
And close your eyes with holy dread,
For he on honey-dew hath fed,
And drunk the milk of Paradise.

(1797)   (1816)

Frost at Midnight

The Frost performs its secret ministry,
Unhelped by any wind. The owlet's cry
Came loud — and hark, again! loud as before.
The inmates of my cottage, all at rest,
5   Have left me to that solitude, which suits
Abstruser musings: save that at my side
My cradled infant slumbers peacefully.
'Tis calm indeed! so calm, that it disturbs
And vexes meditation with its strange
10   And extreme silentness. Sea, hill, and wood,
This populous village! Sea, and hill, and wood,
With all the numberless goings-on of life,
Inaudible as dreams! the thin blue flame
Lies on my low-burnt fire, and quivers not;
15   Only that film,¹ which fluttered on the grate,
Still flutters there, the sole unquiet thing.
Methinks, its motion in this hush of nature
Gives it dim sympathies with me who live,
Making it a companionable form,
20   Whose puny flaps and freaks the idling Spirit
By its own moods interprets, every where

---

1 *a film, or radiation, was believed to signal the arrival of a friend.*

Echo or mirror seeking of itself,
And makes a toy of Thought.
                                    But O! how oft,
How oft, at school, with most believing mind,
25   Presageful, have I gazed upon the bars,
To watch that fluttering *stranger*! and as oft
With unclosed lids, already had I dreamt
Of my sweet birth-place, and the old church-tower,
Whose bells, the poor man's only music, rang
30   From morn to evening, all the hot Fair-day,
So sweetly, that they stirred and haunted me
With a wild pleasure, falling on mine ear
Most like articulate sounds of things to come!
So gazed I, till the soothing things, I dreamt,
35   Lulled me to sleep, and sleep prolonged my dreams!
And so I brooded all the following morn,
Awed by the stern preceptor's[2] face, mine eye
Fixed with mock study on my swimming book:
Save if the door half opened, and I snatched
40   A hasty glance, and still my heart leaped up,
For still I hoped to see the *stranger's* face,
Townsman, or aunt, or sister more beloved,
My play-mate when we both were clothed alike!

Dear Babe, that sleepest cradled by my side,
45   Whose gentle breathings, heard in this deep calm,
Fill up the intersperséd vacancies
And momentary pauses of the thought!
My babe so beautiful! it thrills my heart
With tender gladness, thus to look at thee,
50   And think that thou shalt learn far other lore,
And in far other scenes! For I was reared
In the great city, pent 'mid cloisters dim,
And saw nought lovely but the sky and stars.

2 *teacher's.*

But *thou*, my babe! shalt wander like a breeze
55   By lakes and sandy shores, beneath the crags
Of ancient mountain, and beneath the clouds,
Which image in their bulk both lakes and shores
And mountain crags: so shalt thou see and hear
The lovely shapes and sounds intelligible
60   Of that eternal language, which thy God
Utters, who from eternity doth teach
Himself in all, and all things in himself.
Great universal Teacher! he shall mould
Thy spirit, and by giving make it ask.

65   Therefore all seasons shall be sweet to thee,
Whether the summer clothe the general earth
With greenness, or the redbreast sit and sing
Betwixt the tufts of snow on the bare branch
Of mossy apple-tree, while the nigh thatch
70   Smokes in the sun-thaw; whether the eave-drops fall
Heard only in the trances of the blast,
Or if the secret ministry of frost
Shall hang them up in silent icicles,
Quietly shining to the quiet Moon.

(1798)

The Rime of the Ancient Mariner

PART I

An ancient Mariner meeteth three Gallants bidden to a wedding feast, and detaineth one.

It is an ancient Mariner,
And he stoppeth one of three.
'By thy long grey beard and glittering eye,
Now wherefore stopp'st thou me?

The Bridegroom's doors are opened wide,   5
And I am next of kin;
The guests are met, the feast is set:
May'st hear the merry din.'

He holds him with his skinny hand,
'There was a ship,' quoth he.   10
'Hold off! unhand me, grey-beard loon!'
Eftsoons¹ his hand dropt he.

The Wedding-Guest is spellbound by the eye of the old seafaring man, and constrained to hear his tale.

He holds him with his glittering eye —
The Wedding-Guest stood still,
And listens like a three years' child: 15
The Mariner hath his will.

The Wedding-Guest sat on a stone:
He cannot choose but hear;
And thus spake on that ancient man,
The bright-eyed Mariner.   20

'The ship was cheered, the harbour cleared,
Merrily did we drop
Below the kirk,² below the hill,
Below the lighthouse top.

The Mariner tells how the ship sailed southward with a good wind and fair weather, till it reached the line.

The Sun came up upon the left,   25
Out of the sea came he!
And he shone bright, and on the right
Went down into the sea.

1 *immediately.*
2 *church.*

Higher and higher every day,
Till over the mast at noon — '   30
The Wedding-Guest here beat his breast,
For he heard the loud bassoon.

The Wedding-Guest heareth
the bridal music; but the
Mariner continueth his tale.

The bride hath paced into the hall,
Red as a rose is she;
Nodding their heads before her goes   35
The merry minstrelsy.[3]

The Wedding-Guest he beat his breast,
Yet he cannot choose but hear;
And thus spake on that ancient man,
The bright-eyed Mariner.   40

The ship driven by a storm
toward the south pole.

'And now the STORM-BLAST came, and he
Was tyrannous and strong:
He struck with his o'ertaking wings,
And chased us south along.

With sloping masts and dipping prow,   45
As who pursued with yell and blow
Still treads the shadow of his foe,
And forward bends his head,
The ship drove fast, loud roared the blast,
And southward aye we fled.   50

And now there came both mist and snow,
And it grew wondrous cold:
And ice, mast-high, came floating by,
As green as emerald.

The land of ice, and of fearful
sounds where no living thing
was to be seen.

And through the drifts the snowy clifts   55
Did send a dismal sheen:
Nor shapes of men nor beasts we ken — [4]
The ice was all between.

3 *a group of minstrels.*
4 *know.*

The ice was here, the ice was there,
The ice was all around: 60
It cracked and growled, and roared and howled,
Like noises in a swound!⁵

Till a great sea-bird, called
the Albatross, came through
the snow-fog, and was
received with great joy and
hospitality.

At length did cross an Albatross,
Thorough the fog it came;
As if it had been a Christian soul,   65
We hailed it in God's name.

It ate the food it ne'er had eat,
And round and round it flew.
The ice did split with a thunder-fit;
The helmsman⁶ steered us through!   70

And lo! the Albatross proveth
a bird of good omen, and
followeth the ship as it
returned northward through
fog and floating ice.

And a good south wind sprung up behind;
The Albatross did follow,
And every day, for food or play,
Came to the mariners' hollo!

In mist or cloud, on mast or shroud,   75
It perched for vespers⁷ nine;
Whiles all the night, through fog-smoke white,
Glimmered the white Moon-shine.'

The ancient Mariner
inhospitably killeth the pious
bird of good omen.

'God save thee, ancient Mariner!
From the fiends, that plague thee thus! —   80
Why look'st thou so?' — With my cross-bow
I shot the ALBATROSS.

PART II

The Sun now rose upon the right:
Out of the sea came he,
Still hid in mist, and on the left   85
Went down into the sea.

And the good south wind still blew behind,
But no sweet bird did follow,
Nor any day for food or play
Came to the mariners' hollo!   90

5 *swoon.*
6 *person who steers the ship.*
7 *evening worship; i.e., the bird remained for nine evenings.*

*His shipmates cry out against
the ancient Mariner, for
killing the bird of good luck.*

And I had done a hellish thing,
And it would work 'em woe:
For all averred, I had killed the bird
That made the breeze to blow.
Ah wretch! said they, the bird to slay,   95
That made the breeze to blow!

*But when the fog cleared off,
they justify the same, and
thus make themselves
accomplices in the crime.*

Nor dim nor red, like God's own head,
The glorious Sun uprist:
Then all averred, I had killed the bird
That brought the fog and mist.   100
'Twas right, said they, such birds to slay,
That bring the fog and mist.

*The fair breeze continues; the
ship enters the Pacific Ocean,
and sails northward, even till
it reaches the Line.*

The fair breeze blew, the white foam flew,
The furrow followed free;
We were the first that ever burst   105
Into that silent sea.

*The ship hath been suddenly
becalmed.*

Down dropt the breeze, that sails dropt down,
'Twas sad as sad could be;
And we did speak only to break
The silence of the sea!   110

All in a hot and copper sky,
The bloody Sun, at noon,
Right up above the mast did stand,
No bigger than the Moon.

Day after day, day after day,   115
We stuck, nor breath nor motion;
As idle as a painted ship
Upon a painted ocean.

*And the Albatross begins to
be avenged.*

Water, water, every where,
And all the boards did shrink;   120
Water, water, every where,
Nor any drop to drink.

The very deep did rot: O Christ!
That ever this should be!
Yea, slimy things did crawl with legs   125
Upon the slimy sea.

About, about, in reel and rout
The death-fires danced at night;
The water, like a witch's oils,
Burnt green, and blue and white.   130

A Spirit had followed them;
one of the invisible inhabitants
of this planet, neither departed
souls nor angels; concerning
whom the learned Jew,
Josephus, and the Platonic
Constantinopolitan, Michael
Psellus, may be consulted.
They are very numerous, and
there is no climate or element
without one or more.

And some in dreams assuréd were
Of the Spirit that plagued us so;
Nine fathom deep he had followed us
From the land of mist and snow.

And every tongue, through utter drought,   135
Was withered at the root;
We could not speak, no more than if
We had been choked with soot.

The shipmates, in their sore
distress, would fain throw the
whole guilt on the ancient
Mariner: in sign whereof
they hang the dead sea-bird
round his neck.

Ah! well a-day! what evil looks
Had I from old and young!   140
Instead of the cross, the Albatross
About my neck was hung.

PART III
There passed a weary time. Each throat
Was parched, and glazed each eye.
A weary time! a weary time!   145
How glazed each weary eye,

The ancient Mariner
beholdeth a sign in the
element afar off.

When looking westward, I beheld
A something in the sky.

At first it seemed a little speck,
And then it seemed a mist;   150
It moved and moved, and took at last
A certain shape, I wist.

A speck, a mist, a shape, I wist!
And still it neared and neared:
As if it dodged a water-sprite,[8]   155
It plunged and tacked and veered.

At its nearer approach, it
seemeth him to be a ship; and
at a dear ransom he freeth his
speech from the bonds of
thirst.

With throats unslaked, with black lips baked,
We could nor laugh nor wail:
Through utter drought all dumb we stood!
I bit my arm, I sucked the blood,   160
And cried, A sail! a sail!

With throats unslacked, with black lips baked,
Agape they heard me call:
A flash of joy; Gramercy![9] they for joy did grin,
And all at once their breath drew in,   165
As they were drinking all.

And horror follows. For can
it be a ship that comes
onward without wind or tide?

See! see! (I cried) she tacks no more!
Hither to work us weal;
Without a breeze, without a tide,
She steadies with upright keel!   170

The western wave was all a-flame.
The day was well nigh done!
Almost upon the western wave
Rested the broad bright Sun;
When that strange shape drove suddenly   175
Betwixt us and the Sun.

It seemeth him but the
skeleton of a ship.

And straight the Sun was flecked with bars,
(Heaven's Mother send us grace!)
As if through a dungeon-grate he peered
With broad and burning face.   180

Alas! (thought I, and my heart beat loud)
How fast she nears and nears!
Are those *her* sails that glance in the Sun,
Like restless gossameres?[10]

8 *spirit living in water.*
9 *an expression of surprise or gratitude, literally, "Great thanks."*
10 *cobwebs.*

And the ribs are seen as bars
on the face of the setting Sun.
The Spectre-Woman and her
Death-mate, and no other on
board the skeleton ship.

Are those *her* ribs through which the Sun   185
Did peer, as through a grate?
And is that Woman all her crew?
Is that a DEATH? and are there two?
Is DEATH that woman's mate?

Like vessel, like crew!

Her lips were red, *her* looks were free,   190
Her locks were yellow as gold:
Her skin was as white as leprosy,
The Night-mare LIFE-IN-DEATH was she,
Who thicks man's blood with cold.

Death and Life-in-Death
have diced for the ship's crew,
and she (the latter) winneth
the ancient Mariner.

The naked hulk alongside came,   195
And the twain were casting dice;
'The game is done! I've won! I've won!'
Quoth she, and whistles thrice.

No twilight within the courts
of the Sun.

The Sun's rim dips; the stars rush out:
At one stride comes the dark;   200
With far-heard whisper, o'er the sea,
Off shot the spectre-bark.[11]

At the rising of the Moon,

We listened and looked sideways up!
Fear at my heart, as at a cup,
My life-blood seemed to sip!   205
The stars were dim, and thick the night,
The steersman's face by his lamp gleamed white;
From the sails the dew did drip —
Till clomb above the eastern bar
The hornéd Moon,[12] with one bright star   210
Within the nether tip.

One after another,

One after one, by the star-dogged[13] Moon,
Too quick for groan or sigh,
Each turned his face with a ghastly pang,
And cursed me with his eye.   215

11 *phantom ship.*
12 *crescent moon.*
13 *followed by a star.*

His shipmates drop down
dead.
Four times fifty living men,
(And I heard nor sigh nor groan)
With heavy thump, a lifeless lump,
They dropped down one by one.

But Life-in-Death begins her
work on the ancient Mariner.
The souls did from their bodies fly, —   *220*
They fled to bliss or woe!
And every soul, it passed me by,
Like the whizz of my cross-bow!

Part IV

The Wedding-Guest feareth
that a Spirit is talking to
him;
'I fear thee, ancient Mariner!
I fear thy skinny hand!   *225*
And thou art long, and lank, and brown,
As is the ribbed sea-sand.

I fear thee and thy glittering eye,
And thy skinny hand, so brown.' —
But the ancient Mariner
assureth him of his bodily life,
and proceedeth to relate his
horrible penance.
Fear not, fear not, thou Wedding-Guest!   *230*
This body dropt not down.

Alone, alone, all, all alone,
Alone on a wide wide sea!
And never a saint took pity on
My soul in agony.   *235*

He despiseth the creatures of
the calm,
The many men, so beautiful!
And they all dead did lie:
And a thousand thousand slimy things
Lived on; and so did I.

And envieth that they should
live, and so many lie dead.
I looked upon the rotting sea,   *240*
And drew my eyes away;
I looked upon the rotting deck,
And there the dead men lay.

I looked to heaven, and tried to pray;
But or ever a prayer had gusht,   *245*
A wicked whisper came, and made
My heart as dry as dust.

I closed my lids, and kept them close,
And the balls like pulses beat;
For the sky and the sea, and the sea and the sky   250
Lay like a load on my weary eye,
And the dead were at my feet.

But the curse liveth for him
in the eye of the dead men.

The cold sweat melted from their limbs,
Nor rot nor reek did they:
The look with which they looked on me   255
Had never passed away.

An orphan's curse would drag to hell
A spirit from on high;
But oh! more horrible than that
Is the curse in a dead man's eye!   260
Seven days, seven nights, I saw that curse,
And yet I could not die.

In his loneliness and fixedness
he yearneth towards the
journeying Moon, and the
stars that still sojourn, yet
still move onward; and every
where the blue sky belongs to
them, and is their appointed
rest, and their native country
and their own natural homes,
which they enter
unannounced, as lords that
are certainly expected and yet
there is a silent joy at their
arrival.

The moving Moon went up the sky.
And no where did abide:
Softly she was going up,   265
And a star or two beside —

Her beams bemocked the sultry main,[14]
Like April hoar-frost spread;
But where the ship's huge shadow lay,
The charméd water burnt alway   270
A still and awful red.

By the light of the Moon he
beholdeth God's creatures of
the great calm.

Beyond the shadow of the ship,
I watched the water-snakes:
They moved in tracks of shining white,
And when they reared, the elfish light   275
Fell off in hoary flakes.

Within the shadow of the ship
I watched their rich attire:
Blue, glossy green, and velvet black,
They coiled and swam; and every track   280
Was a flash of golden fire.

14 *sea.*

Their beauty and their happiness.

O happy living things! no tongue
Their beauty might declare:
A spring of love gushed from my heart,

He blesseth them in his heart.

And I blessed them unaware: 285
Sure my kind saint took pity on me,
And I blessed them unaware.

The spell begins to break.

The self-same moment I could pray;
And from my neck so free
The Albatross fell off, and sank   290
Like lead into the sea.

PART V

Oh sleep! it is a gentle thing,
Beloved from pole to pole!
To Mary Queen[15] the praise be given!
She sent the gentle sleep from Heaven,   295
That slid into my soul.

By grace of the holy Mother, the ancient Mariner is refreshed with rain.

The silly buckets on the deck,
That had so long remained,
I dreamt that they were filled with dew;
And when I awoke, it rained.   300

My lips were wet, my throat was cold,
My garments all were dank;
Sure I had drunken in my dreams,
And still my body drank.

I moved, and could not feel my limbs: 305
I was so light — almost
I thought that I had died in sleep,
And was a blesséd ghost.

He heareth sound and seeth strange sights and commotions in the sky and the element.

And soon I heard a roaring wind:
It did not come anear;   310
But with its sound it shook the sails,
That were so thin and sere.

15 *the Virgin Mary, queen of Heaven.*

The upper air burst into life!
And a hundred fire-flags[16] sheen,
To and fro they were hurried about!   315
And to and fro, and in and out,
The wan stars danced between.

And the coming wind did roar more loud,
And the sails did sigh like sedge;
And the rain poured down from one black cloud;   320
The Moon was at its edge.

The thick black cloud was cleft, and still
The Moon was at its side:
Like waters shot from some high crag,
The lightning fell with never a jag,   325
A river steep and wide.

The bodies of the ship's crew
are inspired and the ship
moves on;

The loud wind never reached the ship,
Yet now the ship moved on!
Beneath the lightning and the Moon
The dead men gave a groan.   330

They groaned, they stirred, they all uprose,
Nor spake, nor moved their eyes;
It had been strange, even in a dream,
To have seen those dead men rise.

The helmsman steered, the ship moved on;   335
Yet never a breeze up-blew;
The mariners all 'gan work the ropes,
Where they were wont to do;
They raised their limbs like lifeless tools —
We were a ghastly crew.   340

The body of my brother's son
Stood by me, knee to knee:
The body and I pulled at one rope,
But he said nought to me.

16 *meteors.*

'I fear thee, ancient Mariner!'   345
Be calm, thou Wedding-Guest!
'Twas not those souls that fled in pain,
Which to their corses[17] came again,
But a troop of spirits blest:

But not by the souls of the men, nor by demons of earth or middle air, but by a blessed troop of angelic spirits, sent down by the invocation of the guardian saint.

For when it dawned — they dropped their arms,   350
And clustered round the mast;
Sweet sounds rose slowly through their mouths,
And from their bodies passed.

Around, around, flew each sweet sound,
Then darted to the Sun;   355
Slowly the sounds came back again,
Now mixed, now one by one.

Sometimes a-dropping from the sky
I heard the sky-lark sing;
Sometimes all little birds that are,   360
How they seemed to fill the sea and air
With their sweet jargoning!

And now 'twas like all instruments,
Now like a lonely flute;
And now it is an angel's song,   365
That makes the heavens be mute.

It ceased; yet still the sails made on
A pleasant noise till noon,
A noise like of a hidden brook
In the leafy month of June,   370
That to the sleeping woods all night
Singeth a quiet tune.

Till noon we quietly sailed on,
Yet never a breeze did breathe:
Slowly and smoothly went the ship,   375
Moved onward from beneath.

17 *corpses.*

The lonesome Spirit from the
south-pole carries on the ship
as far as the Line, in
obedience to the angelic troop,
but still requireth vengeance.

Under the keel nine fathom deep,
From the land of mist and snow,
The spirit slid: and it was he
That made the ship to go.   380
The sails at noon left off their tune,
And the ship stood still also.

The Sun, right up above the mast,
Had fixed her to the ocean:
But in a minute she 'gan stir,   385
With a short uneasy motion —
Backwards and forwards half her length
With a short uneasy motion.

Then like a pawing horse let go,
She made a sudden bound: 390
It flung the blood into my head,
And I fell down in a swound.

The Polar Spirit's fellow-
demons, the invisible
inhabitants of the element,
take part in his wrong; and
two of them relate, one to the
other, that penance long and
heavy for the ancient
Mariner hath been accorded
to the Polar Spirit, who
returneth southward.

How long in that same fit I lay,
I have not to declare;
But ere my living life returned,   395
I heard and in my soul discerned
Two voices in the air.

'Is it he?' quoth one, 'Is this the man?
By him who died on cross,[18]
With his cruel bow he laid full low   400
The harmless Albatross.

The spirit who bideth by himself
In the land of mist and snow,
He loved the bird that loved the man
Who shot him with his bow.'   405

The other was a softer voice,
As soft as honey-dew:
Quoth he, 'The man hath penance done,
And penance more will do.'

18 *Christ, who was crucified on a cross.*

PART VI

FIRST VOICE

'But tell me, tell me! speak again,   410
Thy soft response renewing —
What makes that ship drive on so fast?
What is the ocean doing?'

SECOND VOICE

'Still as a slave before his lord,
The ocean hath no blast;   415
His great bright eye most silently
Up to the Moon is cast —

If he may know which way to go;
For she guides him smooth or grim.
See, brother, see! how graciously   420
She looketh down on him.'

FIRST VOICE

The Mariner hath been cast into a trance; for the angelic power causeth the vessel to drive northward faster than human life could endure.

'But why drives on that ship so fast,
Without a wave or wind?'

SECOND VOICE

'The air is cut away before,
And closes from behind.   425

Fly, brother, fly! more high, more high!
Or we shall be belated:
For slow and slow that ship will go,
When the Mariner's trance is abated.'

The supernatural motion is retarded; the Mariner awakes, and his penance begins anew.

I woke, and we were sailing on   430
As in a gentle weather:
'Twas night, calm night, the moon was high;
The dead men stood together.

All stood together on the deck,
For a charnel-dungeon[19] fitter: 435
All fixed on me their stony eyes,
That in the Moon did glitter.

19 *a burial house, or a prison in which people are left to die.*

The pang, the curse, with which they died,
Had never passed away:
I could not draw my eyes from theirs,   440
Nor turn them up to pray.

The curse is finally expiated. And now this spell was snapt: once more
I viewed the ocean green,
And looked far forth, yet little saw
Of what had else been seen —   445

Like one that on a lonesome road
Doth walk in fear and dread,
And having once turned round walks on,
And turns no more his head;
Because he knows, a frightful fiend   450
Doth close behind him tread.

But soon there breathed a wind on me,
Nor sound nor motion made:
Its path was not upon the sea,
In ripple or in shade.   455

It raised my hair, it fanned my cheek
Like a meadow-gale of spring —
It mingled strangely with my fears,
Yet it felt like a welcoming.

Swiftly, swiftly flew the ship,   460
Yet she sailed softly too:
Sweetly, sweetly blew the breeze —
On me alone it blew.

And the ancient Mariner Oh! dream of joy! is this indeed
beholdeth his native country. The light-house top I see?   465
Is this the hill? is this the kirk?
Is this mine own countree?

We drifted o'er the harbour-bar,[20]
And I with sobs did pray —
O let me be awake, my God!   470
Or let me sleep alway.

The harbour-bay was clear as glass,
So smoothly it was strewn!
And on the bay the moonlight lay,
And the shadow of the Moon.   475

The rock shone bright, the kirk no less,
That stands above the rock:
The moonlight steeped in silentness
The steady weathercock.

And the bay was white with silent light,   480
Till rising from the same,
The angelic spirits leave the Full many shapes, that shadows were,
dead bodies, In crimson colours came.

And appear in their own A little distance from the prow
forms of light. Those crimson shadows were: 485
I turned my eyes upon the deck —
Oh, Christ! what saw I there!

Each corse lay flat, lifeless and flat,
And, by the holy rood![21]
A man all light, a seraph-man,[22]   490
On every corse there stood.

This seraph-band, each waved his hand:
It was a heavenly sight!
They stood as signals to the land,
Each one a lovely light;   495

This seraph-band, each waved his hand,
No voice did they impart —
No voice; but oh! the silence sank
Like music on my heart.

20 *a breakwater or sandbar protecting a harbour.*
21 *the cross on which Christ was crucified.*
22 *a fiery angel.*

But soon I heard the dash of oars,   500
I heard the Pilot's[23] cheer;
My head was turned perforce away,
And I saw a boat appear.

The Pilot and the Pilot's boy,
I heard them coming fast: 505
Dear Lord in Heaven! it was a joy
The dead men could not blast.

I saw a third — I heard his voice:
It is the Hermit good!
He singeth loud his godly hymns   510
That he makes in the wood.
He'll shrieve[24] my soul, he'll wash away
The Albatross's blood.

PART VII

The Hermit of the Wood,

This Hermit good lives in that wood
Which slopes down to the sea.   515
How loudly his sweet voice he rears!
He loves to talk with marineres
That come from a far countree.

He kneels at morn, and noon, and eve —
He hath a cushion plump: 520
It is the moss that wholly hides
The rotted old oak-stump.

The skiff-boat neared: I heard them talk,
'Why, this is strange, I trow!
Where are those lights so many and fair,   525
That signal made but now?'

Approacheth the ship with
wonder.

'Strange, by my faith!' the Hermit said —
'And they answered not our cheer!
The planks looked warped! and see those sails,
How thin they are and sere!   530
I never saw aught like to them,
Unless perchance it were

23 *person who steers ships into harbour.*
24 *administer spiritual absolution.*

Brown skeletons of leaves that lag
My forest-brook along;
When the ivy-tod is heavy with snow,   535
And the owlet whoops to the wolf below,
That eats the she-wolf's young.'

'Dear Lord! it hath a fiendish look —
(The Pilot made reply)
I am a-feared' — 'Push on, push on!'   540
Said the Hermit cheerily.

The boat came closer to the ship,
But I nor spake nor stirred;
The boat came close beneath the ship,
And straight a sound was heard.   545

The ship suddenly sinketh.   Under the water it rumbled on,
Still louder and more dread:
It reached the ship, it split the bay;
The ship went down like lead.

The ancient Mariner is saved   Stunned by that loud and dreadful sound,   550
in the Pilot's boat.   Which sky and ocean smote,
Like one that hath been seven days drowned
My body lay afloat;
But swift as dreams, myself I found
Within the Pilot's boat.   555

Upon the whirl, where sank the ship,
The boat spun round and round;
And all was still, save that the hill
Was telling of the sound.

I moved my lips — the Pilot shrieked   560
And fell down in a fit;
The holy Hermit raised his eyes,
And prayed where he did sit.

I took the oars: the Pilot's boy,
Who now doth crazy go,   565
Laughed loud and long, and all the while
His eyes went to and fro.
'Ha! ha!' quoth he, 'full plain I see,
The Devil knows how to row.'

And now, all in my own countree,   570
I stood on the firm land!
The Hermit stepped forth from the boat,
And scarcely he could stand.

The ancient Mariner
earnestly entreateth the
Hermit to shrieve him; and
the penance of life falls on
him.

'O shrieve me, shrieve me, holy man!
The Hermit crossed his brow.   575
'Say quick,' quoth he, 'I bid thee say —
What manner of man art thou?'

Forthwith this frame of mine was wrenched
With a woful agony,
Which forced me to begin my tale;   580
And then it left me free.

And ever and anon
throughout his future life an
agony constraineth him to
travel from land to land;

Since them, at an uncertain hour,
That agony returns:
And till my ghastly tale is told,
This heart within me burns.   585

I pass, like night, from land to land;
I have strange power of speech;
That moment that his face I see,
I know the man that must hear me:
To him my tale I teach.   590

What loud uproar bursts from that door!
The wedding-guests are there:
But in the garden-bower the bride
And bride-maids singing are:
And hark the little vesper bell,[25]   595
Which biddeth me to prayer!

25 *bell calling people to evening worship.*

O Wedding-Guest! this soul hath been
Alone on a wide wide sea:
So lonely 'twas, that God himself
Scarce seeméd there to be.   600

O sweeter than the marriage-feast,
'Tis sweeter far to me,
To walk together to the kirk
With a goodly company! —

To walk together to the kirk,   605
And all together pray,
While each to his great Father bends,
Old men, and babes, and loving friends
And youths and maidens gay!

*And to teach, by his own
example, love and reverence to
all things that God made and
loveth.*

Farewell, farewell! but this I tell   610
To thee, thou Wedding-Guest!
He prayeth well, who loveth well
Both man and bird and beast.

He prayeth best, who loveth best
All things both great and small;   615
For the dear God who loveth us,
He made and loveth all.

The Mariner, whose eye is bright,
Whose beard with age is hoar,[26]
Is gone: and now the Wedding-Guest   620
Turned from the bridegroom's door.

He went like one that hath been stunned,
And is of sense forlorn:
A sadder and a wiser man,
He rose the morrow morn.   625

(1798)

---

26 *greyish-white.*

GEORGE GORDON, LORD BYRON

(1788–1824)

*R*aised in Aberdeen, Scotland, George Gordon became Lord Byron at age *ten, after the death of his uncle. While a student at Cambridge, he became notorious for his flamboyant life. His first major work,* Childe Harold, *cantos I and II (1812), was based in part on his own European travels. An advocate of liberal causes as a member of the House of Lords, he died in Greece while training soldiers for that country's fight for independence. During his life and after, he was regarded as an almost legendary figure: handsome, athletic, proud, talented, but often filled with guilt and remorse. An accomplished craftsman, his works range from the beautiful lyric "She Walks in Beauty," to the long, satirical, and humorous* Don Juan *(1819–24). In "On This Day I Complete My Thirty-Sixth Year," written shortly before his death, Byron portrays himself as a world-weary individual seeking to find meaning in his life through involvement in the political and military struggles of Greece. In "Who kill'd John Keats?", he displays his long-held disdain for literary reviewers, blaming the death of his contemporary on their attacks of his work.*

She Walks in Beauty

I.

She walks in beauty, like the night
  Of cloudless climes and starry skies;
And all that's best of dark and bright
  Meet in her aspect and her eyes:
5 Thus mellow'd to that tender light
  Which heaven to gaudy day denies.

II.

One shade the more, one ray the less,
  Had half impair'd the nameless grace
Which waves in every raven tress,
10 Or softly lightens o'er her face;
Where thoughts serenely sweet express
  How pure, how dear their dwelling-place.

III.

And on that cheek, and o'er that brow,
  So soft, so calm, yet eloquent,
15 The smiles that win, the tints that glow,
  But tell of days in goodness spent,
A mind at peace with all below,
  A heart whose love is innocent!

(1814)   (1815)

Who kill'd John Keats?

Who kill'd John Keats?
  "I," says the Quarterly,[1]
So savage and Tartarly;
  "'Twas one of my feats."

5 Who shot the arrow?
  "The poet-priest Milman[2]
(So ready to kill man),
  Or Southey, or Barrow."[3]

(1821)   (1830)

---

1 *a conservative literary journal that, in 1818, wrote a scathing review of the poetry of John Keats.*
2 *a professor at Oxford.*
3 *Southey was a minor romantic poet; Barrow, an English travel writer.*

On This Day I Complete My Thirty-Sixth Year

MISSOLONGHI, Jan. 22, 1824.

'Tis time this heart should be unmoved,
    Since others it hath ceased to move:
Yet, though I cannot be beloved,
      Still let me love!

5   My days are in the yellow leaf;
    The flowers and fruits of love are gone;
The worm, the canker, and the grief
      Are mine alone!

The fire that on my bosom preys
10   Is lone as some volcanic isle;
No torch is kindled at its blaze —
      A funeral pile.

The hope, the fear, the jealous care,
    The exalted portion of the pain
15   And power of love, I cannot share,
      But wear the chain.

But 'tis not *thus* — and 'tis not *here* —
    Such thoughts should shake my soul, nor *now*,
Where glory decks the hero's bier,
20   Or binds his brow.

The sword, the banner, and the field,
    Glory and Greece, around me see!
The Spartan, borne upon his shield,
      Was not more free.

25   Awake! (not Greece — she *is* awake!)
    Awake, my spirit! Think through *whom*
Thy life-blood tracks its parent lake,
      And then strike home!

Tread those reviving passions down,
30   Unworthy manhood! — unto thee
Indifferent should the smile or frown
        Of beauty be.

If thou regrett'st thy youth, *why live?*
The land of honourable death
35   Is here: — up to the field, and give
        Away thy breath!

Seek out — less often sought than found —
A soldier's grave, for thee the best;
Then look around, and choose thy ground,
40   And take thy rest.

(1824)

PERCY BYSSHE SHELLEY

(1792–1822)

*B*orn in Field Place, Sussex, Percy Bysshe Shelley lived a stormy life. *Expelled from Oxford for writing a pamphlet on atheism, he eloped with sixteen-year-old Harriet Westbrook, whom he later abandoned for Mary Godwin, the daughter of the political radical William Godwin and author of the novel Frankenstein. In 1818, he moved permanently to Italy, but never settled in one place. He drowned after his sailboat was swamped in a squall. Frequently condemned during his life for his highly unconventional moral, political, and antireligious beliefs, Shelley has been praised for his careful craftsmanship as a poet. In "Ozymandias," the words of the pharaoh are juxtaposed with a description of the desert setting and the present condition of the pharaoh's statue to create an implicit satirical comment on the vainglory of tyrants. "Hymn to Intellectual Beauty," "Ode to the West Wind," and "To a Skylark" illustrate the various ways in which Shelley used his observations of nature to present his themes. In "Hymn," which reveals the influence on the poet of the Greek philosopher Plato's ideas about a more perfect realm existing outside of the physical world, the "unseen Power" which human beings can only briefly experience is compared to summer winds, moonbeams, and rainbows. The West Wind becomes a complex symbol representing, among other things, the interrelationship between life and death and the forces of revolution which may create a better world (a new spring) for people. Like John Keats in "Ode to a Nightingale" and Gerard Manley Hopkins in "The Windhover," Shelley, in "To a Skylark," contrasts the freedom of the bird with the limitations of his own life.*

Hymn to Intellectual Beauty

I

The awful shadow of some unseen Power
   Floats tho' unseen amongst us, — visiting
   This various world with as inconstant wing
As summer winds that creep from flower to flower, —
5   Like moonbeams that behind some piny mountain shower,
     It visits with inconstant glance
     Each human heart and countenance;

Like hues and harmonies of evening, —
　　Like clouds in starlight widely spread, —
10　　　Like memory of music fled, —
　　Like aught that for its grace may be
Dear, and yet dearer for its mystery.

II

Spirit of BEAUTY, that dost consecrate
　　With thine own hues all thou dost shine upon
15　　Of human thought or form, — where art thou gone?
Why dost thou pass away and leave our state,
This dim vast vale of tears, vacant and desolate?
　　　Ask why the sunlight not for ever
　　　Weaves rainbows o'er yon mountain river,
20　Why aught should fail and fade that once is shown,
　　　Why fear and dream and death and birth
　　　Cast on the daylight of this earth
　　　Such gloom, — why man has such a scope
For love and hate, despondency and hope?

III

25　No voice from some sublimer world hath ever
　　To sage or poet these responses given —
　　　Therefore the names of Demon, Ghost, and Heaven,
Remain the records of their vain endeavour,
Frail spells — whose uttered charm might not avail to
　　　sever,
30　　　From all we hear and all we see,
　　　Doubt, chance, and mutability.
Thy light alone — like mist o'er mountains driven,
　　　Or music by the night wind sent,
　　　Thro' strings of some still instrument,
35　　　Or moonlight on a midnight stream,
Gives grace and truth to life's unquiet dream.

IV

Love, Hope, and Self-esteem, like clouds depart
　　And come, for some uncertain moments lent,
　　Man were immortal, and omnipotent,

40 Didst thou, unknown and awful as thou art,
Keep with thy glorious train firm state within his heart.
      Thou messenger of sympathies,
      That wax and wane in lovers' eyes —
Thou — that to human thought art nourishment,
45   Like darkness to a dying flame!
      Depart not as thy shadow came,
      Depart not — lest the grave should be,
Like life and fear, a dark reality.

V

When yet a boy I sought for ghosts, and sped
50   Thro' many a listening chamber, cave and ruin,
      And starlight wood, with fearful steps pursuing
Hopes of high talk with the departed dead.
I called on poisonous names with which our youth is fed;
      I was not heardt — I saw them not —
55   When musing deeply on the lot
Of life, at the sweet time when winds are wooing
      All vital things that wake to bring
      News of birds and blossoming, —
      Sudden, thy shadow fell on me;
60 I shrieked, and clasped my hands in ecstasy!

VI

I vowed that I would dedicate my powers
      To thee and thine — have I not kept the vow?
      With beating heart and streaming eyes, even now
I call the phantoms of a thousand hours
65 Each from his voiceless grave: they have in visioned bowers
      Of studious zeal or love's delight
      Outwatched with me the envious night —
They know that never joy illumed my brow
      Unlinked with hope that thou wouldst free
70   This world from its dark slavery,
      That thou — O awful LOVELINESS,
Wouldst give whate'er these words cannot express.

VII

The day becomes more solemn and serene
　　When noon is past — there is a harmony
75　　　In autumn, and a lustre in its sky,
　　Which thro' the summer is not heard or seen,
　　As if it could not be, as if it had not been!
　　　　Thus let thy power, which like the truth
　　　　Of nature on my passive youth
80　　Descended, to my onward life supply
　　　　Its calm — to one who worships thee,
　　　　And every form containing thee,
　　　　Whom, SPIRIT fair, thy spells did bind
To fear himself, and love all human kind.

(1816)   (1819)

Ozymandias[1]

I met a traveller from an antique land
Who said: Two vast and trunkless legs of stone
Stand in the desert. Near them, on the sand,
Half sunk, a shattered visage lies, whose frown,
5　　And wrinkled lip, and sneer of cold command,
Tell that its sculptor well those passions read
Which yet survive, stamped on these lifeless things,
The hand that mocked them and the heart that fed:
And on the pedestal these words appear:
10　　"My name is Ozymandias, king of kings:
Look on my works, ye Mighty, and despair!"
Nothing beside remains. Round the decay
Of that colossal wreck, boundless and bare
The lone and level sands stretch far away.

(1817)   (1818)

---

1 *a Greek variant of the name of the thirteenth-century* B.C. *Egyptian pharaoh, Ramses II.*

Ode to the West Wind

I

O wild West Wind, thou breath of Autumn's being,
Thou, from whose unseen presence the leaves dead
Are driven, like ghosts from an enchanter fleeing,

Yellow, and black, and pale, and hectic red,
5 Pestilence-stricken multitudes: O thou,
Who chariotest to their dark wintry bed

The wingèd seeds, where they lie cold and low,
Each like a corpse within its grave, until
Thine azure sister of the spring shall blow

10 Her clarion o'er the dreaming earth, and fill
(Driving sweet buds like flocks to feed in air)
With living hues and odours plain and hill:

Wild Spirit, which art moving everywhere;
Destroyer and preserver; hear, Oh hear!

II

15 Thou on whose stream, 'mid the steep sky's commotion,
Loose clouds like earth's decaying leaves are shed,
Shook from the tangled boughs of Heaven and Ocean,

Angels of rain and lightning: there are spread
On the blue surface of thine airy surge,
20 Like the bright hair uplifted from the head

Of some fierce Mænad,[1] even from the dim verge
Of the horizon to the zenith's height
The locks of the approaching storm. Thou dirge[2]

Of the dying year, to which this closing night
25 Will be the dome of a vast sepulchre,
Vaulted with all thy congregated might

---

1 *female worshipers of Dionysus, the Greek god of wine.*
2 *song of mourning.*

Of vapours, from whose solid atmosphere
Black rain, and fire, and hail will burst: Oh hear!

III

Thou who didst waken from his summer dreams
30   The blue Mediterranean, where he lay,
Lulled by the coil of his crystàlline streams,

Beside a pumice isle in Baiæ's bay,[3]
And saw in sleep old palaces and towers
Quivering within the wave's intenser day,

35   All overgrown with azure moss and flowers
So sweet, the sense faints picturing them! Thou
For whose path the Atlantic's level powers

Cleave themselves into chasms, while far below
The sea-blooms and the oozy woods which wear
40   The sapless foliage of the ocean, know

Thy voice, and suddenly grow gray with fear,
And tremble and despoil themselves: Oh hear!

IV

If I were a dead leaf thou mightest bear;
If I were a swift cloud to fly with thee;
45   A wave to pant beneath thy power, and share

The impulse of thy strength, only less free
Than thou, O uncontrollable! If even
I were as in my boyhood, and could be

The comrade of thy wanderings over heaven,
50   As then, when to outstrip thy skiey speed
Scarce seemed a vision; I would ne'er have striven

As thus with thee in prayer in my sore need.
Oh lift me as a wave, a leaf, a cloud!
I fall upon the thorns of life! I bleed!

55   A heavy weight of hours has chained and bowed
One too like thee: tameless, and swift, and proud.

---

3 *city in southwestern Italy.*

V

Make me thy lyre, even as the forest is:
What if my leaves are falling like its own!
The tumult of thy mighty harmonies

60 Will take from both a deep, autumnal tone,
Sweet though in sadness. Be thou, spirit fierce,
My spirit! be thou me, impetuous one!

Drive my dead thoughts over the universe
Like withered leaves to quicken a new birth!
65 And, by the incantation of this verse,

Scatter, as from an unextinguished hearth
Ashes and sparks, my words among mankind!
Be through my lips to unawakened earth

The trumpet of a prophecy! O, wind,
70 If Winter comes, can Spring be far behind?

(1819)   (1820)

To a Skylark

Hail to thee, blithe spirit!
    Bird thou never wert,
That from heaven, or near it,
    Pourest thy full heart
5 In profuse strains of unpremeditated art.

Higher still and higher
    From the earth thou springest
Like a cloud of fire;
    The blue deep thou wingest,
10 And singing still dost soar, and soaring ever singest.

In the golden lightning
    Of the sunken sun,
O'er which clouds are brightning,
    Thou dost float and run;
15 Like an unbodied joy whose race is just begun.

The pale purple even
  Melts around thy flight;
Like a star of heaven,
  In the broad daylight
20 Thou art unseen, but yet I hear thy shrill delight,

Keen as are the arrows
  Of that silver sphere,
Whose intense lamp narrows
  In the white dawn clear,
25 Until we hardly see, we feel that it is there.

All the earth and air
  With thy voice is loud,
As, when night is bare,
  From one lonely cloud
30 The moon rains out her beams, and heaven is overflowed.

What thou art we know not;
  What is most like thee?
From rainbow clouds there flow not
  Drops so bright to see,
35 As from thy presence showers a rain of melody.

Like a poet hidden
  In the light of thought,
Singing hymns unbidden,
  Till the world is wrought
40 To sympathy with hopes and fears it heeded not:

Like a high-born maiden
  In a palace-tower,
Soothing her love-laden
  Soul in secret hour
45 With music sweet as love, which overflows her bower:

Like a glow-worm golden
  In a dell of dew,
Scattering unbeholden
  Its aërial hue
50 Among the flowers and grass, which screen it from the
      view:

Like a rose embowered
　　In its own green leaves,
By warm winds deflowered,
　　Till the scent it gives
55　Makes faint with too much sweet these heavy-wingèd
　　　　thieves:

Sound of vernal showers
　　On the twinkling grass,
Rain-awakened flowers,
　　All that ever was
60　Joyous, and clear, and fresh, thy music doth surpass:

Teach us, sprite or bird,
　　What sweet thoughts are thine:
I have never heard
　　Praise of love or wine
65　That panted forth a flood of rapture so divine.

Chorus Hymeneal,[1]
　　Or triumphal chaunt,
Matched with thine would be all
　　But an empty vaunt,
70　A thing wherein we feel there is some hidden want.

What objects are the fountains
　　Of thy happy strain?
What fields, or waves, or mountains?
　　What shapes of sky or plain?
75　What love of thine own kind? what ignorance of pain?

With thy clear keen joyance
　　Languor cannot be:
Shadow of annoyance
　　Never came near thee:
80　Thou lovest; but ne'er knew love's sad satiety.

1　*marriage hymn.*

Waking or asleep,
  Thou of death must deem
Things more true and deep
  Than we mortals dream,
85 Or how could thy notes flow in such a crystal stream?

We look before and after,
  And pine for what is not:
Our sincerest laughter
  With some pain is fraught;
90 Our sweetest songs are those that tell of saddest thought.

Yet if we could scorn
  Hate, and pride, and fear;
If we were things born
  Not to shed a tear,
95 I know not how thy joy we ever should come near.

Better than all measures
  Of delightful sound,
Better than all treasures
  That in books are found,
100 Thy skill to poet were, thou scorner of the ground!

Teach me half the gladness
  That thy brain must know,
Such harmonious madness
  From my lips would flow,
105 The world should listen then, as I am listening now.

(1820)   (1824)

JOHN KEATS

(1795–1821)

orn in London, John Keats was orphaned at age 14. Although he trained as an apothecary-surgeon, he chose to devote his life to the writing of poetry; in his sonnet "On First Looking into Chapman's Homer," he described the inspiration he received on reading the sixteenth-century translation of Homer's Odyssey. His talents matured rapidly, and in 1819, at the age of 24, he wrote his greatest works, "La Belle Dame Sans Merci," his six famous odes, and several sonnets that, along with those of William Wordsworth, are considered the finest of the romantic era. In "Bright Star" and "When I have fears that I may cease to be," his rich, concrete imagery reflects his deep appreciation for the physical world and his awareness that his worsening health would probably result in his dying before he had fulfilled his love for his fiancée, Fanny Brawne, and his poetic ambitions. The theme of the destructive power of death appears again in "La Belle Dame," in which Keats used the form and imagery of medieval ballads. "Ode to a Nightingale," "Ode on a Grecian Urn," and "To Autumn," three of his best-known poems, reveal Keats's poetic talents at their fullest. The melancholy song of the nightingale, a traditional symbol of suffering transformed into beauty; the burial urn decorated with scenes of life; and the physical splendour of autumn are symbols used to evoke meditations on the nature of art, life and death, and permanence and transience. Imagery that evokes several senses, skilful portrayal of the shifting emotions of the speaker of each poem, the penetrating questions and observations, and the tightly unified stanzas are superb vehicles for Keats's themes. Although he died before his pen had gleaned his "teeming brain," the quality of the works Keats did write marks him as one of the greatest of English poets.

On First Looking into Chapman's Homer

> Much have I travell'd in the realms of gold,
>   And many goodly states and kingdoms seen;
>   Round many western islands have I been
> Which bards in fealty to Apollo[1] hold.
> 5   Oft of one wide expanse had I been told
>   That deep-brow'd Homer[2] ruled as his demesne;
>   Yet did I never breathe its pure serene

---

1 Greek god of music and poetry; also the sun.
2 ninth-century B.C. Greek poet, author of the Iliad and the Odyssey.

Till I heard Chapman[3] speak out loud and bold:
Then felt I like some watcher of the skies
10   When a new planet swims into his ken;
Or like stout Cortez[4] when with eagle eyes
      He star'd at the Pacific — and all his men
Look'd at each other with a wild surmise —
      Silent, upon a peak in Darien.[5]

(1816)

When I have fears

When I have fears that I may cease to be
      Before my pen has glean'd my teeming brain,
Before high-piled books, in charact'ry,[1]
      Hold like rich garners the full-ripen'd grain;
5   When I behold, upon the night's starr'd face,
      Huge cloudy symbols of a high romance,
And think that I may never live to trace
      Their shadows, with the magic hand of chance;
And when I feel, fair creature of an hour!
10   That I shall never look upon thee more,
Never have relish in the faery power
      Of unreflecting love! — then on the shore
Of the wide world I stand alone, and think
Till love and fame to nothingness do sink.

(1818)   (1848)

3 George Chapman, late sixteenth-century English translator of Homer.
4 sixteenth-century Spanish conquerer of Mexico whom Keats confused with Balboa, the first European to see the
   Pacific Ocean.
5 former name of the Isthmus of Panama.

1 printed letters.

Bright star!

Bright star! would I were steadfast as thou art —
    Not in lone splendour hung aloft the night
And watching, with eternal lids apart,
    Like nature's patient, sleepless Eremite,[1]
5   The moving waters at their priestlike task
        Of pure ablution round earth's human shores,
    Or gazing on the new soft fallen mask
        Of snow upon the mountains and the moors —
No — yet still steadfast, still unchangeable,
10   Pillow'd upon my fair love's ripening breast,
To feel for ever its soft fall and swell,
    Awake for ever in a sweet unrest,
Still, still to hear her tender-taken breath,
And so live ever — or else swoon to death.

(1819)   (1838)

Ode to a Nightingale

1

My heart aches, and a drowsy numbness pains
    My sense, as though of hemlock[1] I had drunk,
Or emptied some dull opiate to the drains
    One minute past, and Lethe-wards[2] had sunk:
5   'Tis not through envy of thy happy lot,
        But being too happy in thine happiness, —
            That thou, light-winged Dryad[3] of the trees,
                In some melodious plot
        Of beechen green, and shadows numberless,
10   Singest of summer in full-throated ease.

---

1 *a religious hermit.*

1 *a poison derived from a parsnip-like root, not the common hemlock.*
2 *towards Lethe, in Greek mythology, a river in Hades. Drinking its water caused one to forget the past.*
3 *tree nymph.*

2

O, for a draught of vintage! that hath been
　Cool'd a long age in the deep-delved earth,
Tasting of Flora⁴ and the country green,
　Dance, and Provençal song,⁵ and sunburnt mirth!
15　O for a beaker full of the warm South,
　Full of the true, the blushful Hippocrene,⁶
　　With beaded bubbles winking at the brim,
　　　And purple-stained mouth;
That I might drink, and leave the world unseen,
20　And with thee fade away into the forest dim:

3

Fade far away, dissolve, and quite forget
　What thou among the leaves hast never known,
The weariness, the fever, and the fret
　Here, where men sit and hear each other groan;
25　Where palsy shakes a few, sad, last gray hairs,
　Where youth grows pale, and spectre-thin, and dies;
　　Where but to think is to be full of sorrow
　　　And leaden-eyed despairs,
　Where Beauty cannot keep her lustrous eyes,
30　　Or new Love pine at them beyond to-morrow.

4

Away! away! for I will fly to thee,
　Not charioted by Bacchus⁷ and his pards,
But on the viewless wings of Poesy,
　Though the dull brain perplexes and retards:
35　Already with thee! tender is the night,
　And haply the Queen-Moon is on her throne,
　　Cluster'd around by all her starry Fays;⁸
　　　But here there is no light,
Save what from heaven is with the breezes blown
40　　Through verdurous glooms and winding mossy ways.

---

4 *Roman goddess of flowers.*
5 *in the Middle Ages, Provence, in southern France, was famous for its poets and singers.*
6 *in Greek mythology, the sacred fountain of the muses of poetry.*
7 *Roman god of wine, whose chariot was pulled by leopards (pards).*
8 *fairies.*

5

I cannot see what flowers are at my feet,
  Nor what soft incense hangs upon the boughs,
But, in embalmed darkness, guess each sweet
  Wherewith the seasonable month endows
45   The grass, the thicket, and the fruit-tree wild;
    White hawthorn, and the pastoral eglantine;
      Fast fading violets cover'd up in leaves;
        And mid-May's eldest child,
    The coming musk-rose, full of dewy wine,
50   The murmurous haunt of flies on summer eves.

6

Darkling[9] I listen; and, for many a time
  I have been half in love with easeful Death,
Call'd him soft names in many a mused rhyme,
  To take into the air my quiet breath;
55 Now more than ever seems it rich to die,
    To cease upon the midnight with no pain,
      While thou art pouring forth thy soul abroad
        In such an ecstasy!
    Still wouldst thou sing, and I have ears in vain —
60   To thy high requiem[10] become a sod.

7

Thou wast not born for death, immortal Bird!
  No hungry generations tread thee down;
The voice I hear this passing night was heard
  In ancient days by emperor and clown:
65 Perhaps the self-same song that found a path
    Through the sad heart of Ruth,[11] when, sick for home,
      She stood in tears amid the alien corn;
        The same that oft-times hath
    Charm'd magic casements, opening on the foam
70   Of perilous seas, in faery lands forlorn.

9 in the dark.
10 mass performed for the souls of the dead.
11 in the Old Testament, Ruth was a foreigner who gleaned corn in the fields of ancient Israel; see Ruth 2:3.

8

Forlorn! the very word is like a bell
  To toll me back from thee to my sole self!
Adieu! the fancy cannot cheat so well
  As she is fam'd to do, deceiving elf.
75   Adieu! adieu! thy plaintive anthem fades
    Past the near meadows, over the still stream,
      Up the hill-side; and now 'tis buried deep
        In the next valley-glades:
  Was it a vision, or a waking dream?
80   Fled is that music: — Do I wake or sleep?

(1819)   (1820)

Ode on a Grecian Urn

1

Thou still unravish'd bride of quietness,
  Thou foster-child of silence and slow time,
Sylvan[1] historian, who canst thus express
  A flowery tale more sweetly than our rhyme:
5   What leaf-fring'd legend haunts about thy shape
    Of deities or mortals, or of both,
      In Tempe[2] or the dales of Arcady?[3]
What men or gods are these? What maidens loth?
  What mad pursuit? What struggle to escape?
10   What pipes and timbrels?[4] What wild ecstasy?

---

1 belonging to the woods or forests.
2 a quiet valley in Greece, noted for its beauty.
3 a mountainous area in Greece, symbol of an ideal rural area.
4 a tambourine-like musical instrument.

2

Heard melodies are sweet, but those unheard
　Are sweeter; therefore, ye soft pipes, play on;
Not to the sensual ear, but, more endear'd,
　Pipe to the spirit ditties of no tone:
15　Fair youth, beneath the trees, thou canst not leave
　　Thy song, nor ever can those trees be bare;
　　　Bold Lover, never, never canst thou kiss,
Though winning near the goal — yet, do not grieve;
　　She cannot fade, though thou hast not thy bliss,
20　　　For ever wilt thou love, and she be fair!

3

Ah, happy, happy boughs! that cannot shed
　Your leaves, nor ever bid the Spring adieu;
And, happy melodist, unwearied,
　For ever piping songs for ever new;
25　More happy love! more happy, happy love!
　　For ever warm and still to be enjoy'd,
　　　For ever panting, and for ever young;
All breathing human passion far above,
　　That leaves a heart high-sorrowful and cloy'd,
30　　　A burning forehead, and a parching tongue.

4

Who are these coming to the sacrifice?
　To what green altar, O mysterious priest,
Lead'st thou that heifer lowing at the skies,
　And all her silken flanks with garlands drest?
35　What little town by river or sea shore,
　　Or mountain-built with peaceful citadel,
　　　Is emptied of this folk, this pious morn?
And, little town, thy streets for evermore
　　Will silent be; and not a soul to tell
40　　　Why thou art desolate, can e'er return.

5

O Attic[5] shape! Fair attitude! with brede[6]
   Of marble men and maidens overwrought,
With forest branches and the trodden weed;
   Thou, silent form, dost tease us out of thought
45   As doth eternity: Cold Pastoral!
   When old age shall this generation waste,
      Thou shalt remain, in midst of other woe
Than ours, a friend to man, to whom thou say'st,
   'Beauty is truth, truth beauty,' — that is all
50   Ye know on earth, and all ye need to know.

(1819)   (1820)

To Autumn

1

Season of mists and mellow fruitfulness,
   Close bosom-friend of the maturing sun;
Conspiring with him how to load and bless
   With fruit the vines that round the thatch-eves run;
5   To bend with apples the moss'd cottage-trees,
      And fill all fruit with ripeness to the core;
      To swell the gourd, and plump the hazel shells
With a sweet kernel; to set budding more,
   And still more, later flowers for the bees,
10   Until they think warm days will never cease,
      For Summer has o'er-brimm'd their clammy cells.

2

Who hath not seen thee oft amid thy store?
   Sometimes whoever seeks abroad may find
Thee sitting careless on a granary floor,
15   Thy hair soft-lifted by the winnowing wind;

---

5 *belonging to or relating to Attica, whose capital was Athens.*
6 *a pattern of interwoven designs.*

Or on a half-reap'd furrow sound asleep,
   Drows'd with the fume of poppies, while thy hook
      Spares the next swath and all its twined flowers:
And sometimes like a gleaner thou dost keep
20   Steady thy laden head across a brook;
   Or by a cyder-press, with patient look,
      Thou watchest the last oozings hours by hours.

3

Where are the songs of Spring? Ay, where are they?
   Think not of them, thou hast thy music too, —
25 While barred clouds bloom the soft-dying day,
   And touch the stubble-plains with rosy hue;
Then in a wailful choir the small gnats mourn
   Among the river sallows, borne aloft
      Or sinking as the light wind lives or dies;
30 And full-grown lambs loud bleat from hilly bourn;
   Hedge-crickets sing; and now with treble soft
The red-breast whistles from a garden-croft;
   And gathering swallows twitter in the skies.

(1819)   (1820)

La Belle Dame sans Merci[1]

A BALLAD

I

O what can ail thee, knight-at-arms,
   Alone and palely loitering?
The sedge has wither'd from the lake,
   And no birds sing.

II

5 O what can ail thee, knight-at-arms!
   So haggard and so woe-begone?
The squirrel's granary is full,
   And the harvest's done.

1 *the beautiful lady without pity.*

III

I see a lilly on thy brow,
    With anguish moist and fever dew,
And on thy cheeks a fading rose
    Fast withereth too.

IV

I met a lady in the meads,[2]
    Full beautiful — a faery's child,
Her hair was long, her foot was light,
    And her eyes were wild.

V

I made a garland for her head,
    And bracelets too, and fragrant zone;[3]
She look'd at me as she did love,
    And made sweet moan.

VI

I set her on my pacing steed,
    And nothing else saw all day long,
For sidelong would she bend, and sing
    A faery's song.

VII

She found me roots of relish sweet,
    And honey wild, and manna dew,[4]
And sure in language strange she said —
    'I love thee true'.

VIII

She took me to her elfin grot,[5]
    And there she wept, and sigh'd full sore,
And there I shut her wild wild eyes
    With kisses four.

2 *meadows.*
3 *belt.*
4 *food that miraculously fell from heaven.*
5 *a grotto: a cave or cavern.*

IX

And there she lulled me asleep,
   And there I dream'd — Ah! woe betide!
35   The latest dream I ever dream'd
    On the cold hill side.

X

I saw pale kings and princes too,
   Pale warriors, death-pale were they all;
They cried — 'La Belle Dame sans Merci
40   Hath thee in thrall!'[6]

XI

I saw their starved lips in the gloam,[7]
   With horrid warning gaped wide,
And I awoke and found me here,
    On the cold hill's side.

XII

45   And this is why I sojourn here,
   Alone and palely loitering,
Though the sedge has wither'd from the lake,
    And no birds sing.

(1819)   (1820)

6 *in bondage or slavery.*
7 *twilight.*

Elizabeth Barrett Browning

(1806–1861)

B *arrett Browning, a self-educated classical scholar and poet, was an invalid for much of her life. At the age of 40 she left her notoriously tyrannical father and her home in Wimpole Street, London, and eloped with Robert Browning to Italy, where she lived for the remaining fifteen years of her life; the story of this courtship and her gradual growth towards a belief in and an acceptance of love, transformed into poetry, resulted in the sequence of love poems called the* Sonnets from the Portuguese, *the work for which she is still most popularly known, and which, in its adaptation of the sonnet for the female voice, is still considered one of her most notable achievements. Barrett Browning produced an extensive body of work which reveals a wide thematic range and an innovative use of genre: she provides a reworking of Christian myth in "The Seraphim" (1838) and "The Drama of Exile" (1844); a protest against social and political injustices in* Casa Guidi Windows *(1851); a subversive attack on the middle-class Victorian notions concerning "woman's sphere" in a number of romance-ballads; and a more detailed exploration of the problems facing Victorian women in general, as well as the particular troubles encountered by such figures as the woman artist and the fallen woman, in* Aurora Leigh *(1857), a verse novel which had an immense influence upon later women writers and which Barrett Browning considered "the most mature of my works, and the one into which my highest convictions upon Life and Art have entered."*

from Sonnets from the Portuguese[1]

XXII

When our two souls stand up erect and strong,
Face to face, silent, drawing nigh and nigher,
Until the lengthening wings break into fire
At either curvèd point, — what bitter wrong

5   Can the earth do to us, that we should not long
Be here contented? Think. In mounting higher,
The angels would press on us and aspire

---

1 *the title was an attempt to disguise the personal nature of the sonnets by suggesting that they were translations.*

To drop some golden orb of perfect song
Into our deep, dear silence. Let us stay
10   Rather on earth, Belovèd, — where the unfit
Contrarious moods of men recoil away
And isolate pure spirits, and permit
A place to stand and love in for a day,
With darkness and the death-hour rounding it.

(1850)

XLIII

How do I love thee? Let me count the ways.
I love thee to the depth and breadth and height
My soul can reach, when feeling out of sight
For the ends of Being and ideal Grace.
5   I love thee to the level of everyday's
Most quiet need, by sun and candle-light.
I love thee freely, as men strive for Right;
I love thee purely, as they turn from Praise.
I love thee with the passion put to use
10   In my old griefs, and with my childhood's faith.
I love thee with a love I seemed to lose
With my lost saints, — I love with the breath,
Smiles, tears, of all my life! — and, if God choose,
I shall but love thee better after death.

(1850)

ALFRED, LORD TENNYSON

(1809–1892)

*T*ennyson, the son of a clergyman, was born in Lincolnshire and educated at Cambridge. Here he joined a group of young intellectuals called the Apostles and formed the friendship with Arthur Hallam that had such an influence upon his work. In May of 1850 Tennyson published In Memoriam — the elegy prompted by Hallam's death in 1833 which comprised a cycle of 131 linked poems and which established his reputation. In June of the same year Tennyson married Emily Sellwood, and in November he succeeded Wordsworth as Poet Laureate. His other major works include The Princess (1847), an extended narrative, interspersed with lyric, on the question of women's proper sphere, and the Idylls of the King (1859–74), a reworking of the Arthurian legends. The langorous flowing rhythms, which led W.H. Auden to conclude that Tennyson possessed the "finest ear, perhaps, of any English poet," are frequently undercut by sharp dramatic irony. Like Browning, Tennyson is interested in the depiction of varying, sometimes abnormal, psychological states, and often, as in "Ulysses" and "Tithonus," he uses the vehicle of the dramatic monologue to capture these states. And like Arnold, Tennyson repeatedly provides evidence of a divided self; "The Lady of Shalott," probably his best-known and most anthologized work, contains one of the earliest explorations of the dilemma which would continue to trouble him throughout his poetic career: the tension between the artist's desire for aesthetic withdrawal and the recognition of the need for responsible commitment to society.

from In Memoriam A.H.H.[1] Obit MDCCCXXXIII

1

I held it truth, with him[2] who sings
To one clear harp in divers tones,
That men may rise on stepping-stones
Of their dead selves to higher things.

---

1 Arthur Henry Hallam was Tennyson's close friend at Cambridge, and was engaged to Tennyson's sister. Hallam died on the Continent while travelling with his father in 1833. The 131 lyrics which make up this poem were written between 1833 and 1849.
2 Goethe.

5   But who shall so forecast the years
            And find in loss a gain to match?
            Or reach a hand thro' time to catch
      The far-off interest of tears?

      Let Love clasp Grief lest both be drown'd,
10   Let darkness keep her raven gloss.
            Ah, sweeter to be drunk with loss,
      To dance with Death, to beat the ground,

      Than that the victor Hours should scorn
            The long result of love, and boast,
15   'Behold the man that loved and lost,
      But all he was is overworn.'

                    7

      Dark house,[1] by which once more I stand
            Here in the long unlovely street,
            Doors, where my heart was used to beat
      So quickly, waiting for a hand,

5   A hand that can be clasp'd no more —
            Behold me, for I cannot sleep,
            And like a guilty thing I creep
      At earliest morning to the door.

      He is not here; but far away
10   The noise of life begins again,
            And ghastly thro' the drizzling rain
      On the bald street breaks the blank day.

                    95

      By night we linger'd on the lawn,
            For underfoot the herb was dry;
            And genial warmth; and o'er the sky
      The silvery haze of summer drawn;

5   And calm that let the tapers burn
            Unwavering: not a cricket chirr'd;
            The brook alone far-off was heard,
      And on the board the fluttering urn.[1]

1 *Hallam's home in London.*
1 *the boiling kettle.*

And bats went round in fragrant skies,
10   And wheel'd or lit the filmy shapes[2]
     That haunt the dusk, with ermine capes
And woolly breasts and beaded eyes;

While now we sang old songs that peal'd
     From knoll to knoll, where, couch'd at ease,
15   The white kine glimmer'd, and the trees
Laid their dark arms about the field.

But when those others, one by one,
     Withdrew themselves from me and night,
     And in the house light after light
20   Went out, and I was all alone,

A hunger seized my heart; I read
     Of that glad year which once had been,
     In those fallen leaves which kept their green,
The noble letters of the dead.

25   And strangely on the silence broke
     The silent-speaking words, and strange
     Was love's dumb cry defying change
To test his worth; and strangely spoke

The faith, the vigor, bold to dwell
30   On doubts that drive the coward back,
     And keen thro' wordy snares to track
Suggestion to her inmost cell.

So word by word, and line by line,
     The dead man touch'd me from the past,
35   And all at once it seem'd at last
The living soul was flash'd on mine,

2 *moths.*

And mine in this was wound, and whirl'd
   About empyreal heights of thought,
   And came on that which is, and caught
40 The deep pulsations of the world,

Aeonian[3] music measuring out
   The steps of Time — the shocks of Chance —
   The blows of Death. At length my trance
Was cancell'd, stricken thro' with doubt.

45 Vague words! but ah, how hard to frame
   In matter-moulded forms of speech,
   Or even for intellect to reach
Thro' memory that which I became;

Till now the doubtful dusk reveal'd
50   The knolls once more where, couch'd at ease,
   The white kine glimmer'd, and the trees
Laid their dark arms about the field;

And suck'd from out the distant gloom
   A breeze began to tremble o'er
55   The large leaves of the sycamore,
And fluctuate all the still perfume,

And gathering freshlier overhead,
   Rock'd the full-foliaged elms, and swung
   The heavy-folded rose, and flung
60 The lilies to and fro, and said,

'The dawn, the dawn,' and died away;
   And East and West, without a breath,
   Mixt their dim lights, like life and death,
To broaden into boundless day.

118

Contemplate all this work of Time,
   The giant laboring in his youth;
   Nor dream of human love and truth,
As dying Nature's earth and lime;

---

3 *the music of the spheres which has lasted through eons.*

5   But trust that those we call the dead
              Are breathers of an ampler day
              For ever nobler ends. They say,
           The solid earth whereon we tread

           In tracts of fluent heat began,[1]
10   And grew to seeming-random forms,
              The seeming prey of cyclic storms,[2]
           Till at the last arose the man;

           Who throve and branch'd from clime to clime,
              The herald of a higher race,
15   And of himself in higher place,
           If so he type[3] this work of time

           Within himself, from more to more;
              Or, crown'd with attributes of woe
              Like glories, move his course, and show
20   That life is not as idle ore,

           But iron dug from central gloom,
              And heated hot with burning fears,
              And dipt in baths of hissing tears,
           And batter'd with the shocks of doom

25   To shape and use. Arise and fly
              The reeling Faun, the sensual feast;
              Move upward, working out the beast,
           And let the ape and tiger die.

           (1833–49)   (1850)

1 *the nebular hypothesis held that the earth condensed from gaseous matter thrown off from a nebular mass.*
2 *periodic cataclysms, a reference to the theory of geologic change through catastrophe.*
3 *prefigure.*

Tears, idle tears[1] . . .

'Tears, idle tears, I know not what they mean,
Tears from the depth of some divine despair
Rise in the heart, and gather to the eyes,
In looking on the happy autumn-fields,
5   And thinking of the days that are no more.

'Fresh as the first beam glittering on a sail,
That brings our friends up from the underworld,
Sad as the last which reddens over one
That sinks with all we love below the verge;
10   So sad, so fresh, the days that are no more.

'Ah, sad and strange as in dark summer dawns
The earliest pipe of half-awaken'd birds
To dying ears, when unto dying eyes
The casement slowly grows a glimmering square;
15   So sad, so strange, the days that are no more.

'Dear as remember'd kisses after death,
And sweet as those by hopeless fancy feign'd
On lips that are for others; deep as love,
Deep as first love, and wild with all regret;
20   O Death in Life, the days that are no more!'

(1847)

The Eagle. Fragment

He clasps the crag with crooked hands;
Close to the sun in lonely lands,
Ring'd with the azure world, he stands.

The wrinkled sea beneath him crawls;
5   He watches from his mountain walls,
And like a thunderbolt he falls.

(1851)

---

1 song from Tennyson's The Princess.

The Lady of Shalott

PART I

On either side the river lie
Long fields of barly and of rye,
That clothe the wold and meet the sky;
And thro' the field the road runs by
5   To many-tower'd Camelot;[1]
And up and down the people go,
Gazing where the lilies blow
Round an island there below,
   The island of Shalott.

10 Willows whiten,[2] aspens quiver,
Little breezes dusk and shiver
Thro' the wave that runs for ever
By the island in the river
   Flowing down to Camelot.
15 Four gray walls, and four gray towers,
Overlook a space of flowers,
And the silent isle imbowers
   The Lady of Shalott.

By the margin, willow-veil'd,
20 Slide the heavy barges trail'd
By slow horses; and unhail'd
The shallop flitteth silken-sail'd
   Skimming down to Camelot:
But who hath seen her wave her hand?
25 Or at the casement seen her stand?
Or is she known in all the land,
   The Lady of Shalott?

Only reapers, reaping early
In among the bearded barley,
30 Hear a song that echoes cheerly
From the river winding clearly,
   Down to tower'd Camelot:
And by moon the reaper weary,
Piling sheaves in uplands airy,
35 Listening, whispers, "'Tis the fairy
   Lady of Shalott."

1 legendary seat of King Arthur's court. 2 the wind reveals the white underside of the leaves.

PART II

There she weaves by night and day
A magic web with colours gay.
She has heard a whisper say,
40   A curse is on her if she stay
     To look down to Camelot.
She knows not what the curse may be,
And so she weaveth steadily,
And little other care hath she,
45   The Lady of Shalott.

And moving thro' a mirror clear
That hangs before her all the year,
Shadows of the world appear.
There she sees the highway near
50   Winding down to Camelot:
There the river eddy whirls,
And there the surly village-churls,
And the red cloaks of market girls,
     Pass onward from Shalott.

55   Sometimes a troop of damsels glad,
An abbot on an ambling pad,
Sometimes a curly shepherd-lad,
Or long-hair'd page in crimson clad,
     Goes by to tower'd Camelot;
60   And sometimes thro' the mirror blue
The knights come riding two and two:
She hath no loyal knight and true,
     The Lady of Shalott.

But in her web she still delights
65   To weave the mirror's magic sights,
For often thro' the silent nights
A funeral, with plumes and lights
     And music, went to Camelot:
Or when the moon was overhead,
70   Came two young lovers lately wed;
"I am half sick of shadows," said
     The Lady of Shalott.

PART III

A bow-shot from her bower-eaves,
He rode between the barly-sheaves,
The sun came dazzling thro' the leaves,
And flamed upon the brazen greaves
    Of bold Sir Lancelot.
A red-cross knight for ever kneel'd
To a lady in his shield,
That sparkled on the yellow field,
    Beside remote Shalott.

The gemmy bridle glitter'd free,
Like to some branch of stars we see
Hung in the golden Galaxy.[3]
The bridle bells rang merrily
    As he rode down to Camelot:
And from his blazon'd baldric slung
A mighty silver bugle hung,
And as he rode his armour rung,
    Beside remote Shalott.

All in the blue unclouded weather
Thick-jewell'd shone the saddle-leather,
The helmet and the helmet-feather
Burn'd like one burning flame together,
    As he rode down to Camelot.
As often thro' the purple night,
Below the starry clusters bright,
Some bearded meteor, trailing light,
    Moves over still Shalott.

His broad clear brow in sunlight glow'd;
On burnished hooves his war-horse trode;
From underneath his helmet flow'd
His coal-black curls as on he rode,
    As he rode down to Camelot.
From the bank and from the river
He flash'd into the crystal mirror,
"Tirra lirra," by the river
    Sang Sir Lancelot.

75
80
85
90
95
100
105

3 *Milky Way.*

She left the web, she left the loom,
She made three paces thro' the room,
She saw the water-lily bloom,
She saw the helmet and the plume,
    She look'd down to Camelot.
Out flew the web and floated wide;
The mirror crack'd from side to side;
"The curse is come upon me," cried
    The Lady of Shalott.

PART IV

In the stormy east-wind straining,
The pale yellow woods were waning,
The broad stream in his banks complaining,
Heavily the low sky raining
    Over tower'd Camelot;
Down she came and found a boat
Beneath a willow left afloat,
And round about the prow she wrote
    The Lady of Shalott.

And down the river's dim expanse
Like some bold seër in a trance,
Seeing all his own mischance —
With a glassy countenance
    Did she look to Camelot.
And at the closing of the day
She loosed the chain, and down she lay;
The broad stream bore her far away,
    The Lady of Shalott.

Lying, robed in snowy white
That loosely flew to left and right —
The leaves upon her falling light —
Thro' the noises of the night
    She floated down to Camelot;
And as the boat-head wound along
The willowy hills and fields among,
They heard her singing her last song,
    The Lady of Shalott.

145 Heard a carol, mournful, holy,
Chanted loudly, chanted lowly,
Till her blood was frozen slowly,
And her eyes were darken'd wholly,
　　Turn'd to tower'd Camelot.
150 For ere she reach'd upon the tide
The first house by the water-side,
Singing in her song she died,
　　The Lady of Shalott.

Under tower and balcony,
155 By garden-wall and gallery,
A gleaming shape she floated by,
Dead-pale between the houses high,
　　Silent into Camelot.
Out upon the wharfs they came,
160 Knight and burgher, lord and dame,
And round the prow they read her name,
　　The Lady of Shalott.

Who is this? and what is here?
And in the lighted palace near
165 Died the sound of royal cheer;
And they cross'd themselves for fear,
　　All the knights at Camelot:
But Lancelot mused a little space;
He said, "She has a lovely face;
170 God in his mercy lend her grace,
　　The Lady of Shalott."

(1833)　　　　　　　　　　　　　　　(1842)

Ulysses[1]

It little profits that an idle king,
By this still hearth, among these barren crags,
Match'd with an aged wife, I mete and dole
Unequal laws unto a savage race,
5   That hoard, and sleep, and feed, and know not me.
I cannot rest from travel; I will drink
Life to the lees. All times I have enjoy'd
Greatly, have suffer'd greatly, both with those
That loved me, and alone; on shore, and when
10   Thro' scudding drifts the rainy Hyades[2]
Vext the dim sea. I am become a name;
For always roaming with a hungry heart
Much have I seen and known, — cities of men
And manners, climates, councils, governments,
15   Myself not least, but honor'd of them all, —
And drunk delight of battle with my peers,
Far on the ringing plains of windy Troy.
I am a part of all that I have met;
Yet all experience is an arch wherethro'
20   Gleams that untravell'd world whose margin fades
For ever and for ever when I move.
How dull it is to pause, to make an end.
To rust unburnish'd, not to shine in use!
As tho' to breathe were life! Life piled on life
25   Were all too little, and of one to me
Little remains; but every hour is saved
From that eternal silence, something more,
A bringer of new things; and vile it were
For some three suns to store and hoard myself,
30   And this gray spirit yearning in desire
To follow knowledge like a sinking star,
Beyond the utmost bound of human thought.
   This is my son, mine own Telemachus,

---

1 Ulysses (Greek Odysseus) wandered for ten years following the fall of Troy before returning to his island kingdom of Ithaca and to his wife Penelope and son Telemachus. For Tennyson's sources, see particularly Homer's Odyssey XI.100–137 and Dante's Inferno 26.
2 cluster of stars in the constellation Taurus which are associated with the rainy season.

To whom I leave the sceptre and the isle, —
35 Well-loved of me, discerning to fulfil
This labor, by slow prudence to make mild
A rugged people, and thro' soft degrees
Subdue them to the useful and the good.
Most blameless is he, centred in the sphere
40 Of common duties, decent not to fail
In offices of tenderness, and pay
Meet adoration to my household gods,
When I am gone. He works his work, I mine.
    There lies the port; the vessel puffs her sail;
45 There gloom the dark, broad seas. My mariners,
Souls that have toil'd, and wrought, and thought with
        me, —
That ever with a frolic welcome took
The thunder and the sunshine, and opposed
Free hearts, free foreheads, — you and I are old;
50 Old age hath yet his honor and his toil.
Death closes all; but something ere the end,
Some work of noble note, may yet be done,
Not unbecoming men that strove with Gods.
The lights begin to twinkle from the rocks;
55 The long day wanes; the slow moon climbs; the deep
Moans round with many voices. Come, my friends.
'Tis not too late to seek a newer world.
Push off, and sitting well in order smite
The sounding furrows; for my purpose holds
60 To sail beyond the sunset, and the baths
Of all the western stars, until I die.
It may be that the gulfs will wash us down;
It may be we shall touch the Happy Isles,[3]
And see the great Achilles,[4] whom we knew.
65 Tho' much is taken, much abides; and tho'
We are not now that strength which in old days
Moved earth and heaven, that which we are, we are, —
One equal temper of heroic hearts,
Made weak by time and fate, but strong in will
70 To strive, to seek, to find, and not to yield.

(1833)   (1842)

---

3 the abode of dead heroes, also known as Elysium.
4 Greek hero who fought at Troy. Homer's Illiad revolves around the wrath of Achilles.

Tithonus[1]

The woods decay, the woods decay and fall,
The vapours weep their burthen to the ground,
Man comes and tills the fields and lies beneath,
And after many a summer dies the swan.
5   Me only cruel immortality
Consumes; I wither slowly in thine arms,
Here at the quiet limit of the world,
A white-hair'd shadow roaming like a dream
The ever-silent spaces of the East,
10   Far-folded mists, and gleaming halls of morn.

    Alas! for this gray shadow, once a man —
So glorious in his beauty and thy choice,
Who madest him thy chosen, that he seem'd
To his great heart none other than a God!
15   I ask'd thee, "Give me immortality."
Then didst thou grant mine asking with a smile,
Like wealthy men who care not how they give.
But thy strong Hours indignant work'd their wills,
And beat me down, and marr'd and wasted me,
20   And tho' they could not end me, left me maim'd
To dwell in presence of immortal youth,
Immortal age beside immortal youth,
And all I was, in ashes. Can thy love,
Thy beauty, make amends, tho' even now,
25   Close over us, the silver star,[2] thy guide,
Shines in those tremulous eyes that fill with tears
To hear me? Let me go; take back thy gift:
Why should a man desire in any way
To vary from the kindly race of men,
30   Or pass beyond the goal of ordinance[3]
Where all should pause, as is most meet for all?

1 Eos, goddess of the dawn, loved the mortal Tithonus and begged Zeus to grant him eternal life; she forgot to ask
also for eternal youth.
2 the morning star.
3 appointed limit.

A soft air fans the cloud apart; there comes
A glimpse of that dark world where I was born.
Once more the old mysterious glimmer steals
35   From thy pure brows, and from thy shoulders pure,
And bosom beating with a heart renew'd.
Thy cheek begins to redden thro' the gloom,
Thy sweet eyes brighten slowly close to mine,
Ere yet they blind the stars, and the wild team[4]
40   Which love thee, yearning for thy yoke, arise,
And shake the darkness from their loosen'd manes,
And beat the twilight into flakes of fire.

Lo! ever thus thou growest beautiful
In silence, then before thine answer given
45   Departest, and thy tears are on my cheek.
Why wilt thou ever scare me with thy tears,
And make me tremble lest a saying learnt,
In days far-off, on that dark earth, be true?
"The Gods themselves cannot recall their gifts."

50   Ay me! ay me! with what another heart
In days far-off, and with what other eyes
I used to watch — if I be he that watch'd —
The lucid outline forming round thee; saw
The dim curls kindle into sunny rings;
55   Changed with thy mystic change, and felt my blood
Glow with the glow that slowly crimson'd all
Thy presence and thy portals, while I lay,
Mouth, forehead, eyelids, growing dewy-warm
With kisses balmier than half-opening buds
60   Of April, and could hear the lips that kiss'd
Whispering I knew not what of wild and sweet,
Like that strange song I heard Apollo sing,
While Ilion like a mist rose into towers.[5]

4 *horses that draw the chariot of dawn.*
5 *Troy (Ilion) was supposedly built to the music of Apollo's lyre.*

Yet hold me not for ever in thine East:
65 How can my nature longer mix with thine?
Coldly thy rosy shadows bathe me, cold
Are all thy lights, and cold my wrinkled feet
Upon thy glimmering thresholds, when the steam
Floats up from those dim fields about the homes
70 Of happy men that have the power to die,
And grassy barrows of the happier dead.
Release me, and restore me to the ground;
Thou seëst all things, thou wilt see my grave:
Thou wilt renew thy beauty morn by morn;
75 I earth in earth forget these empty courts,
And thee returning on thy silver wheels.

(1833)   (1860)

ROBERT BROWNING

(1812–1889)

$\mathscr{B}$orn in London and educated mostly at home, Browning eloped with Elizabeth Barrett to Italy in 1846 and did not return to live in England until after her death. When his first significant work, Pauline (1833), prompted the philosopher and critic J.S. Mill to remark on his "intense and morbid self-consciousness," Browning turned to the objective dramatic mode. He is best known for his development of the dramatic monologue, a form that focuses on a single character whose personality is exposed — often indirectly and ironically — through his or her speech. The culmination of Browning's experiments with this form is The Ring and the Book *(1869), ten long monologues focusing on a single event, in which he suggests that the only way of knowing "truth" may be through art. His attempt to give this "truth broken into prismatic hues" is represented here by such ironic works as "The Bishop Orders His Tomb" (1845) and by the surrealistic psychological study "Childe Roland to the Dark Tower Came." His dramatic monologues, along with his notably "unpoetic" language and his interests in psychology, philosophy, and arcane learning, had a great influence on modern poetic movements and particularly upon the poetry of Ezra Pound and T.S. Eliot.*

My Last Duchess

FERRARA[1]

That's my last Duchess painted on the wall,
Looking as if she were alive. I call
That piece a wonder, now: Frà Pandolf's[2] hands
Worked busily a day, and there she stands.
5 Will't please you sit and look at her? I said
'Frà Pandolf' by design, for never read
Strangers like you that pictured countenance,
The depth and passion of its earnest glance,
But to myself they turned (since none puts by
10 The curtain I have drawn for you, but I)

---

1 *the Italian town of Ferrara, during the Renaissance. The Duke of Ferrara's first wife died under suspicious circumstances in 1561. Soon after, he began to negotiate for the hand of the niece of the Count of Tyrol.*
2 *Brother Pandolf, an imaginary painter.*

And seemed as they would ask me, if they durst,
How such a glance came there; so, not the first
Are you to turn and ask thus. Sir, 'twas not
Her husband's presence only, called that spot
15 Of joy into the Duchess' cheek: perhaps
Frà Pandolf chanced to say 'Her mantle laps
Over my lady's wrist too much,' or 'Paint
Must never hope to reproduce the faint
Half-flush that dies along her throat': such stuff
20 Was courtesy, she thought, and cause enough
For calling up that spot of joy. She had
A heart — how shall I say? — too soon made glad,
Too easily impressed; she liked whate'er
She looked on, and her looks went everywhere.
25 Sir, 'twas all one! My favour at her breast,
The dropping of the daylight in the West,
The bough of cherries some officious fool
Broke in the orchard for her, the white mule
She rode with round the terrace — all and each
30 Would draw from her alike the approving speech,
Or blush, at least. She thanked men, — good! but thanked
Somehow — I know not how — as if she ranked
My gift of a nine-hundred-years-old name
With anybody's gift. Who'd stoop to blame
35 This sort of trifling? Even had you skill
In speech — (which I have not) — to make your will
Quite clear to such an one, and say, 'Just this
Or that in you disgusts me; here you miss,
Or there exceed the mark' — and if she let
40 Herself be lessoned so, nor plainly set
Her wits to yours, forsooth, and made excuse,
— E'en then would be some stooping; and I choose
Never to stoop. Oh sir, she smiled, no doubt,
Whene'er I passed her; but who passed without
45 Much the same smile? This grew; I gave commands;
Then all smiles stopped together. There she stands
As if alive. Will't please you rise? We'll meet
The company below, then. I repeat,
The Count your master's known munificence

50   Is ample warrant that no just pretence
      Of mine for dowry will be disallowed;
      Though his fair daughter's self, as I avowed
      At starting, is my object. Nay, we'll go
      Together down, sir. Notice Neptune, though,
55   Taming a sea-horse, thought a rarity,
      Which Claus of Innsbruck³ cast in bronze for me!

(1842)

Soliloquy of the Spanish Cloister

I

Gr-r-r — there go, my heart's abhorrence!
    Water your damned flower-pots, do!
If hate killed men, Brother Lawrence,
    God's blood, would not mine kill you!
5   What? your myrtle-bush wants trimming?
    Oh, that rose has prior claims —
Needs its leaden vase filled brimming?
    Hell dry you up with its flames!

II

At the meal we sit together:
10   *Salve tibi!*¹ I must hear
Wise talk of the kind of weather,
    Sort of season, time of year:
Not a plenteous cork-crop: scarcely
    *Dare we hope oak-galls,*² *I doubt:*
15 *What's the Latin name for 'parsley'?*
    What's the Greek name for Swine's Snout?

3 *imaginary sculptor.*

1 *Hail to thee!*
2 *growths on leaves of oaks, valuable for their tannic acid.*

III

Whew! We'll have our platter burnished,
  Laid with care on our own shelf!
With a fire-new spoon we're furnished,
20   And a goblet for ourself,
Rinsed like something sacrificial
  Ere 'tis fit to touch our chaps —
Marked with L. for our initial!
  (He-he! There his lily snaps!)

IV

25 *Saint*, forsooth! While brown Dolores
    Squats outside the Convent³ bank
With Sanchicha, telling stories,
    Steeping tresses in the tank,
Blue-black, lustrous, thick like horsehairs,
30   — Can't I see his dead eye glow,
Bright as 'twere a Barbary corsair's?⁴
    (That is, if he'd let it show!)

V

When he finishes refection,
    Knife and fork he never lays
35 Cross-wise, to my recollection,
    As do I, in Jesu's praise.
I the Trinity illustrate,
    Drinking watered orange-pulp —
In three sips the Arian⁵ frustrate;
40   While he drains his at one gulp.

VI

Oh, those melons? If he's able
    We're to have a feast! so nice!
One goes to the Abbot's table,
    All of us get each a slice.
45 How go on your flowers? None double?
    Not one fruit-sort can you spy?
Strange! — And I, too, at such trouble,
    Keep them close-nipped on the sly!

---

3 *here, a monastery.*
4 *pirate of the North African coast.*
5 *follower of Arius, the fourth-century heretic who denied the doctrine of the Trinity.*

VII

There's a great text in Galatians,[6]
50   Once you trip on it, entails
Twenty-nine distinct damnations,
      One sure, if another fails:
If I trip him just a-dying,
      Sure of heaven as sure can be,
55   Spin him round and send him flying
      Off to hell, a Manichee?[7]

VIII

Or, my scrofulous French novel
      On grey paper with blunt type!
Simply glance at it, you grovel
60   Hand and foot in Belial's[8] gripe:
If I double down its pages
      At the woeful sixteenth print,
When he gathers his greengages,
      Ope a sieve and slip it in't?

IX

65   Or, there's Satan! — one might venture
      Pledge one's soul to him, yet leave
Such a flaw in the indenture
      As he'd miss till, past retrieve,
Blasted lay that rose-acacia
70   We're so proud of! *Hy, Zy, Hine* . . . [9]
'St, there's Vespers! *Plena gratiâ*
      Ave, Virgo![10] Gr-r-r — you swine!

(1842)

---

6 *usually thought to refer to Galatians 3:10, in the New Testament, which in turn refers to Deuteronomy 28, in the Old Testament, where 29 curses are listed. For other possibilities see Galatians 5:14–15; 5:16–24.*
7 *Manicheism was a popular heresy holding that the world was equally divided between good (God) and evil (Satan). Official Christian doctrine holds God omnipotent in his goodness.*
8 *Satan.*
9 *probably the sound of vesper bells.*
10 *Full of grace, hail, Virgin! The monk garbles his prayer.*

The Bishop Orders His Tomb at Saint Praxed's Church[1]

ROME, 15 —

Vanity, saith the preacher, vanity![2]
Draw round my bed: is Anselm keeping back?
Nephews[3] — sons of mine . . . ah God, I know not!
    Well —
She, men would have to be your mother once,
5   Old Gandolf envied me, so fair she was!
What's done is done, and she is dead beside,
Dead long ago, and I am Bishop since,
And as she died so must we die ourselves,
And thence ye may perceive the world's a dream.
10   Life, how and what is it? As here I lie
In this state-chamber, dying by degrees,
Hours and long hours in the dead night, I ask
'Do I live, am I dead?' Peace, peace seems all.
Saint Praxed's ever was the church for peace;
15   And so, about this tomb of mine. I fought
With tooth and nail to save my niche, ye know:
— Old Gandolf cozened me, despite my care;
Shrewd was that snatch from out the corner South
He graced his carrion with, God curse the same!
20   Yet still my niche is not so cramped but thence
One sees the pulpit o' the epistle-side,[4]
And somewhat of the choir, those silent seats,
And up into the airy dome where live
The angels, and a sunbeam's sure to lurk:
25   And I shall fill my slab of basalt there,
And 'neath my tabernacle[5] take my rest,
With those nine columns round me, two and two,
The odd one at my feet where Anselm stands:

1 Church of Santa Prassede, in Rome.
2 Ecclesiastes 1:2. "Vanity of vanities, saith the Preacher, vanity of vanities."
3 conventional euphemism for illegitimate sons.
4 the right-hand side as one faces the altar.
5 canopy over his tomb.

Peach-blossom marble all, the rare, the ripe
30   As fresh-poured red wine of a mighty pulse.
— Old Gandolf with his paltry onion-stone,[6]
Put me where I may look at him! True peach,
Rosy and flawless: how I earned the prize!
Draw close: that conflagration of my church
35   — What then? So much was saved if aught were missed!
My sons, ye would not be my death? Go dig
The white-grape vineyard where the oil-press stood,
Drop water gently till the surface sink,
And if ye find . . . Ah God, I know not, I! . . .
40   Bedded in store of rotten fig-leaves soft,
And corded up in a tight olive-frail,[7]
Some lump, ah God, of *lapis lazuli*,
Big as a Jew's head cut off at the nape,
Blue as a vein o'er the Madonna's breast . . .
45   Sons, all have I bequeathed you, villas, all,
That brave Frascati[8] villa with its bath,
So, let the blue lump poise between my knees,
Like God the Father's globe on both his hands
Ye worship in the Jesu Church[9] so gay,
50   For Gandolf shall not choose but see and burst!
Swift as a weaver's shuttle fleet our years:
Man goeth to the grave, and where is he?
Did I say basalt for my slab, sons? Black —
'Twas ever antique-black I meant! How else
55   Shall ye contrast my frieze to come beneath?
The bas-relief in bronze ye promised me,
Those Pans and Nymphs ye wot of, and perchance
Some tripod, thyrsus,[10] with a vase or so,
The Saviour at his sermon on the mount,
60   Saint Praxed in a glory,[11] and one Pan
Ready to twitch the Nymph's last garment off,
And Moses with the tables . . . but I know
Ye mark me not! What do they whisper thee,
Child of my bowels, Anselm? Ah, ye hope

---

6 *inferior grade of marble.* 7 *olive basket.* 8 *fashionable resort town in the mountains.* 9 *Church of Il Gesu in Rome.* 10 *classical and pagan ornamentation. The tripod is associated with the priestess of Apollo at Delphi; the thyrsus is the staff carried by Dionysus.* 11 *with a halo.*

65 To revel down my villas while I gasp
    Bricked o'er with beggar's mouldy travertine[12]
    Which Gandolf from his tomb-top chuckles at!
    Nay, boys, ye love me — all of jasper, then!
    'Tis jasper ye stand pledged to, lest I grieve
70 My bath must needs be left behind, alas!
    One block, pure green as a pistachio-nut,
    There's plenty jasper somewhere in the world —
    And have I not Saint Praxed's ear to pray
    Horses for ye, and brown Greek manuscripts,
75 And mistresses with great smooth marbly limbs?
    — That's if ye carve my epitaph aright,
    Choice Latin, picked phrase, Tully's[13] every word,
    No gaudy ware like Gandolf's second line —
    Tully, my masters? Ulpian[14] serves his need!
80 And then how I shall lie through centuries,
    And hear the blessed mutter of the mass,
    And see God made and eaten all day long,[15]
    And feel the steady candle-flame, and taste
    Good strong thick stupefying incense-smoke!
85 For as I lie here, hours of the dead night,
    Dying in state and by such slow degrees,
    I fold my arms as if they clasped a crook,
    And stretch my feet forth straight as stone can point,
    And let the bedclothes, for a mortcloth,[16] drop
90 Into great laps and folds of sculptor's-work:
    And as yon tapers dwindle, and strange thoughts
    Grow, with a certain humming in my ears,
    About the life before I lived this life,
    And this life too, popes, cardinals and priests,
95 Saint Praxed at his sermon on the mount,[17]
    Your tall pale mother with her talking eyes,
    And new-found agate urns as fresh as day,
    And marble's language, Latin pure, discreet,
    — Aha, ELUCESCEBAT[18] quoth our friend?

12 *ordinary limestone.* 13 *Cicero.* 14 *the decadent Latin of Ulpianus was far inferior to that of Cicero.* 15 *reference to doctrine of transubstantiation, the conversion of bread and wine into the body and blood of Christ which is thought to occur during mass.* 16 *funeral pall.* 17 *the Bishop is confusing Praxed with Christ.* 18 "*He was illustrious.*" *Phrase in Ulpianus's Latin, which is part of inscription on Gandalf's tomb. The Ciceronian form would be* elucebat.

100 No Tully, said I, Ulpian at the best!
Evil and brief hath been my pilgrimage.
All *lapis*, all, sons! Else I give the Pope
My villas! Will ye ever eat my heart?
Ever your eyes were as a lizard's quick,
105 They glitter like your mother's for my soul,
Or ye would heighten my impoverished frieze,
Piece out its starved design, and fill my vase
With grapes, and add a vizor and a Term,[19]
And to the tripod ye would tie a lynx
110 That in his struggle throws the thyrsus down,
To comfort me on my entablature
Whereon I am to lie till I must ask
'Do I live, am I dead?' There, leave me, there!
For ye have stabbed me with ingratitude
115 To death — ye wish it — God, ye wish it! Stone —
Gritstone,[20] a-crumble! Clammy squares which sweat
As if the corpse they keep were oozing through —
And no more *lapis* to delight the world!
Well go! I bless ye. Fewer tapers there,
120 But in a row: and, going, turn your backs
— Ay, like departing altar-ministrants,
And leave me in my church, the church for peace,
That I may watch at leisure if he leers —
Old Gandolf, at me, from his onion-stone,
125 As still he envied me, so fair she was!

(1845)

---

19 *a vizor is the eye covering of a helmet; Term is an abbreviation of Terminus, the Roman god of boundaries, and thus, a common symbol of mortality. A term was also the tapered pedestal on which a bust, such as that of Terminus, would be placed.*
20 *sandstone.*

'Childe Roland to the Dark Tower Came'[1]

I

My first thought was, he lied in every word,
    That hoary cripple, with malicious eye
    Askance to watch the working of his lie
On mine, and mouth scarce able to afford
5   Suppression of the glee, that pursed and scored
    Its edge, at one more victim gained thereby.

II

What else should he be set for, with his staff?
    What, save to waylay with his lies, ensnare
    All travellers who might find him posted there,
10   And ask the road? I guessed what skull-like laugh
Would break, what crutch 'gin write my epitaph
    For pastime in the dusty thoroughfare,

III

If at his counsel I should turn aside
    Into that ominous tract which, all agree,
15   Hides the Dark Tower. Yet acquiescingly
I did turn as he pointed: neither pride
Nor hope rekindling at the end descried,
    So much as gladness that some end might be.

IV

For, what with my whole world-wide wandering,
20   What with my search drawn out through years, my hope
    Dwindled into a ghost not fit to cope
With that obstreperous joy success would bring, —
I hardly tried now to rebuke the spring
    My heart made, finding failure in its scope.

---

1 see Edgar's mad song in Shakespeare's King Lear 3.4:171–73. "Child Rowland to the dark tower came, / His word was still — Fie, foh, and fum / I smell the blood of a British man." A childe is a young knight who has not yet proved himself.

V

25   As when a sick man very near to death
       Seems dead indeed, and feels begin and end
       The tears and takes the farewell of each friend,
   And hears one bid the other go, draw breath
   Freelier outside, ('since all is o'er,' he saith,
30   'And the blow fallen no grieving can amend';)

VI

While some discuss if near the other graves
       Be room enough for this, and when a day
       Suits best for carrying the corpse away,
With care about the banners, scarves and staves:
35   And still the man hears all, and only craves
       He may not shame such tender love and stay.

VII

Thus, I had so long suffered in this quest,
       Heard failure prophesied so oft, been writ
       So many times among 'The Band' — to wit,
40   The knights who to the Dark Tower's search addressed
Their steps — that just to fail as they, seemed best,
       And all the doubt was now — should I be fit?

VIII

So, quiet as despair, I turned from him,
       That hateful cripple, out of his highway
45   Into the path he pointed. All the day
Had been a dreary one at best, and dim
Was settling to its close, yet shot one grim
       Red leer to see the plain catch its estray.[2]

IX

For mark! no sooner was I fairly found
50   Pledged to the plain, after a pace or two,
       Than, pausing to throw backward a last view
O'er the safe road, 'twas gone; grey plain all around:
Nothing but plain to the horizon's bound.
       I might go on; naught else remained to do.

2 *someone who has strayed.*

X

55 So, on I went. I think I never saw
        Such starved ignoble nature; nothing throve:
        For flowers — as well expect a cedar grove!
    But cockle, spurge,[3] according to their law
    Might propagate their kind, with none to awe,
60   You'd think; a burr had been a treasure-trove.

XI

    No! penury, inertness and grimace,
        In some strange sort, were the land's portion. 'See
        Or shut your eyes,' said Nature peevishly,
    'It nothing skills: I cannot help my case:
65   'Tis the Last Judgement's fire must cure this place,
        Calcine[4] its clods and set my prisoners free.'

XII

    If there pushed any ragged thistle-stalk
        Above its mates, the head was chopped; the bents
        Were jealous else. What made those holes and rents
70 In the dock's harsh swarth leaves, bruised as to balk
    All hope of greenness? 'tis a brute must walk
        Pashing their life out, with a brute's intents.

XIII

    As for the grass, it grew as scant as hair
        In leprosy; thin dry blades pricked the mud
75   Which underneath looked kneaded up with blood.
    One stiff blind horse, his every bone a-stare,
    Stood stupefied, however he came there:
        Thrust out past service from the devil's stud!

XIV

    Alive? he might be dead for aught I know,
80   With that red gaunt and colloped[5] neck a-strain,
        And shut eyes underneath the rusty mane;
    Seldom went such grotesqueness with such woe;
    I never saw a brute I hated so;
        He must be wicked to deserve such pain.

---

3 cockle is any of several weeds that grow in wheat fields; some of the varieties belong to the spurge family and have an acrid milky juice with purgative properties.
4 pulverize by heat.
5 in folds or ridges.

XV

⁸⁵ I shut my eyes and turned them on my heart.
As a man calls for wine before he fights,
I asked one draught of earlier, happier sights,
Ere fitly I could hope to play my part.
Think first, fight afterwards — the soldier's art:
⁹⁰ One taste of the old time sets all to rights.

XVI

Not it! I fancied Cuthbert's reddening face
Beneath its garniture of curly gold,
Dear fellow, till I almost felt him fold
An arm in mine to fix me to the place,
⁹⁵ That way he used. Alas, one night's disgrace!
Out went my heart's new fire and left it cold.

XVII

Giles then, the soul of honour — there he stands
Frank as ten years ago when knighted first.
What honest man should dare (he said) he durst.
¹⁰⁰ Good — but the scene shifts — faugh! what hangman-
hands
Pin to his breast a parchment? His own bands
Read it. Poor traitor, spit upon and curst!

XVIII

Better this present than a past like that;
Back therefore to my darkening path again!
¹⁰⁵ No sound, no sight as far as eye could strain.
Will the night send a howler[6] or a bat?
I asked: when something on the dismal flat
Came to arrest my thoughts and change their train.

XIX

A sudden little river crossed my path
¹¹⁰ As unexpected as a serpent comes.
No sluggish tide congenial to the glooms;
This, as it frothed by, might have been a bath
For the fiend's glowing hoof — to see the wrath
Of its black eddy bespate with flakes and spumes.

6 *owl.*

XX

115 So petty yet so spiteful! All along,
    Low scrubby alders kneeled down over it;
    Drenched willows flung them headlong in a fit
Of mute despair, a suicidal throng:
The river which had done them all the wrong,
120   Whate'er that was, rolled by, deterred no whit.

XXI

Which, while I forded, — good saints, how I feared
    To set my foot upon a dead man's cheek,
    Each step, or feel the spear I thrust to seek
For hollows, tangled in his hair or beard!
125 — It may have been a water-rat I speared,
    But, ugh! it sounded like a baby's shriek.

XXII

Glad was I when I reached the other bank.
    Now for a better country. Vain presage!
    Who were the strugglers; what war did they wage,
130 Whose savage trample thus could pad the dank
Soil to a plash? Toads in a poisoned tank,
    Or wild cats in a red-hot iron cage —

XXIII

The fight must so have seemed in that fell cirque.
    What penned them there, with all the plain to choose?
135   No foot-print leading to that horrid mews,
None out of it. Mad brewage set to work
Their brains, no doubt, like galley-slaves the Turk
    Pits for his pastime, Christians against Jews.

XXIV

And more than that — a furlong on — why, there!
140   What bad use was that engine for, that wheel,
    Or brake, not wheel — that harrow fit to reel
Men's bodies out like silk? with all the air
Of Tophet's tool,[7] on earth left unaware,
    Or brought to sharpen its rusty teeth of steel.

---

7 *hell's tool.*

XXV

145   Then came a bit of stubbed ground, once a wood,
        Next a marsh, it would seem, and now mere earth
        Desperate and done with; (so a fool finds mirth,
    Makes a thing and then mars it, till his mood
    Changes and off he goes!) within a rood —
150   Bog, clay and rubble, sand and stark black dearth.

XXVI

    Now blotches rankling, coloured gay and grim,
        Now patches where some leanness of the soil's
        Broke into moss or substances like boils;
    Then came some palsied oak, a cleft in him
155   Like a distorted mouth that splits its rim
        Gaping at death, and dies while it recoils.

XXVII

    And just as far as ever from the end!
        Naught in the distance but the evening, naught
        To point my footsteps further! At the thought,
160   A great black bird, Apollyon's bosom-friend,[8]
    Sailed past, nor beat his wide wing dragon-penned[9]
        That brushed my cap — perchance the guide I sought.

XXVIII

    For, looking up, aware I somehow grew,
        'Spite of the dusk, the plain had given place
165   All round to mountains — with such name to grace
    Mere ugly heights and heaps now stolen in view.
    How thus they had surprised me, — solve it, you!
        How to get from them was no clearer case.

XXIX

    Yet half I seemed to recognize some trick
170   Of mischief happened to me, God knows when —
        In a bad dream perhaps. Here ended, then,
    Progress this way. When, in the very nick
    Of giving up, one time more, came a click
        As when a trap shuts — you're inside the den!

8 in Revelations 9:11, the devil is called Apollyon, the destroyer.
9 with pinions like a dragon.

XXX

175 Burningly it came on me all at once,
    This was the place! those two hills on the right,
    Crouched like two bulls locked horn in horn in fight;
While to the left, a tall scalped mountain . . . Dunce,
Dotard, a-dozing at the very nonce,
180   After a life spent training for the sight!

XXXI

What in the midst lay but the Tower itself?
    The round squat turret, blind as the fool's heart,
    Built of brown stone, without a counterpart
In the whole world. The tempest's mocking elf
185 Points to the shipman thus the unseen shelf
    He strikes on, only when the timbers start.

XXXII

Not see? because of night perhaps? — why, day
    Came back again for that! before it left,
    The dying sunset kindled through a cleft:
190 The hills, like giants at a hunting, lay,
Chin upon hand, to see the game at bay, —
    'Now stab and end the creature — to the heft!'

XXXIII

Not hear? when noise was everywhere! it tolled
    Increasing like a bell. Names in my ears
    Of all the lost adventurers my peers, —
195 How such a one was strong, and such was bold,
And such was fortunate, yet each of old
    Lost, lost! one moment knelled the woe of years.

XXXIV

There they stood, ranged along the hill-sides, met
200   To view the last of me, a living frame
    For one more picture! in a sheet of flame
I saw them and I knew them all. And yet
Dauntless the slug-horn[10] to my lips I set,
    And blew. *'Childe Roland to the Dark Tower came.'*

(1855)

10 *trumpet.*

WALT WHITMAN

(1819–1892)

*orn on Long Island, New York (referred to by its native name, Pau-
manok, in many of his poems), Walt Whitman worked as a labourer,
teacher, printer, journalist, and, during the American Civil War, as a nurse.
Leaves of Grass, first published in 1855 and revised and expanded several
times during his life, was the first major collection by an American poet, and
influenced such twentieth-century American poets as Hart Crane and Allen Gins-
berg. Celebrating the diversity of the United States and the dignity of the common
person, the poems were praised by the poet-essayist Ralph Waldo Emerson, but
often criticized by reviewers for what they considered obscene passages. Their central
figure is a speaker who embodies the diversity and greatness of American life.
While many of Whitman's poems have justly been described as massive and form-
less, others, such as "Out of the Cradle Endlessly Rocking" and "While Lilacs Last
in the Dooryard Bloom'd," are tightly knit and intricately developed. In the former,
the speaker traces his birth as a poet back to his childhood when he heard a mock-
ingbird mourning for its lost mate. In the latter, the death and funeral procession of
Abraham Lincoln are the occasion for an elegy examining the interrelationships
between life, death, and love. Whitman introduces his major symbols (the mocking-
bird, the sea, and the moon in "Out of the Cradle," and the hermit thrush, lilac
leaf, and evening star in "When Lilacs") early in the poems and develops their
meanings in succeeding sections.*

There Was a Child Went Forth

There was a child went forth every day,
And the first object he look'd upon, that object he became,
And that object became part of him for the day or a certain
      part of the day,
Or for many years or stretching cycles of years.

5   The early lilacs became part of this child,
And grass and white and red morning-glories, and white
      and red clover, and the song of the phœbe-bird,
And the Third-month[1] lambs and the sow's pink-faint
      litter, and the mare's foal and the cow's calf,

---

1 *Quaker name for March.*

And the noisy brood of the barnyard or by the mire of the
pond-side,

And the fish suspending themselves so curiously below
there, and the beautiful curious liquid,

10   And the water-plants with their graceful flat heads, all
became part of him.

The field-sprouts; of Fourth-month and Fifth-month[2]
became part of him,

Winter-grain sprouts and those of the light-yellow corn,
and the esculent roots of the garden,

And the apple-trees cover'd with blossoms and the fruit
afterward, and wood-berries, and the commonest
weeds by the road,

And the old drunkard staggering home from the outhouse
of the tavern whence he had lately risen,

15   And the schoolmistress that pass'd on her way to the
school,

And the friendly boys that pass'd, and the quarrelsome
boys,

And the tidy and fresh-cheek'd girls, and the barefoot
negro boy and girl,

And all the changes of city and country wherever he went.

His own parents, he that had father'd him and she that had
conceiv'd him in her womb and birth'd him,

20   They gave this child more of themselves than that,

They gave him afterward every day, they became part of
him.

The mother at home quietly placing the dishes on the
supper-table,

The mother with mild words, clean her cap and gown, and
wholesome odor falling off her person and clothes
as she walks by,

The father, strong, self-sufficient, manly, mean, anger'd,
unjust,

2 *Quaker names for April and May.*

25   The blow, the quick loud word, the tight bargain, the crafty
        lure,

The family usages, the language, the company, the
        furniture, the yearning and swelling heart,

Affection that will not be gainsay'd, the sense of what is
        real, the thought if after all it should prove unreal,

The doubts of day-time and the doubts of night-time, the
        curious whether and how,

Whether that which appears so is so, or is it all flashes and
        specks?

30   Men and women crowding fast in the streets, if they are
        not flashes and specks what are they?

The streets themselves and the façades of houses, and
        goods in the windows,

Vehicles, teams, the heavy-plank'd wharves, the huge
        crossing at the ferries,

The village on the highland seen from afar at sunset, the
        river between,

Shadows, aureola and mist, the light falling on roofs and
        gables of white or brown two miles off,

35   The schooner near by sleepily dropping down the tide, the
        little boat slack-tow'd astern,

The hurrying tumbling waves, quick-broken crests,
        slapping,

The strata of color'd clouds, the long bar of maroon-tint
        away solitary by itself, the spread of purity it lies
        motionless in,

The horizon's edge, the flying sea-crow, the fragrance of
        salt marsh and shore mud,

These became part of that child who went forth every day,
        and who now goes, and will always go forth every
        day.

(1855)   (1871)

Out of the Cradle Endlessly Rocking

Out of the cradle endlessly rocking,
Out of the mocking-bird's[1] throat, the musical shuttle,
Out of the Ninth-month[2] midnight,
Over the sterile sands and the fields beyond, where the
    child leaving his bed wander'd alone, bareheaded,
    barefoot,
5   Down from the shower'd halo,
Up from the mystic play of shadows twining and twisting
    as if they were alive,
Out from the patches of briers and blackberries,
From the memories of the bird that chanted to me,
From your memories sad brother, from the fitful risings
    and fallings I heard,
10   From under that yellow half-moon late-risen and swollen
    as if with tears,
From those beginning notes of yearning and love there in
    the mist,
From the thousand responses of my heart never to cease,
From the myriad thence-arous'd words,
From the word stronger and more delicious than any,
15   From such as now they start the scene revisiting,
As a flock, twittering, rising, or overhead passing,
Borne hither, ere all eludes me, hurriedly,
A man, yet by these tears a little boy again,
Throwing myself on the sand, confronting the waves,
20   I, chanter of pains and joys, uniter of here and hereafter,
Taking all hints to use them, but swiftly leaping beyond
    them,
A reminiscence sing.

---

1 *a small American bird which can imitate the songs of other birds.*
2 *Quaker name for September.*

Once Paumanok,[3]
When the lilac-scent was in the air and Fifth-month[4] grass
    was growing,
25   Up this seashore in some briers,
Two feather'd guests from Alabama, two together,
And their nest, and four light-green eggs spotted with
    brown,
And every day the he-bird to and fro near at hand,
And every day the she-bird crouch'd on her nest, silent,
    with bright eyes,
30   And every day I, a curious boy, never too close, never
    disturbing them,
Cautiously peering, absorbing, translating.

Shine! shine! shine!
Pour down your warmth, great sun!
While we bask, we two together.

35   *Two together!*
Winds blow south, or winds blow north,
Day come white, or night come black,
Home, or rivers and mountains from home,
Singing all time, minding no time,
40   *While we two keep together.*

Till of a sudden,
May-be kill'd, unknown to her mate,
One forenoon the she-bird crouch'd not on the nest,
Nor return'd that afternoon, nor the next,
45   Nor ever appear'd again.

And thenceforward all summer in the sound of the sea,
And at night under the full of the moon in calmer weather,
Over the hoarse surging of the sea,
Or flitting from brier to brier by day,
50   I saw, I heard at intervals the remaining one, the he-bird,
The solitary guest from Alabama.

3   *native name for Long Island.*
4   *Quaker name for May.*

Blow! blow! blow!
Blow up sea-winds along Paumanok's shore;
I wait and I wait till you blow my mate to me.

55   Yes, when the stars glisten'd,
All night long on the prong of a moss-scallop'd stake,
Down almost amid the slapping waves,
Sat the lone singer wonderful causing tears.

He call'd on his mate,
60   He pour'd forth the meanings which I of all men know.

Yes my brother I know,
The rest might not, but I have treasur'd every note,
For more than once dimly down to the beach gliding,
Silent, avoiding the moonbeams, blending myself with the
       shadows,
65   Recalling now the obscure shapes, the echoes, the sounds
       and sights after their sorts,
The white arms out in the breakers tirelessly tossing,
I, with bare feet, a child, the wind wafting my hair,
Listen'd long and long.

Listen'd to keep, to sing, now translating the notes,
70   Following you my brother.

Soothe! soothe! soothe!
Close on its wave soothes the wave behind,
And again another behind embracing and lapping, every one close,
But my love soothes not me, not me.

75   *Low hangs the moon, it rose late,*
It is lagging — O I think it is heavy with love, with love.

O madly the sea pushes upon the land,
With love, with love.

O night! do I not see my love fluttering out among the breakers?
80   *What is that little black thing I see there in the white?*

Loud! loud! loud!
Loud I call to you, my love!

High and clear I shoot my voice over the waves,
85 *Surely you must know who is here, is here,*
You must know who I am, my love.

Low-hanging moon!
What is that dusky spot in your brown yellow?
O it is the shape, the shape of my mate!
O moon do not keep her from me any longer.

90 *Land! land! O land!*
Whichever way I turn, O I think you could give me my mate back
        again if you only would,
For I am almost sure I see her dimly whichever way I look.

O rising stars!
Perhaps the one I want so much will rise, will rise with some of you.

95 *O throat! O trembling throat!*
Sound clearer through the atmosphere!
Pierce the woods, the earth,
Somewhere listening to catch you must be the one I want.

Shake out carols!
100 *Solitary here, the night's carols!*
Carols of lonesome love! death's carols!
Carols under that lagging, yellow, waning moon!
O under that moon where she droops almost down into the sea!
O reckless despairing carols.

105 *But soft! sink low!*
Soft! let me just murmur,
And do you wait a moment you husky-nois'd sea,
For somewhere I believe I heard my mate responding to me,
So faint, I must be still, be still to listen,
110 *But not altogether still, for then she might not come immediately to me.*

Hither my love!
Here I am! here!
With this just-sustain'd note I announce myself to you,
This gentle call is for you my love, for you.

115 *Do not be decoy'd elsewhere,*
That is the whistle of the wind, it is not my voice,
That is the fluttering, the fluttering of the spray,
Those are the shadows of leaves.

O darkness! O in vain!
120 *O I am very sick and sorrowful.*

O brown halo in the sky near the moon, drooping upon the sea!
O troubled reflection in the sea!
O throat! O throbbing heart!
And I singing uselessly, uselessly all the night.

125 *O past! O happy life! O songs of joy!*
In the air, in the woods, over fields,
Loved! loved! loved! loved! loved!
But my mate no more, no more with me!
We two together no more.

130 The aria[5] sinking,
All else continuing, the stars shining,
The winds blowing, the notes of the bird continuous
  echoing,
With angry moans the fierce old mother incessantly
  moaning,
On the sands of Paumanok's shore gray and rustling,
135 The yellow half-moon enlarged, sagging down, drooping,
  the face of the sea almost touching,
The boy ecstatic, with his bare feet the waves, with his hair
  the atmosphere dallying,
The love in the heart long pent, now loose, now at last
  tumultuously bursting,

5 *an extended melody sung in an opera.*

The aria's meaning, the ears, the soul, swiftly depositing,
The strange tears down the cheeks coursing,
140   The colloquy[6] there, the trio, each uttering,
The undertone, the savage old mother incessantly crying,
To the boy's soul's questions sullenly timing, some
       drown'd secret hissing,
To the outsetting bard.[7]

Demon or bird! (said the boy's soul,)
145   Is it indeed toward your mate you sing? or is it really to
       me?
For I, that was a child, my tongue's use sleeping, now I
       have heard you,
Now in a moment I know what I am for, I awake,
And already a thousand singers, a thousand songs, clearer,
       louder and more sorrowful than yours,
A thousand warbling echoes have started to life within me,
       never to die.

150   O you singer solitary, singing by yourself, projecting me,
O solitary me listening, never more shall I cease
       perpetuating you,
Never more shall I escape, never more the reverberations,
Never more the cries of unsatisfied love be absent from
       me,
Never again leave me to be the peaceful child I was before
       what there in the night,
155   By the sea under the yellow and sagging moon,
The messenger there arous'd, the fire, the sweet hell
       within,
The unknown want, the destiny of me.

O give me the clew! (it lurks in the night here somewhere,)
O if I am to have so much, let me have more!

6 *a conversation.*
7 *a poet.*

160   A word then, (for I will conquer it,)
The word final, superior to all,
Subtle, sent-up — what is it? — I listen;
Are you whispering it, and have been all the time, you sea-
    waves?
Is that it from your liquid rims and wet sands?

165   Whereto answering, the sea,
Delaying not, hurrying not,
Whisper'd me through the night, and very plainly before
    daybreak,
Lisp'd to me the low and delicious word death,
And again death, death, death, death.
170   Hissing melodious, neither like the bird nor like my arous'd
    child's heart,
But edging near as privately for me rustling at my feet,
Creeping thence steadily up to my ears and laving me
    softly all over,
Death, death, death, death, death.

Which I do not forget,
175   But fuse the song of my dusky demon and brother,
That he sang to me in the moonlight on Paumanok's gray
    beach,
With the thousand responsive songs at random,
My own songs awaked from that hour,
And with them the key, the word up from the waves,
180   The word of the sweetest song and all songs,
That strong and delicious word which, creeping to my feet,
(Or like some old crone rocking the cradle, swathed in
    sweet garments, bending aside,)
The sea whisper'd me.

(1859)   (1881)

When Lilacs Last in the Dooryard Bloom'd

1

When lilacs last in the dooryard bloom'd,
And the great star early droop'd in the western sky in the
      night,
I mourn'd, and yet shall mourn with ever-returning spring.

Ever-returning spring, trinity sure to me you bring,
Lilac blooming perennial and drooping star in the west,
And thought of him[1] I love.

2

O powerful western fallen star!
O shades of night — O moody, tearful night!
O great star disappear'd — O the black murk that hides the
      star!
O cruel hands that hold me powerless — O helpless soul
      of me!
O harsh surrounding cloud that will not free my soul.

3

In the dooryard fronting an old farm-house near the white-
      wash'd palings,
Stands the lilac-bush tall-growing with heart-shaped leaves
      of rich green,
With many a pointed blossom rising delicate, with the
      perfume strong I love,
With every leaf a miracle — and from this bush in the
      dooryard,
With delicate-color'd blossoms and heart-shaped leaves of
      rich green,
A sprig with its flower I break.

4

In the swamp in secluded recesses,
A shy and hidden bird is warbling a song.

1 *Abraham Lincoln, American president assassinated April 14, 1865.*

20 Solitary the thrush,[2]
The hermit withdrawn to himself, avoiding the
    settlements,
Sings by himself a song.

Song of the bleeding throat,
Death's outlet song of life, (for well dear brother I know,
25 If thou wast not granted to sing thou would'st surely die.)

5

Over the breast of the spring, the land, amid cities,
Amid lanes and through old woods, where lately the violets
    peep'd from the ground, spotting the gray debris,
Amid the grass in the fields each side of the lanes, passing
    the endless grass,
Passing the yellow-spear'd wheat, every grain from its
    shroud in the dark-brown fields uprisen,
30 Passing the apple-tree blows of white and pink in the
    orchards,
Carrying a corpse to where it shall rest in the grave,
Night and day journeys a coffin.[3]

6

Coffin that passes through lanes and streets,
Through day and night with the great cloud darkening the
    land,
35 With the pomp of the inloop'd flags with the cities draped
    in black,
With the show of the States themselves as of crape-veil'd
    women standing,
With processions long and winding and the flambeaus of
    the night,
With the countless torches lit, with the silent sea of faces
    and the unbared heads,
With the waiting depot, the arriving coffin, and the sombre
    faces,
40 With dirges through the night, with the thousand voices
    rising strong and solemn,

---

2 *a thrush, seldom seen, but whose beautiful song is often heard in the spring.*
3 *Lincoln's coffin was carried from Washington, D.C., to Springfield, Illinois.*

With all the mournful voices of the dirges pour'd around
the coffin,
The dim-lit churches and the shuddering organs — where
amid these you journey,
With the tolling tolling bells' perpetual clang,
Here, coffin that slowly passes,
45   I give you my sprig of lilac.

7

(Nor for you, for one alone,
Blossoms and branches green to coffins all I bring,
For fresh as the morning, thus would I chant a song for
you O sane and sacred death.

All over bouquets of roses,
50   O death, I cover you over with roses and early lilies,
But mostly and now the lilac that blooms the first,
Copious I break, I break the sprigs from the bushes,
With loaded arms I come, pouring for you,
For you and the coffins all of you O death.)

8

55   O western orb sailing the heaven,
Now I know what you must have meant as a month since I
walk'd,
As I walk'd in silence the transparent shadowy night,
As I saw you had something to tell as you bent to me night
after night,
As you droop'd from the sky low down as if to my side,
(while the other stars all look'd on,)
60   As we wander'd together the solemn night, (for something
I know not what kept me from sleep,)
As the night advanced, and I saw on the rim of the west
how full you were of woe,
As I stood on the rising ground in the breeze in the cool
transparent night,
As I watch'd where you pass'd and was lost in the
netherward black of the night,
As my soul in its trouble dissatisfied sank, as where you
sad orb,
65   Concluded, dropt in the night, and was gone.

9

Sing on there in the swamp,
O singer bashful and tender, I hear your notes, I hear your
    call,
I hear, I come presently, I understand you,
But a moment I linger, for the lustrous star has detain'd
    me,
70   The star my departing comrade holds and detains me.

10

O how shall I warble myself for the dead one there I
    loved?
And how shall I deck my song for the large sweet soul that
    has gone?
And what shall my perfume be for the grave of him I love?

Sea-winds blown from east and west,
75   Blown from the Eastern sea and blown from the Western
    sea, till there on the prairies meeting,
These and with these and the breath of my chant,
I'll perfume the grave of him I love.

11

O what shall I hang on the chamber walls?
And what shall the pictures be that I hang on the walls,
80   To adorn the burial-house of him I love?

Pictures of growing spring and farms and homes,
With the Fourth-month[4] eve at sundown, and the gray
    smoke lucid and bright,
With floods of the yellow gold of the gorgeous, indolent,
    sinking sun, burning, expanding the air,
With the fresh sweet herbage under foot, and the pale
    green leaves of the trees prolific,
85   In the distance the flowing glaze, the breast of the river,
    with a wind-dapple here and there,
With ranging hills on the banks, with many a line against
    the sky, and shadows,

4 *Quaker name for April.*

And the city at hand with dwellings so dense, and stacks of
chimneys,
And all the scenes of life and the workshops, and the
workmen homeward returning.

12

Lo, body and soul — this land,
My own Manhattan with spires, and the sparkling and
hurrying tides, and the ships,
The varied and ample land, the South and the North in the
light,
Ohio's shores and flashing Missouri,
And ever the far-spreading prairies cover'd with grass and
corn.

Lo, the most excellent sun so calm and haughty,
The violet and purple morn with just-felt breezes,
The gentle soft-born measureless light,
The miracle spreading bathing all, the fulfill'd noon,
The coming eve delicious, the welcome night and the stars,
Over my cities shining all, enveloping man and land.

13

Sing on, sing on you gray-brown bird,
Sing from the swamps, the recesses, pour your chant from
the bushes,
Limitless out of the dusk, out of the cedars and pines.

Sing on dearest brother, warble your reedy song,
Loud human song, with voice of uttermost woe.

O liquid and free and tender!
O wild and loose to my soul — O wondrous singer!
You only I hear — yet the star holds me, (but will soon
depart,)
Yet the lilac with mastering odor holds me.

14

Now while I sat in the day and look'd forth,
In the close of the day with its light and the fields of
    spring, and the farmers preparing their crops,
110   In the large unconscious scenery of my land with its lakes
    and forests,
In the heavenly aerial beauty, (after the perturb'd winds
    and the storms,)
Under the arching heavens of the afternoon swift passing,
    and the voices of children and women,
The many-moving sea-tides, and I saw the ships how they
    sail'd,
And the summer approaching with richness, and the fields
    all busy with labor,
115   And the infinite separate houses, how they all went on,
    each with its meals and minutia of daily usages,
And the streets how their throbbings throbb'd, and the
    cities pent — lo, then and there,
Falling upon them all and among them all, enveloping me
    with the rest,
Appear'd the cloud, appear'd the long black trail,
And I knew death, its thought, and the sacred knowledge
    of death.

120   Then with the knowledge of death as walking one side of
    me,
And the thought of death close-walking the other side of
    me,
And I in the middle as with companions, and as holding
    the hands of companions,
I fled forth to the hiding receiving night that talks not,
Down to the shores of the water, the path by the swamp in
    the dimness,
125   To the solemn shadowy cedars and ghostly pines so still.

And the singer so shy to the rest receiv'd me,
The gray-brown bird I know receiv'd us comrades three,
And he sang the carol of death, and a verse for him I love.

From deep secluded recesses,
From the fragrant cedars and the ghostly pines so still,
Came the carol of the bird.

And the charm of the carol rapt me,
As I held as if by their hands my comrades in the night,
And the voice of my spirit tallied the song of the bird.

Come lovely and soothing death,
Undulate round the world, serenely arriving, arriving,
In the day, in the night, to all, to each,
Sooner or later delicate death.

Prais'd be the fathomless universe,
For life and joy, and for objects and knowledge curious,
And for love, sweet love — but praise! praise! praise!
For the sure-enwinding arms of cool-enfolding death.

Dark mother always gliding near with soft feet,
Have none chanted for thee a chant of fullest welcome?
Then I chant it for thee, I glorify thee above all,
I bring thee a song that when thou must indeed come, come
*   unfalteringly.*

Approach strong deliveress,
When it is so, when thou hast taken them I joyously sing the dead,
Lost in the loving floating ocean of thee,
Laved in the flood of thy bliss O death.

From me to thee glad serenades,
Dances for thee I propose saluting thee, adornments and feastings for
*   thee,*
And the sights of the open landscape and the high-spread sky are fitting,
And life and the fields, and the huge and thoughtful night.

The night in silence under many a star,
The ocean shore and the husky whispering wave whose voice I know,
And the soul turning to thee O vast and well-veil'd death,
And the body gratefully nestling close to thee.

Over the tree-tops I float thee a song,

160   *Over the rising and sinking waves, over the myriad fields and the*
                prairies wide,

Over the dense-pack'd cities all and the teeming wharves and ways,

I float this carol with joy, with joy to thee O death.

15

To the tally[5] of my soul,

Loud and strong kept up the gray-brown bird,

165   With pure deliberate notes spreading filling the night.

Loud in the pines and cedars dim,

Clear in the freshness moist and the swamp-perfume,

And I with my comrades there in the night.

While my sight that was bound in my eyes unclosed,

170   As to long panoramas of visions.

And I saw askant the armies,[6]

I saw as in noiseless dreams hundreds of battle-flags,

Borne through the smoke of the battles and pierc'd with
            missiles I saw them,

And carried hither and yon through the smoke, and torn
            and bloody,

175   And at last but a few shreds left on the staffs, (and all in
            silence,)

And the staffs all splinter'd and broken.

I saw battle-corpses, myriads of them,

And the white skeletons of young men, I saw them,

I saw the debris and debris of all the slain soldiers of the
            war,

180   But I saw they were not as was thought,

They themselves were fully at rest, they suffer'd not,

The living remain'd and suffer'd, the mother suffer'd,

And the wife and the child and the musing comrade
            suffer'd,

And the armies that remain'd suffer'd.

5 *record or account.*
6 *armies of the American Civil War.*

16

185 Passing the visions, passing the night,
Passing, unloosing the hold of my comrades' hands,
Passing the song of the hermit bird and the tallying song
    of my soul,
Victorious song, death's outlet song, yet varying ever-
    altering song,
As low and wailing, yet clear the notes, rising and falling,
    flooding the night,
190 Sadly sinking and fainting, as warning and warning, and
    yet again bursting with joy,
Covering the earth and filling the spread of the heaven,
As that powerful psalm in the night I heard from recesses,
Passing, I leave thee lilac with heart-shaped leaves,
I leave thee there in the door-yard, blooming, returning
    with spring.

195 I cease from my song for thee,
From my gaze on thee in the west, fronting the west,
    communing with thee,
O comrade lustrous with silver face in the night.

Yet each to keep and all, retrievements out of the night,
The song, the wondrous chant of the gray-brown bird,
200 And the tallying chant, the echo arous'd in my soul,
With the lustrous and drooping star with the countenance
    full of woe,
With the holders holding my hand nearing the call of the
    bird,
Comrades mine and I in the midst, and their memory ever
    to keep, for the dead I loved so well,
For the sweetest, wisest soul of all my days and lands —
    and this for his dear sake,
205 Lilac and star and bird twined with the chant of my soul,
There in the fragrant pines and the cedars dusk and dim.

(1865–66)   (1881)

One's-Self I Sing

One's-Self I sing, a simple separate person,
Yet utter the word Democratic, the word En-Masse.[1]

Of physiology from top to toe I sing,
Not physiognomy[2] alone nor brain alone is worthy for the
      Muse, I say the Form complete is worthier far,
The Female equally with the Male I sing.

Of Life immense in passion, pulse, and power,
Cheerful, for freest action form'd under the laws divine,
The Modern Man I sing.

(1867)   (1871)

1 *in a group.*
2 *facial features.*

Matthew Arnold

(1822–1888)

*rnold, the eldest son of Thomas Arnold, headmaster of Rugby, was edu-
cated at Oxford, stayed on as professor of poetry for ten years, and was
subsequently appointed an inspector of schools in 1851. He became one of the lead-
ing social and literary critics of the age, and such critical works as* Culture and
Anarchy *(1869), an investigation into the question of whether the anarchy of
individualism should be checked by the authority of culture, are now often consid-
ered to be of greater significance than his poetical works. The two genres of poetry
and criticism come together in his once-influential theory of critical "touchstones" in
"The Study of Poetry" (1888), an attempt to establish standards for distinguishing
poetry of "high seriousness." Frequently referred to as the poet of alienation, Arnold
is preoccupied with the isolation of the individual and the difficulty of knowing the
self. His work is suffused with a sense of frustration, a sharp awareness of the fail-
ings of his age, and a poignant nostalgia for a basically illusory earlier age when
questions of faith and moral integrity were more easily answered. At the same
time, Arnold reveals an unfailing optimistic belief in the efficacy of man's cultural
institutions in bringing about change. The resulting self-division is aptly captured
in the haunting lyricism of both "Dover Beach" and the* Switzerland *sequence.
In both looking back to a better time and yet still believing in human progress,
Arnold is quintessentially Victorian, a man, as he so memorably says in "Stanzas
from the Grande Chartreuse" (1855), "Wandering between two worlds, one dead,
/ The other powerless to be born."*

Isolation: To Marguerite[1]

We were apart; yet, day by day,
I bade my heart more constant be.
I bade it keep the world away,
And grow a home for only thee;
5   Nor fear'd but thy love likewise grew,
Like mine, each day, more tried, more true.

---

1 *from* Switzerland, *a sequence of seven poems.*

The fault was grave! I might have known,
What far too soon, alas! I learn'd —
The heart can bind itself alone,
And faith my oft be unreturn'd.
Self-sway'd our feelings ebb and swell —
Thou lov'st no more; — Farewell! Farewell!

Farewell! — and thou, thou lonely heart,
Which never yet without remorse
Even for a moment didst depart
From thy remote and spheréd course
To haunt the place where passions reign —
Back to thy solitude again!

Back! with the conscious thrill of shame
Which Luna² felt, that summer-night,
Flash through her pure immortal frame,
When she forsook the starry height
To hang over Endymion's sleep
Upon the pine-grown Latmian steep.

Yet she, chaste queen, had never proved
How vain a thing is mortal love,
Wandering in Heaven, far removed.
But thou hast long had place to prove
This truth — to prove, and make thine own:
'Thou hast been, shalt be, art, alone.'

Or, if not quite alone, yet they
Which touch thee are unmating things —
Ocean and clouds and night and day;
Lorn autumns and triumphant springs;
And life, and others' joy and pain,
And love, if love, of happier men.

---

2 *goddess of the moon who fell in love with the shepherd Endymion when she saw him sleeping on Mt. Latmos.*

Of happier men — for they, at least,
Have *dream'd* two human hearts might blend
In one, and were through faith released
40   From isolation without end
Prolong'd; nor knew, although not less
Alone than thou, their loneliness.

(1857)

Dover Beach

The sea is calm to-night.
The tide is full, the moon lies fair,
Upon the straits; — on the French coast the light
Gleams and is gone; the cliffs of England stand,
5   Glimmering and vast, out in the tranquil bay.
Come to the window, sweet is the night-air!
Only, from the long line of spray
Where the sea meets the moon-blanch'd land,
Listen! you hear the grating roar
10   Of pebbles which the waves draw back, and fling,
At their return, up the high strand,
Begin, and cease, and then again begin,
With tremulous cadence slow, and bring
The eternal note of sadness in.

15   Sophocles long ago
Heard it on the Aegæn, and it brought
Into his mind the turbid ebb and flow
Of human misery,[1] we
Find also in the sound a thought,
20   Hearing it by this distant northern sea.

The Sea of Faith
Was once, too, at the full, and round earth's shore
Lay like the folds of a bright girdle furl'd.

---

1 *see Sophocles*, Antigone 2.583*ff.*

But now I only hear
₂₅ Its melancholy, long, withdrawing roar,
Retreating, to the breath
Of the night-wind, down the vast edges drear
And naked shingles² of the world.

Ah, love, let us be true
₃₀ To one another! for the world, which seems
To lie before us like a land of dreams,
So various, so beautiful, so new,
Hath really neither joy, nor love, nor light,
Nor certitude, nor peace, nor help for pain;
₃₅ And we are here as on a darkling plain
Swept with confused alarms of struggle and flight,
Where ignorant armies clash by night.

(1867)

---

2 *pebbled beaches.*

DANTE GABRIEL ROSSETTI

(1828–1882)

orn in London, the son of an exiled Italian patriot, the poet-painter Rossetti was the central figure in the Pre-Raphaelite Brotherhood; this group of youthful artists, which included John Everett Millais and William Holman Hunt, was critical of contemporary art and the Academy and determined to recapture the spirit of medieval art through a return to an insistence on the primacy of nature and a rejection of the stifling rules of classicism. In 1860 Rossetti married his model, Elizabeth Siddal, and when she committed suicide two years later, the remorseful Rossetti buried all his manuscripts in her coffin; as a result, most of his early work was not published until he decided to exhume the manuscripts in 1870. Rossetti's poetry, which like his art frequently reveals the influence of Dante and the medieval world, is carefully crafted and highly stylized, and it had, in its turn, a great influence on the aesthetic and symbolist movements of the later nineteenth century, in particular on such writers as Oscar Wilde and Arthur Symons. The eroticized Christian symbolism so prevalent in both his paintings and his poetry can be found in such works as "The Blessed Damozel" (1850), one of the subjects Rossetti captured in both mediums. The highly pictoral poetry and literary art that he produced provide a concrete reflection of Rossetti's belief that supreme perfection in art lies at that point where the visual and the verbal begin to merge.

The Blessed Damozel[1]

The blessed damozel leaned out
    From the gold bar of Heaven;
Her eyes were deeper than the depth
    Of waters stilled at even;
5   She had three lilies in her hand,
    And the stars in her hair were seven.

Her robe, ungirt from clasp to hem,
    No wrought flowers did adorn,
But a white rose of Mary's gift,
10   For service meetly worn;
Her hair that lay along her back
    Was yellow like ripe corn.

---

1 *young unmarried lady.*

Herseemed[2] she scarce had been a day
  One of God's choristers;
15 The wonder was not yet quite gone
  From that still look of hers;
Albeit, to them she left, her day
  Had counted as ten years.

(To one, it is ten years of years.
20   . . . Yet now, and in this place,
Surely she leaned o'er me — her hair
  Fell all about my face. . . .
Nothing: the autumn-fall of leaves.
  The whole year sets apace.)

25 It was the rampart of God's house
  That she was standing on;
By God built over the sheer depth
  The which is Space begun;
So high, that looking downward thence
30 She scarce could see the sun.

It lies in Heaven, across the flood
  Of ether, as a bridge.
Beneath, the tides of day and night
  With flame and darkness ridge
35 The void, as low as where this earth
  Spins like a fretful midge.

Around her, lovers, newly met
  'Mid deathless love's acclaims,
Spoke evermore among themselves
40 Their heart-remembered names;
And the souls mounting up to God
  Went by her like thin flames.

And still she bowed herself and stooped
  Out of the circling charm;
45 Until her bosom must have made
  The bar she leaned on warm,
And the lilies lay as if asleep
  Along her bended arm.

---

2 *it seemed to her.*

From the fixed place of Heaven she saw
50   Time like a pulse shake fierce
Through all the worlds. Her gaze still strove
     Within the gulf to pierce
Its path; and now she spoke as when
     The stars sang in their spheres.[3]

55   The sun was gone now; the curled moon
     Was like a little feather
Fluttering far down the gulf; and now
     She spoke through the still weather.
Her voice was like the voice the stars
60   Had when they sang together.

(Ah sweet! Even now, in that bird's song,
     Strove not her accents there,
Fain to be hearkened? When those bells
     Possessed the mid-day air,
65   Strove not her steps to reach my side
     Down all the echoing stair?)

"I wish that he were come to me,
     For he will come," she said.
"Have I not prayed in Heaven? — on earth,
70   Lord, Lord, has he not pray'd?
Are not two prayers a perfect strength?
     And shall I feel afraid?

"When round his head the aureole clings,
     And he is clothed in white,
75   I'll take his hand and go with him
     To the deep wells of light;
As unto a stream we will step down,
     And bathe there in God's sight.

---

3 *according to ancient belief, the stars made a singing noise as they moved in their spheres. The music could only be heard by the dead.*

"We two will stand beside that shrine,
80   Occult, withheld, untrod,
Whose lamps are stirred continually
      With prayer sent up to God;
And see our old prayers, granted, melt
      Each like a little cloud.

85   "We two will lie i' the shadow of
      That living mystic tree
Within whose secret growth the Dove[4]
      Is sometimes felt to be,
While every leaf that His plumes touch
90   Saith His Name audibly.

"And I myself will teach to him,
      I myself, lying so,
The songs I sing here; which his voice
      Shall pause in, hushed and slow,
95   And find some knowledge at each pause,
      Or some new thing to know."

(Alas! we two, we two, thou say'st!
      Yea, one wast thou with me
That once of old. But shall God lift
100   To endless unity
The soul whose likeness with thy soul
      Was but its love for thee?)

"We two," she said, "will seek the groves
      Where the lady Mary is,
105   With her five handmaidens, whose names
      Are five sweet symphonies,
Cecily, Gertrude, Magdalen,
      Margaret and Rosalys.

"Circlewise sit they, with bound locks
110   And foreheads garlanded;
Into the fine cloth white like flame
      Weaving the golden thread,
To fashion the birth-robes for them
      Who are just born, being dead.

4 *Holy Ghost.*

115 "He shall fear, haply, and be dumb
        Then will I lay my cheek
To his, and tell about our love,
        Not once abashed or weak:
And the dear Mother will approve
120   My pride, and let me speak.

"Herself shall bring us, hand in hand,
        To Him round whom all souls
Kneel, the clear-ranged unnumbered heads
        Bowed with their aureoles:
125 And angels meeting us shall sing
        To their citherns and citoles.[5]

"There will I ask of Christ the Lord
        Thus much for him and me: —
Only to live as once on earth
130   With Love, — only to be,
As then awhile, for ever now
        Together, I and he."

She gazed and listened and then said,
        Less sad of speech than mild, —
135 "All this is when he comes." She ceased.
        The light thrilled towards her, fill'd
With angels in strong level flight.
        Her eyes prayed, and she smil'd.

(I saw her smile.) But soon their path
140   Was vague in distant spheres:
And then she cast her arms along
        The golden barriers,
And laid her face between her hands,
        And wept. (I heard her tears.)

(1850)

5 *medieval musical instruments.*

The Woodspurge

The wind flapped loose, the wind was still,
Shaken out dead from tree and hill:
I had walked on at the wind's will, —
I sat now, for the wind was still.

5   Between my knees my forehead was, —
My lips, drawn in, said not Alas!
My hair was over in the grass,
My naked ears heard the day pass.

My eyes, wide open, had the run
10   Of some ten weeds to fix upon;
Among those few, out of the sun,
The woodspurge flowered, three cups in one.

From perfect grief there need not be
Wisdom or even memory:
15   One thing then learnt remains to me, —
The woodspurge has a cup of three.

(1856)   (1870)

CHRISTINA ROSSETTI

(1830–1894)

R ossetti, younger sister of the poet-painter Dante Gabriel Rossetti, was edu-
cated at home and lived with her family in London for most of her life.
*Like her mother and sister, she was a devout High Anglican with a great interest
in the Oxford Movement which attempted to merge Catholic doctrine and ritual
with the Anglican faith. In 1862 she established her reputation as a poet with the
publication of her most famous work, "Goblin Market." Rossetti was the only
woman in the Pre-Raphaelite circle to achieve recognition for her own work, to be
the creative rather than simply the inspirational force, and she is also the only Brit-
ish woman poet of the nineteenth century to have consistently drawn critical acclaim
right up until the present day. She wrote much religious poetry and many chil-
dren's rhymes, as well as numerous ballads and lyrics that reveal a deep ambiva-
lence towards romantic love and the conventional roles of women; they have a
strong critical subtext rejecting the limitations imposed upon women by society.
Unhappy or frustrated love between men and the women they betray is often the
focus of her frequently melancholy works, and the women she depicts find their only
consolation in resignation, postponement, and the love of God.*

Song

When I am dead, my dearest,
   Sing no sad songs for me;
Plant thou no roses at my head,
   Nor shady cypress tree:
5   Be the green grass above me
     With showers and dewdrops wet;
And if thou wilt, remember,
   And if thou wilt, forget.

I shall not see the shadows,
10   I shall not feel the rain;
I shall not hear the nightingale
    Sing on as if in pain:
And dreaming through the twilight
    That doth not rise nor set,
15   Haply I may remember,
    And haply may forget.

(1848)   (1862)

The World

By day she woos me, soft, exceeding fair:
    But all night as the moon so changeth she;
    Loathsome and foul with hideous leprosy,
And subtle serpents gliding in her hair.
5   By day she woos me to the outer air,
    Ripe fruits, sweet flowers, and full satiety:
    But thro' the night a beast she grins at me,
A very monster void of love and prayer.
By day she stands a lie: by night she stands
10   In all the naked horror of the truth,
With pushing horns and clawed and clutching hands.
Is this a friend indeed, that I should sell
    My soul to her, give her my life and youth,
Till my feet, cloven too, take hold on hell?

(1854)   (1862)

In an Artist's Studio[1]

One face looks out from all his canvases,
   One selfsame figure sits or walks or leans:
   We found her hidden just behind those screens,
That mirror gave back all her loveliness.
5   A queen in opal or in ruby dress,
   A nameless girl in freshest summer-greens,
   A saint, an angel — every canvas means
The same one meaning, neither more nor less.
He feeds upon her face by day and night,
10   And she with true kind eyes looks back on him,
Fair as the moon and joyful as the light:
   Not wan with waiting, not with sorrow dim;
Not as she is, but was when hope shone bright;
   Not as she is, but as she fills his dream.

(1856)   (1896)

1 the poem was probably prompted by D.G. Rossetti's obsessive use of his wife and model, Elizabeth Siddal, in his paintings.

EMILY DICKINSON

(1830–1886)

orn in Amherst, Massachusetts, where she lived all her life, Emily Dickinson spent her last 25 years, those of her greatest poetic creativity, a relative recluse. For several decades after her death she was regarded as a timid hermit. However, recent studies reveal that, while she seldom ventured outside the family home, she read widely in the classics, contemporary philosophy, and particularly the works of major nineteenth-century women poets and novelists. At a time when intellectual activity was considered detrimental to the emotional and physical health of women and their greatest fulfilment was believed to be found in domestic life, Emily Dickinson was a truly radical woman in her attitudes about religion, society, and art. Although she thought, as she said, "New Englandly," her ideas anticipate by nearly a century those of many modern feminists. During her lifetime, only a handful of her over seventeen hundred poems were published. Today, she is one of the most widely read and studied American writers. None of her poems is long; most are written within a pattern resembling the four-line stanza characteristic of New England hymns, with alternating lines containing 4, 3, 4, and 3 strong beats. Yet within this limitation, Dickinson achieved tremendous variety of poetic effect and complexity of theme. Using dashes to indicate breath pauses, incomplete and inverted syntax, startling images of nature, and homely domestic images, she depicted the individual consciousness questioning itself in relation to other people, society at large, nature, and death.

258

There's a certain Slant of light
Winter Afternoons —
That oppresses, like the Heft[1]
Of Cathedral Tunes —

5   Heavenly Hurt, it gives us —
We can find no scar,
But internal difference,
Where the Meanings, are —

1 *heaviness.*

None may teach it — Any —
10   'Tis the Seal Despair —
And imperial affliction
Sent us of the Air —

When it comes, the Landscape listens —
Shadows — hold their breath —
15   When it goes, 'tis like the Distance
On the look of Death —

(c. 1861)   (1890)

288

I'm Nobody! Who are you?
Are you — Nobody — Too?
Then there's a pair of us?
Don't tell! they'd advertise — you know!

5   How dreary — to be — Somebody!
How public — like a Frog —
To tell one's name — the livelong June —
To an admiring Bog!

(c. 1861)   (1891)

303

The Soul selects her own Society —
Then — shuts the Door —
To her divine Majority —
Present no more —

₅ Unmoved — she notes the Chariots — pausing —
At her low Gate —
Unmoved — and Emperor be kneeling
Upon her Mat —

₁₀ I've known her — from an ample nation —
Choose One —
Then — close the Valves of her attention —
Like Stone —

(c. 1862)   (1890)

328

A Bird came down the Walk —
He did not know I saw —
He bit an Angleworm in halves
And ate the fellow, raw,

₅ And then he drank a Dew
From a convenient Grass —
And then hopped sidewise to the Wall
To let a Beetle pass —

He glanced with rapid eyes
₁₀ That hurried all around —
They looked like frightened Beads, I thought —
He stirred his Velvet Head

Like one in danger, Cautious,
I offered him a Crumb
₁₅ And he unrolled his feathers
And rowed him softer home —

Than Oars divide the Ocean,
Too silver for a seam —
Or Butterflies, off Banks of Noon
₂₀ Leap, plashless as they swim.

(c. 1862)   (1891)

465

I heard a Fly buzz — when I died —
The Stillness in the Room
Was like the Stillness in the Air —
Between the Heaves of Storm —

5   The Eyes around — had wrung them dry —
And Breaths were gathering firm
For that last Onset — when the King
Be witnessed — in the Room —

I willed my Keepsakes — Signed away
10   What portion of me be
Assignable — and then it was
There interposed a Fly —

With Blue — uncertain stumbling Buzz —
Between the light — and me —
15   And then the Windows failed — and then
I could not see to see —

(c. 1862)   (1896)

520

I started Early — Took my Dog —
And visited the Sea —
The Mermaids in the Basement
Came out to look at me —

5   And Frigates[1] — in the Upper Floor
Extended Hempen Hands —
Presuming Me to be a Mouse —
Aground — upon the Sands —

1 *armed naval vessels.*

But no Man moved Me — till the Tide
Went past my simple Shoe —
And past my Apron — and my Belt
And past my Bodice² — too —

And made as He would eat me up —
As wholly as a Dew
Upon a Dandelion's Sleeve —
And then — I started — too —

And He — He followed — close behind —
I felt His Silver Heel
Upon my Ankle — Then my Shoes
Would overflow with Pearl —

Until We met the Solid Town —
No One He seemed to know —
And bowing — with a Mighty look —
At me — The Sea withdrew —

(c. 1862)   (1891)

1540

As imperceptibly as Grief
The Summer lapsed away —
Too imperceptible at last
To seem like Perfidy —
A Quietness distilled
As Twilight long begun,
Or Nature spending with herself
Sequestered Afternoon —

---

2 *laced garment that fits over a blouse.*

The Dusk drew earlier in —
10   The Morning foreign shone —
A courteous, yet harrowing Grace,
As Guest, that would be gone —
And thus, without a Wing
Or service of a Keel
15   Our Summer made her light escape
Into the Beautiful.

(c. 1865)   (1891)

THOMAS HARDY

(1840–1928)

*B*orn in rural Dorsetshire, the part of southwestern England upon which he based the fictional world of Wessex he created in his writing, Hardy was articled to an architect at sixteen, but soon achieved the critical and popular success as a novelist that allowed him to devote himself fully to writing. He published a number of collections of short stories and fifteen novels, including The Mayor of Casterbridge *(1885) and* Tess of the D'Urbervilles *(1891), and he contributed much to the development of the novel as a medium in which to promote social awareness. Following the hostile reception of* Jude the Obscure *in 1895, however, he wrote no more novels and turned to poetry, where he himself considered his true vocation to lie. Both Hardy's poems and his novels are primarily concerned with the problems and ironies of love and life. Like many earlier Victorians, he felt trapped in a world without faith or stability, but with Hardy this develops into a more characteristically modern despair. His belief in the basic futility and waste of human life is grimly reflected in works like "Hap" where he paints the picture of a bleak, unforgiving universe, a universe which contains no God, only an unconscious force which blindly determines all. Stylistically, Hardy had a great influence upon the poets of the first decades of this century. Ezra Pound said upon reading the* Collected Poems *in 1937, "Now there is clarity." Hardy's rugged idiosyncratic style and his often colloquial directness reveal his reaction against what he saw as the excesses of Victorian poetry and his determined effort to avoid what he called the "jewelled line."*

Hap

If but some vengeful god would call to me
From up the sky, and laugh: 'Thou suffering thing,
Know that thy sorrow is my ecstasy,
That thy love's loss is my hate's profiting!'

5   Then would I bear it, clench myself, and die,
Steeled by the sense of ire unmerited;
Half-eased in that a Powerfuller than I
Had willed and meted me the tears I shed.

But not so. How arrives it joy lies slain,
10   And why unblooms the best hope ever sown?
— Crass Casualty obstructs the sun and rain,
And dicing Time for gladness casts a moan. . . .
These purblind Doomsters had as readily strown
Blisses about my pilgrimage as pain.

(1866)

The Ruined Maid

'O 'Melia, my dear, this does everything crown!
Who could have supposed I should meet you in Town?
And whence such fair garments, such prosperi-ty?' —
'O didn't you know I'd been ruined?' said she.

5   — 'You left us in tatters, without shoes or socks,
Tired of digging potatoes, and spudding up docks;[1]
And now you've gay bracelets and bright feathers three!' —
'Yes: that's how we dress when we're ruined,' said she.

— 'At home in the barton[2] you said "thee" and "thou",
10   And "thik oon", and "theäs oon", and "t'other"; but now
Your talking quite fits 'ee for high compa-ny!' —
'Some polish is gained with one's ruin,' said she.

— 'Your hands were like paws then, your face blue and
bleak
But now I'm bewitched by your delicate cheek,
15   And your little gloves fit as on any la-dy!' —
'We never do work when we're ruined,' said she.

---

1 *digging up weeds.*
2 *farmyard.*

— 'You used to call home-life a hag-ridden dream,
And you'd sigh, and you'd sock; but at present you seem
To know not of megrims[3] or melancho-ly!' —
20   'True. One's pretty lively when ruined,' said she.

— 'I wish I had feathers, a fine sweeping gown,
And a delicate face, and could strut about Town!' —
'My dear — a raw country girl, such as you be,
Cannot quite expect that. You ain't ruined,' said she.

(1866)   (1902)

The Darkling Thrush

I leant upon a coppice gate
      When Frost was spectre-gray,
And Winter's dregs made desolate
      The weakening eye of day.
5   The tangled bine-stems scored the sky
      Like strings of broken lyres,
And all mankind that haunted nigh
      Had sought their household fires.

The land's sharp features seemed to be
10   The Century's corpse[1] outleant,
His crypt the cloudy canopy,
      The wind his death-lament.
The ancient pulse of germ and birth
      Was shrunken hard and dry,
15   And every spirit upon earth
      Seemed fervourless as I.

At once a voice arose among
      The bleak twigs overhead
In a full-hearted evensong
20   Of joy illimited;

3 *depression.*
1 *Hardy originally dated this poem December 31, 1900.*

An aged thrush, frail, gaunt, and small,
   In blast-beruffled plume,
Had chosen thus to fling his soul
   Upon the growing gloom.

25   So little cause for carolings
          Of such ecstatic sound
       Was written on terrestrial things
          Afar or nigh around,
       That I could think there trembled through
30   His happy good-night air
       Some blessed Hope, whereof he knew
          And I was unaware.

(1902)

New Year's Eve

'I have finished another year,' said God,
   'In grey, green, white, and brown;
I have strewn the leaf upon the sod,
Sealed up the worm within the clod,
5   And let the last sun down.'

'And what's the good of it?' I said,
   'What reasons made you call
From formless void this earth we tread,
When nine-and-ninety can be read
10   Why nought should be at all?

'Yea, Sire; why shaped you us, "who in
   This tabernacle groan"[1] —
If ever a joy be found herein,
Such joy no man had wished to win
15   If he had never known!'

---

1 II Corinthians 5:4: "For we that are in this tabernacle do groan, being burdened; not for that we would be unclothed, but clothed upon, that mortality might be swallowed up of life."

Then he: 'My labours — logicless —
　　You may explain; not I:
Sense-sealed I have wrought, without a guess
That I evolved a Consciousness
20　　　To ask for reasons why.

'Strange that ephemeral creatures who
　　By my own ordering are,
Should see the shortness of my view,
Use ethic tests I never knew,
25　　　Or made provision for!'

He sank to raptness as of yore,
　　And opening New Year's Day
Wove it by rote as theretofore,
And went on working evermore
30　　　In his unweeting[2] way.

(1907)

The Convergence of the Twain

(*Lines on the loss of the 'Titanic'*)[1]

I

In a solitude of the sea
Deep from human vanity,
And the Pride of Life that planned her, stilly couches she.

II

Steel chambers, late the pyres
5　　Of her salamandrine[2] fires,
Cold currents thrid,[3] and turn to rhythmic tidal lyres.

2 *unknowing.*

1 *the* Titanic, *largest and most advanced ship of the day, struck an iceberg on her maiden voyage across the Atlantic in April 1912 and went down with a loss of 1513 lives.*
2 *the salamander, according to fable, could live in fire.*
3 *thread.*

III

Over the mirrors meant
To glass the opulent
The sea-worm crawls — grotesque, slimed, dumb,
    indifferent.

IV

10   Jewels in joy designed
To ravish the sensuous mind
Lie lightless, all their sparkles bleared and black and blind.

V

Dim moon-eyed fishes near
Gaze at the gilded gear
15   And query: 'What does this vaingloriousness down
    here?' . . .

VI

Well: while was fashioning
This creature of cleaving wing,
The Immanent Will⁴ that stirs and urges everything

VII

Prepared a sinister mate
20   For her — so gaily great —
A Shape of Ice, for the time far and dissociate.

VIII

And as the smart ship grew
In stature, grace, and hue,
In shadowy silent distance grew the Iceberg too.

IX

25   Alien they seemed to be:
No mortal eye could see
The intimate welding of their later history,

---

4 *the unconscious force behind the universe. Hardy also refers to this as the "Spinner of the Years."*

X

Or sign that they were bent
By paths coincident
30   On being anon twin halves of one august event,

XI

Till the Spinner of the Years
Said 'Now!' And each one hears,
And consummation comes, and jars two hemispheres.

(1912)

Afterwards

When the Present has latched its postern[1] behind my
        tremulous stay,
    And the May month flaps its glad green leaves like
        wings,
    Delicate-filmed as new-spun silk, will the neighbours say,
    'He was a man who used to notice such things'?

5   If it be in the dusk when, like an eyelid's soundless blink,
        The dewfall-hawk comes crossing the shades to alight
    Upon the wind-warped upland thorn, a gazer may think,
    'To him this must have been a familiar sight.'

If I pass during some nocturnal blackness, mothy and
        warm,
10   When the hedgehog travels furtively over the lawn,
    One may say, 'He strove that such innocent creatures
        should come to no harm,
    But he could do little for them; and now he is gone.'

1 *backdoor.*

If, when hearing that I have been stilled at last, they stand
    at the door,
  Watching the full-starred heavens that winter sees,

15   Will this thought rise on those who will meet my face no
    more,
  'He was one who had an eye for such mysteries'?

And will any say when my bell of quittance is heard in the
    gloom,
  And a crossing breeze cuts a pause in its outrollings,
Till they rise again, as they were a new bell's boom,

20   'He hears it not now, but used to notice such things'?

(1917)

GERARD MANLEY HOPKINS

(1844–1889)

*H*opkins was born near London and educated at Oxford during a time of
violent religious controversy. He converted to Catholicism in 1866, became
a Jesuit priest, and spent the remainder of his life serving the order. Hopkins is
generally considered one of the most powerful of the religious poets and one of the
most daring innovators in poetic technique. Two notions central to his work are
what he calls "inscape," the unique quality that distinguishes one thing from every
other, and "instress," the response evoked by the perception of inscape. The attempt
to capture these elements in his work can be seen in the lyrically powerful "The
Windhover." Hopkins was also one of the most effective practitioners of the sonnet
during this age, and in the articulation of his struggles with his faith in the "dark"
or "terrible" sonnets, including "No worst, there is none," he is typically Victorian.

Pied Beauty[1]

Glory be to God for dappled things —
    For skies of couple-colour as a brinded[2] cow;
        For rose-moles all in stipple[3] upon trout that swim;
Fresh-firecoal chestnut-falls;[4] finches' wings;
5   Landscape plotted and pieced — fold, fallow, and plough;
        And áll trádes, their gear and tackle and trim.
All things counter, original, spare, strange;
    Whatever is fickle, freckled (who knows how?)
        With swift, slow; sweet, sour; adazzle, dim;
10   He fathers-forth whose beauty is past change:
                        Praise him.

(1877)   (1918)

---

1 *having two or more colours; in patches or blotches.*
2 *streaked.*
3 *method in painting of applying colour in dots.*
4 *chestnuts dappling the dark ground like bright coals.*

No worst, there is none

No worst, there is none. Pitched past pitch of grief,
More pangs will, schooled at forepangs, wilder wring.
Comforter, where, where is your comforting?
Mary, mother of us, where is your relief?
5   My cries heave, herds-long;[1] huddle in a main, a chief-
woe, world-sorrow; on an age-old anvil wince and sing —
Then lull, then leave off. Fury had shrieked 'No ling-
ering! Let me be fell:[2] force I must be brief'.
O the mind, mind has mountains; cliffs of fall
10   Frightful, sheer, no-man-fathomed. Hold them cheap
May who ne'er hung there. Nor does long our small
Durance deal with that steep or deep. Here! creep,
Wretch, under a comfort serves in a whirlwind: all
Life death does end and each day dies with sleep.

(1885?)   (1918)

God's Grandeur

The world is charged with the grandeur of God.
    It will flame out, like shining from shook foil;[1]
    It gathers to a greatness, like the ooze of oil
Crushed.[2] Why do men then now not reck his rod?
5   Generations have trod, have trod, have trod;
    And all is seared with trade; bleared, smeared with toil;
    And wears man's smudge and shares man's smell: the soil
Is bare now, nor can foot feel, being shod.

1 *like the successive cries of a herd.*
2 *fierce.*

1 *foil leaf or tinsel.*
2 *like oil crushed out of olives or seeds.*

10   And for all this, nature is never spent;
       There lives the dearest freshness deep down things;
And though the last lights off the black West went
       Oh, morning, at the brown brink eastward, springs —
Because the Holy Ghost over the bent
       World broods with warm breast and with ah! bright wings.

(1877)   (1917)

The Windhover:[1]
To Christ our Lord

I caught this morning morning's minion,[2] king-
dom of daylight's dauphin,[3] dapple-dawn-drawn Falcon, in
       his riding
       Of the rolling level underneath him steady air, and striding
High there, how he rung upon the rein of a wimpling wing[4]
In his ecstasy! then off, off forth on swing,
5   As a skate's heel sweeps smooth on a bow-bend: the hurl and
       gliding
       Rebuffed the big wind. My heart in hiding
Stirred for a bird, — the achieve of, the mastery of the thing!

1 *a small hawk.*
2 *a favourite.*
3 *name given to the heir to the French throne.*
4 *in falconry, to ring means to rise in the air spirally.*

Brute beauty and valour and act, oh, air, pride, plume, here
   Buckle!⁵ AND the fire that breaks from thee then, a billion
10   Times told lovelier, more dangerous, O my chevalier!⁶

   No wonder of it: shéer plód makes plough down sillion⁷
Shine, and blue-bleak embers, ah my dear,
   Fall, gall themselves, and gash gold-vermilion.

(1877)   (1918)

---

5 buckle *has many possible meanings: fasten, join, enclose, grapple, submit, bend, and crumple.*
6 *knight, nobleman, champion.*
7 *furrow.*

A.E. HOUSMAN

(1859–1936)

orn in Worcestershire and educated at Oxford, Housman failed his final examinations and subsequently worked for ten years as a civil servant before becoming professor of Latin at University College, London. A Shropshire Lad (1896), from which the following selections are taken, initially met with little interest, but became immensely popular during the First World War, probably because of the recurrent intermingled themes of mutability, pessimism, and patriotism, and the recurrent theme of doomed youth. Housman's output was limited: he published only two small volumes during his lifetime, A Shropshire Lad and Last Poems (1922), and another, More Poems (1936), appeared after his death. Housman is important as a link between the Victorian and the modern world, and he is at his best when he avoids the rather artificial decadent style that influenced him in his youth and produces the finely crafted, concentrated poems marked by a vigorous, deceptive simplicity for which he is best known. Revealing the influence of the classical lyric and the popular ballad, these works skilfully exploit balance and opposition and frequently close with a pervasive gentle melancholy undercut by the sudden introduction of irony or bathos.

Loveliest of trees, the cherry now

Loveliest of trees, the cherry now
Is hung with bloom along the bough,
And stands about the woodland ride
Wearing white for Eastertide.

5   Now, of my threescore years and ten,
Twenty will not come again,
And take from seventy springs a score,
It only leaves me fifty more.

And since to look at things in bloom
10   Fifty springs are little room
About the woodlands I will go
To see the cherry hung with snow.

(1896)

When I was one-and-twenty

When I was one-and-twenty
  I heard a wise man say,
'Give crowns and pounds and guineas
  But not your heart away;
5 Give pearls away and rubies
    But keep your fancy free.'
But I was one-and-twenty,
  No use to talk to me.

When I was one-and-twenty
10 I heard him say again,
'The heart out of the bosom
  Was never given in vain;
'Tis paid with sighs a plenty
  And sold for endless rue.'
15 And I am two-and-twenty,
  And oh, 'tis true, 'tis true.

(1896)

To an Athlete Dying Young

The time you won your town the race
We chaired you through the market-place;
Man and boy stood cheering by,
And home we brought you shoulder-high.

5 To-day, the road all runners come,
Shoulder-high we bring you home,
And set you at your threshold down,
Townsman of a stiller town.

Smart lad, to slip betimes away
10   From fields where glory does not stay
And early though the laurel[1] grows
It withers quicker than the rose.[2]

Eyes the shady night has shut
Cannot see the record cut,
15   And silence sounds no worse than cheers
After earth has stopped the ears:

Now you will not swell the rout
Of lads that wore their honours out,
Runners whom renown outran
20   And the name died before the man.

So set, before its echoes fade,
The fleet foot on the sill of shade,
And hold to the low lintel up
The still-defended challenge-cup.

25   And round that early-laurelled head
Will flock to gaze the strengthless dead
And find unwithered on its curls
The garland briefer than a girl's.

(1896)

1 symbol of victory, traditionally awarded by the Greeks to the victor in the Pythian Games.
2 symbol of beauty.

SIR CHARLES G.D. ROBERTS

(1860–1943)

*C*redited with creating the first truly Canadian literary form, the realistic animal tale, Charles George Douglas Roberts also played a significant role in the development of Canadian poetry. His first volume, Orion and Other Poems *(1880), inspired both his cousin, Bliss Carman, and Archibald Lamp-man, who, together with D.C. Scott and Roberts, formed the Confederation Poets, a group that consciously sought to create a distinctive Canadian poetry. Born in Douglas, New Brunswick, Roberts worked as an editor and then an English pro-fessor, but after 1897 he earned his living by writing prose, living in New York, London, and Europe until his return to Canada in 1925. Paradoxically, his most enduring and universal poems are not the obtrusively moralizing ones in which he deliberately tried to be universal, but the early ones in which he was most regional in subject. These poems show three major influences: his classical training, in the highly organized form and choice of allusions; the English Romantics, especially Wordsworth, in the presentation of sharply detailed landscapes in language that avoids consciously poetic diction; and the Victorian intellectual poets, particularly Matthew Arnold, in the probing for spiritual or philosophic significance. These poems support his claim in "The Poetry of Nature" that "nature-poetry is not mere description of landscape in metrical form, but the expression of one or another of many vital relationships between external nature and 'the deep heart of man.'"*

Tantramar[1] Revisited

Summers and summers have come, and gone with the
    flight of the swallow;
Sunshine and thunder have been, storm, and winter, and
    frost;
Many and many a sorrow has all but died from
    remembrance,
Many a dream of joy fall'n in the shadow of pain.
Hands of chance and change have marred, or moulded, or
    broken,
Busy with spirit or flesh, all I most have adored;
Even the bosom of Earth is strewn with heavier
    shadows, —

5

---

1 saltwater tidal marshes along the New Brunswick coast of the Bay of Fundy, where Roberts spent his childhood. Minudie (line 25) is across the bay in Nova Scotia.

Only in these green hills, aslant to the sea, no change!
Here where the road that has climbed from the inland
    valleys and woodlands,
10   Dips from the hill-tops down, straight to the base of the
    hills, —
Here, from my vantage-ground, I can see the scattering
    houses,
Stained with time, set warm in orchards, meadows, and
    wheat,
Dotting the broad bright slopes outspread to southward
    and eastward,
Wind-swept all day long, blown by the south-east wind.

15   Skirting the sunbright uplands stretches a riband[2] of
    meadow,
Shorn of the labouring grass, bulwarked well from the sea,
Fenced on its seaward border with long clay dykes from the
    turbid
Surge and flow of the tides vexing the Westmoreland
    shores.
Yonder, toward the left, lie broad the Westmoreland
    marshes, —
20   Miles on miles they extend, level, and grassy, and dim,
Clear from the long red sweep of flats to the sky in the
    distance,
Save for the outlying heights, green-rampired[3] Cumberland
    Point;
Miles on miles outrolled, and the river-channels divide
    them, —
Miles on miles of green, barred by the hurtling gusts.

25   Miles on miles beyond the tawny bay is Minudie.
There are the low blue hills; villages gleam at their feet.
Nearer a white sail shines across the water, and nearer
Still are the slim, grey masts of fishing boats dry on the
    flats.

---

2 *ribbon.*
3 *containing ramparts (protective embankments).*

Ah, how well I remember those wide red flats, above tide-
mark

30 Pale with scurf[4] of the salt, seamed and baked in the sun!

Well I remember the piles of blocks and ropes, and the net-
reels

Wound with the beaded nets, dripping and dark from the
sea!

Now at this season the nets are unwound; they hang from
the rafters

Over the fresh-stowed hay in upland barns, and the wind

35 Blows all day through the chinks, with the streaks of
sunlight, and sways them

Softly at will; or they lie heaped in the gloom of a loft.

Now at this season the reels are empty and idle; I see them

Over the lines of the dykes, over the gossiping grass,

Now at this season they swing in the long strong wind,
thro' the lonesome

40 Golden afternoon, shunned by the foraging gulls.

Near about sunset the crane will journey homeward above
them;

Round them, under the moon, all the calm night long,

Winnowing soft grey wings of marsh-owls wander and
wander,

Now to the broad, lit marsh, now to the dusk of the dike.

45 Soon, thro' their dew-wet frames, in the live keen
freshness of morning,

Out of the teeth of the dawn blows back the awakening
wind.

Then, as the blue day mounts, and the low-shot shafts of
the sunlight

Glance from the tide to the shore, gossamers jewelled with
dew

Sparkle and wave, where late sea-spoiling fathoms of drift-
net

50 Myriad-meshed, uploomed sombrely over the land.

4 *scales.*

Well I remember it all. The salt, raw scent of the margin;
Surging in ponderous lengths, uprose and coiled in its
    station;
Then each man to his home, — well I remember it all!

Yet, as I sit and watch, this present peace of the
    landscape, —
55 Stranded boats, these reels empty and idle, the hush,
One grey hawk slow-wheeling above yon cluster of
    haystacks, —
More than the old-time stir this stillness welcomes me
    home.
Ah, the old-time stir, how once it stung me with
    rapture, —
Old-time sweetness, the winds freighted with honey and
    salt!
60 Yet will I stay my steps and not go down to the
    marshland, —
Muse and recall far off, rather remember than see, —
Lest on too close sight I miss the darling illusion,
Spy at their task even here the hands of chance and
    change.

(1883)

The Potato Harvest

A high bare field, brown from the plough, and borne
    Aslant from sunset; amber wastes of sky
    Washing the ridge; a clamour of crows that fly
In from the wide flats where the spent tides mourn
5   To yon their rocking roosts in pines wind-torn;
    A line of grey snake-fence that zigzags by
    A pond and cattle; from the homestead nigh
The long deep summonings of the supper horn.

Black on the ridge, against that lonely flush,
10   A cart, and stoop-necked oxen; ranged beside
Some barrels; and the day-worn harvest-folk,
Here emptying their baskets, jar the hush
With hollow thunders. Down the dusk hillside
Lumbers the wain;[1] and day fades out like smoke.

(1886)

The Winter Fields

Winds here, and sleet, and frost that bites like steel.
The low bleak hill rounds under the low sky.
Naked of flock and fold the fallows lie,
Thin streaked with meagre drift. The gusts reveal
5   By fits the dim grey snakes of fence, that steal
Through the white dusk. The hill-foot poplars sigh,
While storm and death with winter trample by,
And the iron fields ring sharp, and blind lights reel.
Yet in the lonely ridges, wrenched with pain,
10   Harsh solitary hillocks, bound and dumb,
Grave glebes[1] close-lipped beneath the scourge and chain,
Lurks hid the germ of ecstasy — the sum
Of life that waits on summer, till the rain
Whisper in April and the crocus come.

(1890)

1 *wagon.*
1 *fields.*

The Herring Weir

Back to the green deeps of the outer bay
   The red and amber currents glide and cringe,
   Diminishing behind a luminous fringe
Of cream-white surf and wandering wraiths of spray.
5   Stealthily, in the old reluctant way,
   The red flats are uncovered, mile on mile,
   To glitter in the sun a golden while.
Far down the flats, a phantom sharply grey,

The herring weir[1] emerges, quick with spoil.
10   Slowly the tide forsakes it. Then draws near,
   Descending from the farm-house on the height,
A cart, with gaping tubs. The oxen toil
   Sombrely o'er the level to the weir,
   And drag a long black trail across the light.

(1893)

---

1 *a fence of stakes erected to catch fish.*

Archibald Lampman

(1861–1899)

orn in 1861 in Morpeth, Canada West (Ontario), Lampman graduated from the University of Toronto in 1882 and spent his working life as a clerk with the Post Office Department, Ottawa. The most accomplished of the Confederation Poets — a group of literary nationalists intent on developing a distinctive Canadian literature — he had a talent for precise observation of nature. Lampman refined his knowledge of nature with walking tours in the countryside and canoe trips into the wilderness with his friend and fellow poet, D.C. Scott. Not surprisingly, perhaps, his poetry was heavily influenced by the English Romantics, who recorded in poetry their responses to similar excursions. The influence of Keats is especially prominent in Lampman's characteristic device: a detailed description of nature leads to the focus on a solitary observer who begins to "dream," to experience a state of transcendent harmony. It is also evident in his concern for exploiting the musical possibilities of language. Romantic reverie represents only one side of Lampman's poetry, however. He sometimes shows an ambivalence about Canadian nature, presenting it as both beautiful and frightening. In darker poems, he completely replaces the dream of romantic harmony with a vision of modern industrial society as a dehumanizing nightmare.

Heat

From plains that reel to southward, dim,
    The road runs by me white and bare;
Up the steep hill it seems to swim
    Beyond, and melt into the glare.
5   Upward half-way, or it may be
    Nearer the summit, slowly steals
A hay-cart, moving dustily
    With idly clacking wheels.

By his cart's side the wagoner
10   Is slouching slowly at his ease,
Half-hidden in the windless blur
    Of white dust puffing to his knees.

This wagon on the height above,
  From sky to sky on either hand,
15 Is the sole thing that seems to move
  In all the heat-held land.

Beyond me in the fields the sun
  Soaks in the grass and hath his will;
I count the marguerites one by one;
20   Even the buttercups are still.
On the brook yonder not a breath
  Disturbs the spider or the midge.
The water-bugs draw close beneath
  The cool gloom of the bridge.

25 Where the far elm-tree shadows flood
  Dark patches in the burning grass,
The cows, each with her peaceful cud,
  Lie waiting for the heat to pass.
From somewhere on the slope near by
30   Into the pale depth of the noon
A wandering thrush slides leisurely
  His thin revolving tune.

In intervals of dreams I hear
  The cricket from the droughty ground;
35 The grasshoppers spin into mine ear
  A small innumerable sound.
I lift mine eyes sometimes to gaze:
  The burning sky-line blinds my sight:
The woods far off are blue with haze:
40   The hills are drenched in light.

And yet to me not this or that
  Is always sharp or always sweet;
In the sloped shadow of my hat
  I lean at rest, and drain the heat;
45 Nay more, I think some blessèd power
  Hath brought me wandering idly here:
In the full furnace of this hour
  My thoughts grow keen and clear.

(1888)

In November[1]

The hills and leafless forests slowly yield
  To the thick-driving snow. A little while
  And night shall darken down. In shouting file
The woodmen's carts go by me homeward-wheeled,
5   Past the thin fading stubbles, half concealed,
    Now golden-gray, sowed softly through with snow,
    Where the last ploughman follows still his row,
Turning black furrows through the whitening field.
Far off the village lamps begin to gleam,
10   Fast drives the snow, and no man comes this way;
    The hills grow wintry white, and bleak winds moan
    About the naked uplands. I alone
Am neither sad, nor shelterless, nor gray,
Wrapped round with thought, content to watch and dream.

(1888)

In November

With loitering step and quiet eye,
Beneath the low November sky,
I wandered in the woods, and found
A clearing, where the broken ground
5   Was scattered with black stumps and briers,
And the old wreck of forest fires.
It was a bleak and sandy spot,
And, all about, the vacant plot,
Was peopled and inhabited
10   By scores of mulleins[1] long since dead.
A silent and forsaken brood
In that mute opening of the wood,
So shrivelled and so thin they were,

---

1 sometimes called "Late November" to distinguish it from the longer 1895 poem with the same title.
1 tall plants with coarse, woolly leaves and dense spikes of flowers.

So gray, so haggard, and austere,
15   Not plants at all they seemed to me,
But rather some spare company
Of hermit folk, who long ago,
Wandering in bodies to and fro,
Had chanced upon this lonely way,
20   And rested thus, till death one day
Surprised them at their compline² prayer,
And left them standing lifeless there.

There was no sound about the wood
Save the wind's secret stir. I stood
25   Among the mullein-stalks as still
As if myself had grown to be
One of their sombre company,
A body without wish or will.
And as I stood, quite suddenly,
30   Down from a furrow in the sky
The sun shone out a little space
Across that silent sober place,
Over the sand heaps and brown sod,
The mulleins and dead goldenrod,
35   And passed beyond the thickets gray,
And lit the fallen leaves that lay,
Level and deep within the wood,
A rustling yellow multitude.

All around me the thin light,
40   So sere, so melancholy bright,
Fell like the half-reflected gleam
Or shadow of some former dream;
A moment's golden reverie
Poured out on every plant and tree
45   A semblance of weird joy, or less,
A sort of spectral happiness;
And I, too, standing idly there,
With muffled hands in the chill air,

2 *the last of seven canonical hours; the last service of the day.*

Felt the warm glow about my feet,
50   And shuddering betwixt cold and heat,
Drew my thoughts closer, like a cloak,
While something in my blood awoke,
A nameless and unnatural cheer,
A pleasure secret and austere.

(1895)

Winter Evening

To-night the very horses springing by
Toss gold from whitened nostrils. In a dream
The streets that narrow to the westward gleam
Like rows of golden palaces; and high
5   From all the crowded chimneys tower and die
A thousand aureoles. Down in the west
The brimming plains beneath the sunset rest,
One burning sea of gold. Soon, soon shall fly
The glorious vision, and the hours shall feel
10   A mightier master; soon from height to height,
With silence and the sharp unpitying stars,
Stern creeping frosts, and winds that touch like steel,
Out of the depth beyond the eastern bars,
Glittering and still shall come the awful night.

(1899)

The City of the End of Things

Beside the pounding cataracts
Of midnight streams unknown to us
'Tis builded in the leafless tracts
And valleys huge of Tartarus.[1]

---

1 *the lowest, gloomiest region of Hades, into which Zeus hurled the Titans and Giants; hell.*

5   Lurid and lofty and vast it seems;
     It hath no rounded name that rings,
     But I have heard it called in dreams
     The City of the End of Things.

     Its roofs and iron towers have grown
10   None knoweth how high within the night,
     But in its murky streets far down
     A flaming terrible and bright
     Shakes all the stalking shadows there,
     Across the walls, across the floors,
15   And shifts upon the upper air
     From out a thousand furnace doors;
     And all the while an awful sound
     Keeps roaring on continually,
     And crashes in the ceaseless round
20   Of a gigantic harmony.
     Through its grim depths re-echoing
     And all its weary height of walls,
     With measured roar and iron ring,
     The inhuman music lifts and falls.
25   Where no thing rests and no man is,
     And only fire and night hold sway;
     The beat, the thunder and the hiss
     Cease not, and change not, night nor day.
     And moving at unheard commands,
30   The abysses and vast fires between,
     Flit figures that with clanking hands
     Obey a hideous routine;
     They are not flesh, they are not bone,
     They see not with the human eye,
35   And from their iron lips is blown
     A dreadful and monotonous cry;
     And whoso of our mortal race
     Should find that city unaware,
     Lean Death would smite him face to face,
40   And blanch him with its venomed air:
     Or caught by the terrific spell,
     Each thread of memory snapt and cut,

His soul would shrivel and its shell
Go rattling like an empty nut.

45 It was not always so, but once,
In days that no man thinks upon,
Fair voices echoed from its stones,
The light above it leaped and shone:
Once there were multitudes of men,
50 That built that city in their pride,
Until its might was made, and then
They withered age by age and died.
But now of that prodigious race,
Three only in an iron tower,
55 Set like carved idols face to face,
Remain the masters of its power;
And at the city gate a fourth,
Gigantic and with dreadful eyes,
Sits looking toward the lightness north,
60 Beyond the reach of memories;
Fast rooted to the lurid floor,
A bulk that never moves a jot,
In his pale body dwells no more,
Or mind or soul, — an idiot!
65 But sometime in the end those three
Shall perish and their hands be still,
And with the master's touch shall flee
Their incommunicable skill.
A stillness absolute as death
70 Along the slacking wheels shall lie,
And, flagging at a single breath,
The fires that moulder out and die.
The roar shall vanish at its height,
And over that tremendous town
75 The silence of eternal night
Shall gather close and settle down.
All its grim grandeur, tower and hall,
Shall be abandoned utterly,
And into rust and dust shall fall
80 From century to century;

Nor ever living thing shall grow,
Nor trunk of tree, nor blade of grass;
No drop shall fall, no wind shall blow,
Nor sound of any foot shall pass:
85   Alone of its accursèd state,
One thing the hand of Time shall spare,
For the grim Idiot at the gate
Is deathless and eternal there.

(1899)

Duncan Campbell Scott

(1862–1947)

*O*ne of the Confederation Poets, a group inspired by the success of Charles
G.D. Roberts to work towards a distinctly Canadian poetry, D.C. Scott
often substituted for the pastoral subjects that characterized the work of his col-
leagues portraits of the indigenous peoples and of wilderness landscapes. Born in
Ottawa, Scott was a life-long civil servant who rose to be deputy superintendent
general in the Department of Indian Affairs. As a consequence of his duties, which
enabled him to travel throughout the Canadian North and West, he came to
believe that the native peoples were doomed to extinction as separate peoples, a belief
evident in a number of his poems. His experiences also developed in him a deep
feeling for the wilderness, which he described as a replacement for the church of his
youth. Scott was both lyrical and intellectual. He declared in "An Autobiographi-
cal Note" that "Everything I write starts with its rhythmical life . . ." and that "I
value brain power at the bottom of everything." As a lyric poet, he organized this
"rhythmical life" through carefully developed metres, rhymes, and repetition; as an
intellectual poet, he characteristically exercised "brain power" by organizing poems
according to dialectic oppositions or paired terms.*

The Onondaga[1] Madonna

> She stands full-throated and with careless pose,
> This woman of a weird and waning race,
> The tragic savage lurking in her face,
> Where all her pagan passion burns and glows;
> 5   Her blood is mingled with her ancient foes,
> And thrills with war and wildness in her veins;
> Her rebel lips are dabbled with the stains
> Of feuds and forays and her father's woes.

---

1 one of the five groups forming what became known as the League of Five Nations, or the Iroquois Confederacy, the
Onondaga originated in upper New York State; many moved to Canada after the American Revolution, and now
form part of the Six Nations Reserve near Brantford, Ontario.

And closer in the shawl about her breast,
10   The latest promise of her nation's doom,
Paler than she her baby clings and lies,
The primal warrior gleaming from his eyes;
He sulks, and burdened with his infant gloom,
He draws his heavy brows and will not rest.

(1898)

The Forsaken

I

Once in the winter
Out on a lake
In the heart of the north-land,
Far from the Fort
5   And far from the hunters,
A Chippewa woman
With her sick baby,
Crouched in the last hours
Of a great storm.
10   Frozen and hungry,
She fished through the ice
With a line of the twisted
Bark of the cedar,
And a rabbit-bone hook
15   Polished and barbed;
Fished with the bare hook
All through the wild day,
Fished and caught nothing;
While the young chieftain
20   Tugged at her breasts,
Or slept in the lacings
Of the warm *tikanagan*.[1]

1 *a cradle-board to which is fastened a moss-bag for carrying an infant.*

All the lake-surface
Streamed with the hissing
25   Of millions of iceflakes
Hurled by the wind;
Behind her the round
Of a lonely island
Roared like a fire
30   With the voice of the storm
In the deeps of the cedars.
Valiant, unshaken,
She took of her own flesh,
Baited the fish-hook,
35   Drew in a gray-trout,
Drew in his fellows,
Heaped them beside her,
Dead in the snow.
Valiant, unshaken,
40   She faced the long distance,
Wolf-haunted and lonely,
Sure of her goal
And the life of her dear one:
Tramped for two days,
45   On the third in the morning,
Saw the strong bulk
Of the Fort by the river,
Saw the wood-smoke
Hang soft in the spruces,
50   Heard the keen yelp
Of the ravenous huskies
Fighting for whitefish:
Then she had rest.

II

Years and years after,
55   When she was old and withered,
When her son was an old man
And his children filled with vigour,
They came in their northern tour on the verge of winter,
To an island in a lonely lake.

60 There one night they camped, and on the morrow
Gathered their kettles and birch-bark
Their rabbit-skin robes and their mink-traps,
Launched their canoes and slunk away through the islands,
Left her alone forever,
65 Without a word of farewell,
Because she was old and useless,
Like a paddle broken and warped,
Or a pole that was splintered.
Then, without a sigh,
70 Valiant, unshaken,
She smoothed her dark locks under her kerchief,
Composed her shawl in state,
Then folded her hands rigid with sinews and corded with
veins,
Folded them across her breasts spent with the nourishing
of children,
75 Gazed at the sky past the tops of the cedars,
Saw two spangled nights arise out of the twilight,
Saw two days go by filled with the tranquil sunshine,
Saw, without pain, or dread, or even a moment of longing:
Then on the third great night there came thronging and
thronging
80 Millions of snowflakes out of a windless cloud;
They covered her close with a beautiful crystal shroud,
Covered her deep and silent.
But in the frost of the dawn,
Up from the life below,
85 Rose a column of breath
Through a tiny cleft in the snow,
Fragile, delicately drawn,
Wavering with its own weakness,
In the wilderness a sign of the spirit,
90 Persisting still in the sight of the sun
Till day was done.
Then all light was gathered up by the hand of God and hid
in His breast,
Then there was born a silence deeper than silence,
Then she had rest.

(1905)

Night Hymns on Lake Nipigon

Here in the midnight, where the dark mainland and island
Shadows mingle in shadow deeper, profounder,
Sing we the hymns of the churches, while the dead water
    Whispers before us.

5   Thunder is travelling slow on the path of the lightning;
One after one the stars and the beaming planets
Look serene in the lake from the edge of the storm-cloud,
    Then have they vanished.

While our canoe, that floats dumb in the bursting thunder,
10   Gathers her voice in the quiet and thrills and whispers,
Presses her prow in the star-gleam, and all her ripple
    Lapses in blackness.

Sing we the sacred ancient hymns of the churches,
Chanted first in old-world nooks of the desert,
15   While in the wild, pellucid Nipigon reaches
    Hunted the savage.

Now have the ages met in the Northern midnight,
And on the lonely, loon-haunted Nipigon reaches
Rises the hymn of triumph and courage and comfort,
20   Adeste Fideles.[1]

Tones that were fashioned when the faith brooded in
    darkness,
Joined with sonorous vowels in the noble Latin,
Now are married with the long-drawn Ojibwa,
    Uncouth and mournful.

25   Soft with the silver drip of the regular paddles
Falling in rhythm, timed with the liquid, plangent
Sounds from the blades where the whirlpools break and
    are carried
    Down into darkness;

---

1 *"O Come All Ye Faithful."*

Each long cadence, flying like a dove from her shelter
30 Deep in the shadow, wheels for a throbbing moment,
Poises in utterance, returning in circles of silver
      To nest in the silence.

All wild nature stirs with the infinite, tender
Plaint of a bygone age whose soul is eternal,
35 Bound in the lonely phrases that thrill and falter
      Back into quiet.

Back they falter as the deep storm overtakes them,
Whelms them in splendid hollows of booming thunder,
Wraps them in rain, that, sweeping, breaks and on-rushes
40   Ringing like cymbals.

(1905)

WILLIAM BUTLER YEATS

(1865–1939)

orn and raised in Dublin, Ireland, William Butler Yeats became one of the leaders in the Irish nationalist movement in the late nineteenth and early twentieth centuries, and was influential in the formation of the Irish Literary Society and the Irish National Theatre Company. Many of his poems and plays are based on Irish legends and folklore. Yeats rejected conventional religious beliefs and studied a variety of religious and philosophical systems, out of which he developed his own poetic mythology, published in A Vision (1925, revised in 1937). He believed that history was divided into 2000-year cycles. The classical age had begun with the union of the god Zeus (who assumed the form of a swan) and a human being, Leda. The Christian age, which ended the classical, commenced with the union of the Holy Spirit (in the form of a dove) and the Virgin Mary. The period of the Byzantine Empire, between the fifth and fifteenth centuries, represented the Christian age's era of greatest artistic achievement, while the twentieth century marked the final phase of its destruction. Many of the ideas in his system are complex and obscure and are dismissed by some as muddle-headed and foolish; however, it provided him with a number of symbols which, in "The Second Coming," "Sailing to Byzantium," and "Among School Children," are used to present the individual's quest for meaning in the chaotic modern world. In such poems as "Easter 1919," Yeats commented on the tumultuous and often tragic conflicts between the Irish and the British. "Crazy Jane Talks with the Bishop" embodies his belief that great wisdom can be found in the words of old, common, or apparently crazy people.

The Old Men Admiring Themselves in the Water

I heard the old, old men say,
'Everything alters,
And one by one we drop away.'
They had hands like claws, and their knees
5   Were twisted like the old thorn-trees
By the waters.
I heard the old, old men say,
'All that's beautiful drifts away
Like the waters.'

(1904)

Easter 1916[1]

I have met them at close of day
Coming with vivid faces
From counter or desk among grey
Eighteenth-century houses.
5   I have passed with a nod of the head
Or polite meaningless words,
Or have lingered awhile and said
Polite meaningless words,
And thought before I had done
10   Of a mocking tale or a gibe
To please a companion
Around the fire at the club,
Being certain that they and I
But lived where motley[2] is worn:
15   All changed, changed utterly:
A terrible beauty is born.

That woman's days were spent
In ignorant good-will,
Her nights in argument
20   Until her voice grew shrill.
What voice more sweet that hers
When, young and beautiful,
She rode to harriers?[3]
This man had kept a school
25   And rode our wingèd horse;[4]
This other his helper and friend
Was coming into his force;
He might have won fame in the end,
So sensitive his nature seemed,
30   So daring and sweet his thought.

---

1 *at Easter 1916, Irish nationalists unsuccessfully rebelled against the British government. Many nationalists were executed.*
2 *many-coloured cloth often used in the clothing of court jesters.*
3 *i.e., on a hunt with hounds.*
4 *Pegasus, the wingèd horse associated with poetry in Greek mythology.*

This other man I had dreamed
A drunken, vainglorious lout.
He had done most bitter wrong
To some who are near my heart,
35 Yet I number him in the song;
He, too, has resigned his part
In the casual comedy;
He, too, has been changed in his turn,
Transformed utterly:
40 A terrible beauty is born.

Hearts with one purpose alone
Through summer and winter seem
Enchanted to a stone
To trouble the living stream.
45 The horse that comes from the road,
The rider, the birds that range
From cloud to tumbling cloud,
Minute by minute they change;
A shadow of cloud on the stream
50 Changes minute by minute;
A horse-hoof slides on the brim,
And a horse plashes within it;
The long-legged moor-hens dive,
And hens to moor-cocks call;
55 Minute by minute they live:
The stone's in the midst of all.

Too long a sacrifice
Can make a stone of the heart.
O when may it suffice?
60 That is Heaven's part, our part
To murmur name upon name,
As a mother names her child
When sleep at last has come
On limbs that had run wild.
65 What is it but nightfall?
No, no, not night but death;
Was it needless death after all?
For England may keep faith

For all that is done and said.
70   We know their dream; enough
To know they dreamed and are dead;
And what if excess of love
Bewildered them till they died?
I write it out in a verse —
75   MacDonagh and MacBride
And Connolly and Pearse⁵
Now and in time to be,
Wherever green is worn,
Are changed, changed utterly:
80   A terrible beauty is born.

(1916)   (1921)

The Second Coming¹

Turning and turning in the widening gyre²
The falcon cannot hear the falconer;
Things fall apart; the centre cannot hold;
Mere anarchy is loosed upon the world,
5   The blood-dimmed tide is loosed, and everywhere
The ceremony of innocence is drowned;
The best lack all conviction, while the worst
Are full of passionate intensity.

Surely some revelation is at hand;
10   Surely the Second Coming is at hand.
The Second Coming! Hardly are those words out
When a vast image out of *Spiritus Mundi*³
Troubles my sight; somewhere in sands of the desert
A shape with lion body and the head of a man,

---

5 *four Irish patriots who were executed by the British after the Easter uprising.*

1 *traditionally, the coming of Jesus Christ on the Day of Judgement.*
2 *a spiral.*
3 *the Spirit of the Universe.*

15   A gaze blank and pitiless as the sun,
   Is moving its slow thighs, while all about it
   Reel shadows of the indignant desert birds.
   The darkness drops again; but now I know
   That twenty centuries of stony sleep
20   Were vexed to nightmare by a rocking cradle,
   And what rough beast, its hour come round at last,
   Slouches towards Bethlehem[4] to be born?

(1919)   (1920)

Sailing to Byzantium[1]

I

That is no country for old men. The young
In one another's arms, birds in the trees
— Those dying generations — at their song,
The salmon-falls, the mackerel-crowded seas,
5 Fish, flesh, or fowl, commend all summer long
Whatever is begotten, born, and dies.
Caught in that sensual music all neglect
Monuments of unageing intellect.

II

An aged man is but a paltry thing,
10 A tattered coat upon a stick, unless
Soul clap its hands and sing, and louder sing
For every tatter in its mortal dress,
Nor is there singing school but studying
Monuments of its own magnificence;
15 And therefore I have sailed the seas and come
To the holy city of Byzantium.

---

4 birthplace of Jesus Christ.

1 a Greek city on whose site was built the city of Constantinople (now known as Istanbul), noted for its exceptional art.

III

O sages standing in God's holy fire
As in the gold mosaic of a wall,
Come from the holy fire, perne in a gyre,[2]
20   And be the singing-masters of my soul.
Consume my heart away; sick with desire
And fastened to a dying animal
It knows not what it is; and gather me
Into the artifice of eternity.

IV

25   Once out of nature I shall never take
My bodily form from any natural thing,
But such a form as Grecian goldsmiths make
Of hammered gold and gold enamelling
To keep a drowsy Emperor awake;
30   Or set upon a golden bough to sing
To lords and ladies of Byzantium
Of what is past, or passing, or to come.

(1926)   (1927)

Among School Children

I

I walk through the long schoolroom questioning;
A kind old nun in a white hood replies;
The children learn to cipher and to sing,
To study reading-books and histories,
5   To cut and sew, be neat in everything
In the best modern way — the children's eyes
In momentary wonder stare upon
A sixty-year-old smiling public man.

2 *spin in a spiral motion.*

II

I dream of a Ledaean[1] body, bent
Above a sinking fire, a tale that she
Told of a harsh reproof, or trivial event
That changed some childish day to tragedy —
Told, and it seemed that our two natures blent
Into a sphere from youthful sympathy,
Or else, to alter Plato's parable,[2]
Into the yolk and white of the one shell.

III

And thinking of that fit of grief or rage
I look upon one child or t'other there
And wonder if she stood so at that age —
For even daughters of the swan can share
Something of every paddler's heritage —
And had that colour upon cheek or hair,
And thereupon my heart is driven wild:
She stands before me as a living child.

IV

Here present image floats into the mind —
Did Quattrocento[3] finger fashion it
Hollow of cheek as though it drank the wind
And took a mess of shadows for its meat?
And I though never of Ledaean kind
Had pretty plumage once — enough of that,
Better to smile on all that smile, and show
There is a comfortable kind of old scarecrow.

V

What youthful mother, a shape upon her lap
Honey of generation had betrayed,
And that must sleep, shriek, struggle to escape
As recollection or the drug decide,
Would think her son, did she but see that shape
With sixty or more winters on its head,
A compensation for the pang of his birth,
Or the uncertainty of his setting forth?

1 like Leda, a beautiful woman in Greek mythology.
2 in this legend, human beings originally had four legs, four arms, and two faces. This body later split into two.
   The embrace of love was an attempt to become reunified.
3 fifteenth century. The term usually refers to Italian painting of the period.

VI

Plato thought nature but a spume that plays
Upon a ghostly paradigm of things;
Solider Aristotle played the taws
Upon the bottom of a king of kings;
45 World-famous golden-thighed Pythagoras[4]
Fingered upon a fiddle-stick or strings
What a star sang and careless Muses heard:
Old clothes upon old sticks to scare a bird.

VII

Both nuns and mothers worship images,
50 But those the candles light are not as those
That animate a mother's reveries,
But keep a marble or a bronze repose.
And yet they too break hearts — O Presences
That passion, piety or affection knows,
55 And that all heavenly glory symbolise —
O self-born mockers of man's enterprise;

VIII

Labour is blossoming or dancing where
The body is not bruised to pleasure soul,
Nor beauty born out of its own despair,
60 Nor blear-eyed wisdom out of midnight oil.
O chestnut-tree, great-rooted blossomer,
Are you the leaf, the blossom or the bole?
O body swayed to music, O brightening glance,
How can we know the dancer from the dance?

(1926)   (1927)

---

4 *Plato, Aristotle, and Pythagoras were ancient Greek philosophers.*

Crazy Jane Talks with the Bishop

I met the Bishop on the road
And much said he and I.
'Those breasts are flat and fallen now,
Those veins must soon be dry;
5   Live in a heavenly mansion,
Not in some foul sty.'

'Fair and foul are near of kin,
And fair needs foul,' I cried.
'My friends are gone, but that's a truth
10   Nor grave nor bed denied,
Learned in bodily lowliness
And in the heart's pride.

'A woman can be proud and stiff
When on love intent;
15   But Love has pitched his mansion in
The place of excrement;
For nothing can be sole or whole
That has not been rent.'

(1931)   (1932)

Lapis Lazuli[1]

(For Harry Clifton)

I have heard that hysterical women say
They are sick of the palette and fiddle-bow,
Of poets that are always gay,
For everybody knows or else should know

1 a blue semi-precious stone.

5   That if nothing drastic is done
       Aeroplane and Zeppelin² will come out,
       Pitch like King Billy bomb-balls³ in
       Until the town lie beaten flat.

       All perform their tragic play,
10   There struts Hamlet, there is Lear,
       That's Ophelia, that Cordelia;⁴
       Yet they, should the last scene be there,
       The great stage curtain about to drop,
       If worthy their prominent part in the play,
15   Do not break up their lines to weep.
       They know that Hamlet and Lear are gay;
       Gaiety transfiguring all that dread.
       All men have aimed at, found and lost;
       Black out;⁵ Heaven blazing into the head:
20   Tragedy wrought to its uttermost.
       Though Hamlet rambles and Lear rages,
       And all the drop-scenes⁶ drop at once
       Upon a hundred thousand stages,
       It cannot grow by an inch or an ounce.

25   On their own feet they came, or on shipboard,
       Camel-back, horse-back, ass-back, mule-back,
       Old civilisations put to the sword.
       Then they and their wisdom went to rack:
       No handiwork of Callimachus,⁷
30   Who handled marble as if it were bronze,
       Made draperies that seemed to rise
       When sea-wind swept the corner, stands;
       His long lamp-chimney shaped like the stem
       Of a slender palm, stood but a day;
35   All things fall and are built again,
       And those that build them again are gay.

2 *blimp-like German airship.*
3 *bombs.*
4 *Ophelia is Hamlet's lover in Shakespeare's* Hamlet *and Cordelia is Lear's daughter in Shakespeare's* King
  Lear.
5 *darkening the stage during a play.*
6 *curtain on which a scene is painted.*
7 *ancient Greek sculptor.*

Two Chinamen, behind them a third,
Are carved in lapis lazuli,
Over them flies a long-legged bird,[8]
A symbol of longevity;
The third, doubtless a serving-man,
Carries a musical instrument.

40

Every discoloration of the stone,
Every accidental crack or dent,
Seems a water-course or an avalanche,
Or lofty slope where it still snows
Though doubtless plum or cherry-branch
Sweetens the little half-way house
Those Chinamen climb towards, and I
Delight to imagine them seated there;
There, on the mountain and the sky,
On all the tragic scene they stare.
One asks for mournful melodies;
Accomplished fingers begin to play.
Their eyes mid many wrinkles, their eyes,
Their ancient, glittering eyes, are gay.

45

50

55

(1936)   (1938)

The Circus Animals' Desertion

I

I sought a theme and sought for it in vain,
I sought it daily for six weeks or so.
Maybe at last, being but a broken man,
I must be satisfied with my heart, although
Winter and summer till old age began
My circus animals were all on show,
Those stilted boys, that burnished chariot,
Lion and woman and the Lord knows what.

5

8 *a crane.*

II

What can I but enumerate old themes?
10   First that sea-rider Oisin[1] led by the nose
Through three enchanted islands, allegorical dreams,
Vain gaiety, vain battle, vain repose,
Themes of the embittered heart, or so it seems,
That might adorn old songs or courtly shows;
15   But what cared I that set him on to ride,
I, starved for the bosom of his faery bride?

And then a counter-truth filled out its play,
The Countess Cathleen[2] was the name I gave it;
She, pity-crazed, had given her soul away,
20   But masterful Heaven had intervened to save it.
I thought my dear must her own soul destroy,
So did fanaticism and hate enslave it,
And this brought forth a dream and soon enough
This dream itself had all my thought and love.

25   And when the Fool and Blind Man[3] stole the bread
Cuchulain fought the ungovernable sea;
Heart-mysteries there, and yet when all is said
It was the dream itself enchanted me:
Character isolated by a deed
30   To engross the present and dominate memory.
Players and painted stage took all my love,
And not those things that they were emblems of.

III

Those masterful images because complete
Grew in pure mind, but out of what began?
35   A mound of refuse or the sweepings of a street,
Old kettles, old bottles, and a broken can,
Old iron, old bones, old rags, that raving slut
Who keeps the till. Now that my ladder's gone,
I must lie down where all the ladders start,
40   In the foul rag-and-bone shop of the heart.

(1939)

---

1 *legendary Irish hero who was taken into fairyland for 150 years.*
2 *in this play by Yeats, the heroine sold her soul to the devil to aid starving people.*
3 *characters in a play by Yeats about the conflict between Cuchulain, who strives for individuality, and Conchubae, who wants strong government.*

EDWIN ARLINGTON ROBINSON

(1869–1935)

*orn into a distinguished New England family in decline, Edwin Arling-
ton Robinson was raised in Maine, and his work shows an old-fashioned
New England concern with ethical conflict and individual responsibility. Robinson's
poetry presents a bleak, somewhat fatalistic view of life. Little in his life would have
encouraged optimism. As a youth, he was shy and often ill. A scholar by nature,
he was later forced by his family's misfortunes to abandon his studies at Harvard.
Although his poetry eventually won both popular and critical acclaim, this success
came only after decades of frustration and disappointment. During his lifetime,
Robinson's most popular works were his book-length rewritings of Arthurian leg-
ends — Tristram (1927) won a Pulitzer Prize and sold over 100 000 copies —
but he is remembered today mainly for the concentrated psychological studies of
New England characters, usually eccentrics or failures, which he wrote earlier in
his career.*

Richard Cory

Whenever Richard Cory went down town,
We people on the pavement looked at him:
He was a gentleman from sole to crown,
Clean favored, and imperially slim.

5   And he was always quietly arrayed,
And he was always human when he talked;
But still he fluttered pulses when he said,
"Good-morning," and he glittered when he walked.

And he was rich — yes, richer than a king —
10   And admirably schooled in every grace:
In fine, we thought that he was everything
To make us wish that we were in his place.

So on we worked, and waited for the light,
And went without the meat, and cursed the bread;
15   And Richard Cory, one calm summer night,
Went home and put a bullet through his head.

(1897)

Mr. Flood's Party

Old Eben Flood, climbing alone one night
Over the hill between the town below
And the forsaken upland hermitage
That held as much as he should ever know
5   On earth again of home, paused warily.
The road was his with not a native near;
And Eben, having leisure, said aloud,
For no man else in Tilbury Town[1] to hear:

"Well, Mr. Flood, we have the harvest moon
10   Again, and we may not have many more;
The bird is on the wing, the poet says,[2]
And you and I have said it here before.
Drink to the bird." He raised up to the light
The jug that he had gone so far to fill,
15   And answered huskily: "Well, Mr. Flood,
Since you propose it, I believe I will."

Alone, as if enduring to the end
A valiant armor of scarred hopes outworn,
He stood there in the middle of the road
20   Like Roland's ghost winding a silent horn.[3]
Below him, in the town among the trees,
Where friends of other days had honored him,
A phantom salutation of the dead
Rang thinly till old Eben's eyes were dim.

25   Then, as a mother lays her sleeping child
Down tenderly, fearing it may awake,
He set the jug down slowly at his feet
With trembling care, knowing that most things break;

---

1 *used by Robinson in various poems to represent Gardiner, Maine, where he grew up.*
2 *echoes English poet Edward Fitzgerald's (1809–83) version of* The Rubáiyát of Omar Khayyám *(1859).*
3 *in the medieval* Song of Roland, *Roland refuses to blow his horn for help, even though his force is greatly outnumbered, until he is at the point of death.*

And only when assured that on firm earth
30   It stood, as the uncertain lives of men
Assuredly did not, he paced away,
And with his hand extended paused again:

"Well, Mr. Flood, we have not met like this
In a long time; and many a change has come
35   To both of us, I fear, since last it was
We had a drop together. Welcome home!"
Convivially returning with himself,
Again he raised the jug up to the light;
And with an acquiescent quaver said:
40   "Well, Mr. Flood, if you insist, I might.

"Only a very little, Mr. Flood —
For auld lang syne. No more, sir; that will do."
So, for the time, apparently it did,
And Eben evidently thought so too;
45   For soon amid the silver loneliness
Of night he lifted up his voice and sang,
Secure, with only two moons listening,
Until the whole harmonious landscape rang —

"For auld lang syne." The weary throat gave out,
50   The last word wavered, and the song was done.
He raised again the jug regretfully
And shook his head, and was again alone.
There was not much that was ahead of him,
And there was nothing in the town below —
55   Where strangers would have shut the many doors
That many friends had opened long ago.

(1921)

Eros Turannos¹

She fears him, and will always ask
   What fated her to choose him;
She meets in his engaging mask
   All reasons to refuse him;
5 But what she meets and what she fears
Are less than are the downward years,
Drawn slowly to the foamless weirs
   Of age, were she to lose him.

Between a blurred sagacity
10   That once had power to sound him,
And Love, that will not let him be
   The Judas that she found him,
Her pride assuages her almost,
As if it were alone the cost. —
15 He sees that he will not be lost,
   And waits and looks around him.

A sense of ocean and old trees
   Envelops and allures him;
Tradition, touching all he sees,
20   Beguiles and reassures him;
And all her doubts of what he says
Are dimmed with what she knows of days —
Till even prejudice delays
   And fades, and she secures him.

25 The falling leaf inaugurates
   The reign of her confusion;
The pounding wave reverberates
   The dirge of her illusion;
And home, where passion lived and died,
30 Becomes a place where she can hide,
While all the town and harbor side
   Vibrate with her seclusion.

1 *"Love, the Tyrant" (Greek).*

We tell you, tapping on our brows,
   The story as it should be, —
35   As if the story of a house
   Were told, or ever could be;
We'll have no kindly veil between
Her visions and those we have seen, —
As if we guessed what hers have been,
40   Or what they are or would be.

Meanwhile we do no harm; for they
   That with a god have striven,
Not hearing much of what we say,
   Take what the god has given;
45   Though like waves breaking it may be,
Or like a changed familiar tree,
Or like a stairway to the sea
   Where down the blind are driven.

(1916)

WALTER DE LA MARE

(1873–1956)

Although best known as a writer and editor of children's works, Walter de la Mare published more than 80 books of prose and poetry for adults. Born in Charlton, Kent, and educated at St. Paul's Choir School, he published his first collection of verse under a pseudonym in 1902. De la Mare was especially concerned with the aural qualities of poetry. "We can, . . . " he said, "particularly when we are young, delight in the sound of the words of a poem . . . without realizing its full meaning." Because they possess strong musical qualities, contain some narrative elements, and treat childhood, fantastic events, or the mystery within apparently commonplace things, many of his best poems are suitable for and have been favourites of both adults and children.

The Listeners

'Is there anybody there?' said the Traveller,
   Knocking on the moonlit door;
And his horse in the silence champed the grasses
   Of the forest's ferny floor:
5   And a bird flew up out of the turret,
   Above the Traveller's head:
And he smote upon the door again a second time;
   'Is anybody there?' he said.
But no one descended to the Traveller;
10   No head from the leaf-fringed sill
Leaned over and looked into his grey eyes,
   Where he stood perplexed and still.
But only a host of phantom listeners
   That dwelt in the lone house then
15   Stood listening in the quiet of the moonlight
   To that voice from the world of men:
Stood thronging the faint moonbeams on the dark stair,
   That goes down to the empty hall,
Hearkening in an air stirred and shaken
20   By the lonely Traveller's call.

And he felt in his heart their strangeness,
　　Their stillness answering his cry,
While his horse moved, cropping the dark turf,
　　'Neath the starred and leafy sky;
25　For he suddenly smote on the door, even
　　Louder, and lifted his head: —
'Tell them I came, and no one answered,
　　That I kept my word,' he said.
Never the least stir made the listeners,
30　　Though every word he spake
Fell echoing through the shadowiness of the still house
　　From the one man left awake:
Ay, they heard his foot upon the stirrup,
　　And the sound of iron on stone,
35　And how the silence surged softly backward,
　　When the plunging hoofs were gone.

(1912)

ROBERT FROST

(1874–1963)

*T*hough born in California, Robert Frost wrote most of his poetry about life in New England, where his family originated and where he moved at eleven with his widowed mother. Frost had the ability, rare in modern times, to appeal to both sophisticated and unsophisticated audiences with the same poems, and he eventually became the most popular serious poet of his country. But success did not come easily. He wrote in obscurity until middle age, supporting his family mainly by farming and teaching, and received recognition in his own country only after his first two books, A Boy's Will (1913) and North of Boston (1914), had been published and praised in England.

Although Frost was learned and intellectual, and taught in various universities after 1915, he preferred to present himself as a rustic sage whose wisdom was derived from common sense and the everyday experiences he explored in his poetry. Despite its wide appeal, this public persona, together with Frost's reliance on traditional forms and his treatment of homely subjects, gives many of his best-known poems the deceptive appearance of slightness, but Frost confronts the darkness and philosophical uncertainty of modern life as honestly as any of his contemporaries, and his work is highly innovative in its use of vernacular speech and conversational rhythms.

After Apple-Picking

My long two-pointed ladder's sticking through a tree
Toward heaven still,
And there's a barrel that I didn't fill
Beside it, and there may be two or three
5   Apples I didn't pick upon some bough.
But I am done with apple-picking now.
Essence of winter sleep is on the night,
The scent of apples: I am drowsing off.
I cannot rub the strangeness from my sight
10   I got from looking through a pane of glass
I skimmed this morning from the drinking trough
And held against the world of hoary grass.
It melted, and I let it fall and break.

But I was well
15   Upon my way to sleep before it fell,
And I could tell
What form my dreaming was about to take.
Magnified apples appear and disappear,
Stem end and blossom end,
20   And every fleck of russet showing clear.
My instep arch not only keeps the ache,
It keeps the pressure of a ladder-round.
I feel the ladder sway as the boughs bend.
And I keep hearing from the cellar bin
25   The rumbling sound
Of load on load of apples coming in.
For I have had too much
Of apple-picking: I am overtired
Of the great harvest I myself desired.
30   There were ten thousand thousand fruit to touch,
Cherish in hand, lift down, and not let fall.
For all
That struck the earth,
No matter if not bruised or spiked with stubble,
35   Went surely to the cider-apple heap
As of no worth.
One can see what will trouble
This sleep of mine, whatever sleep it is.
Were he not gone,
40   The woodchuck could say whether it's like his
Long sleep, as I describe its coming on,
Or just some human sleep.

(1914)

An Old Man's Winter Night

All out-of-doors looked darkly in at him
Through the thin frost, almost in separate stars,
That gathers on the pane in empty rooms.
What kept his eyes from giving back the gaze

5   Was the lamp tilted near them in his hand.
What kept him from remembering what it was
That brought him to that creaking room was age.
He stood with barrels round him — At a loss.
And having scared the cellar under him
10 In clomping here, he scared it once again
In clomping off; — and scared the outer night,
Which has its sounds, familiar, like the roar
Of trees and crack of branches, common things,
But nothing so like beating on a box.
15 A light he was to no one but himself
Where now he sat, concerned with he knew what,
A quiet light, and then not even that.
He consigned to the moon, such as she was,
So late-arising, to the broken moon
20 As better than the sun in any case
For such a charge, his snow upon the roof,
His icicles along the wall to keep;
And slept. The log that shifted with a jolt
Once in the stove, disturbed him and he shifted,
25 And eased his heavy breathing, but still slept.
One aged man — one man — can't keep a house,
A farm, a countryside, or if he can,
It's thus he does it of a winter night.

(1916)

For Once, Then, Something

Others taunt me with having knelt at well-curbs
Always wrong to the light, so never seeing
Deeper down in the well than where the water
Gives me back in a shining surface picture
5   Me myself in the summer heaven godlike
Looking out of a wreath of fern and cloud puffs.
Once, when trying with chin against a well-curb,
I discerned, as I thought, beyond the picture,

Through the picture, a something white, uncertain,
10   Something more of the depths — and then I lost it.
Water came to rebuke the too clear water.
One drop fell from a fern, and lo, a ripple
Shook whatever it was lay there at bottom,
Blurred it, blotted it out. What was that whiteness?
15   Truth? A pebble of quartz? For once, then, something.

(1923)

Stopping by Woods on a Snowy Evening

Whose woods these are I think I know.
His house is in the village though;
He will not see me stopping here
To watch his woods fill up with snow.

5   My little horse must think it queer
To stop without a farmhouse near
Between the woods and frozen lake
The darkest evening of the year.

He gives his harness bells a shake
10   To ask if there is some mistake.
The only other sound's the sweep
Of easy wind and downy flake.

The woods are lovely, dark and deep,
But I have promises to keep,
15   And miles to go before I sleep,
And miles to go before I sleep.

(1923)

Acquainted with the Night

I have been one acquainted with the night.
I have walked out in rain — and back in rain.
I have outwalked the furthest city light.

I have looked down the saddest city lane.
5   I have passed by the watchman on his beat
And dropped my eyes, unwilling to explain.

I have stood still and stopped the sound of feet
When far away an interrupted cry
Came over houses from another street,

10   But not to call me back or say good-by;
And further still at an unearthly height,
One luminary clock against the sky

Proclaimed the time was neither wrong nor right.
I have been one acquainted with the night.

(1928)

Design

I found a dimpled spider, fat and white,
On a white heal-all,[1] holding up a moth
Like a white piece of rigid satin cloth —
Assorted characters of death and blight
5   Mixed ready to begin the morning right,
Like the ingredients of a witches' broth —
A snow-drop spider, a flower like a froth,
And dead wings carried like a paper kite.

---

1 *a plant (*Prunella vulgaris, *also called woundwort), normally with blue flowers, thought to have healing power.*

What had that flower to do with being white,
10   The wayside blue and innocent heal-all?
What brought the kindred spider to that height,
Then steered the white moth thither in the night?
What but design of darkness to appall? —
If design govern in a thing so small.

(1936)

WALLACE STEVENS

(1879–1955)

Born in Pennsylvania and educated at Harvard and the New York Law School, Wallace Stevens lived most of his adult life in Hartford, Connecticut, where he advanced to the rank of vice-president with the Hartford Accident and Indemnity Company. Although Stevens began writing poetry seriously when at university, he devoted much of his energy to law and business in the years that followed and was 44 when his first collection of poems, Harmonium *(1923), was published. From late middle age on, having become financially secure, Stevens devoted himself increasingly to his poetry. Although he is a philosophical poet, much concerned with ideas of order and the relationship between imagination and reality, Stevens is also a master at evoking complex sensuous experience; his poems are distinguished by the originality of their opulent, intricate images and their subtle, deftly controlled rhythms.*

Sunday Morning

I

Complacencies of the peignoir,[1] and late
Coffee and oranges in a sunny chair,
And the green freedom of a cockatoo
Upon a rug mingle to dissipate
5   The holy hush of ancient sacrifice.
She dreams a little, and she feels the dark
Encroachment of that old catastrophe,
As a calm darkens among water-lights.
The pungent oranges and bright, green wings
10   Seem things in some procession of the dead,
Winding across wide water, without sound.
The day is like wide water, without sound,
Stilled for the passing of her dreaming feet
Over the seas, to silent Palestine,
15   Dominion of the blood and sepulchre.

---

1 *a loose, often sheer robe.*

II

Why should she give her bounty to the dead?
What is divinity if it can come
Only in silent shadows and in dreams?
Shall she not find in comforts of the sun,
In pungent fruit and bright, green wings, or else
In any balm or beauty of the earth,
Things to be cherished like the thought of heaven?
Divinity must live within herself:
Passions of rain, or moods in falling snow;
Grievings in loneliness, or unsubdued
Elations when the forest blooms; gusty
Emotions on wet roads on autumn nights;
All pleasures and all pains, remembering
The bough of summer and the winter branch.
These are the measures destined for her soul.

III

Jove in the clouds had his inhuman birth.
No mother suckled him, no sweet land gave
Large-mannered motions to his mythy mind
He moved among us, as a muttering king,
Magnificent, would move among his hinds,[2]
Until our blood, commingling, virginal,
With heaven, brought such requital to desire
The very hinds discerned it, in a star.
Shall our blood fail? Or shall it come to be
The blood of paradise? And shall the earth
Seem all of paradise that we shall know?
The sky will be much friendlier then than now,
A part of labor and a part of pain,
And next in glory to enduring love,
Not this dividing and indifferent blue.

IV

She says, "I am content when wakened birds,
Before they fly, test the reality
Of misty fields, by their sweet questionings;

2 *farmhands or shepherds.*

But when the birds are gone, and their warm fields
50   Return no more, where, then, is paradise?"
There is not any haunt of prophecy,
Nor any old chimera³ of the grave,
Neither the golden underground, nor isle
Melodious, where spirits gat them home,
55   Nor visionary south, nor cloudy palm
Remote on heaven's hill, that has endured
As April's green endures; or will endure
Like her remembrance of awakened birds,
Or her desire for June and evening, tipped
60   By the consummation of the swallow's wings.

V

She says, "But in contentment I still feel
The need of some imperishable bliss."
Death is the mother of beauty; hence from her,
Alone, shall come fulfilment to our dreams
65   And our desires. Although she strews the leaves
Of sure obliteration on our paths,
The path sick sorrow took, the many paths
Where triumph rang its brassy phrase, or love
Whispered a little out of tenderness,
70   She makes the willow shiver in the sun
For maidens who were wont to sit and gaze
Upon the grass, relinquished to their feet.
She causes boys to pile new plums and pears
On disregarded plate. The maidens taste
75   And stray impassioned in the littering leaves.

VI

Is there no change of death in paradise?
Does ripe fruit never fall? Or do the boughs
Hang always heavy in that perfect sky,
Unchanging, yet so like our perishing earth,
80   With rivers like our own that seek for seas
They never find, the same receding shores
That never touch with inarticulate pang?
Why set the pear upon those river-banks

---

3 *a horrible but imaginary monster.*

Or spice the shores with odors of the plum?
85   Alas, that they should wear our colors there,
The silken weavings of our afternoons,
And pick the strings of our insipid lutes!
Death is the mother of beauty, mystical,
Within whose burning bosom we devise
90   Our earthly mothers waiting, sleeplessly.

VII

Supple and turbulent, a ring of men
Shall chant in orgy on a summer morn
Their boisterous devotion to the sun,
Not as a god, but as a god might be,
95   Naked among them, like a savage source.
Their chant shall be a chant of paradise,
Out of their blood, returning to the sky;
And in their chant shall enter, voice by voice,
The windy lake wherein their lord delights,
100   The trees, like serafin,[4] and echoing hills,
That choir among themselves long afterward.
They shall know well the heavenly fellowship
Of men that perish and of summer morn.
And whence they came and whither they shall go
105   The dew upon their feet shall manifest.

VIII

She hears, upon that water without sound,
A voice that cries, "The tomb in Palestine
Is not the porch of spirits lingering.
It is the grave of Jesus, where he lay."
110   We live in an old chaos of the sun,
Or old dependency of day and night,
Or island solitude, unsponsored, free,
Of that wide water, inescapable.
Deer walk upon our mountains, and the quail
115   Whistle about us their spontaneous cries;
Sweet berries ripen in the wilderness;

4 *high-ranking angels.*

And, in the isolation of the sky,
At evening, casual flocks of pigeons make
Ambiguous undulations as they sink,
120   Downward to darkness, on extended wings.

(1915)   (1923)

Thirteen Ways of Looking at a Blackbird

I

Among twenty snowy mountains,
The only moving thing
Was the eye of the blackbird.

II

I was of three minds,
5   Like a tree
In which there are three blackbirds.

III

The blackbird whirled in the autumn winds.
It was a small part of the pantomime.

IV

A man and a woman
10   Are one.
A man and a woman and a blackbird
Are one.

V

I do not know which to prefer,
The beauty of inflections
15   Or the beauty of innuendoes,
The blackbird whistling
Or just after.

VI

Icicles filled the long window
With barbaric glass.
20 The shadow of the blackbird
Crossed it, to and fro.
The mood
Traced in the shadow
An indecipherable cause.

VII

25 O thin men of Haddam,[1]
Why do you imagine golden birds?
Do you not see how the blackbird
Walks around the feet
Of the women about you?

VIII

30 I know noble accents
And lucid, inescapable rhythms;
But I know, too,
That the blackbird is involved
In what I know.

IX

35 When the blackbird flew out of sight,
It marked the edge
Of one of many circles.

X

At the sight of blackbirds
Flying in a green light,
40 Even the bawds of euphony
Would cry out sharply.

XI

He rode over Connecticut
In a glass coach.
Once, a fear pierced him,

---

1 *a town in Connecticut.*

45   In that he mistook
       The shadow of his equipage
       For blackbirds.

XII

       The river is moving.
       The blackbird must be flying.

XIII

50   It was evening all afternoon.
       It was snowing
       And it was going to snow.
       The blackbird sat
       In the cedar-limbs.

                                                    (1931)

The Idea of Order at Key West

       She sang beyond the genius of the sea.
       The water never formed to mind or voice,
       Like a body wholly body, fluttering
       Its empty sleeves; and yet its mimic motion
5   Made constant cry, caused constantly a cry,
       That was not ours although we understood,
       Inhuman, of the veritable ocean.

       The sea was not a mask. No more was she.
       The song and water were not medleyed sound
10   Even if what she sang was what she heard,
       Since what she sang was uttered word by word.
       It may be that in all her phrases stirred
       The grinding water and the gasping wind;
       But it was she and not the sea we heard.

15   For she was the maker of the song she sang.
      The ever-hooded, tragic-gestured sea
      Was merely a place by which she walked to sing.
      Whose spirit is this? we said, because we knew
      It was the spirit that we sought and knew
20   That we should ask this often as she sang.

      If it was only the dark voice of the sea
      That rose, or even colored by many waves;
      If it was only the outer voice of sky
      And cloud, of the sunken coral water-walled,
25   However clear, it would have been deep air,
      The heaving speech of air, a summer sound
      Repeated in a summer without end
      And sound alone. But it was more than that,
      More even than her voice, and ours, among
30   The meaningless plungings of water and the wind,
      Theatrical distances, bronze shadows heaped
      On high horizons, mountainous atmospheres
      Of sky and sea.

                    It was her voice that made
      The sky acutest at its vanishing.
35   She measured to the hour its solitude.
      She was the single artificer of the world
      In which she sang. And when she sang, the sea,
      Whatever self it had, became the self
      That was her song, for she was the maker. Then we,
40   As we beheld her striding there alone,
      Knew that there never was a world for her
      Except the one she sang and, singing, made.

      Ramon Fernandez,[1] tell me, if you know,
      Why, when the singing ended and we turned
45   Toward the town, tell why the glassy lights,
      The lights in the fishing boats at anchor there,
      As the night descended, tilting in the air,
      Mastered the night and portioned out the sea,
      Fixing emblazoned zones and fiery poles,
50   Arranging, deepening, enchanting night.

---

1 *Stevens said he simply made this name up with no actual person in mind.*

Oh! Blessed rage for order, pale Ramon,
The maker's rage to order words of the sea,
Words of the fragrant portals, dimly-starred,
And of ourselves and of our origins,
55   In ghostlier demarcations, keener sounds.

(1935)

Study of Two Pears

I

Opusculum paedagogum.[1]
The pears are not viols,
Nudes or bottles.
They resemble nothing else.

II

5   They are yellow forms
Composed of curves
Bulging toward the base.
They are touched red.

III

They are not flat surfaces
10   Having curved outlines.
They are round
Tapering toward the top.

IV

In the way they are modelled
There are bits of blue.
15   A hard dry leaf hangs
From the stem.

---

1 *a little instructional work (Latin).*

V

The yellow glistens.
It glistens with various yellows,
Citrons, oranges and greens
20   Flowering over the skin.

VI

The shadows of the pears
Are blobs on the green cloth.
The pears are not seen
As the observer wills.

(1942)

E.J. PRATT

(1882–1964)

dwin John Pratt, son of a Methodist minister, was born in Western Bay, Newfoundland. After graduating from St. John's Methodist College and serving as both a teacher and a preacher in several outport villages, he attended Victoria College, University of Toronto, receiving his B.A. (1911), M.A. (1912), B.D. (1913), and Ph.D. (1917). Although ordained in 1913, Pratt never served as a minister. Instead, he became a member of the Victoria College English Department in 1920. He is best known for his lengthy narratives, such as The Titanic *(1935),* Brébeuf and His Brethren *(1940), and* Towards the Last Spike *(1952), the latter two of which won the Governor General's Award. Pratt's concern for scientific and technological matters, ranging from evolution to communication, is evident throughout his work. His religious background and ethical ideas are embodied in biblical references and images of individuals sacrificing themselves for the common good or enduring inevitable suffering.*

From Stone to Steel

From stone to bronze, from bronze to steel
Along the road-dust of the sun,
Two revolutions of the wheel
From Java[1] to Geneva[2] run.

5   The snarl Neanderthal[3] is worn
Close to the smiling Aryan[4] lips,
The civil polish of the horn
Gleams from our praying finger tips.

---

1 *the site of the discovery in 1891 of the fossil remains of an early type of human, Pithecanthropus, or, as he was popularly called, "Java Ape Man."*

2 *a city long identified with advocating humane and reasonable conduct — the Geneva Convention of 1864 codified rules of war, for example — it was chosen as headquarters for the League of Nations in 1919.*

3 *a cave-dwelling early human of the Upper Pleistocene Age, whose remains were first located in sites in Europe.*

4 *even before Hitler assumed power in 1933, the term, originally describing a prehistoric group of peoples whose language was presumed to be the basis of most Indo-European languages, was being used to refer to non-Jews of European, especially Nordic, descent.*

The evolution of desire

10   Has but matured a toxic wine,
      Drunk long before its heady fire
      Reddened Euphrates or the Rhine.[5]

      Between the temple and the cave
      The boundary lies tissue-thin:

15   The yearlings still the altars crave
      As satisfaction for a sin.

      The road goes up, the road goes down —
      Let Java or Geneva be —
      But whether to the cross or crown,

20   The path lies through Gethsemane.[6]

(1932)

The Truant

      "What have you there?" the great Panjandrum[1] said
      To the Master of the Revels who had led
      A bucking truant with a stiff backbone
      Close to the foot of the Almighty's throne.

5   "Right Reverend, most adored,
      And forcibly acknowledged Lord
      By the keen logic of your two-edged sword!
      This creature has presumed to classify
      Himself — a biped, rational, six feet high

10   And two feet wide; weighs fourteen stone;[2]

---

5 the Euphrates, a major river in southwest Asia, and the Rhine, the principal waterway of Europe, were influential in developing civilizations and were sites of numerous wars.

6 a garden outside the walls of Jerusalem, it was the site of what is known as the agony of Christ: the sorrowing Christ prayed that his coming trials might be removed, yet also resigned himself, saying that God's will, not his own, should prevail. Shortly afterwards, Judas betrayed Christ in this garden.

1 coined by the English dramatist Samuel Foote (1720–77), this is a mock title for a pompous official of exaggerated importance or power.

2 a British unit of weight equal to fourteen pounds or about six kilograms.

Is guilty of a multitude of sins.
He has abjured his choric origins,
And like an undomesticated slattern,
Walks with tangential step unknown
15   Within the weave of the atomic pattern.
He has developed concepts, grins
Obscenely at your Royal bulletins,
Possesses what he calls a will
Which challenges your power to kill."

20   "What is his pedigree?"

"The base is guaranteed, your Majesty —
Calcium, carbon, phosphorus, vapour
And other fundamentals spun
From the umbilicus of the sun,
25   And yet he says he will not caper
Around your throne, nor toe the rules
For the ballet of the fiery molecules."
"His concepts and denials — scrap them, burn them —
To the chemists with them promptly."
                                              "Sire,
30   The stuff is not amenable to fire.
Nothing but their own kind can overturn them.
The chemists have sent back the same old story —
'With our extreme gelatinous apology,
We beg to inform your Imperial Majesty,
35   Unto whom be dominion and power and glory,
There still remains that strange precipitate
Which has the quality to resist
Our oldest and most trusted catalyst.
It is a substance we cannot cremate
40   By temperatures known to our Laboratory.'"

And the great Panjandrum's face grew dark —
"I'll put those chemists to their annual purge,
And I myself shall be the thaumaturge[3]
To find the nature of this fellow's spark.
45   Come, bring him nearer by yon halter rope:

---

3 *a worker of miracles or wonders.*

I'll analyse him with the cosmoscope."
Pulled forward with his neck awry,
The little fellow six feet short,
Aware he was about to die,
50   Committed grave contempt of court
By answering with a flinchless stare
The Awful Presence seated there.

The ALL HIGH swore until his face was black.
He called him a coprophagite,[4]
55   A genus *homo*, egomaniac,
Third cousin to the family of worms,
A sporozoan[5] from the ooze of night,
Spawn of a spavined[6] troglodyte:[7]
He swore by all the catalogue of terms
60   Known since the slang of carboniferous[8] Time.
He said that he could trace him back
To pollywogs and earwigs in the slime.
And in his shrillest tenor he began
Reciting his indictment of the man,
65   Until he closed upon this capital crime —
"You are accused of singing out of key,
(A foul unmitigated dissonance)
Of shuffling in the measures of the dance,
Then walking out with that defiant, free
70   Toss of your head, banging the doors,
Leaving a stench upon the jacinth[9] floors.
You have fallen like a curse
On the mechanics of my Universe.

"Herewith I measure out your penalty —
75   Hearken while you hear, look while you see:
I send you now upon your homeward route
Where you shall find

---

4 *one who eats dung.* 5 *a class of parasitic protozoans.* 6 *suffering from spavin, a disease of horses in which the hock joint becomes inflamed; by extension, lame or broken down.* 7 *cave-dweller.* 8 *a geological period, beginning about 315 million years ago, during which conditions produced a lush growth of vegetation, the remains of which formed the great coal beds.* 9 *a reddish-orange gem.*

Humiliation for your pride of mind.
I shall make deaf the ear, and dim the eye,
80   Put palsy in your touch, make mute
Your speech, intoxicate your cells and dry
Your blood and marrow, shoot
Arthritic needles through your cartilage,
And having parched you with old age,
85   I'll pass you wormwise through the mire;
And when your rebel will
Is mouldered, all desire
Shrivelled, all your concepts broken,
Backward in dust I'll blow you till
90   You join my spiral festival of fire.
Go, Master of the Revels — I have spoken."

And the little genus *homo*, six feet high,
Standing erect, countered with this reply —
"You dumb insouciant invertebrate,
95   You rule a lower than a feudal state —
A realm of flunkey decimals that run,
Return; return and run; again return,
Each group around its little sun,
And every sun a satellite.
100   There they go by day and night,
Nothing to do but run and burn,
Taking turn and turn about,
Light-year in and light-year out,
Dancing, dancing in quadrillions,
105   Never leaving their pavilions.

"Your astronomical conceit
Of bulk and power is anserine.[10]
Your ignorance so thick,
You did not know your own arithmetic.
110   We flung the graphs about your flying feet;
We measured your diameter —
Merely a line
Of zeros prefaced by an integer.

10 *goose-like; thus, stupid or foolish.*

Before we came
115   You had no name.
You did not know direction or your pace;
We taught you all you ever knew
Of motion, time and space.
We healed you of your vertigo
120   And put you in our kindergarten show,
Perambulated you through prisms, drew
Your mileage through the Milky Way,
Lassoed your comets when they ran astray,
Yoked Leo, Taurus, and your team of Bears[11]
125   To pull our kiddy cars of inverse squares.

"Boast not about your harmony,
Your perfect curves, your rings
Of *pure and endless light*[12] — 'Twas we
Who pinned upon your Seraphim[13] their wings,
130   And when your brassy heavens rang
With joy that morning while the planets sang
Their choruses of archangelic lore,
'Twas we who ordered the notes upon their score
Out of our winds and strings.
135   Yes! all your shapely forms
Are ours — parabolas of silver light,
Those blueprints of your spiral stairs
From nadir depth to zenith height,
Coronas, rainbows after storms,
140   Auroras on your eastern tapestries
And constellations over western seas.

"And when, one day, grown conscious of your age,
While pondering an eolith,[14]
We turned a human page
145   And blotted out a cosmic myth
With all its baby symbols to explain

11 *constellations: Leo, the lion; Taurus, the bull; and Ursa Major and Ursa Minor, the big bear and little bear,*
respectively.
12 *a phrase from the opening of "The World" (1650) by Henry Vaughn (1621–95):*
    I saw eternity the other night
    Like a great ring of pure and endless light.
13 *one of the highest orders of angels.*
14 *a roughly shaped tool from the earliest stone age.*

The sunlight in Apollo's eyes,[15]
Our rising pulses and the birth of pain,
Fear, and that fern-and-fungus breath
150 Stalking our nostrils to our caves of death —
That day we learned how to anatomize
Your body, calibrate your size
And set a mirror up before your face
To show you what you really were — a rain
155 Of dull Lucretian atoms[16] crowding space,
A series of concentric waves which any fool
Might make by dropping stones within a pool,
Or an exploding bomb forever in flight
Bursting like hell through Chaos and Old Night.[17]

160 "You oldest of the hierarchs
Composed of electronic sparks,
We grant you speed,
We grant you power, and fire
That ends in ash, but we concede
165 To you no pain nor joy nor love nor hate,
No final tableau of desire,
No causes won or lost, no free
Adventure at the outposts — only
The degradation of your energy[18]
170 When at some late
Slow number of your dance your sergeant-major Fate
Will catch you blind and groping and will send
You reeling on that long and lonely
Lockstep of your wave-lengths towards your end.

---

15 *Apollo, the Greek god of music, poetry, archery, healing, and prophecy, was often identified with Helios, the sun god, and given the epithet Phoebus ("Shining One").*

16 *in* De Rerum Natura *(On the Nature of Things), the Roman poet and philosopher Lucretius (c. 96–55 B.C.) sought to provide a reasonable explanation for natural phenomena. He argued that, since nothing can come from nothing, all being has its source in minuscule seeds of matter that rain down from a void.*

17 *in* Paradise Lost *(I.54–43), Milton says of the fallen angels:*
 . . . *the universal host up sent*
 A shout that tore Hell's concave, and beyond
 Frighted the reign of Chaos and Old Night.
In Milton's schema, Chaos and Dark Night represent the first materials of the cosmos.

18 *entropy, one of the concepts of thermodynamics, suggests that the universe must eventually lose all of its energy.*

175   "We who have met
       With stubborn calm the dawn's hot fusillades;[19]
       Who have seen the forehead sweat
       Under the tug of pulleys on the joints,
       Under the liquidating tally
180   Of the cat-and-truncheon bastinades;[20]
       Who have taught our souls to rally
       To mountain horns and the sea's rockets
       When the needle ran demented through the points;
       We who have learned to clench
185   Our fists and raise our lightless sockets
       To morning skies after the midnight raids,
       Yet cocked our ears to bugles on the barricades,
       And in cathedral rubble found a way to quench
       A dying thirst within a Galilean valley — [21]
190   No! by the Rood,[22] we will not join your ballet."

(1943)

---

19 a simultaneous discharge of firearms.
20 beatings with whips (cat-o'-nine-tails) and sticks or clubs (truncheons).
21 Galilee was a Roman province in northern Palestine during the time of Christ, who began his ministry there
    and was sometimes called the Galilean.
22 the cross upon which Christ died.

WILLIAM CARLOS WILLIAMS

(1883–1963)

A medical doctor as well as a writer, William Carlos Williams spent most of his life in Rutherford, New Jersey, where he maintained a busy practice as a pediatrician. Williams worked in various genres, producing more than two dozen volumes of poetry, fiction, essays, plays, and autobiography, but he was most influential as a poet. While studying at the University of Pennsylvania, he developed a lasting friendship with Ezra Pound, and through Pound was influenced by imagism, an Anglo-American poetic movement stressing concentration, freedom in form and subject matter, and especially precise, concrete images. Working from imagism, Williams developed a distinctive style of free verse, characterized by careful observation, vivid images, and a reliance on the rhythms and diction of common American speech. Although initially overshadowed by other modernist poets, Williams's influence on American poets since World War II has equalled that of any of his contemporaries.

Portrait of a Lady

Your thighs are appletrees
whose blossoms touch the sky.
Which sky? The sky
where Watteau[1] hung a lady's
5   slipper. Your knees
are a southern breeze — or
a gust of snow. Agh! what
sort of man was Fragonard?[2]
— as if that answered
10   anything. Ah, yes — below
the knees, since the tune
drops that way, it is
one of those white summer days,
the tall grass of your ankles
15   flickers upon the shore —
Which shore? —

---

1 French painter Jean-Antoine Watteau (1684–1721).
2 French painter Jean-Honoré Fragonard (1732–1806). Like Watteau, Fragonard specialized in painting love scenes.

the sand clings to my lips —
Which shore?
Agh, petals maybe. How
20   should I know?
Which shore? Which shore?
I said petals from an appletree.

(1915)

Tract

I will teach you my townspeople
how to perform a funeral —
for you have it over a troop
of artists —
5   unless one should scour the world —
you have the ground sense necessary.

See! the hearse leads.
I begin with a design for a hearse.
For Christ's sake not black —
10   nor white either — and not polished!
Let it be weathered — like a farm wagon —
with gilt wheels (this could be
applied fresh at small expense)
or no wheels at all:
15   a rough dray to drag over the ground.

Knock the glass out!
My God — glass, my townspeople!
For what purpose? Is it for the dead
to look out or for us to see
20   how well he is housed or to see
the flowers or the lack of them —
or what?
To keep the rain and snow from him?
He will have a heavier rain soon:

25   pebbles and dirt and what not.
Let there be no glass —
and no upholstery, phew!
and no little brass rollers
and small easy wheels on the bottom —
30   my townspeople what are you thinking of?

A rough plain hearse then
with gilt wheels and no top at all.
On this the coffin lies
by its own weight.

            No wreaths please —
35   especially no hot-house flowers.
Some common memento is better,
something he prized and is known by:
his old clothes — a few books perhaps —
God knows what! You realize
40   how we are about these things,
my townspeople —
something will be found — anything —
even flowers if he had come to that.
So much for the hearse.

45   For heaven's sake though see to the driver!
Take off the silk hat! In fact
that's no place at all for him
up there unceremoniously
dragging our friend out to his own dignity!
50   Bring him down — bring him down!
Low and inconspicuous! I'd not have him ride
on the wagon at all — damn him —
the undertaker's understrapper![1]
Let him hold the reins
55   and walk at the side
and inconspicuously too!

---

1 *subordinate; underling.*

Then briefly as to yourselves:
Walk behind — as they do in France,
seventh class, or if you ride
60   Hell take curtains! Go with some show
of inconvenience; sit openly —
to the weather as to grief.

Or do you think you can shut grief in?
What — from us? We who have perhaps
65   nothing to lose? Share with us
share with us — it will be money
in your pockets.
                Go now
I think you are ready.

                              (1917)

The Red Wheelbarrow

so much depends
upon

a red wheel
barrow

5   glazed with rain
water

beside the white
chickens.

                              (1923)

Spring and All

By the road to the contagious hospital
under the surge of the blue
mottled clouds driven from the
northeast — a cold wind. Beyond, the
5   waste of broad, muddy fields
brown with dried weeds, standing and fallen

patches of standing water
the scattering of tall trees

All along the road the reddish
10   purplish, forked, upstanding, twiggy
stuff of bushes and small trees
with dead, brown leaves under them
leafless vines —

Lifeless in appearance, sluggish
15   dazed spring approaches —

They enter the new world naked,
cold, uncertain of all
save that they enter. All about them
the cold, familiar wind —

20   Now the grass, tomorrow
the stiff curl of wildcarrot leaf
One by one objects are defined —
It quickens: clarity, outline of leaf

But now the stark dignity of
25   entrance — Still, the profound change
has come upon them: rooted, they
grip down and begin to awaken.

(1923)

D.H. LAWRENCE

(1885–1930)

he son of a miner, David Herbert Lawrence was born in Eastwood, Nottinghamshire, and was educated at Nottingham University, where he obtained a teacher's certificate in 1908. He gave up teaching in 1912 after falling in love with Frieda von Richthofen, the wife of one of his former professors. They went to Germany and, after her divorce, married in 1914. Lawrence returned to England during World War I, but he travelled extensively during the rest of his life, living for varying periods in Italy, Ceylon, Australia, the United States, Mexico, and France. Frequently ill, he died of tuberculosis in southern France. Lawrence is one of the twentieth century's greatest novelists, a rebel against conformity whose books were often attacked for their frank treatment of sexuality. His first published works, however, were poems printed in the English Review in 1909. Although not as obviously an innovator in his poetry, Lawrence rejected traditional forms, believing that each poem should find its own form. In his poetry, as in much of his fiction, Lawrence celebrated the free expression of emotions as a natural part of human identity; he believed that modern civilization was artificial, that it had separated humanity from nature, and that it sought to repress natural and healthy feelings. A symbolist who frequently gave dramatic intensity to descriptive passages, Lawrence was a careful craftsman. Combining natural speech with subtle and controlled rhythms, he created poems that convey powerful feelings without being sentimental or self-indulgent.

Piano

Softly, in the dusk, a woman is singing to me;
Taking me back down the vista of years, till I see
A child sitting under the piano, in the boom of the tingling
    strings
And pressing the small, poised feet of a mother who smiles
    as she sings.

5   In spite of myself, the insidious mastery of song
Betrays me back, till the heart of me weeps to belong
To the old Sunday evenings at home, with winter outside
And hymns in the cosy parlour, the tinkling piano our
    guide.

So now it is vain for the singer to burst into clamour
10 With the great black piano appassionato.[1] The glamour
Of childish days is upon me, my manhood is cast
Down in the flood of remembrance, I weep like a child for
  the past.

(1918)

Snake

A snake came to my water-trough
On a hot, hot day, and I in pyjamas for the heat,
To drink there.

In the deep, strange-scented shade of the great dark carob-
  tree
5 I came down the steps with my pitcher
And must wait, must stand and wait, for there he was at
  the trough before me.

He reached down from a fissure in the earth-wall in the
  gloom
And trailed his yellow-brown slackness soft-bellied down,
  over the edge of the stone trough
And rested his throat upon the stone bottom,
10 And where the water had dripped from the tap, in a small
  clearness,
He sipped with his straight mouth,
Softly drank through his straight gums, into his slack long
  body,
Silently.

Someone was before me at my water-trough,
15 And I, like a second comer, waiting.

---

1. *impassioned, passionately (Italian).*

He lifted his head from his drinking, as cattle do,
And looked at me vaguely, as drinking cattle do,
And flickered his two-forked tongue from his lips, and
      mused a moment,
And stooped and drank a little more,
20   Being earth-brown, earth-golden from the burning bowels
      of the earth
On the day of Sicilian July, with Etna smoking.

The voice of my education said to me
He must be killed,
For in Sicily the black, black snakes are innocent, the gold
      are venomous.

25   And voices in me said, If you were a man
You would take a stick and break him now, and finish him
      off.

But must I confess how I liked him,
How glad I was he had come like a guest in quiet, to drink
      at my water-trough
And depart peaceful, pacified, and thankless,
30   Into the burning bowels of this earth?

Was it cowardice, that I dared not kill him?
Was it perversity, that I longed to talk to him?
Was it humility, to feel so honoured?
I felt so honoured.

35   And yet those voices:
If you were not afraid, you would kill him!

And truly I was afraid, I was most afraid,
But even so, honoured still more
That he should seek my hospitality
40   From out of the dark door of the secret earth.

He drank enough
And lifted his head, dreamily, as one who has drunken,
And flickered his tongue like a forked night on the air, so
      black,

Seeming to lick his lips,

45 And looked around like a god, unseeing, into the air,
And slowly turned his head,
And slowly, very slowly, as if thrice adream,
Proceeded to draw his slow length curving round
And climb again the broken bank of my wall-face.

50 And as he put his head into that dreadful hole,
And as he slowly drew up, snake-easing his shoulders, and
      entered farther,
A sort of horror, a sort of protest against his withdrawing
      into that horrid black hole,
Deliberately going into the blackness, and slowly drawing
      himself after,
Overcame me now his back was turned.

55 I looked round, I put down my pitcher,
I picked up a clumsy log
And threw it at the water-trough with a clatter.

I think it did not hit him,
But suddenly that part of him that was left behind
      convulsed in undignified haste,
60 Writhed like lightening, and was gone
Into the black hole, the earth-lipped fissure in the wall-
      front,
At which, in the intense still noon, I stared with
      fascination.

And immediately I regretted it.
I thought how paltry, how vulgar, what a mean act!
65 I despised myself and the voices of my accursed human
      education.

And I thought of the albatross,[1]
And I wished he would come back, my snake.

---

1 *see Coleridge's "The Rime of the Ancient Mariner," in which the mariner wantonly slays an albatross, which is then hung around his neck as a symbol of his guilt.*

For he seemed to me again like a king,
Like a king in exile, uncrowned in the underworld,
70   Now due to be crowned again.

And so, I missed my chance with one of the lords
Of life.
And I have something to expiate;
A pettiness.

(1923)

Ezra Pound

(1885–1972)

Ezra Pound was born in Idaho but grew up in Pennsylvania. He specialized in Romance languages and literature at the University of Pennsylvania and received a master's degree in 1906. Considering his native country intellectually oppressive, Pound lived most of the rest of his life in Europe. A leader in the modernist revolution in literature, Pound influenced and assisted dozens of modern writers, including James Joyce, W.B. Yeats, Ernest Hemingway, and T.S. Eliot, whose famous poem "The Waste Land" he edited. Early in his poetic career, he advocated the concentration, free forms, and precise, concrete images of the imagist movement, and while he soon moved away from imagism to write erudite, esoterically allusive poems that all but specialists find daunting, his early insistence on unforced rhythms and clear detail had a pervasive, lasting effect on twentieth-century poetry.

Critical opinion of Pound's own work is divided, partly because it varies in quality and is sometimes extremely difficult, and partly because it reflects his unpopular social and political views. Living in Italy between the world wars and increasingly convinced that art prospered in stable societies with strong leaders, Pound actively supported Italian dictator Benito Mussolini. He became stridently anti-Semitic and attacked the American political and economic system in both writing and radio broadcasts. Charged with treason at the end of World War II, he was caged at Pisa and brought to the United States only after his mental condition had deteriorated to the point where he was judged unfit to stand trial. He was confined at St. Elizabeth's Hospital for the criminally insane in Washington until efforts by American writers led to his release in 1958, after which he lived the remainder of his life in Italy.

An Immorality

Sing we for love and idleness,
Naught else is worth the having.

Though I have been in many a land,
There is naught else in living.

5   And I would rather have my sweet,
     Though rose-leaves die of grieving,

     Than do high deeds in Hungary
     To pass all men's believing.

(1912)

The River-Merchant's Wife: A Letter[1]

While my hair was still cut straight across my forehead
I played about the front gate, pulling flowers.
You came by on bamboo stilts, playing horse,
You walked about my seat, playing with blue plums.
5   And we went on living in the village of Chokan:[2]
Two small people, without dislike or suspicion.

At fourteen I married My Lord you.
I never laughed, being bashful.
Lowering my head, I looked at the wall.
10   Called to, a thousand times, I never looked back.

At fifteen I stopped scowling,
I desired my dust to be mingled with yours
Forever and forever and forever.
Why should I climb the look out?

15   At sixteen you departed,
You went into far Ku-to-yen,[3] by the river of swirling
          eddies,
And you have been gone five months.
The monkeys make sorrowful noise overhead.

1 adapted from a translation of the Chinese poet Li Po (701?–62), called Rihaku in Japanese.
2 a suburb of Nanjing, China.
3 an island hundreds of miles up the Kiang River from Nanjing.

You dragged your feet when you went out.
20   By the gate now, the moss is grown, the different mosses,
Too deep to clear them away!
The leaves fall early this autumn, in wind.
The paired butterflies are already yellow with August
Over the grass in the West garden;
25   They hurt me. I grow older.
If you are coming down through the narrows of the river
   Kiang,
Please let me know beforehand,
And I will come out to meet you
   As far as Cho-fu-Sa.[4]

          (1915)

In a Station of the Metro

The apparition of these faces in the crowd;
Petals on a wet, black bough.

          (1916)

Ancient Music[1]

Winter is icummen in,
Lhude sing Goddamm,
Raineth drop and staineth slop,
And how the wind doth ramm!
5   Sing: Goddamm.
Skiddeth bus and sloppeth us,
An ague hath my ham.
Freezeth river, turneth liver,
    Damn you, sing: Goddamm.

4 *a beach on the Kiang River not far from Ku-to-yen.*

1 *a parody of the medieval lyric "The Cuckoo Song." (See page 74.)*

10   Goddamm, Goddamm, 'tis why I am, Goddamm.
       So 'gainst the winter's balm.
Sing goddamm, damm, sing Goddamm,
Sing goddamm, sing goddamm, DAMM.

(1917)

from E.P. Ode pour l'Élection de Son Sépulchre[1]

IV

These fought in any case,
and some believing,
                    pro domo,[2] in any case . . .

Some quick to arm,
some for adventure,
5   some from fear of weakness,
some from fear of censure,
some for love of slaughter, in imagination,
learning later . . .
some in fear, learning love of slaughter;

10   Died some, pro patria,
                    non 'dulce' non 'et decor'[3] . . .
walked eye-deep in hell
believing in old men's lies, then unbelieving
came home, home to a lie,
home to many deceits,

---

1 "*E.P. Ode on the Choice of His Tomb*" — *the opening section of* Hugh Selwyn Mauberley (Life and Contracts) *(1920). The title is adapted from the title of a poem, "On the Selection of His Tomb," Odes IV.5, by the French poet Pierre de Ronsard (1524–85).*
2 *for the home (Latin).*
3 *"for the native land, not 'sweetly,' not 'and fittingly'" (Latin); adapted from Horace's Odes (III.2.13): "Dulce et decorum est pro patria mori" or "It is sweet and fitting to die for one's native land." (See also Wilfred Owen, "Dulce et Decorum Est," page 468.)*

15   home to old lies and new infamy;
      usury age-old and age-thick
      and liars in public places.

      Daring as never before, wastage as never before.
      Young blood and high blood,
20   fair cheeks, and fine bodies;

      fortitude as never before

      frankness as never before,
25   disillusions as never told in the old days,
      hysterias, trench confessions,
      laughter out of dead bellies.

                    V
      There died a myriad,
      And of the best, among them,
30   For an old bitch gone in the teeth,
      For a botched civilization,

      Charm, smiling at the good mouth,
      Quick eyes gone under earth's lid,

      For two gross of broken statues,
35   For a few thousand battered books.

                                    (1920)

SIEGFRIED SASSOON

(1886–1967)

*E*ducated at Cambridge University, Siegfried Sassoon, before seeing action in
World War I, enjoyed the life of a wealthy country gentleman and dilet-
tante poet. Twice wounded in the war, Sassoon publicly protested what he consid-
ered the unnecessary prolongation of the fighting and threw his Military Cross into
the Mersey River. Although he wrote poetry throughout his life, much of it reli-
gious, he is chiefly remembered for those poems which grew out of his experiences
in the trenches. He vividly portrayed the physical and emotional horrors of the war
and bitterly criticized the attitudes of commanding officers and people at home, most
of whom held idealized notions of the glory and justness of the fighting. In "Drea-
mers," Sassoon uses the conventional form of the sonnet to contrast the stark reality
faced by the soldiers and their visions of a simple, ordinary way of life at home.

Dreamers

Soldiers are citizens of death's gray land,
   Drawing no dividend from time's to-morrows.
In the great hour of destiny they stand,
   Each with his feuds and jealousies and sorrows.
5 Soldiers are sworn to action; they must win
   Some flaming fatal climax with their lives.
Soldiers are dreamers; when the guns begin
   They think of firelit homes, clean beds, and wives.

I see them in foul dug-outs, gnawed by rats,
10   And in the ruined trenches, lashed with rain,
Dreaming of things they did with balls and bats,
   And mocked by hopeless longing to regain
Bank-holidays,[1] and picture-shows, and spats,
   And going to the office in the train.

(1917)

---

1 *first Monday in August.*

T.S. ELIOT

(1888–1965)

homas Stearns Eliot grew up in St. Louis, Missouri, where his grand-
father had founded Washington University. His parents were well-to-do;
his mother wrote poetry and supported cultural activities. Eliot attended Harvard,
from which he received an M.A., the Sorbonne in Paris, and Oxford. After
1914, he lived mainly in England and became a British subject in 1927. While
he first made his living as a teacher, then from 1917 to 1925 as a banker, and
later as an editor with the British publisher Faber and Faber, Eliot also devoted
himself to writing criticism. In his essays, no less than in his poetry, he had an
immense influence on the literature of his time.

The development of Eliot's poetry reflects his personal struggle to find meaning
and order in an age that seemed to many to deny them. Such early poems as "The
Love Song of J. Alfred Prufrock" and "The Waste Land" captured the mood of
doubt, the loss of confidence in Western traditions and religion, that followed World
War I. The Four Quartets *and his verse plays, written after his conversion to*
Anglo-Catholicism in the late 1920s, reflect his personal solutions to this earlier
doubt. Despite its changing perspective, however, most of Eliot's poetry, early and
late, shows his concern with literary and religious tradition, which is reflected in a
wealth of allusions; his interest in symbols, not only as literary devices but as man-
ifestations of culture as well; and his facility for capturing speaking voices. Eliot's
achievements were recognized with the Nobel Prize for literature in 1948.

The Love Song of J. Alfred Prufrock

S'io credesse che mia risposta fosse
A persona che mai tornasse al mondo,
Questa fiamma staria senza piu scosse.
Ma perciocche giammai di questo fondo
Non torno vivo alcun, s'i'odo il vero,
Senza tema d'infamia ti rispondo.[1]

---

1 *in Dante's* Inferno *XXXVII.61–66, Guido da Montefeltro answers Dante through the tongue of flame that*
imprisons him: "If I thought I were answering someone who could ever return to the world, this flame would be
still; but since no one has returned alive from this depth, if what I hear is true, I respond without fear of ill
repute."

Let us go then, you and I,
When the evening is spread out against the sky
Like a patient etherised upon a table;
Let us go, through certain half-deserted streets,
5 The muttering retreats
Of restless nights in one-night cheap hotels
And sawdust restaurants with oyster-shells:
Streets that follow like a tedious argument
Of insidious intent
10 To lead you to an overwhelming question . . .
Oh, do not ask, "What is it?"
Let us go and make our visit.

In the room the women come and go
Talking of Michelangelo.

15 The yellow fog that rubs its back upon the window-
panes,
The yellow smoke that rubs its muzzle on the window-
panes
Licked its tongue into the corners of the evening,
Lingered upon the pools that stand in drains,
Let fall upon its back the soot that falls from chimneys,
20 Slipped by the terrace, made a sudden leap,
And seeing that it was a soft October night,
Curled once about the house, and fell asleep.

And indeed there will be time
For the yellow smoke that slides along the street,
25 Rubbing its back upon the window-panes;
There will be time, there will be time
To prepare a face to meet the faces that you meet;
There will be time to murder and create,
And time for all the works and days of hands
30 That lift and drop a question on your plate;
Time for you and time for me,
And time yet for a hundred indecisions,
And for a hundred visions and revisions,
Before the taking of a toast and tea.

35   In the room the women come and go
Talking of Michelangelo.

And indeed there will be time
To wonder, "Do I dare?" and, "Do I dare?"
Time to turn back and descend the stair,
40   With a bald spot in the middle of my hair —
(They will say: "How his hair is growing thin!")
My morning coat, my collar mounting firmly to the chin,
My necktie rich and modest, but asserted by a simple
            pin —
[They will say: "But how his arms and legs are thin!"]
45   Do I dare
Disturb the universe?
In a minute there is time
For decisions and revisions which a minute will reverse.

For I have known them all already, known them all —
50   Have known the evenings, mornings, afternoons,
I have measured out my life with coffee spoons;
I know the voices dying with a dying fall
Beneath the music from a farther room.
So how should I presume?

55   And I have known the eyes already, known them all —
The eyes that fix you in a formulated phrase,
And when I am formulated, sprawling on a pin,
When I am pinned and wriggling on the wall,
Then how should I begin
60   To spit out all the butt-ends of my days and ways?
And how should I presume?

And I have known the arms already, known them all —
Arms that are braceleted and white and bare
(But in the lamplight, downed with light brown hair!)
65   Is it perfume from a dress
That makes me so digress?
Arms that lie along a table, or wrap about a shawl.
And should I then presume?
And how should I begin?

. . . . .

70 Shall I say, I have gone at dusk through narrow streets
And watched the smoke that rises from the pipes
Of lonely men in shirt-sleeves, leaning out of
     windows? . . .

I should have been a pair of ragged claws
Scuttling across the floors of silent seas.

    . . . . .

75 And the afternoon, the evening, sleeps so peacefully!
Smoothed by long fingers,
Asleep — tired — or it malingers,
Stretched on the floor, here beside you and me.
Should I, after tea and cakes and ices,
80 Have the strength to force the moment to its crisis?
But though I have wept and fasted, wept and prayed,
Though I have seen my head [grown slightly bald] brought
     in upon a platter,[2]
I am no prophet — and here's no great matter;
I have seen the moment of my greatness flicker,
85 And I have seen the eternal Footman hold my coat, and
     snicker,
And in short, I was afraid.

    And would it have been worth it, after all,
After the cups, the marmalade, the tea,
Among the porcelain, among some talk of you and me,
90 Would it have been worth while,
To have bitten off the matter with a smile,
To have squeezed the universe into a ball
To roll it toward some overwhelming question,
To say: "I am Lazarus, come from the dead,[3]
95 Come back to tell you all, I shall tell you all" —
If one, settling a pillow by her head,
    Should say: "That is not what I meant at all.
    That is not it, at all."

2 the head of John the Baptist was presented on a platter to Queen Herodias (see Matthew 14; Mark 6).
3 see John 11.

And would it have been worth it, after all,
100 Would it have been worth while,
After the sunsets and the dooryards and the sprinkled
    streets,
After the novels, after the teacups, after the skirts that trail
    along the floor —
And this, and so much more? —
It is impossible to say just what I mean!
105 But as if a magic lantern threw the nerves in patterns on a
    screen:
Would it have been worth while
If one, settling a pillow or throwing off a shawl,
And turning toward the window, should say:
    "That is not it at all,
110   That is not what I meant, at all."

    . . . . .

No! I am not Prince Hamlet, nor was meant to be;
Am an attendant lord, one that will do
To swell a progress, start a scene or two,
Advise the prince; no doubt, an easy tool,
115 Deferential, glad to be of use,
Politic, cautious, and meticulous;
Full of high sentence, but a bit obtuse;
At times, indeed, almost ridiculous —
Almost, at times, the Fool.

120   I grow old . . . I grow old . . .
I shall wear the bottoms of my trousers rolled.

Shall I part my hair behind? Do I dare to eat a peach?
I shall wear white flannel trousers, and walk upon the
    beach.
I have heard the mermaids singing, each to each.

125   I do not think that they will sing to me.

I have seen them riding seaward on the waves
Combing the white hair of the waves blown back
When the wind blows the water white and black.

We have lingered in the chambers of the sea
130   By sea-girls wreathed with seaweed red and brown
Till human voices wake us, and we drown.

(1915)

Preludes

I

The winter evening settles down
With smell of steaks in passageways.
Six o'clock.
The burnt-out ends of smoky days.
5   And now a gusty shower wraps
The grimy scraps
Of withered leaves about your feet
And newspapers from vacant lots;
The showers beat
10   On broken blinds and chimney-pots,
And at the corner of the street
A lonely cab-horse steams and stamps.
And then the lighting of the lamps.

II

The morning comes to consciousness
15   Of faint stale smells of beer
From the sawdust-trampled street
With all its muddy feet that press
To early coffee-stands.
With the other masquerades
20   That time resumes,
One thinks of all the hands
That are raising dingy shades
In a thousand furnished rooms.

III

You tossed a blanket from the bed,
You lay upon your back, and waited;
You dozed, and watched the night revealing
The thousand sordid images
Of which your soul was constituted;
They flickered against the ceiling.
And when all the world came back
And the light crept up between the shutters
And you heard the sparrows in the gutters,
You had such a vision of the street
As the street hardly understands;
Sitting along the bed's edge, where
You curled the papers from your hair,
Or clasped the yellow soles of feet
In the palms of both soiled hands.

IV

His soul stretched tight across the skies
That fade behind a city block,
Or trampled by insistent feet
At four and five and six o'clock;
And short square fingers stuffing pipes,
And evening newspapers, and eyes
Assured of certain certainties,
The conscience of a blackened street
Impatient to assume the world.

I am moved by fancies that are curled
Around these images, and cling:
The notion of some infinitely gentle
Infinitely suffering thing.

Wipe your hand across your mouth, and laugh;
The worlds revolve like ancient women
Gathering fuel in vacant lots.

(1917)

The Hollow Men

Mistah Kurtz — he dead.[1]

A penny for the Old Guy[2]

I

We are the hollow men
We are the stuffed men
Leaning together
Headpiece filled with straw. Alas!
5   Our dried voices, when
We whisper together
Are quiet and meaningless
As wind in dry grass
Or rats' feet over broken glass
10   In our dry cellar

Shape without form, shade without colour,
Paralysed force, gesture without motion;

Those who have crossed
With direct eyes, to death's other Kingdom
15   Remember us — if at all — not as lost
Violent souls, but only
As the hollow men
The stuffed men.

II

Eyes I dare not meet in dreams
20   In death's dream kingdom
These do not appear:
There, the eyes are
Sunlight on a broken column

---

1 in Joseph Conrad's Heart of Darkness, *Kurtz's European cultural values fail him in the African jungle and he dies insane.*
2 *refers to an English children's custom of begging on Guy Fawkes Day (November 5), the anniversary of the execution of the leading conspirator in the plot to blow up the Houses of Parliament in 1605.*

There, is a tree swinging
25   And voices are
In the wind's singing
More distant and more solemn
Than a fading star.

Let me be no nearer
30   In death's dream kingdom
Let me also wear
Such deliberate disguises
Rat's coat, crowskin, crossed staves
In a field
35   Behaving as the wind behaves
No nearer —

Not that final meeting
In the twilight kingdom

III

This is the dead land
40   This is cactus land
Here the stone images
Are raised, here they receive
The supplication of a dead man's hand
Under the twinkle of a fading star.

45   Is it like this
In death's other kingdom
Waking alone
At the hour when we are
Trembling with tenderness
50   Lips that would kiss
Form prayers to broken stone.

IV

The eyes are not here
There are no eyes here
In this valley of dying stars
55   In this hollow valley
This broken jaw of our lost kingdoms

In this last of meeting places
We grope together
And avoid speech
60 Gathered on this beach of the tumid river

Sightless, unless
The eyes reappear
As the perpetual star
Multifoliate rose
65 Of death's twilight kingdom
The hope only
Of empty men.

V

Here we go round the prickly pear
Prickly pear prickly pear
70 *Here we go round the prickly pear*
At five o'clock in the morning.

Between the idea
And the reality
75 Between the motion
And the act
Falls the Shadow
            For Thine is the Kingdom

Between the conception
80 And the creation
Between the emotion
And the response
Falls the Shadow
            Life is very long

85 Between the desire
And the spasm
Between the potency
And the existence
Between the essence
90 And the descent
Falls the Shadow
            For Thine is the Kingdom

                For Thine is
                Life is
95   For Thine is the

                This is the way the world ends
                This is the way the world ends
                This is the way the world ends
                Not with a bang but a whimper.

                                                    (1925)

Journey of the Magi[1]

                'A cold coming we had of it,
                Just the worst time of the year
                For a journey, and such a long journey:
                The ways deep and the weather sharp,
5   The very dead of winter.'[2]
                And the camels galled, sore-footed, refractory,
                Lying down in the melting snow.
                There were times we regretted
                The summer palaces on slopes, the terraces,
10   And the silken girls bringing sherbet.
                Then the camel men cursing and grumbling
                And running away, and wanting their liquor and women,
                And the night-fires going out, and the lack of shelters,
                And the cities hostile and the towns unfriendly
15   And the villages dirty and charging high prices:
                A hard time we had of it.
                At the end we preferred to travel all night,
                Sleeping in snatches,
                With the voices singing in our ears, saying
20   That this was all folly.

1 *the wise men who brought gifts to the infant Jesus (see Matthew 2).*
2 *adapted from a Christmas sermon by Bishop Lancelot Andrewes (1555–1626), who helped prepare the 1611*
   King James version of the Bible.

Then at dawn we came down to a temperate valley,
Wet, below the snow line, smelling of vegetation;
With a running stream and a water-mill beating the
    darkness,
And three trees on the low sky,
25   And an old white horse galloped away in the meadow.
Then we came to a tavern with vine-leaves over the lintel,
Six hands at an open door dicing for pieces of silver,
And feet kicking the empty wine-skins.
But there was no information, and so we continued
30   And arrived at evening, not a moment too soon
Finding the place; it was (you may say) satisfactory.

All this was a long time ago, I remember,
And I would do it again, but set down
This set down
35   This: were we led all that way for
Birth or Death? There was a Birth, certainly,
We had evidence and no doubt. I had seen birth and death,
But had thought they were different; this Birth was
Hard and bitter agony for us, like Death, our death.
40   We returned to our places, these Kingdoms,
But no longer at ease here, in the old dispensation,
With an alien people clutching their gods.
I should be glad of another death.

(1927)

ISAAC ROSENBERG

(1890–1918)

orn in Bristol and raised in London, Isaac Rosenberg, the son of poor Russian émigrés, attracted early attention for his talents as a poet and painter. His many months of service in World War I sapped his physical health and spiritual vitality; he was eventually killed in action. "Break of Day in the Trenches" embodies his view that "poetry should be definite thought and clear expression." Focusing on the red poppy and the scavenging rat, he depicts the soldier's love of life in the face of almost inevitable death.

Break of Day in the Trenches

The darkness crumbles away —
It is the same old druid Time as ever.
Only a live thing leaps my hand —
A queer sardonic rat —
5   As I pull the parapet's poppy
To stick behind my ear.
Droll rat, they would shoot you if they knew
Your cosmopolitan sympathies.
Now you have touched this English hand
10   You will do the same to a German —
Soon, no doubt, if it be your pleasure
To cross the sleeping green between.
It seems you inwardly grin as you pass
Strong eyes, fine limbs, haughty athletes
15   Less chanced than you for life,
Bonds to the whims of murder,
Sprawled in the bowels of the earth,
The torn fields of France.
What do you see in our eyes
20   At the shrieking iron and flame
Hurled through still heavens?

What quaver — what heart aghast?
Poppies whose roots are in man's veins
Drop, and are ever dropping;
25   But mine in my ear is safe,
Just a little white with the dust.

(1916)   (1922)

WILFRED OWEN

(1893–1918)

Although his best poems were written in the year before his death in action during World War I, Wilfred Owen had decided to become a poet while a boy in Shropshire, England. He was critical of conventional religious beliefs before the war and had written many war poems before his 1917 meeting with Siegfried Sassoon; however, the meeting was the catalyst for the creation of the works for which he is now remembered, many of which were included in the libretto of composer Benjamin Britten's War Requiem *(1962). In the Preface to his* Collected Poems, *Owen stated: "My subject is War, and the pity of War. The Poetry is in the pity." He achieves his startling, moving effects through the sharp contrasts of his language and the careful modulation of rhythms, rhyme schemes, and sound patterns. In "Dulce et Decorum Est," the Latin motto, with its conventional notions of glorious, patriotic death, is set against vivid, realistic details of a gas attack. "Anthem for Doomed Youth" juxtaposes the noises of war with the quietness of mourning. In "Strange Meeting," the speaker escapes from the terrors of war into a place marked by the muted sadness of lives ended before their time.*

Anthem[1] for Doomed Youth

What passing-bells[2] for these who die as cattle?
   — Only the monstrous anger of the guns.
   Only the stuttering rifles' rapid rattle
Can patter out their hasty orisons.[3]
5   No mockeries now for them; no prayers nor bells;
   Nor any voice of mourning save the choirs, —
The shrill, demented choirs of wailing shells;
   And bugles calling for them from sad shires.[4]

---

1 *song of praise.*
2 *church bells rung to announce a death.*
3 *prayers.*
4 *districts, counties.*

What candles may be held to speed them all?
10   Not in the hands of boys but in their eyes
Shall shine the holy glimmers of goodbyes.
     The pallor of girls' brows shall be their pall;
Their flowers the tenderness of patient minds,
And each slow dusk a drawing-down of blinds.

(1917)   (1920)

Dulce et Decorum Est[1]

Bent double, like old beggars under sacks,
Knock-kneed, coughing like hags, we cursed through
     sludge,
Till on the haunting flares we turned our backs
And towards our distant rest began to trudge.
5   Men marched asleep. Many had lost their boots
But limped on, blood-shod. All went lame; all blind;
Drunk with fatigue; deaf even to the hoots
Of tired, outstripped Five-Nines[2] that dropped behind.

Gas! GAS! Quick, boys! — An ecstasy of fumbling,
10   Fitting the clumsy helmets just in time;
But someone still was yelling out and stumbling,
And flound'ring like a man in fire or lime . . .
Dim, through the misty panes and thick green light,
As under a green sea, I saw him drowning.

15   In all my dreams, before my helpless sight,
He plunges at me, guttering, choking, drowning.

---

1 "It is sweet and fitting [to die for one's country]" (Horace Odes III.2.13). (See also Ezra Pound, "Ode pour
l'Élection de Son Sépulchre," p. 450.)
2 shells that are 5.9 inches (or 150 mm) in diameter.

If in some smothering dreams you too could pace
Behind the wagon that we flung him in,
And watch the white eyes writhing in his face,
20 His hanging face, like a devil's sick of sin;
If you could hear, at every jolt, the blood
Come gargling from the froth-corrupted lungs,
Obscene as cancer, bitter as the cud
Of vile, incurable sores on innocent tongues, —
25 My friend, you would not tell with such high zest
To children ardent for some desperate glory,
The old Lie: Dulce et decorum est
Pro patria mori.

(1917)   (1920)

Strange Meeting

It seemed that out of battle I escaped
Down some profound dull tunnel, long since scooped
Through granites which titanic wars had groined.

Yet also there encumbered sleepers groaned,
5   Too fast in thought or death to be bestirred.
Then, as I probed them, one sprang up, and stared
With piteous recognition in fixed eyes,
Lifting distressful hands, as if to bless.
And by his smile, I knew that sullen hall,
10   By his dead smile I knew we stood in Hell.

With a thousand pains that vision's face was grained;
Yet no blood reached there from the upper ground,
And no guns thumped, or down the flues made moan.
'Strange friend,' I said, 'here is no cause to mourn,'
15   'None,' said that other, 'save the undone years,
The hopelessness. Whatever hope is yours,
Was my life also; I went hunting wild

After the wildest beauty in the world,
Which lies not calm in eyes, or braided hair,
20   But mocks the steady running of the hour,
And if it grieves, grieves richlier than here.
For by my glee might many men have laughed,
And of my weeping something had been left,
Which must die now. I mean the truth untold,
25   The pity of war, the pity war distilled.
Now men will go content with what we spoiled,
Or, discontent, boil bloody, and be spilled.
They will be swift with swiftness of the tigress.
None will break ranks, though nations trek from progress.
30   Courage was mine, and I had mystery,
Wisdom was mine, and I had mastery:
To miss the march of this retreating world
Into vain citadels that are not walled.
Then, when much blood had clogged their chariot-wheels,
35   I would go up and wash them from sweet wells,
Even with truths that lie too deep for taint.
I would have poured my spirit without stint
But not through wounds; not on the cess of war.
Foreheads of men have bled where no wounds were.

40   'I am the enemy you killed, my friend.
I knew you in this dark: for so you frowned
Yesterday through me as you jabbed and killed.
I parried; but my hands were loath and cold.
Let us sleep now. . . . '

(1918)   (1920)

E.E. CUMMINGS

(1894–1962)

*B*orn in Cambridge, Massachusetts, and educated at Harvard, Edward
Estlin Cummings became one of the most unconventional of modern
American poets. Cummings was a successful painter and wrote both fiction and
drama, but his greatest artistic achievement was his poetry. Sometimes lyric, some-
times satirical, Cummings's poetry celebrates spontaneous feeling, individualism, the
love of nature, and erotic love; it attacks institutions, formality, and stuffiness gener-
ally. He has sometimes been criticized for being exhibitionist and overly playful in
his manipulations of diction, syntax, stanzaic forms, and typography, but, notwith-
standing his eccentricities, Cummings was always a careful craftsman and serious
artist. His ardent rebellion against both poetic conventions and what he considered
the complacent, middle-class narrowness of his country gave him considerable
influence with poets after World War II.

it may not always be so; and i say

it may not always be so; and i say
that if your lips, which i have loved, should touch
another's, and your dear strong fingers clutch
his heart, as mine in time not far away;
5   if on another's face your sweet hair lay
in such a silence as i know, or such
great writhing words as, uttering overmuch,
stand helplessly before the spirit at bay;

if this should be, i say if this should be —
10   you of my heart, send me a little word;
that i may go unto him, and take his hands,
saying, Accept all happiness from me.
Then shall i turn my face, and hear one bird
sing terribly afar in the lost lands.

(1923)

in Just-   spring

in Just-
spring   when the world is mud-
luscious the little
lame balloonman

5   whistles   far   and wee

and eddieandbill come
running from marbles and
piracies and it's
spring

10   when the world is puddle-wonderful

the queer
old balloonman whistles
far   and   wee
and bettyandisbel come dancing

15   from hop-scotch and jump-rope and

it's
spring
and
      the

20   goat-footed

balloonMan   whistles
far
and
wee

(1923)

next to of course god america i

"next to of course god america i
love you land of the pilgrims' and so forth oh
say can you see by the dawn's early my
country 'tis of centuries come and go
and are no more what of it we should worry
in every language even deafanddumb
thy sons acclaim your glorious name by gorry
by jingo by gee by gosh by gum
why talk of beauty what could be more beaut-
iful than these heroic happy dead
who rushed like lions to the roaring slaughter
they did not stop to think they died instead
then shall the voice of liberty be mute?"

He spoke. And drank rapidly a glass of water

(1926)

anyone lived in a pretty how town

anyone lived in a pretty how town
(with up so floating many bells down)
spring summer autumn winter
he sang his didn't he danced his did.

Women and men(both little and small)
cared for anyone not at all
they sowed their isn't they reaped their same
sun moon stars rain

children guessed(but only a few
and down they forgot as up they grew
autumn winter spring summer)
that noone loved him more by more

when by now and tree by leaf
she laughed his joy she cried his grief
bird by snow and stir by still
anyone's any was all to her

someones married their everyones
laughed their cryings and did their dance
(sleep wake hope and then)they
said their nevers they slept their dream

stars rain sun moon
(and only the snow can begin to explain
how children are apt to forget to remember
with up so floating many bells down)

one day anyone died i guess
(and noone stooped to kiss his face)
busy folk buried them side by side
little by little and was by was

all by all and deep by deep
and more by more they dream their sleep
noone and anyone earth by april
wish by spirit and if by yes.

Women and men(both dong and ding)
summer autumn winter spring
reaped their sowing and went their came
sun moon stars rain

(1940)

ROBERT GRAVES

(1895–1985)

orn in London, Graves served in the British army during World War I before attending Oxford. Publication of his first novel, Goodbye to All That (1929), enabled him to move to Majorca, where, with only a few interruptions, he spent the rest of his life as a writer. Graves published numerous historical novels including I, Claudius (1934), poetry collections, essays, and such specialized works as The White Goddess (1948), a mythological study in which he seeks to analyze the poetic impulse. Graves was not a revolutionary poet, preferring to refine traditional metrical patterns and verse forms. In fact, he often viewed himself as a poet's poet, declaring in the Foreword to Poems 1938–45: "To write poems for other than poets is wasteful." Certainly, other poets must admire his metrical skill and the careful craftsmanship with which he combined emotional expression, intellectual analysis, and ironic observation. As technically sophisticated as they often are, his poems seldom advertise their complexity: they exhibit classical grace and ease of expression, frequently combining colloquial diction with traditional metrical forms. Although Graves wrote many poems about personal relationships, he is most notable as an intellectual whose poems often crackle with the energy of original ideas presented in witty or unusual images.

The Cool Web

Children are dumb to say how hot the day is,
How hot the scent is of the summer rose,
How dreadful the black wastes of evening sky,
How dreadful the tall soldiers drumming by.

5   But we have speech, to chill the angry day,
And speech, to dull the rose's cruel scent.
We spell away the overhanging night,
We spell away the soldiers and the fright.

There's a cool web of language winds us in,
10   Retreat from too much joy or too much fear:
We grow sea-green at last and coldly die
In brininess and volubility.

But if we let our tongues lose self-possession,
Throwing off language and its watery clasp
15   Before our death, instead of when death comes,
Facing the wide glare of the children's day,
Facing the rose, the dark sky and the drums,
We shall go mad no doubt and die that way.

(1927)

The Naked and the Nude

For me, the naked and the nude
(By lexicographers[1] construed
As synonyms that should express
The same deficiency of dress
5   Or shelter) stand as wide apart
As love from lies, or truth from art.

Lovers without reproach will gaze
On bodies naked and ablaze;
The Hippocratic[2] eye will see
10   In nakedness, anatomy;
And naked shines the Goddess when
She mounts her lion among men.[3]

The nude are bold, the nude are sly
To hold each treasonable eye.
15   While draping by a showman's trick
Their dishabille[4] in rhetoric,
They grin a mock-religious grin
Of scorn at those of naked skin.

1 those who write or compile dictionaries.
2 medical: Hippocrates (c. 460–c. 375 B.C.) was a Greek physician often considered to be the father of scientific medicine.
3 in The White Goddess, Graves uses the term Goddess to mean "the White Goddess, or Muse, the Mother of All Living," the supreme creative deity who ruled prior to the triumph of patriarchy; ancient images of the Goddess showed her riding a lion, and Graves cites the example of Hera astride a lion as indicative of the sexual dominance of the Goddess.
4 the state of being undressed or carelessly dressed.

The naked, therefore, who compete
20   Against the nude may know defeat;
Yet when they both together tread
The briary pastures of the dead,
By Gorgons[5] with long whips pursued,
How naked go the sometime nude!

(1958)

5 in Greek mythology, hideous females who had snakes on their heads instead of hair and whose glance could turn mortals to stone.

F.R. Scott

(1899–1985)

*T*he son of Frederick George Scott (1861–1944), an Anglican clergyman and minor poet of the Confederation group, Francis Reginald Scott made remarkable contributions to Canadian life in several areas. Born in Quebec City, he was educated at Bishop's College, Oxford University, where he was a Rhodes Scholar, and McGill University, where he eventually became dean of the law school. As a social reformer, he was active in founding the Co-operative Commonwealth Federation, the forerunner of the New Democratic Party. As a lawyer, he defended civil liberties in several important court cases. As a professor of constitutional law, he promoted the cause of social justice and served as a member of the Royal Commission on Bilingualism and Biculturalism. As a poet and anthologist, he was a leader in the fight against romantic and traditional poetry as outmoded and insincere forms of verse. He began writing while still a student, but his first collection was not published until 1945. His Collected Poems (1981) won the Governor General's Award. Often sharply satirical, his poetry is notable for its precision and grace of expression, its unpretentious allusions, and its wit.

The Canadian Authors Meet[1]

Expansive puppets percolate self-unction
Beneath a portrait of the Prince of Wales.[2]
Miss Crotchet's muse has somehow failed to function,
Yet she's a poetess. Beaming, she sails

5   From group to chattering group, with such a dear
Victorian saintliness, as is her fashion,
Greeting the other unknowns with a cheer —
Virgins of sixty who still write of passion.

---

1 *an earlier version of this poem appeared in the* McGill Fortnightly Review *in April 1927, shortly after Scott had attended a meeting of the Canadian Authors' Association. Scott viewed the CAA as a group smugly content with the clichés and forms of the past and incapable of appreciating or promoting meaningful writing of the present.*

2 *Edward, Prince of Wales when the poem was written, became King Edward VIII on January 21, 1936, and abdicated on December 11, 1936, in order to marry an American divorcée, Wallis Warfield Simpson.*

The air is heavy with Canadian topics,
10   And Carman, Lampman, Roberts, Campbell, Scott,
Are measured for their faith and philanthropics,
Their zeal for God and King, their earnest thought.

The cakes are sweet, but sweeter is the feeling
That one is mixing with the *literati*;[3]
15   It warms the old, and melts the most congealing.
Really, it is a most delightful party.

Shall we go round the mulberry bush, or shall
We gather at the river, or shall we
Appoint a Poet Laureate this fall,
20   Or shall we have another cup of tea?

O Canada, O Canada, Oh can
A day go by without new authors springing
To paint the native maple, and to plan
More ways to set the selfsame welkin[4] ringing?

(1927)   (1945)

Saturday Sundae

The triple-decker and the double-cone
I side-swipe swiftly, suck the coke-straws dry.
Ride toadstool seat behind the slab of morgue —
Sweet corner drug-store, sweet pie in the sky.

5   Him of the front-flap apron, him I sing,
The counter-clockwise clerk in underalls.
Swing low, sweet chocolate, Oh swing, swing,
While cheek by juke the jitter chatter falls.

3 *people of letters; the learned.*
4 *sky, or vault of heaven; a poetic archaism.*

I swivel on my axle and survey

10   The latex tintex kotex cutex land.

Soft kingdoms sell for dimes, Life Pic Look Click[1]

Inflate the male with conquest girly grand.

My brothers and my sisters, two by two,

Sit sipping succulence and sighing sex.

15   Each tiny adolescent universe

A world the vested interests annex.

Such bread and circuses[2] these times allow,

Opium most popular, life so small and slick,

Perhaps with candy is the new world born

20   And cellophane shall wrap the heretic.

(1945)

Trans Canada

Pulled from our ruts by the made-to-order gale

We sprang upward into a wider prairie

And dropped Regina below like a pile of bones.[1]

Sky tumbled upon us in waterfalls,

5   But we were smarter than a Skeena[2] salmon

And shot our silver body over the lip of air

To rest in a pool of space

On the top storey of our adventure.

A solar peace

10   And a six-way choice.

1 *popular pictorial magazines.*
2 *Juvenal (c. 50–c. 130 A.D.) declared in his* Satires *that the Roman people, who "once bestowed commands, consulships, legions, and all else," were now only concerned with bread and circuses, that is, with free food and entertainment.*

1 *because of a huge pile of bones left after buffalo hunts, Regina was originally known as Pile of Bones Creek.*
2 *the Skeena River, which empties into the Pacific Ocean near Prince Rupert, British Columbia, has been an important salmon fishery for well over a hundred years.*

Clouds, now, are the solid substance,
A floor of wool roughed by the wind
Standing in waves that halt in their fall.
A still of troughs.

15   The plane, our planet,
Travels on roads that are not seen or laid
But sound in instruments on pilots' ears,
While underneath
The sure wings
20   Are the everlasting arms of science.

Man, the lofty worm, tunnels his latest clay,
And bores his new career.

This frontier, too, is ours.
This everywhere whose life can only be led
25   At the pace of a rocket
Is common to man and man,
And every country below is an I land.

The sun sets on its top shelf,
And stars seem farther from our nearer grasp.

30   I have sat by night beside a cold lake
And touched things smoother than moonlight on still
          water,
But the moon on this cloud sea is not human,
And here is no shore, no intimacy,
Only the start of space, the road to suns.

                                        (1945)

Yvor Winters

(1900–1968)

orn in Chicago, Yvor Winters taught English after 1928 at Stanford University in California. During his lifetime, he was known mainly for his criticism, which stressed the value of order and morality in literature and argued against the emphasis on individual feelings he found in much modern poetry. Winters's own poetry displays the comparative formality he stressed in his criticism, but it is less conservative than many of his critical essays would suggest and reveals that he shared many of the same concerns as the modern writers whom he criticized harshly. Moreover, the intensity and depth of perception in Winters's best poems prove that, at least for him, what many modern writers would consider the excessive restraint demanded in his criticism did not prove unduly limiting.

The Slow Pacific Swell

Far out of sight forever stands the sea,
Bounding the land with pale tranquillity.
When a small child, I watched it from a hill
At thirty miles or more. The vision still
Lies in the eye, soft blue and far away:
The rain has washed the dust from April day;
Paint-brush and lupine lie against the ground;
The wind above the hill-top has the sound
Of distant water in unbroken sky;
Dark and precise the little steamers ply —
Firm in direction they seem not to stir.
That is illusion. The artificer
Of quiet, distance holds me in a vise
And holds the ocean steady to my eyes.

Once when I rounded Flattery,[1] the sea
Hove its loose weight like sand to tangle me
Upon the washing deck, to crush the hull;
Subsiding, dragged flesh at the bone. The skull

5

10

15

---

1 *Cape Flattery in the State of Washington.*

Felt the retreating wash of dreaming hair.
20   Half drenched in dissolution, I lay bare.
I scarcely pulled myself erect; I came
Back slowly, slowly knew myself the same.
That was the ocean. From the ship we saw
Gray whales for miles: the long sweep of the jaw,
25   The blunt head plunging clean above the wave.
And one rose in a tent of sea and gave
A darkening shudder; water fell away;
The whale stood shining, and then sank in spray.

A landsman, I. The sea is but a sound.
30   I would be near it on a sandy mound,
And hear the steady rushing of the deep
While I lay stinging in the sand with sleep.
I have lived inland long. The land is numb.
It stands beneath the feet, and one may come
35   Walking securely, till the sea extends
Its limber margin, and precision ends.
By night a chaos of commingling power,
The whole Pacific hovers hour by hour.
The slow Pacific swell stirs on the sand,
40   Sleeping to sink away, withdrawing land,
Heaving and wrinkled in the moon, and blind;
Or gathers seaward, ebbing out of mind.

(1931)

By the Road to the Air-Base

The calloused grass lies hard
Against the cracking plain:
Life is a grayish stain;
The salt-marsh hems my yard.

5   Dry dikes rise hill on hill:
In sloughs of tidal slime
Shell-fish deposit lime,
Wild sea-fowl creep at will.

The highway, like a beach,
10   Turns whiter, shadowy, dry:
Loud, pale against the sky,
The bombing planes hold speech.

Yet fruit grows on the trees;
Here scholars pause to speak;
15   Through gardens bare and Greek,
I hear my neighbor's bees.

(1940)

STEVIE SMITH

(1902–1971)

*F*lorence Margaret Smith was born in Hull, England. She later moved to the home of an aunt in London, where she lived the rest of her life. Her first book, Novel on Yellow Paper, *appeared in 1936, and her first poetry collection,* A Good Time Was Had by All, *the following year. She published two more novels and eight collections of verse. Smith's poetry belongs to no particular school or movement: it stands apart as the unique utterance of a unique voice. Although she did on occasion use traditional poetic or elevated language, much of her poetry is informal or conversational. Much of it is also highly musical, and Smith herself sang many poems to tunes she based on Gregorian chant and hymns. The most distinctive characteristic of her poetry, however, is its wit, evident even in poems dealing with death, a frequent topic in her collections.*

Our Bog Is Dood

Our Bog is dood, our Bog is dood,
They lisped in accents mild,
But when I asked them to explain
They grew a little wild.
5   How do you know your Bog is dood
My darling little child?

We know because we wish it so
That is enough, they cried,
And straight within each infant eye
10   Stood up the flame of pride,
And if you do not think it so
You shall be crucified.

Then tell me, darling little ones,
What's dood, suppose Bog is?
15   Just what we think, the answer came,
Just what we think it is.
They bowed their heads. Our Bog is ours
And we are wholly his.

But when they raised them up again
20   They had forgotten me
Each one upon each other glared
In pride and misery
For what was dood, and what their Bog
They never could agree.

25   Oh sweet it was to leave them then,
And sweeter not to see,
And sweetest of all to walk alone
Beside the encroaching sea,
The sea that soon should drown them all,
30   That never yet drowned me.

(1950)

Not Waving but Drowning

Nobody heard him, the dead man,
But still he lay moaning:
I was much further out than you thought
And not waving but drowning.

5   Poor chap, he always loved larking
And now he's dead
It must have been too cold for him his heart gave way,
They said.

Oh, no no no, it was too cold always
10   (Still the dead one lay moaning)
I was much too far out all my life
And not waving but drowning.

(1957)

EARLE BIRNEY

(1904–   )

*B*orn *in Calgary, Birney grew up on a farm in the British Columbia interior and in Banff. He studied at British Columbia and Toronto before completing a Ph.D. in Chaucer's irony at the University of Toronto in 1938. He spent most of his academic career at the University of British Columbia. Twice winner of the Governor General's Award, for his first volume,* David and Other Poems *(1942), and for* Now Is Time *(1945), he has also written two novels, the first of which,* Turvey *(1949), won the Leacock Medal for humour.*

Literally and figuratively, Birney is a peripatetic poet. He has for much of his life travelled throughout the world, writing poems about his observations. He has also journeyed widely through poetic forms, producing everything from poems based on Anglo-Saxon metrics (see "Mappemounde" and "Anglosaxon Street") to concrete poetry mobiles. Not surprisingly, journeys of various kinds are prominent thematic elements in much of his poetry. In fact, for Birney life itself is a journey, and his poems are "signals out of the loneliness into which all of us are born and in which we die, affirmations of kinship with other wayfarers. . . ."

Vancouver Lights

About me the night   moonless   wimples¹ the mountains
wraps ocean   land   air   and mounting
sucks at the stars   The city   throbbing below
webs the sable peninsula   The golden
5   strands overleap the seajet   by bridge and buoy
vault the shears of the inlet   climb the woods
toward me   falter   and halt   Across to the firefly
haze of a ship on the gulf's erased horizon
roll the lambent spokes of a lighthouse

10   Through the feckless years we have come to the time
when to look on this quilt of lamps is a troubling delight
Welling from Europe's bog   through Africa flowing
and Asia   drowning the lonely lumes² on the oceans

1 *veils.*
2 *lights.*

tiding up over Halifax   now to this winking
15   outpost comes flooding the primal ink[3]

On this mountain's brutish forehead with terror of space
I stir   of the changeless night and the stark ranges
of nothing   pulsing down from beyond and between
the fragile planets   We are a spark beleaguered
20   by darkness   this twinkle we make in a corner of emptiness
how shall we utter our fear that the black Experimentress
will never in the range of her microscope find it?   Our Phoebus[4]
himself is a bubble that dries on Her slide   while the Nubian[5]
wears for an evening's whim a necklace of nebulae

25   Yet we must speak   we the unique glowworms
Out of the waters and rocks of our little world
we conjured these flames   hooped these sparks
by our will   From blankness and cold we fashioned stars
to our size   and signalled Aldebaran[6]
30   This must we say   whoever may be to hear us
if murk devour   and none weave again in gossamer:

These rays were ours
we made and unmade them   Not the shudder of continents
doused us   the moon's passion   nor crash of comets
35   In the fathomless heat of our dwarfdom   our dream's combustion
we contrived the power   the blast that snuffed us
No one bound Prometheus   Himself he chained
and consumed his own bright liver[7]   O stranger
Plutonian[8]   descendant   or beast in the stretching night —
40   there was light

(1941)   (1942)

<hr />

3 in The Cow Jumped Over the Moon (1972), Birney explains that this stanza describes the spreading of
blackouts during World War II. 4 Phoebus Apollo, the sun. 5 a black native from Nubia, in northeastern
Africa. 6 the brightest star in the constellation Taurus. 7 Prometheus stole fire for mankind, and Zeus punished
him by chaining him to a rock, where every day an eagle ate his liver, which was renewed each night. 8 pertaining
to Pluto, god of the dead, or to the dark lower world where the souls of the dead lived.

Anglosaxon Street

Dawndrizzle ended   dampness steams from
blotching brick and   blank plasterwaste
Faded housepatterns   hoary and finicky
unfold stuttering   stick like a phonograph

5   Here is a ghetto   gotton for goyim[1]
O with care denuded   of nigger and kike
No coonsmell rankles   reeks only cellarrot
attar of carexhaust   catcorpse and cookinggrease
Imperial hearts   heave in this haven
10   Cracks across windows   are welded with slogans
There'll Always Be An England   enhances geraniums
and V's for Victory   vanquish the housefly

Ho! with climbing sun   march the bleached beldames
festooned with shopping bags   farded[2] flatarched
15   bigthewed Saxonwives[3]   stepping over buttrivers
waddling back wienerladen   to suckle smallfry

Hoy! with sunslope   shrieking over hydrants
flood from learninghall   the lean fingerlings
Nordic nobblecheeked[4]   not all clean of nose
20   leaping Commandowise   into leprous lanes

What! after whistleblow!   spewed from wheelboat
after daylong doughtiness   dire handplay
in sewertrench or sandpit   come Saxonthegns[5]
Junebrown Jutekings   jawslack for meat

25   Sit after supper   on smeared doorsteps
not humbly swearing   hatedeeds on Huns[6]
profiteers politicians   pacifists Jews

1 *Gentiles; non-Jews.*
2 *painted, here with cosmetics.*
3 *the Saxons were one of three Germanic tribes, the others — mentioned later in the poem — being the Jutes and the Angles, who conquered Britain in the fifth century.*
4 *ulcerous or pimpled.*
5 *a thegn was a freeman who held land by virtue of military service.*
6 *a fierce Asiatic tribe of nomads who conquered much of eastern and central Europe; a derogatory appellation for Germans during the two world wars.*

Then by twobit magic   to muse in movie
unlock picturehoard   or lope to alehall
30   soaking bleakly   in beer skittleless

Home again to hotbox   and humid husbandhood
in slumbertrough adding   sleepily to Anglekin
Alongside the lanenooks   carling[7] and leman[8]
caterwaul and clip   careless of Saxonry
35   with moonglow and haste   and a higher heartbeat

Slumbers now slumtrack   unstinks cooling
waiting brief for milkmaid   mornstar and worldrise

(*Toronto 1942*)   (1966)

Mappemounde[1]

No not this old   whalehall[2] can whelm us
shiptamed gullgraced   soft to our glidings
Harrows that mere[3] more   which squares our map
See in its north   where scribe has marked *mermen*
5   shore-sneakers who croon   to the seafarer's girl
next year's gleewords   East and west *nadders*[4]
flamefanged bale-twisters[5]   their breath dries up tears
chars in the breast-hoard[6]   the brave picture-faces
Southward *Cetegrande*[7] that   sly beast who sucks in
10   with whirlwind also   the wanderer's pledges

That sea is hight[8] Time   it hems all hearts' landtrace
Men say the redeless[9]   reaching its bounds
topple in maelstrom   tread back never
Adread in that mere   we drift to map's end

(*Hospital Ship* El Nil, *Atlantic 1945*)   (1948)

---

7 *woman.* 8 *lover.* 1 *"Map of the world." This poem is based on old maps of the world, which pictured the land as totally surrounded by the sea. The corners of such maps contain decorative illustrations.* 2 *an Anglo-Saxon kenning (poetic compound) for the sea.* 3 *sea.* 4 *an obscure form of adders; thus, sea-serpents.* 5 *"bale" means actively evil, as in destroying or tormenting; in Middle English poetic use it could mean the results of evil, such as pain, torment, woe, or death. Here, the phrase "bale-twister" has the double meaning of destruction-maker and sorrow-maker.* 6 *a kenning for memory.* 7 *a great whale.* 8 *named or called.* 9 *those without counsel.*

Bushed

He invented a rainbow but lightning struck it
shattered it into the lake-lap of a mountain
so big his mind slowed when he looked at it

Yet he built a shack on the shore
5 learned to roast porcupine belly and
wore the quills on his hatband

At first he was out with the dawn
whether it yellowed bright as wood-columbine
or was only a fuzzed moth in a flannel of storm
10 But he found the mountain was clearly alive
sent messages whizzing down every hot morning
boomed proclamations at noon and spread out
a white guard of goat
before falling asleep on its feet at sundown

15 When he tried his eyes on the lake   ospreys
would fall like valkyries[1]
choosing the cut-throat[2]
He took then to waiting
till the night smoke rose from the boil of the sunset

20 But the moon carved unknown totems
out of the lakeshore
owls in the beardusky woods derided him
moosehorned cedars circled his swamps and tossed
their antlers up to the stars
25 then he knew   though the mountain slept   the winds
were shaping its peak to an arrowhead
poised

And now he could only
bar himself in and wait
30 for the great flint to come singing into his heart

(*Wreck Beach 1951*)   (1952)

---

1 *in Norse mythology, the Valkyries (Choosers of the Slain) were handmaidens of Odin who hovered over battlefields in order to choose the heroes killed in battle and escort them to Valhalla.*
2 *this pun points to both the slain warriors awaiting the Valkyries and a kind of large trout found in the Rocky Mountain region.*

JOHN BETJEMAN

(1906–1984)

ir John Betjeman, appointed Britain's Poet Laureate in 1972, was a journalist, broadcaster, author of travel guides and books on architecture, and a poet who, according to Philip Larkin, "re-established the link with the common reader." Born in Highgate, he was educated at Oxford, where he came into contact with W.H. Auden and other influential poets. He published his first volume of verse in 1931. From a technical point of view, his poetry uses regular rhythms and common rhymes, but for all that it is not mere versifying. His work is notable for its urbane wit and trenchant satire. His use of place names and topographical description testifies to his love of his English heritage. A vocal opponent of many modern developments, Betjeman once declared that he would "continue to use poetry in the cause of preserving the countryside."

In Westminster Abbey

Let me take this other glove off
   As the *vox humana*[1] swells,
And the beauteous fields of Eden
   Bask beneath the Abbey bells.
5 Here, where England's statesmen lie,
Listen to a lady's cry.

Gracious Lord, oh bomb the Germans.
   Spare their women for Thy Sake,
And if that is not too easy
10   We will pardon Thy Mistake.
But, gracious Lord, whate'er shall be,
Don't let anyone bomb me.

Keep our Empire undismembered
   Guide our Forces by Thy Hand,
15 Gallant blacks from far Jamaica,
   Honduras and Togoland;
Protect them Lord in all their fights,
And, even more, protect the whites.

---

1 *an organ reed stop intended to imitate the human voice.*

Think of what our Nation stands for,
20   Books from Boots'[2] and country lanes,
Free speech, free passes, class distinction,
      Democracy and proper drains.
Lord, put beneath Thy special care
One-eighty-nine Cadogan Square.

25   Although dear Lord I am a sinner,
      I have done no major crime;
Now I'll come to Evening Service
      Whensoever I have the time.
So, Lord, reserve for me a crown,
30   And do not let my shares go down.

I will labour for Thy Kingdom,
      Help our lads to win the war,
Send white feathers to the cowards[3]
      Join the Women's Army Corps,
35   Then wash the Steps around Thy Throne
In the Eternal Safety Zone.

Now I feel a little better,
      What a treat to hear Thy Word,
Where the bones of leading statesmen,
40   Have so often been interr'd.
And now, dear Lord, I cannot wait
Because I have a luncheon date.

(1940)

---

2 *Boots the Chemist is a chain of British pharmacies.*
3 *she promises, that is, to send white feathers, traditional symbols of cowardice, to men not in uniform.*

Upper Lambourne[1]

Up the ash-tree climbs the ivy,
  Up the ivy climbs the sun,
With a twenty-thousand pattering
  Has a valley breeze begun,
5   Feathery ash, neglected elder,
  Shift the shade and make it run —

Shift the shade toward the nettles,
  And the nettles set it free
To streak the stained Carrara[2] headstone
10   Where, in nineteen-twenty-three,
He who trained a hundred winners
  Paid the Final Entrance Fee.

Leathery limbs of Upper Lambourne,
  Leathery skin from sun and wind,
15   Leathery breeches, spreading stables,
  Shining saddles left behind —
To the down the string of horses
  Moving out of sight and mind.

Feathery ash in leathery Lambourne
20   Waves above the sarsen stone,[3]
And Edwardian[4] plantations
  So coniferously moan
As to make the swelling downland,
  Far-surrounding, seem their own.

(1940)

1 town in Berkshire, an area in which a number of trainers maintained stables in order to train race horses on the downs.
2 a distinctive kind of marble quarried in Carrara, Italy.
3 large boulders of sandstone scattered over chalk downs.
4 dating from the reign of King Edward VII (1901–10).

W.H. AUDEN

(1907–1973)

*T*hough born in Britain and educated at Oxford, Wystan Hugh Auden lived in America much of the time after 1939 and became an American citizen in 1946. He began writing poetry in school, revealed a remarkable talent for handling various styles, and established himself as a leader among the younger poets in Britain while he was still in his twenties. Early in his career, Auden was influenced by Marxism and was much concerned with satirizing the British middle class. Later, however, while still showing an ironic bent, his work became more generally philosophical as it explored the need for meaning in modern life. Typically less personal and more analytical than most modern poets, Auden demonstrated an unsurpassed gift for capturing the political and intellectual temper of the times in which he lived.

Primarily a poet, Auden also produced a body of non-poetic work, including travel literature, philosophical writings, plays, and criticism, that is impressive both in its extent and its variety.

Lullaby

Lay your sleeping head, my love,
Human on my faithless arm;
Time and fevers burn away
Individual beauty from
5   Thoughtful children, and the grave
Proves the child ephemeral:
But in my arms till break of day
Let the living creature lie,
Mortal, guilty, but to me
10   The entirely beautiful.

Soul and body have no bounds:
To lovers as they lie upon
Her tolerant enchanted slope
In their ordinary swoon,
15   Grave the vision Venus sends

Of supernatural sympathy,
Universal love and hope;
While an abstract insight wakes
Among the glaciers and the rocks
20 The hermit's carnal ecstasy.

Certainty, fidelity
On the stroke of midnight pass
Like vibrations of a bell
And fashionable madmen raise
25 Their pedantic boring cry:
Every farthing of the cost,
All the dreaded cards foretell,
Shall be paid, but from this night
Not a whisper, not a thought,
30 Not a kiss nor look be lost.

Beauty, midnight, vision dies:
Let the winds of dawn that blow
Softly round your dreaming head
Such a day of welcome show
35 Eye and knocking heart may bless,
Find our mortal world enough;
Noons of dryness find you fed
By the involuntary powers,
Nights of insult let you pass
40 Watched by every human love.

(1937)

The Unknown Citizen

(*TO JS/07/M/378*
THIS MARBLE MONUMENT
IS ERECTED BY THE STATE)

He was found by the Bureau of Statistics to be
One against whom there was no official complaint,
And all the reports on his conduct agree
That, in the modern sense of an old-fashioned word, he
    was a saint,
5   For in everything he did he served the Greater
    Community.
Except for the War till the day he retired
He worked in a factory and never got fired,
But satisfied his employers, Fudge Motors Inc.
Yet he wasn't a scab or odd in his views,
10   For his Union reports that he paid his dues,
(Our report on his Union shows it was sound)
And our Social Psychology workers found
That he was popular with his mates and liked a drink.
The Press are convinced that he bought a paper every day
15   And that his reactions to advertisements were normal in
    every way.
Policies taken out in his name prove that he was fully
    insured,
And his Health-card shows he was once in hospital but left
    it cured.
Both Producers Research and High-Grade Living declare
He was fully sensible to the advantages of the Instalment
    Plan
20   And had everything necessary to the Modern Man,
A phonograph, a radio, a car and a frigidaire.
Our researchers into Public Opinion are content
That he held the proper opinions for the time of year;
When there was peace, he was for peace; when there was
    war, he went.

25   He was married and added five children to the population,
Which our Eugenist says was the right number for a parent
        of his generation,
And our teachers report that he never interfered with their
        education.
Was he free? Was he happy? The question is absurd:
Had anything been wrong, we should certainly have heard.

(1939)

In Memory of W.B. Yeats

(D. JAN. 1939)

I

He disappeared in the dead of winter:
The brooks were frozen, the airports almost deserted,
And snow disfigured the public statues;
The mercury sank in the mouth of the dying day.
5   What instruments we have agree
The day of his death was a dark cold day.

Far from his illness
The wolves ran on through the evergreen forests,
The peasant river was untempted by the fashionable quays;
10   By mourning tongues
The death of the poet was kept from his poems.

But for him it was his last afternoon as himself,
An afternoon of nurses and rumours;
The provinces of his body revolted,
15   The squares of his mind were empty,
Silence invaded the suburbs,
The current of his feeling failed; he became his admirers.

Now he is scattered among a hundred cities
And wholly given over to unfamiliar affections,
20 To find his happiness in another kind of wood
And be punished under a foreign code of conscience.
The words of a dead man
Are modified in the guts of the living.

But in the importance and noise of to-morrow
25 When the brokers are roaring like beasts on the floor of
the Bourse,[1]
And the poor have the sufferings to which they are fairly
accustomed,
And each in the cell of himself is almost convinced of his
freedom,
A few thousand will think of this day
As one thinks of a day when one did something slightly
unusual.
30 What instruments we have agree
The day of his death was a dark cold day.

II

You were silly like us; your gift survived it all:
The parish of rich women, physical decay,
Yourself. Mad Ireland hurt you into poetry.
35 Now Ireland has her madness and her weather still,
For poetry makes nothing happen: it survives
In the valley of its making where executives
Would never want to tamper, flows on south
From ranches of isolation and the busy griefs,
40 Raw towns that we believe and die in; its survives,
A way of happening, a mouth.

III

Earth, receive an honoured guest:
William Yeats is laid to rest.
Let the Irish vessel lie
45 Emptied of its poetry.[2]

---

1 *French Stock Exchange.*
2 *in the original version written in 1939, Auden included three more stanzas here in which Time, while indifferent to other gifts and virtues, is said to pardon the failings of those who write well.*

In the nightmare of the dark
All the dogs of Europe bark,
And the living nations wait,
Each sequestered in its hate;

50   Intellectual disgrace
Stares from every human face,
And the seas of pity lie
Locked and frozen in each eye.

Follow, poet, follow right
55   To the bottom of the night,
With your unconstraining voice
Still persuade us to rejoice;

With the farming of a verse
Make a vineyard of the curse,
60   Sing of human unsuccess
In a rapture of distress;

In the deserts of the heart
Let the healing fountain start,
In the prison of his days
65   Teach the free man how to praise.

(1939)   (1966)

Musée des Beaux Arts[1]

About suffering they were never wrong,
The Old Masters: how well they understood
Its human position; how it takes place
While someone else is eating or opening a window or just
        walking dully along;

---

1 *This refers to the Museum of Fine Arts in Brussels, Belgium, where* The Fall of Icarus, *a painting by Flemish painter Pieter Brueghel the Elder (c. 1525–69) still hangs.*

₅ How, when the aged are reverently, passionately waiting
For the miraculous birth, there always must be
Children who did not specially want it to happen, skating
On a pond at the edge of the wood:

They never forgot
₁₀ That even the dreadful martyrdom must run its course
Anyhow in a corner, some untidy spot
Where the dogs go on with their doggy life and the
    torturer's horse
Scratches its innocent behind on a tree.

In Brueghel's *Icarus*,[2] for instance: how everything turns
    away
₁₅ Quite leisurely from the disaster; the ploughman may
Have heard the splash, the forsaken cry,
But for him it was not an important failure; the sun shone
As it had to on the white legs disappearing into the green
Water; and the expensive delicate ship that must have seen
₂₀ Something amazing, a boy falling out of the sky,
Had somewhere to get to and sailed calmly on.

                                 (1940)

The Shield of Achilles[1]

    She looked over his shoulder
      For vines and olive trees,
    Marble well-governed cities
      And ships upon untamed seas,
₅   But there on the shining metal
      His hands had put instead
    An artificial wilderness
      And a sky like lead.

2 in Greek myth, the skilled craftsman Daedalus makes wings of wax and feathers in order to escape with Icarus,
his son, from the Cretan labyrinth, which he himself had designed. When Icarus flies too near the sun, the wax
melts and he falls into the sea.

1 In Book XVIII of the Iliad, the goddess Thetis, mother of the Greek hero Achilles, persuades Hephaestus, the god
of fire and metalworking, to make armour for her son. The shield carries a depiction of the universe and scenes
representing human life at the time.

A plain without a feature, bare and brown,
10   No blade of grass, no sign of neighbourhood,
Nothing to eat and nowhere to sit down,
        Yet, congregated on its blankness, stood
        An unintelligible multitude,
A million eyes, a million boots in line,
15   Without expression, waiting for a sign.

Out of the air a voice without a face
    Proved by statistics that some cause was just
In tones as dry and level as the place:
        No one was cheered and nothing was discussed;
20   Column by column in a cloud of dust
They marched away enduring a belief
Whose logic brought them, somewhere else, to grief.

                She looked over his shoulder
                    For ritual pieties,
25   White flower-garlanded heifers,
                    Libation and sacrifice,
                But there on the shining metal
                    Where the altar should have been,
                She saw by his flickering forge-light
30   Quite another scene.

Barbed wire enclosed an arbitrary spot
    Where bored officials lounged (one cracked a joke)
And sentries sweated for the day was hot:
        A crowd of ordinary decent folk
35   Watched from without and neither moved nor spoke
As three pale figures were led forth and bound
To three posts driven upright in the ground.

The mass and majesty of this world, all
    That carries weight and always weighs the same
40 Lay in the hands of others; they were small
        And could not hope for help and no help came:
        What their foes liked to do was done, their shame
Was all the worst could wish; they lost their pride
And died as men before their bodies died.

45   She looked over his shoulder
          For athletes at their games,
      Men and women in a dance
          Moving their sweet limbs
      Quick, quick, to music,
50   But there on the shining shield
      His hands had set no dancing-floor
      But a weed-choked field.

A ragged urchin, aimless and alone,
    Loitered about that vacancy, a bird
55 Flew up to safety from his well-aimed stone:
    That girls are raped, that two boys knife a third,
    Were axioms to him, who'd never heard
Of any world where promises were kept,
Or one could weep because another wept.

60   The thin-lipped armourer,
          Hephaestos hobbled away,
      Thetis of the shining breasts
          Cried out in dismay
      At what the god had wrought
65   To please her son, the strong
      Iron-hearted man-slaying Achilles
      Who would not live long.

(1952)

After Reading a Child's Guide to Modern Physics

    If all a top physicist knows
    About the Truth be true.
    Then, for all the so-and-so's,
    Futility and grime,
5   Our common world contains,
    We have a better time
    Than the Greater Nebulae do,
    Or the atoms in our brains.

Marriage is rarely bliss
10   But, surely it would be worse
As particles to pelt
At thousands of miles per sec
About a universe
In which a lover's kiss
15   Would either not be felt
Or break the loved one's neck.

Though the face at which I stare
While shaving it be cruel
For, year after year, it repels
20   An ageing suitor, it has,
Thank God, sufficient mass
To be altogether there.
Not an indeterminate gruel
Which is partly somewhere else.

25   Our eyes prefer to suppose
That a habitable place
Has a geocentric view.
That architects enclose
A quiet Euclidean space:
30   Exploded myths — but who
Would feel at home astraddle
An ever expanding saddle?

This passion of our kind
For the process of finding out
35   Is a fact one can hardly doubt,
But I would rejoice in it more
If I knew more clearly what
We wanted the knowledge for,
Felt certain still that the mind
40   Is free to know or not.

It has chosen once, it seems,
And whether our concern
For magnitude's extremes
Really become a creature
45   Who comes in a median size,
Or politicizing Nature
Be altogether wise,
Is something we shall learn.

(1962)

THEODORE ROETHKE

(1908–1963)

*T*heodore Roethke's family operated greenhouses in Saginaw, Michigan, and, growing up surrounded by plants, he developed the almost mystical sympathy with primitive life that characterized his early nature lyrics. He received a master's degree from the University of Michigan, did graduate work at Harvard, and devoted his working life to college teaching as well as writing poetry.

During much of his adult life, Roethke suffered from alcoholism and mental illness, which caused him to experience alternating bouts of manic energy and depression. He managed to turn these problems to poetic advantage, however, by exploring his changing mental states as poetic journeys through interior psychic landscapes.

Root Cellar

Nothing would sleep in that cellar, dank as a ditch,
Bulbs broke out of boxes hunting for chinks in the dark,
Shoots dangled and drooped,
Lolling obscenely from mildewed crates,
5   Hung down long yellow evil necks, like tropical snakes.
And what a congress of stinks! —
Roots ripe as old bait,
Pulpy stems, rank, silo-rich,
Leaf-mold, manure, lime, piled against slippery planks.
10   Nothing would give up life:
Even the dirt kept breathing a small breath.

(1948)

My Papa's Waltz

The whiskey on your breath
Could make a small boy dizzy;
But I hung on like death:
Such waltzing was not easy.

5 We romped until the pans
Slid from the kitchen shelf;
My mother's countenance
Could not unfrown itself.

The hand that held my wrist
10 Was battered on one knuckle;
At every step you missed
My right ear scraped a buckle.

You beat time on my head
With a palm caked hard by dirt,
15 Then waltzed me off to bed
Still clinging to your shirt.

(1948)

The Minimal

I study the lives on a leaf: the little
Sleepers, numb nudgers in cold dimensions,
Beetles in caves, newts, stone-deaf fishes,
Lice tethered to long limp subterranean weeds,
5 Squirmers in bogs,
And bacterial creepers
Wriggling through wounds
Like elvers[1] in ponds,
Their wan mouths kissing the warm sutures,
10 Cleaning and caressing,
Creeping and healing.

(1948)

1 *young eels.*

The Waking

I strolled across
An open field;
The sun was out;
Heat was happy.

5   This way! This way!
The wren's throat shimmered,
Either to other,
The blossoms sang.

The stones sang,
10   The little ones did,
And flowers jumped
Like small goats.

A ragged fringe
Of daisies waved;
15   I wasn't alone
In a grove of apples.

Far in the wood
A nestling sighed;
The dew loosened
20   Its morning smells.

I came where the river
Ran over stones:
My ears knew
An early joy.

25   And all the waters
Of all the streams
Sang in my veins
That summer day.

(1953)

A.M. KLEIN

(1909–1972)

*A*braham Moses Klein was born in Ratno, Ukraine, and came to Montreal with his parents in 1910. After receiving a B.A. from McGill University in 1930, he studied law at the Université de Montréal and was admitted to the bar in 1933. A mental breakdown and several suicide attempts forced his retirement in 1956. Klein became reclusive and completely abandoned all writing, but he had already made a permanent literary contribution as one of the leading figures in the development of modern poetry in Canada.

Jewish themes dominate Klein's writing: his first book, Hath Not a Jew . . . (1940), celebrates the rich heritage and customs of the Jewish people, and much of his later work treats Jewish suffering. The Rocking Chair (1948), winner of the Governor General's Award for poetry, contained poems about Quebec, as well as his finest work, "Portrait of the Poet as Landscape." He returned to Jewish themes in his complex visionary novel, The Second Scroll (1951). Klein's poetry is both intellectual and witty; it is characterized by learned allusions, metaphors, puns, archaisms, and words derived from several languages.

Heirloom

My father bequeathed me no wide estates;
No keys and ledgers were my heritage;
Only some holy books with *yahrzeit* dates[1]
Writ mournfully upon a blank front page —

5   Books of the Baal Shem Tov,[2] and of his wonders;
Pamphlets upon the devil and his crew;
Prayers against road demons, witches, thunders;
And sundry other tomes for a good Jew.

1 anniversary dates of the death of ancestors.
2 the eighteenth-century rabbi who founded Hasidism, a Jewish movement that emphasizes communion with God through joyful prayer, encourages religious expression in song and dance, and values the experience of the natural world and a simple delight in service to God more than the legal dialectic of traditional study of the Torah.

Beautiful: though no pictures on them, save
10   The scorpion crawling on a printed track;
The Virgin floating on a scriptural wave,
Square letters twinkling in the Zodiac.[3]

The snuff left on this page, now brown and old,
The tallow stains of midnight liturgy —
15   These are my coat of arms, and these unfold
My noble lineage, my proud ancestry!

And my tears, too, have stained this heirloomed ground,
When reading in these treatises some weird
Miracle, I turned a leaf and found
20   A white hair fallen from my father's beard.

(1940)

Portrait of the Poet as Landscape

i

Not an editorial-writer, bereaved with bartlett,[1]
mourns him, the shelved Lycidas.[2]
No actress squeezes a glycerine[3] tear for him.
The radio broadcast lets his passing pass.
5   And with the police, no record. Nobody, it appears,
either under his real name or his alias,
missed him enough to report.

3 in a letter to A.J.M. Smith dated January 21, 1943, Klein explained that "Hebrew prayer books are never
    illustrated. The only drawings that appear in the liturgy are the signs of the Zodiac illustrating the prayers for
    rain and fertility."

1 Familiar Quotations, first published in 1855 by John Bartlett and frequently updated.
2 "Lycidas" (1637), a pastoral elegy by John Milton, mourns the drowning of Edward King, a young poet. See
    page 120.
3 used to simulate tears on stage.

It is possible that he is dead, and not discovered.
It is possible that he can be found some place
in a narrow closet, like the corpse in a detective story,
standing, his eyes staring, and ready to fall on his face.
It is also possible that he is alive
and amnesiac, or mad, or in retired disgrace,
or beyond recognition lost in love.

We are sure only that from our real society
he has disappeared; he simply does not count,
except in the pullulation⁴ of vital statistics —
somebody's vote, perhaps, an anonymous taunt
of the Gallup poll, a dot in a government table —
but not felt, and certainly far from eminent —
in a shouting mob, somebody's sigh.

O, he who unrolled our culture from his scroll —
the prince's quote, the rostrum-rounding roar —
who under one name made articulate
heaven, and under another the seven-circled air,⁵
is, if he is at all, a number, an x,
a Mr. Smith in a hotel register, —
incognito, lost, lacunal.⁶

ii

The truth is he's not dead, but only ignored —
like the mirroring lenses forgotten on a brow
that shine with the guilt of their unnoticed world.
The truth is he lives among neighbours, who, though they
    will allow
him a passable fellow, think him eccentric, not solid,
a type that one can forgive, and for that matter, forgo.

4 *teeming; rapid sprouting or breeding.*
5 *before Nicolaus Copernicus (1473–1543), people believed that the earth was the fixed centre of the universe and that it was surrounded by seven concentric circles.*
6 *a lacuna is a blank space or missing portion.*

35 Himself he has his moods, just like a poet.
Sometimes, depressed to nadir,[7] he will think all lost,
will see himself as throwback, relict,[8] freak
his mother's miscarriage, his great-grandfather's ghost,
and he will curse his quintuplet senses, and their tutors
40 in whom he put, as he should not have put, his trust.

Then he will remember his travels over that body —
the torso verb, the beautiful face of the noun,
and all those shaped and warm auxiliaries!
A first love it was, the recognition of his own.
45 Dear limbs adverbial, complexion of adjective,
dimple and dip of conjugation!

And then remember how this made a change in him
affecting for always the glow and growth of his being;
how suddenly was aware of the air, like shaken tinfoil,[9]
50 of the patents of nature, the shock of belated seeing,
the loneliness peering from the eyes of crowds;
the integers of thought; the cube-roots of feeling.

Thus, zoomed to zenith, sometimes he hopes again,
and sees himself as a character, with a rehearsed role:
55 the Count of Monte Cristo,[10] come for his revenges;
the unsuspecting heir, with papers; the risen soul;
or the chloroformed prince awakening from his flowers;
or — deflated again — the convict on parole.

iii

He is alone; yet not completely alone.
60 Pins on a map of a colour similar to his,
each city has one, sometimes more than one;
here, caretakers of art, in colleges;
in offices, there, with arm-bands, and green-shaded;
and there, pounding their catalogued beats in libraries, —

---

7 *the lowest point; the point opposite the zenith.*
8 *a plant or animal surviving from a previous age.*
9 *see line 2 of "God's Grandeur," by Gerard Manley Hopkins, page 368.*
10 in The Count of Monte Cristo *(1844–45), by Alexandre Dumas* père *(1802–70), Edmond Dantes
elaborately plots the ruin of those whose false accusations led to his prolonged imprisonment.*

65 everywhere menial, a shadow's shadow.
And always for their egos — their outmoded art.
Thus, having lost the bevel[11] in the ear,
they know neither up nor down, mistake the part
for the whole, curl themselves in a comma,
70 talk technics, make a colon their eyes. They distort —
such is the pain of their frustration — truth
to something convolute and cerebral.
How they do fear the slap of the flat of the platitude!
Now Pavlov's victims[12] their mouths water at bell,
75 the platter empty.
     See they set twenty-one jewels
into their watches; the time they do not tell!

Some, patagonian[13] in their own esteem,
and longing for the multiplying word,
join party and wear pins, now have a message,
80 an ear, and the convention-hall's regard.
Upon the knees of ventriloquists, they own,
of their dandled[14] brightness, only the paint and board.

And some go mystical, and some go mad.
One stares at a mirror all day long, as if
85 to recognize himself; another courts
angels, — for here he does not fear rebuff;
and a third, alone, and sick with sex, and rapt,
doodles him symbols convex and concave.

O schizoid solitudes! O purities
90 curdling upon themselves! Who live for themselves,
or for each other, but for nobody else;
desire affection, private and public loves;
are friendly, and then quarrel and surmise
the secret perversions of each other's lives.

---

11 *an instrument for determining angles; thus, the sense of balance.*
12 *Ivan Petrovich Pavlov (1849–1936), a Russian physiologist, studied conditioned reflexes by ringing a bell when he provided food to dogs. Later, even if he did not serve them food, the dogs salivated when he rang the bell.*
13 *the natives of Patagonia, at the extreme southern tip of South America, were reputed to be the tallest people in the world; figuratively, patagonian means gigantic.*
14 *to be moved up and down on one's knee, as with a child.*

iv

95   He suspects that something has happened, a law
    been passed, a nightmare ordered. Set apart,
    he finds himself, with special haircut and dress,
    as on a reservation. Introvert.
    He does not understand this; sad conjecture
100   muscles and palls thrombotic on his heart.

    He thinks an impostor, having studied his personal
          biography,
    his gestures, his moods, now has come forward to pose
    in the shivering vacuums his absence leaves.
    Wigged with his laurel, that other, and faked with his face,
105   he pats the heads of his children, pecks his wife,
    and is at home, and slippered, in his house.

    So he guesses at the impertinent silhouette
    that talks to his phone-piece and slits open his mail.
    Is it the local tycoon who for a hobby
110   plays poet, he so epical in steel?
    The orator, making a pause? Or is that man
    he who blows his flash of brass in the jittering hall?

    Or is he cuckolded by the troubadour
    rich and successful out of celluloid?
115   Or by the don who unrhymes atoms? Or
    the chemist death built up? Pride, lost impostor'd pride,
    it is another, another, whoever he is,
    who rides where he should ride.

v

    Fame, the adrenalin:[15] to be talked about;
120   to be a verb; to be introduced as *The:*
    to smile with endorsement from slick paper; make
    caprices anecdotal; to nod to the world; to see
    one's name like a song upon the marquees played;
    to be forgotten with embarrassment; to be —
125   to be.

15 Milton's "Lycidas" also argues about a poet's motivation, first declaring that "Fame is the spur" (line 70) and
    then rejecting this notion.

It has its attractions, but is not the thing;
nor is it the ape mimesis[16] who speaks from the tree
ancestral; nor the merkin[17] joy . . .
Rather it is stark infelicity
130   which stirs him from his sleep, undressed, asleep
to walk upon roofs and window-sills and defy
the gape of gravity.

vi

Therefore he seeds illusions. Look, he is
the nth Adam taking a green inventory
135   in world[18] but scarcely uttered, naming, praising,
the flowering fiats in the meadow, the
syllabled fur, stars aspirate, the pollen
whose sweet collusion sounds eternally.
For to praise

140   the world — he, solitary man — is breath
to him. Until it has been praised, that part
has not been. Item by exciting item —
air to his lungs, and pressured blood to his heart —
they are pulsated, and breathed, until they map,
145   not the world's, but his own body's chart!

And now in imagination he has climbed
another planet, the better to look
with single camera view upon this earth —
its total scope,and each afflated[19] tick,
150   its talk, its trick, its tracklessness — and this,
this, he would like to write down in a book!

To find a new function for the *déclassé*[20] craft
archaic like the fletcher's;[21] to make a new thing;
to say the word that will become sixth sense;

---

16 *imitation.*
17 *a false hairpiece for the female genitalia.*
18 *in Genesis 2:19–20, Adam names the animals.*
19 *inspired.*
20 *outmoded.*
21 *arrow-maker's*

155   perhaps by necessity and indirection bring
new forms to life, anonymously, new creeds —
O, somehow pay back the daily larcenies of the lung!

These are not mean ambitions. It is already something
merely to entertain them. Meanwhile, he
160   makes of his status as zero a rich garland,
a halo of his anonymity,
and lives alone, and in his secret shines
like phosphorus. At the bottom of the sea.

(1948)

STEPHEN SPENDER

(1909–   )

ovelist, playwright, essayist, and poet, Stephen Spender was born in London. He attended but did not graduate from Oxford, where, like many others, he briefly turned to communism. He printed his first poems himself in 1928. The exceptionally favourable notices his Poems *(1933) received in both England and America established his reputation as a poet who was both sensitive and intense. Particularly sensitive to suffering and victimization, he gave social concerns a prominent part in his works. "The only true hope for civilization," he once said, is "the conviction of the individual that his inner life can affect outward events and that, whether or not he does so, he is responsible for them."*

The Truly Great[1]

I think continually of those who were truly great.
Who, from the womb, remembered the soul's history
Through corridors of light where the hours are suns,
Endless and singing. Whose lovely ambition
5   Was that their lips, still touched with fire,
Should tell of the Spirit, clothed from head to foot in song.
And who hoarded from the Spring branches
The desires falling across their bodies like blossoms.

What is precious, is never to forget
10   The essential delight of the blood drawn from ageless
            springs
Breaking through rocks in worlds before our earth.
Never to deny its pleasure in the morning simple light
Nor its grave evening demand for love.
Never to allow gradually the traffic to smother
15   With noise and fog, the flowering of the Spirit.

---

1 *This is the revised version of one of Spender's best-known works: he altered the original version by making minor changes in the punctuation and by capitalizing* Spirit *at the end of the second stanza.*

Near the snow, near the sun, in the highest fields,
See how these names are fêted by the waving grass
And by the streamers of white cloud
And whispers of wind in the listening sky.
20   The names of those who in their lives fought for life,
Who wore at their hearts the fire's centre.
Born of the sun, they travelled a short while toward the
        sun
And left the vivid air signed with their honour.

(1933)   (1954)

An Elementary School Classroom in a Slum

Far far from the gusty waves these children's faces.
Like rootless weeds, the hair torn round their pallor.
The tall girl with her weighed-down head. The paper-
seeming boy, with rat's eyes. The stunted, unlucky heir
5   Of twisted bones, reciting a father's gnarled disease,
His lesson from his desk. At back of the dim class
One unnoted, sweet and young. His eyes live in a dream
Of squirrel's game, in tree room, other than this.

On sour cream walls, donations. Shakespeare's head,
10   Cloudless at dawn, civilized dome riding all cities.
Belled, flowery, Tyrolese valley. Open-handed map
Awarding the world its world. And yet, for these
Children, these windows, not this world, are world,
Where all their future's painted with a fog,
15   A narrow street sealed in with a lead sky,
Far far from rivers, capes, and stars of words.

Surely, Shakespeare is wicked, the map a bad example
With ships and sun and love tempting them to steal —
For lives that slyly turn in their cramped holes
20   From fog to endless night? On their slag heap, these
        children
Wear skins peeped through by bones and spectacles of steel
With mended glass, like bottle bits on stones.
All of their time and space are foggy slum.
So blot their maps with slums as big as doom.

25   Unless, governor, teacher, inspector, visitor,
This map becomes their window and these windows
That shut upon their lives like catacombs,
Break O break open till they break the town
And show the children to green fields, and make their
        world
30   Run azure on gold sands, and let their tongues
Run naked into books, the white and green leaves open
History theirs whose language is the sun.

(1939)

DOROTHY LIVESAY

(1909–   )

*D*orothy Livesay's poetry has developed through a number of distinct phases. Born in Winnipeg, Livesay began her career while an undergraduate at the University of Toronto. Thematically, her first book, Green Pitcher *(1928)*, displayed her sensitivity to nature and its relationship to people; technically, it showed the influence of the imagists. After studying at the Sorbonne and returning to Toronto for a degree in social work, she joined the Communist Party and was active as an organizer. Her poetry during the Depression and war years was dominated by political issues and her concern for workers' rights. Two collections of her leftist poetry won the Governor General's Award — Day and Night *(1944)* and Poems for People *(1947)*. Livesay served as a teacher in Zambia *(1960–63)* and earned her M.Ed. at the University of British Columbia in *1964*. After this, her career entered a new phase. With the publication of The Unquiet Bed *(1967)*, she established herself as a lyric poet capable of giving fresh, sensitive, and forceful expression to issues of female identity and sexuality.

Bartok[1] and the Geranium

She lifts her green umbrellas
Towards the pane
Seeking her fill of sunlight
Or of rain;
5   Whatever falls
She has no commentary
Accepts, extends,
Blows out her furbelows,[2]
Her bustling boughs;

10   And all the while he whirls
Explodes in space,
Never content with this small room:
Not even can he be
Confined to sky

---

1 Béla Bartók *(1881–1945), a Hungarian composer of intense, passionate music, exerted a profound influence on modern music through his efforts to free himself from strict tonality and the bar-measure system.*
2 *ornamental pleats or flounces.*

15 But must speed high and higher still
From galaxy to galaxy,
Wrench from the stars their momentary notes
Steal music from the moon.

She's daylight
20 He is dark
She's heaven-held breath
He storms and crackles
Spits with hell's own spark.

Yet in this room, this moment now
25 These together breathe and be:
She, essence of serenity,
He in a mad intensity
Soars beyond sight
Then hurls, lost Lucifer,
30 From heaven's height.

And when he's done, he's out:
She leans a lip against the glass
And preens herself in light.

(1955)

The Three Emilys[1]

These women crying in my head
Walk alone, uncomforted:
The Emilys, these three
Cry to be set free —
5 And others whom I will not name
Each different, each the same.

---

1 *a note identifying the three as Emily Brontë, Emily Dickinson, and Emily Carr appeared with first publication of this poem in* The Canadian Forum *(September 1953). Emily Brontë (1818–48) was a British poet and author of the novel* Wuthering Heights *(1848); Emily Dickinson (1830–86) was an American poet (some of her work is included in this anthology); Emily Carr (1871–1945) was a Canadian painter and author.*

Yet they had liberty!
Their kingdom was the sky:
They batted clouds with easy hand,
10   Found a mountain for their stand;
From wandering lonely they could catch
The inner magic of a heath —
A lake their palette, any tree
Their brush could be.

15   And still they cry to me
As in reproach —
I, born to hear their inner storm
Of separate man in woman's form,
I yet possess another kingdom, barred
20   To them, these three, this Emily.[2]
I move as mother in a frame,
My arteries
Flow the immemorial way
Towards the child, the man;
25   And only for brief span
Am I an Emily on mountain snows
And one of these.

And so the whole that I possess
Is still much less —
30   They move triumphant through my head:
I am the one
Uncomforted.

(1953)   (1972)

---

2   *none of the three Emilys married or gave birth, whereas Livesay married and raised two children.*

CHARLES OLSON

(1910–1970)

*C*harles Olson grew up in the fishing town of Gloucester, Massachusetts, which he explored, along with the formation of his own identity, in his *Maximus* poems. Educated at Harvard, Yale, and Wesleyan University, Olson taught at various American colleges and made his mark as a critic before he became known as a poet; his statements about poetry were as widely influential on younger American poets as the poetry he wrote. At the experimental Black Mountain College in North Carolina in the early 1950s, Olson became a leader of the Black Mountain movement in poetry, which included Robert Duncan and Robert Creeley. Believing that poetry in the 1940s had become too intellectual and restrained, Olson promoted a freer, more energetic verse in which the arrangement of lines and spaces on the typed page would reflect what he termed the breath units of individual poets, rather than artificial metrics or printing conventions of left-aligned margins. In his own poetry, Olson strove to reach and expose the primal sources and deepest meanings of his experience.

Maximus, to himself

I have had to learn the simplest things
last. Which made for difficulties.
Even at sea I was slow, to get the hand out, or to cross
a wet deck.
5   The sea was not, finally, my trade.
But even my trade, at it, I stood estranged
from that which was most familiar. Was delayed,
and not content with the man's argument
that such postponement
10 is now the nature of
obedience,
                that we are all late
                in a slow time,
                that we grow up many
15   And the single
                is not easily
                known

It could be, though the sharpness (the *achiote*)[1]
I note in others,
makes more sense
than my own distances. The agilities

      they show daily
      who do the world's
      businesses
      And who do nature's
      as I have no sense
      I have done either

I have made dialogues,
have discussed ancient texts,
have thrown what light I could, offered
what pleasures
doceat[2] allows

      But the known?
This, I have had to be given,
a life, love, and from one man
the world.

      Tokens.
      But sitting here
      I look out as a wind
      and water man, testing
      And missing
      some proof

I know the quarters
of the weather, where it comes from,
where it goes. But the stem of me,
this I took from their welcome,
or their rejection, of me

      And my arrogance
      was neither diminished
      nor increased,
      by the communication

---

1 *the seeds of the arnatto plant and the red dye obtained from them (Spanish).*
2 *teaching (Latin).*

2
It is undone business
I speak of, this morning,
with the sea
55   stretching out
from my feet

(1960)

Irving Layton

(1912-   )

orn in Rumania, Layton (originally Lazarovitch) came to Montreal as an infant. He was educated at Macdonald College and McGill University, taught parochial school in Montreal, and eventually became an English professor at York University. A prolific writer, he published his first book in 1945. A Red Carpet for the Sun (1959) won the Governor General's Award. Layton is probably as well known for his controversial attacks on those who disagree with him or criticize him as he is for his poetry. The guardians of official morality, intellectuals, women resistant to his charms, and Christians — all of whom he has grouped among the forces of repression — have felt his deliberately outrageous assaults. In spite of the provocations and bombast in his public statements, his poetry is not always acerbic: it can express tenderness, pathos, humour, and complex ideas, often in elegantly memorable language. Furthermore, Layton has a lofty vision of his calling, which he expresses in terms of his Jewish heritage. He believes that the true poet is, like the Hebrew prophets, one who knows truth, one whose work is of extreme importance: "Poetry, by giving dignity and utterance to our distress, enables us to hope, makes compassion reasonable."

The Birth of Tragedy [1]

And me happiest when I compose poems.
Love, power, the huzza of battle
are something, are much;
yet a poem includes them like a pool
5   water and reflection.
In me, nature's divided things —
tree, mould on tree —
have their fruition;
I am their core. Let them swap,
10   bandy, like a flame swerve
I am their mouth; as a mouth I serve.

---

1 in The Birth of Tragedy (1872), the German philosopher Friedrich Nietzsche (1844–1900) sought to explain the origins of Greek tragedy in a fusion of opposite tendencies. One, the Apollonian, stood for order and idealism; the other, the Dionysian, represented energy and actual experience.

And I observe how the sensual moths
      big with odour and sunshine
      dart into the perilous shrubbery;
or drop their visiting shadows
      upon the garden I one year made
of flowering stone to be a footstool
      for the perfect gods:
      who, friends to the ascending orders,
sustain all passionate meditations
and call down pardons
for the insurgent blood.

A quiet madman, never far from tears,
      I lie like a slain thing
      under the green air the trees
inhabit, or rest upon a chair
      towards which the inflammable air
tumbles on many robins' wings;
      noting how seasonably
      leaf and blossom uncurl
and living things arrange their death,
while someone from afar off
blows birthday candles for the world.

(1954)

Keine Lazarovitch 1870–1959

When I saw my mother's head on the cold pillow,
Her white waterfalling hair in the cheeks' hollows,
I thought, quietly circling my grief, of how
She had loved God but cursed extravagantly his creatures.

5   For her final mouth was not water but a curse,
A small black hole, a black rent in the universe,
Which damned the green earth, stars and trees in its
    stillness
And the inescapable lousiness of growing old.

And I record she was comfortless, vituperative,
10   Ignorant, glad, and much else besides; I believe
She endlessly praised her black eyebrows, their thick
    weave,
Till plagiarizing Death leaned down and took them for his
    mould.

And spoiled a dignity I shall not again find,
And the fury of her stubborn limited mind;
15   Now none will shake her amber beads and call God blind,
Or wear them upon a breast so radiantly.

O fierce she was, mean and unaccommodating;
But I think now of the toss of her gold earrings,
Their proud carnal assertion, and her youngest sings
20   While all the rivers of her red veins move into the sea.

(1961)

DOUGLAS LEPAN

(1914–   )

*W*inner of the Governor General's Award for both poetry and fiction, Douglas LePan has been a professor and a member of the diplomatic service. Born in Toronto, he was educated at the University of Toronto and Oxford. His first published volume, The Wounded Prince (1948), contains some of his best-known and most important work, including "A Country without a Mythology." A significant contribution to the tradition that stretches at least as far back as Charles G.D. Roberts and the Confederation Poets — the attempt to create a distinctly Canadian poetry through treatment of the Canadian landscape — this poem contains sharply rendered scenes of external nature. It is not, however, simply another romantic landscape poem: its concern with myth transforms it into a compelling mental landscape and gives it an ironic edge as a comment on the traditions and possibilities of Canadian poetry.

A Country without a Mythology

No monuments or landmarks guide the stranger
Going among this savage people, masks
Taciturn or babbling out an alien jargon
And moody as barbaric skies are moody.

5   Berries must be his food. Hurriedly
He shakes the bushes, plucks pickerel from the river,
Forgetting every grace and ceremony,
Feeds like an Indian, and is on his way.

And yet, for all his haste, time is worth nothing.
10   The abbey clock, the dial in the garden,
Fade like saint's days and festivals.
Months, years, are here unbroken virgin forests.

There is no law — even no atmosphere
To smooth the anger of the flagrant sun.
15   November skies sting sting like icicles.
The land is open to all violent weathers.

Passion is not more quick. Lightnings in August
Stagger, rocks split, tongues in the forest hiss,
As fire drinks up the lovely sea-dream coolness.
20   This is the land the passionate man must travel.

Sometimes — perhaps at the tentative fall of twilight —
A belief will settle that waiting around the bend
Are sanctities of childhood, that melting birds
Will sing him into a limpid gracious Presence.

25   The hills will fall in folds, the wilderness
Will be a garment innocent and lustrous
To wear upon a birthday, under a light
That curls and smiles, a golden-haired Archangel.

And now the channel opens. But nothing alters.
30   Mile after mile of tangled struggling roots,
Wild-rice, stumps, weeds, that clutch at the canoe,
Wild birds hysterical in tangled trees.

And not a sign, no emblem in the sky
Or boughs to friend him as he goes; for who
35   Will stop where, clumsily constructed, daubed
With war-paint, teeters some lust-red manitou?[1]

(1948)

---

1 *the spirit worshipped as a force of nature by Algonquin Indians.*

DYLAN THOMAS

(1914–1953)

*G*ifted with a richly expressive voice, Dylan Thomas attracted many who had never previously felt the beauty and emotional power of poetry. At the same time, he often repelled those who met him because of his excessive drinking and blunt, irreverent wit. Born in Swansea, Wales, Thomas earned fame with his first collection, Eighteen Poems *(1934). Later collections, such as* The Map of Love *(1939) and* Deaths and Entrances *(1946), consolidated his reputation as the leading lyric poet of his generation. Thomas, who worked at the beginning of his career as a script-writer and broadcaster for the* BBC, *was also an accomplished prose writer, his best-known works being the novel* Portrait of the Artist as a Young Dog *(1940), the radio drama* Under Milk Wood *(1954), and his reminiscence,* A Child's Christmas in Wales *(1954). Much of his popularity, however, came because of performances — readings of poems by himself and others, phonograph recordings, and three American tours. His readings stressed the musical and oral qualities of the poetry. His own poems are distinctive in employing a profusion of sonorous images, for, as he once said, "A poem by myself* needs *a host of images, because its centre is a host of images." Although his sequences of images can sometimes seem an incoherent, surrealistic jumble, his best work unifies the abundant imagery through theme. His major themes are childhood experience, the cycle of nature, religious sensibility, sex, and death.*

And Death Shall Have No Dominion[1]

And death shall have no dominion.
Dead men naked they shall be one
With the man in the wind and the west moon;
When their bones are picked clean and the clean bones
    gone,
5   They shall have stars at elbow and foot;
Though they go mad they shall be sane,
Though they sink through the sea they shall rise again;
Though lovers be lost love shall not;
And death shall have no dominion.

---

1 *an echo of Romans 6:9: "Knowing that Christ being raised from the dead dieth no more; death hath no more dominion over him."*

10   And death shall have no dominion.
Under the windings of the sea
They lying long shall not die windily;
Twisting on racks when sinews give way,
Strapped to a wheel, yet they shall not break;
15   Faith in their hands shall snap in two,
And the unicorn evils run them through;
Split all ends up they shan't crack;
And death shall have no dominion.

And death shall have no dominion.
20   No more may gulls cry at their ears
Or waves break loud on the seashores;
Where blew a flower may a flower no more
Lift its head to the blows of the rain;
Though they be mad and dead as nails,
25   Heads of the characters hammer through daisies;
Break in the sun till the sun breaks down,
And death shall have no dominion.

(1934)

The Force That through the Green Fuse Drives the Flower

The force that through the green fuse drives the flower
Drives my green age; that blasts the roots of trees
Is my destroyer.
And I am dumb to tell the crooked rose
5   My youth is bent by the same wintry fever.

The force that drives the water through the rocks
Drives my red blood; that dries the mouthing streams
Turns mine to wax.
And I am dumb to mouth unto my veins
10   How at the mountain spring the same mouth sucks.

The hand that whirls the water in the pool
Stirs the quicksand; that ropes the blowing wind
Hauls my shroud sail.
And I am dumb to tell the hanging man
15   How of my clay is made the hangman's lime.

The lips of time leech to the fountain head;
Love drips and gathers, but the fallen blood
Shall calm her sores.
And I am dumb to tell a weather's wind
20   How time has ticked a heaven round the stars.

And I am dumb to tell the lover's tomb
How at my sheet goes the same crooked worm.

(1934)

The Hunchback in the Park

The hunchback in the park
A solitary mister
Propped between trees and water
From the opening of the garden lock
5   That lets the trees and water enter
Until the Sunday sombre bell at dark

Eating bread from a newspaper
Drinking water from the chained cup
That the children filled with gravel
10   In the fountain basin where I sailed my ship
Slept at night in a dog kennel
But nobody chained him up.

Like the park birds he came early
Like the water he sat down
15   And Mister they called Hey mister
The truant boys from the town
Running when he had heard them clearly
On out of sound

Past lake and rockery
20   Laughing when he shook his paper
Hunchbacked in mockery
Through the loud zoo of the willow groves
Dodging the park keeper
With his stick that picked up leaves.

25   And the old dog sleeper
Alone between nurses and swans
While the boys among willows
Made the tigers jump out of their eyes
To roar on the rockery stones
30   And the groves were blue with sailors

Made all day until bell time
A woman figure without fault
Straight as a young elm
Straight and tall from his crooked bones
35   That she might stand in the night
After the locks and chains

All night in the unmade park
After the railings and shrubberies
The birds the grass the trees the lake
40   And the wild boys innocent as strawberries
Had followed the hunchback
To his kennel in the dark.

(1942)

Fern Hill[1]

Now as I was young and easy under the apple boughs
About the lilting house and happy as the grass was green,
   The night above the dingle[2] starry,
     Time let me hail and climb
5   Golden in the heydays of his eyes,
And honoured among wagons I was prince of the apple towns
And once below a time I lordly had the trees and leaves
   Trail with daisies and barley
   Down the rivers of the windfall[3] light.

10 And as I was green and carefree, famous among the barns
About the happy yard and singing as the farm was home,
   In the sun that is young once only,
     Time let me play and be
   Golden in the mercy of his means,
15 And green and golden I was huntsman and herdsman, the calves
Sang to my horn, the foxes on the hills barked clear and cold,
   And the sabbath rang slowly
   In the pebbles of the holy streams.

All the sun long it was running, it was lovely, the hay
20 Fields high as the house, the tunes from the chimneys, it was air
   And playing, lovely and watery
     And fire green as grass.
     And nightly under the simple stars
As I rode to sleep the owls were bearing the farm away,
25 All the moon long I heard, blessed among stables, the nightjars[4]
   Flying with the ricks,[5] and the horses
     Flashing into the dark.

---

1 *the Welsh farm of Ann Jones, the aunt with whom Thomas spent holidays away from Swansea.*
2 *a deep dell or hollow, usually wooded.*
3 *a transferred epithet: windfall apples are those blown down by the wind.*
4 *a common nocturnal bird.*
5 *stacks of hay.*

And then to awake, and the farm, like a wanderer white
With the dew, come back, the cock on his shoulder: it was all
30   Shining, it was Adam and maiden,
         The sky gathered again
And the sun grew round that very day.
So it must have been after the birth of the simple light
In the first, spinning place, the spellbound horses walking warm
35   Out of the whinnying green stable
         On to the fields of praise.

And honoured among foxes and pheasants by the gay house
Under the new made clouds and happy as the heart was long,
         In the sun born over and over,
40   I ran my heedless ways,
         My wishes raced through the house high hay
And nothing I cared, at my sky blue trades, that time allows
In all his tuneful turning so few and such morning songs
         Before the children green and golden
45   Follow him out of grace,

Nothing I cared, in the lamb white days, that time would take me
Up to the swallow thronged loft by the shadow of my hand,
         In the moon that is always rising,
         Nor that riding to sleep
50   I should hear him fly with the high fields
And wake to the farm forever fled from the childless land.
Oh as I was young and easy in the mercy of his means,
         Time held me green and dying
55   Though I sang in my chains like the sea.

                                                    (1946)

In My Craft or Sullen Art

In my craft or sullen art
Exercised in the still night
When only the moon rages
And the lovers lie abed
5   With all their griefs in their arms,
I labour by singing light
Not for ambition or bread
Or the strut and trade of charms
On the ivory stages
10   But for the common wages
Of their most secret heart.

Not for the proud man apart
From the raging moon I write
On these spindrift[1] pages
15   Nor for the towering dead
With their nightingales and psalms
But for the lovers, their arms
Round the griefs of the ages,
Who pay no praise or wages
20   Nor heed my craft or art.

(1946)

Do Not Go Gentle into That Good Night[1]

Do not go gentle into that good night,
Old age should burn and rave at close of day;
Rage, rage against the dying of the light.

1 spray blown up from the waves.
1 written in 1951 and addressed to his dying father.

Though wise men at their end know dark is right,
Because their words had forked no lightning they
Do not go gentle into that good night.

Good men, the last wave by, crying how bright
Their frail deeds might have danced in a green bay,
Rage, rage against the dying of the light.

Wild men who caught and sang the sun in flight,
And learn, too late, they grieved it on its way,
Do not gentle into that good night.

Grave men, near death, who see with blinding sight
Blind eyes could blaze like meteors and be gay,
Rage, rage against the dying of the light.

And you, my father, there on the sad height,
Curse, bless, me now with your fierce tears, I pray.
Do not go gentle into that good night.
Rage, rage against the dying of the light.

(1952)

P.K. Page

(1916–   )

Patricia Kathleen Page was born in Swanage, England, but came to Red Deer, Alberta, when she was three. She began her career as a poet in Montreal, where she was associated with the founders of Preview, *a literary journal that championed formally sophisticated and intellectually demanding poetry. Her first collection, published in 1946, showed concern with both social issues and psychology. Page is also a graphic artist, and the abundant imagery and profusion of metaphors in her poetry are signs of her intensely visual sensibility. Nevertheless, Page tries to present more than surface appearance. In doing so, especially in her later work, she has been influenced by Sufism, a Muslim movement that emphasizes turning away from the world in order to see only God and to achieve a union of the soul with God. Thus in her poetry, Page is a mystic seeking, with what she calls her "two-dimensional consciousness," a glimpse of the three-dimensional unity beyond mundane appearances.*

The Stenographers

After the brief bivouac of Sunday,
their eyes, in the forced march of Monday to Saturday,
hoist the white flag, flutter in the snow-storm of paper,
haul it down and crack in the mid-sun of temper.

5 In the pause between the first draft and the carbon
they glimpse the smooth hours when they were children —
the ride in the ice-cart, the ice-man's name,
the end of the route and the long walk home;

remember the sea where floats at high tide
10 were sea marrows growing on the scatter-green vine
or spools of grey toffee, or wasps' nests on water;
remember the sand and the leaves of the country.

Bell rings and they go and the voice draws their pencil
like a sled across snow; when its runners are frozen
15   rope snaps and the voice then is pulling no burden
but runs like a dog on the winter of paper.

Their climates are winter and summer — no wind
for the kits of their hearts — no wind for a flight;
a breeze at the most, to tumble them over
20   and leave them like rubbish — the boy-friends of blood.

In the inch of the noon as they move they are stagnant.
The terrible calm of the noon is their anguish;
the lip of the counter, the shapes of the straws
like icicles breaking their tongues, are invaders.

25   Their beds are their oceans — salt water of weeping
the waves that they know — the tide before sleep;
and fighting to drown they assemble their sheep
in columns and watch them leap desks for their fences
and stare at them with their own mirror-worn faces.

30   In the felt of the morning the calico-minded,
sufficiently starched, insert papers, hit keys,
efficient and sure as their adding machines;
yet they weep in the vault, they are taut as net curtains
stretched upon frames. In their eyes I have seen
35   the pin men of madness in marathon trim
race round the track of the stadium pupil.

(1946)

Stories of Snow

Those in the vegetable rain retain
an area behind their sprouting eyes
held soft and rounded with the dream of snow
precious and reminiscent as those globes —

5   souvenir of some never-nether land —
which hold their snow-storms circular, complete,
high in a tall and teakwood cabinet.

In countries where the leaves are large as hands
where flowers protrude their fleshy chins
10   and call their colours,
an imaginary snow-storm sometimes falls
among the lilies.
And in the early morning one will waken
to think the glowing linen of his pillow
15   a northern drift, will find himself mistaken
and lie back weeping.
And there the story shifts from head to head,
of how in Holland, from their feather beds
hunters arise and part the flakes and go
20   forth to the frozen lakes in search of swans —
the snow-light falling white along their guns,
their breath in plumes.
While tethered in the wind like sleeping gulls
ice-boats wait the raising of their wings
25   to skim the electric ice at such a speed
they leap jet strips of naked water,
and how these flying, sailing hunters feel
air in their mouths as terrible as ether.
And on the story runs that even drinks
30   in that white landscape dare to be no colour;
how flasked and water clear, the liquor slips
silver against the hunters' moving hips.
And of the swan in death these dreamers tell
of its last flight and how it falls, a plummet,
35   pierced by the freezing bullet
and how three feathers, loosened by the shot,
descend like snow upon it.
While hunters plunge their fingers in its down
deep as a drift, and dive their hands
40   up to the neck of the wrist
in that warm metamorphosis of snow
as gentle as the sort that woodsmen know

who, lost in the white circle, fall at last
and dream their way to death.

45   And stories of this kind are often told
in countries where great flowers bar the roads
with reds and blues which seal the route to snow —
as if, in telling, raconteurs unlock
the colour with its complement and go
50   through to the area behind the eyes
where silent, unrefractive whiteness lies.

(1946)

Photos of a Salt Mine

How innocent their lives look,
how like a child's
dream of caves and winter, both combined;
the steep descent to whiteness
5   and the stope[1]
with its striated walls
their folds all leaning as if pointing to
the greater whiteness still,
that great white bank
10   with its decisive front,
that seam upon a slope,
salt's lovely ice.

And wonderful underfoot the snow of salt
the fine
15   particles a broom could sweep,
one thinks
muckers might make angels in its drifts
as children do in snow,
lovers in sheets,
20   lie down and leave imprinted where they lay
a feathered creature holier than they.

---

1 *a mine excavation designed to remove ore made accessible by the sinking of shafts.*

And in the outworked stopes
with lamps and ropes
up miniature matterhorns[2]

25   the miners climb
probe with their lights
the ancient folds of rock —
syncline and anticline — [3]
and scoop from darkness an Aladdin's cave:

30   rubies and opals glitter from its walls.

But hoses douse the brilliance of these jewels,
melt fire to brine.
Salt's bitter water trickles thin and forms,
slow fathoms down,

35   a lake within a cave,
lacquered with jet —
white's opposite.
There grey on black the boating miners float
to mend the stays and struts of that old stope

40   and deeply underground
their words resound,
are multiplied by echo, swell and grow
and make a climate of a miner's voice.

So all the photographs like children's wishes

45   are filled with caves or winter,
innocence
has acted as a filter,
selected only beauty from the mine.
Except in the last picture,

50   it is shot
from an acute high angle. In a pit
figures the size of pins are strangely lit
and might be dancing but you know they're not.
Like Dante's vision of the nether hell[4]

55   men struggle with the bright cold fires of salt,
locked in the black inferno of the rock:
the filter here, not innocence but guilt.

(1954)

---

2 *the Matterhorn is a mountain in the Swiss Alps.* 3 *a syncline is a trough formed by a fold in the rocks; and anticline is the opposite, a fold of rock strata bending downward from its centre.* 4 *in Dante's* Inferno, *the ninth and final circle of hell is a deep pit, Cocytus, a region of ice where Satan is confined.*

ROBERT LOWELL

(1917–1977)

*D*escended from distinguished Boston families, Robert Lowell was critical of much of his heritage. As a young man, he rebelled against his family's expectations for him by becoming a conscientious objector in World War II and by converting for a time to Catholicism. Showing the benefits of a good education at Harvard and Kenyon College, Lowell's poetry is richly allusive. His early work was heavily rhetorical, rhymed, and metrically formal, but in the mid-1950s he became interested in psychoanalysis and began writing what has commonly come to be called "confessional" poetry. His forms became more relaxed, and he began drawing directly upon his private problems to represent the problems of his time. Although Lowell's earlier poetry has been widely praised, it is the work of his confessional phase that has most influenced younger poets, notably Anne Sexton and Sylvia Plath.

After the Surprising Conversions[1]

September twenty-second, Sir: today
I answer. In the latter part of May,
Hard on our Lord's Ascension, it began
To be more sensible. A gentleman
5   Of more than common understanding, strict
In morals, pious in behaviour, kicked
Against our goad. A man of some renown,
An useful, honored person in the town,
He came of melancholy parents; prone
10   To secret spells, for years they kept alone —
His uncle, I believe, was killed of it:
Good people, but of too much or little wit.
I preached one Sabbath on a text from Kings;
He showed concernment for his soul. Some things
15   In his experience were hopeful. He
Would sit and watch the wind knocking a tree
And praise this countryside our Lord has made.

---

1 based on accounts by American theologian, preacher, and educator Jonathan Edwards (1703–58) of a religious revival that took place in Massachusetts in 1734 and 1735.

Once when a poor man's heifer died, he laid
A shilling on the doorsill; though a thirst
20 For loving shook him like a snake, he durst
Not entertain much hope of his estate
In heaven. Once we saw him sitting late
Behind his attic window by a light
That guttered on his Bible; through that night
25 He meditated terror, and he seemed
Beyond advice or reason, for he dreamed
That he was called to trumpet Judgment Day
To Concord. In the latter part of May
He cut his throat. And though the coroner
30 Judged him delirious, soon a noisome stir
Palsied our village. At Jehovah's nod
Satan seemed more let loose amongst us: God
Abandoned us to Satan, and he pressed
Us hard, until we thought we could not rest
35 Till we had done with life. Content was gone.
All the good work was quashed. We were undone.
The breath of God had carried out a planned
And sensible withdrawal from this land;
The multitude, once unconcerned with doubt,
40 Once neither callous, curious nor devout,
Jumped at broad noon, as though some peddler groaned
At it in its familiar twang: "My friend,
Cut your own throat. Cut your own throat. Now! Now!"
September twenty-second, Sir, the bough
45 Cracks with the unpicked apples, and at dawn
The small-mouth bass breaks water, gorged with spawn.

(1946)

Skunk Hour

[FOR ELIZABETH BISHOP] [1]

Nautilus Island's hermit
heiress still lives through winter in her Spartan cottage;
her sheep still graze above the sea.
Her son's a bishop. Her farmer
5   is first selectman in our village;
she's in her dotage.

Thirsting for
the hierarchic privacy
of Queen Victoria's century,
10   she buys up all
the eyesores facing her shore,
and lets them fall.

The season's ill —
we've lost our summer millionaire,
15   who seemed to leap from an L.L. Bean [2]
catalogue. His nine-knot yawl
was auctioned off to lobstermen.
A red fox stain covers Blue Hill.

And now our fairy
20   decorator brightens his shop for fall;
his fishnet's filled with orange cork,
orange, his cobbler's bench and awl;
there is no money in his work,
he'd rather marry.

25   One dark night,
my Tudor Ford climbed the hill's skull;
I watched for love-cars. Lights turned down,
they lay together, hull to hull,
where the graveyard shelves on the town. . . .
30   My mind's not right.

---

1 *American poet, 1911–79.*
2 *a Maine mail-order business specializing in sporting supplies and clothing.*

A car radio bleats,
"Love, O careless love. . . . " I hear
my ill-spirit sob in each blood cell,
as if my hand were at its throat. . . .

35   I myself am hell;
nobody's here —

only skunks, that search
in the moonlight for a bite to eat.
They march on their soles up Main Street:
40   white stripes, moonstruck eyes' red fire
under the chalk-dry and spar spire
of the Trinitarian Church.

I stand on top
of our back steps and breathe the rich air —
45   a mother skunk with her column of kittens swills the
garbage pail.
She jabs her wedge-head in a cup
of sour cream, drops her ostrich tail,
and will not scare.

(1959)

MIRIAM WADDINGTON

(1917–   )

he daughter of Russian immigrants, Miriam Waddington was born in Winnipeg. She attended the University of Toronto (B.A., 1939; diploma in social work, 1942) and the University of Pennsylvania (M.S.W., 1945). Her first book of poems, Green World *(1945), appeared in the same year that she moved to Montreal to begin her career in social work. Waddington later changed careers: she earned an M.A. in English at the University of Toronto (1968) and became an associate professor of English at York University, where she taught until her retirement in 1983. Her poems touch on a variety of public and private topics, such as social injustices, her roots as a European Jew, her attempt to define her Canadian identity, divorce and the search for new lovers, and life as an aging woman. Nevertheless, two themes dominate: the pain of the solitary or alienated individual and the discrepancies between imaginative desire and mundane fulfilment.*

Conserving

On November afternoons
the harem girls are out
walking their dogs.

They have eaten pineapples
5   and drunk white wine,
they have heard murmurings

From enchanted palaces,
they have dreamed of sultans
with turbans of gold.

10   The frost pinches their faces,
the wind teases their hair,
their eyes have the blinds down,

They don't want anyone to see
behind their shuttered eyes
15   where they are working hard

To conserve the small heat
in the rooms of their lives;
they are husbanding warmth

For their annointed lords
who will return from travels
at difficult sundown,

After dangerous journeys
on highways and throughways,
after hand-to-hand fighting

In offices and corridors;
what more can harem girls do?
They have walked their dogs

And eaten the pineapples,
they have combed out their hair
and buffed up their nails,

They have chopped up the day
for firewood, hating November,
and now they are burning the sultans

With the turbans of gold,
they are burning their dreams
in suburban fireplaces.

Perhaps the harem girls are angry,
for it is not always possible
to be beautiful or to walk the dogs;

And they have to work so hard,
they have to burn more dreams
than they really have

In order to conserve the heat
in the small rooms
where they live.

(1981)

AL PURDY

(1918–   )

orn in Wooler, Ontario, Alfred Purdy left school after Grade 10, riding freight trains to Vancouver, where he worked in a mattress factory and at other manual labour. Purdy published his first book in 1944 and won the Governor General's Award for The Cariboo Horses *(1965). Much of his early poetry relies upon his experiences as a labourer and uses the voice of a "common person." This voice combines colloquial expressions, vulgarity, and poetic sentimentality. This conversational voice is frequently an effective vehicle for philosophic thought and social criticism because it casts ideas into unexpected forms. Purdy has travelled widely and written about his travels throughout Canada, including the Arctic, and such places as Cuba, Mexico, South America, Greece, and Japan. Nevertheless, he is quintessentially the poet of a single place, the area around his home of Ameliasburg, Ontario. Purdy conveys his love of Canada, of ordinary working people, and of tradition in these poems, which mingle past and present and thereby transform the area into a mythic landscape.*

The Country North of Belleville

Bush land scrub land —
    Cashel Township and Wollaston
Elzevir McClure and Dungannon
green lands of Weslemkoon Lake
5   where a man might have some
      opinion of what beauty
is and none deny him
        for miles —

Yet this is the country of defeat
10   where Sisyphus[1] rolls a big stone
year after year up the ancient hills
picnicking glaciers have left strewn
with centuries' rubble
      backbreaking days
15   in the sun and rain

---

1 *a king of Corinth whose punishment in Hades was to roll a heavy stone up a hill, only to have it roll down again when it neared the top.*

when realization seeps slow in the mind
without grandeur or self deception in
                              noble struggle
of being a fool —

20   A country of quiescence and still distance
        lean land
                        not like the fat south
        with inches of black soil on
                          earth's round belly —
25   And where the farms are
                          it's as if a man stuck
        both thumbs in the stony earth and pulled

                          it apart
                          to make room
30   enough between the trees
        for a wife
                          and maybe some cows and
                          room for some
        of the more easily kept illusions —
35   And where the farms have gone back
        to forest
                          and only soft outlines
                          shadowy differences —
        Old fences drift vaguely among the trees
40   a pile of moss-covered stones
        gathered for some ghost purpose
        has lost meaning under the meaningless sky
                          — they are like cities under water
        and the undulating green waves of time
45   are laid on them —

        This is the country of our defeat
                          and yet
        during the fall plowing a man
        might stop and stand in a brown valley of the furrows
50   and shade his eyes to watch for the same

red patch mixed with gold
that appears on the same
spot in the hills
year after year
55   and grow old
plowing and plowing a ten-acre field until
the convolutions run parallel with his own brain —

And this is a country where the young
           leave quickly
60   unwilling to know what their fathers know
or think the words their mothers do not say —

Herschel Monteagle and Faraday
lakeland rockland and hill country
a little adjacent to where the world is
65   a little north of where the cities are and
sometime
we may go back there
                   to the country of our defeat
Wollaston Elzevir and Dungannon
70   and Weslemkoon lake land
where the high townships of Cashel
                   McClure and Marmora once were —
But it's been a long time since
and we must enquire the way
75   of strangers —

(1965)   (1972)

Lament for the Dorsets

(ESKIMOS EXTINCT IN THE 14TH CENTURY AD)[1]

Animal bones and some mossy tent rings
scrapers and spearheads   carved ivory swans
all that remains of the Dorset giants
who drove the Vikings back to their long ships
5   talked to spirits of earth and water
— a picture of terrifying old men
so large they broke the backs of bears
so small they lurk behind bone rafters
in the brain of modern hunters
10   among good thoughts and warm things
and come out at night
to spit on the stars

The big men with clever fingers
who had no dogs and hauled their sleds
15   over the frozen northern oceans
awkward giants
        killers of seal
they couldn't compete with little men
who came from the west with dogs
20   Or else in a warm climatic cycle
the seals went back to cold waters
and the puzzled Dorsets scratched their heads
with hairy thumbs around 1350 A.D.
— couldn't figure it out
25   went around saying to each other
plaintively
        "What's wrong? What happened?
        Where are the seals gone?"
And died

1 *in about A.D. 1000, the Dorset people were displaced from most of the Arctic regions by Thule Inuit from Alaska, but they continued to live in northern Quebec and Labrador until about A.D. 1500, when they disappeared.*

30   Twentieth-century people
      apartment dwellers
      executives of neon death
      warmakers with things that explode
      — they have never imagined us in their future
35   how could we imagine them in the past
      squatting among the moving glaciers
      six hundred years ago
      with glowing lamps?
      As remote or nearly
40   as the trilobites and swamps
      when coal became
      or the last great reptile hissed
      at a mammal the size of a mouse
      that squeaked and fled

45   Did they ever realize at all
      what was happening to them?
      Some old hunter with one lame leg
      a bear had chewed
      sitting in a caribou-skin tent
50   — the last Dorset?
      Let's say his name was Kudluk
      and watch him sitting there
      carving 2-inch ivory swans
      for a dead grand-daughter
55   taking them out of his mind
      the places in his mind
      where pictures are

      He selects a sharp stone tool
      to gouge a parallel pattern of lines
60   on both sides of the swan
      holding it with his left hand
      bearing down and transmitting
      his body's weight
      from brain to arm and right hand
65   and one of his thoughts
      turns to ivory

The carving is laid aside
in beginning darkness
at the end of hunger
70   and after a while wind
blows down the tent and snow
begins to cover him

After 600 years
the ivory thought
75   is still warm

(1968)

LAWRENCE FERLINGHETTI

(1919–   )

*A*lthough Lawrence Ferlinghetti has long been associated with San Francisco, he was actually born in Yonkers, New York. He lost both his parents early, but survived a precarious childhood to receive a good education, including an M.A. from Columbia and a doctorate from the Sorbonne in Paris. As one of the older, better educated, and more practical members of the beat movement, which in the 1950s rejected conventional American society as corrupt, materialistic, and shallow and prized states of personal beatitude, Ferlinghetti's guiding influence was vital. In addition to providing the example of his own anti-establishment poetry, he encouraged younger poets by founding in 1952 City Lights Books, which began as the first all-paperbound bookstore in the United States and quickly expanded into an influential publishing company of avant-garde poets. Notwithstanding his learned background, Ferlinghetti is far from bookish; he writes for a broad audience and designs his poems to be read aloud.

Constantly risking absurdity

Constantly risking absurdity
                            and death
            whenever he performs
                        above the heads
5   of his audience
        the poet like an acrobat
                climbs on rime
                        to a high wire of his own making
        and balancing on eyebeams
10   above a sea of faces
                paces his way
                        to the other side of day
        performing entrechats[1]
                            and sleight-of-foot tricks
15   and other high theatrics
                            and all without mistaking
                any thing
                        for what it may not be

1 ballet leaps during which the legs are repeatedly crossed and sometimes beaten together.

For he's the super realist

20.   who must perforce perceive

taut truth

before the taking of each stance or step

in his supposed advance

toward that still higher perch

25   where Beauty stands and waits

with gravity

to start her death-defying leap

And he

a little charleychaplin[2] man

30   who may or may not catch

her fair eternal form

spreadeagled in the empty air

of existence

(1958)

---

2 Charlie Chaplin (1889–1977) was a British comic genius who wrote, starred in, and directed numerous silent
   films. He is most famous for his development of the kind-hearted Little Tramp, a character who allowed Chaplin
   to display his considerable talents for acrobatic physical comedy.

ROBERT DUNCAN

(1919–   )

lthough Robert Duncan has lived in Europe and in various parts of the United States, his home is in California where he was born. Like the other members of the Black Mountain movement in poetry, Duncan formed his mature poetic voice under the influence of Ezra Pound and William Carlos Williams and the poetic theories of Charles Olson. He wrote poems expressing his objection to the Vietnam War, but the main impulse behind his poetry is mystical rather than social, a quest for spiritual meaning through a study of the self.

Bending the Bow

We've our business to attend Day's duties,
bend back the bow in dreams as we may
til the end rimes in the taut string
with the sending. Reveries are rivers and flow
5   where the cold light gleams reflecting the window upon
      the surface of the table,
the presst-glass creamer, the pewter sugar bowl, the litter
      of coffee cups and saucers,
carnations painted growing upon whose surfaces. The whole
composition of surfaces leads into the other
          current disturbing
what I would take hold of. I'd been

10   in the course of a letter — I am still
in the course of a letter — to a friend,
who comes close in to my thought so that
the day is hers. My hand writing here
there shakes in the currents of . . . of air?
15   of an inner anticipation of . . . ? reaching to touch
ghostly exhilarations in the thought of her.

At the extremity of this
design
"there is a connexion working in both directions, as in
the bow and the lyre" —
only in that swift fulfillment of the wish
that sleep
20   can illustrate my hand
sweeps the string.

You stand behind the where-I-am.
The deep tones and shadows I will call a woman.
The quick high notes . . . You are a girl there too,
having something of sister and of wife,
25   inconsolate,
and I would play Orpheus for you again,

recall the arrow or song
to the trembling daylight
from which it sprang.

(1968)

My Mother Would Be a Falconress

My mother would be a falconress,
And I, her gay falcon treading her wrist,
would fly to bring back
from the blue of the sky to her, bleeding, a prize,
5   where I dream in my little hood with many bells
jangling when I'd turn my head.

My mother would be a falconress,
and she sends me as far as her will goes.
She lets me ride to the end of her curb
10   where I fall back in anguish.
I dread that she will cast me away,
for I fall, I mis-take, I fail in her mission.

She would bring down the little birds.
And I would bring down the little birds.
15 When will she let me bring down the little birds,
pierced from their flight with their necks broken,
their heads like flowers limp from the stem?

I tread my mother's wrist and would draw blood.
Behind the little hood my eyes are hooded.
20 I have gone back into my hooded silence,
talking to myself and dropping off to sleep.

For she has muffled my dreams in the hood she has made
        me,
sewn round with bells, jangling when I move.
She rides with her little falcon upon her wrist.
25 She uses a barb that brings me to cower.
She sends me abroad to try my wings
and I come back to her. I would bring down
the little birds to her
I may not tear into, I must bring back perfectly.

30 I tear at her wrist with my beak to draw blood,
and her eye holds me, anguisht, terrifying.
She draws a limit to my flight.
Never beyond my sight, she says.
She trains me to fetch and to limit myself in fetching.
35 She rewards me with meat for my dinner.
But I must never eat what she sends me to bring her.

Yet it would have been beautiful, if she would have carried
        me,
always, in a little hood with the bells ringing,
at her wrist, and her riding
40 to the great falcon hunt, and me
flying up to the curb of my heart from her heart
to bring down the skylark from the blue to her feet,
straining, and then released for the flight.

My mother would be a falconress,
45   and I her gerfalcon, raised at her will,
from her wrist sent flying, as if I were her own
pride, as if her pride
knew no limits, as if her mind
sought in me flight beyond the horizon.

50   Ah, but high, high in the air I flew.
And far, far beyond the curb of her will,
were the blue hills where the falcons nest.
And then I saw west to the dying sun —
it seemd my human soul went down in flames.

55   I tore at her wrist, at the hold she had for me,
until the blood ran hot and I heard her cry out,
far, far beyond the curb of her will

to horizons of stars beyond the ringing hills of the world
        where the falcons nest
I saw, and I tore at her wrist with my savage beak.
60   I flew, as if sight flew from the anguish in her eye beyond
        her sight,
sent from my striking loose, from the cruel strike at her
        wrist,
striking out from the blood to be free of her.

My mother would be a falconress,
and even now, years after this,
65   when the wounds I left her had surely heald,
and the woman is dead,
her fierce eyes closed, and if her heart
were broken, it is stilld.

I would be a falcon and go free.
70   I tread her wrist and wear the hood,
talking to myself, and would draw blood.

                                    (1968)

LOUISE BENNETT

(1919–   )

*L*ouise Bennett has achieved success in a variety of artistic forms. She is a leading actor, singer, and performer in Jamaica, a notable folklorist who has preserved and popularized traditional tales, and a poet who helped to usher in a new age of Caribbean poetry. Born in Kingston, she moved to England in the 1940s, first studying social work, then studying drama at the Royal Academy of Dramatic Arts. In England, she worked for the BBC Overseas Service and various repertory theatres. Her poetry, which first appeared in Jamaican newspapers and on Jamaican radio, was collected in the volume Dialect Verses, published in 1942. She also began studying folklore, eventually publishing four collections of tales about Anansi, the Caribbean (and West African) trickster-hero, between 1944 and 1970. In 1955, she returned to Jamaica to work as a drama specialist with the Jamaica Social Welfare Commission. Although she was not the first to use dialect in poetry, her success stimulated others to use the popular speech of Jamaica and to explore new ways of presenting the Caribbean experience. Her most famous volume is Jamaica Labrish (1966) — the term is dialect for "gossip" — in which her animated colloquial language and sharp wit deliver biting commentary on Jamaican life.

Colonization in Reverse[1]

Wat a joyful news, Miss Mattie,[2]
I feel like me heart gwine burs'
Jamaica people colonizin
Englan in reverse.

5   By de hundred, by de t'ousan
From country and from town,
By de ship-load, by de plane-load
Jamaica is Englan boun.

---

1 as citizens of a Commonwealth country, Jamaicans once had almost automatic admission to England. During the 1960s, thousands took advantage of their passports to flee poor economic conditions and settle in England, the mother country of those who colonized Jamaica.
2 a character frequently addressed in Bennett's dramatic monologues.

Dem a-pour out o' Jamaica,
10 Everybody future plan
Is fe get a big-time job
An settle in de mother lan.

What a islan! What a people!
Man an woman, old an young
15 Jusa pack dem bag an baggage
An tun history upside dung!

Some people don't like travel,
But fe show dem loyalty
Dem all a-open up cheap-fare-
20 To-Englan agency.

An week by week dem shippin off
Dem countryman like fire,
Fe immigrate an populate
De seat o' de Empire.

25 Oonoo see how life is funny,
Oonoo see de tunabout,
Jamaica live fe box bread
Outa English people mout'.

For wen dem catch a Englan,
30 An start play dem different role,
Some will settle down to work
And some will settle fe de dole.

Jane say de dole is not too bad
Because dey payin' she
35 Two pounds a week fe seek a job
Dat suit her dignity.

Me say Jane will never find work
At the rate how she dah-look,
For all day she stay pon Aunt Fan couch
40 An read love-story book.

Wat a devilment a Englan!
Dem face war an brave de worse,
But I'm wonderin' how dem gwine stan'
Colonizin' in reverse.

(1966)

OODGEROO OF THE TRIBE NOONUCCAL (KATH WALKER)

(1919–   )

*T*he first prominent Aboriginal poet and protest writer in Australia, Kath Walker, who now uses her Aboriginal name, Oodgeroo of the tribe Noonuccal, was born on Stradbroke Island, off the Queensland coast near Brisbane. At the age of thirteen, she began work as a domestic servant. When she was sixteen, she encountered a powerful example of official discrimination: because she was part Aboriginal, she was denied admission to nursing studies. A leading advocate of Aboriginal rights, she was involved in the campaign that led to the 1967 repeal of constitutional discrimination against Aborigines. The title of her first volume of poetry, We Are Going (1964), she has said, was "a warning to the white people: we can go out of existence, or with proper help we could also go on and live in this world in peace and harmony. . . . " She has also said that her poems are "sloganistic, civil rightish, plain and simple." At their best, however, they are powerfully emotional presentations of the culture and history of the Aborigines; they clearly portray the abuses whites have inflicted, the dignity of Aborigines, and the value of an ancient way of life lived close to the land.

We Are Going

FOR GRANNIE COOLWELL

They came in to the little town
A semi-naked band subdued and silent,
All that remained of their tribe.
They came here to the place of their old bora ground[1]
5   Where now the many white men hurry about like ants.
Notice of estate agent reads: 'Rubbish May Be Tipped
    Here'.
Now it half covers the traces of the old bora ring.
They sit and are confused, they cannot say their thoughts:
'We are as strangers here now, but the white tribe are the
    strangers.

---

1 the term bora is applied both to the most solemn of Aboriginal rites, in which a young boy is admitted to the rights of manhood, and to the site of the ceremony. The bora ground is usually called a bora ring because it is most often a circular earthen bank or an area marked off by a ring of stones.

10   We belong here, we are of the old ways.
We are the corroboree[2] and the bora ground,
We are the old sacred ceremonies, the laws of the elders.
We are the wonder tales of Dream Time,[3] the tribal legends
     told.
We are the past, the hunts and the laughing games, the
     wandering camp fires.
15   We are the lightning-bolt over Gaphembah Hill[4]
Quick and terrible,
And the Thunderer[5] after him, that loud fellow.
We are the quiet daybreak paling the dark lagoon.
We are the shadow-ghosts creeping back as the camp fires
     burn low.
20   We are nature and the past, all the old ways
Gone now and scattered.
The scrubs are gone, the hunting and the laughter.
The eagle is gone, the emu[6] and the kangaroo are gone
     from this place.
The bora ring is gone.
25   The corroboree is gone.
And we are going.'

(1964)

2 an Aboriginal dance ceremony, sometimes sacred and sometimes secular, involving singing and rhythmical musical
  accompaniment.
3 the time of mythic events; the time of the first ancestors or the time, beyond living memory, in which the physical,
  spiritual, and moral world was developed.
4 on Stradbroke Island, behind Myora Springs and near Moongalba, where the author, also known as Oodgeroo
  Noonuccal Moongalba, lives.
5 thunder; Aboriginal beliefs tend to be localized, rather than universal among the various tribes, and mythic
  figures, such as Thunderer, are often attached to specific sites or regions.
6 a large, flightless bird that can run at a speed of approximately 50 kilometres per hour.

Nona

At the happy chattering evening meal
Nona the lithe and lovely,
Liked by all,
Came out of her mother's gunya,[1]
5   Naked like the rest, and like the rest
Unconscious of her body
As the dingo pup rolling about in play.
All eyes turned, men and women, all
Had smiles for Nona.
10   And what did the women see? They saw
The white head-band above her forehead,
The gay little feather-tuft in her hair
Fixed with gum, and how she wore it.
They saw the necklet of red berries
15   And the plaited and painted reed arm-band
Jarri had made her.
And what did the men see? Ah, the men.
They did not see armlet or band
Or the bright little feather-tuft in her hair.
20   They had no eye for the red berries,
They did not look at these things at all.

(1966)

---

1 *a temporary shelter made from bark, branches, or both.*

Philip Larkin

(1922–1985)

orn at Coventry and educated at Oxford, Larkin led a quiet and unre-markable life. He worked as a librarian in several places, completing his career as head librarian at the University of Hull, a post he took up in 1955. His first poetry collection was The North Ship *(1945), but it was* The Less Deceived *(1955) that established him as one of the most popular British poets of the post-war era. Larkin was opposed to what he considered the overly complex tech-niques of modernist and academic poetry, such as that written by Eliot and Pound. Instead, he favoured carefully crafted works that speak directly to people who may not have a specialized understanding of literature and literary tradition. Poetry should be, he said, "emotional in nature and theatrical in operation, a skilled re-creation of emotion in other people." Therefore, like Thomas Hardy, whose poems obviously influenced him, he used traditional forms and techniques, employed the language of ordinary people, and used his own experiences, rather than other poetry or works of art, as the basis for most of his poems. Larkin's range was narrow, but people responded favourably because his poetry was both witty and accessible.*

Lines on a Young Lady's Photograph Album

At last you yielded up the album, which,
Once open, sent me distracted. All your ages
Matt and glossy on the thick black pages!
Too much confectionery, too rich:
5   I choke on such nutritious images.

My swivel eye hungers from pose to pose —
In pigtails, clutching a reluctant cat;
Or furred yourself, a sweet girl-graduate;
Or lifting a heavy-headed rose
10   Beneath a trellis, or in a trilby hat[1]

---

1 *a hat of soft felt with an indented crown.*

(Faintly disturbing, that, in several ways) —
From every side you strike at my control,
Not least through these disquieting chaps who loll
At ease about your earlier days:

15   Not quite your class, I'd say, dear, on the whole.

But o, photography! as no art is,
Faithful and disappointing! that records
Dull days as dull, and hold-it smiles as frauds,
And will not censor blemishes

20   Like washing-lines, and Hall's-Distemper boards,

But shows the cat as disinclined, and shades
A chin as doubled when it is, what grace
Your candour thus confers upon her face!
How overwhelmingly persuades

25   That this is a real girl in a real place,

In every sense empirically true!
Or is it just *the past*? Those flowers, that gate,
These misty parks and motors,[2] lacerate
Simply by being over; you

30   Contract my heart by looking out of date.

Yes, true; but in the end, surely, we cry
Not only at exclusion, but because
It leaves us free to cry. We know *what was*
Won't call on us to justify

35   Our grief, however hard we yowl across

The gap from eye to page. So I am left
To mourn (without a chance of consequence)
You, balanced on a bike against a fence;
To wonder if you'd spot the theft

40   Of this one of you bathing; to condense,

2 *automobiles.*

In short, a past that no one now can share,
No matter whose your future; calm and dry,
It holds you like a heaven, and you lie
Unvariably lovely there,
45   Smaller and clearer as the years go by.

(1955)

Next, Please

Always too eager for the future, we
Pick up bad habits of expectancy.
Something is always approaching; every day
Till then we say,

5   Watching from a bluff the tiny, clear,
Sparkling armada[1] of promises draw near.
How slow they are! And how much time they waste,
Refusing to make haste!

Yet still they leave us holding wretched stalks
10   Of disappointment, for, though nothing balks,
Each big approach, leaning with brasswork prinked,[2]
Each rope distinct,

Flagged, and the figurehead with golden tits
Arching our way, it never anchors; it's
15   No sooner present than it turns to past.
Right to the last

We think each one will heave to and unload
All good into our lives, all we are owed
For waiting so devoutly and so long.
20   But we are wrong:

1 *a large fleet.*
2 *spruced up, shined.*

Only one ship is seeking us, a black-
Sailed unfamiliar, towing at her back
A huge and birdless silence. In her wake
No waters breed or break.

(1955)

Church Going

Once I am sure there's nothing going on
I step inside, letting the door thud shut.
Another church: matting, seats, and stone,
And little books; sprawlings of flowers, cut
5   For Sunday, brownish now; some brass and stuff
Up at the holy end; the small neat organ;
And a tense, musty, unignorable silence,
Brewed God knows how long. Hatless, I take off
My cycle-clips in awkward reverence,

10   Move forward, run my hand around the font.
From where I stand, the roof looks almost new —
Cleaned, or restored? Someone would know: I don't.
Mounting the lectern, I peruse a few
Hectoring large-scale verses, and pronounce
15   'Here endeth' much more loudly than I'd meant.
The echoes snigger briefly. Back at the door
I sign the book, donate an Irish sixpence,
Reflect the place was not worth stopping for.

Yet stop I did: in fact I often do,
20   And always end much at a loss like this,
Wondering what to look for; wondering, too,
When churches fall completely out of use
What we shall turn them into, if we shall keep
A few cathedrals chronically on show,
25   Their parchment, plate and pyx[1] in locked cases,
And let the rest rent-free to rain and sheep.
Shall we avoid them as unlucky places?

---

1 *a vessel in which the consecrated Host is reserved.*

Or, after dark, will dubious women come
To make their children touch a particular stone;
30   Pick simples² for a cancer; or on some
Advised night see walking a dead one?
Power of some sort or other will go on
In games, in riddles, seemingly at random;
But superstition, like belief, must die,
35   And what remains when disbelief has gone?
Grass, weedy pavement, brambles, buttress, sky,

A shape less recognisable each week,
A purpose more obscure. I wonder who
Will be the last, the very last, to seek
40   This place for what it was; one of the crew
That tap and jot and know what rood-lofts³ were?
Some ruin-bibber,⁴ randy for antique,
Or Christmas-addict, counting on a whiff
Of gowns-and-bands and organ-pipes and myrrh?
45   Or will he be my representative,

Bored, uninformed, knowing the ghostly silt
Dispersed, yet tending to this cross of ground
Through suburb scrub because it held unspilt
So long and equably what since is found
50   Only in separation — marriage, and birth,
And death, and thoughts of these — for which was built
This special shell? For, though I've no idea
What this accoutred frowsty⁵ barn is worth,
It pleases me to stand in silence here;

55   A serious house on serious earth it is,
In whose blent air all our compulsions meet,
Are recognised, and robed as destinies.
And that much never can be obsolete,

2 *herbs or plants used for medicinal purposes.*
3 *loft or gallery over a rood-screen, a screen with a cross on top separating the nave from the choir or chancel.*
4 *a bibber is one who drinks frequently; hence, a ruin-bibber frequents ruins or antiquities.*
5 *musty, or stale-smelling.*

Since someone will forever be surprising
60   A hunger in himself to be more serious,
And gravitating with it to this ground,
Which, he once heard, was proper to grow wise in,
If only that so many dead lie around.

(1955)

Toads

Why should I let the toad *work*
    Squat on my life?
Can't I use my wit as a pitchfork
    And drive the brute off?

5   Six days of the week it soils
    With its sickening poison —
Just for paying a few bills!
    That's out of proportion.

Lots of folk live on their wits:
10   Lecturers, lispers,
Losels, loblolly-men,¹ louts —
    They don't end as paupers;

Lots of folk live up lanes
    With fires in a bucket,
15   Eat windfalls and tinned sardines —
    They seem to like it.

Their nippers² have got bare feet,
    Their unspeakable wives
Are skinny as whippets³ — and yet
20   No one actually *starves*.

1 *losels are worthless persons, scoundrels, or rakes; loblolly-men are bumpkins or rustics.*
2 *children.*
3 *short-haired dogs, resembling but smaller than greyhounds, that are bred for speed.*

Ah, were I courageous enough
   To shout *Stuff your pension!*
But I know, all too well, that's the stuff
   That dreams are made on:

25   For something sufficiently toad-like
   Squats in me, too;
Its hunkers are heavy as hard luck,
   And cold as snow,

And will never allow me to blarney
30   My way to getting
The fame and the girl and the money
   All at one sitting.

I don't say, one bodies the other
   One's spiritual truth;
35   But I do say it's hard to lose either,
   When you have both.

(1955)

An Arundel Tomb[1]

Side by side, their faces blurred,
The earl and countess lie in stone,
Their proper habits vaguely shown
As jointed armour, stiffened pleat,
5   And that faint hint of the absurd —
The little dogs under their feet.

1 located *near Chichester Cathedral, this is the tomb of the Howard family, currently dukes and duchesses of Norfolk, but once earls and countesses of Arundel. Most figures on monuments do not, as these do, hold hands.*

Such plainness of the pre-baroque[2]
Hardly involves the eye, until
It meets his left-hand gauntlet,[3] still
10   Clasped empty in the other; and
One sees, with a sharp tender shock,
His hand withdrawn, holding her hand.

They would not think to lie so long.
Such faithfulness in effigy
15   Was just a detail friends would see:
A sculptor's sweet commissioned grace
Thrown off in helping to prolong
The Latin names around the base.

They would not guess how early in
20   Their supine stationary voyage
The air would change to soundless damage,
Turn the old tenantry away;
How soon succeeding eyes begin
To look, not read. Rigidly they

25   Persisted, linked, through lengths and breadths
Of time. Snow fell, undated. Light
Each summer thronged the glass. A bright
Litter of birdcalls strewed the same
Bone-riddled ground. And up the paths
30   The endless altered people came,

Washing at their identity.
Now, helpless in the hollow of
An unarmorial age, a trough
Of smoke in slow suspended skeins
35   Above their scrap of history,
Only an attitude remains:

2 *baroque style, which flourished in the arts during the seventeenth and first half of the eighteenth centuries, was notable for its elaborate ornamentation.*
3 *a glove of mail or armour plate worn to protect the hand during medieval times.*

Time has transfigured them into
Untruth. The stone fidelity
They hardly meant has come to be
40   Their final blazon,[4] and to prove
Our almost-instinct almost true:
What will survive of us is love.

(1964)

4 *coat of arms.*

ANTHONY HECHT

(1923–   )

*A*nthony Hecht was born in New York City and educated at Bard College and Columbia University, from which he received his M.A. in 1950. In 1967, he was appointed the John H. Deane Professor of Poetry and Rhetoric at the University of Rochester. Hecht's first poetry collection, A Summoning of Stones (1954), established him as a traditionalist in his use of language and form, but it also showed him to be an erudite and often witty poet. Later poems among his relatively small body of work show his skill in sensitively handling personal, philosophic, and Jewish themes. His stinging wit is evident in his most popular poem, "The Dover Bitch," an accomplished parody of Matthew Arnold's "Dover Beach."

The Dover Bitch
A Criticism of Life

FOR ANDREWS WANNING

So there stood Matthew Arnold and this girl
With the cliffs of England crumbling away behind them,
And he said to her, "Try to be true to me,
And I'll do the same for you, for things are bad
5   All over, etc., etc."
Well now, I knew this girl. It's true she had read
Sophocles in a fairly good translation
And caught that bitter allusion to the sea,
But all the time he was talking she had in mind
10   The notion of what his whiskers would feel like
On the back of her neck. She told me later on
That after a while she got to looking out
At the lights across the channel, and really felt sad,
Thinking of all the wine and enormous beds
15   And blandishments in French and the perfumes.
And then she got really angry. To have been brought
All the way down from London, and then be addressed

As a sort of mournful cosmic last resort
Is really tough on a girl, and she was pretty.
20   Anyway, she watched him pace the room
And finger his watch-chain and seem to sweat a bit,
And then she said one or two unprintable things.
But you mustn't judge her by that. What I mean to say is,
She's really all right. I still see her once in a while
25   And she always treats me right. We have a drink
And I give her a good time, and perhaps it's a year
Before I see her again, but there she is,
Running to fat, but dependable as they come.
And sometimes I bring her a bottle of *Nuit d'Amour*.

(1968)

DENISE LEVERTOV

(1923–   )

enise Levertov grew up in England and published one fairly conventional book of poetry there before moving to the United States in 1948. She developed her mature poetic style under the influence of American poetry, perhaps most notably William Carlos Williams's stress on immediate experience and the language of common speech. Although Levertov has commonly been associated with the Black Mountain poets, particularly Robert Duncan and Robert Creeley, with whom she shares a belief in free forms and a stress on the deeper meanings available in apparently trivial, mundane experience, her connection with the movement itself is tenuous. Levertov became active in protesting the Vietnam War in the late 1960s and, without abandoning her interest in non-political subjects and her interior experiences, she has continued since then to voice her liberal activism in her poetry.

The Ache of Marriage

The ache of marriage:

thigh and tongue, beloved,
are heavy with it,
it throbs in the teeth

5   We look for communion
and are turned away, beloved,
each and each

It is leviathan and we
in its belly
10   looking for joy, some joy
not to be known outside it

two by two in the ark of
the ache of it.

(1964)

What Were They Like?

    1) Did the people of Viet Nam
       use lanterns of stone?
    2) Did they hold ceremonies
       to reverence the opening of buds?
    3) Were they inclined to quiet laughter?
    4) Did they use bone and ivory,
       jade and silver, for ornament?
    5) Had they an epic poem?
    6) Did they distinguish between speech and singing?

    1) Sir, their light hearts turned to stone.
       It is not remembered whether in gardens
       stone lanterns illumined pleasant ways.
    2) Perhaps they gathered once to delight in blossom,
       but after the children were killed
       there were no more buds.
    3) Sir, laughter is bitter to the burned mouth.
    4) A dream ago, perhaps. Ornament is for joy.
       All the bones were charred.
    5) It is not remembered. Remember,
       most were peasants; their life
       was in rice and bamboo.
       When peaceful clouds were reflected in the paddies
       and the water buffalo stepped surely along terraces,
       maybe fathers told their sons old tales.

25   When bombs smashed those mirrors
          there was time only to scream.
    6) There is an echo yet
          of their speech which was like a song.
          It was reported their singing resembled
30   the flight of moths in moonlight.
          Who can say? It is silent now.

(1966)

A.R. Ammons

(1926–   )

A. R. Ammons grew up in rural North Carolina, where he developed a habit of observing nature closely. He began writing poetry while in the navy during World War II, but took a degree in science rather than English after the war. He later did graduate work in English at the University of California but left without a degree. In 1964, after more than a decade as an executive in a New Jersey glass-manufacturing company, Ammons began a long association with Cornell University, where he teaches mainly creative writing.

Ammons writes about nature with a scientist's eye for detail, but he sees the natural world as emblematic of spiritual meaning. His language is plain, but his purpose is ambitious — exploring humanity's relationship with nature in hopes of glimpsing the underlying principles of existence.

Dunes

Taking root in windy sand
   is not an easy
way
to go about
5   finding a place to stay.

A ditchbank or wood's-edge
   has firmer ground.

In a loose world though
   something can be started —
10 a root touch water,
   a tip break sand —

Mounds from that can rise
   on held mounds,
a gesture of building, keeping,
15   a trapping
into shape.

Firm ground is not available ground.

(1965)

ROBERT CREELEY

(1926–   )

orn in Massachusetts, Robert Creeley has lived in various regions of the United States as well as Central America, East Asia, and Europe. Creeley taught briefly at Black Mountain College and became one of the leaders of the poetic movement associated with that school. Influenced by William Carlos Williams as well as the other members of the Black Mountain group, he concentrates on recording the details of actual experiences, rather than supplying carefully organized intellectual analyses of experience. While he has maintained that form is no more than an extension of content, Creeley's work is generally more formal than that of the other leading poets of the Black Mountain group.

Ballad of the Despairing Husband

My wife and I lived all alone,
contention was our only bone.
I fought with her, she fought with me,
and things went on right merrily.

5   But now I live here by myself
with hardly a damn thing on the shelf,
and pass my days with little cheer
since I have parted from my dear.

O come home soon, I write to her.
10   Go fuck yourself, is her answer.
Now what is that, for Christian word?
I hope she feeds on dried goose turd.

But still I love her, yes I do.
I love her and the children too.
15   I only think it fit that she
should quickly come right back to me.

Ah no, she says, and she is tough,
and smacks me down with her rebuff.
Ah no, she says, I will not come
20   after the bloody things you've done.

Oh wife, oh wife — I tell you true,
I never loved no one but you.
I never will, it cannot be
another woman is for me.

25   That may be right, she will say then,
but as for me, there's other men.
And I will tell you I propose
to catch them firmly by the nose.

And I will wear what dresses I choose!
30   And I will dance, and what's to lose!
I'm free of you, you little prick,
And I'm the one can make it stick.

Was this the darling I did love?
Was this that mercy from above
35   did open violets in the spring —
and made my own worn self to sing?

She was. I know. And she is still,
and if I love her? then so I will.
And I will tell her, and tell her right . . .

40   Oh lovely lady, morning or evening or afternoon.
Oh lovely lady, eating with or without a spoon.
Oh most lovely lady, whether dressed or undressed or
         partly.
Oh most lovely lady, getting up or going to bed or sitting
         only.

Oh loveliest of ladies, than whom none is more fair, more
gracious, more beautiful.

45 Oh loveliest of ladies, whether you are just or unjust,
merciful, indifferent, or cruel.

Oh most loveliest of ladies, doing whatever, seeing
whatever, being whatever.

Oh most loveliest of ladies, in rain, in shine, in any
weather.

Oh lady, grant me time,
please, to finish my rhyme.

(1956)

The Rhythm

It is all a rhythm,
from the shutting
door, to the window
opening,

5 the seasons, the sun's
light, the moon,
the oceans, the
growing of things,

the mind in men
10 personal, recurring
in them again,
thinking the end

is not the end, the
time returning,
15 themselves dead but
someone else coming.

If in death I am dead,
then in life also
dying, dying . . .
20   And the women cry and die.

The little children
grow only to old men.
The grass dries,
the force goes.

25   But is met by another
returning, oh not mine,
not mine, and
in turn dies.

The rhythm which projects
30   from itself continuity
bending all to its force
from window to door,
from ceiling to floor,
light at the opening,
35   dark at the closing.

(1962)

ALLEN GINSBERG

(1926–   )

*T*he best-known poet identified with the beat movement of the 1950s, Allen
Ginsberg became a controversial public figure at the forefront of various
protest movements in the 1960s. After growing up in the industrial city of Pater-
son, New Jersey, Ginsberg received a B.A. from Columbia University, where he
wrote poems based on traditional models. Soon, however, he rebelled against both
poetic convention and the staid norms of post-war America, and his long poem
"Howl," published in Lawrence Ferlinghetti's City Lights Pocket Poet Series in
1956, survived charges of obscenity to become the best-selling poem of the decade.
Ginsberg's poetry is characterized by long, declamatory lines of free verse, rhetori-
cally charged diction, and a blending of social comment and self-revelation. He is
an accomplished performer and his poems are most effective when read aloud.

A Supermarket in California

What thoughts I have of you tonight, Walt Whitman,[1]
for I walked down the sidestreets under the trees with a
headache self-conscious looking at the full moon.

In my hungry fatigue, and shopping for images, I went
into the neon fruit supermarket, dreaming of your
enumerations!

What peaches and what penumbras! Whole families
shopping at night! Aisles full of husbands! Wives in the
avocados, babies in the tomatoes! — and you, Garcia
Lorca,[2] what were you doing down by the watermelons?

I saw you, Walt Whitman, childless, lonely old
grubber, poking among the meats in the refrigerator and
eyeing the grocery boys.

5   I heard you asking questions of each: Who killed the
pork chops? What price bananas? Are you my Angel?

I wandered in and out of the brilliant stacks of cans
following you, and followed in my imagination by the store
detective.

---

1 the experiments with free verse of American poet Walt Whitman (1819–92) influenced many twentieth-century
poets, including Ginsberg, who in this poem also identifies with Whitman's homosexuality.
2 Spanish poet and dramatist (1899–1936), who wrote an "Ode to Walt Whitman."

We strode down the open corridors together in our
solitary fancy tasting artichokes, possessing every frozen
delicacy, and never passing the cashier.

Where are we going, Walt Whitman? The doors close
in an hour. Which way does your beard point tonight?
(I touch your book and dream of our odyssey in the
supermarket and feel absurd.)

10   Will we walk all night through solitary streets? The
trees add shade to shade, lights out in the houses, we'll
both be lonely.

Will we stroll dreaming of the lost America of love
past blue automobiles in driveways, home to our silent
cottage?

Ah, dear father, graybeard, lonely old courage-teacher,
what America did you have when Charon quit poling his
ferry and you got out on a smoking bank and stood
watching the boat disappear on the black waters of Lethe?[3]

(Berkeley, 1955)   (1956)

---

3 in Greek mythology, the dead drank from the Lethe, the river of forgetfulness, before being ferried by Charon
across the river Styx to the underworld.

PHYLLIS WEBB

(1927–   )

orn in Victoria, B.C., Phyllis Webb received her B.A. from the Univer-
sity of British Columbia and studied briefly at McGill. She has taught
at UBC and the University of Victoria and was writer in residence at the Univer-
sity of Alberta. She has also been a producer for the Canadian Broadcasting Cor-
poration. Her first book of poetry was Trio *(1954), which also featured the work*
of two other poets. The Vision Tree: Selected Poems *(1982) won the Gov-*
ernor General's Award. An intellectual with an often bleak vision of the world,
Webb develops ideas carefully through complex structures and careful arrangements
of sounds, creating what she calls "the dance of the intellect in the syllables."

Marvell's Garden[1]

Marvell's garden, that place of solitude,
is not where I'd choose to live
yet is the fixed sundial
that turns me round
5   unwillingly
in a hot glade
as closer, closer I come to contradiction
to the shade green within the green shade.[2]

The garden where Marvell scorned love's solicitude —
10   that dream — and played instead an arcane solitaire,
shuffling his thoughts like shadowy chance
across the shrubs of ecstasy,
and cast the myths away to flowering hours[3]
and yes, his mind, that sea,[4] caught at green
15   thoughts shadowing a green infinity.

1 see Andrew Marvell's "The Garden" (p. 135), in which a garden symbolizes the solitary contemplative life.
2 in "The Garden," Marvell speaks of "a green thought in a green shade" (line 48). Green symbolizes a cool
detachment from human concerns.
3 the fourth stanza of "The Garden" recounts the stories of Daphne and Syrinx, maidens who escaped seduction
when they were transformed into, respectively, a laurel and a reed.
4 Marvell's poem (lines 44–45) refers to the mind as an ocean because, like the ocean, which was thought to
contain a form of everything on land, the mind contains a resemblance of everything on earth.

And yet Marvell's garden was not Plato's[5]
garden — and yet — he did care more for the form
of things than for the thing itself —
ideas and visions,
20   resemblances and echoes,
things seeming and being
not quite what they were.

That was his garden, a kind of attitude
struck out of an earth too carefully attended,
25   wanting to be left alone.
And I don't blame him for that.
God knows, too many fences fence us out
and his garden closed in on Paradise.[6]

On Paradise! When I think of his hymning
30   Puritans in the Bermudas, the bright oranges
lighting up that night![7] When I recall
his rustling tinsel hopes
beneath the cold decree of steel,
Oh, I have wept for some new convulsion
35   to tear together this world and his.[8]

But then I saw his luminous plumèd Wings
prepared for flight,
and then I heard him singing glory
in a green tree,
40   and then I caught the vest he'd laid aside
all blest with fire.[9]

---

5 *Plato argued that any earthly thing was but a pale reflection or shadow of the ideal form or idea of that thing.*

6 *Marvell compared his garden, a solitary place — and thus free from sexual passion — to Eden before the creation of Eve: "Two paradises 'twere in one / To live in paradise alone" (lines 63–64).*

7 *in "Bermudas" (see page 137), Marvell wrote of Puritans seeking refuge from English bishops in a land "far kinder than our own" (line 8). In praising God, who gave the Puritans such a beautiful refuge, he says God "hangs in shades the orange bright, / Like golden lamps in a green night" (lines 17–18).*

8 *in "The Definition of Love" (1681), a poem about a lover's despair because he can never consummate his love, Marvell speaks of "feeble hope," which "vainly flapped its tinsel wing." Fate's "decrees of steel" separate the lovers as if they were the poles of the earth. He declares that they will remain apart "Unless the giddy heaven fall / And earth some new convulsion tear," joining the lovers by flattening the globe.*

9 *in the seventh stanza of "The Garden," Marvell speaks of his soul casting off "the body's vest" to fly like a bird into the trees.*

And I have gone walking slowly in
his garden of necessity
leaving brothers, lovers, Christ
45 outside my walls
where they have wept without
and I within.

(1956)

The Glass Castle

The glass castle is my image for the mind
that if outmoded has its public beauty.
It can contain both talisman and leaf,
and private action, homely disbelief.
5 And I have lived there as you must
and scratched with diamond and gathered diamond dust,
have signed the castle's tense and fragile glass
and heard the antique whores and stoned Cassandras[1]
call me, and I answered in the one voice I knew,
10 "I am here. I do not know . . . "
but moved the symbols and polished up the view.
For who can refrain from action —
there is always a princely kiss for the Sleeping Beauty —
when even to put out the light takes a steady hand,
15 for the reward of darkness in a glass castle
is starry and full of glory.

I do not mean I shall not crack the pane.
I merely make a statement, judicious and polite,
that in this poise of crystal space
20 I balance and I claim the five gods of reality
to bless and keep me sane.

(1962)

---

1 the daughter of King Priam of Troy, Cassandra had the gift of prophecy, but she lived under Apollo's curse that no one would believe her.

Treblinka[1] Gas Chamber

> Klostermayer ordered another count of the children.
> Then their stars were snipped off and thrown into
> the center of the courtyard. It looked like a field of
> buttercups. — JOSEPH HYAMS, *A Field of Buttercups*

fallingstars

    'a field of

        buttercups'

    yellow stars

5   of David

          falling

the prisoners

    the children

      falling

10   in heaps

      on one another

        they go down

Thanatos[2]

    showers

15   his dirty breath

        they must breathe

          him in

    they see stars

      behind their

20   eyes

David's

    'a field of

      buttercups'

    a metaphor

25   where all that's

        left lies down

(1980)

---

1 *extermination camp in Poland where the Nazis gassed thousands of Jews during World War II.*
2 *the ancient Greek personification of Death.*

ANNE SEXTON

(1928–1974)

*A*nne Sexton grew up in Massachusetts and eventually studied with Robert Lowell at Boston University. There she became friends with other poets who, like herself, are sometimes assigned to the "confessional school" — poets using their personal lives to represent larger social and spiritual problems. Sexton, however, went beyond most in her frankness. In an epigraph to an early book, Sexton quoted Franz Kafka's observation that " . . . a book should serve as the ax for the frozen sea within us," and throughout her career she strove to meet this prescription. Sexton's poems are distinguished by their courageous honesty, their depth of feeling, and their insight into the falseness and foolishness of social mores, especially those restricting women; they also benefit from her fine, dark sense of humour.

You All Know the Story of the Other Woman

It's a little Walden.[1]
She is private in her breathbed
as his body takes off and flies,
flies straight as an arrow.
5   But it's a bad translation.
Daylight is nobody's friend.
God comes in like a landlord
and flashes on his brassy lamp.
Now she is just so-so.
10   He puts his bones back on,
turning the clock back an hour.
She knows flesh, that skin balloon,
the unbound limbs, the boards,
the roof, the removable roof.

1 the pond in Massachusetts to which American poet and philosopher Henry David Thoreau retired in 1845 to live a simple life near nature, an experience he later recounted in Walden, or Life in the Woods (1854).

15 She is his selection, part time.
You know the story too! Look,
when it is over he places her,
like a phone, back on the hook.

(1969)

Rumpelstiltskin[1]

Inside many of us
is a small old man
who wants to get out.
No bigger than a two-year-old
5   whom you'd call lamb chop
yet this one is old and malformed.
His head is okay
but the rest of him wasn't Sanforized.[2]
He is a monster of despair.
10 He is all decay.
He speaks up as tiny as an earphone
with Truman's asexual voice:
I am your dwarf.
I am the enemy within.
15 I am the boss of your dreams.
No. I am not the law in your mind,
the grandfather of watchfulness.
I am the law of your members,
the kindred of blackness and impulse.
20 See. Your hand shakes.
It is not palsy or booze.
It is your Doppelgänger[3]
trying to get out.
Beware . . . Beware . . .

1 this poem is a retelling of a fairy tale collected by German folklorists Jacob Grimm (1785–1863) and Wilhelm Grimm (1786–1859)
2 a process by which cotton cloth is shrunk before being made into clothing.
3 a ghostly double of a living person.

25 There once was a miller
with a daughter as lovely as a grape.
He told the king that she could
spin gold out of common straw.
The king summoned the girl
30 and locked her in a room full of straw
and told her to spin it into gold
or she would die like a criminal.
Poor grape with no one to pick.
Luscious and round and sleek.
35 Poor thing.
To die and never see Brooklyn.

She wept,
of course, huge aquamarine tears.
The door opened and in popped a dwarf.
40 He was as ugly as a wart.
Little thing, what are you? she cried.
With his tiny no-sex voice he replied:
I am a dwarf.
I have been exhibited on Bond Street[4]
45 and no child will ever call me Papa.
I have no private life.
If I'm in my cups
the whole town knows by breakfast
and no child will ever call me Papa.
50 I am eighteen inches high.
I am no bigger than a partridge.
I am your evil eye
and no child will ever call me Papa.
Stop this Papa foolishness,
55 she cried. Can you perhaps
spin straw into gold?
Yes indeed, he said,
that I can do.
He spun the straw into gold
60 and she gave him her necklace
as a small reward.

4 *a street in London famous for its shops.*

When the king saw what she had done
he put her in a bigger room of straw
and threatened death once more.
65   Again she cried.
Again the dwarf came.
Again he spun the straw into gold.
She gave him her ring
as a small reward.
70   The king put her in an even bigger room
but this time he promised
to marry her if she succeeded.
Again she cried.
Again the dwarf came.
75   But she had nothing to give him.
Without a reward the dwarf would not spin.
He was on the scent of something bigger.
He was a regular bird dog.
Give me your first-born
80   and I will spin.
She thought: Piffle!
He is a silly little man.
And so she agreed.
So he did the trick.
85   Gold as good as Fort Knox.[5]

The king married her
and within a year
a son was born.
He was like most new babies,
90   as ugly as an artichoke
but the queen thought him a pearl.
She gave him her dumb lactation,
delicate, trembling, hidden,
warm, etc.
95   And then the dwarf appeared
to claim his prize.
Indeed! I have become a papa!
cried the little man.

5 *the U.S. gold depository in Kentucky.*

She offered him all the kingdom
100   but he wanted only this —
a living thing
to call his own.
And being mortal
who can blame him?

105   The queen cried two pails of sea water.
She was as persistent
as a Jehovah's Witness.
And the dwarf took pity.
He said: I will give you
110   three days to guess my name
and if you cannot do it
I will collect your child.
The queen sent messengers
throughout the land to find names
115   of the most unusual sort.
When he appeared the next day
she asked: Melchior?
Balthazar?
But each time the dwarf replied:
120   No! No! That's not my name.
The next day she asked:
Spindleshanks? Spiderlegs?
But it was still no-no.
On the third day the messenger
125   came back with a strange story.
He told her:
As I came around the corner of the wood
where the fox says good night to the hare
I saw a little house with a fire
130   burning in front of it.
Around that fire a ridiculous little man
was leaping on one leg and singing:
Today I bake.
Tomorrow I brew my beer.
135   The next day the queen's only child will be mine.
Not even the census taker knows
that Rumpelstiltskin is my name . . .

The queen was delighted.
She had the name!
140   Her breath blew bubbles.

When the dwarf returned
she called out:
Is your name by any chance Rumpelstiltskin?
He cried: The devil told you that!
145   He stamped his right foot into the ground
and sank in up to his waist.
Then he tore himself in two.
Somewhat like a split broiler.
He laid his two sides down on the floor,
150   one part soft as a woman,
one part a barbed hook,
one part papa,
one part Doppelgänger.

(1971)

ADRIENNE RICH

(1929–   )

A drienne Rich grew up in Baltimore, Maryland, where she began writing poetry as a girl. While formal and restrained compared with her later work, her first book, A Change of World *(1951), showed remarkable maturity of thought and technique for a 22 year old and won the Yale Series of Younger Poets award. Only after marrying early and having three sons in quick succession did Rich begin breaking away from stereotypical female roles. In her third book,* Snapshots of a Daughter-in-Law *(1963), her forms are freer, her voice is more personal, and her growing resentment of the limitations she sees imposed on her in a male-dominated society is made plain. Beginning with her opposition to the Vietnam War in the 1960s, Rich — guided always by a strong feminist commitment — has become increasingly involved in various liberal political movements. In 1986, she became professor of English and feminist studies at Stanford University.*

Aunt Jennifer's Tigers

Aunt Jennifer's tigers prance across a screen,
Bright topaz denizens of a world of green.
They do not fear the men beneath the tree;
They pace in sleek chivalric certainty.

5   Aunt Jennifer's fingers fluttering through her wool
Find even the ivory needle hard to pull.
The massive weight of Uncle's wedding band
Sits heavily upon Aunt Jennifer's hand.

When Aunt is dead, her terrified hands will lie
10   Still ringed with ordeals she was mastered by.
The tigers in the panel that she made
Will go on prancing, proud and unafraid.

(1951)

Living in Sin

She had thought the studio would keep itself;
no dust upon the furniture of love.
Half heresy, to wish the taps less vocal,
the panes relieved of grime. A plate of pears,
5   a piano with a Persian shawl, a cat
stalking the picturesque amusing mouse
had risen at his urging.
Not that at five each separate stair would writhe
under the milkman's tramp; that morning light
10   so coldly would delineate the scraps
of last night's cheese and three sepulchral bottles;
that on the kitchen shelf among the saucers
a pair of beetle-eyes would fix her own —
envoy from some village in the moldings . . .
15   Meanwhile, he, with a yawn,
sounded a dozen notes upon the keyboard,
declared it out of tune, shrugged at the mirror,
rubbed at his beard, went out for cigarettes;
while she, jeered by the minor demons,
20   pulled back the sheets and made the bed and found
a towel to dust the table-top,
and let the coffee-pot boil over on the stove.
By evening she was back in love again,
though not so wholly but throughout the night
25   she woke sometimes to feel the daylight coming
like a relentless milkman up the stairs.

(1955)

Snapshots of a Daughter-in-Law

1.

You, once a belle in Shreveport,[1]
with henna-colored hair, skin like a peachbud,
still have your dresses copied from that time,
and play a Chopin[2] prelude
called by Cortot:[3] *"Delicious recollections*
float like perfume through the memory."

Your mind now, moldering like wedding-cake,
heavy with useless experience, rich
with suspicion, rumor, fantasy,
crumbling to pieces under the knife-edge
of mere fact. In the prime of your life.

Nervy, glowering, your daughter
wipes the teaspoons, grows another way.

2.

Banging the coffee-pot into the sink
she hears the angels chiding, and looks out
past the raked gardens to the sloppy sky.
Only a week since They said: *Have no patience.*

The next time it was: *Be insatiable.*
Then: *Save yourself; others you cannot save.*
Sometimes she's let the tapstream scald her arm,
a match burn to her thumbnail,

or held her hand above the kettle's snout
right in the woolly steam. They are probably angels,

---

1 *city in Louisiana.*
2 *Frédéric Chopin (1810–49), Polish-French pianist and composer.*
3 *Alfred Cortot (1877–1962), French pianist.*

since nothing hurts her anymore, except
₂₅ each morning's grit blowing into her eyes.

3.

A thinking woman sleeps with monsters.
The beak that grips her, she becomes. And Nature,
that sprung-lidded, still commodious
steamer-trunk of *tempora* and *mores*[4]
₃₀ gets stuffed with it all: the mildewed orange-flowers,
the female pills, the terrible breasts
of Boadicea[5] beneath flat foxes' heads and orchids.

Two handsome women, gripped in argument,
each proud, acute, subtle, I hear scream
₃₅ across the cut glass and majolica
like Furies cornered from their prey:
The argument *ad feminam*,[6] all the old knives
that have rusted in my back, I drive in yours,
ma semblable, ma soeur![7]

4.

₄₀ Knowing themselves too well in one another:
their gifts no pure fruition, but a thorn,
the prick filed sharp against a hint of scorn . . .
Reading while waiting
for the iron to heat,
₄₅ writing, *My Life had stood — a Loaded Gun —* [8]
in that Amherst pantry while the jellies boil and scum,
or, more often,
iron-eyed and beaked and purposed as a bird,
dusting everything on the whatnot every day of life.

---

4 *times and customs (Latin).*
5 *British queen whose revolt against the Romans was put down in A.D. 61.*
6 *feminine version of the* ad hominem *fallacy of reasoning, in which one appeals to the audience's prejudices or attacks the character of an opponent rather than replying logically to opposing arguments.*
7 *"my double, my sister" — adapted from the introductory poem of* Les Fleurs du Mal *by French poet Charles Baudelaire (1821–67).*
8 *opening line of a poem by Emily Dickinson (1830–86), who lived, her talent unrecognized during her lifetime, in Amherst, Massachusetts.*

5.

50   *Dulce ridens, dulce loquens,*[9]
she shaves her legs until they gleam
like petrified mammoth-tusk.

6.

When to her lute Corinna sings[10]
neither words nor music are her own;
55   only the long hair dipping
over her cheek, only the song
of silk against her knees
and these
adjusted in reflections of an eye.

60   Poised, trembling and unsatisfied, before
an unlocked door, that cage of cages,
tell us, you bird, you tragical machine —
is this *fertilisante douleur?*[11] Pinned down
by love, for you the only natural action,
65   are you edged more keen
to prise the secrets of the vault? has Nature shown
her household books to you, daughter-in-law,
that her sons never saw?

7.

"To have in this uncertain world some stay
70   *which cannot be undermined, is*
of the utmost consequence."[12]

                    Thus wrote
a woman, partly brave and partly good,
who fought with what she partly understood.
Few men about her would or could do more,
75   hence she was labeled harpy, shrew and whore.

---

9 *"Sweetly laughing, sweetly prattling" (Latin) — adapted from Horace's* Odes *I.22.*
10 *the opening line of an Elizabethan love lyric by Thomas Campion (1567–1620).*
11 *fertilizing pain or sorrow (French).*
12 *from* Thoughts on the Education of Daughters *(1787) by Mary Wollstonecraft (1759–97).*

8.
"You all die at fifteen," said Diderot,[13]
and turn part legend, part convention.
Still, eyes inaccurately dream
behind closed windows blankening with steam.
80   Deliciously, all that we might have been,
all that we were — fire, tears,
wit, taste, martyred ambition —
stirs like the memory of refused adultery
the drained and flagging bosom of our middle years.

9.
85   *Not that it is done well, but*
that it is done at all?[14] Yes, think
of the odds! or shrug them off forever.
This luxury of the precocious child,
Time's precious chronic invalid, —
90   would we, darlings, resign it if we could?
Our blight has been our sinecure:
mere talent was enough for us —
glitter in fragments and rough drafts.

Sigh no more, ladies:
               Time is male
95   and in his cups drinks to the fair.
Bemused by gallantry, we hear
our mediocrities over-praised,
indolence read as abnegation,
slattern thought styled intuition,
100   every lapse forgiven, our crime
only to cast too bold a shadow
or smash the mold straight off.

For that, solitary confinement,
tear gas, attrition shelling.
105   Few applicants for that honor.

---

13 *from* Lettres à Sophie Volland *by French Enlightenment writer and philosopher Denis Diderot (1713–84).*
14 *echo of Samuel Johnson's comment, recorded by James Boswell (1740–95) in* The Life of Samuel Johnson
   (1791), that a woman preaching is like a dog walking on its hind legs.

10.
                              Well,
she's long about her coming, who must be
more merciless to herself than history.
Her mind full to the wind, I see her plunge
breasted and glancing through the currents,
110   taking the light upon her
at least as beautiful as any boy
or helicopter,
                    poised, still coming,
her fine blades making the air wince

but her cargo
115   no promise then:
delivered
palpable
ours.

(1963)

Diving into the Wreck

First having read the book of myths,
and loaded the camera,
and checked the edge of the knife-blade,
I put on
5   the body-armor of black rubber
the absurd flippers
the grave and awkward mask.
I am having to do this
not like Cousteau[1] with his
10   assiduous team
aboard the sun-flooded schooner
but here alone.

---

1 Jacques Cousteau, contemporary French author, filmmaker, and underwater explorer.

There is a ladder.
The ladder is always there

15   hanging innocently
close to the side of the schooner.
We know what it is for,
we who have used it.
Otherwise

20   it's a piece of maritime floss
some sundry equipment.

I go down.
Rung after rung and still
the oxygen immerses me

25   the blue light
the clear atoms
of our human air.
I go down.
My flippers cripple me,

30   I crawl like an insect down the ladder
and there is no one
to tell me when the ocean
will begin.

First the air is blue and then

35   it is bluer and then green and then
black I am blacking out and yet
my mask is powerful
it pumps my blood with power
the sea is another story

40   the sea is not a question of power
I have to learn alone
to turn my body without force
in the deep element.

And now: it is easy to forget

45   what I came for
among so many who have always
lived here
swaying their crenellated fans
between the reefs

50   and besides
you breathe differently down here.

I came to explore the wreck.
The words are purposes.
The words are maps.
55 I came to see the damage that was done
and the treasures that prevail.
I stroke the beam of my lamp
slowly along the flank
of something more permanent
60 than fish or weed.

the thing I came for:
the wreck and not the story of the wreck
the thing itself and not the myth
the drowned face always staring
65 toward the sun
the evidence of damage
worn by salt and sway into this threadbare beauty
the ribs of the disaster
curving their assertion
70 among the tentative haunters.

This is the place.
And I am here, the mermaid whose dark hair
streams black, the merman in his armored body
We circle silently
75 about the wreck
we dive into the hold.
I am she: I am he

whose drowned face sleeps with open eyes
whose breasts still bear the stress
80 whose silver, copper, vermeil cargo lies
obscurely inside barrels
half-wedged and left to rot
we are the half-destroyed instruments
that once held to a course
85 the water-eaten log
the fouled compass

We are, I am, you are
by cowardice or courage
the one who find our way
90   back to this scene
carrying a knife, a camera
a book of myths
in which
our names do not appear.

(1973)

Transit

When I meet the skier she is always
walking, skis and poles shouldered, toward the mountain
free-swinging in worn boots
over the path new-sifted with fresh snow
5   her greying dark hair almost hidden by
a cap of many colors
her fifty-year-old, strong, impatient body
dressed for cold and speed
her eyes level with mine

10   And when we pass each other I look into her face
wondering what we have in common
where our minds converge
for we do not pass each other, she passes me
as I halt beside the fence tangled in snow,
15   she passes me as I shall never pass her
in this life

Yet I remember us together
climbing Chocorua,[1] summer nineteen-forty-five
details of vegetation beyond the timberline
20   lichens, wildflowers, birds,

_____

1 _a small mountain near Conway, New Hampshire._

amazement when the trail broke out onto the granite ledge
sloped over blue lakes, green pines, giddy air
like dreams of flying

When sisters separate they haunt each other
25   as she, who I might once have been, haunts me
or is it I who do the haunting
halting and watching on the path
how she appears again through lightly-blowing
crystals, how her strong knees carry her,
30   how unaware she is, how simple
this is for her, how without let or hindrance
she travels in her body
until the point of passing, where the skier
and the cripple must decide
35   to recognize each other?

(1981)

THOM GUNN

(1929–   )

*B*orn in Gravesend, Kent, Thom Gunn received a B.A. from Cambridge in 1954 and an M.A. from Stanford in 1958. Long a resident of San Francisco, Gunn has been influenced by both English and American poetic practices. Much of his early work shows a deliberately tough attitude: the themes focus on danger, destruction, alienation, and purposelessness. Other work shows the formal and intellectual influences of Yvor Winters, under whom he studied at Stanford. Gunn himself has said that he is following a tradition in which "a poem should balance the emotion with the intellect."

On the Move[1]

The blue jay scuffling in the bushes follows
Some hidden purpose, and the gust of birds
That spurts across the field, the wheeling swallows,
Have nested in the trees and undergrowth.
5   Seeking their instinct, or their poise, or both,
One moves with an uncertain violence
Under the dust thrown by a baffled sense
Or the dull thunder of approximate words.

On motorcycles, up the road, they come:
10   Small, black, as flies hanging in heat, the Boys,
Until the distance throws them forth, their hum
Bulges to thunder held by calf and thigh.
In goggles, donned impersonality,
In gleaming jackets trophied with the dust,
15   They strap in doubt — by hiding it, robust —
And almost hear a meaning in their noise.

1 *the version of this poem printed in* Selected Poems 1950–1975 (1979), *the source of our text, omits the epigraph included in earlier printings:* "'Man, you gotta Go.'"

Exact conclusion of their hardiness
Has no shape yet, but from known whereabouts
They ride, direction where the tires press.
20   They scare a flight of birds across the field:
Much that is natural, to the will must yield.
Men manufacture both machine and soul,
And use what they imperfectly control
To dare a future from the taken routes.

25   It is a part solution, after all.
One is not necessarily discord
On earth; or damned because, half animal,
One lacks direct instinct, because one wakes
Afloat on movement that divides and breaks.
30   One joins the movement in a valueless world,
Choosing it, till, both hurler and the hurled,
One moves as well, always toward, toward.

A minute holds them, who have come to go:
The self-defined, astride the created will
35   They burst away; the towns they travel through
Are home for neither bird nor holiness,
For birds and saints complete their purposes.
At worst, one is in motion; and at best,
Reaching no absolute, in which to rest,
40   One is always nearer by not keeping still.

(California)   (1957)

To Yvor Winters, 1955[1]

I leave you in your garden.
                                    In the yard
Behind it, run the Airedales you have reared
With boxer's vigilance and poet's rigor:
Dog generations you have trained the vigor
5   That few can breed to train and fewer still
Control with the deliberate human will.
And in the house there rest, piled shelf on shelf,
The accumulations that compose the self —
Poem and history: for if we use
10   Words to maintain the actions that we choose,
Our words, with slow defining influence,
Stay to mark out our chosen lineaments.

Continual temptation waits on each
To renounce his empire over thought and speech,
15   Till he submit his passive faculties
To evening, come where no resistance is;
The unmotivated sadness of the air
Filling the human with his own despair.
Where now lies power to hold the evening back?
20   Implicit in the gray is total black:
Denial of the discriminating brain
Brings the neurotic vision, and the vein
Of necromancy. All as relative
For mind as for the sense, we have to live
25   In a half world, not ours nor history's,
And learn the false from half-true premises.

But sitting in the dusk — though shapes combine,
Vague mass replacing edge and flickering line,
You keep both Rule and Energy in view,

---

1 *Gunn's teacher at Stanford, Yvor Winters (1900–68) was an influential American literary critic and poet who
developed a rigorous analysis of poetry, especially British poetry of the sixteenth and seventeenth centuries.*

30   Much power in each, most in the balanced two:
Ferocity existing in the fence
Built by an exercised intelligence.
Though night is always close, complete negation
Ready to drop on wisdom and emotion,
35   Night from air or the carnivorous breath,
Still it is right to know the force of death,
And, as you do, persistent, tough in will,
Raise from the excellent the better still.

(1957)

Moly[1]

Nightmare of beasthood, snorting, how to wake.
I woke. What beasthood skin she made me take?

Leathery toad that ruts for days on end,
Or cringing dribbling dog, man's servile friend,

5   Or cat that prettily pounces on its meat,
Tortures it hours, then does not care to eat:

Parrot, moth, shark, wolf, crocodile, ass, flea.
What germs, what jostling mobs there were in me.

These seem like bristles, and the hide is tough.
10   No claw or web here: each foot ends in hoof.

Into what bulk has method disappeared?
Like ham, streaked. I am gross — gray, gross, flap-eared.

The pale-lashed eyes my only human feature.
My teeth tear, tear. I am the snouted creature

1 *a magical herb that Hermes gave to Odysseus to protect him from the enchantment of Circe, who turned Odysseus's crew into swine.*

15   That bites through anything, root, wire, or can.
       If I was not afraid I'd eat a man.

       Oh a man's flesh already is in mine.
       Hand and foot poised for risk. Buried in swine.

           I root and root, you think that it is greed,
20   It is, but I seek out a plant I need.

       Direct me, gods, whose changes are all holy,
       To where it flickers deep in grass, the moly:

       Cool flesh of magic in each leaf and shoot,
       From milky flower to the black forked root.

25   From this fat dungeon I could rise to skin
       And human title, putting pig within.

       I push my big gray wet snout through the green,
       Dreaming the flower I have never seen.

                                        (1971)

TED HUGHES

(1930–   )

orn in the small Yorkshire town of Mytholmroyd, Hughes received B.A. and M.A. degrees from Cambridge. His first wife was the American poet Sylvia Plath. Hughes achieved critical respect with his very first volume of poems, The Hawk in the Rain *(1957), which introduced one of his dominant subjects, animal life. Although some critics contend that Hughes celebrates raw power and brutality in his animal poems, even accusing him of presenting the figure of a fascist in "Hawk Roosting," Hughes contends that he is presenting "Nature thinking. Simply Nature." Hughes says: "What excites my imagination is the war between vitality and death, and my poems may be said to celebrate the exploits of the warriors of either side." For him, animals combine "the arrogance of blood and bone" with "an energy too strong for death." Hughes compares his poetic technique to that of a composer. He says that he turns each of his combatants "into a bit of music" and then resolves "the whole uproar into as formal and balanced a figure of melody and rhythm as I can."*

Wind

This house has been far out at sea all night,
The woods crashing through darkness, the booming hills,
Winds stampeding the fields under the window
Floundering black astride and blinding wet

5   Till day rose; then under an orange sky
The hills had new places, and wind wielded
Blade-light, luminous black and emerald,
Flexing like the lens of a mad eye.

At noon I scaled along the house-side as far as
10   The coal-house door. Once I looked up —
Through the brunt wind that dented the balls of my eyes
The tent of the hills drummed and strained its guy rope,

The fields quivering, the skyline a grimace,
At any second to bang and vanish with a flap:
15 The wind flung a magpie away and a black-
Back gull bent like an iron bar slowly. The house

Rang like some fine green goblet in the note
That any second would shatter it. Now deep
In chairs, in front of the great fire, we grip
20 Our hearts and cannot entertain book, thought,

Or each other. We watch the fire blazing,
And feel the roots of the house move, but sit on,
Seeing the window tremble to come in,
Hearing the stones cry out under the horizons.

(1957)

Pike

Pike, three inches long, perfect
Pike in all parts, green tigering the gold.
Killers from the egg: the malevolent aged grin.
They dance on the surface among the flies.

5 Or move, stunned by their own grandeur,
Over a bed of emerald, silhouette
Of submarine delicacy and horror.
A hundred feet long in their world.

In ponds, under the heat-struck lily pads —
10 Gloom of their stillness:
Logged on last year's black leaves, watching upwards.
Or hung in an amber cavern of weeds

The jaws' hooked clamp and fangs
Not to be changed at this date;
15 A life subdued to its instrument;
The gills kneading quietly, and the pectorals.

Three we kept behind glass,
Jungled in weed: three inches, four,
And four and a half: fed fry to them —
20 Suddenly there were two. Finally one.

With a sag belly and the grin it was born with.
And indeed they spare nobody.
Two, six pounds each, over two feet long,
High and dry and dead in the willow-herb —

25 One jammed past its gills down the other's gullet:
The outside eye stared: as a vice locks —
The same iron in this eye
Though its film shrank in death.

A pond I fished, fifty yards across,
30 Whose lilies and muscular tench[1]
Had outlasted every visible stone
Of the monastery that planted them —

Stilled legendary depth:
It was as deep as England. It held
35 Pike too immense to stir, so immense and old
That past nightfall I dared not cast

But silently cast and fished
With the hair frozen on my head
For what might move, for what eye might move.
40 The still splashes on the dark pond,

Owls hushing the floating woods
Frail on my ear against the dream
Darkness beneath night's darkness had freed,
That rose slowly towards me, watching.

(1960)

1 *a fresh-water fish that inhabits still, deep waters.*

Hawk Roosting

I sit in the top of the wood, my eyes closed.
Inaction, no falsifying dream
Between my hooked head and hooked feet:
Or in sleep rehearse perfect kills and eat.

5   The convenience of the high trees!
The air's buoyancy and the sun's ray
Are of advantage to me;
And the earth's face upward for my inspection.

My feet are locked upon the rough bark.
10   It took the whole of Creation
To produce my foot, my each feather:
Now I hold Creation in my foot

Or fly up, and revolve it all slowly —
I kill where I please because it is all mine.
15   There is no sophistry in my body:
My manners are tearing off heads —

The allotment of death.
For the one path of my flight is direct
Through the bones of the living.
20   No arguments assert my right:

The sun is behind me.
Nothing has changed since I began.
My eye has permitted no change.
I am going to keep things like this.

(1960)

SYLVIA PLATH

(1932–1963)

he daughter of German and Austrian parents who taught at Boston University, Sylvia Plath was both precocious and ambitious. She excelled at school and college, began writing as a child, and was publishing in popular magazines while still in her teens. She was also manic-depressive and suffered emotionally from the pressure she felt to succeed at everything. Married to English poet Ted Hughes and living in England with her two young children, she committed suicide at age thirty.

Plath's early poems are deftly controlled but fairly conventional, and it is mainly to her later work, most of which appeared in book form only after her death, that she owes her reputation. Writing under the influence of Robert Lowell's confessional poetry, Plath turned inward to confront the darker side of her psyche — her anger at her parents, her resentment at the cost to her art of motherhood, her sense of evil in modern society, and her obsession with self-destruction as a means of escape — in powerful, highly original, intensely disturbing poems.

Spider

Anansi,[1] black busybody of the folktales,
You scuttle out on impulse
Blunt in self-interest
As a sledge hammer, as a man's bunched fist,
5 Yet of devils the cleverest
To get your carousals told:
You spun the cosmic web: you squint from center field.

Last summer I came upon your Spanish cousin,
Notable robber baron,
10 Behind a goatherd's hut:
Near his small stonehenge above the ants' route,
One-third ant-size, a leggy spot,
He tripped an ant with a rope
Scarcely visible. About and about the slope

1 *the Twi word for spider. Anansi appears commonly in West African and West Indian folktales as a trickster figure.*

15   Of his redoubt he ran his nimble filament,
      Each time round winding that ant
      Tighter to the cocoon
      Already veiling the gray spool of stone
      From which coils, caught ants waved legs in
20   Torpid warning, or lay still
      And suffered their livelier fellows to struggle.

      Then briskly scaled his altar tiered with tethered ants,
      Nodding in a somnolence
      Appalling to witness,
25   To the barbarous outlook, from there chose
      His next martyr to the gross cause
      Of concupiscence. Once more
      With black alacrity bound round his prisoner.

      The ants — a file of comers, a file of goers —
30   Persevered on a set course
      No scruple could disrupt,
      Obeying orders of instinct till swept
      Off-stage and infamously wrapped
      Up by a spry black deus
35   Ex machina. Nor did they seem deterred by this.

      (1956)   (1981)

Daddy[1]

      You do not do, you do not do
      Any more, black shoe
      In which I have lived like a foot
      For thirty years, poor and white,
5   Barely daring to breathe or Achoo.

---

1 Plath's father was of German descent but came to America from Poland at age fifteen. He was an expert on bees
and taught at Boston University until his early death in 1940.

Daddy, I have had to kill you.
You died before I had time —
Marble-heavy, a bag full of God,
Ghastly statue with one gray toe[2]
Big as a Frisco seal

And a head in the freakish Atlantic
Where it pours bean green over blue
In the waters off beautiful Nauset.
I used to pray to recover you.
Ach, du.[3]

In the German tongue, in the Polish town
Scraped flat by the roller
O wars, wars, wars.
But the name of the town is common.
My Polack friend

Says there are a dozen or two.
So I never could tell where you
Put your foot, your root,
I never could talk to you.
The tongue stuck in my jaw.

It stuck in a barb wire snare.
Ich, ich, ich, ich,[4]
I could hardly speak.
I thought every German was you.
And the language obscene

An engine, an engine
Chuffing me off like a Jew.
A Jew to Dachau, Auschwitz, Belsen.[5]
I began to talk like a Jew.
I think I may well be a Jew.

2 *Plath's father died of blood poisoning when his diabetes led to gangrene in a toe.*
3 *Ah, you (German).*
4 *I, I, I, I (German).*
5 *Nazi concentration camps.*

The snows of the Tyrol, the clear beer of Vienna
Are not very pure or true.
With my gipsy ancestress and my weird luck
And my Taroc pack and my Taroc pack
40   I may be a bit of a Jew.

I have always been scared of *you*,
With your Luftwaffe, your gobbledygoo.
And your neat mustache
And your Aryan eye, bright blue.
45   Panzer-man, panzer-man, O You —

Not God but a swastika
So black no sky could squeak through.
Every woman adores a Fascist,
The boot in the face, the brute
50   Brute heart of a brute like you.

You stand at the blackboard, daddy,
In the picture I have of you,
A cleft in your chin instead of your foot
But no less a devil for that, no not
55   Any less the black man who

Bit my pretty red heart in two.
I was ten when they buried you.
At twenty I tried to die
And get back, back, back to you.
60   I thought even the bones would do.

But they pulled me out of the sack,
And they stuck me together with glue.
And then I knew what to do.
I made a model of you,
65   A man in black with a Meinkampf[6] look

6 *before coming to power, Adolf Hitler (1889–1945) outlined his plans for world domination in* Mein Kampf,
"my struggle" in German.

And a love of the rack and the screw.
And I said I do, I do.
So daddy, I'm finally through.
The black telephone's off at the root,
70 The voices just can't worm through.

If I've killed one man, I've killed two —
The vampire who said he was you
And drank my blood for a year,
Seven years, if you want to know.
75 Daddy, you can lie back now.

There's a stake in your fat black heart
And the villagers never liked you.
They are dancing and stamping on you.
They always *knew* it was you.
80 Daddy, daddy, you bastard, I'm through.

(1965)

Lady Lazarus[1]

I have done it again.
One year in every ten
I manage it —

A sort of walking miracle, my skin
5 Bright as a Nazi lampshade,
My right foot

A paperweight,
My face a featureless, fine
Jew linen.

1 *Lazarus was brought back from death by Jesus (John 11).*

10   Peel off the napkin
      O my enemy.
      Do I terrify? —

      The nose, the eye pits, the full set of teeth?
      The sour breath
15   Will vanish in a day.

      Soon, soon the flesh
      The grave cave ate will be
      At home on me

      And I a smiling woman.
20   I am only thirty.
      And like the cat I have nine times to die.

      This is Number Three.
      What a trash
      To annihilate each decade.

25   What a million filaments.
      The peanut-crunching crowd
      Shoves in to see

      Them unwrap me hand and foot —
      The big strip tease.
30   Gentlemen, ladies

      These are my hands
      My knees.
      I may be skin and bone,

      Nevertheless, I am the same, identical woman.
35   The first time it happened I was ten.
      It was an accident.

      The second time I meant
      To last it out and not come back at all.
      I rocked shut

40 As a seashell.
They had to call and call
And pick the worms off me like sticky pearls.

Dying
Is an art, like everything else.
45 I do it exceptionally well.

I do it so it feels like hell.
I do it so it feels real.
I guess you could say I've a call.

It's easy enough to do it in a cell.
50 It's easy enough to do it and stay put.
It's the theatrical

Comeback in broad day
To the same place, the same face, the same brute
Amused shout:

55 'A miracle!'
That knocks me out.
There is a charge

For the eyeing of my scars, there is a charge
For the hearing of my heart —
60 It really goes.

And there is a charge, a very large charge
For a word or a touch
Or a bit of blood

Or a piece of my hair or my clothes.
65 So, so, Herr Doktor.
So, Herr Enemy.

I am your opus,
I am your valuable,
The pure gold baby

70   That melts to a shriek.
     I turn and burn.
     Do not think I underestimate your great concern.

     Ash, ash —
     You poke and stir.
75   Flesh, bone, there is nothing there —

     A cake of soap,
     A wedding ring,
     A gold filling.

     Herr God, Herr Lucifer
80   Beware
     Beware.

     Out of the ash
     I rise with my red hair
     And I eat men like air.

(1965)

ALDEN NOWLAN

(1933–1983)

lthough he had a limited formal education — he left school after Grade 5 — Nowlan became one of the leading literary figures in Atlantic Canada. Born in Windsor, Nova Scotia, he held various jobs as a manual labourer until he moved to New Brunswick to work as a journalist. He began his literary career as a poet, publishing his first collection in 1958. Bread, Wine and Salt *(1967) won the Governor General's Award. Later, he turned his hand to other genres, producing plays, stories, and a novel. Although he is a regionalist painting relatively realistic pictures of nature and society in Atlantic Canada, Nowlan infuses his poems with universal significance. He can also, like a backwoods storyteller, be by turns sentimental and ironic. "The Bull Moose," his most famous poem, shows his most characteristic attitudes; he evokes sympathy for victims and imbues even the most mundane of events with religious or spiritual importance.*

The Bull Moose

Down from the purple mist of trees on the mountain,
lurching through forests of white spruce and cedar,
stumbling through tamarack swamps,
came the bull moose
5   to be stopped at last by a pole-fenced pasture.

Too tired to turn or, perhaps, aware
there was no place left to go, he stood with the cattle.
They, scenting the musk of death, seeing his great head
like the ritual mask of a blood god, moved to the other end
10   of the field, and waited.

The neighbours heard of it, and by afternoon
cars lined the road. The children teased him
with alder switches and he gazed at them
like an old, tolerant collie. The women asked
15   if he could have escaped from a Fair.

The oldest man in the parish remembered seeing
a gelded moose yoked with an ox for plowing.
The young men snickered and tried to pour beer
down his throat, while their girlfriends took their pictures.

20   And the bull moose let them stroke his tick-ravaged flanks,
let them pry open his jaws with bottles, let a giggling girl
plant a little purple cap
of thistles on his head.

When the wardens came, everyone agreed it was a shame
25   to shoot anything so shaggy and cuddlesome.
He looked like the kind of pet
women put to bed with their sons.

So they held their fire. But just as the sun dropped in the
        river
the bull moose gathered his strength
30   like a scaffolded king, straightened and lifted his horns
so that even the wardens backed away as they raised their
        rifles.
When he roared, people ran to their cars. All the young
        men
leaned on their automobile horns as he toppled.

(1962)

LEONARD COHEN

(1934–   )

*B*orn into a wealthy Montreal family in 1934, Cohen received a B.A.
from McGill University in 1955. Since then, he has moved freely
between literature and popular culture, becoming an internationally successful poet
and singer during the 1960s, and a controversial experimental novelist. He won,
but refused to accept, the Governor General's Award for Selected Poems
(1968).

In much of Cohen's work, traditional poetic elements contrast with the con-
temporary subject matter. That is to say, their lush imagery and abundant musical
qualities mark his poems as conventionally romantic and deliberately "poetic"
works. However, their bleakness and shocking assaults on conventional moral
assumptions make them thoroughly modern. Cohen frequently combines images
from classical mythology or religion (drawing on both his own Jewish heritage and
that of the dominant Catholic culture of Quebec) with images of sex, suffering, vio-
lence, and death. In this way he attempts to create an informal mythology to replace
what he considers the worn-out myths of the past. The exact meaning of Cohen's
poems is often elusive, but one figure is central. The "saint" renounces the ordinary
world, enduring consequent suffering and even destruction of the self in order to
achieve the purity necessary to attain a higher state. In Cohen's mythic world, the
only winners are beautiful losers.

I Have Not Lingered in European Monasteries

I have not lingered in European monasteries
and discovered among the tall grasses tombs of knights
who fell as beautifully as their ballads tell;
I have not parted the grasses
5   or purposefully left them thatched.

I have not released my mind to wander and wait
in those great distances
between the snowy mountains and the fishermen,
like a moon,
10   or a shell beneath the moving water.

I have not held my breath
so that I might hear the breathing of God,
or tamed my heartbeat with an exercise,
or starved for visions.
15   Although I have watched him often
I have not become the heron,
leaving my body on the shore,
and I have not become the luminous trout,
leaving my body in the air.

20   I have not worshipped wounds and relics,
or combs of iron,
or bodies wrapped and burnt in scrolls.

I have not been unhappy for ten thousand years.
During the day I laugh and during the night I sleep.
25   My favourite cooks prepare my meals,
my body cleans and repairs itself,
and all my work goes well.

(1961)

For E.J.P.[1]

I once believed a single line
    in a Chinese poem could change
        forever how blossoms fell
and that the moon itself climbed on
5   the grief of concise weeping men
            to journey over cups of wine
I thought invasions were begun for crows
    to pick at a skeleton
        dynasties sown and spent

1 E.J. Pratt (see page 429).

10   to serve the language of a fine lament
       I thought governors ended their lives
          as sweetly drunken monks
    telling time by rain and candles
       instructed by an insect's pilgrimage
15   across the page — all this
    so one might send an exile's perfect letter
    to an ancient home-town friend

    I chose a lonely country
       broke from love
20   scorned the fraternity of war
    I polished my tongue against the pumice moon
       floated my soul in cherry wine
          a perfumed barge for Lords of Memory
    to languish on to drink to whisper out
25   their store of strength
          as if beyond the mist along the shore
    their girls their power still obeyed
       like clocks wound for a thousand years
    I waited until my tongue was sore

30   Brown petals wind like fire around my poems
       I aimed them at the stars but
          like rainbows they were bent
    before they sawed the world in half
       Who can trace the canyoned paths
35   cattle have carved out of time
    wandering from meadowlands to feasts
       Layer after layer of autumn leaves
          are swept away
    Something forgets us perfectly.

(1964)

Suzanne Takes You Down

Suzanne takes you down
to her place near the river,
you can hear the boats go by
you can stay the night beside her.
5   And you know that she's half crazy
but that's why you want to be there
and she feeds you tea and oranges
that come all the way from China.
Just when you mean to tell her
10   that you have no gifts to give her,
she gets you on her wave-length
and she lets the river answer
that you've always been her lover.
    And you want to travel with her,
15   you want to travel blind
    and you know that she can trust you
    because you've touched her perfect body
    with your mind.

Jesus was a sailor
20   when he walked upon the water
and he spent a long time watching
from a lonely wooden tower
and when he knew for certain
only drowning men could see him
25   he said All men will be sailors then
until the sea shall free them,
but he himself was broken
long before the sky would open,
forsaken, almost human,
30   he sank beneath your wisdom like a stone.
    And you want to travel with him,
    you want to travel blind
    and you think maybe you'll trust him
    because he touched your perfect body
35   with his mind.

Suzanne takes your hand
and she leads you to the river,
she is wearing rags and feathers
from Salvation Army counters.
40 The sun pours down like honey
on our lady of the harbour
as she shows you where to look
among the garbage and the flowers,
there are heroes in the seaweed
45 there are children in the morning,
they are leaning out for love
they will lean that way forever
while Suzanne she holds the mirror.
    And you want to travel with her
50 and you want to travel blind
and you're sure that she can find you
because she's touched her perfect body
with her mind.

(1966)

SEAMUS HEANEY

(1939–   )

O *ne of the most widely read of contemporary poets, Seamus Heaney has been praised for his evocative language and for the integrity of his treatment of the troubles in Northern Ireland. Born in County Derry in Northern Ireland, he graduated from Queen's University, Belfast, in 1961 and obtained a teacher's diploma the next year. He has held a number of teaching appointments, including positions at his alma mater and at Harvard University. He published his first full-length collection,* Death of a Naturalist, *to critical acclaim in 1966. A Roman Catholic increasingly upset by the conflict in Northern Ireland, Heaney moved to the Irish Republic in 1972 in order, he said, "to put the practice of poetry more deliberately at the centre of my life." Ireland — its traditions, its rural landscape, and its political and religious difficulties — is at the centre of Heaney's poetry, but he also explores universal themes, such as the role of the poet and the nature of art. A poet whose unobtrusive craftsmanship produces works that are immediately accessible but also deeply moving and memorable, he has described poetry "as a point of entry into the buried life of the feelings or as a point of exit for it."*

Death of a Naturalist

All year the flax-dam festered in the heart
Of the townland; green and heavy headed
Flax had rotted there, weighted down by huge sods.
Daily it sweltered in the punishing sun.
5   Bubbles gargled delicately, bluebottles
Wove a strong gauze of sound around the smell.
There were dragon-flies, spotted butterflies,
But best of all was the warm thick slobber
Of frogspawn that grew like clotted water
10   In the shade of the banks. Here, every spring
I would fill jampotfuls of the jellied
Specks to range on window-sills at home,
On shelves at school, and wait and watch until
The fattening dots burst into nimble-
15   Swimming tadpoles. Miss Walls would tell us how
The daddy frog was called a bullfrog

And how he croaked and how the mammy frog
Laid hundreds of little eggs and this was
Frogspawn. You could tell the weather by frogs too
20   For they were yellow in the sun and brown
In rain.

Then one hot day when fields were rank
With cowdung in the grass the angry frogs
Invaded the flax-dam; I ducked through hedges
25   To a coarse croaking that I had not heard
Before. The air was thick with a bass chorus.
Right down the dam gross-bellied frogs were cocked
On sods; their loose necks pulsed like sails. Some hopped:
The slap and plop were obscene threats. Some sat
30   Poised like mud grenades, their blunt heads farting.
I sickened, turned, and ran. The great slime kings
Were gathered there for vengeance and I knew
That if I dipped my hand the spawn would clutch it.

(1966)

Personal Helicon[1]

FOR MICHAEL LONGLEY[2]

As a child, they could not keep me from wells
And old pumps with buckets and windlasses.
I loved the dark drop, the trapped sky, the smells
Of waterweed, fungus and dank moss.

5   One, in a brickyard, with a rotted board top.
I savoured the rich crash when a bucket
Plummeted down at the end of a rope.
So deep you saw no reflection in it.

---

1 *a mountain sacred to the Muses and location of the fountains of Aganippe and Hippocrene, which provided inspiration for anyone drinking there.*
2 *a Northern Irish poet.*

A shallow one under a dry stone ditch
10   Fructified like any aquarium.
When you dragged out long roots from the soft mulch
A white face hovered over the bottom.

Others had echoes, gave back your own call
With a clean new music in it. And one
15   Was scaresome for there, out of ferns and tall
Foxgloves, a rat slapped across my reflection.

Now, to pry into roots, to finger slime,
To stare, big-eyed Narcissus,[3] into some spring
Is beneath all adult dignity. I rhyme
20   To see myself, to set the darkness echoing.

(1966)

The Otter

When you plunged
The light of Tuscany wavered
And swung through the pool
From top to bottom.

5   I loved your wet head and smashing crawl,
Your fine swimmer's back and shoulders
Surfacing and surfacing again
This year and every year since.

I sat dry-throated on the warm stones.
10   You were beyond me.
The mellowed clarities, the grape-deep air
Thinned and disappointed.

3   in Greek mythology a beautiful youth who fell in love with his own reflection.

Thank God for the slow loadening,
When I hold you now
15   We are close and deep
As the atmosphere on water.

My two hands are plumbed water.
You are my palpable, lithe
Otter of memory
20   In the pool of the moment,

Turning to swim on your back,
Each silent, thigh-shaking kick
Re-tilting the light,
Heaving the cool at your neck.

25   And suddenly you're out,
Back again, intent as ever,
Heavy and frisky in your freshened pelt,
Printing the stones.

(1979)

The Singer's House

When they said *Carrickfergus*[1] I could hear
the frosty echo of saltminers' picks.
I imagined it, chambered and glinting,
a township built of light.

5   What do we say any more
to conjure the salt of our earth?
So much comes and is gone
that should be crystal and kept

---

1 *Northern Irish salt-mining area and seaport, the subject of a popular Irish folksong.*

and amicable weathers
10 that bring up the grain of things,
their tang of season and store,
are all the packing we'll get.

So I say to myself *Gweebarra*[2]
and its music hits off the place
15 like water hitting off granite.
I see the glittering sound

framed in your window,
knives and forks set on oilcloth,
and the seals' heads, suddenly outlined,
20 scanning everything.

People here used to believe
that drowned souls lived in the seals.
At spring tides they might change shape.
They loved music and swam in for a singer

25 who might stand at the end of summer
in the mouth of a whitewashed turf-shed,
his shoulder to the jamb, his song
a rowboat far out in evening.

When I came here first you were always singing,
30 a hint of the clip of the pick
in your winnowing climb and attack.
Raise it again, man. We still believe what we hear.

(1979)

---

2 *the bay in County Donegal in the Irish Republic.*

The Harvest Bow

As you plaited the harvest bow
You implicated the mellowed silence in you
In wheat that does not rust
But brightens as it tightens twist by twist
Into a knowable corona,
A throwaway love-knot of straw.

Hands that aged round ashplants and cane sticks
And lapped the spurs on a lifetime of game cocks
Harked to their gift and worked with fine intent
Until your fingers moved somnambulant:
I tell and finger it like braille,
Gleaning the unsaid off the palpable,

And if I spy into its golden loops
I see us walk between the railway slopes
Into an evening of long grass and midges,
Blue smoke straight up, old beds and ploughs in hedges,
An auction notice on an outhouse wall —
You with a harvest bow in your lapel,

Me with the fishing rod, already homesick
For the big lift of these evenings, as your stick
Whacking the tips off weeds and bushes
Beats out of time, and beats, but flushes
Nothing: that original townland
Still tongue-tied in the straw tied by your hand.

The end of art is peace
Could be the motto of this frail device
That I have pinned up on our deal dresser —
Like a drawn snare
Slipped lately by the spirit of the corn
Yet burnished by its passage, and still warm.

(1979)

Casualty[1]

I

He would drink by himself
And raise a weathered thumb
Towards the high shelf,
Calling another rum
5   And blackcurrant, without
Having to raise his voice,
Or order a quick stout
By a lifting of the eyes
And a discreet dumb-show
10   Of pulling off the top;
At closing time would go
In waders and peaked cap
Into the showery dark,
A dole-kept[2] breadwinner
15   But a natural for work.
I loved his whole manner,
Sure-footed but too sly,
His deadpan sidling tact,
His fisherman's quick eye
20   And turned observant back.

Incomprehensible
To him, my other life.
Sometimes, on his high stool,
Too busy with his knife
25   At a tobacco plug
And not meeting my eye,
In the pause after a slug
He mentioned poetry.
We would be on our own

---

1 *Heaney has identified the subject of this poem as Louis O'Neill, who frequented a pub owned by Heaney's father-in-law in County Tyrone. An alcoholic, O'Neill defied a curfew imposed by Catholics who were mourning the thirteen men shot dead by British soldiers on "Bloody Sunday," January 30, 1972. The men were killed after violence erupted during an illegal march organized by the Derry Civil Rights Association. As Heaney noted, O'Neill was killed by a bomb "planted by his own people."*
2 *one who lives on social assistance payments "doled out" by the government.*

30   And, always politic
        And shy of condescension,
        I would manage by some trick
        To switch the talk to eels
        Or lore of the horse and cart
35   Or the Provisionals.[3]

        But my tentative art
        His turned back watches too:
        He was blown to bits
        Out drinking in a curfew
40   Others obeyed, three nights
        After they shot dead
        The thirteen men in Derry.
        PARAS THIRTEEN, the walls said,
        BOGSIDE NIL.[4] That Wednesday
45   Everybody held
        His breath and trembled.

                    II
        It was a day of cold
        Raw silence, wind-blown
        Surplice and soutane:[5]
50   Rained-on, flower-laden
        Coffin after coffin
        Seemed to float from the door
        Of the packed cathedral
        Like blossoms on slow water.
55   The common funeral
        Unrolled its swaddling band,
        Lapping, tightening
        Till we were braced and bound
        Like brothers in a ring.

---

3 the Provisional Irish Republican Army, a militant group that split off from the IRA in December 1969 when the IRA decided to give at least token recognition to three parliaments: Westminster, Dublin, and Stormont.
4 the slogan on the wall is like a football score. Paras are the members of the First Parachute Regiment, who had killed the thirteen men on Bloody Sunday; Bogside is the working-class Catholic district in which the killings occurred.
5 a soutane, or cassock, is a long, loose-fitting garment worn by priests, altar boys, and choristers; a surplice is a loose-fitting, wide-sleeved white vestment worn over the soutane.

60   But he would not be held
At home by his own crowd
Whatever threats were phoned,
Whatever black flags waved.
I see him as he turned
65   In that bombed offending place,
Remorse fused with terror
In his still knowable face,
His cornered outfaced stare
Blinding in the flash.

70   He had gone miles away
For he drank like a fish
Nightly, naturally
Swimming towards the lure
Of warm lit-up places,
75   The blurred mesh and murmur
Drifting among glasses
In the gregarious smoke.
How culpable was he
That last night when he broke
80   Our tribe's complicity?
'Now you're supposed to be
An educated man,'
I hear him say. 'Puzzle me
The right answer to that one.'

III

85   I missed his funeral,
Those quiet walkers
And sideways talkers
Shoaling out of his lane
To the respectable
90   Purring of the hearse . . .
They move in equal pace
With the habitual
Slow consolation
Of a dawdling engine,

95   The line lifted, hand
Over fist, cold sunshine
On the water, the land
Banked under fog: that morning
I was taken in his boat,
100   The screw purling,[6] turning
Indolent fathoms white,
I tasted freedom with him.
To get out early, haul
Steadily off the bottom,
105   Dispraise the catch, and smile
As you find a rhythm
Working you, slow mile by mile,
Into your proper haunt
Somewhere, well out, beyond . . .

110   Dawn-sniffing revenant,[7]
Plodder through midnight rain,
Question me again.

(1979)

6 *the boat's propeller, or screw, is making a murmuring sound.*
7 *one who returns, such as a ghost or spirit after death.*

Margaret Atwood

(1939–   )

Internationally successful as both a poet and novelist, Margaret Atwood was born in Ottawa and educated at the University of Toronto and Radcliffe College, Harvard. She has worked as a book editor, has taught English at several universities, and has been a university writer in residence. Her first book was a thin volume of poems, Double Persephone *(1961). Her second collection,* The Circle Game *(1966), won the Governor General's Award. Her novels include* Surfacing *(1972) and* The Handmaid's Tale *(1985), winner of the Governor General's Award for fiction.* Survival *(1972) is a controversial study of Canadian literature in which she expands upon Northrop Frye's analysis of the "garrison mentality" and argues that Canadian literature is dominated by images of victims. In her own poetry, she often explores victimization and liberation, dissecting the personal, psychological, cultural, political, and sexual ideas or myths confining the individual. This exploration frequently challenges both conventional perceptions of reality and conventional logic. Although she has said that sound and phrasing are important elements in her poetry, Atwood does not indulge in verbal pyrotechnics. Typically, her narrators employ startlingly provocative and often violent images, but they make thematic pronouncements in a flat, unemotional voice. In this way, she conveys both the violence of the modern world and the alienation of its victims.*

Progressive Insanities of a Pioneer

i
He stood, a point
on a sheet of green paper
proclaiming himself the centre,

with no walls, no borders
anywhere; the sky no height
above him, totally un-
enclosed
and shouted:

Let me out!

ii

10　He dug the soil in rows,
imposed himself with shovels
He asserted
into the furrows, I
am not random.

15　The ground
replied with aphorisms:

a tree-sprout, a nameless
weed, words
he couldn't understand.

iii

20　The house pitched
the plot staked
in the middle of nowhere.

At night the mind
inside, in the middle
25　of nowhere.

The idea of an animal
patters across the roof.

In the darkness the fields
defend themselves with fences
30　in vain:
everything
is getting in.

iv

By daylight he resisted.
He said, disgusted
35　with the swamp's clamourings and the outbursts
of rocks,
This is not order
but the absence
of order.

40   He was wrong, the unanswering
      forest implied:

            It was
            an ordered absence

      v
      For many years
45   he fished for a great vision,
      dangling the hooks of sown
      roots under the surface
      of the shallow earth.

      It was like
50   enticing whales with a bent
      pin. Besides he thought

      in that country
      only the worms were biting.

      vi
      If he had known unstructured
55   space is a deluge
      and stocked his log house-
      boat with all the animals

      even the wolves,

      he might have floated.

60   But obstinate he
      stated, The land is solid
      and stamped,

      watching his foot sink
      down through stone
65   up to the knee.

vii
Things
refused to name themselves; refused
to let him name them.

The wolves hunted
70   outside.

On his beaches, his clearings,
by the surf of under-
growth breaking
at his feet, he foresaw
75   disintegration
             and in the end
through eyes
made ragged by his
effort, the tension
between subject and object,

80   the green
vision, the unnamed
whale invaded.

(1968)

The Animals in That Country

In that country the animals
have the faces of people:

the ceremonial
cats possessing the streets

5   the fox run
politely to earth, the huntsmen
standing around him, fixed
in their tapestry of manners

the bull, embroidered
10   with blood and given
an elegant death, trumpets, his name
stamped on him, heraldic brand
because

(when he rolled
15   on the sand, sword in his heart, the teeth
in his blue mouth were human)

he is really a man

even the wolves, holding resonant
conversations in their
20   forests thickened with legend.

In this country the animals
have the faces of
animals.

Their eyes
25   flash once in car headlights
and are gone.

Their deaths are not elegant.

They have the faces of
no-one.

(1968)

Further Arrivals[1]

After we had crossed the long illness
that was the ocean, we sailed up-river

On the first island
the immigrants threw off their clothes
5   and danced like sandflies

We left behind one by one
the cities rotting with cholera,
one by one our civilized
distinctions

10   and entered a large darkness.

It was our own
ignorance we entered.

I have not come out yet

My brain gropes nervous
15   tentacles in the night, sends out
fears hairy as bears,
demands lamps; or waiting

for my shadowy husband, hears
malice in the trees' whispers.

20   I need wolf's eyes to see
the truth.

---

1 *the speaker in this poem is Susanna Moodie (1803–85), a pioneer settler and author. Atwood based events in this and the other poems in* The Journals of Susanna Moodie *(1970) on Mrs. Moodie's accounts of her life in* Roughing It in the Bush *(1852) and* Life in the Clearings *(1853).*

I refuse to look in a mirror.

Whether the wilderness is
real or not
25   depends on who lives there.

(1970)

you fit into me

you fit into me
like a hook into an eye

a fish hook
an open eye

(1973)

Variations on the Word *Love*

This is a word we use to plug
holes with. It's the right size for those warm
blanks in speech, for those red heart-
shaped vacancies on the page that look nothing
5   like real hearts. Add lace
and you can sell
it. We insert it also in the one empty
space on the printed form
that comes with no instructions. There are whole
10   magazines with not much in them
but the word *love*, you can
rub it all over your body and you
can cook with it too. How do we know
it isn't what goes on at the cool
15   debaucheries of slugs under damp

pieces of cardboard? As for the weed-
seedlings nosing their tough snouts up
among the lettuces, they shout it.
Love! Love! sing the soldiers, raising
20   their glittering knives in salute.

Then there's the two
of us. This word
is far too short for us, it has only
four letters, too sparse
25   to fill those deep bare
vacuums between the stars
that press on us with their deafness.
It's not love we don't wish
to fall into, but that fear.
30   This word is not enough but it will
have to do. It's a single
vowel in this metallic
silence, a mouth that says
O again and again in wonder
35   and pain, a breath, a finger-
grip on a cliffside. You can
hold on or let go.

(1981)

A Women's Issue

The woman in the spiked device
that locks around the waist and between
the legs, with holes in it like a tea strainer
is Exhibit A.

5   The woman in black with a net window
to see through and a four-inch
wooden peg jammed up
between her legs so she can't be raped
is Exhibit B.

10   Exhibit C is the young girl
dragged into the bush by the midwives
and made to sing while they scrape the flesh
from between her legs, then tie her thighs
till she scabs over and is called healed.

15   Now she can be married.
For each childbirth they'll cut her
open, then sew her up.
Men like tight women.
The ones that die are carefully buried.

20   The next exhibit lies flat on her back
while eighty men a night
move through her, ten an hour.
She looks at the ceiling, listens
to the door open and close.
25   A bell keeps ringing.
Nobody knows how she got here.

You'll notice that what they have in common
is between the legs. Is this
why wars are fought?
30   Enemy territory, no man's
land, to be entered furtively,
fenced, owned but never surely,
scene of these desperate forays
at midnight, captures
35   and sticky murders, doctors' rubber gloves
greasy with blood, flesh made inert, the surge
of your own uneasy power.

This is no museum.
Who invented the word *love*?

(1981)

Interlunar[1]

Darkness waits apart from any occasion for it;
like sorrow it is always available.
This is only one kind,

the kind in which there are stars
5   above the leaves, brilliant as steel nails
and countless and without regard.

We are walking together
on dead wet leaves in the intermoon
among the looming nocturnal rocks
10   which would be pinkish grey
in daylight, gnawed and softened
by moss and ferns, which would be green,
in the musty fresh yeast smell
of trees rotting, each returning
15   itself to itself

and I take your hand, which is the shape a hand
would be if you existed truly.
I wish to show you the darkness
you are so afraid of.

20   Trust me. This darkness
is a place you can enter and be
as safe in as you are anywhere;
you can put one foot in front of the other
and believe the sides of your eyes.
25   Memorize it. You will know it
again in your own time.
When the appearances of things have left you,
you will still have this darkness.
Something of your own you can carry with you.

---

1 *the period between the old and the new moon.*

30 We have come to the edge:
the lake gives off its hush;
in the outer night there is a barred owl
calling, like a moth
against the ear, from the far shore
35 which is invisible.
The lake, vast and dimensionless,
doubles everything, the stars,
the boulders, itself, even the darkness
that you can walk so long in
40 it becomes light.

(1984)

GWENDOLYN MACEWEN

(1941–1987)

orn in Toronto, Gwendolyn MacEwen grew up there and in Winnipeg. She discovered her calling as a writer early: at the age of seventeen she published her first poem, and she left school the next year to pursue her career. In addition to poetry, MacEwen wrote two novels, a collection of short stories, two children's books, and a number of radio plays and documentaries. Her books of poetry include A Breakfast for Barbarians *(1966),* The Shadow-Maker *(1969), winner of the Governor General's Award, and* The T.E. Lawrence Poems *(1982). MacEwen said of her work: "I write basically to communicate joy, mystery, passion . . . not the joy that naively exists without knowledge of pain, but that joy which arises out of and conquers pain. I want to construct a myth." MacEwen constructs her myth, which celebrates the triumph of the human spirit, with materials borrowed from a variety of traditions. Lush, even exotic, imagery establishes the dualities that are central to her mythic vision. Throughout her poetry, she explores meaningful relationships between spiritual and physical worlds, archetypal and mundane experience, waking and dreaming consciousness, past and present times, painful and joyful events, and male and female lives.*

Dark Pines under Water

This land like a mirror turns you inward
And you become a forest in a furtive lake;
The dark pines of your mind reach downward,
You dream in the green of your time,
5   Your memory is a row of sinking pines.

Explorer, you tell yourself this is not what you came for
Although it is good here, and green;
You had meant to move with a kind of largeness,
You had planned a heavy grace, an anguished dream.

10   But the dark pines of your mind dip deeper
And you are sinking, sinking, sleeper
In an elementary world;
There is something down there and you want it told.

(1969)

The Real Enemies[1]

In that land where the soul aged long before the body,
My nameless men, my glamorous bodyguards,
                                        died for me.
My deadly friends with their rouged lips and pretty eyes
    died for me; *my bed of tulips* I called them,
5   who wore every colour but the white
    that was mine alone to wear.

But they could not guard me against the real enemies —
Omnipotence, and the Infinite —
                    those beasts the soul invents
    and then bows down before.
10   The real enemies were not the men of Fakhri Pasha,[2] nor
Were they even of this world.
                        One could never conquer them,
Never. Hope was another of them, Hope, most brutal of all.

For those who thought clearly, failure was the only goal.
Only failure could redeem you, there where the soul aged
    long before the body.
15   You failed at last, you fell into the delicious light
    and were free.

---

1 *the speaker in this poem from* The T.E. Lawrence Poems *is Thomas Edward Lawrence (1888–1935), a British archaeologist, soldier, and adventurer, who became known as Lawrence of Arabia. Working for British intelligence in Egypt during World War I, he joined the Arab forces and became a leader in their revolt against Turkish rule. A nearly legendary figure, he recorded his Arabian exploits in* The Seven Pillars of Wisdom *(1935).*

2 *notoriously ruthless commander of the Turkish forces.*

And there was much honour in this;

it was a worthy defeat.

Islam is surrender[3] — the passionate surrender of the self,
the puny self, to God.

We declared a Holy War upon Him and were victors as He won.

(1982)

But

Out there in the large dark and in the long light is the breathless
Poem,
As ruthless and beautiful and amoral as the world is,
As nature is.

5   In the end there's just me and the bloody Poem and the murderous
Tongues of the trees,
Their glossy green syllables licking my mind (the green
Work of the wind).

Out there in the night between two trees is the Poem saying:
10   Do not hate me
Because I peeled the veil from your eyes and tore your world
To shreds, and brought

The darkness down upon your head. Here is a book of tongues,
Take it. (Dark leaves invade the air.)
15   *Beware! Now I know a language so beautiful and lethal*
My mouth bleeds when I speak it.

(1987)

---

3 *Islam, the religion whose prophet was Muhammad (570–632), means, in Arabic, surrender or submission to*
God.

MICHAEL ONDAATJE

(1943–   )

orn in Colombo, Ceylon (now Sri Lanka), Ondaatje moved to England when he was eleven and came to Canada in 1962. He received a B.A. from the University of Toronto and an M.A. from Queen's. He currently teaches at York University. Ondaatje began his career as a poet, publishing his first book in 1967. He has also produced novels, films, criticism, and anthologies. He has won the Governor General's Award twice: for The Collected Works of Billy the Kid *(1970), in which he combined poetry and prose, and for* There's a Trick with a Knife I'm Learning to Do: Poems 1973–1978 *(1979). Ondaatje most frequently explores the tensions between the subjective inner vision and the supposedly objective and logical realm of outward reality. Dissatisfied with traditional classifications and methods, he challenges both conventional perceptions and literary forms by mixing prose and poetry, fact and fiction, realism and surrealism, lyricism and violence.*

Elizabeth[1]

Catch, my Uncle Jack[2] said
and oh I caught this huge apple
red as Mrs Kelly's[3] bum.
It's red as Mrs Kelly's bum, I said
5   and Daddy[4] roared
and swung me on his stomach with a heave.
Then I hid the apple in my room
till it shrunk like a face
growing eyes and teeth ribs.

10   Then Daddy took me to the zoo
he knew the man there
they put a snake around my neck
and it crawled down the front of my dress.

---

1 *the speaker is Elizabeth I (1533–1603).*
2 *a fictitious character, probably not an actual uncle but a man given that title because of familiarity with the child.*
3 *a fictitious character, probably a nurse.*
4 *Elizabeth's father, Henry VIII (1491–1547).*

I felt its flicking tongue
15   dripping onto me like a shower.
Daddy laughed and said Smart Snake
and Mrs Kelly with us scowled.

In the pond where they kept the goldfish
Philip[5] and I broke the ice with spades
20   and tried to spear the fishes;
we killed one and Philip ate it,
then he kissed me
with raw saltless fish in his mouth.

My sister Mary's got bad teeth
25   and said I was lucky, then she said
I had big teeth, but Philip said I was pretty.
He had big hands that smelled.

I would speak of Tom,[6] soft laughing,
who danced in the mornings round the sundial
30   teaching me the steps from France, turning
with the rhythm of the sun on the warped branches,
who'd hold my breast and watch it move like a snail
leaving his quick urgent love in my palm.
And I kept his love in my palm till it blistered.

35   When they axed his shoulders and neck
the blood moved like a branch into the crowd.
And he staggered with his hanging shoulder
cursing their thrilled cry, wheeling,
waltzing in the French style to his knees
40   holding his head with the ground,
blood settling on his clothes like a blush;
this way
when they aimed the thud into his back.

---

5 *Philip II of Spain (1527–98) married Elizabeth's sister Mary Tudor (1515–58) in 1554. After Mary's death, he unsuccessfully sought to marry Elizabeth.*

6 *Lord Thomas Seymour of Sudeley (c. 1508–49) was executed for intriguing against his brother, Edward, Duke of Somerset, Lord Protector of the Realm. He vainly sought the hand of Elizabeth, having treated her with marked indelicacy when she stayed at his house.*

And I find cool entertainment now
45   with white young Essex,[7] and my nimble rhymes.[8]

(1967)

White Dwarfs[1]

This is for people who disappear
for those who descend into the code
and make their room a fridge for Superman
— who exhaust costume and bones that could perform
        flight,
5   who shave their moral so raw
they can tear themselves through the eye of a needle
this is for those people
that hover and hover
and die in the ether peripheries

10   There is my fear
of no words   of
falling without words
over and over   of
mouthing the silence
15   Why do I love most
among my heroes those
who sail to that perfect edge
where there is no social fuel
Release of sandbags
20   to understand their altitude —

that silence of the third cross[2]
3rd man hung so high and lonely
we don't hear him say

7 Robert Devereux (1566–1601), the second Earl of Essex and one of Elizabeth's confidants, was executed for
attempting to raise a rebellion.
8 Elizabeth wrote lyric poetry.

1 whitish stars of the average mass but of such small dimensions that their density is enormous.
2 according to Luke 23:39–43, one of the two malefactors crucified with Christ called on Christ to save himself
and them; the other rebuked him, saying that they deserved their punishment, whereas Christ was innocent. He
then asked Christ to remember him in his kingdom, but the other criminal said nothing more.

say his pain, say his unbrotherhood
25   What has he to do with the smell of ladies
can they eat off his skeleton of pain?

The Gurkhas[3] in Malaya
cut the tongues of mules
so they were silent beasts of burden
30   in enemy territories
after such cruelty what could they speak of anyway
And Dashiell Hammett[4] in success
suffered conversation and moved
to the perfect white between the words

35   This white that can grow
is fridge, bed,
is an egg — most beautiful
when unbroken, where
what we cannot see is growing
40   in all the colours we cannot see

there are those burned out stars
who implode into silence
after parading in the sky
after such choreography what would they wish to speak of anyway

(1973)

---

3 Nepalese mercenary soldiers in the service of the British army.
4 an American novelist (1894–1961), Hammett was the originator of the "hard-boiled" school of detective fiction
and wrote such popular works as The Maltese Falcon (1930) and The Thin Man (1932), which became
successful Hollywood films.

Letters & Other Worlds

"for there was no more darkness for him and, no doubt
like Adam before the fall, he could see in the dark"[1]

My father's body was a globe of fear
His body was a town we never knew
He hid that he had been where we were going
His letters were a room he seldom lived in
In them the logic of his love could grow

My father's body was a town of fear
He was the only witness to its fear dance
He hid where he had been that we might lose him
His letters were a room his body scared

He came to death with his mind drowning.
On the last day he enclosed himself
in a room with two bottles of gin, later
fell the length of his body
so that brain blood moved
to new compartments
that never knew the wash of fluid
and he died in minutes of a new equilibrium.

His early life was a terrifying comedy
and my mother divorced him again and again.
He would rush into tunnels magnetized
by the white eye of trains
and once, gaining instant fame,
managed to stop a Perahara[2] in Ceylon
— the whole procession of elephants dancers
local dignitaries — by falling
dead drunk onto the street.

1 *from* "Descendit ad infernos" *(He Descends to the Underworld), a chapter for Alfred Jarry's* La dragonne
(1943), quoted in Roger Shattuck's The Banquet Years: The Arts in France, 1885–1918 *(1955). The*
clause immediately preceding the section Ondaatje quotes is "But soon he could drink no more."
2 *Sinhalese for* procession; *a perahara was most frequently associated with a religious celebration or marriage.*

As a semi-official, and semi-white at that,
the act was seen as a crucial
turning point in the Home Rule Movement
30   and led to Ceylon's independence in 1948.

(My mother had done her share too —
her driving so bad
she was stoned by villagers
whenever her car was recognized)

35   For 14 years of marriage
each of them claimed he or she
was the injured party.
Once on the Colombo docks
saying goodbye to a recently married couple
40   my father, jealous
at my mother's articulate emotion,
dove into the waters of the harbour
and swam after the ship waving farewell.
My mother pretending no affiliation
45   mingled with the crowd back to the hotel.

Once again he made the papers
though this time my mother
with a note to the editor
corrected the report — saying he was drunk
50   rather than broken hearted at the parting of friends.
The married couple received both editions
of *The Ceylon Times* when their ship reached Aden.³

And then in his last years
he was the silent drinker,
55   the man who once a week
disappeared into his room with bottles
and stayed there until he was drunk
and until he was sober.

---

3 *the capital of the British colony of Aden and later the capital of the People's Democratic Republic of Yemen; port
of call on voyages through the Suez Canal.*

There speeches, head dreams, apologies,
60   the gentle letters, were composed.
With the clarity of architects
he would write of the row of blue flowers
his new wife had planted,
the plans for electricity in the house,
65   how my half-sister fell near a snake
and it had awakened and not touched her.
Letters in a clear hand of the most complete empathy
his heart widening and widening and widening
to all manner of change in his children and friends
70   while he himself edged
into the terrible acute hatred
of his own privacy
till he balanced and fell
the length of his body
75   the blood screaming in
the empty reservoir of bones
the blood searching in his head without metaphor

(1973)

Bearhug

Griffin calls to come and kiss him goodnight
I yell ok. Finish something I'm doing,
then something else, walk slowly round
the corner to my son's room.
5   He is standing arms outstretched
waiting for a bearhug. Grinning.

Why do I give my emotion an animal's name,
give it that dark squeeze of death?
This is the hug which collects

10   all his small bones and his warm neck against me.
      The thin tough body under the pyjamas
      locks to me like a magnet of blood.

      How long was he standing there
      like that, before I came?

                                                    (1979)

The Cinnamon Peeler[1]

      If I were a cinnamon peeler
      I would ride your bed
      and leave the yellow bark dust
      on your pillow.

5   Your breasts and shoulders would reek
      you could never walk through markets
      without the profession of my fingers
      floating over you. The blind would
      stumble certain of whom they approached
10   though you might bathe
      under rain gutters, monsoon.

      Here on the upper thigh
      at this smooth pasture
      neighbour to your hair
15   or the crease
      that cuts your back. This ankle.
      You will be known among strangers
      as the cinnamon peeler's wife.

      I could hardly glance at you
20   before marriage
      never touch you
      — your keen nosed mother, your rough brothers.

---

1 *one who peels from the cinnamon tree the bark whose inner layer provides the aromatic spice.*

I buried my hands
in saffron, disguised them
25   over smoking tar,
helped the honey gatherers . . .

*

When we swam once
I touched you in water
and our bodies remained free,
30   you could hold me and be blind of smell.
You climbed the bank and said

        this is how you touch other women
the grass cutter's wife, the lime burner's daughter.
And you searched your arms
35   for the missing perfume
        and knew

        what good is it
to be the lime burner's daughter
left with no trace
40   as if not spoken to in the act of love
as if wounded without the pleasure of a scar.

You touched
your belly to my hands
in the dry air and said
I am the cinnamon
45   peeler's wife. Smell me.

                                        (1982)

To a Sad Daughter

All night long the hockey pictures
gaze down at you
sleeping in your tracksuit.
Belligerent goalies are your ideal.

5 Threats of being traded
cuts and wounds
— all this pleases you.
O my god! you say at breakfast
reading the sports page over the Alpen[1]
10 as another player breaks his ankle
or assaults the coach.

When I thought of daughters
I wasn't expecting this
but I like this more.
15 I like all your faults
even your purple moods
when you retreat from everyone
to sit in bed under a quilt.
And when I say 'like'
20 I mean of course 'love'
but that embarrasses you.
You who feel superior to black and white movies
(coaxed for hours to see *Casablanca*)[2]
though you were moved
25 by *Creature from the Black Lagoon.*[3]

One day I'll come swimming
beside your ship or someone will
and if you hear the siren[4]
listen to it. For if you close your ears
30 only nothing happens. You will never change.

I don't care if you risk
your life to angry goalies
creatures with webbed feet.
You can enter their caves and castles
35 their glass laboratories. Just
don't be fooled by anyone but yourself.

1 *a brand of breakfast cereal.*
2 *celebrated 1942 film starring Humphrey Bogart and Ingrid Bergman.*
3 *1954 monster film starring Richard Carlson.*
4 *sirens were mythical creatures, half-woman and half-bird, who used their sweet song to lure sailors. In the*
   Odyssey, Odysseus (Ulysses) escaped by stopping the ears of the members of his crew with wax and then lashing
   himself to the ship's mast.

This is the first lecture I've given you.
You're 'sweet sixteen' you said.
I'd rather be your closest friend
40 than your father. I'm not good at advice
you know that, but ride
the ceremonies
until they grow dark.

Sometimes you are so busy
45 discovering your friends
I ache with a loss
— but that is greed.
And sometimes I've gone
into *my* purple world
50 and lost you.

One afternoon I stepped
into your room. You were sitting
at the desk where I now write this.
Forsythia outside the window
55 and sun spilled over you
like a thick yellow miracle
as if another planet
was coaxing you out of the house
— all those possible worlds! —
60 and you, meanwhile, busy with mathematics.

I cannot look at forsythia now
without loss, or joy for you.
You step delicately
into the wild world
65 and your real prize will be
the frantic search.
Want everything. If you break
break going out not in.
How you live your life I don't care
70 but I'll sell my arms for you,
hold your secrets forever.

If I speak of death
which you fear now, greatly,
it is without answers,
75   except that each
one we know is
in our blood.
Don't recall graves.
Memory is permanent.
80   Remember the afternoon's
yellow suburban annunciation.
Your goalie
in his frightening mask
dreams perhaps
85   of gentleness.

(1984)

When you drive the Queensborough roads at midnight

do not look at a star
or full moon. Look out for frogs.
And not the venerable ones who recline
on gravel parallel to the highway
5   but the foolhardy, bored on a country night
dazzled by the adventure of passing beams.

We know their type of course, local heroes
who take off their bandanas and leap naked,
night green, seduced
10   by the whispers of michelin.

To them we are distinct death.
I am fond of these foolish things
more than the moon.

They welcome me after absence.
15 One of them is my youth
still jumping into rivers
take care and beware of him.

Knowing you love this landscape
there are few rules.
20 Do not gaze at moons.
Nuzzle the heat in granite.
Swim toward pictographs.[1]
Touch only reflections.

(1984)

---

1 *pictures used as symbols or as records, as in early native Canadian rock paintings.*

LINDA HOGAN

(1947–   )

inda Hogan says that the fact that her father was a Chickasaw and her mother a white has had a profound impact on her poetry: "This created a natural tension that surfaces in my work and strengthens it." Born in Denver but raised on Chickasaw "relocation land" in Oklahoma, she grew up listening to the tales of her father's family, something that she says affected the oral quality and organization of her poetry. Hogan received an M.A. in English and creative writing from the University of Colorado. She taught for several years at the University of Minnesota but now is an associate professor of native American studies at the University of Colorado, Boulder. Hogan's published works include Calling Myself Home *(1978) and* Seeing through the Sun *(1985) — both volumes of poetry — and* Mean Spirit *(1990), a novel. Although she writes effectively of the ordinary experiences of motherhood and city life, many of her finest poems draw on her sense of her native heritage as a living force and on her feelings of connection to the land. Hogan's poetry is often allusive and intellectual, drawing on elements of native American history and tradition, but the quality she prizes most is the naturalness that comes when "the earth writes through me. . . ."*

The Sand Roses

They lie down in the fields,
what labor,
born of nothing,
the geology of flowers
5   sifting together.
I hear them forming
as once I heard
invisible hooves of elk
rumbling over the land,
10   and heard the breastplate of Crazy Horse,[1]
a man who listened to stones,

---

1 *Crazy Horse (c. 1840–77) was a chief of the Oglala Sioux. He led the resistance against the whites trying to settle the mineral-rich Black Hills of South Dakota, which had been granted to the Sioux by treaty. Highly revered by natives, he was known to have visions — as a youth, he saw himself as a warrior wearing a sacred stone in his ear, his body streaked with the marks of lightning and hailstones, riding a horse through battle, with arrows and bullets missing him — and he regarded this world as a dream world separated from the real world of spirit. A clever tactician, he was instrumental in the defeat of George Armstrong Custer at the Battle of the Little Bighorn, June 25, 1876. Crazy Horse was killed while resisting arrest at Fort Robinson, Nebraska. His parents buried his heart in a secret spot in the Black Hills.*

singing a museum back to life,
singing to breathless animals
the song of all people.

15   It was on his breast,
that song
that bone plate
that thin flesh
over lungs and heart, on skin
20   moving across the land,
the song of all people in a stone
he wore beneath his arm.

Beyond time,
beyond space
25   Nijinski[2] heard that stone
and danced his body into the shape
of Guernica[3] and war.
Who didn't know
gods live in stone and in our bodies,
30   that inside each other's skin
we hear voices
in the solar plexus
the heart
the ancient ones that burn inside us
35   rising up from nothing
in the dark fields of ourselves
like roses.

Beyond skin and stone and nations
all of earth's creations dance together
40   drawing together
the songs of warriors
drawing the dances
all over the globe
like a magnet

2   *Vaslav Nijinsky (1890–1950) was a Russian ballet dancer noted for spectacular leaps and sensitive interpretation. As both dancer and choreographer, he ushered in a new era of dance. He retired from the stage in 1914 as the result of a breakdown that was diagnosed as schizophrenia.*
3   *Guernica y Luno, a city in the Basque province of Vizcaya (Biscay) in northern Spain, led the agitation for Basque statehood and was bombed in 1937, during the Spanish Civil War, by German planes. This inspired Pablo Picasso's (1881–1973)* Guernica, *a painting protesting war and fascism.*

with her iron roses,
45   sand roses of America,
Indian roses,
the Russian dancing roses of flesh,
Africa,
the opening roses of the eye's pupil,
50   the singing mouth,
genital roses
heart roses pounding
breaking into the world
the tiny pieces of life coming together
55   where the mysteries in the ruins
of the dead
are speaking
in the red temples of the living.

(1985)

DIONNE BRAND

(1953–   )

orn in Guayguayare, Trinidad, Dionne Brand moved to Toronto in 1970 to study at the University of Toronto, where she earned an honours degree in English and drama. She published her first volume of poetry, 'Fore Day Morning, in 1978. Chronicles of the Hostile Sun *(1984) records her experiences in Grenada in the months leading up to the American invasion in October 1983. A vocal feminist and advocate for black rights, Brand frequently attacks imperialism and patriarchy in her poetry. Impassioned and allusive, these poems focus on the abuses suffered and the heroism displayed by both blacks and women.*

Eurocentric

There are things you do not believe
there are things you cannot believe
(in fairness i do not mean women here except
jean kirkpatrick¹ and the like)
5   these things
they include such items as
revolutions, when they are made by people of colour
truth, when it is told by your privilege
percussive piano solos, squawking saxophones
10   rosa parks'² life, bessie smith's³ life and any life
which is not your own,
ripe oranges with green skins,
blacks lynched in the american way,

1 Jeane Kirkpatrick (1926–   ), a conservative political scientist and professor, was the U.S. permanent representative to the United Nations (1981–85).
2 Rosa Parks (1913–77) is sometimes cited as "the Mother of the Modern Civil Rights Movement" because her arrest when she refused to relinquish a bus seat to a white passenger initiated the Montgomery, Alabama, bus boycott in 1955, a boycott that itself marked the beginning of concerted civil rights actions throughout the American South.
3 Bessie Smith (1898?–1937), known as the "Empress of the Blues," was one of the greatest blues singers. She died in an automobile accident: many people believe that had she been white she would have received medical attention earlier and would have survived.

Orange Free State,[4] bantustans,[5]

15 people waking up in the morning, in any place where you
do not live,
people anywhere other than where you live wanting
freedom
instead of your charity and coca-cola,

20 the truth about ITT[6] or AFL-CIO[7]
until it is a blithe expose in your newspaper,
women, who do not need men
(even male revolutionaries refuse to radicalise their balls)

25 housework
massacres more in number than 1 american officer
4 american nuns,[8]
sugar apples, cutlass mangoes, sapodillas,[9]
and an assortment of fruit

30 which having never rested on your tongue
you name exotic,
chains other than ornamental ones,
war, unless you see burning children;
hunger, unless you see burning children;

35 hibiscus flowers and anthurium lilies
rain, on a beach in the caribbean.

(1984)

---

4 *the smallest of the four provinces of the Republic of South Africa and a stronghold for Afrikaner culture and the policy of apartheid, the official system of segregation in effect at the time the poem was written.*

5 *officially called Bantu Homelands, these were the segregated territories set aside for South Africa's "Bantus," the term the government of the day officially designated to replace the terms "native" or "African" when speaking of blacks. The Bantustans were organized according to tribal groupings, the actual Bantu being but one of these groups.*

6 *ITT Corporation was known until 1983 as IT&T (International Telephone and Telegraph). Incorporated in 1920 from several Caribbean telephone and telegraph companies, it established its headquarters in New York and became known for the manufacture of telecommunications, electronic, and defence equipment. In 1987, ITT divested itself of these in order to concentrate on food, hotel, publishing, and insurance businesses.*

7 *American Federation of Labor and Congress of Industrial Organizations, the leading voice in American trade unionism, formed by the merger of the AFL and CIO in 1955.*

8 *in December 1980, three nuns and a laywoman were murdered by National Guardsmen in El Salvador, an action that caused the American public and many politicians to call for a re-evaluation of support for that country's government.*

9 *the rusty-brown-coloured fruit of the sapodilla tree has a sweet, pear-like taste.*

ERIN MOURÉ

(1955–   )

A *supervisor for VIA Rail, Erin Mouré is notable as one of the few working-class female poets to have earned critical respect in Canada. Born and educated in Calgary, she published her first book,* Empire, York Street, *in 1979. In 1982 she won the DuMaurier Award for Poetry. The railroad, current events, and social issues figure prominently in her poems, which often develop themes of social and political criticism. Whether looking at the way popular culture and economic forces shape individual lives, especially those of women, or portraying universal experiences such as love and loneliness, Mouré typically moves from physical perception and emotion to an attempt at intellectual comprehension.*

Bends[1]

What the heart is is not enough.
That I can open it &
let you enter
an ocean so dense
5 you'll get the bends if you surface.
That you will be open to the love of every being:
I crave this,
it makes me possible, anarchic, calling
your attention,
10 your fingers' madness on my ear or soft neck,
the light on each side of your face, altered
as you speak to me.

Oh speak to me
I have a friend who says the heart's
15 a shovel, do you believe this?
My heart is a wild muscle, that's all,
open as the ocean
at the end of the railway,
a cross-country line pulled by four engines

---

1 *the bends, or nitrogen narcosis, occurs when nitrogen bubbles form in the blood. It is a condition experienced by divers ascending from a deep dive too swiftly and can cause pain, paralysis, and even death.*

20   Whatever it is I don't care, it is not enough
      unless you see it
      unless I can make you
      embrace & breathe it, its light that knows you,
      unless you cry out in it, & swim

                                                        (1985)

Safety

      Far off in the washroom, the light comes thru, the sound
      of him throwing up dinner,
      his sickness,
      his body so hard it won't digest,
5   won't welcome food
      In the newspaper, a picture of Gilles Villeneuve[1]
      in the last second of his life,
      his car already demolished,
      his body in the air
10   turned-over
      about to slam its bones into the wall
      So many kilometres per hour,
      with or without the Ferrari.
      & the small man in the washroom, who admires
15   but will not listen
      to the fast man who says death is boring.
      I can't drive slower, he says.
      I drive at my limits, for
      the pleasure, purely

20   & you, in this house, listening to the small man's body
      turn over its cylinders,
      refusing its food
      What part you play here, the pattern,
      the man sick with alcohol,

1 *Villeneuve (1950–82), a member of the famous Ferrari racing car team and Canada's most successful driver, was killed on May 9, 1982, during a qualifying race for the Belgian Grand Prix.*

25 who wants boredom,
    who wants to be a dead man in your arms'
    bent safety without cure
    or derision
    the way Villeneuve held his body in the air,
30 so fast only the camera stopped him

(1985)

Miss Chatelaine[1]

In the movie, the horse almost dies.
A classic for children, where the small girl pushes a thin
knife into the horse's side.
Later I am sitting in brightness with the women
5 I went to high school with in Calgary,
fifteen years later we are all feminist, talking of the girl
in the film.
The horse who has some parasite & is afraid of the storm,
& the girl who goes out to save him.
10 We are in a baggage car on VIA Rail around a huge table,
its varnish light & cold,
as if inside the board rooms of the corporation;
the baggage door is open
to the smell of dark prairie,
15 we are fifteen years older, serious
about women, these images:
the girl running at night between the house & the barn,
& the noise of the horse's fear mixed in with the rain.

Finally there are no men between us.
20 Finally none of us are passing or failing according to
Miss Chatelaine.
I wish I could tell you how much I love you,
my friends with your odd looks, our odd looks,

---

1 Miss Chatelaine *(now published as* Flare*) was a magazine of fashion, beauty, and lifestyles for young Canadian women.*

our nervousness with each other,
25   the girl crying out as she runs in the darkness,
our decoration we wore, so many years ago, high school
boys watching from another table.

Finally I can love you.
Wherever you have gone to, in your secret marriages.
30   When the knife goes so deeply into the horse's side, a
few seconds & the rush of air.
In the morning, the rain is over.
The space between the house & barn is just a space again.
Finally I can meet with you & talk this over.
35   Finally I can see us meeting, & our true tenderness,
    emerge.

(1988)

The Producers

What the producers do to meat, you pay for in your cells.
It is your cells I have come to speak about.
Only a certain thickness separates me from the air in this
    room.
Density. Its whirligig[1] spinning
5   to the tune of bouzouki[2] music.
My body the street fair offers you the altered clothing of
    the cells.
It offers you the chance to read a novel by a famous
    woman
in which other women reproduce, & their
value is this:
10   reproduction.

---

1 *a spinning toy, such as a top.*
2 *fretted musical instrument, something like a mandolin, having three or four courses of double metal strings and*
    traditionally used in Greece to play music for dancing and social entertainment.

It is because of this I have come to speak to you:
because it is possible that
the meaning of a woman is the meaning of a single cell.

A certain thickness prevents me from saying what I might
    say.
15 The difference between a human cell & the atoms in this
    table.
I lean my head against the wood.
Where are you, I want to speak to you.
What the producers do to lettuce, you pay for in your cells.
Everything they do, you will pay for.
20 Your cells will not recognize what they are to become.
It is on behalf of your cells.
I speak to you without election because the cells know
    nothing
of democracy.
They think not of the good of the whole, but of
    themselves.
25 They think of their thin unguarded border.
The illusion of wholeness captivates us, as a kind of
    slavery.
I asked a woman with cancer, who told me.
Now she has died because some cells wanted to go
someplace else.
30 Before she died, she thought about the producers
of x-rays,
& how we once believed we could see thru anything,
we humans.

(1988)

WRITING ESSAYS ABOUT LITERATURE

PUTTING THE JOB IN PERSPECTIVE

*W*riting well on any academic subject is demanding work, and writing about literature is among the most demanding kinds of academic writing. It helps to remember, however, that confronting the task seriously will improve not only the way you express what you think but your ability to think, as well. Mastering the critical and interpretive essays required in English courses will prepare you to handle other writing jobs with comparative ease. Whether you are committed to specializing in English or interested mainly in doing as well as you can in a required English course before going on to other areas of study, the advice that follows will help you make your choices sensibly and get the most from the work you do.

Writing about literature often starts with a feeling — you either like something or not — or an intuition about how a piece of writing works. In expressing these inklings in writing, you clarify them for yourself, identify the assumptions behind them, and learn how well they are grounded in the work you are considering. In the process, you not only come to understand better how literature works, but you also discover a good deal about how you think. Writing about literature is challenging for the same reasons it is rewarding — because it requires you to confront yourself as well as what you read.

When you explore literature in essays, you will rarely be looking for answers that are absolutely right or wrong. Depending on the approach taken and the questions asked, a wide variety of conclusions can be drawn about an individual work of literature, and because of the personal element in responses, even writers approaching questions in similar ways will often come up with quite different answers. Think of your essays about literature as part of an ongoing search for understanding, a process that begins when an author, poet, or playwright confronts his or her perceptions about the world in writing and continues as long as somebody is reading and writing about the original creation. Remembering that you are taking part in a continuing dialogue rather than solving a problem with a single, predetermined answer will help you resist obvious conclusions and make your confrontation with a demanding subject less intimidating.

But again, "less intimidating" does not mean easy. The lack of pat answers, though reassuring in some ways, is no excuse for either slack thinking or sloppy writing. On the contrary, because your essays will be judged more by the quality of thought and expression they demonstrate than by how close they come to some established position, care is especially important.

Originality is a start, but your original perceptions have to be supported scrupulously with evidence from the work in question; you must impress you audience by convincing it.

PREPARING TO WRITE

An essay about a literary work should say something illuminating about it, and an illumination depends on focus as well as initial brilliance. Thoughtful insights take time to develop, and an essential step in writing about literature involves clarifying for yourself what it is you want to say. Only when you are sure of your message can you decide how best to present it clearly and convincingly to your readers. The work cannot be rushed at this stage, so it is essential to leave yourself adequate time, not only to draft and revise, but to think, to plan, and to criticize your own ideas, as well.

PROCESS IN SUMMARY

PREPARING TO WRITE

Step 1: Prepare for writing assignments in advance by reading all assigned texts in a course as early as possible and by including speculation about potential lines of argument in your notes.

Step 2: Once you receive a writing assignment, evaluate it carefully to determine special requirements and anticipate problems.

Step 3: Choose a subject that interests you.

Step 4: Choose a topic you can handle well in the time available.

Step 5: If you are confused about any aspect of an assignment or if you anticipate deviating in any way from the directions, check with your instructor.

Step 6: Review the primary works you are writing about carefully, taking notes and identifying key passages as you read.

Step 7: Read whatever background material you consider necessary.

DRAFTING

Step 1: Begin generating ideas in writing while you still have more time than you need to complete your essay.

Step 2: Focus your ideas into a manageable thesis and state this thesis clearly in a single sentence.

Step 3:   Prepare a simple, tentative outline. Do not spend a lot of time on this outline because it will probably have to be modified later. Repeat Step 2 if necessary.

Step 4:   Working from your outline and keeping your thesis statement clearly in mind, complete a rough draft of the entire essay without stopping to revise.

REVISING AND EDITING

Step 1:   Review your essay to identify any parts that do not relate clearly to your thesis; cut or adapt these as necessary.

Step 2:   Add support at any point where your conclusions seem to need it.

Step 3:   Revise your opening to ensure that the main points of your essay are clear and supply any additional information your reader may need to follow your approach.

Step 4:   When you are satisfied with the content of your essay, continue revising it for clarity and style until you are satisfied that it is the best you can make it or until the deadline requires you to commit yourself to a final version.

Step 5:   When you are rested and free from distractions, proofread your essay carefully, making neat changes on the manuscript where necessary.

READING WITH AWARENESS

The most fundamental preparation for writing about literature is reading. Read the piece you intend to write about, and then reread it. Read not just superficially to get a basic idea of what the piece says, but carefully, with an awareness of implications beneath the surface and of how the way it is written determines the way it affects you. Taking English courses and studying what others write about literature will teach you the kinds of things to look for, but you will need more. Serious reading, like serious writing, takes practice and cannot be rushed: putting off thinking about literature in general until you are required to write about a particular piece is like putting off training for a race until just before you have to run it. Developing the habit of reading seriously will put you far ahead of students who read only when forced to by an assignment, and it will also yield a great deal of satisfaction in itself.

TAKING NOTES

While reading thoughtfully is essential, it is not enough. You will find that your reading translates more readily into essays if you record your responses. Take notes as you read, perhaps on the text itself if it is your own copy and an inexpensive one. Marking particularly interesting passages will be a great help when you come back later to sort out evidence for an idea you are developing in an essay. When taking notes in class, record not only what your instructor says but the ideas that occur to you as well. If what is said about one work suggests comparison with another, take note of the possibility. Remark contradictions and unanswered questions. Your dissenting opinions, which you might well forget if you neglected to write them down at the time, will often provide the foundation for your most original essays and may in the long run prove to be the most valuable material you record in class.

An excellent practice for bridging the gap between the sketchy notes you write in class and fully developed essays is to extend your notes in a journal. Rather than reviewing class notes only when you are preparing for an exam, take time between classes to review and expand on the ideas your notes record. Consider which of your ideas may yield topics for essays, and test the manageability of these topics by sketching outlines. Elaborate in a paragraph or two on ideas you have had time to record in only a sentence. If you have recorded questions in your notes, attempt to answer them yourself in writing. The best time to develop your notes into something more useful occurs when the ideas they record are still fresh in your mind. While keeping a literary journal is not so different from taking notes, it allows you time to develop your ideas more thoughtfully and provides practice that will help you become more comfortable with critical writing.

EVALUATING ASSIGNMENTS

Before attempting a writing assignment, you must first determine exactly what it requires and whether you can carry out any approach you are considering in the time available. The time you invest in evaluating assignments is rarely wasted. However eager you may be to get started, be cautious; enthusiasm is great, but you will win few races by sprinting off in the wrong direction.

Be especially careful when choosing topics from a list, a point at which the work of a few minutes can make the difference between success and failure. While you can assume that your instructor considers all suggested topics suitable for some students in your class, you cannot assume that all the topics will be suitable for all the students. Resist the temptation to commit yourself to the first topic that catches your interest. Evaluate all your options, eliminating the obvious impossibilities first. It will usually be clear that some works and some approaches are too difficult for you to manage. Personal taste is also an important consideration: until you gain more experience as a critic, you will rarely write successful essays about literary works you dislike. Once you have narrowed the choice to a few possibilities, sketch brief outlines to give yourself a better idea of where you might go with each topic. Determine whether you can meet all the requirements in each case. For example, even though you admire a certain poem, you may not be capable of handling a topic that requires you to produce a successful essay about how that poem's metrical patterns reinforce its meaning. While there can be long-term benefits in taking the extra time required to prepare for specialized topics, be sure you can manage the workload. Be wary of ambitious failures.

Once you find an assignment you think you can handle well, consider its wording carefully. Are you sure what all the terms mean? If not, ask your instructor to explain. Is there anything about the approach you are considering that seems at odds with the assignment as stated? Perhaps, for example, an assignment asks you to compare characterization in two stories, only one of which particularly impresses you. It may be permissible to concentrate on the one you like while using the other to illuminate by contrast what you admire in your favourite, but, then again, your instructor may want a more balanced comparison. Find out before you devote a lot of time to a questionable approach. Similarly, even though you plan no deviations from the stated requirements, you may find an assignment ambiguous in some respect. If you are told to compare two poems, for example, does this mean you are obligated to consider all aspects of the two poems? Or will you be permitted to devote most of your comparison to some aspect that seems especially revealing? While the more focused approach may seem more interesting to you, your instructor may have left the comparison general to test your understanding of a variety of elements in the poems. Any number of misunderstandings can occur, and you will be wise to anticipate them while you still have plenty of time to adapt.

Think early. Check early. Doing so can save you time, effort, and disappointment.

RESEARCH

In a very limited sense, any essay you write on a literary subject will involve research: you will have to read the works you intend to write about very carefully, probably a number of times, and even with an assignment that does not formally require research, you will often read other works by the same writer and explore his or her personal and historical background.

In a formal research paper, however, you will also be expected to find and evaluate what others have written about your subject. In this case, finding and properly acknowledging your debt to secondary material — writings about literature rather than the literature itself — will be a major part of your job. A detailed explanation of research methods and the format for acknowledging sources is beyond the scope of this chapter, but most college-level writing textbooks cover such material thoroughly. If you plan to take more than a few English courses, *The MLA Handbook for Writers of Research Papers*, which provides an exhaustive guide to the standard format used in English essays, is a good investment. Here it will suffice to provide a few general hints that can save you a lot of time and trouble.

Many students get into difficulty by confusing random sampling with research. They find the call number of a book on their topic, go to the specified shelf in the library, pull out several books on the same general subject, and consider their search complete. The one advantage of this approach — speed — cannot compensate for the problems it will almost certainly create. Books chosen at random rarely provide more than brief, general comment on an essay topic; what relevant comment they do include is often slanted according to their focal concerns. In addition, books stay on library shelves long after what they say has been qualified by later observations, and the material you find in a random selection will certainly not be the most recent available. This is not to say that books are of no value; the point is that books must be chosen carefully and supplemented by reference to up-to-date articles from scholarly journals.

The annotated bibliographies and the periodical indexes available in reference libraries will allow you to find material relevant to your topic quickly, and they will also give you an overview of the kinds of approaches to the work in question that others have found useful. But, as valuable as they are in saving you the trouble of reviewing irrelevant or barely relevant material, these resources will not solve all your problems. Often, they will list far more apparently relevant resources than you have time to consult. How are you to choose? In some cases your instructor will make suggestions, but such advice may still leave you guessing about which comments are most important and influential. One of the easiest ways into ongoing critical debates is to look first at the most recent writings you can find on your topic, taking careful note of the earlier works these cite. When two or three recent sources refer to an older one, it will usually be worth your while to check what it says directly. No method of sampling is a substitute for an exhaustive review of criticism, but methods that allow you to make an informed selection should be sufficient for most of your essays. They will certainly serve you better than random choice.

Seeking out the most pertinent material is not the only challenge in research, however. When you set out to research critical comment, remember that you are in at least as much danger from what you find as from what you miss. Discovering a source that carries on your line of argument so well that it leaves you little to add will take the satisfaction out of your work as well as the challenge, and you will learn little from basing your essay on such a source. Moreover, depending heavily on a source increases the chances of unintentional plagiarism — not making it entirely clear which ideas are really yours and which are borrowed. Thus, finding a published essay that covers much of what you intend to say about a topic is a good reason to consider changing topics or at least modifying your approach.

Much more serious than occasional reliance on secondary sources for ideas is developing a habit of dependency. It is all too easy to drift into a pattern of reviewing criticism before you begin to form your own ideas, thereby allowing others to shape your views. Always keep in mind when dealing with critical opinions that they are just that — opinions. Be impressed if you like, but never be intimidated. Even the best critics are human and therefore fallible. They are influenced by the prevailing critical assumptions of their times and often by specific theoretical affiliations. You have every right to disagree with published critics or, for that matter, with your instructors, provided you state your case clearly and support it conscientiously with references to the text in question. Consider other views carefully and with the respect any honest effort to advance understanding deserves, but then, when writing your essays, think for yourself.

STARTING TO WRITE

In contrast with the many difficulties involved in completing a good critical essay on time, putting off getting started is one of the easiest things you will ever do — easy and risky. It is human nature to put off the more difficult of competing tasks until the straightforward ones are out of the way, but with writing, the difficult jobs are precisely the ones to start first. Start early. Leave yourself time to explore blind alleys and, when you feel you are getting nowhere, to allow your subconscious mind to work on the problem while you are consciously engaged with other concerns. You will almost always find that ten hours invested in a writing project over a week will yield better results than a single ten-hour stretch of writing immediately before the deadline for submission.

WRITER'S BLOCK

Unfortunately, even when you are well aware of the advantages of an early start, you may be held up by a psychological quirk commonly referred to as "writer's block."

Writer's block usually sets in at the earliest stages of a project, making it impossible to begin writing at all or, at best, to carry on past the first page or two. Because fear of failure is part of the cause, writer's block often strikes when you can least afford it — when you are involved in an especially important project or working under pressure. If you have never experienced writer's block, you may find the idea amusing, but sooner or later it affects most writers, and when it does, it can be both unpleasant and costly. Moreover, the anxiety created by one experience can lead to others, creating a steadily worsening problem. It makes sense, therefore, to prepare for writer's block before it strikes by experimenting with methods of resistance in order to determine which work best for you.

The methods described below are primarily intended to help you generate and shape ideas, but because they also encourage you to start writing early, not just when you have time to complete a project but when you have time to waste, they help eliminate writer's block as well. So, even if you find it fairly easy to think of things to say without writing, writing will usually help, and it will certainly make your work no harder.

QUESTIONS

Perhaps the most straightforward way to clarify what you think about a subject is to ask yourself questions about it. In order to avoid writer's block, not to mention loss and confusion, keep a record of your questions and answers in writing.

Beginning with very general questions, such as why you like or dislike something, progress gradually to questions that are more specific, quickly abandoning lines of inquiry that lead away from manageable topics. If you need help devising questions, you will find the lists included in writing textbooks many and varied, and most of them will work adequately up to a point. Watch for that point. At first, any question that forces you to examine your ideas will be better than none, but the further you carry on with a ready-made list, the more likely the questions are to limit your answers. As soon as a suggested line of inquiry begins to get in the way of your developing ideas, abandon it and strike off on your own. Such lists are generally more useful for getting started than for leading you to conclusions.

Be wary also of lists of questions not designed for students of literature. For example, lists are often based on the journalistic standard: Who? What? Where? When? Why? How? While such lists encourage thoroughness in getting at the facts of a situation, an essay about literature is, of course, far more subtle than a news story. Normally, your readers will be familiar with the facts of the works you are discussing and will not require a review. Thus you will be wise to pass quickly over the Who? What? Where? and When? and concentrate on questions concerned with Why? and How? More often than not, you will begin forming a useful argument only when you begin addressing these last two.

INTERACTION

If asking and answering questions by yourself seems lonely work, you may prefer to involve others. Approaches vary according to circumstances and temperament.

One common method of generating ideas, sometimes called brainstorming, involves gathering a group together, with tape recorder running or one member taking notes, and throwing out ideas. The exchange is kept as informal as possible to avoid inhibiting creativity. This sort of exercise works better in developing advertising slogans than critical essays, and a lot of what results will be useless, but finding and rejecting inappropriate approaches to a subject will often help you progress towards forming better ones. At least such an exchange of ideas will get you started.

If you lack the informed group required for brainstorming, you can sometimes develop ideas and free yourself from writer's block by talking to a single listener. Even if this person knows little about your subject, his or her responses can help you decide where your views lack clarity or need support. Remember, however, that in the end it should be you who judges and refines the ideas: using another person as a sounding board for your own ideas is not the same thing as allowing another person to tell you what to think. For the sake of honesty and your development as a critical thinker, avoid working with someone whose superior knowledge of your subject may make it hard to rely on your own judgement.

FREE WRITING

One of the most reliable ways of breaking writer's block is called "free writing." Free writing is a way of freeing yourself from worry about imperfections in expression that can inhibit the flow of ideas early in a project. It involves committing yourself to writing for a predetermined period of time. You simply sit down in a place where you will not be interrupted and, keeping your subject in mind, write until the time is up. Resist pausing for reflection or stopping to revise. At best, you will be well into a rough draft by the time you finish. At worst, what you produce will be only vaguely relevant to your subject, but, even if the written result is of little value, you will still have broken your writer's block and moved closer to understanding what you want to say. You can always begin a second session of free writing by reacting to the shortcomings of your first.

FOCUSING

Once you put your early inhibitions behind you and begin accumulating ideas, you will soon find yourself with more than you can hope to bring together in a paper. This is the time to turn your attention from generating ideas to pruning and focusing. Handling the focusing stage of a writing project well can save you a great deal of time later on, but it takes discipline. Piling up ideas becomes so easy once you get started that it is tempting to carry on too long, deluding yourself that you are accomplishing something when in fact you are rambling out of control. While writing anything is better than writing nothing at the start of the writing process, this does not remain true throughout. Avoid the common mistake of trying to substitute quantity for quality.

You can approach the job of focusing from two general directions — working from a thesis or toward one. If you are lucky, you will discover one particularly interesting line of argument early along. Stating your main ideas as a proposition to be proved — a proposition often referred to as a "thesis" and commonly announced near the beginning of an essay in a sentence termed a "thesis statement" — will provide you with a guide as you write, a premise to refer to as you choose which of your secondary ideas to expand, which to subordinate, and which to cut. If no clear thesis has emerged by the time you are ready to start focusing, you can develop one by grouping the most promising ideas and then pruning obvious loose ends. The more loose ends you cut, the more clearly you will see the best potential lines of argument. By the time you have narrowed the possibilities to two or three, you will not only be in a good position to choose the best, but you will also have developed a general idea of how best to support the one you choose.

Be certain, however, that you do not stop before the job is done. Just as it is important to begin focusing before you are overwhelmed with an unmanageable accumulation of ideas, it is also vital to carry on to the desired end — a single, supportable thesis:

> **Not** *"Although Andrew Marvell's 'To His Coy Mistress' is manip-ulative to some extent in taking advantage of flattery, sophistry, and shocking images of mutability, it sometimes reveals a genuine regard for the object of passion and leaves the reader wondering how fully the object of Marvell's affection — or lust — would be capable of appreciating what is going on in the poem."*

> **But** *"In 'To His Coy Mistress,' Andrew Marvell is addressing a well-educated woman whose intelligence he respects."*

> **Or** *"Andrew Marvell's most compelling means of seduction in 'To His Coy Mistress' is neither flattery nor shock, but logic."*

The first statement above has more than its share of interesting ideas, but it would likely yield either two or three papers tacked loosely together or, worse still, a muddled blend. Parting with ideas can be hard, but attempting to fit more notions into an essay than you can explain and support adequately will be much harder. Saving a few minutes by rushing the focusing stage can cost you many hours later on.

OUTLINES

Quite a few writing textbooks advise preparing a detailed outline before attempting the first draft, a practice that is usually less effective for critical arguments than expository essays. In essays devoted mainly to reviewing large amounts of factual information, information that is readily gathered and organized in advance of writing, a detailed outline will prove an invaluable tool, one that can greatly speed the process of writing and revision. In more speculative essays, however, the kind of essays commonly written about literature, the difficulty of deciding what you are going to say in what order without a certain amount of groping on paper will often make a detailed outline harder to produce than a draft.

Therefore, using outlines for essays on literature requires flexibility. If planning is one of your strengths, beginning your writing with an outline will definitely speed the work that follows. But if you find preparing outlines more difficult than diving in and writing a draft without one, you will be wise not to spend too much time struggling to follow advice that is more appropriate for some types of writers and for some types of writing than others. Do what works for you.

TREE-DIAGRAMMING

If you like working from an outline yet find outlines difficult to organize while you are still generating ideas, try "tree-diagramming," a method that can help you form an outline in something the same way free writing helps you progress towards a first draft. Place a word or phrase representing your central idea in the middle of a large sheet of paper and work outward, connecting related ideas through a series of branches. Though the result of this exercise will rarely resemble a tree, it will provide you with an overview of relationships, revealing both dead ends and useful lines of inquiry quickly. (See figures 1 and 2.)

WRITING AND REVISING

If you start early and use your time efficiently, you should have developed and focused your ideas several days before your essay is due. At this point, you will have at least a general idea of how your essay will be organized to support your thesis, and you will have probably done some drafting. The next step, completing your first draft, should be fairly straightforward if you resist the temptation to stop and polish style.

Once you have a completed draft that makes sense and includes all your main points, distance yourself from what you have written by leaving it alone for a day or two. Then, coming back to the project relatively fresh, you will be able to decide more quickly and reliably whether what you have written needs cutting, expansion, or restructuring. After you are satisfied with the form and the essential content, it will be time for polishing style and fine-tuning your argument.

Remember: an essay you write over a week or ten days will almost always be better than one you produce in a single marathon effort, even though you invest the same number of hours in total.

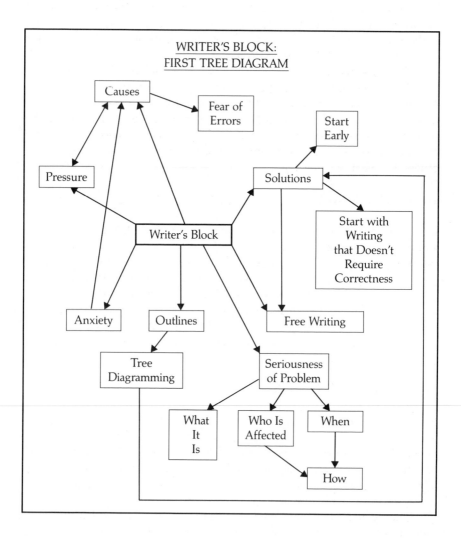

AUDIENCE

As you revise your essay, you will have two main concerns — making your argument clear and forceful, and maintaining one consistent appropriate style throughout. Style can be the trickier of the two, especially when you try to affect it. Do not assume an overly sophisticated, erudite style which may not be appropriate even for literary critics. You will find that an unnatural

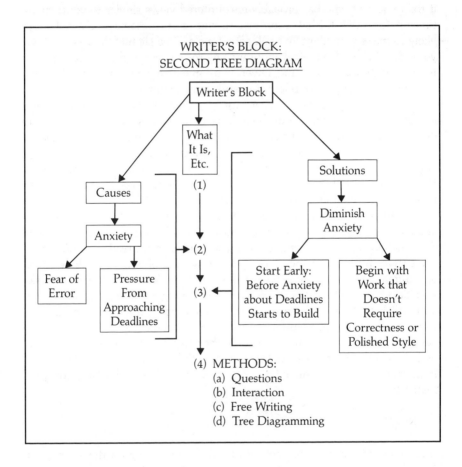

style will be very difficult to maintain for an entire essay. A much easier and more reliable approach is to let your audience and your relationship with it control your style automatically, as they would your voice if you were speaking.

What audience do you write for? The answer is less obvious than you might think. While you probably want most to impress the instructor who will eventually give your work a grade, you may well find that writing with another audience in mind makes this easier. Consider the unnaturalness of explicating literature for someone who knows a great deal more about it than you and who has probably encountered views similar to yours many times before. Will this situation inspire you with confidence? Or is it more likely to make you adopt an apologetic tone and be slightly dismissive about your ideas? How do you feel about writing for someone who can be expected to note technical errors and lower your grade in consequence? Will this audience encourage a confident, forceful style? Hardly.

It makes more sense to write for an audience you can persuade and enlighten, one at about your own level of ability. An audience made up of the better students in your class is a sensible choice. You know this audience well, you can assume it will be familiar with the works you are considering, and you can be confident that it will find your insights fresh and interesting. Writing for an audience of equals will also make it easier for you to adopt a natural, unpretentious style — your own.

In addition to helping you find an appropriate style, writing for an audience of equals will also help you decide what needs to be explained and what does not. For example, since your audience has read and understood the surface meaning of the works you are writing about, you will not need to summarize plot or review other obvious facts. When you need to make specific references to plot or character in support of your developing argument, you will keep these references brief — reminders, rather than revelations. On the other hand, you cannot assume that your audience has seen reasoning similar to yours before, and you should therefore make your line of thinking and the connections between evidence and the conclusions you draw from it more explicit than you might if you were writing exclusively for your instructor.

OPENINGS

Inexperienced writers often get into trouble by working on the assumption that the parts of an essay should be finished one at a time from first to last. This assumption is wrong on two counts. First, if you have the time, it is almost always easier to improve all the parts of an essay at about the same rate as you work through a series of drafts. Second, when lack of time makes a series of drafts impossible and you have to finish sections in sequence, it is usually easier to write the rest of the essay before you put the finishing touches on the opening.

If you are like most student writers, you have more difficulty with openings than with any other part of your essays. Your opening paragraphs may be wordy, vague, and repetitive, even though they receive more attention line for line than other sections. The problem is poor timing. While good essays generally require several drafts, inexperienced writers working under pressure hope to arrive at a final version in as few drafts as possible. In this hope, they attempt to produce a final, polished version when they have only an incomplete or very rough draft to revise, and they naturally start with the opening, struggling to introduce what they will say before they are sure of precisely what this will be. The time-consuming tinkering with wording and groping for ideas that ensue can take more time than revising the whole essay less meticulously. Even worse, having put so much effort into the opening, they are reluctant to make necessary changes once they finish the rest of the essay. The result: a vague, inflated introduction followed by a hastily composed argument that had to be dashed off because of all the time wasted in introducing it. There is nothing wrong with including an opening paragraph containing a clear thesis statement in your first draft; in fact it helps to keep your argument on topic. But, having done that, you will usually find it easiest to leave the opening rough until the rest of your essay is polished to its conclusion. At this point, you will have a much more certain idea of what you want to introduce in the opening, and you will find writing it much easier in consequence.

Keep in mind as you complete your opening that it should actually accomplish something — excite your reader's interest, persuade your reader of the value of your approach, prepare your reader to grasp what follows. You can achieve these aims only when you yourself fully understand where your essay is going.

REVISING FOR CORRECTNESS

While your first concerns throughout most of the writing process should be to make sense and express yourself in an appropriate, consistent style, you cannot afford to ignore correctness — following the accepted conventions of grammar, punctuation, and spelling. While correctness cannot in itself guarantee success, carelessness or incompetence in handling basic writing will certainly ensure failure.

Fortunately, whether they believe it or not, most students who are penalized for errors know enough about grammar and punctuation to write correctly. Attitude more than ignorance is the cause. If you tend to make a lot of mistakes, do not let discouragement or frustration exaggerate your weakness. Convincing yourself that you lack the ability to write correctly is simply an excuse for not investing the time and the work required to master correctness. Seriously confronted, the job of revising for correctness will become easier and less time-consuming with practice.

TEN COMMON MISTAKES TO AVOID IN WRITING ABOUT LITERATURE

Occasionally, even when you start early and work conscientiously, you will still get into difficulty in writing an essay about literature. More often than not this stems from one of the common errors below. While being on guard against these mistakes cannot guarantee success, it will greatly increase your chances.

1. TAKING ON UNREALISTICALLY AMBITIOUS PROJECTS

Be realistic in choosing topics. Avoid topics that will take more space, time, specialized knowledge, or research than you can put into them. If you are not sure whether your plans are manageable, check with your instructor.

2. PLAGIARIZING BY MISTAKE

Be careful not to drift into plagiarism by keeping sloppy records of your research. Record complete information for references immediately upon encountering a source you may want to refer to later. When taking notes, make a clear distinction between recorded information, paraphrases, and quotations.

3. RETAINING IRRELEVANT MATERIAL FROM EARLY DRAFTS

If sections of an essay seem loosely connected with each other or with the controlling thesis, try to put the essay in order by supplying clear transitions showing the reader how each part relates to the whole. If you find it difficult to justify a section, cut or shorten it. The ideas that could produce two or three good essays will usually make one bad one.

4. ATTEMPTING TO POLISH STYLE TOO EARLY

Do not attempt to perfect style while you are still unsure of what you want to say. Be especially wary of polishing openings before you have a clear idea of what will follow.

5. WRITING ABOUT YOURSELF RATHER THAN YOUR TOPIC

Concentrate on your topic rather than your feelings, doubts, or difficulties as you write. Avoid such redundant insertions as "it seems to me that" and "I think that"; your reader will know you are doing the thinking that goes into your essay without constantly being reminded.

Time is the key factor. To write correctly you must know your limitations and allow yourself time to compensate for them. If you find yourself penalized

6. SUMMARIZING PLOT AND EXPLAINING THE OBVIOUS

Avoid boring your reader by summarizing what happens in literary works and reviewing obvious facts at length. Assume an audience of intelligent readers familiar with the works you are analyzing and supply only the information this audience will need to evaluate your argument.

Do not be influenced by the summaries provided in various publications termed "notes." These summaries do not constitute serious criticism and should not be imitated.

7. CONFUSING VERB TENSES

Keep the sequences of verb tenses within long sentences as simple as possible, and avoid shifting tenses unnecessarily. Using the conventional present tense to describe characters, circumstances, and events in literary works will help greatly.

8. INFLATING STYLE

Inflated style is no substitute for good ideas. Impress your readers with the clarity and sense of your thinking rather than the sophistication of your presentation. Strive to write in your own voice; keep your sentence structure as straightforward as you can without being choppy and repetitive; use only those literary terms that you understand. If you work with a thesaurus, use it to find the most accurate and readily understood terms available rather than as a shortcut to pretentiousness and obscurity.

9. FAILING TO FOLLOW CONVENTIONS OF MANUSCRIPT FORM

Follow the accepted conventions for presenting your work on the page and acknowledging sources. It helps to remember that these conventions are not merely decorative; rather, they are an essential code for communicating information efficiently and accurately.

10. PROOFREADING INATTENTIVELY

Proofread when you are rested, preferably after a good night's sleep, rather than immediately after you finish an essay. Proofread in a place free from distractions, and give the job the full attention it requires. The half hour or so you take to proofread an essay properly will often have more effect on the grade than any other half hour of work you invest in the project.

for errors regularly, understand why. Is it carelessness in the final stages of writing? Or do you lack the background in the basics of writing? If you know what you are doing but make careless mistakes, you need merely improve your proofreading skills and find an appropriate proofreading time, which is to say a time when you will not be too tired to concentrate or likely to be distracted. If your problem is more serious and you are uncertain of what is correct in some cases, budget the extra time you will need to check. Checking your own work is a good way to learn, and you will probably find once you confront the problem of errors that you know more than you think you do. Like most students who are penalized for errors, you probably make the same types of errors again and again, although you handle most elements correctly. Take note of the types of things that go wrong and concentrate on these. Make a checklist of things to watch for. Review the relevant rules as you approach the final stages of writing. Ignorance, in this case, is no excuse: all the information you need about grammar and punctuation can be found easily in writing handbooks, and spelling can, of course, be checked in a dictionary — provided you allow yourself time to do the work.

Once you are satisfied that your own writing is correct, turn your attention to another aspect of your essay that requires care. Most instructors consider the format and accuracy of quotations and references to be just as important as the correctness of your own writing, so check these carefully before submitting your essay. Have you provided all the requirements, such as a title and title page, that are mentioned in the assignment? Are all your quotations recorded exactly? Have you consistently followed the correct format in supplying notes and bibliographical references? Taking care with such details shows that you are serious about your work; allowing even a few mistakes can call the accuracy of all your work into question.

One further word of warning, however: remember that timing is just as important as taking time in correcting your essays. It is as serious a mistake to let your concern with correctness preoccupy you during the earlier stages of writing as it is to neglect correctness later on. Worrying about errors early along will distract you from the important work of forming ideas, and it may also encourage you to adopt an overly cautious style aimed more at avoiding errors than communicating. So leave the job of checking for correctness till the end of your project, and then take it seriously.

*   *   *

While you cannot avoid the basic fact that writing well about literature involves hard work, you can, by following the advice supplied here, avoid wasting the work you do and ensure that your hard work yields the good results it deserves. But be skeptical: this advice is a basis, not a formula, for success. Keep in mind that writing is a personal endeavour and that no one method will work best for every person and every occasion. Treat this and all advice on writing critically, measuring its usefulness against your experience of what works best for you as you continue to grow as a writer.

GLOSSARY OF LITERARY TERMS

ACCENT: The stress that makes a syllable more emphatic or prominent in pronunciation than neighbouring syllables.

ACT: A main division of a drama.

ACTION: What happens in a drama; the physical activity represented on the stage, but also the mental activity stimulated in a reader or audience.

ALLITERATION: The repetition of consonant sounds, particularly at the beginning of words close to one another.

ALLUSION: A reference to characters, places, events, or objects from history, religion, mythology, or literature, which the reader is supposed to recognize and connect to the subject of the work in which the allusion appears.

AMBIGUITY: The presence of multiple meanings in a word or phrase, whether intentional or accidental.

AMPHIBRACH (AMPHIBRACHIC): A poetic foot of three syllables, only the middle one being accented. See FOOT and Figure 1, "The Metrical Feet," in the Introduction to Poetry.

AMPHIMACER (AMPHIMACRIC): A poetic foot of three syllables, the first and last being accented; also called a cretic. See FOOT and Figure 1, "The Metrical Feet," in the Introduction to Poetry.

ANAPEST (ANAPESTIC): A poetic foot of three syllables, only the last being accented. See FOOT and Figure 1, "The Metrical Feet," in the Introduction to Poetry.

ANTAGONIST: Any character who opposes another; most often applied to one opposing the main character (the protagonist).

APOSTROPHE: An address to an absent or dead person, to an object, or to an abstraction.

ARCHETYPE: A character type, symbol, plot, or theme that appears frequently in works of literature and therefore seems to have universal meaning.

ASIDE: Words delivered by one character to another or to the audience, and understood not to be heard by other characters on the stage.

ASSONANCE: Repetition of similar vowel sounds.

BALLAD: A form of narrative poetry used continuously since medieval times, consisting of four-line stanzas usually alternating iambic tetrameter and iambic trimeter and rhyming *abcb*, often characterized by repetition and repeated refrains. Ballads are usually classed as either popular or literary ballads. Popular ballads were transmitted orally and were frequently intended to be sung; they originated with anonymous authors among the folk, or common people of rural society. Literary ballads are conscious imitations of these popular ballads and are intended to be read or recited, not sung. Because they are often composed by individuals familiar with literary traditions, however, they may employ complex symbolism lacking in the popular ballads.

BLANK VERSE: Lines of unrhymed iambic pentameter.

BLOCKING: The planning of movement on the stage for a production of a drama.

CAESURA: A pause within a poetic line, created by punctuation, by the phrasing of ideas, or by the manipulation of metre.

CARPE DIEM: A Latin phrase, meaning "seize the day," often used to describe poems that urge the enjoyment of the moment because time is fleeting.

CHARACTER: A person in a work of literature or one of the *dramatis personae* of a play; also the moral, psychological, and intellectual traits of such a person. A *round* character possesses the complexities, contradictions, and subtle depths of personality associated with actual human beings. A *flat* character, in contrast, seems relatively two dimensional: the character is presented briefly and has little depth of personality. Both kinds may be *dynamic* — a character who changes, for better or worse, during the course of a literary work — or *static*, a character who undergoes no development.

CHARACTERIZATION: The techniques used to depict the traits of a character in a literary work. See CHARACTER.

CHORUS: In ancient Greek drama, a group of characters who comment in unison upon and sometimes take part in the action of a drama.

CLASSIC: A work considered to be the best of its class.

CLASSICAL LITERATURE: The literature of ancient Greece and Rome.

CLASSICISM: The application of artistic principles supposedly derived from the classical literatures of Greece and Rome, including formal control, proportion, simplicity, unity, and rationality. Classicism emerged in the Continent and England among the humanists of the fifteenth and sixteenth centuries. See NEOCLASSICISM.

CLIMAX: The crucial or high point of tension, understanding, or recognition in a plot and the turning point of the action.

CLOSED COUPLET: See COUPLET.

COMEDY: A literary mode, especially in drama, that ends happily, with the resolution of difficulties, the restoration of fortunes, and the unity of the community, often symbolized by one or more marriages. Comedy can celebrate or satirize the values of a society or individual, but it affirms life through its presentation of good fortune, positive pleasures, meaningful societal values, and individuals as significant parts of society.

COMPLICATION: The problem near the beginning of a story or drama that causes the conflict.

CONCEIT: An elaborate or extended comparison, whether simile or metaphor; known as Petrarchan conceits (after Petrarch, the poet who popularized them in his sonnets) when they are conventional, as with the comparison of a lover to a ship, and as metaphysical conceits (after the metaphysical poets of the seventeenth century) when they are elaborate or ingenious comparisons of things not traditionally linked, as with the comparison of separated lovers to a compass.

CONFLICT: The opposition of forces within a character, or the struggles either between characters (protagonists) and other characters (antagonists) or between characters and natural or supernatural forces.

CONNOTATION: The implications of a word; that is, the feelings, ideas, or associations suggested by a word in addition to its denotation, or dictionary meaning.

CONSONANCE: Repetition of consonants within or at the end of words.

CONTEXTUAL SYMBOL: See SYMBOL.

CONVENTION: A technique or feature included frequently in specific types of literature or in literature from a particular historical period. The Petrarchan conceit is a conventional feature in some Renaissance poetry; the use of heroic couplets is a conventional technique in eighteenth-century poetry.

CONVENTIONAL SYMBOL: See SYMBOL.

COUPLET: Two adjacent lines of poetry that rhyme; called a closed couplet when the pair is end-stopped by significant punctuation and contains a complete thought; called heroic couplet when the rhymed lines are in iambic pentameter.

CRETIC: See AMPHIMACER.

DACTYL (DACTYLIC): A poetic foot of three syllables, only the first being accented. See FOOT and Figure 1, "The Metrical Feet," in the Introduction to Poetry.

DACTYLIC RHYME: See RHYME.

DENOTATION: The dictionary meaning of a word, which depends significantly on context, without reference to its implications and associations.

DÉNOUEMENT: See RESOLUTION.

DEUS EX MACHINA: Literally, "the god out of the machine"; the descent of a god, represented by an actor lowered to the main level of the stage in a mechanical device, to intercede and conclude an ancient Greek drama; by extension, any contrived and improbable ending.

DIALOGUE: The direct presentation of the spoken words of characters in a story or play.

DICTION: The choice of types of words, specific words, and levels of language. Levels may be formal (lofty language such as that used in epics and in the speeches of nobles in Shakespearean drama), informal (the speech and idiom of daily life), or colloquial (the speech and idioms of particular social classes or groups, such as the Cockneys in England).

DIMETER: A term of poetic measurement indicating a line containing two feet. See FOOT, METRE, and Figure 2, "Line Lengths," in the Introduction to Poetry.

DOUBLE RHYME: See RHYME.

DRAMATIC MONOLOGUE: A form of poetry in which a character speaks to a definite but silent listener and thereby reveals his or her own character.

DRAMATIS PERSONAE: Literally, "the characters of the drama"; a descriptive list of characters prefixed to a drama; see CHARACTER.

DYNAMIC CHARACTER: See CHARACTER.

ELEGY: In classical Greece, a poem on any serious theme that was written in a couplet form known as elegiac metre; since the Renaissance, used to refer to a lyric that laments a death.

END RHYME: See RHYME.

END-STOPPED LINE: A line terminated with a relatively strong pause, usually indicated by the presence of a comma, semicolon, dash, or period; the opposite of enjambment.

ENJAMBMENT: The running over of meaning from one line to another unhindered by punctuation or syntactical pauses; opposite of an end-stopped line.

EPIC: A long narrative poem recounting in elevated language the deeds of heroes; settings are vast, sometimes extending beyond earth, and episodes may involve the gods or other supernatural beings.

EPILOGUE: The concluding, summarizing section of a drama in which all the strands of the plot are drawn together; sometimes the epilogue is an actual addition.

EPIPHANY: A religious term meaning a "manifestation" or "showing forth"; western Christianity celebrates the Feast of the Epiphany on January 6 to mark Christ's manifestation of divinity to the Magi; James Joyce applied the term to short fiction to describe the moment when events show forth their meaning, bringing illumination or revelation to a character.

EXEUNT: The plural form of the Latin "*exit*"; literally, "they go out"; a stage direction signalling the exit of all characters in a scene; sometimes expressed as "*exeunt omnes*" ("all go out"); when names or categories follow the term, as in "*exeunt* Lords," only the named group leaves the stage.

EXPOSITION: The presentation, usually at or near the beginning of a narrative or drama, of necessary background information about characters and situations.

EXPRESSIONISM: An early twentieth-century artistic movement that emphasized the inner world of emotions and thought and projected this inner world through distortions of real-world objects; unlike impressionism, expressionist literature and drama distorts and abstracts the external world, creating works that are symbolic, anti-realistic, and often nightmarish in vision; in prose, stream of consciousness narration is one of its major techniques.

EYE RHYME: See RHYME.

FEMININE RHYME: See RHYME.

FIGURATIVE LANGUAGE: Language that uses figures of speech (such as metaphors or similes) so that it means more than the simple denotation of the words and, therefore, must be understood in more than a literal way.

FLASHBACK: An interruption of the chronological sequence of events to present an event that occurred at an earlier time.

FLAT CHARACTER: See CHARACTER.

FOOT: The basic metrical unit in poetry, consisting of one or more syllables, usually with one stressed or accented; a basic pattern of stressed and unstressed syllables commonly identified by names derived from Greek poetics, the most common being the iamb, the trochee, the dactyl, the anapest, and the spondee. See METRE and Glossary entries for each kind, or see Figure 1, "The Metrical Feet," in the Introduction to Poetry for a list.

FORESHADOWING: The presentation of incidents, characters, or objects that hint at important events that will occur later.

FREE VERSE: Poetry that is free of regular rhythm, rhyme pattern, and verse form; often called *vers libre*.

FREYTAG'S PYRAMID: A structural diagram, resembling a pyramid in shape, devised by the nineteenth-century German playwright and critic Gustav Freytag to illustrate the rising and falling action of a five-act drama:

3. Climax
2. Rising Action 4. Falling Action
1. Exposition   5. Resolution

GENRE: A classification of literature into separate kinds, such as drama, poetry, and prose fiction; a major literary form that sometimes contains other related forms, which are known as subgenres.

HEPTAMETER: A term of poetic measurement indicating a line containing seven feet. See FOOT, METRE, and Figure 2, "Line Lengths," in the Introduction to Poetry.

HEROIC COUPLET: See COUPLET.

HEROIC QUATRAIN: See QUATRAIN.

HEXAMETER: A term of poetic measurement indicating a line containing six feet. See FOOT, METRE, and Figure 2, "Line Lengths," in the Introduction to Poetry.

HYPERBOLE: A figure of speech depending on exaggeration, the overstatement of the literal situation, to achieve dramatic or comic effects.

IAMB (IAMBIC): A poetic foot of two syllables, the second being accented. See FOOT and Figure 1, "The Metrical Feet," in the Introduction to Poetry.

IMAGE: See IMAGERY.

IMAGERY: At its most basic, the verbal creation of images, or pictures, in the imagination; also applied to verbal appeals to any of the senses.

IMPERFECT RHYME: See RHYME.

INTERNAL RHYME: See RHYME.

IRONY: A figure of speech that creates a discrepancy between appearance and reality, expectation and result, or surface meaning and implied meaning; traditionally categorized as verbal irony (a reversal of denotative meaning in which the thing stated is not the thing meant), dramatic irony (in which the discrepancy is between what a character believes or says and the truth possessed by the reader or audience), and situational irony (in which the result of a situation is the reverse of what a character expects).

ITALIAN SONNET: See SONNET and SONNET, PETRARCHAN.

LEITMOTIF: A recurring word, phrase, situation, or theme running through a literary work. Also see MOTIF.

LINE LENGTH: See Figure 2, "Line Lengths," in the Introduction to Poetry for a list; consult this Glossary for descriptions of individual kinds.

LYRIC: A form of poetry that is relatively short and that emphasizes emotions, moods, and thoughts, rather than story.

MASCULINE RHYME: See RHYME.

METAPHOR: A figure of speech that makes a comparison by equating things, as in "His heart is a stone."

METAPHYSICAL CONCEIT: See CONCEIT.

METAPHYSICAL POETS: Seventeenth-century poets who linked physical with metaphysical or spiritual elements in their poetry.

METONYMY: A figure of speech that substitutes one idea or object for a related one, such as saying "the Crown" when referring to the monarchy or the government.

METRE: A measure of the feet in a line of poetry, and thus a term expressing the number of feet in a line and the pattern of the predominant feet in that line; the rhythmic pattern of a line. See Figure 1, "The Metrical Feet," in the Introduction to Poetry.

MODERNISM: An artistic movement of the early twentieth century that deliberately broke from the reliance on established forms and insisted that individual consciousness, not something objective or external, was the source of truth; modernist literature may be structurally fragmented; its themes tend to emphasize the philosophy of existentialism, the alienation of the individual, and the despair inherent in modern life.

MONOMETER: A term of poetic measurement indicating a line containing one foot. See FOOT, METRE, and Figure 2, "Line Lengths," in the Introduction to Poetry.

MOOD: A general emotional atmosphere created by the characters and setting and by the language chosen to present these.

MOTIF: An image, character, object, setting, situation, or theme recurring in many works. Also see LEITMOTIF.

MOTIVATION: The psychological reason behind a character's words or actions.

MYTH: A traditional story embodying ideas or beliefs of a people; also a story setting forth the ideas or beliefs of an individual writer.

NARRATION: The recounting, in summarized form, of events and conversations.

NARRATIVE POEM: A poem that tells a story.

NARRATOR: The person telling a story, either a fictional character or the implied author of the work; see POINT OF VIEW.

NATURALISM: A literary movement based on philosophical determinism, the belief that the lives of ordinary people are determined by biological, economic, and social factors; naturalists tend to use the techniques of realism in order to present a tragic vision of the fate of individuals crushed by forces they cannot control.

NEAR RHYME: See RHYME.

NEOCLASSICISM: The principles of those writers who emerged with the restoration of Charles II to the throne of England in 1660 and who sought to restore classical restraint in all areas of life. The literature of the Neoclassical Period, which extends until about the 1798 publication of Wordsworth and Coleridge's *Lyrical Ballads*, was highly formal (frequently being based on the heroic couplet), praised reason over emotion, and often used satire and irony to criticize deviations from decorum and propriety. See CLASSICISM.

OBLIQUE RHYME: See RHYME.

OCTAMETER: A term of poetic measurement indicating a line containing eight feet. See FOOT, METRE, and Figure 2, "Line Lengths," in the Introduction to Poetry.

OCTAVE: An eight-line stanza in any metre or any rhyme scheme; any eight-line unit of poetry, rhymed or unrhymed; the initial eight lines of a sonnet united by the rhyme scheme.

ODE: A long, often elaborate, lyric poem that uses a dignified tone and style in treating a lofty or serious theme; regular forms not frequently used in English include the Greek Pindaric ode, which was divided into three repeated types of stanzas (strophe, antistrophe, and epode), each with its own metrical pattern, and the Horatian ode, which retained a single pattern throughout every stanza.

OFF RHYME: See RHYME.

ONOMATOPOEIA: Words that imitate the sounds that they describe.

OXYMORON: An ironic figure of speech containing an overt contradiction, as in the word *oxymoron* itself, which means "sharp stupidity" in Greek, or in such phrases as "fearful joy" or "paper coin"; see IRONY and PARADOX.

PARADOX: An apparent contradiction that, upon deeper analysis, contains a degree of truth.

PARODY: A humorous imitation that mocks a given literary work by exaggerating or distorting some of its salient features.

PENTAMETER: A term of poetic measurement indicating a line containing five feet. See FOOT, METRE, and Figure 2, "Line Lengths," in the Introduction to Poetry.

PERSONA: Literally, the mask; the speaking personality through which the author delivers the words in a poem or other literary work; the fictional "I" who acts as the actual author's mouthpiece in a literary work.

PERSONIFICATION: The attribution of human traits to inanimate objects or abstract concepts.

PETRARCHAN CONCEIT: See CONCEIT.

PETRARCHAN SONNET: See SONNET and SONNET, PETRARCHAN.

PLOT: The arrangement of actions in a drama or story, often in a sequence according to cause and effect.

POINT OF VIEW: The angle of vision or perspective from which a story is told. The point of view may be first person (in which the narrator is a character within the story), third person (a character or an implied author outside the story), or very rarely, second person (in which the narrator, as in "choose-your-adventure" books, addresses the reader as "you"). Narrative point of view also involves questions of knowledge and reliability. Narrators may be omniscient, knowing both external events and internal thoughts and motivations, or they may be limited to some degree, knowing only some external details. Reliable narrators (a category that includes omniscient narrators) tell the truth completely. Unreliable narrators have personal limitations, such as youth or lack of education, that make them misunderstand what they narrate.

PROLOGUE: The preface or introduction to a play, often containing a plot summary.

PROTAGONIST: The main character of a drama or story.

PYRRHIC: A poetic foot of two syllables, neither of which is accented. See FOOT and Figure 1, "The Metrical Feet," in the Introduction to Poetry.

QUATRAIN: A four-line stanza in any metre or any rhyme scheme, except the heroic quatrain, which is in iambic pentameter and rhymes *abab*; any four-line unit of poetry, rhymed or unrhymed; four lines of a sonnet united by the rhyme scheme.

QUINTET: A five-line stanza in any metre or any rhyme scheme; any five-line unit of poetry, rhymed or unrhymed.

REALISM: The attempt to represent accurately the actual world; a literary movement that developed in reaction to the artificialities of romantic literature and melodramatic drama and that tended to focus on the lives of ordinary people, to use the language of daily speech, and to develop themes that offered social criticism and explored the problems of mundane life.

RESOLUTION: A portion of a story or drama occurring after the climax that reveals the consequences of the plot and resolves conflicts.

RHYME (RIME): The repetition of identical or similar final sounds in words, particularly at the end of lines of poetry. Single, or masculine, rhymes repeat only the last syllable of the words; double, or feminine, rhymes (also sometimes called trochaic rhymes) repeat identical sounds in both an accented syllable and the following unaccented syllable; triple, or dactylic, rhymes repeat identical sounds in an accented syllable and the two following unaccented syllables. End rhyme occurs when the rhyming words are at the end of their respective lines; internal rhyme occurs when one or both of the rhyming words are within a line. Most rhyme involves the exact repetition of sounds; near rhyme (also known as slant, off, imperfect, or oblique rhyme) depends upon the approximation, rather than duplication, of sounds: it repeats either the final consonant (but not the preceding vowels) or the vowels (but not the following consonants) of the words. Eye, or sight, rhyme depends on the similar spelling of words, not their pronunciation, as in *gone* and *lone*.

RHYTHM: The flow of stressed and unstressed syllables; the patterned repetition of beats.

RISING ACTION: The progression of events and development of the conflict of a story or play up to the point of the climax.

ROMANTICISM: A literary movement that began in England sometime around the 1798 publication of Wordsworth and Coleridge's *Lyrical Ballads* and was a reaction to the restraint and order of neoclassicism. The Romantics praised emotion over reason and celebrated the imagination; their literature used a diction that was less formal and elevated than that of the classicists (see CLASSICISM), employed themes based on the supernatural, nature and nature's influence on human beings, and the power of the liberated imagination. "Romantic" and "romanticism" are applied to works that exhibit emotional and imaginative exuberance or that use such themes, whether or not written during the Romantic period.

ROUND CHARACTER: See CHARACTER.

SATIRE: A literary form that uses wit and humour to ridicule persons, things, and ideas, frequently with the declared purpose of effecting a reformation of vices or follies.

SCANSION: The analysis and marking of the metres and feet in a poem; see METRE and FOOT; see also Figure 1, "The Metrical Feet," and Figure 2, "Line Lengths," in the Introduction to Poetry.

SEPTET: A seven-line stanza in any metre or any rhyme scheme; any seven-line unit of poetry, rhymed or unrhymed.

SESTET: A six-line stanza in any metre or any rhyme scheme; any six-line unit of poetry, rhymed or unrhymed; the final six lines of a Petrarchan sonnet, which are united by the rhyme scheme.

SETTING: Emotional, physical, temporal, and cultural context in which the action of the story or play takes place.

SHAKESPEAREAN SONNET: See SONNET and SONNET, ENGLISH.

SIGHT RHYME: See RHYME.

SIMILE: A figure of speech making a direct comparison between things by using *like* or *as* or similar words, as in "His heart is like a stone."

SINGLE RHYME: See RHYME.

SLANT RHYME: See RHYME.

SOLILOQUY: The thoughts and impulses of a character, voiced aloud on stage and shared with the audience.

SONNET: A lyric form of fourteen lines, traditionally of iambic pentameter and following one of several established rhyme schemes; see SONNET, ENGLISH; SONNET, MILTONIC; SONNET, PETRARCHAN.

SONNET, ENGLISH: Also called the Shakespearean sonnet; a sonnet consisting of three quatrains and a couplet, rhyming *abab cdcd efef gg*; when the quatrains employ linked rhyme (*abab bcbc cdcd ee*), known as the Spenserian Sonnet.

SONNET, MILTONIC: A variation of the Petrarchan sonnet that eliminates the pause at the end of the octave; thus, the *volta*, when it occurs, usually appears in the middle of the ninth line.

SONNET, PETRARCHAN: Also called the Italian sonnet: the first eight lines (the octave) state a problem, and the final six lines (the sestet) frequently begin with a *volta*, or turn, such as *but*, *yet*, or *however*, and resolve or comment on the problem; originally limited to five rhymes, with the rhyme scheme of the octave usually being *abba abba* (thus dividing into two quatrains), and the rhyme scheme of the sestet varying, but generally being either *cde cde* (thus dividing into two tercets, or three-line units) or *cdcdcd*.

SPONDEE (SPONDAIC): A poetic foot of two syllables, both of which are accented. See FOOT and Figure 1, "The Metrical Feet," in the Introduction to Poetry.

STANZA: A division of a poem into a group of lines; traditionally, a grouping of lines according to rhyme scheme, number of lines, or metrical pattern that frequently is repeated in each stanza; a unit of two or more lines that are grouped together visually in any poem by being separated from preceding and following lines. See Figure 3, "Names of Stanzas and Line Groupings," and Figure 4, "Notable Fixed and Complex Forms," in the Introduction to Poetry.

STATIC CHARACTER: See CHARACTER.

STREAM OF CONSCIOUSNESS: A narrative presenting the flow of thoughts and emotions of a character.

STRUCTURE: The arrangement of elements within a work; the organization of and relationship between parts of a work; the plan, design, or form of a work.

STYLE: A writer's selection and arrangement of words.

SUSPENSE: The anxiety created by a situation in which the outcome is uncertain.

SYMBOL: A figure of speech that links a person, place, object, or action to a meaning that is not necessarily inherent in it; a word so charged with implication that it means itself and also suggests additional meanings, which are the product of convention (the culture traditionally associates a particular image with a particular meaning) or of context (the placement of the image in a work and the details and emphases within that work add suggestiveness to the image, making it symbolic).

SYNECDOCHE: A figure of speech in which a part stands for the whole or the whole stands for the part, as when the term "hands" signifies "sailors."

TERCET: A three-line stanza in any metre or any rhyme scheme, but usually called a triplet when all three lines rhyme; any three-line unit of poetry, rhymed or unrhymed; three lines united by the rhyme scheme in the sestet or a Petrarchan sonnet.

TETRAMETER: A term of poetic measurement indicating a line containing four feet. See FOOT, METRE, and Figure 2, "Line Lengths," in the Introduction to Poetry.

THEME: The central idea or meaning of a work; a generalization, or statement of underlying ideas, suggested by the concrete details of language, character, setting, and action in a work.

TONE: The speaker's attitude towards the subject matter or audience, as revealed by the choice of language and the rhythms of speech.

TRAGEDY: A literary work, especially a drama, presenting the failure and downfall of a character. Tragedy is a serious form demonstrating moral choice, error of judgement, and, in many cases, heroic death, as well as the enlightened understanding resulting from such considerations. Tragedy tends to deal with right and wrong, life and death, and the remorselessness of the universe in relationship to the puniness of human beings.

TRIMETER: A term of poetic measurement indicating a line containing three feet. See FOOT, METRE, and Figure 2, "Line Lengths," in the Introduction to Poetry.

TRIPLE RHYME: See RHYME.

TRIPLET: A tercet; usually applied to one in which all three lines rhyme.

TROCHAIC RHYME: See RHYME.

TROCHEE (TROCHAIC): A poetic foot of two syllables, the first being accented. See FOOT and Figure 1, "The Metrical Feet," in the Introduction to Poetry.

UNDERSTATEMENT: A figure of speech, the opposite of exaggeration, that intensifies meaning ironically by deliberately minimizing, or underemphasizing, the importance of ideas, emotions, and situations.

UNITY: The cohesiveness of a literary work in which all the parts and elements harmonize.

VERS LIBRE: See FREE VERSE.

VOLTA: The turn of thought in a poem, especially after the octave of a Petrarchan sonnet.

INDEX OF AUTHORS, TITLES, AND FIRST LINES OF POETRY

To the Owner of this Book:

We are interested in your reaction to *The Harbrace Anthology of Literature* by Rick Bowers, Raymond E. Jones, and Jon C. Stott. With your comments, we can improve this book in future editions. Please help us by completing this questionnaire.

1. Please indicate which version of this anthology you used: Literature
    Poetry
    Drama
    Short Fiction

2. What was your reason for using this book?
    _____ university course
    _____ college course
    _____ continuing education course
    _____ personal interest
    _____ other (specify)

3. If you used this text for a program, what was the name of that program?

4. Which school do you attend?

5. Approximately how much of the book did you use?
    _____ ¼ _____ ½ _____ ¾ _____ all

6. Which chapters or sections were omitted from your course?

7. What is the best aspect of this book?

8. Is there anything that should be added?

9. Please add any comments or suggestions.

(fold here)

(fold here and tape shut)

0116870399-M8Z4X6-BR01

Heather McWhinney
Publisher, College Division
HARCOURT BRACE & COMPANY, CANADA
55 HORNER AVENUE
TORONTO, ONTARIO
M8Z 9Z9